AFRICA *84-85*

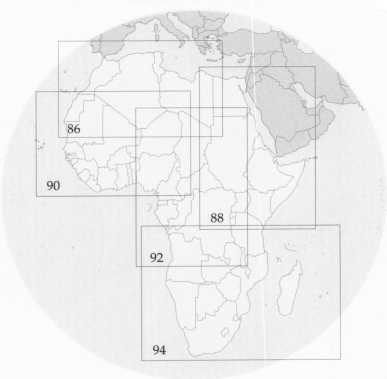

86
90
88
92
94

EUROPE *96-97*

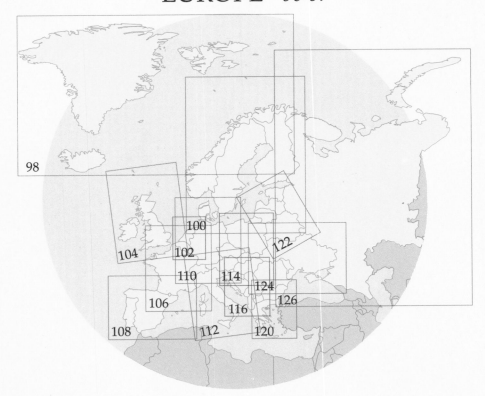

98
100
104
102
122
110
114
124
106
116
126
108
112
120

FAMILY
ATLAS

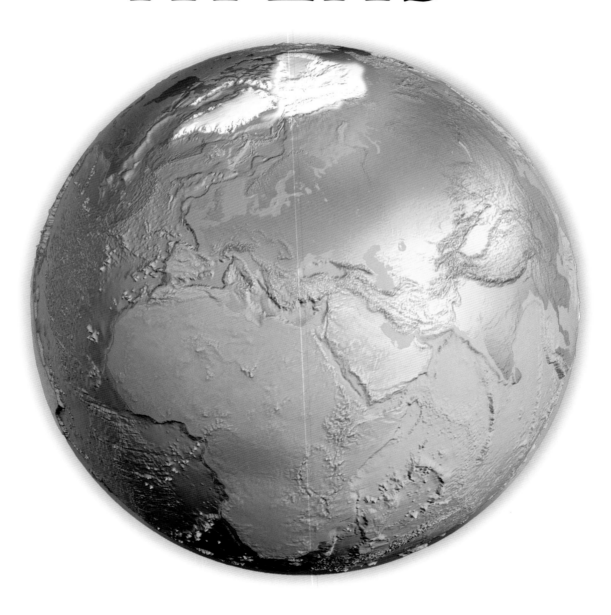

FAMILY ATLAS

THE COMPREHENSIVE ATLAS FOR THE WHOLE FAMILY

FAMILY LEARNING

A DORLING KINDERSLEY BOOK

EDITORIAL DIRECTION
Andrew Heritage

CARTOGRAPHERS
James Anderson, Sarah Baker-Ede,
Dale Buckton, Roger Bullen, Jan Clark,
Martin Darlison, Sally Gable, Jeremy Hepworth,
Julia Lunn, Simon Mumford, John Plumer,
David Roberts, Jane Voss

DIGITAL CARTOGRAPHY CREATED IN DK CARTOPIA BY
Phil Rowles, Rob Stokes

DESIGN
David Douglas, Paul Williams

DESIGN ASSISTANCE
Anthony Cutting, Nicola Liddiard

INDEX-GAZETTEER
Natalie Clarkson, Ruth Duxbury,
Simon Lewis, Julia Lynch

DTP SYSTEM MANAGER
Tokiko Morishima

MANAGING EDITOR
Lisa Thomas

MANAGING ART EDITOR
Philip Lord

PRODUCTION
David Proffit

First published in Great Britain in 1998
by Dorling Kindersley Limited
9 Henrietta Street, London WC2E 8PS

Copyright © 1998 Dorling Kindersley Limited, London
Visit us on the World Wide Web at http://www.dk.com

A CIP catalogue record for this book is available from the
British Library

ISBN 0-7513-0639-8

Film output by Graphical Innovations, UK
Printed and bound in China by L.Rex Printing Co.. Ltd.

PICTURE CREDITS

The publisher would like to thank the following for their kind
permission to reproduce the photographs.

t =top, b= bottom, a=above, c= centre, l= left, r= right.

Adams Picture Library: 220cr; **G Andrews:** 223cl;
Aspect Picture Library: K Naylor 190cr; F Nichols 220cl;
B Seed 197cr; D Donne **Bryant Stock Picture Agency:** 186cl;
J Allan Cash: 179cr, 194cl, 195cl, 212cr, 218cr; **Bruce Coleman
Ltd:** 17bc, 182cr; M Berge 224cl; G Cubitt 188cr, 196cl;
M P Kahl 186cr; G Langesbury 192cl; O Langrand 187cr;
Luiz C Marigo 17cl (below); F Prenzel 222cr; **Colorific:**
J Howard 222cl; Lehtikuva 18bc (above); Reza/Black Star 19tl;
M Rogers 188cl; **Comstock:** 218cl; T Eigeland 191cl;
Compix: 224cr; J Leach 223cr; B McGrath 198cr; **James Davis
Travel Photography:** 181cr, 185cl, 200cr, 202cr, 204cl, 205cr,
212cl, 213cl, 225cr; Chris Fairclough **Colour Library:** 206cl;
J Guest 219cr; **Finnish Tourist Board:** 201cl; **Robert Harding
Picture Library:** 14c, 15tr, 17tr, 18cr (below), 19tc, 178cr, 182cl,
199cr, 206cr, 207cr, 210cr, 216cl; David Atchison-Jones 225cl;
Robert Francis 17cl(above); G Hellier 207cl; **Photri:** 14br,
14cr (above), 14tr; R Rainford 203cr; C Rennie 215cl; J Ross
211cr; G Roli 200cl; A Woolfitt 214cl; **Hutchison Library:** 193cl,
197cl; Robert Francis 196cr; Christine Pemberton 180cr; Bernard
Regent 195cr; **Image Bank:** 13ccl; Melchior Di Giacomo 19bl;
G Jung 211cl; T Madison 221cr; ME Newman 205cl;
Images Colour Library: 217cl; **Impact:** G J Norman 214cr;

C Penn 189cl; **Frank Lane Picture Agency:** D Hoadley 16tr;
Lorna Stanton: 57tr; **N.A.S.A.:** 11tl; **Oxford Scientific Films:**
Lon E Lauber 15br; **Panos Pictures:** N Cooper 179cl; R Giling
184cr; J Hartley 193cr; D Hulcher 219cl; S Sprague 185cr, 190cl;
Photo Access: Pat de la Harpe 52br; **Pictor International:**
16tr(below), 17tl, 17cr, 18c; **Planet Earth Pictures:** John
Eastcott/Yva Momatiuk 17tc; **REX Features:** 216cr; **Science
Photo Library:** Martin Bond 13ccr; Ray Ellis 17br;
David Parker 13cr; **South American Pictures:** J Berrange 180cl;
Frank Spooner Pictures: Iliona-Figaro Magazine 181cl; N Jallot
209cr; **Tony Stone Images:** 14cr(below), 16tc(below), 199cl;
Doug Armand 178cl; Oliver Benn 183cl; Joe Cornish 203cl;
Shaun Egan 204cr; Rosemary Evans 209cl; H Richard Johnston
15cr (above); Hideo Kirshara 202cl; Peter/Steph Lamberti 15cr
(below); Angus M Makillop 19bc; Steven Rothfeld 18br, 191cr;
Alan Smith 201cr; Dennis Stone 189cr; **J Tempest:** 213cr;
Topham Picturepoint: 194cr; **Trip:** T Goodman 192cr;
V Shuba 210cl; V Sidoropolev 215cr; **Tony Waltham:** 13cl; P
Woods: 217cr; **World Pictures:** 186cl, 221cl; **ZEFA Picture
Library:** 183cr, 208cr; Everts 208cl; F Lanting 198cl; Sunak 184cl.

Jacket
BACK COVER: **Bruce Coleman:** crb; **Colorific:** br; **James Davis
Travel Photography:** tr and cra; **Getty Images:** clb; **Robert
Harding Picture Library:** tl and cla; **Peter Woods:** bl.
FRONT COVER: **James Davis Travel Photography:** tl; **Robert
Harding Picture Library:** cla/T. Gervis clb; **Oxford Scientfic
Films:** bl; **Pictor International:** tr; **Image Bank:** cra; **Trip:** crb;
Getty Images: br; INSIDE FRONT COVER: **Science Photo Library**

KEY TO MAP SYMBOLS

BOUNDARIES

▬▬▬	Full international border
▬ ▬ ▬	Disputed *de facto* border
· · · · · ·	Territorial claim border
x — x — x	Ceasefire line
▬ ▬ ▬	Undefined boundary
——	Internal administrative boundary

COMMUNICATION FEATURES

———	Major road
———	Minor road
———	Railway
✈	International airport

DRAINAGE FEATURES

———	Major perennial river
———	Minor perennial river
– – –	Seasonal river
———	Canal
ǀ	Waterfall
⬭	Perennial lake
⬭	Seasonal lake
▨	Wetland

ICE FEATURES

▢	Permanent ice cap/ice shelf
▲▲▲	Summer limit of pack ice
△	Winter limit of pack ice

LANDSCAPE FEATURES

▨	Sandy desert
△	Mountain
▽	Depression depth
⌂	Volcano
)(	Pass/tunnel
+	Site of interest

ADMINISTRATIVE CENTRES

●	Capital
◎	Internal administrative capital

NAMES

TAIWAN	Country
JERSEY (to UK)	Dependent territory
PARIS	Capital
KANSAS	Administrative region
Dordogne	Cultural region
Sahara	Landscape feature
Mont Blanc 4807m	Mountain/pass
Blue Nile	Drainage feature
Sulu Sea	Ocean feature
Chile Rise	Underwater feature

INSET MAP SYMBOLS

▢	Urban area
▢	City
▢	Park
▫	Place of interest
▫	Suburb/district

CONTENTS

ASIA (NORTH & WEST)   128–129

ASIA (SOUTH & EAST)   140–141

AUSTRALASIA & OCEANIA 158–159

WORLD FACTFILE
pages 172–225

HOW THE
WORLD
WORKS

THE WORLD WE INHABIT IS ANCIENT,
yet dynamic, and is constantly being
shaped and moulded by natural forces.
This section looks at the nature of these
forces, and shows how humans have
populated and organized its surface.

THE EARTH IN SPACE

THE EARTH IS ONE OF NINE PLANETS that orbit a large star – the Sun. Together they form the solar system. All life on Earth – plant, animal and human – depends on the Sun. Its energy warms our planet's surface, powers the wind and waves, drives the ocean currents and weather systems, and recycles water. Sunlight also gives plants the power to photo-synthesize – to make the foods and oxygen on which organisms rely. The fact that the Earth is habitable at all is due to its precise position in the solar system, its daily spin, and an annual journey round the Sun at a constant tilt. Without these, and the breathable atmosphere that cloaks and protects the Earth, it would be as barren as our near-neighbours Venus and Mars.

Asteroid belt
Mars
687 days
Mercury
88 days
Jupiter
12 years
Uranus
84 years
Earth
365 days
(1 year)
Venus
225 days
Neptune
165 years
Saturn
29 years
Pluto
248 years

THE SOLAR SYSTEM
Although the planets move at great speeds, they do not fly off in all directions into space because the Sun's gravity holds them in place. This keeps the planets circling the Sun. A planet's 'year' is the time it takes to make one complete trip round the Sun. The diagram shows the length of the planet's year in Earth-days or Earth-years.

THE RELATIVE SIZES OF THE SUN AND PLANETS
WITH THEIR AVERAGE TEMPERATURE

THE LIFE ZONE

MANY
VERY
EAGER
MOUNTAINEERS
JOG
SWIFTLY
UP
NEW
PEAKS

You can use this sentence to remember the sequence of planets:

MERCURY
Day 430°C
Night -180°C

VENUS
465°C

EARTH
15°C

MARS
-23°C

The Earth seems to be the only habitable planet in our solar system. Mercury and Venus, which are closer to the Sun, are hotter than an oven. Mars, and planets still farther out, are colder than a deep freeze.

JUPITER
-150°C

SATURN
-180°C

URANUS
-210°C

NEPTUNE
-220°C

PLUTO
-230°C

THE PLANETS AND THEIR DISTANCES FROM THE SUN

MARS
227,940,000 km
(141,600,000 miles)

SATURN
1,426,980,000 km
(886,700,000 miles)

URANUS
2,870,990,000 km
(1,783,000,000 miles)

NEPTUNE
4,497,070,000 km
(2,800,000,000 miles)

PLUTO
5,913,520,000 km
(3,670,000,000 miles)

JUPITER
778,330,000 km
(483,000,000 miles)

EARTH
149,500,000 km
(92,900,000 miles)

VENUS
108,200,000 km
(67,200,000 miles)

MERCURY
57,910,000 km
(36,000,000 miles)

Huge solar flares, up to 200,000 km (125,000 miles) long, lick out into space

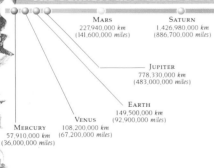

THE FOUR SEASONS

The Earth always tilts in the same direction on its 950 million-km (590 million-mile) journey around the Sun. This means that each hemisphere in turn leans towards the Sun, then leans away from it. This is what causes summer and winter.

THE EARTH TRAVELS AROUND THE SUN AT 66,000 MILES PER HOUR (107,244 KM/H)

MARCH 21
EQUINOX
Spring in the Northern hemisphere; autumn in the Southern hemisphere. At noon, the Sun is overhead at the Equator. Everywhere on Earth has 12 hours of daylight, 12 hours of darkness.

DECEMBER 21 SOLSTICE
Summer in the Southern hemisphere; winter in the Northern hemisphere. At noon, the Sun is overhead at the Tropic of Capricorn. The South Pole is in sunlight for 24 hours, and the North Pole is in darkness for 24 hours.

SEPTEMBER 21 EQUINOX
Autumn in the Northern hemisphere; spring in the Southern hemisphere. At noon, the Sun is overhead at the Equator. Everywhere on Earth has 12 hours of daylight, 12 hours of darkness.

SUN

To North Star

IT TAKES 23 HOURS, 56 MINUTES AND 4 SECONDS FOR THE EARTH TO ROTATE ONCE ON ITS AXIS. THIS IS THE TRUE LENGTH OF AN EARTH 'DAY'.

JUNE 21 SOLSTICE
Summer in the Northern hemisphere; winter in the Southern hemisphere. At noon, the Sun is overhead at the Tropic of Cancer. The North Pole is in sunlight for 24 hours, and the South Pole is in darkness for 24 hours.

IT TAKES 365 DAYS, 6 HOURS, 9 MINUTES AND 9 SECONDS FOR THE EARTH TO REVOLVE ONCE AROUND THE SUN. THIS IS THE TRUE LENGTH OF AN EARTH YEAR.

South Pole

24 HOURS IN THE LIFE OF PLANET EARTH

The Earth turns a complete circle (360°) in 24 hours, or 15° in one hour. Countries on a similar line of longitude (or 'meridian') usually share the same time. They set their clocks in relation to Greenwich Mean Time (GMT). This is the time at Greenwich (London, England), on longitude 0°. Countries east of Greenwich are ahead of GMT. Countries to the west are behind GMT.

NOON AT GMT	GREENWICH 1200 HRS	DAKAR 1100 HRS	E. GREENLAND 1000 HRS	RIO DE JANEIRO 0900 HRS	CARACAS 0800 HRS	NEW YORK 0700 HRS	MEXICO CITY 0600 HRS	CALGARY 0500 HRS	LOS ANGELES 0400 HRS	E. ALASKA 0300 HRS	HONOLULU 0200 HRS	Pacific Ocean 0100 HRS
Noon everywhere on this meridian	0°	15°W	30°W	45°W	60°W	75°W	90°W	105°W	120°W	135°W	150°W	165°W

MOON AND EARTH

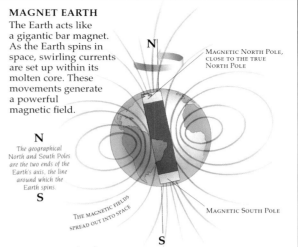

Craters made by collision with meteors

The Moon is a ball of barren rock 3,476 km (2,156 miles) across. It orbits the Earth every 27.3 days at an average distance of 384,400 km (238,700 miles). The Moon's gravity is only one-sixth that of Earth – too small to keep an atmosphere around itself, but strong enough to exert a powerful pull on the Earth. The Moon and Sun together create tides in the Earth's oceans. The period between successive high tides is 12 hours 25 minutes. The highest (or 'spring') tides occur twice a month, when the Moon, Sun and Earth are in line.

THE MOON'S SURFACE TEMPERATURE FALLS FROM 220°F (105°C) IN SUNLIGHT TO –247°F (–155°C) WHEN IT TURNS AWAY FROM THE SUN

MAGNET EARTH

The Earth acts like a gigantic bar magnet. As the Earth spins in space, swirling currents are set up within its molten core. These movements generate a powerful magnetic field.

MAGNETIC NORTH POLE, CLOSE TO THE TRUE NORTH POLE

The geographical North and South Poles are the two ends of the Earth's axis, the line around which the Earth spins.

THE MAGNETIC FIELDS SPREAD OUT INTO SPACE

MAGNETIC SOUTH POLE

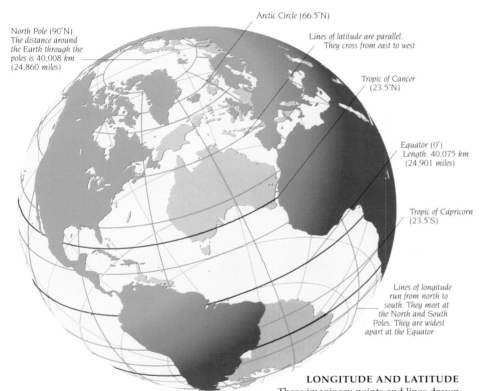

Arctic Circle (66.5°N)

North Pole (90°N) *The distance around the Earth through the poles is 40,008 km (24,860 miles)*

Lines of latitude are parallel. They cross from east to west

Tropic of Cancer (23.5°N)

Equator (0°) Length: 40,075 km (24,901 miles)

Tropic of Capricorn (23.5°S)

Lines of longitude run from north to south. They meet at the North and South Poles. They are widest apart at the Equator

LONGITUDE AND LATITUDE

These imaginary points and lines drawn on the Earth's surface help locate places on a map or globe. The Earth spins around an axis drawn between the North and South Poles through the centre of the planet. Lines of longitude are vertical lines running through the Poles. Lines of latitude are horizontal lines drawn parallel to the Equator, the line around the middle of the Earth.

DIAMETER OF EARTH AT EQUATOR 12,756 KM (7,927 miles)

DIAMETER FROM POLE TO POLE 12,714 KM (7,900 miles)

MASS 5,988 million, million million tonnes (tons)

THE ATMOSPHERE

An envelope of gases such as nitrogen and oxygen surrounds our planet. It provides us with breathable air, filters the Sun's rays and retains heat at night.

HEIGHT IN KM (MILES)

INTERPLANETARY SPACE

COMMUNICATIONS AND SOME ASTRONOMICAL SATELLITES 35,880 km (22,295 miles)

EXOSPHERE 500–2,000 km (300–1,240 miles) Outer limit of atmosphere

40,000 (25,000)

SPACE STATION 300 km (186 miles)

SPACE SHUTTLE 300–600 km (186–372 miles)

THERMOSPHERE 80–500 km (50–300 miles)

500 (300)

MESOSPHERE 50–80 km (31–50 miles)

WEATHER BALLOON up to 50 km (31 miles)

80 (50)

STRATOSPHERE 15–50 km (9–31 miles)

PASSENGER AIRCRAFT 8–16 km (5–10 miles)

OZONE LAYER 15–30 km (9–18 miles)

CLOUDS Usually below 10 km (6 miles)

50 (31)

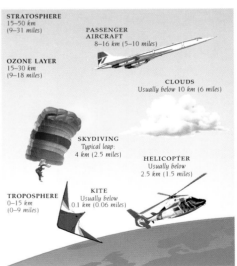

SKYDIVING Typical leap: 4 km (2.5 miles)

HELICOPTER Usually below 2.5 km (1.5 miles)

TROPOSPHERE 0–15 km (0–9 miles)

KITE Usually below 0.1 km (0.06 miles)

SEA LEVEL

WINDS AND CURRENTS

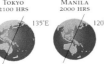

Cold air descends from the poles towards the Equator

Warm air and water travel to the poles from the Equator

Air circulates between the poles and the Equator in stages called 'cells'

Winds and currents do not move in straight lines because the Earth spins

The world's winds and ocean currents are caused by the way the Sun heats the Earth's surface. More heat energy arrives at the Equator than at the poles because the Earth is curved and tilted. Warm air and warm water carry much of this energy towards the Poles, heating up the higher latitudes. Meanwhile cool air and water moves back towards the Equator, lowering its temperature.

WELLINGTON 2400 HRS	Pacific Ocean 2300 HRS	SYDNEY 2200 HRS	TOKYO 2100 HRS	MANILA 2000 HRS	JAKARTA 1900 HRS	DACCA 1800 HRS	KARACHI 1700 HRS	MUSCAT 1600 HRS	BAGHDAD 1500 HRS	CAIRO 1400 HRS	BERLIN 1300 HRS	GREENWICH 1200 HRS
180°	165°E	150°E	135°E	120°E	105°E	90°E	75°E	60°E	45°E	30°E	15°E	0°

THE EARTH'S STRUCTURE

THE EARTH IS IN SOME WAYS like an egg, with a thin shell around a soft interior. Its hard, rocky outer layer – the crust – is up to 70 km (45 miles) thick under the continents, but less than 8 km (5 miles) thick under the oceans. This crust is broken into gigantic slabs, called 'plates', in which the continents are embedded. Below the hard crust is the mantle, a layer of rocks so hot that some melt and flow in huge swirling currents. The Earth's plates do not stay in the same place. Instead, they move, carried along like rafts on the currents in the mantle. This motion is very slow – usually less than 5 cm (2 in) a year – but enormously powerful. Plate movement makes the Earth quake and volcanoes erupt, causes immense mountain ranges such as the Himalayas to grow where plates collide, and explains how over millions of years whole continents have drifted across the face of the planet.

DRIFTING CONTINENTS
CURRENTS OF MOLTEN ROCK DEEP WITHIN THE MANTLE SLOWLY MOVE THE CONTINENTS. OVER TIME, THEY APPEAR TO 'DRIFT' ACROSS THE EARTH'S SURFACE.

Pangaea

200 MILLION YEARS AGO

All of today's continents were joined in one supercontinent, called Pangaea. It began to break up about 180 million years ago.

'Africa'
'India'
'Atlantic Ocean' opening up

120 MILLION YEARS AGO

The Atlantic Ocean splits Pangaea into two. India has broken away from Africa.

'North America'
'Asia'
'India'
'Australia'
'Antarctica'

40 MILLION YEARS AGO

India is moving closer to Asia. Australia and Antarctica have separated.

North America
Europe
Asia
India
Australia
Africa
Antarctica
South America

TODAY
India has collided with Asia, pushing up the Himalaya Mountains.

Great Rift Valley, now sea

50 MILLION YEARS IN THE FUTURE ?

If today's plate movements continue, the Atlantic Ocean will be 1,250 km (775 miles) wider. Africa and Europe will fuse, the Americas will separate again, and Africa east of the Great Rift Valley will be an island.

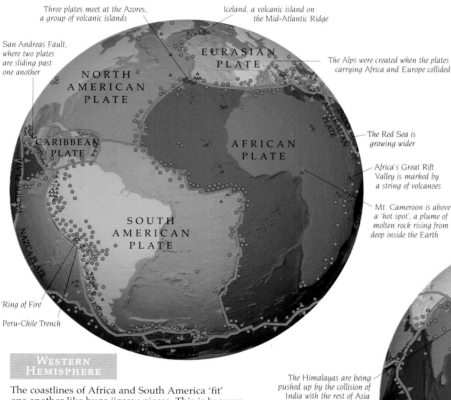

Three plates meet at the Azores, a group of volcanic islands

Iceland, a volcanic island on the Mid-Atlantic Ridge

San Andreas Fault, where two plates are sliding past one another

EURASIAN PLATE

The Alps were created when the plates carrying Africa and Europe collided

NORTH AMERICAN PLATE

CARIBBEAN PLATE

AFRICAN PLATE

The Red Sea is growing wider

Africa's Great Rift Valley is marked by a string of volcanoes

SOUTH AMERICAN PLATE

Mt. Cameroon is above a 'hot spot', a plume of molten rock rising from deep inside the Earth

'Ring of Fire'

Peru-Chile Trench

NAZCA PLATE

PACIFIC PLATE

WESTERN HEMISPHERE

The coastlines of Africa and South America 'fit' one another like huge jigsaw pieces. This is because they were once joined. Then, about 180 million years ago, a crack appeared in the Earth's crust. Hot liquid rock (magma) rose through the crack and cooled, forming new oceanic crust on either side. As the ocean grew wider, the continents moved apart. The process continues today.

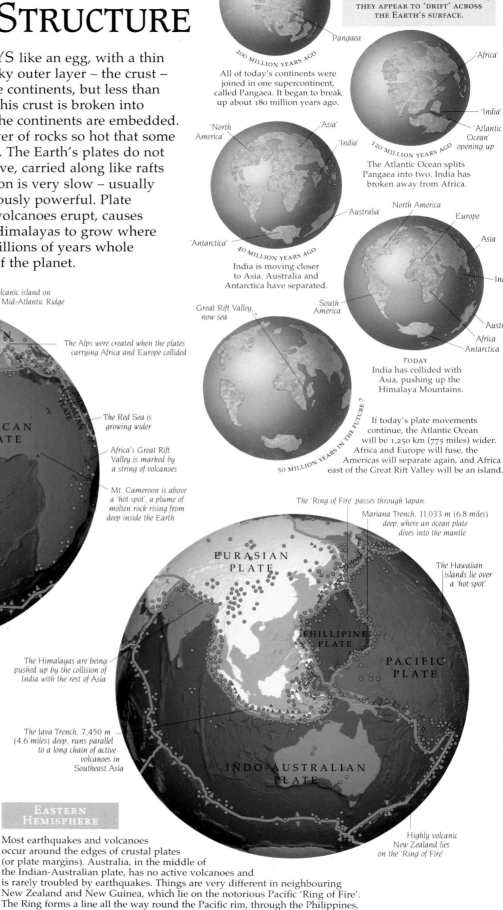

The 'Ring of Fire' passes through Japan.

Mariana Trench, 11,033 m (6.8 miles) deep, where an ocean plate dives into the mantle

The Hawaiian islands lie over a 'hot spot'

EURASIAN PLATE

PHILLIPINE PLATE

PACIFIC PLATE

The Himalayas are being pushed up by the collision of India with the rest of Asia

The Java Trench, 7,450 m (4.6 miles) deep, runs parallel to a long chain of active volcanoes in Southeast Asia

INDO-AUSTRALIAN PLATE

Highly volcanic New Zealand lies on the 'Ring of Fire'

EASTERN HEMISPHERE

Most earthquakes and volcanoes occur around the edges of crustal plates (or plate margins). Australia, in the middle of the Indian-Australian plate, has no active volcanoes and is rarely troubled by earthquakes. Things are very different in neighbouring New Zealand and New Guinea, which lie on the notorious Pacific 'Ring of Fire'. The Ring forms a line all the way round the Pacific rim, through the Philippines, Japan and North America, and down the coast of South America to New Zealand.

KEYBOX

▲	MAJOR ACTIVE VOLCANO
●	MAJOR EARTHQUAKE
▶◀	SPREADING PLATES
▼	SLIDING PLATES
▶	COLLIDING PLATES

THE ATLANTIC OCEAN IS GROWING WIDER BY 2.5 CM (1 IN) A YEAR – ABOUT THE SAME SPEED THAT FINGERNAILS GROW. THE NAZCA PLATE IS SLIDING THREE TIMES FASTER UNDER SOUTH AMERICA, PUSHING UP THE ANDES.

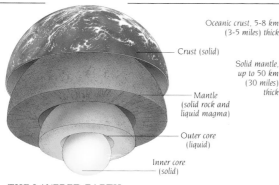

Crust (solid)

Mantle
(solid rock and
liquid magma)

Outer core
(liquid)

Inner core
(solid)

THE LAYERED EARTH
The Earth has layers, like an egg. The core is made of metals such as iron and nickel. This is surrounded by a rocky mantle and a thin crust.

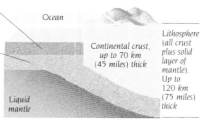

Oceanic crust, 5-8 km (3-5 miles) thick

Ocean

Continental crust, up to 70 km (45 miles) thick

Lithosphere (all crust plus solid layer of mantle). Up to 120 km (75 miles) thick

Solid mantle, up to 50 miles (30 miles) thick

Liquid mantle

CRUST
Crust is of two kinds: continental and oceanic. Continental crust is older, thicker and less dense. Beneath the crust is a solid layer of mantle. Together, these form the lithosphere, which is broken into several plates. These float on the liquid mantle layer.

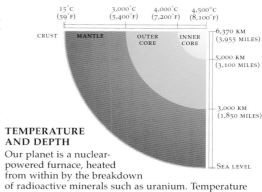

	15°C (59°F)	3,000°C (5,400°F)	4,000°C (7,200°F)	4,500°C (8,100°F)	
CRUST	MANTLE		OUTER CORE	INNER CORE	6,370 KM (3,955 MILES)

5,000 KM (3,100 MILES)

3,000 KM (1,850 MILES)

SEA LEVEL

TEMPERATURE AND DEPTH
Our planet is a nuclear-powered furnace, heated from within by the breakdown of radioactive minerals such as uranium. Temperature increases with depth: 100 km (60 miles) down it is 1,350°C (2,460°F), hot enough for rocks to melt.

Magma rising along centre of ridge

Ocean

Magma from molten mantle

Solid mantle

SPREADING PLATES
When two plates move apart, molten rock (magma) rises from the mantle and cools, forming new crust. This is called a constructive margin. Most are found in oceans.

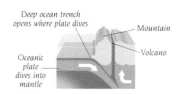

Deep ocean trench opens where plate dives

Mountain

Volcano

Oceanic plate dives into mantle

COLLIDING PLATES THAT DIVE
When two ocean plates or an ocean plate and a continent plate collide, the denser plate is forced under the other, diving down into the mantle. These are destructive margins.

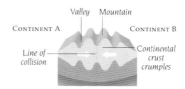

Valley   Mountain

CONTINENT A   CONTINENT B

Line of collision

Continental crust crumples

COLLIDING PLATES THAT BUCKLE
When two continents collide, their plates fuse, crumple and push upwards. Mountain ranges such as the Himalayas and the Urals have been formed in this way.

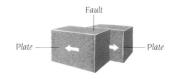

Fault

Plate   Plate

SLIDING PLATES
When two plates slide past one another, intense friction is created along the 'fault line' between them, causing earthquakes. These are called conservative margins.

MID-ATLANTIC RIDGE ICELAND
Most constructive margins are found beneath oceans, but here in volcanic Iceland one comes to the surface.

VOLCANO JAVA
Diving plates often build volcanic islands and mountain chains. Deep ocean trenches form offshore.

FOLDING STRATA ENGLAND
The clash of continental plates may cause the Earth to buckle and twist far from the collision zone.

SAN ANDREAS FAULT
A huge earthquake is expected soon somewhere along California's San Andreas Fault, seen here.

EXPLOSIVE VOLCANO
About 50 of the world's 600 or so active volcanoes erupt each year. Explosive pressure is created by the build-up of magma, gases, or super-heated steam.

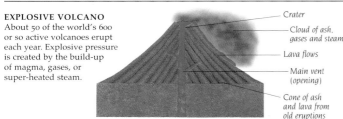

Crater

Cloud of ash, gases and steam

Lava flows

Main vent (opening)

Cone of ash and lava from old eruptions

DIRECTION OF OCEAN PLATE MOVEMENT

HOT SPOT HAWAII
Hawaii is on a 'hot spot' in the Earth's crust. This is a plume of hot magma that rises from the mantle and breaks through the thin ocean crust to feed a volcano. As the crust moves, the volcano is carried away, but the hot spot stays, forming a new volcano.

Maui

Hawaii rises more than 10,000 m (33,000 ft) from the ocean floor

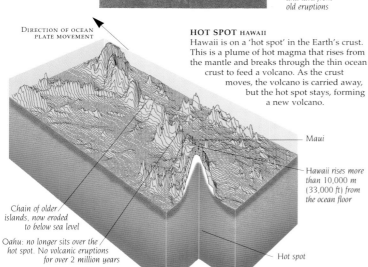

Chain of older islands, now eroded to below sea level

Oahu: no longer sits over the hot spot. No volcanic eruptions for over 2 million years

Hot spot

This map shows some of the worst natural disasters in recorded history. Over one million earthquakes and about 50 volcanic eruptions are detected every year. Most are minor or occur where there are few people, so there is no loss of human life or great damage to property. But crowded cities and poorly-constructed buildings are putting ever-greater numbers at risk.

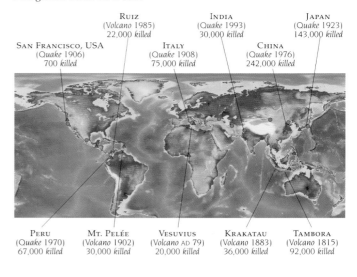

RUIZ (Volcano 1985) 22,000 killed

INDIA (Quake 1993) 30,000 killed

JAPAN (Quake 1923) 143,000 killed

SAN FRANCISCO, USA (Quake 1906) 700 killed

ITALY (Quake 1908) 75,000 killed

CHINA (Quake 1976) 242,000 killed

PERU (Quake 1970) 67,000 killed

MT. PELÉE (Volcano 1902) 30,000 killed

VESUVIUS (Volcano AD 79) 20,000 killed

KRAKATAU (Volcano 1883) 36,000 killed

TAMBORA (Volcano 1815) 92,000 killed

SHAPING THE LANDSCAPE

LANDSCAPES ARE CREATED and changed – even destroyed – in a continuous cycle. Over millions of years, constant movements of the Earth's plates have built its continents, islands and mountains. But as soon as new land is formed, it is shaped (or 'eroded') by the forces of wind, water, ice and heat. Sometimes change is quick, as when a river floods and cuts a new channel, or a landslide cascades down a mountain slope. But usually change is so slow that it is invisible to the human eye. Extremes of heat and cold crack open rocks and expose them to attack by wind and water. Rivers and glaciers scour out valleys, the wind piles up sand dunes, and the sea attacks shorelines and cliffs. Eroded materials are blown away or carried along by rivers, piling up as sediments on valley floors or the sea bed. Over millions of years these may be compressed into rock and pushed up to form new land. As soon as the land is exposed to the elements, the cycle of erosion begins again.

KEY TO ALL MAPS

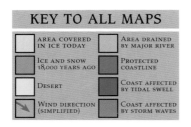

☐	AREA COVERED IN ICE TODAY	☐	AREA DRAINED BY MAJOR RIVER
☐	ICE AND SNOW 18,000 YEARS AGO	☐	PROTECTED COASTLINE
☐	DESERT	☐	COAST AFFECTED BY TIDAL SWELL
➔	WIND DIRECTION (SIMPLIFIED)	☐	COAST AFFECTED BY STORM WAVES

THIS GLOBE SHOWS NORTH AMERICA AND THE DIFFERENT FORCES WORKING ON ITS LANDSCAPE. THE LANDSCAPE IN EVERY PART OF THE WORLD IS CHANGED BY THE ACTION OF ICE, SEA, WIND AND WATER

THE 'ROOF OF NORTH AMERICA'

Steeply-sloping Denali (also called Mt. McKinley), Alaska, is North America's highest mountain at 6,194 m (20,320 ft). It is a fairly 'young' mountain, less than 70 million years old. The gently sloping Appalachians in the east of the continent are very much older. Once, they were probably higher than Denali is today. But more than 300 million years of ice, rain and wind have ground them down.

GREENLAND IS the world's largest island, and is not at all green as its name suggests – consisting mainly of ice and snow. In AD 982 the Norwegian Erik the Red, who had been banished to the island for three years, named it Greenland in an effort to make people go there.

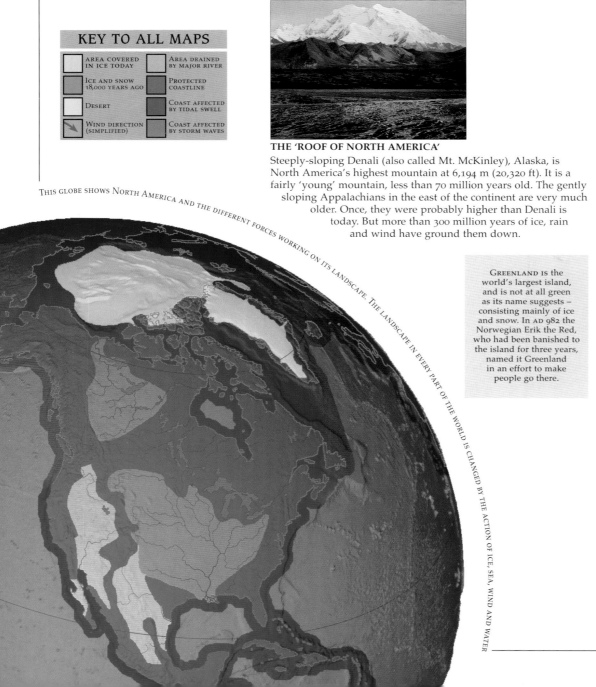

ALASKA

☐ Areas close to the North Pole are permanently covered in snow and ice. Glaciers are rivers of ice that flow towards the sea. Some glaciers are more than 60 km (40 miles) long.

CAPE COD

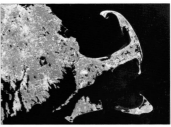

☐ Cape Cod, a sandy peninsula 105 km (65 miles) long, juts out like a beckoning finger into the Atlantic Ocean. Its strangely-curved coastline has been shaped by wave action.

DEATH VALLEY

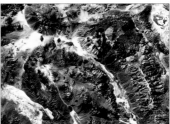

☐ Death Valley is the hottest, driest place in North America. Its floor is covered in sand and salt. Winds sweeping across the valley endlessly reshape the loose surface.

MISSISSIPPI RIVER

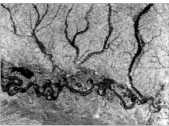

☐ The Mississippi River and its many tributaries frequently change course. Where two loops are close together, the river may cut a new path between them, leaving an 'ox-bow lake'.

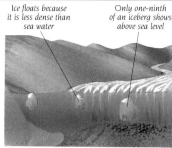

Ice floats because it is less dense than sea water

Only one-ninth of an iceberg shows above sea level

A GLACIER REACHES THE SEA

When a glacier enters the sea, its front edge or 'snout' breaks up and forms icebergs – a process called calving. These 'ice mountains' are then carried away by ocean currents.

ICE COVER
key on opposite page

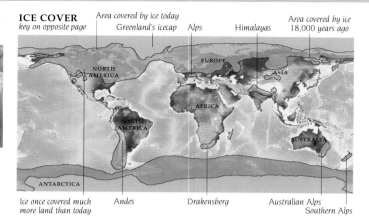

Area covered by ice today
Greenland's icecap
Alps
Himalayas
Area covered by ice 18,000 years ago

NORTH AMERICA
EUROPE
ASIA
AFRICA
SOUTH AMERICA
AUSTRALIA
ANTARCTICA

Ice once covered much more land than today
Andes
Drakensberg
Australian Alps
Southern Alps

NORDFJORD NORWAY

One sign of glacial action on the landscape is the fjord. These long, narrow, steep-sided inlets are found along the coasts of Norway, Alaska, Chile and New Zealand. They mark the points where glaciers once entered the sea.

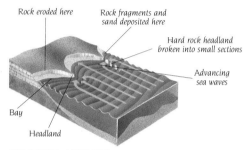

Rock eroded here
Rock fragments and sand deposited here
Hard rock headland broken into small sections
Advancing sea waves
Bay
Headland

COASTAL ATTACK

The ceaseless push and pull of waves on a shore can destroy even the hardest rocks. The softest rocks are eroded first, leaving headlands of hard rock that survive a little longer.

COASTAL EROSION
key on opposite page

Northwest Europe's shorelines are heavily eroded by Atlantic storms

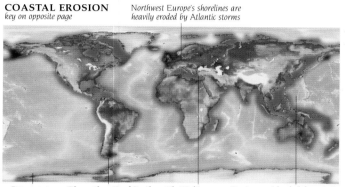

Permanent ice protects Antarctica's shores
The southern tip of South America is notorious for its devastating storms
The Mediterranean Sea is enclosed by land, so there is little coastal erosion
Islands help protect Asia's mainland from advancing waves

WAVE POWER

The powerful action of waves on an exposed coast can erode a coastline by several metres (feet) a year.

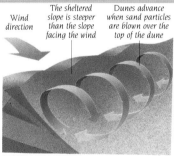

Wind direction
The sheltered slope is steeper than the slope facing the wind
Dunes advance when sand particles are blown over the top of the dune

DESERT DUNE

Dunes are slow-moving mounds or ridges of sand found in deserts and along some coastlines. They only form when the wind's direction and speed is fairly constant.

THE GREAT DESERTS
key on opposite page

Kara Kum
Sahara
Arabian
Takla Makan

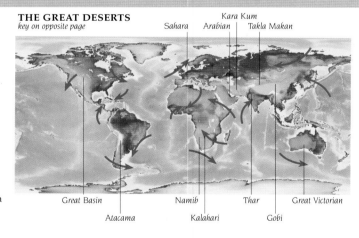

Great Basin
Atacama
Namib
Kalahari
Thar
Gobi
Great Victorian

NAMIB DESERT SOUTHERN AFRICA

The sand dunes seen in the centre of the picture are about 50 m (160 feet) high. Winds are driving them slowly but relentlessly towards the right. Not all deserts are sandy. Wind may blow away all the loose sand and gravel, leaving bare rock.

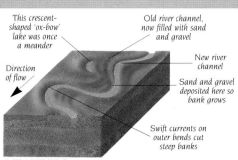

This crescent-shaped 'ox-bow' lake was once a meander
Old river channel, now filled with sand and gravel
Direction of flow
New river channel
Sand and gravel deposited here so bank grows
Swift currents on outer bends cut steep banks

MEANDERS

River banks are worn away most on the outside of bends, where water flows fastest. Eroded sand and gravel are built up into banks on the inside of bends, in slower-moving water.

THE LARGEST RIVER BASINS
key on opposite page

Lena
Ob'
Yenisey
Amur

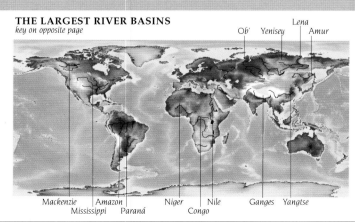

Mackenzie
Mississippi
Amazon
Paraná
Niger
Congo
Nile
Ganges
Yangtse

WINDING RIVER ALASKA

The more a river winds across a plain, the longer it becomes and the more slowly it flows.

CLIMATE AND VEGETATION

THE EARTH IS the only planet in our solar system which supports life. Most of our planet has a breathable atmosphere, and sufficient light, heat and water to support a wide range of plants and animals. The main influences on an area's climate are the amount of sunshine it receives (which varies with latitude and season), how close it is to the influence of ocean currents, and its height above sea level. Since there is more sunlight at the Equator than elsewhere, and rainfall is highest here too, this is where we find the habitats which have more species of plants and animals than anywhere else: rain-forests, coral reefs and mangrove swamps. Where rainfall is very low, and where it is either too hot, such as in deserts, or too cold, few plants and animals can survive. Only the icy North and South Poles, and the frozen tops of high mountains, are practically without life.

WEATHER EXTREMES

Weather is a powerful influence on how we feel, the clothes we wear, the buildings we live in, the colour of our skin, the plants that grow around us, and what we eat and drink. Extreme weather events such as heatwaves, hurricanes, blizzards, tornadoes, sandstorms, droughts and floods, can be terrifyingly destructive.

TORNADO
Tornadoes are whirlwinds of cold air that develop when thunderclouds cross warm land. They are extremely violent and unpredictable. Windspeeds often exceed 300 km (180 miles) per hour.

TROPICAL STORMS
These devastating winds develop when air spirals upwards above warm seas. More air is sucked in and the storm begins to move. They bring torrential rain, thunder and lightning and destruction.

DROUGHT
Long periods without water kill plants. Stripped of its protective covering of vegetation, the soil is easily blown away.

OCEAN CURRENTS

Currents are a powerful influence on climates. They are like great rivers in the ocean that carry warm water (orange) away from the Equator and cold water (blue) towards the Equator.

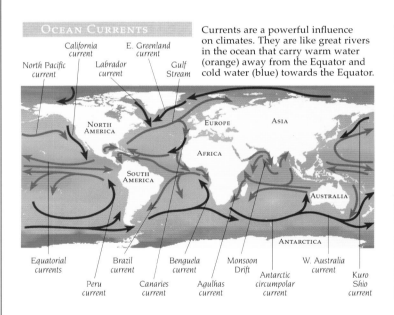

California current
E. Greenland current
North Pacific current
Labrador current
Gulf Stream
NORTH AMERICA
EUROPE
ASIA
AFRICA
SOUTH AMERICA
AUSTRALIA
ANTARCTICA

Equatorial currents
Brazil current
Peru current
Canaries current
Benguela current
Agulhas current
Monsoon Drift
Antarctic circumpolar current
W. Australia current
Kuro Shio current

MAIN STORM ZONES

Storms combine very high winds with heavy rainfall (tropical storms) or driving snow (blizzards). Typhoons, cyclones, hurricanes and willy-willies are regional names for tropical storms.

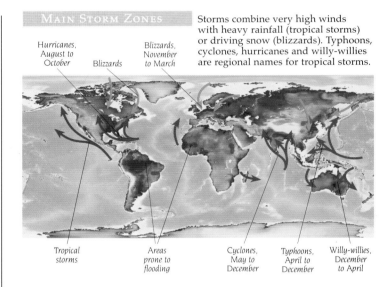

Hurricanes, August to October
Blizzards
Blizzards, November to March

Tropical storms
Areas prone to flooding
Cyclones, May to December
Typhoons, April to December
Willy-willies, December to April

TEMPERATURE

Average temperatures are very different around the world. Areas close to the Equator are usually hot (orange on the map); those close to the Poles usually cold (deep blue). The hottest areas move during the year from the Southern to the Northern hemispheres.

AVERAGE JANUARY TEMPERATURE

AVERAGE JULY TEMPERATURE

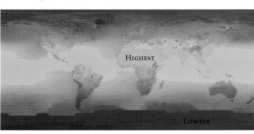

Arctic Circle
Tropic of Cancer
Equator
Tropic of Capricorn
Antarctic Circle

HIGHEST
LOWEST

HIGHEST: 58°C (136°F), Sahara

LOWEST: -89°C (-129°F), Antarctica

RAINFALL

The wettest areas (grey) lie near the Equator. The driest are found close to the tropics, in the centre of continents, or at the Poles. Elsewhere, rainfall varies with the season, but it is usually highest in summer. Asia's wet season is known as the monsoon.

AVERAGE JANUARY RAINFALL

AVERAGE JULY RAINFALL

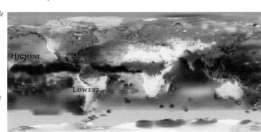

Arctic Circle
Tropic of Cancer
Equator
Tropic of Capricorn
Antarctic Circle

HIGHEST
LOWEST

HIGHEST IN 1 YEAR: 11.68 m (460 in), Hawaii

LOWEST: No rain in more than 14 years, Atacama

BROADLEAF FOREST

Temperate climates have no great extremes of temperature, and plentiful rainfall. Drought is very unusual. Forests usually contain a wide variety of broad-leaved or deciduous trees, such as beech, oak and maple, that shed their leaves in autumn.

TUNDRA

As long as frozen soil melts for at least two months of the year, mosses, lichens and ground-hugging shrubs can survive. They are found around the Arctic Circle and on mountains.

NEEDLELEAF FOREST

Forests of cone-bearing, needleleaf trees such as pine and fir cover much of northern North America, Europe and Asia. They are evergreen and can survive long frozen winters. Most have tall, straight trunks and down-pointing branches. This reduces the amount of snow that can settle on them. The forest floor is dark because leaves absorb most of the incoming sunlight.

MEDITERRANEAN

Hot dry summers and warm wet winters typical of this region are also found in small areas of Southern Africa, the Americas and Australia. Mediterranean-type vegetation can vary from dense forest to thinly spread evergreen shrubs.

TRAVELLING SOUTHWARD FROM THE NORTH POLE, A NUMBER OF DISTINCTIVE LIFE ZONES OR 'BIOMES' CAN BE SEEN. PLANT AND ANIMAL LIFE IS CLOSELY ADAPTED TO LOCAL CLIMATE

NORTH POLE Ⓐ
Arctic Circle
Needleleaf Forest
Tundra
NORTH AMERICA
Needleleaf Forest
Broadleaf Forest
EUROPE
Mediterranean
MEDITERRANEAN SEA
Tropic of Cancer
CARIBBEAN SEA
Hot Desert
AFRICA
ATLANTIC
Dry woodland
Tropical Grassland
Equator
Tropical Rainforest
Tropical Rainforest
Dry Woodland
OCEAN
SOUTH AMERICA
Mountain
PACIFIC OCEAN
Tropical Grassland
Tropic of Capricorn
Antarctic Circle
ANTARCTICA
SOUTH POLE

MOUNTAIN

Vegetation changes with height because the temperature drops and wind increases. Even on the Equator, mountain peaks can be covered in snow. Although trees may cloak the lower slopes, at higher altitudes they give way to sparser vegetation. Near the top, only tundra-type plants can survive.

TROPICAL RAINFOREST

The lush forests found near the Equator depend on year-round high temperatures and heavy rainfall. Worldwide, they may contain 50,000 different kinds of trees and support several million other plant and animal species. Trees are often festooned with climbing plants, or covered with ferns and orchids that have rooted in pockets of water and soil on trunks and branches.

DRY WOODLAND

Plants in many parts of the tropics have to cope with high temperatures and long periods without rain. Some store water in enlarged stems or trunks, or limit water losses by having small, spiny leaves. In dry (but not desert) conditions, trees are widely spaced, with expanses of grassland between, called savannah.

HOT DESERT

Very few plants and animals can survive in hot deserts. Rainfall is low – under 10 cm (4 in) a year. Temperatures often rise above 40°C (104°F) during the day, but drop to freezing point at night. High winds and shifting sands can be a further hazard to life. Only specially adapted plants, such as cacti, can survive.

NORTH-SOUTH CROSS-SECTION THROUGH EUROPE AND AFRICA

5,000 m (16,404 ft)

THE LINE RUNNING BETWEEN POINTS A AND B ON THE MAP IS THE LINE OF THE CROSS-SECTION

Tundra-type vegetation
Mediterranean-type vegetation
Needleleaf forest
Tundra-type vegetation
Temperate rainforest
Tundra-type vegetation
Tropical rainforest
Dry woodland
Tropical grassland
Mediterranean-type vegetation
Tundra
Needleleaf forest
Broadleaf forest
Temperate grassland
Mediterranean-type vegetation
Hot desert
Tropical grassland

SEA LEVEL Ⓐ
Arctic Ocean
Lappland
Black Sea
Mediterranean Sea
Turkey
TROPIC OF CANCER
Ruwenzori Range
TROPIC OF CAPRICORN
Drakensberg
Ⓑ
Indian Ocean

-4,000 m (-13,123) ft

PEOPLE AND PLANET

SOON, THERE WILL BE 6,000 million people on Earth, and numbers are rising at the rate of about one million every week. People are not distributed evenly. Some areas, such as parts of Europe, India and China, are very densely populated. Other areas – particularly deserts, polar regions and mountains – can support very few people. Almost half of the world's population now lives in towns or cities. This is quite a recent development. Until 1800, most people lived in small villages in the countryside, and worked on the land. But since then more and more people have lived and worked in much larger settlements. A century ago, most of the world's largest cities were in Europe and North America, where new industries and businesses were flourishing. Today, the most rapidly-growing cities are in Asia, South America and Africa. People who move to these cities are usually young adults, so the birth rate amongst these new populations is very high.

A CROWDED PLANET?

If the 5.5 billion people alive today stood close together, they could all fit into an area no larger than the small Caribbean island of Jamaica. Of course, so many people could not live in such a small place. Areas with few people are usually very cold, such as land near the poles and in mountains, or very dry, such as deserts. Areas with large populations often have fertile land and a good climate for crops. Cities support huge populations because they are wealthy enough to buy in everything they need.

THERE ARE JUST OVER 400 MILLION PEOPLE IN NORTH AMERICA. NEARLY 7 IN 10 LIVE IN A CITY

NORTH AMERICA

New York
14.6 million

Los Angeles
10.1 million

JAMAICA

Mexico City
20.9 million

THERE ARE JUST OVER 300 MILLION PEOPLE IN SOUTH AMERICA. MORE THAN 7 IN 10 LIVE IN A CITY

SOUTH AMERICA

Rio de Janeiro
11.7 million

São Paulo
18.7 million

Buenos Aires
11.7 million

MAIN MAP KEY

	ORANGE REPRESENTS TOWNS AND CITIES
•	CITY WITH MORE THAN 1 MILLION PEOPLE.
•	CITY WITH MORE THAN 10 MILLION PEOPLE

LONDON

MILLIONAIRE CITIES 1900

Less than a century ago there were only 13 cities with more than one million people living in them. All the cities were in the northern hemisphere. The largest was London, with seven million people.

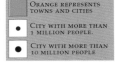

NEW YORK

MILLIONAIRE CITIES 1950

By 1950, there were nearly 70 cities with more than one million inhabitants. The largest was New York.

SAHARA AFRICA

The Sahara, like all deserts, is thinly populated. The Tuareg of the northern Sahara are nomads. They travel in small groups because food sources are scarce. Their homes have to be portable.

MONGOLIA ASIA

Traditionally, Mongolia's nomadic people lived by herding their animals across the steppe. Today, their felt tents, or gers, are often set up next to more permanent houses.

AMAZONIA SOUTH AMERICA

The Yanomami people gather plants in the rainforest and hunt game, but they also grow crops in small forest gardens. Several families live together in a 'village' under one huge roof.

MALI AFRICA

The Dogon people of Mali use mud to construct their elaborate villages. Every family has its own huts and walled areas in which their animals are penned for the night.

The world's population in 1500 was about 425 million

The world's population in 1600 was about 545 million

The world's population in 1700 was about 610 million

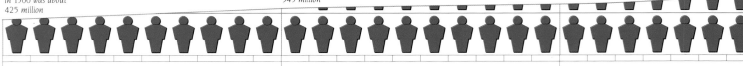

1500

1600

1700

EACH FIGURE ON THE GRAPH REPRESENTS 500 MILLION PEOPLE

POOR SUBURB
Densely-populated 'shanty towns' have grown on the fringes of many cities in the developing world. Houses are usually built from discarded materials.

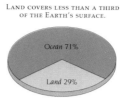

RICH SUBURB
Cities are often surrounded by areas where the richest people live. Population densities are low, and the houses may be luxurious, with large gardens or swimming pools. People in these suburbs rely on their cars for transport. This allows them to live a great distance from places of work and leisure in the city centre.

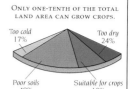

LAND COVERS LESS THAN A THIRD OF THE EARTH'S SURFACE.

Ocean 71%
Land 29%

ONLY ONE-TENTH OF THE TOTAL LAND AREA CAN GROW CROPS.

Too cold 17%
Too dry 24%
Poor soils 49%
Suitable for crops 10%

CULTIVATION
Only a small proportion of the Earth's surface can grow crops. It may be possible to bring more land – such as deserts – into production, but yields may be low and costly.

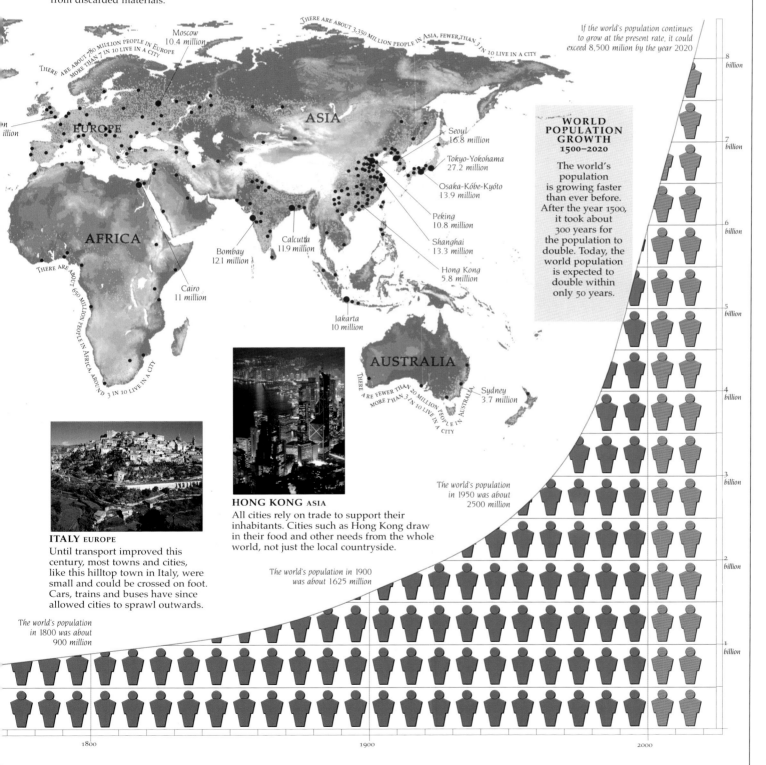

THERE ARE ABOUT 3,350 MILLION PEOPLE IN ASIA, FEWER THAN 3 IN 10 LIVE IN A CITY

THERE ARE ABOUT 780 MILLION PEOPLE IN EUROPE MORE THAN 7 IN 10 LIVE IN A CITY

Moscow 10.4 million

EUROPE

ASIA

Seoul 16.8 million

Tokyo-Yokohama 27.2 million

Osaka-Kóbe-Kyóto 13.9 million

Peking 10.8 million

Shanghai 13.3 million

Hong Kong 5.8 million

AFRICA

THERE ARE ABOUT 650 MILLION PEOPLE IN AFRICA, AROUND 3 IN 10 LIVE IN A CITY

Bombay 12.1 million

Calcutta 11.9 million

Cairo 11 million

Jakarta 10 million

AUSTRALIA

THERE ARE FEWER THAN 20 MILLION PEOPLE IN AUSTRALIA, MORE THAN 3 IN 10 LIVE IN A CITY

Sydney 3.7 million

If the world's population continues to grow at the present rate, it could exceed 8,500 million by the year 2020

8 billion

7 billion

6 billion

WORLD POPULATION GROWTH 1500–2020

The world's population is growing faster than ever before. After the year 1500, it took about 300 years for the population to double. Today, the world population is expected to double within only 50 years.

5 billion

4 billion

3 billion

2 billion

1 billion

The world's population in 1950 was about 2500 million

HONG KONG ASIA
All cities rely on trade to support their inhabitants. Cities such as Hong Kong draw in their food and other needs from the whole world, not just the local countryside.

The world's population in 1900 was about 1625 million

ITALY EUROPE
Until transport improved this century, most towns and cities, like this hilltop town in Italy, were small and could be crossed on foot. Cars, trains and buses have since allowed cities to sprawl outwards.

The world's population in 1800 was about 900 million

1800

1900

2000

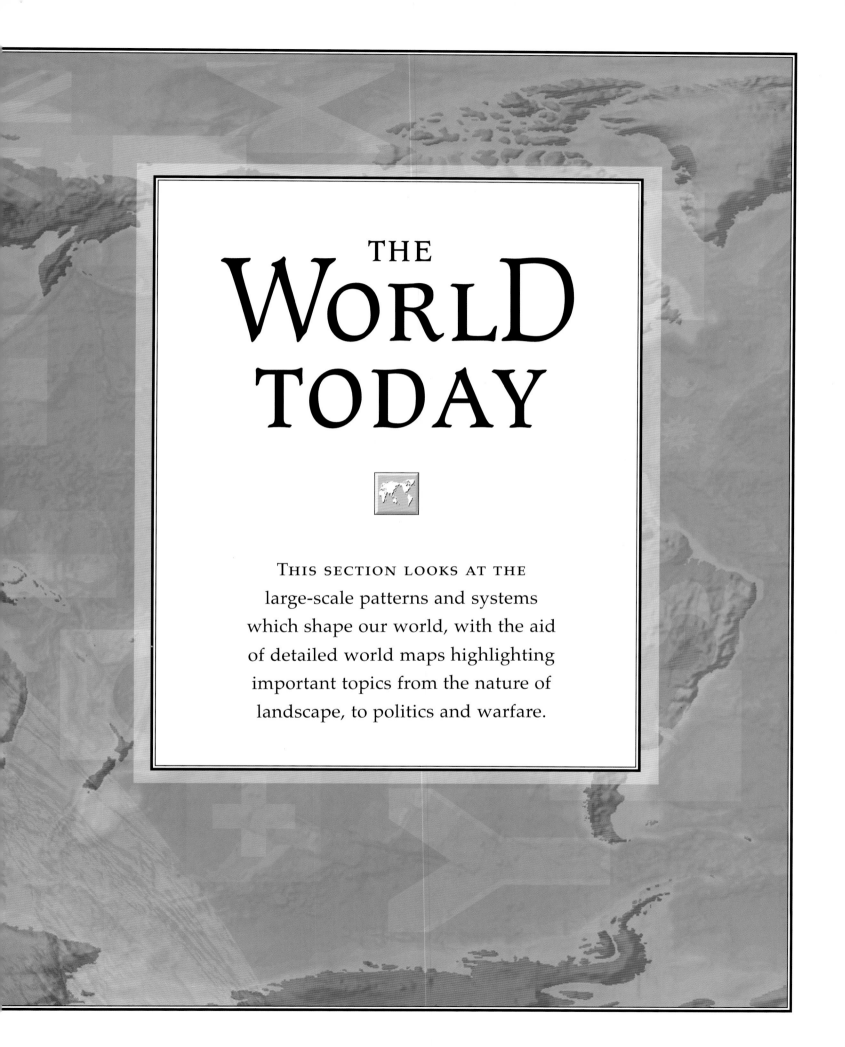

THE
WORLD
TODAY

THIS SECTION LOOKS AT THE
large-scale patterns and systems
which shape our world, with the aid
of detailed world maps highlighting
important topics from the nature of
landscape, to politics and warfare.

THE POLITICAL WORLD

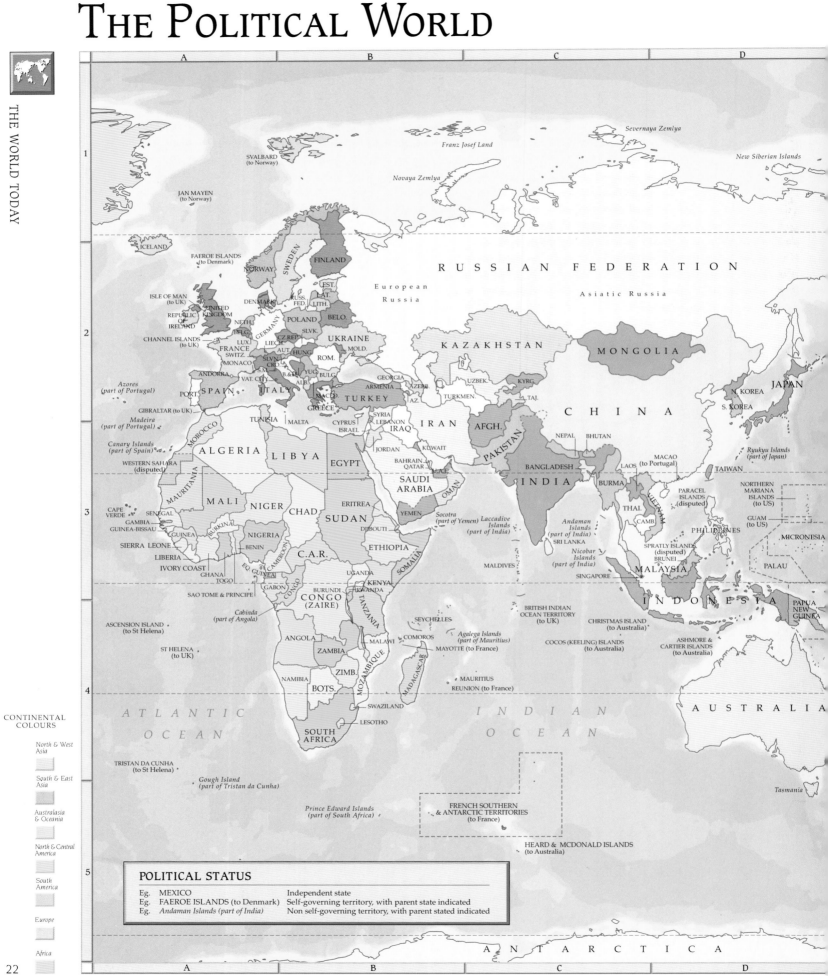

A B C D

1

SVALBARD
(to Norway)

Franz Josef Land

Severnaya Zemlya

New Siberian Islands

Novaya Zemlya

JAN MAYEN
(to Norway)

ICELAND

FAEROE ISLANDS
(to Denmark)

NORWAY

SWEDEN

FINLAND

RUSSIAN FEDERATION

European
Russia

Asiatic Russia

ISLE OF MAN
(to UK)

EST.
LAT.
LITH.

DENMARK

RUSS.
FED.

UNITED
KINGDOM

REPUBLIC
OF
IRELAND

NETH.

POLAND

BELO.

KAZAKHSTAN

MONGOLIA

2

CHANNEL ISLANDS
(to UK)

BELG.
LUX.
FRANCE
SWITZ.

GERMANY

LIECH.

CZ.REP.

SLVK.

UKRAINE

MOLD.

AUT. HUNG.

ROM.

UZBEK.

KYRG.

JAPAN

ANDORRA

S.M.
MONACO
VAT. CITY

SLVN
CRO.

B.&H.
YUG.

BULG.

ALB.

GEORGIA

ARMENIA

AZERB.

TURKMEN.

TAJ.

N. KOREA

S. KOREA

CHINA

Azores
(part of Portugal)

PORT.

SPAIN

ITALY

MACD.

GREECE

TURKEY

AZ.

GIBRALTAR (to UK)

Madeira
(part of Portugal)

TUNISIA

MALTA

CYPRUS
ISRAEL

SYRIA
LEBANON

IRAQ

IRAN

AFGH.

NEPAL

BHUTAN

MACAO
(to Portugal)

Ryukyu Islands
(part of Japan)

Canary Islands
(part of Spain)

MOROCCO

JORDAN

KUWAIT

PAKISTAN

BANGLADESH

LAOS

TAIWAN

WESTERN SAHARA
(disputed)

ALGERIA

LIBYA

EGYPT

BAHRAIN
QATAR

U.A.E.

INDIA

BURMA

NORTHERN
MARIANA
ISLANDS
(to US)

3

MAURITANIA

SAUDI
ARABIA

OMAN

THAIL.

PARACEL
ISLANDS
(disputed)

GUAM
(to US)

MALI

NIGER

CHAD

ERITREA

YEMEN

Socotra
(part of Yemen)

Laccadive
Islands
(part of India)

Andaman
Islands
(part of India)

CAMB.

VIETNAM

PHILIPPINES

MICRONESIA

CAPE
VERDE

SENEGAL

SUDAN

DJIBOUTI

SRI LANKA

SPRATLY ISLANDS
(disputed)

GAMBIA
GUINEA-BISSAU

BURKINA

NIGERIA

Nicobar
Islands
(part of India)

BRUNEI

GUINEA

BENIN

ETHIOPIA

MALDIVES

SINGAPORE

MALAYSIA

PALAU

SIERRA LEONE

C.A.R.

LIBERIA

CAMEROON

IVORY COAST

UGANDA

SOMALIA

INDONESIA

PAPUA
NEW
GUINEA

GHANA
TOGO

EQ. GUINEA

GABON

CONGO

BURUNDI

RWANDA

KENYA

BRITISH INDIAN
OCEAN TERRITORY
(to UK)

CHRISTMAS ISLAND
(to Australia)

SAO TOME & PRINCIPE

CONGO
(ZAIRE)

TANZANIA

SEYCHELLES

Agalega Islands
(part of Mauritius)

COCOS (KEELING) ISLANDS
(to Australia)

ASHMORE &
CARTIER ISLANDS
(to Australia)

Cabinda
(part of Angola)

ASCENSION ISLAND
(to St Helena)

ANGOLA

MALAWI

COMOROS

MAYOTTE (to France)

ST HELENA
(to UK)

ZAMBIA

MOZAMBIQUE

MADAGASCAR

MAURITIUS

REUNION (to France)

NAMIBIA

ZIMB.

4

BOTS.

SWAZILAND

AUSTRALIA

ATLANTIC
OCEAN

LESOTHO

INDIAN
OCEAN

SOUTH
AFRICA

TRISTAN DA CUNHA
(to St Helena)

Gough Island
(part of Tristan da Cunha)

Tasmania

Prince Edward Islands
(part of South Africa)

FRENCH SOUTHERN
& ANTARCTIC TERRITORIES
(to France)

HEARD & MCDONALD ISLANDS
(to Australia)

5

POLITICAL STATUS

Eg.	MEXICO	Independent state
Eg.	FAEROE ISLANDS (to Denmark)	Self-governing territory, with parent state indicated
Eg.	Andaman Islands (part of India)	Non self-governing territory, with parent stated indicated

ANTARCTICA

A B C D

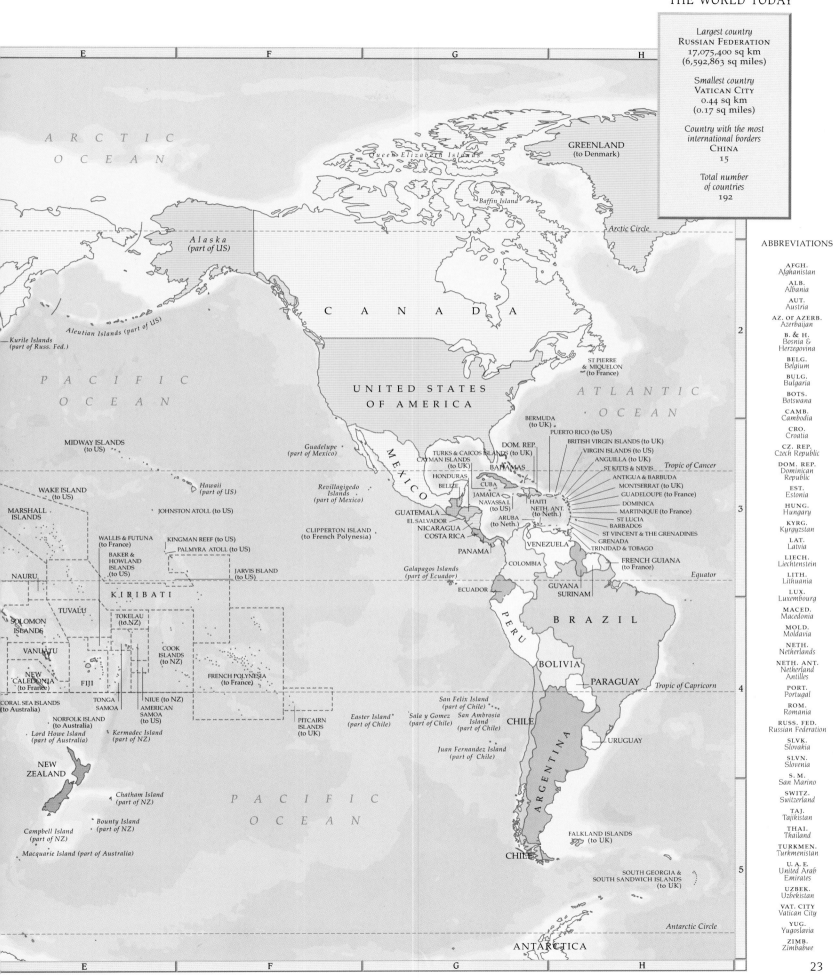

Largest country
RUSSIAN FEDERATION
17,075,400 sq km
(6,592,863 sq miles)

Smallest country
VATICAN CITY
0.44 sq km
(0.17 sq miles)

Country with the most
international borders
CHINA
15

Total number
of countries
192

A R C T I C

O C E A N

GREENLAND
(to Denmark)

Queen Elizabeth Islands

Baffin Island

Arctic Circle

*Alaska
(part of US)*

Aleutian Islands (part of US)

*Kurile Islands
(part of Russ. Fed.)*

C A N A D A

2

ST PIERRE
& MIQUELON
(to France)

P A C I F I C

O C E A N

A T L A N T I C

O C E A N

UNITED STATES
OF AMERICA

MIDWAY ISLANDS
(to US)

*Guadelupe
(part of Mexico)*

BERMUDA
(to UK)

PUERTO RICO (to US)
BRITISH VIRGIN ISLANDS (to UK)
VIRGIN ISLANDS (to US)
ANGUILLA (to UK)
ST KITTS & NEVIS

DOM. REP.

TURKS & CAICOS ISLANDS (to UK)
CAYMAN ISLANDS
(to UK)
BAHAMAS

Tropic of Cancer

WAKE ISLAND
(to US)

*Hawaii
(part of US)*

*Revillagigedo
Islands
(part of Mexico)*

HONDURAS
BELIZE

CUBA

ANTIGUA & BARBUDA
MONTSERRAT (to UK)
GUADELOUPE (to France)
DOMINICA
MARTINIQUE (to France)
ST LUCIA
BARBADOS
ST VINCENT & THE GRENADINES
GRENADA
TRINIDAD & TOBAGO

MARSHALL
ISLANDS

JOHNSTON ATOLL (to US)

JAMAICA
NAVASSA I.
(to US)

HAITI
NETH. ANT.
(to Neth.)

3

GUATEMALA
EL SALVADOR
NICARAGUA
COSTA RICA

ARUBA
(to Neth.)

WALLIS & FUTUNA
(to France)

KINGMAN REEF (to US)
PALMYRA ATOLL (to US)

*CLIPPERTON ISLAND
(to French Polynesia)*

PANAMA

VENEZUELA

FRENCH GUIANA
(to France)

NAURU

BAKER &
HOWLAND
ISLANDS
(to US)

JARVIS ISLAND
(to US)

COLOMBIA

*Galapagos Islands
(part of Ecuador)*

Equator

K I R I B A T I

ECUADOR

GUYANA
SURINAM

SOLOMON
ISLANDS

TUVALU

TOKELAU
(to NZ)

B R A Z I L

VANUATU

COOK
ISLANDS
(to NZ)

P E R U

*FRENCH POLYNESIA
(to France)*

BOLIVIA

NEW
CALEDONIA
(to France)

FIJI

PARAGUAY

Tropic of Capricorn

4

CORAL SEA ISLANDS
(to Australia)

TONGA
SAMOA

NIUE (to NZ)

AMERICAN
SAMOA
(to US)

*San Felix Island
(part of Chile)*

CHILE

NORFOLK ISLAND
(to Australia)

*Lord Howe Island
(part of Australia)*

*Kermadec Island
(part of NZ)*

PITCAIRN
ISLANDS
(to UK)

*Easter Island
(part of Chile)*

*Sala y Gomez
(part of Chile)*

*San Ambrosia
Island
(part of Chile)*

A R G E N T I N A

URUGUAY

NEW
ZEALAND

*Juan Fernandez Island
(part of Chile)*

*Chatham Island
(part of NZ)*

P A C I F I C

*Bounty Island
(part of NZ)*

O C E A N

*Campbell Island
(part of NZ)*

FALKLAND ISLANDS
(to UK)

Macquarie Island (part of Australia)

5

SOUTH GEORGIA &
SOUTH SANDWICH ISLANDS
(to UK)

CHILE

Antarctic Circle

ANTARCTICA

ABBREVIATIONS

AFGH.
Afghanistan

ALB.
Albania

AUT.
Austria

AZ. or AZERB.
Azerbaijan

B. & H.
Bosnia &
Herzegovina

BELG.
Belgium

BULG.
Bulgaria

BOTS.
Botswana

CAMB.
Cambodia

CRO.
Croatia

CZ. REP.
Czech Republic

DOM. REP.
Dominican
Republic

EST.
Estonia

HUNG.
Hungary

KYRG.
Kyrgyzstan

LAT.
Latvia

LIECH.
Liechtenstein

LITH.
Lithuania

LUX.
Luxembourg

MACED.
Macedonia

MOLD.
Moldavia

NETH.
Netherlands

NETH. ANT.
Netherland
Antilles

PORT.
Portugal

ROM.
Romania

RUSS. FED.
Russian Federation

SLVK.
Slovakia

SLVN.
Slovenia

S. M.
San Marino

SWITZ.
Switzerland

TAJ.
Tajikistan

THAI.
Thailand

TURKMEN.
Turkmenistan

U. A. E.
United Arab
Emirates

UZBEK.
Uzbekistan

VAT. CITY
Vatican City

YUG.
Yugoslavia

ZIMB.
Zimbabwe

E   F   G   H

THE PHYSICAL WORLD

Greenland Sea

Spitsbergen

Franz Josef Land

Severnaya Zemlya

New Siberian Islands

Novaya Zemlya

Laptev Sea

Barents Sea

Kara Sea

Denmark Strait

Norwegian Sea

Iceland

Scandinavia

Ural Mountains

West Siberian Plain

Ob'

Central Siberian Plateau

Lena

Khrebet Cherskogo

British Isles

North Sea

Baltic Sea

North European Plain

Volga

Yenisey

S i b e r i a

Sea of Okhotsk

Bay of Biscay

E U R O P E

Alps

Carpathian Mts

Danube

Balkans Mts

Black Sea

Caucasus

Aral Sea

Lake Balkhash

A S I A

Altai Mountains

Lake Baikal

Amur

Sakhalin

Manchurian Plain

Azores

Iberian Peninsula

Mediterranean Sea

Anatolia

Caspian Sea

Zagros Mountains

Pamirs

Tien Shan

Gobi

Yellow River

Sea of Japan

Hokkaido

Maderia

Atlas Mts

Syrian Desert

Iranian Plateau

Hindu Kush

Indus

Kunlun Mountains

K2 8611m

Plateau of Tibet

Himalayas

Mount Everest 8848m

Yellow Sea

Yangtze

East China Sea

Japan

Honshū

Kyūshū

Ryukyu Islands

Canary Islands

S a h a r a

Ahaggar

Libyan Desert

Nile

Red Sea

The Gulf

Arabian Peninsula

Thar Desert

Ganges

Taiwan

Cape Verde Islands

Tibesti

A F R I C A

S a h e l

Niger

Lake Chad

Deccan

Western Ghats

Eastern Ghats

Bay of Bengal

Philippine Sea

Mariana Islands

Mariana Trench

Arabian Sea

Arabian Basin

Andaman Islands

Sri Lanka

Nicobar Islands

Mekong

South China Sea

Philippine Islands

Philippine Trench

Carolin

Gulf of Guinea

Adamawa Highlands

Ethiopian Highlands

Gulf of Aden

Horn of Africa

Maldive Islands

Malay Peninsula

Congo

Congo Basin

Great Rift Valley

Lake Victoria

Kilimanjaro 5895m

Somali Basin

Sumatra

Borneo

Celebes

East Indies

New Guinea

ATLANTIC

Ascension Island

Angola Basin

St Helena

Lake Tanganyika

Lake Nyasa

Seychelles

Java Sea

Java

Java Trench

Arafura Sea

Timor Sea

Great Barrier Re

Great Dividing

OCEAN

Zambezi

Mazambique Channel

Madagascar

INDIAN

Ninetyeast Ridge

Great Sandy Desert

Namib Desert

Kalahari Desert

Drakensberg

OCEAN

Mauritius

Réunion

AUSTRALIA

Great Victoria Desert

Nullarbor Plain

Darling

Mid-Atlantic Ridge

Cape Basin

Cape of Good Hope

Bass Strait

Tasmania

Tristan da Cunha

Gough Island

Southwest Indian Ridge

Kerguelen

Southeast Indian Ridge

Winter limit of pack ice

South Indian Basin

Summer limit of pack ice

A N T A R C T I C A

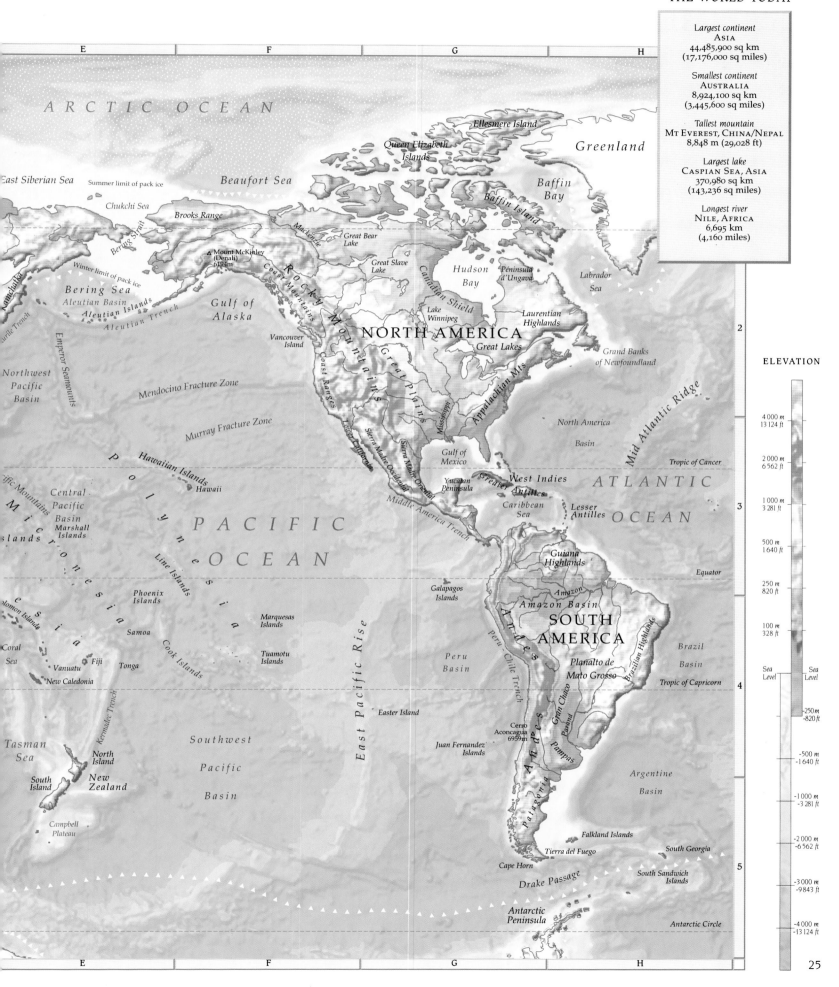

Largest continent
ASIA
44,485,900 sq km
(17,176,000 sq miles)

Smallest continent
AUSTRALIA
8,924,100 sq km
(3,445,600 sq miles)

Tallest mountain
MT EVEREST, CHINA/NEPAL
8,848 m (29,028 ft)

Largest lake
CASPIAN SEA, ASIA
370,980 sq km
(143,236 sq miles)

Longest river
NILE, AFRICA
6,695 km
(4,160 miles)

ARCTIC OCEAN

East Siberian Sea

Summer limit of pack ice

Beaufort Sea

Ellesmere Island

Queen Elizabeth Islands

Greenland

Chukchi Sea

Brooks Range

Bering Strait

△ Mount McKinley
(Denali)
6194m

Mackenzie

Great Bear Lake

Great Slave Lake

Baffin Island

Baffin Bay

Winter limit of pack ice

Bering Sea

Aleutian Basin
Aleutian Islands

Aleutian Trench

Gulf of Alaska

Vancouver Island

Hudson Bay

Péninsule d'Ungava

Labrador Sea

Kurile Trench

Kamchatka

Northwest Pacific Basin

Emperor Seamounts

Mendocino Fracture Zone

Coast Ranges

Rocky Mountains

Great Plains

NORTH AMERICA

Lake Winnipeg

Canadian Shield

Great Lakes

Laurentian Highlands

Grand Banks of Newfoundland

ELEVATION

Murray Fracture Zone

Hawaiian Islands

Hawaii

Sierra Nevada
Sierra Madre Occidental

Appalachian Mts

North America Basin

Mid Atlantic Ridge

4 000 m
13 124 ft

2 000 m
6 562 ft

Central Pacific Basin
Marshall Islands

Lower California

Sierra Madre Oriental

Gulf of Mexico

Yucatan Peninsula

West Indies
Greater Antilles

Tropic of Cancer

ATLANTIC

1 000 m
3 281 ft

Pacific Mountains

Micronesia

Islands

PACIFIC

Line Islands

Middle America Trench

Caribbean Sea

Lesser Antilles

OCEAN

500 m
1 640 ft

Phoenix Islands

OCEAN

Galapagos Islands

Guiana Highlands

Amazon

250 m
820 ft

Polynesia

Marquesas Islands

Amazon Basin

SOUTH AMERICA

Equator

Solomon Islands
Samoa

Cook Islands

Tuamotu Islands

Peru Basin

Andes

Brazilian Highlands

Brazil Basin

100 m
328 ft

Coral Sea
Vanuatu Fiji Tonga

Peru-Chile Trench

Planalto de Mato Grosso

New Caledonia

East Pacific Rise

Tropic of Capricorn

Sea Level

Sea Level

Tasman Sea

Southwest

Easter Island

△ Cerro Aconcagua
6959m

Gran Chaco

Paraná

−250 m
−820 ft

North Island

Pacific

Juan Fernandez Islands

Pampas

Argentine Basin

South Island

New Zealand

Basin

Andes

Patagonia

−500 m
−1 640 ft

−1 000 m
−3 281 ft

Campbell Plateau

Kermadec Trench

Falkland Islands

South Georgia

−2 000 m
−6 562 ft

Tierra del Fuego

South Sandwich Islands

Cape Horn

Drake Passage

−3 000 m
−9 843 ft

Antarctic Peninsula

Antarctic Circle

−4 000 m
−13 124 ft

TIME ZONES

A   B   C   D

Severnaya Zemlya

Franz Josef Land   *New Siberian Islands*

1

SVALBARD
(to Norway)   **+1**

Novaya Zemlya **+5**   **+11**

JAN MAYEN
(to Norway)

Arctic Circle

−1

ICELAND
0   FAEROE ISLANDS
(to Denmark)   **+1**   **+2**   RUSSIAN FEDERATION   **+10**

NORWAY   SWEDEN   FINLAND   **+3**   European
Russia   **+4**   **+9**

2   ISLE OF MAN
(to UK)   UNITED
KINGDOM   DENMARK   EST.
LTH.   RUSS.
FED.   **+5**   **+7** Asiatic Russia

REPUBLIC
OF
IRELAND   **0**   NETH.   POLAND   BELO.   **+4**   **+8**   **+8**

CHANNEL ISLANDS
(to UK)   BELG.   GERMANY   CZ. REP.   SLVK.   UKRAINE   KAZAKHSTAN   MONGOLIA

LUX.   LIECH.   AUT.   HUNG.   **+2**   MOLD.   **+4**   **+4**

FRANCE
SWITZ.   SLVN.   ROM.

MONACO   S.M.   CRO.   **+2**   GEORGIA   AZERB.   UZBEK.   KYRG.   JAPAN   **+8**

ANDORRA   **+1**   VAT. CITY   B.&H.   BULG.   ARMENIA   **+2** AZ.   TURKMEN.   **+5**   TAJ.   N. KOREA

*Azores
(part of Portugal)*   PORT.   SPAIN   ITALY   MACED.   TURKEY   **+2**   **+8**   S. KOREA   **+8**

0   GREECE   **+2**   SYRIA   IRAN   CHINA

GIBRALTAR (to UK)   ALB.   CYPRUS   LEBANON   **+3½**   AFGH.   **+5**

*Madeira
(part of Portugal)*   −   TUNISIA   MALTA   ISRAEL   IRAQ   **+4½**   NEPAL   BHUTAN   MACAO
(to Portugal)   TAIWAN

*Canary Islands
(part of Spain)*   MOROCCO   JORDAN   KUWAIT   PAKISTAN   **+5¾**   **+6**   LAOS

WESTERN SAHARA   ALGERIA   LIBYA   EGYPT   BAHRAIN   OMAN   BANGLADESH   **+6½**   NORTHERN
MARIANA
ISLANDS
(to US)

Tropic of Cancer   **+1**   SAUDI
ARABIA   QATAR   U.A.E.   INDIA   **+6**   BURMA   **+8**   GUAM
(to US)

MAURITANIA   MALI   NIGER   CHAD   **+2**   ERITREA   **+5½**   THAI.   **+7**   PARACEL
ISLANDS
(disputed)   **+10**

CAPE
VERDE   **0**   SUDAN   YEMEN   *Laccadive
Islands
(part of India)*   *Andaman
Islands
(part of India)*   VIETNAM   CAMB.   PHILIPPINES

−1   SENEGAL   BURKINA   NIGERIA   BENIN   DJIBOUTI   MICRONESIA

GAMBIA   GUINEA   C.A.R.   ETHIOPIA   SPRATLY ISLANDS
(disputed)   **+8**   **+10**

GUINEA-BISSAU   SIERRA LEONE   LIBERIA   IVORY COAST   GHANA   TOGO   EQ. GUINEA   CAMEROON   **+3**   SOMALIA   SRI LANKA   BRUNEI   **+9**   PALAU

Equator   **0**   GABON   CONGO   UGANDA   KENYA   MALDIVES   SINGAPORE   MALAYSIA

SAO TOME & PRINCIPE   RWANDA   BURUNDI   **+7**   INDONESIA

*Cabinda
(part of Angola)*   CONGO
(ZAIRE)   TANZANIA   SEYCHELLES   *BRITISH INDIAN
OCEAN TERRITORY
(to UK)*   **+8**   PAPUA
NEW
GUINEA

ASCENSION ISLAND ·
(to St Helena)   ANGOLA   ZAMBIA   MALAWI   COMOROS   MAYOTTE (to France)   CHRISTMAS ISLAND
(to Australia)·   **+6½**   ASHMORE &
CARTIER ISLANDS
(to Australia)

ST HELENA
(to UK)   ZIMB.   MOZAMBIQUE   **+3**   COCOS (KEELING) ISLANDS
(to Australia)

NAMIBIA   BOTS.   MADAGASCAR   *MAURITIUS
REUNION (to France)*   **+9½**

Tropic of Capricorn   **+1**   **+2**   SWAZILAND   *INDIAN*   **+8**   AUSTRALIA   **+10**

ATLANTIC   SOUTH
AFRICA   LESOTHO   *OCEAN*   **+10½**

OCEAN   **+11**

TRISTAN DA CUNHA
(to St Helena)   Greenwich Meridian   *Prince Edward Islands
(part of South Africa)*   **+5**   *Tasmania*

*Gough Island
(part of Tristan da Cunha)*

FRENCH SOUTHERN
& ANTARCTIC TERRITORIES
(to France)   **+5**   **+5**

HEARD & MCDONALD ISLANDS
(to Australia)

*The numbers
represented
thus: +2/−2,
indicate the
number of
hours ahead or
behind GMT
(Greenwich
Mean Time)
of each
time zone.*

−2	**−1**	**0**	**+1**	**+2**	**+3**	**+4**	**+5**	**+6**	**+7**	**+8**	**+9**	**+10**
	11:00	12:00	13:00	14:00	15:00	16:00	17:00	18:00	19:00	20:00	21:00	22:00

Antarctic Circle

ANTARCTICA
(except for Graham Land, Antarctica is not subject to any time zone)

A   B   C   D

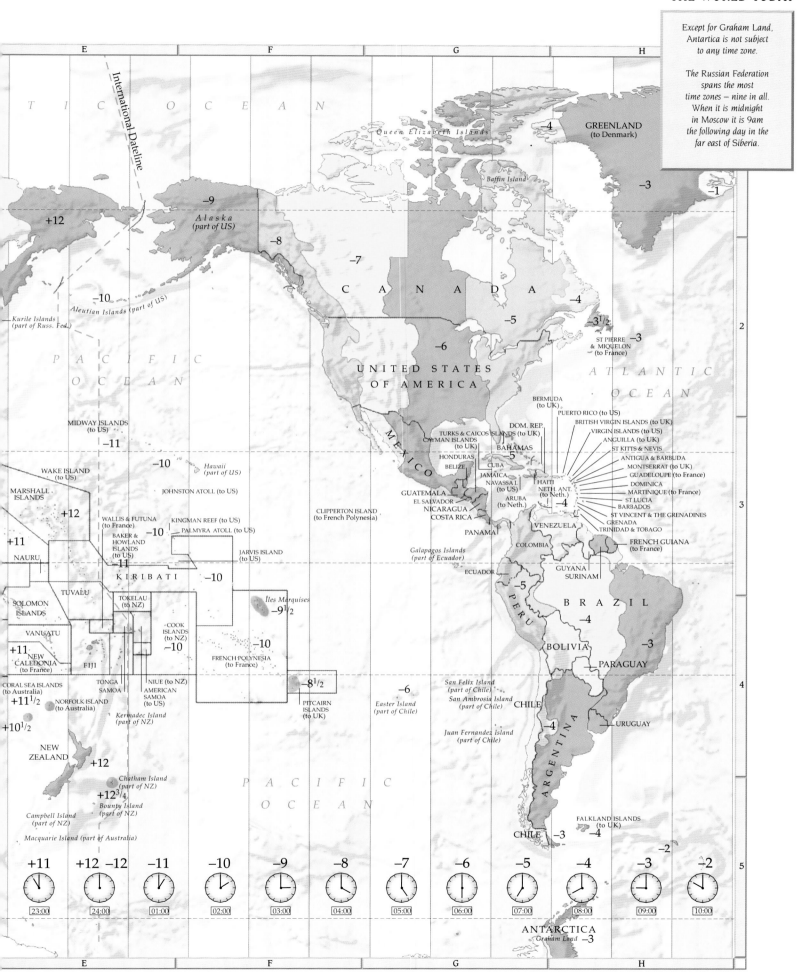

Except for Graham Land,
Antartica is not subject
to any time zone.

The Russian Federation
spans the most
time zones – nine in all.
When it is midnight
in Moscow it is 9am
the following day in the
far east of Siberia.

International Dateline

Queen Elizabeth Islands

GREENLAND
(to Denmark)

−4

Baffin Island

−3

−1

−9

Alaska
(part of US)

−8

−7

C A N A D A

−4

+12

−10

Aleutian Islands (part of US)

−5

−3¹⁄₂

Kurile Islands
(part of Russ. Fed.)

ST PIERRE
& MIQUELON
(to France)

−3

P A C I F I C

O C E A N

−6

UNITED STATES
OF AMERICA

A T L A N T I C

O C E A N

MIDWAY ISLANDS
(to US)

−11

BERMUDA
(to UK)

PUERTO RICO (to US)
BRITISH VIRGIN ISLANDS (to UK)

−10

Hawaii
(part of US)

TURKS & CAICOS ISLANDS (to UK)
CAYMAN ISLANDS
(to UK)

VIRGIN ISLANDS (to US)
ANGUILLA (to UK)
ST KITTS & NEVIS

WAKE ISLAND
(to US)

JOHNSTON ATOLL (to US)

BAHAMAS

−5

ANTIGUA & BARBUDA
MONTSERRAT (to UK)

MARSHALL
ISLANDS

HONDURAS
BELIZE

CUBA

GUADELOUPE (to France)
DOMINICA

+12

WALLIS & FUTUNA
(to France)

KINGMAN REEF (to US)

CLIPPERTON ISLAND
(to French Polynesia)

GUATEMALA

JAMAICA

NAVASSA I.
(to US)

HAITI

DOM. REP.

MARTINIQUE (to France)
ST LUCIA

−10

PALMYRA ATOLL (to US)

EL SALVADOR
NICARAGUA

NETH. ANT.
(to Neth.)

BARBADOS
ST VINCENT & THE GRENADINES

+11

BAKER &
HOWLAND
ISLANDS
(to US)

JARVIS ISLAND
(to US)

COSTA RICA

ARUBA
(to Neth.)

−4

GRENADA
TRINIDAD & TOBAGO

NAURU

−11

PANAMA

VENEZUELA

FRENCH GUIANA
(to France)

K I R I B A T I

−10

Galapagos Islands
(part of Ecuador)

COLOMBIA

GUYANA
SURINAM

TUVALU

ECUADOR

TOKELAU
(to NZ)

−5

B R A Z I L

SOLOMON
ISLANDS

Îles Marquises

−9¹⁄₂

P
E
R
U

VANUATU

COOK
ISLANDS
(to NZ)

−10

−4

+11

NEW
CALEDONIA
(to France)

FIJI

FRENCH POLYNESIA
(to France)

BOLIVIA

−3

PARAGUAY

CORAL SEA ISLANDS
(to Australia)

TONGA

NIUE (to NZ)

−8¹⁄₂

San Felix Island
(part of Chile)

+11¹⁄₂

SAMOA

AMERICAN
SAMOA
(to US)

PITCAIRN
ISLANDS
(to UK)

Easter Island
(part of Chile)

−6

San Ambrosia Island
(part of Chile)

CHILE

A
R
G
E
N
T
I
N
A

NORFOLK ISLAND
(to Australia)

Kermadec Island
(part of NZ)

−4

+10¹⁄₂

Juan Fernandez Island
(part of Chile)

URUGUAY

NEW
ZEALAND

+12

Chatham Island
(part of NZ)

P A C I F I C

O C E A N

+12³⁄₄

Bounty Island
(part of NZ)

Campbell Island
(part of NZ)

FALKLAND ISLANDS
(to UK)

Macquarie Island (part of Australia)

CHILE

−3

−4

−2

+11	+12	−12	−11	−10	−9	−8	−7	−6	−5	−4	−3	−2
23:00	24:00	01:00	02:00	03:00	04:00	05:00	06:00	07:00	08:00	09:00	10:00	

ANTARCTICA
Graham Land −3

27

GEOLOGY & STRUCTURE

A   B   C   D

1

Ural Mountains

EURASIAN PLATE

2

Alps

ANATOLIAN
PLATE

IRANIAN
PLATE

Himalayas

ARABIAN
PLATE

PHILIPPINE
PLATE

3

AFRICAN
PLATE

INDO-

AUSTRALIAN

PLATE

4

ANTARCTIC PLATE

5

GEOLOGICAL
REGIONS

*Continental
Shield*

*Sedimentary
Rocks*

*Igneous
Rock Types*

*Coral
Formation*

MOUNTAIN
RANGES

*Formation expressed as
millions of years ago*

*Alpine
(5 to 23 M)*

*Hercynian
(290 to 362 M)*

*Caledonian
(386 to 439 M)*

A   B   C   D

THE WORLD TODAY

Worst landslide
YUNGAY, PERU
31 May, 1970
17,500 killed

Worst volcanic eruption
MT PELÉE, MARTINIQUE
8 May 1902
40,000 killed

Worst earthquake
TANGSHAN, CHINA
28 JULY 1976
242,419 killed

Arctic Circle

NORTH AMERICAN
PLATE

Rocky Mountains

JUAN DE FUCA
PLATE

Tropic of Cancer

CAROLINE
PLATE

PACIFIC PLATE

COCOS
PLATE

CARIBBEAN
PLATE

Andes

Equator

BISMARCK
PLATE

SOLOMON
PLATE

FIJI PLATE

NAZCA
PLATE

SOUTH
AMERICAN
PLATE

Andes

Tropic of Capricorn

Andes

SCOTIA PLATE

ANTARCTIC

PLATE

Antarctic Circle

TECTONIC
FEATURES

Earthquake
Zone

Hot
Spot

Volcanic
Zone

Rift
Valleys

PLATE
BOUNDARIES

Sliding
Plates

Spreading
Plates

Colliding
Plates

Uncertain
Plate
Boundary

29

WORLD CLIMATE

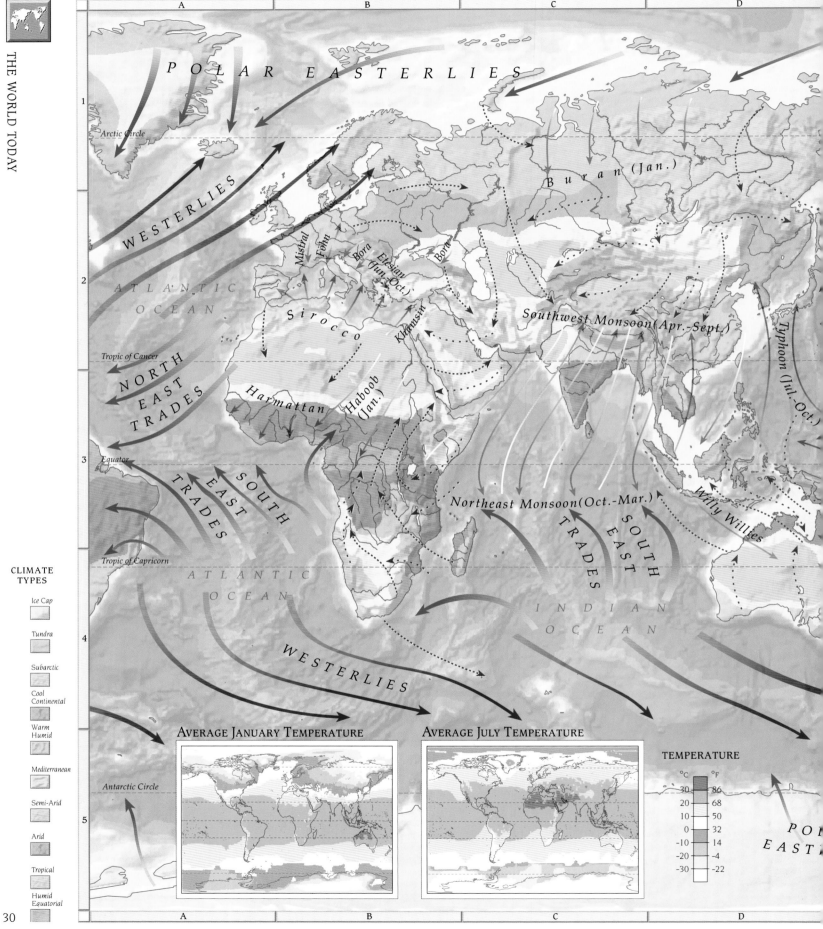

P O L A R   E A S T E R L I E S

Arctic Circle

1

WESTERLIES

ATLANTIC
OCEAN

Buran (Jan.)

Mistral

Föhn

Bora

Etesian
(Jun.-Oct.)

Bora

2

Sirocco

Khamsin

Southwest Monsoon(Apr.-Sept.)

Typhoon (Jul.-Oct.)

Tropic of Cancer

NORTH
EAST
TRADES

Harmattan

Haboob
(Jan.)

3

Equator

SOUTH
EAST
TRADES

Northeast Monsoon(Oct.-Mar.)

SOUTH
EAST
TRADES

Willy Willies

Tropic of Capricorn

ATLANTIC
OCEAN

INDIAN
OCEAN

4

WESTERLIES

AVERAGE JANUARY TEMPERATURE

AVERAGE JULY TEMPERATURE

TEMPERATURE

Antarctic Circle

5

°C	°F
30	86
20	68
10	50
0	32
-10	14
-20	-4
-30	-22

PO
EAST

**CLIMATE
TYPES**

Ice Cap

Tundra

Subarctic

Cool
Continental

Warm
Humid

Mediterranean

Semi-Arid

Arid

Tropical

Humid
Equatorial

A

B

C

D

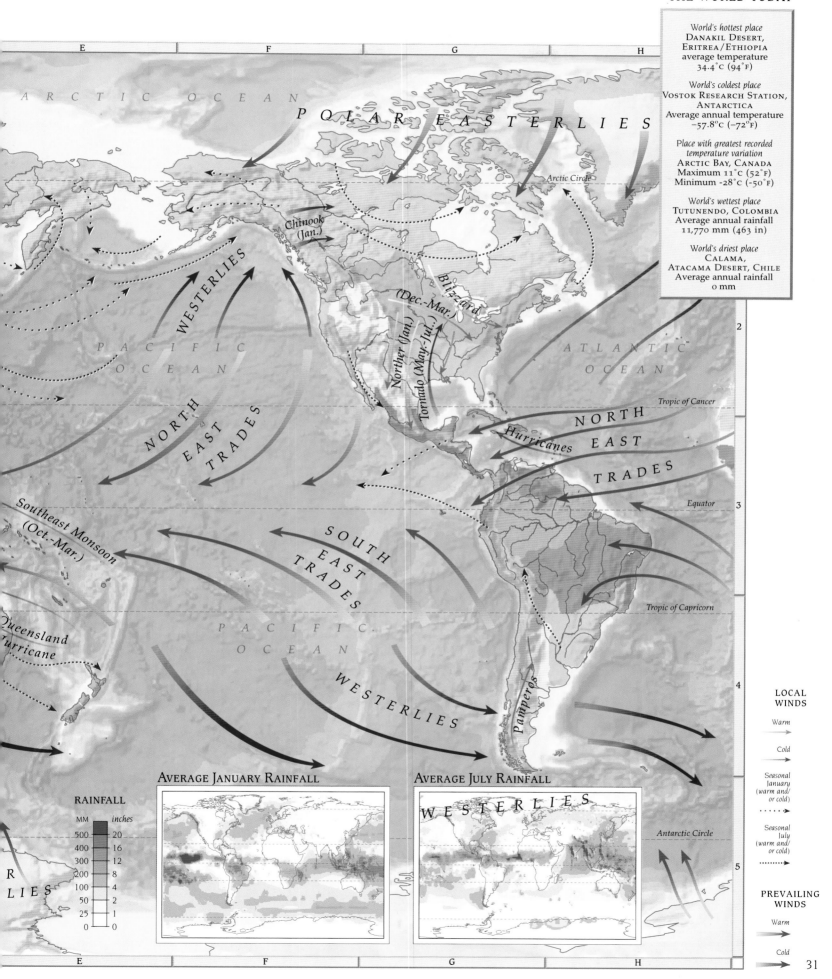

POLAR EASTERLIES

ARCTIC OCEAN

Arctic Circle

WESTERLIES

Chinook
(Jan.)

Blizzard
(Dec.–Mar.)

Norther (Jan.)

Tornado (May–Jul.)

PACIFIC
OCEAN

ATLANTIC
OCEAN

NORTH

EAST

TRADES

Tropic of Cancer

NORTH

EAST

TRADES

Hurricanes

Southeast Monsoon
(Oct.–Mar.)

SOUTH

EAST

TRADES

Equator

Queensland
Hurricane

Tropic of Capricorn

PACIFIC
OCEAN

WESTERLIES

Pamperos

World's hottest place
Danakil Desert,
Eritrea / Ethiopia
average temperature
34.4°C (94°F)

World's coldest place
Vostok Research Station,
Antarctica
Average annual temperature
−57.8°C (−72°F)

Place with greatest recorded
temperature variation
Arctic Bay, Canada
Maximum 11°C (52°F)
Minimum -28°C (-50°F)

World's wettest place
Tutunendo, Colombia
Average annual rainfall
11,770 mm (463 in)

World's driest place
Calama,
Atacama Desert, Chile
Average annual rainfall
0 mm

AVERAGE JANUARY RAINFALL

AVERAGE JULY RAINFALL

WESTERLIES

Antarctic Circle

RAINFALL

MM	inches
500	20
400	16
300	12
200	8
100	4
50	2
25	1
0	0

LIES

LOCAL
WINDS

Warm

Cold

Seasonal
January
(warm and/
or cold)

Seasonal
July
(warm and/
or cold)

PREVAILING
WINDS

Warm

Cold

OCEAN CURRENTS

ANNUAL
MEAN
OCEAN
TEMPERATURE

20 to 30°C
68° to 86°F

10 to 20°C
50° to 68°F

0 to 10°C
32° to 50°F

-2° to 0°C
28° to 32°F

Annual mean
extent of sea ice
below -2°C/28°F

Permanent
ice shelf

Prevailing warm
Ocean current

Prevailing cold
Ocean current

Greenland
Sea

Summer limit of pack ice

Winter limit of pack ice

Laptev
Sea

Denmark Strait

Barents Sea

Kara
Sea

North Atlantic Drift

North
Sea

Baltic Sea

EUROPE

ASIA

Sea of
Okhotsk

Black Sea

Sea of
Japan

Canary Current

Mediterranean Sea

Yellow
Sea

East
China
Sea

Kuro Siwo Current

AFRICA

Red Sea

The
Gulf

Gulf of Aden

Arabian
Sea

Bay of
Bengal

Philippine
Sea

Equatorial
Counter-
current

Gulf of Guinea

South
China
Sea

Doldrums

Doldrums

Celebes
Sea

South Equatorial
Current

South Equatorial Current

Java Sea

Banda Sea

Benguela Current

Timor
Sea

Arafura
Sea

Mozambique Channel

ATLANTIC
OCEAN

INDIAN
OCEAN

West Australian Current

AUSTRALIA

Winter limit of pack ice

Summer limit of pack ice

ANTARCTICA

32

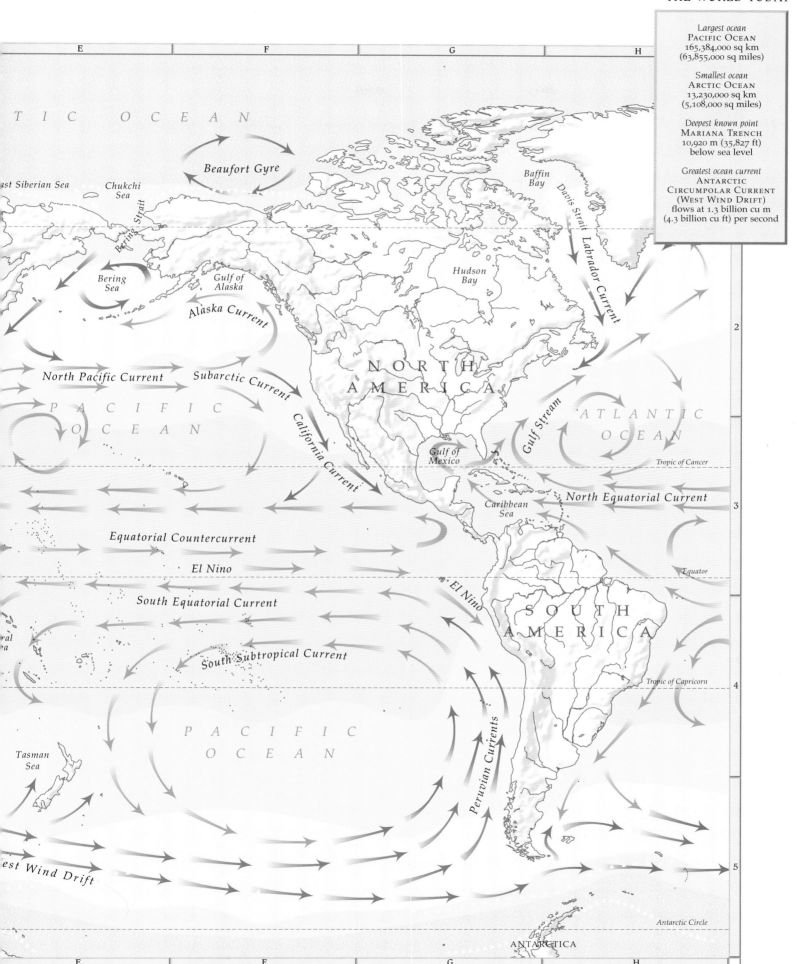

Largest ocean
PACIFIC OCEAN
165,384,000 sq km
(63,855,000 sq miles)

Smallest ocean
ARCTIC OCEAN
13,230,000 sq km
(5,108,000 sq miles)

Deepest known point
MARIANA TRENCH
10,920 m (35,827 ft)
below sea level

Greatest ocean current
ANTARCTIC
CIRCUMPOLAR CURRENT
(WEST WIND DRIFT)
flows at 1.3 billion cu m
(4.3 billion cu ft) per second

TIC O C E A N

Beaufort Gyre

ast Siberian Sea

Chukchi
Sea

Baffin
Bay

Bering Strait

Bering
Sea

Gulf of
Alaska

Hudson
Bay

Davis Strait Labrador Current

Alaska Current

North Pacific Current

Subarctic Current

NORTH
AMERICA

P A C I F I C
O C E A N

California Current

Gulf Stream

ATLANTIC
OCEAN

Gulf of
Mexico

Tropic of Cancer

Caribbean
Sea

North Equatorial Current

Equatorial Countercurrent

El Nino

Equator

El Nino

South Equatorial Current

SOUTH
AMERICA

South Subtropical Current

Tropic of Capricorn

P A C I F I C
O C E A N

Tasman
Sea

Peruvian Currents

ral
a

est Wind Drift

Antarctic Circle

ANTARCTICA

LIFE ZONES

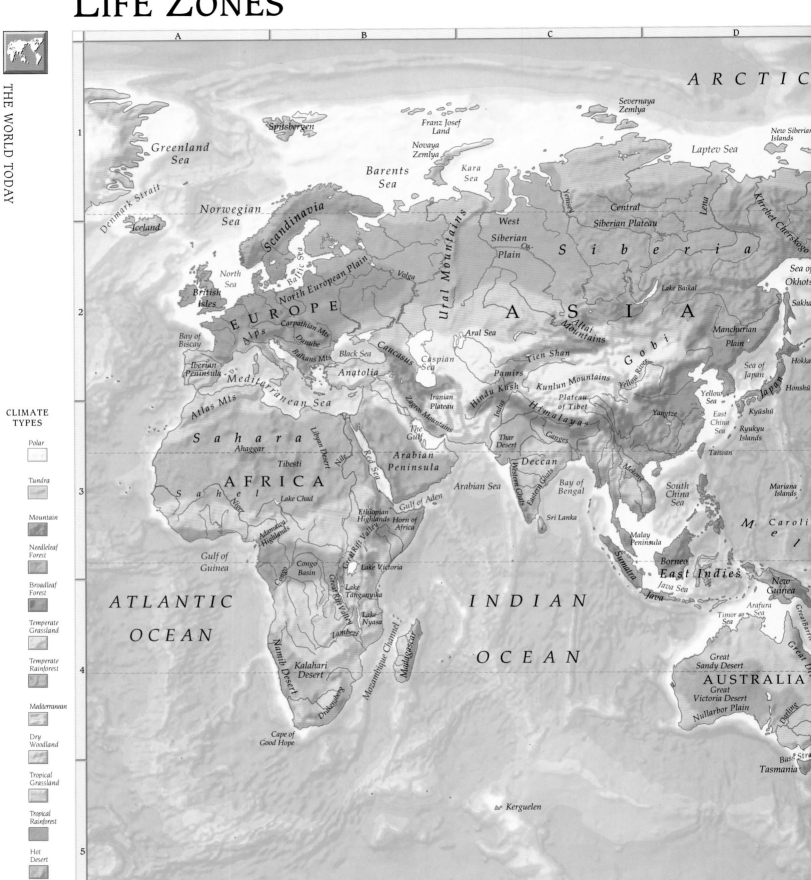

CLIMATE TYPES

Polar

Tundra

Mountain

Needleleaf Forest

Broadleaf Forest

Temperate Grassland

Temperate Rainforest

Mediterranean

Dry Woodland

Tropical Grassland

Tropical Rainforest

Hot Desert

Cold Desert

Wetland

A   B   C   D

1

2

3

4

5

ARCTIC

Greenland Sea

Denmark Strait

Iceland

Spitsbergen

Franz Josef Land

Severnaya Zemlya

New Siberian Islands

Laptev Sea

Khrebet Cherskogo

Barents Sea

Novaya Zemlya

Kara Sea

Norwegian Sea

Scandinavia

North Sea

British Isles

Baltic Sea

EUROPE

North European Plain

Alps

Carpathian Mts

Danube

Balkans Mts

Bay of Biscay

Iberian Peninsula

Mediterranean Sea

Atlas Mts

Black Sea

Caucasus

Anatolia

Caspian Sea

Volga

Ural Mountains

West Siberian Plain

Ob'

Yenisey

Central Siberian Plateau

Lena

Siberia

ASIA

Aral Sea

Pamirs

Tien Shan

Altai Mountains

Gobi

Lake Baikal

Manchurian Plain

Sea of Okhotsk

Sakha

Zagros Mountains

Iranian Plateau

Hindu Kush

Kunlun Mountains

Plateau of Tibet

Himalayas

Yellow River

Yangtze

Yellow Sea

Sea of Japan

Japan

Hokka

Honshū

The Gulf

Arabian Peninsula

Red Sea

Nile

Libyan Desert

Sahara

Ahaggar

Tibesti

AFRICA

Sahel

Niger

Lake Chad

Gulf of Aden

Ethiopian Highlands

Horn of Africa

Arabian Sea

Thar Desert

Ganges

Indus

Deccan

Western Ghats

Eastern Ghats

Bay of Bengal

Sri Lanka

Mekong

South China Sea

East China Sea

Ryukyu Islands

Taiwan

Kyūshū

Mariana Islands

Caroli

M

e

Adamawa Highlands

Gulf of Guinea

Congo

Congo Basin

Great Rift Valley

Lake Victoria

Lake Tanganyika

Great Rift Valley

Lake Nyasa

Zambezi

Mozambique Channel

Madagascar

ATLANTIC OCEAN

Namib Desert

Kalahari Desert

Drakensberg

Cape of Good Hope

INDIAN OCEAN

Malay Peninsula

Sumatra

Borneo

East Indies

Java Sea

Java

Timor Sea

New Guinea

Arafura Sea

GreatBarri

Great Di

Great Sandy Desert

AUSTRALIA

Great Victoria Desert

Nullarbor Plain

Darling

Kerguelen

Bass Str

Tasmania

ANTARCTICA

34

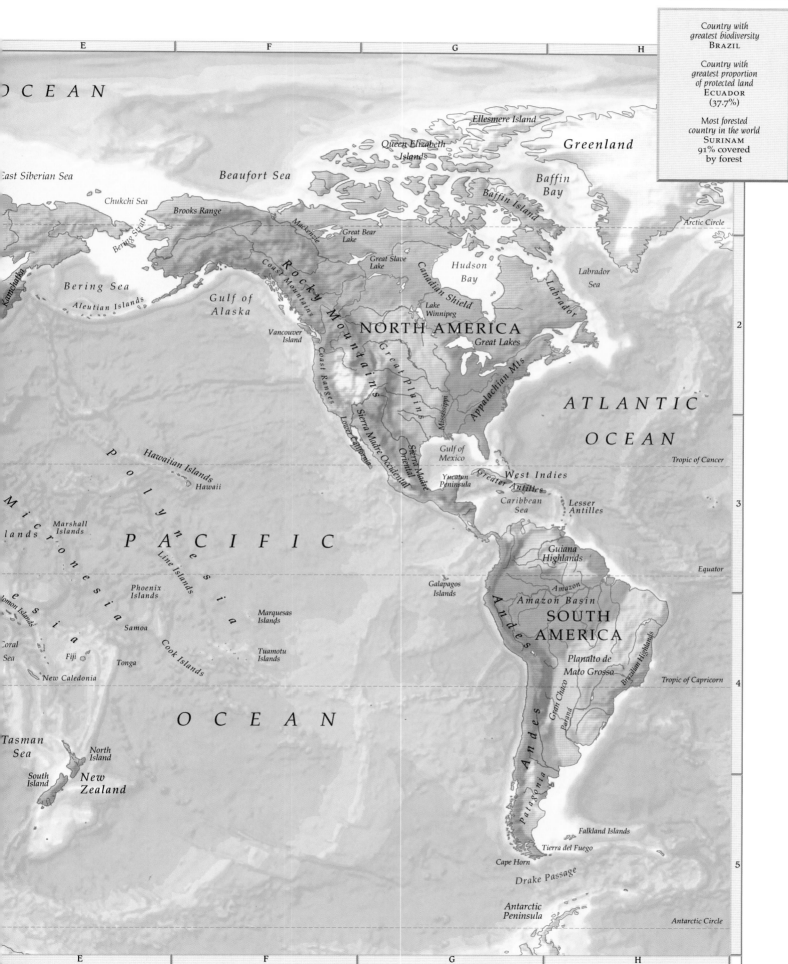

Country with
greatest biodiversity
BRAZIL

Country with
greatest proportion
of protected land
ECUADOR
(37.7%)

Most forested
country in the world
SURINAM
91% covered
by forest

OCEAN

East Siberian Sea

Chukchi Sea

Brooks Range

Bering Strait

Kamchatka

Bering Sea

Aleutian Islands

Gulf of
Alaska

Vancouver
Island

Coast Mountains

Coast Ranges

Rocky Mountains

Lower California

Sierra Madre Occidental

Sierra Madre Oriental

Great Plains

Mississippi

Great Basin

Ellesmere Island

Queen Elizabeth
Islands

Beaufort Sea

Mackenzie

Great Bear
Lake

Great Slave
Lake

Hudson
Bay

Canadian Shield

Lake
Winnipeg

NORTH AMERICA

Great Lakes

Appalachian Mts

Gulf of
Mexico

Yucatan
Peninsula

Greenland

Baffin
Bay

Baffin Island

Arctic Circle

Labrador
Sea

Labrador

ATLANTIC

OCEAN

Tropic of Cancer

West Indies

Greater Antilles

Caribbean
Sea

Lesser
Antilles

Polynesia

Hawaiian Islands

Hawaii

PACIFIC

Micronesia

Marshall
Islands

lands

Line Islands

Phoenix
Islands

Marquesas
Islands

Galapagos
Islands

Guiana
Highlands

Amazon

Amazon Basin

SOUTH
AMERICA

Andes

Equator

esia

Solomon Islands

Coral
Sea

Fiji

Samoa

Tonga

Cook Islands

Tuamotu
Islands

Planalto de
Mato Grosso

Gran Chaco

Paraná

Brazilian Highlands

Tropic of Capricorn

New Caledonia

OCEAN

Tasman
Sea

North
Island

South
Island

New
Zealand

Andes

Patagonia

Falkland Islands

Tierra del Fuego

Cape Horn

Drake Passage

Antarctic
Peninsula

Antarctic Circle

POPULATION

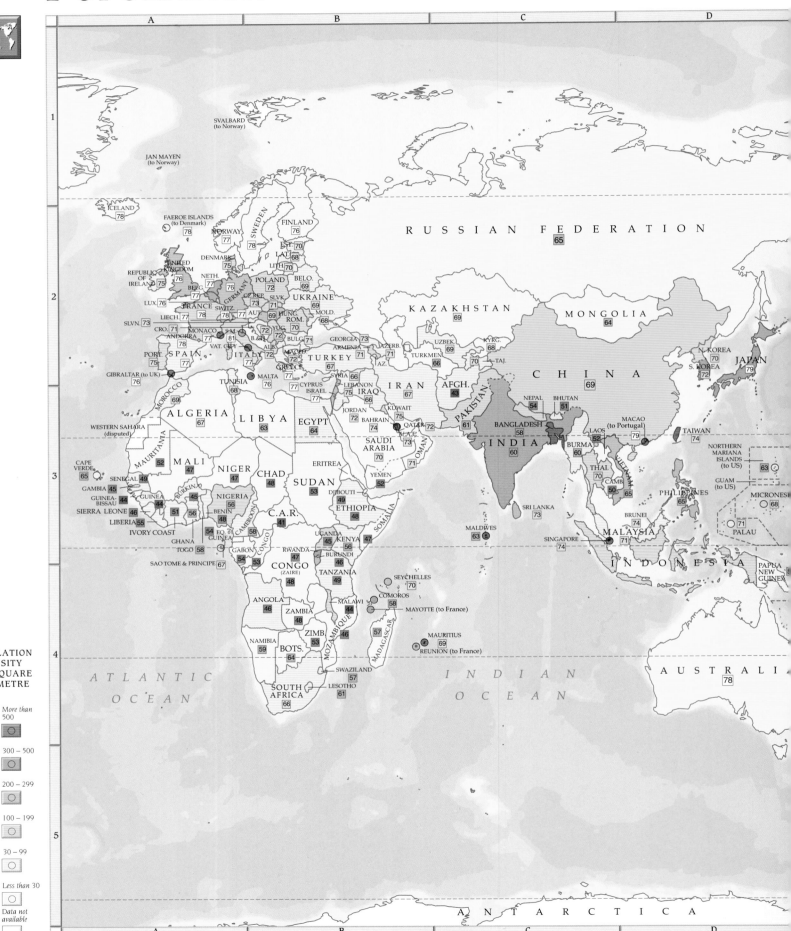

	A	B	C	D

1

SVALBARD
(to Norway)

JAN MAYEN
(to Norway)

RUSSIAN FEDERATION
65

KAZAKHSTAN
69

MONGOLIA
64

ICELAND
78

FAEROE ISLANDS
(to Denmark)
78

NORWAY
77

SWEDEN
78

FINLAND
76

EST. 70
LAT. 68
LITH. 70

2

DENMARK
75

UNITED
KINGDOM
76

REPUBLIC
OF
IRELAND 75

NETH. 77
BELG. 77

LUX. 76

FRANCE
78

POLAND
72

BELO.
69

UKRAINE
69

GERMANY 76

CZ. REP. 73
SLVK 69

AUT. 69

HUNG. 70
ROM. 70

MOLD. 68

LIECH. 77
SLVN. 73
CRO. 71
ANDORRA 78
MONACO 77
S-M 81
VAT. CITY
PORT. 75
SPAIN

ITALY 77

B.&H. 72
YUG. 72
BULG. 71

ALB. 72
MACED. 72
GREECE 77

GEORGIA 73
ARMENIA 71
AZ.

AZERB. 71

UZBEK
69

KYRG.
68

TURKMEN.
66

TAJ.

KYRG. 68

SWITZ. 78

N. KOREA
70

S. KOREA
72

JAPAN
79

CHINA
69

GIBRALTAR (to UK)
76

TUNISIA
68

MALTA
76

CYPRUS 77

MOROCCO
69

ALGERIA
67

LIBYA
63

EGYPT
64

TURKEY
67

SYRIA 66
LEBANON 75
ISRAEL 77
JORDAN 72
IRAQ 66

IRAN
67

AFGH.
43

PAKISTAN
61

NEPAL
54

BHUTAN
51

BANGLADESH
58

INDIA
60

BURMA
60

LAOS
52

TAIWAN
74

MACAO
(to Portugal)
79

NORTHERN
MARIANA
ISLANDS
(to US)
63

WESTERN SAHARA
(disputed)

KUWAIT 75
BAHRAIN 74
QATAR 72
U.A.E. 73
OMAN 71

SAUDI
ARABIA
70

YEMEN
52

ERITREA

CAPE
VERDE
65

MAURITANIA
52

MALI
47

NIGER
47

CHAD
48

SUDAN
53

DJIBOUTI 49

3

SENEGAL 49
GAMBIA 45
GUINEA-
BISSAU 44
GUINEA 44
SIERRA LEONE 46
LIBERIA 55

BURKINA 45

NIGERIA
48

BENIN 56
TOGO 58
GHANA 58
IVORY COAST 54

CAMEROON 58
EQ.
GUINEA 54

C.A.R.
41

ETHIOPIA
48

SOMALIA

UGANDA 45
KENYA 56
47

SAO TOME & PRINCIPE
67

GABON 47
CONGO 54
53

RWANDA 56
BURUNDI 46

SRI LANKA
73

MALDIVES
63

SEYCHELLES
70

SINGAPORE
74

MALAYSIA
71

BRUNEI
74

PHILIPPINES
65

GUAM
(to US)
71

MICRONES

PALAU
71

INDONESIA

PAPUA
NEW
GUINEA

THAI.
70

CAMB.
50
65

VIETNAM

CONGO
(ZAIRE)
48

TANZANIA
49

ANGOLA
46

ZAMBIA
48

MALAWI
44

COMOROS
58

MAYOTTE (to France)

SEYCHELLES

MADAGASCAR
57

MAURITIUS
69
REUNION (to France)

NAMIBIA
59

BOTS.
64

ZIMB.

MOZAMBIQUE
46

4

SWAZILAND 57
SOUTH
AFRICA
66

LESOTHO
61

ATLANTIC
OCEAN

INDIAN
OCEAN

AUSTRALIA
78

5

ANTARCTICA

POPULATION
DENSITY
PER SQUARE
KILOMETRE

*More than
500*

300 – 500

200 – 299

100 – 199

30 – 99

Less than 30

*Data not
available*

	A	B	C	D

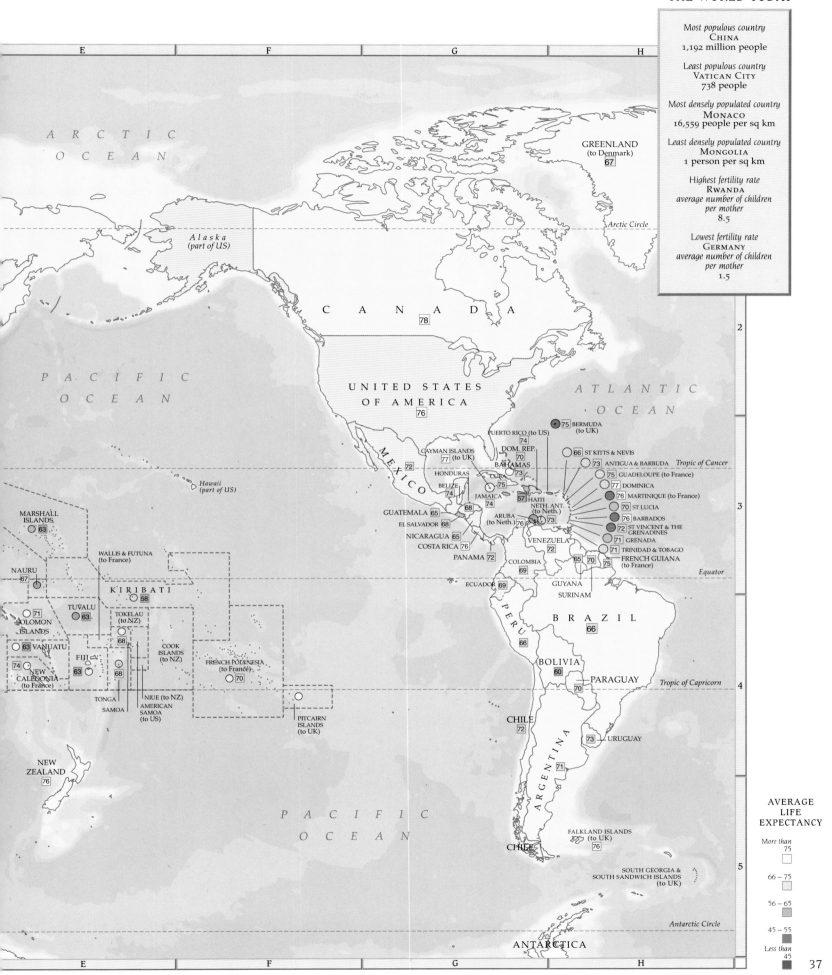

Most populous country
CHINA
1,192 million people

Least populous country
VATICAN CITY
738 people

Most densely populated country
MONACO
16,559 people per sq km

Least densely populated country
MONGOLIA
1 person per sq km

Highest fertility rate
RWANDA
average number of children
per mother
8.5

Lowest fertility rate
GERMANY
average number of children
per mother
1.5

ARCTIC OCEAN

Alaska (part of US)

Arctic Circle

GREENLAND
(to Denmark)
67

C A N A D A
78

PACIFIC OCEAN

UNITED STATES OF AMERICA
76

ATLANTIC OCEAN

Hawaii (part of US)

75 BERMUDA
(to UK)

PUERTO RICO (to US)
74

MEXICO
72

CAYMAN ISLANDS
(to UK)
77

DOM. REP.
70

Tropic of Cancer

66 ST KITTS & NEVIS

BAHAMAS

73 ANTIGUA & BARBUDA

HONDURAS

BELIZE
72

CUBA
75

73

75 GUADELOUPE (to France)

77 DOMINICA

MARSHALL ISLANDS
63

JAMAICA
74

HAITI
57

76 MARTINIQUE (to France)

GUATEMALA
65

68

NETH. ANT.
(to Neth.)

70 ST LUCIA

EL SALVADOR
68

ARUBA
(to Neth.)
76

73

76 BARBADOS

NAURU
67

NICARAGUA
65

72 ST VINCENT & THE
GRENADINES

COSTA RICA
76

VENEZUELA
72

71 GRENADA

SOLOMON
ISLANDS
71

PANAMA
72

71 TRINIDAD & TOBAGO

KIRIBATI
58

COLOMBIA
69

65

70

75 FRENCH GUIANA
(to France)

Equator

WALLIS & FUTUNA
(to France)

TUVALU
63

ECUADOR
69

GUYANA

SURINAM

TOKELAU
(to NZ)
68

VANUATU
63

COOK
ISLANDS
(to NZ)

FRENCH POLYNESIA
(to France)

PERU
66

B R A Z I L
66

FIJI
63

68

70

BOLIVIA
60

NEW
CALEDONIA
(to France)
74

TONGA

SAMOA

NIUE (to NZ)

AMERICAN
SAMOA
(to US)

PARAGUAY
70

Tropic of Capricorn

PITCAIRN
ISLANDS
(to UK)

CHILE
72

73 URUGUAY

NEW
ZEALAND
76

A
R
G
E
N
T
I
N
A
71

PACIFIC OCEAN

CHILE

FALKLAND ISLANDS
(to UK)
76

SOUTH GEORGIA &
SOUTH SANDWICH ISLANDS
(to UK)

Antarctic Circle

ANTARCTICA

AVERAGE
LIFE
EXPECTANCY

More than
75

66 – 75

56 – 65

45 – 55

Less than
45

37

LANGUAGES

MAIN
INTERNATIONAL
LANGUAGES

Chinese

Spanish

Arabic

Hindi

English

French

Russian

Portuguese

Arabic/French

French/other

English/other

Arabic/other

Hindi/English/
Other

Chinese/Other

Russian/Other

English/French

English/
Spanish

Spanish/Other

Portuguese/
Other

Other
Language

Language
Group
B a n t u

Other
Language
H a u s a

Uninhabited
Land

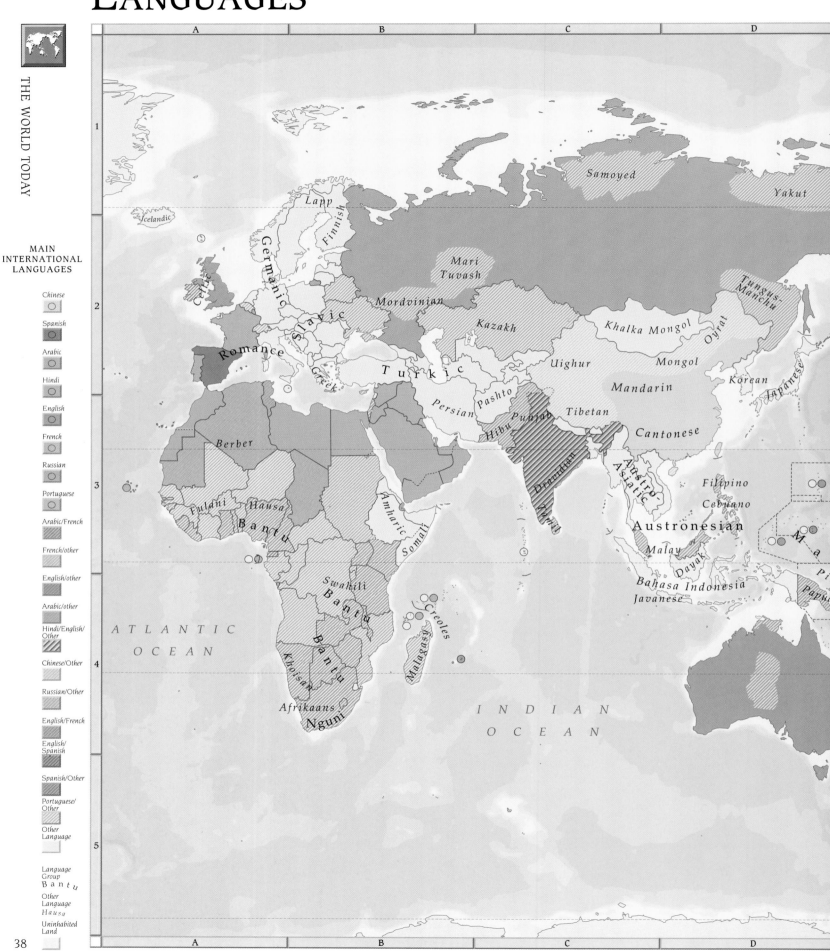

Languages spoken by
greatest number of people

MANDARIN CHINESE
931,100,000 speakers

ENGLISH
463,000,000 speakers

HINDI
400,000,000 speakers

SPANISH
371,000,000 speakers

RUSSIAN
290,000,000 speakers

ARCTIC OCEAN

Greenlandic

Danish

Arctic Circle

Eskimo - Aleut

Aleut

American Indian

Athabascan

Algonquin

PACIFIC OCEAN

Nahuatl

Maya

Creoles

Tropic of Cancer

Carib

Arawak

Equator

Quechua

Aymara

Tropic of Capricorn

Polynesian

Maori

PACIFIC OCEAN

Antarctic Circle

39

RELIGION

MAJORITY
RELIGIONS

Chinese

Protestant
Christianity

Catholic
Christianity

Orthodox
Christianity

Shi'a Islam

Sunni Islam

Hinduism

Judaism

Theravada
Buddhism

Mahayana
Buddhism

Tibetan
Buddhism

Other

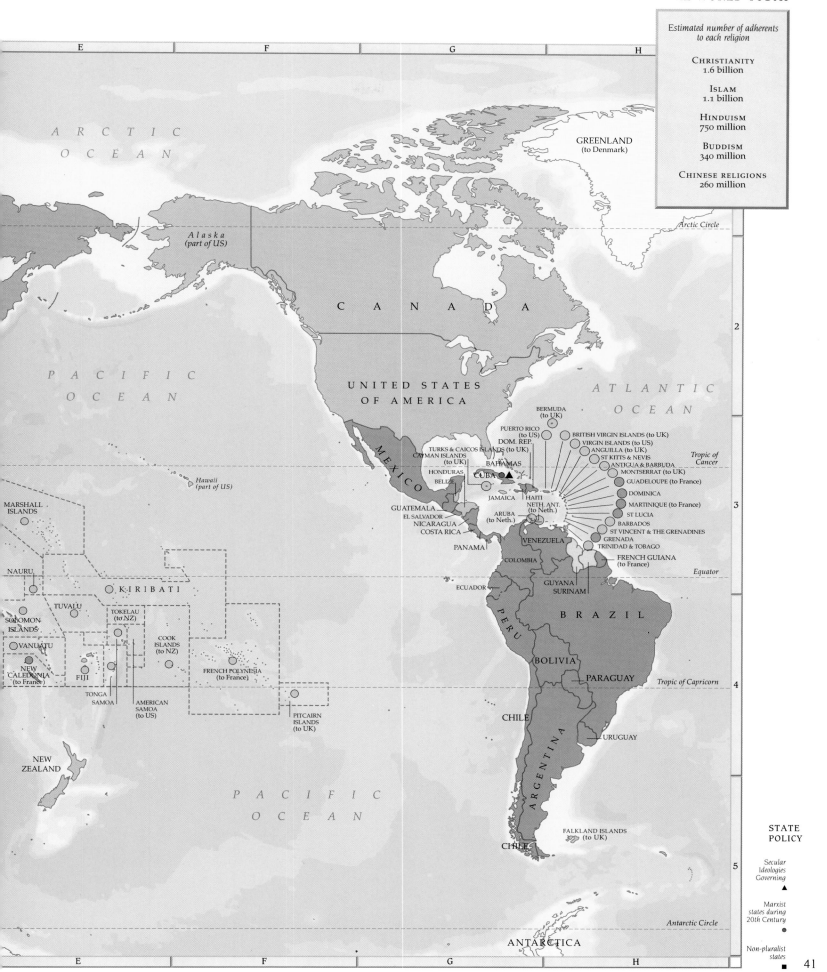

Estimated number of adherents
to each religion

CHRISTIANITY
1.6 billion

ISLAM
1.1 billion

HINDUISM
750 million

BUDDISM
340 million

CHINESE RELIGIONS
260 million

ARCTIC
OCEAN

GREENLAND
(to Denmark)

Arctic Circle

Alaska
(part of US)

C A N A D A

2

PACIFIC
OCEAN

UNITED STATES
OF AMERICA

A T L A N T I C
OCEAN

BERMUDA
(to UK)

PUERTO RICO
(to US)
DOM. REP.

BRITISH VIRGIN ISLANDS (to UK)
VIRGIN ISLANDS (to US)
ANGUILLA (to UK)
ST KITTS & NEVIS
ANTIGUA & BARBUDA
MONTSERRAT (to UK)

Tropic of
Cancer

TURKS & CAICOS ISLANDS (to UK)
CAYMAN ISLANDS
(to UK)

BAHAMAS

Hawaii
(part of US)

HONDURAS

CUBA ▲

GUADELOUPE (to France)

MARSHALL
ISLANDS

MEXICO

BELIZE

JAMAICA

HAITI
NETH. ANT.
(to Neth.)

DOMINICA

MARTINIQUE (to France)

3

GUATEMALA
EL SALVADOR
NICARAGUA
COSTA RICA

ARUBA
(to Neth.)

ST LUCIA
BARBADOS
ST VINCENT & THE GRENADINES
GRENADA
TRINIDAD & TOBAGO

PANAMA

VENEZUELA

COLOMBIA

FRENCH GUIANA
(to France)

Equator

NAURU

K·I·R·I·B·A·T·I

ECUADOR

GUYANA
SURINAM

TUVALU

SOLOMON
ISLANDS

TOKELAU
(to NZ)

PERU

B R A Z I L

VANUATU

COOK
ISLANDS
(to NZ)

FIJI

FRENCH POLYNESIA
(to France)

BOLIVIA

NEW
CALEDONIA
(to France)

PARAGUAY

Tropic of Capricorn

4

TONGA
SAMOA

AMERICAN
SAMOA
(to US)

PITCAIRN
ISLANDS
(to UK)

CHILE

URUGUAY

NEW
ZEALAND

ARGENTINA

PACIFIC

OCEAN

FALKLAND ISLANDS
(to UK)

STATE
POLICY

CHILE

5

Secular
Ideologies
Governing ▲

Marxist
states during
20th Century ●

Antarctic Circle

ANTARCTICA

Non-pluralist
states ■

E   F   G   H   41

THE GLOBAL ECONOMY

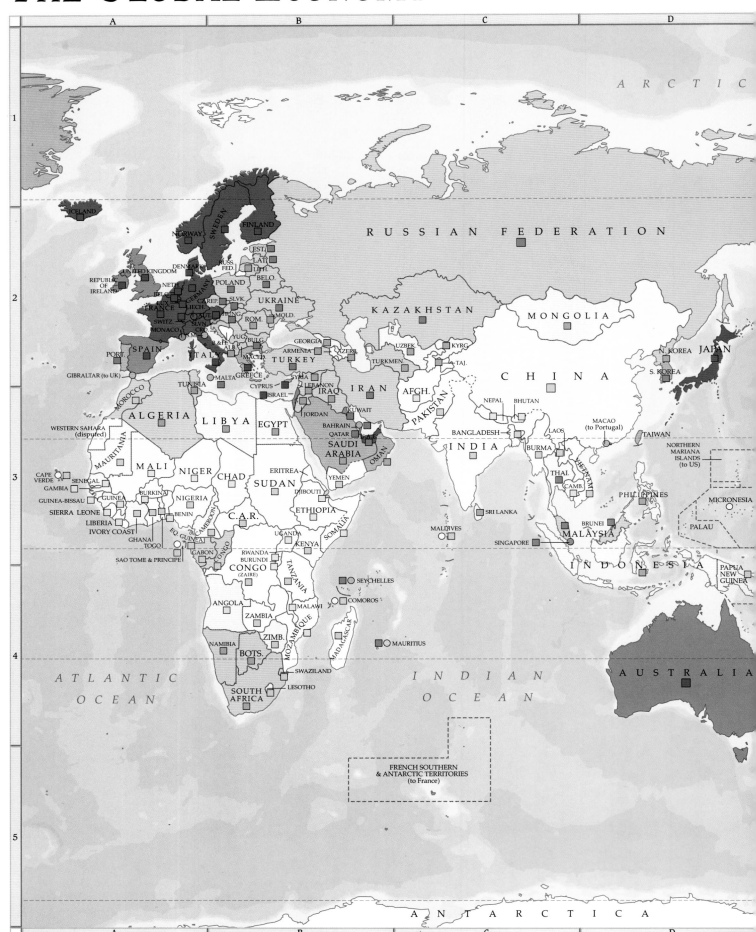

	A	B	C	D

ARCTIC

1

ICELAND

RUSSIAN FEDERATION

NORWAY SWEDEN FINLAND

EST.
LAT.
RUSS. LITH.
DENMARK FED.
UNITED KINGDOM BELO.
REPUBLIC NETH. POLAND
OF BELG. GERMANY
IRELAND LUX. C.REP.
FRANCE LIECH. SLVK. UKRAINE
AUT. HUNG. KAZAKHSTAN
SWITZ. SLVN. ROM. MOLD. MONGOLIA
MONACO CRO.
B.&H. YUG. BULG. GEORGIA
S.M. ALB. ARMENIA AZERB. UZBEK. KYRG.
PORT. SPAIN ITALY MACED. TURKMEN. TAJ.
GIBRALTAR (to UK) MALTA GREECE TURKEY CHINA
TUNISIA CYPRUS SYRIA AFGH.
MOROCCO ISRAEL LEBANON IRAQ IRAN PAKISTAN NEPAL BHUTAN
JORDAN NEPAL BANGLADESH

2

N. KOREA JAPAN
S. KOREA

MACAO
(to Portugal) TAIWAN

3

WESTERN SAHARA
(disputed)
ALGERIA LIBYA EGYPT KUWAIT
BAHRAIN
QATAR U.A.E.
MAURITANIA SAUDI OMAN INDIA LAOS NORTHERN
ARABIA BURMA MARIANA
CAPE MALI NIGER CHAD ERITREA YEMEN THAI. ISLANDS
VERDE SUDAN DJIBOUTI CAMB. (to US)
GAMBIA SENEGAL PHILIPPINES
GUINEA-BISSAU GUINEA BURKINA NIGERIA ETHIOPIA SRI LANKA MICRONESIA
SIERRA LEONE BENIN C.A.R. SOMALIA BRUNEI
LIBERIA CAMEROON MALDIVES MALAYSIA PALAU
IVORY COAST GHANA EQ. GUINEA UGANDA SINGAPORE
TOGO GABON CONGO KENYA INDONESIA
SAO TOME & PRINCIPE CONGO RWANDA PAPUA
(ZAIRE) BURUNDI NEW
TANZANIA GUINEA

SEYCHELLES

ANGOLA MALAWI COMOROS
ZAMBIA
NAMIBIA MOZAMBIQUE MADAGASCAR MAURITIUS

4

ZIMB.
BOTS. SWAZILAND INDIAN AUSTRALIA
ATLANTIC LESOTHO OCEAN
OCEAN SOUTH
AFRICA

FRENCH SOUTHERN
& ANTARCTIC TERRITORIES
(to France)

5

ANTARCTICA

ECONOMIC PERFORMANCE
GNP *per capita*
1995 $US

More than
20 000

10 000
to 20 000

5000
to 10 000

1000
to 5000

500
to 1000

250
to 500

Less than
250

Data not
availablr

45% of world trade
is accounted for by
FRANCE
GERMANY
JAPAN
UK
USA

Highest GNP *per capita*
SWITZERLAND
US$ 36,230

Lowest GNP *per capita*
MOZAMBIQUE
US$ 70

OCEAN

GREENLAND
(to Denmark)

Arctic Circle

*Alaska
(part of US)*

*PACIFIC

OCEAN*

C A N A D A

UNITED STATES
OF AMERICA

*ATLANTIC

OCEAN*

BERMUDA
(to UK)

*Hawaii
(part of US)*

DOM. REP.
PUERTO RICO
(to US)

TURKS & CAICOS ISLANDS (to UK)
ST KITTS & NEVIS
ANTIGUA & BARBUDA

Tropic of Cancer

CAYMAN ISLANDS
(to UK)
BAHAMAS
GUADELOUPE (to France)

HONDURAS
CUBA
DOMINICA

BELIZE
MARTINIQUE (to France)

JAMAICA
ST LUCIA

MARSHALL
ISLANDS

HAITI
BARBADOS

GUATEMALA
NETH. ANT.
(to Neth.)
ST VINCENT &
THE GRENADINES

EL SALVADOR
ARUBA
(to Neth.)
GRENADA

NICARAGUA
TRINIDAD & TOBAGO

COSTA RICA
FRENCH GUIANA
(to France)

PANAMA
VENEZUELA

NAURU
COLOMBIA

K I R I B A T I
ECUADOR
GUYANA

Equator

SURINAM

TUVALU

SOLOMON
ISLANDS
TOKELAU
(to NZ)
P E R U
B R A Z I L

SAMOA

VANUATU
TONGA
BOLIVIA

NEW
CALEDONIA
(to France)
FIJI
FRENCH POLYNESIA
(to France)
PARAGUAY
Tropic of Capricorn

HUMAN
DEVELOPMENT
INDEX (HDI)

PITCAIRN
ISLANDS
(to UK)
CHILE

High HDI

A R G E N T I N A
URUGUAY

NEW
ZEALAND

*PACIFIC

OCEAN*

Low HDI

HDI is one
of the best
indicators of
economic
development.
The single
index is
reached by
measuring life
expectancy
at birth,
per capita
purchasing
power, literacy
rates and
years of
schooling

FALKLAND ISLANDS
(to UK)

CHILE

Antarctic Circle

ANTARCTICA

43

GLOBAL CONFLICT

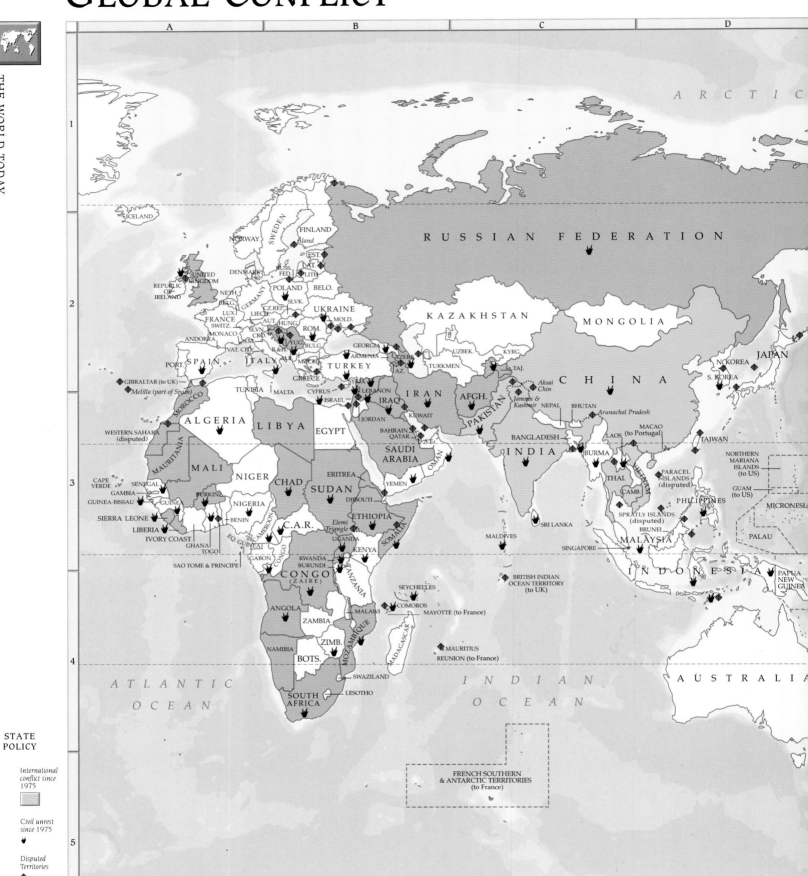

ARCTIC

ICELAND

NORWAY

SWEDEN

FINLAND
Åland

RUSSIAN FEDERATION

EST.
LAT.
LITH.

UNITED
KINGDOM
REPUBLIC
OF
IRELAND

DENMARK

RUSS.
FED.

POLAND
BELO.

NETH.
BELG.
LUX.
FRANCE
SWITZ.
GERMANY
LIECH.
CZ.REP.
AUT.
SLVK.
HUNG.
UKRAINE

KAZAKHSTAN

MONGOLIA

ANDORRA
MONACO
SLVN.
CRO.
S.M.
VAT. CITY
B &H.
BULG.
ROM.
MOLD.

UZBEK.
KYRG.

N. KOREA
S. KOREA
JAPAN

PORT.
SPAIN
ITALY
YUG.
ALB.
MACED.
GREECE
TURKEY
GEORGIA
ARMENIA
AZERB.
AZ.
TURKMEN.
TAJ.

CHINA

GIBRALTAR (to UK)
Melilla (part of Spain)
TUNISIA
MALTA
CYPRUS
SYRIA
LEBANON
ISRAEL
IRAQ
JORDAN
IRAN
AFGH.
Aksai
Chin
Jammu &
Kashmir
NEPAL
BHUTAN
Arunachal Pradesh

MOROCCO
WESTERN SAHARA
(disputed)
ALGERIA
LIBYA
EGYPT
KUWAIT
BAHRAIN
QATAR
U.A.E.
SAUDI
ARABIA
PAKISTAN
MACAO
(to Portugal)
TAIWAN

MAURITANIA
MALI
NIGER
CHAD
ERITREA
SUDAN
YEMEN
OMAN
BANGLADESH
INDIA
BURMA
LAOS
THAI.
VIETNAM
NORTHERN
MARIANA
ISLANDS
(to US)

CAPE
VERDE
SENEGAL
GAMBIA
GUINEA-BISSAU
GUINEA
BURKINA
NIGERIA
BENIN
DJIBOUTI
ETHIOPIA
Elemi
Triangle
UGANDA
SOMALIA
CAMB.
PARACEL
ISLANDS
(disputed)
GUAM
(to US)
MICRONESIA

SIERRA LEONE
LIBERIA
IVORY COAST
GHANA
TOGO
EQ. GUINEA
CAMEROON
C.A.R.
KENYA
SRI LANKA
SPRATLY ISLANDS
(disputed)
PHILIPPINES
BRUNEI
MALAYSIA
PALAU

SAO TOME & PRINCIPE
GABON
CONGO
RWANDA
BURUNDI
TANZANIA
MALDIVES
SINGAPORE

CONGO
(ZAIRE)
SEYCHELLES
BRITISH INDIAN
OCEAN TERRITORY
(to UK)
INDONESIA
PAPUA
NEW
GUINEA

ANGOLA
ZAMBIA
MALAWI
COMOROS
MAYOTTE (to France)

NAMIBIA
ZIMB.
MOZAMBIQUE
MADAGASCAR
MAURITIUS
REUNION (to France)

BOTS.
SWAZILAND
INDIAN
OCEAN

ATLANTIC
OCEAN
SOUTH
AFRICA
LESOTHO
AUSTRALIA

FRENCH SOUTHERN
& ANTARCTIC TERRITORIES
(to France)

ANTARCTICA

STATE
POLICY

International
conflict since
1975

Civil unrest
since 1975

Disputed
Territories

Disputed
Territories

Disputed
Territories

Origins of major
refugee populations (1997)

AFGHANISTAN
2,350,000

RWANDA
1,700,000

BOSNIA & HERZEGOVINA
1,330,000

LIBERIA
750,000

OCEAN

GREENLAND
(to Denmark)

Arctic Circle

*Alaska
(part of US)*

~ *Kurile Islands
(part of Russ.Fed.)*

C A N A D A

2

*P A C I F I C

O C E A N*

ST PIERRE
& MIQUELON
(to France)

U N I T E D   S T A T E S
O F   A M E R I C A

*A T L A N T I C

O C E A N*

BERMUDA
(to UK)

PUERTO RICO (to US)

BRITISH VIRGIN ISLANDS (to UK)

DOM. REP.

VIRGIN ISLANDS (to US)

TURKS & CAICOS ISLANDS (to UK)

ANGUILLA (to UK)

CAYMAN ISLANDS
(to UK)

BAHAMAS

ST KITTS & NEVIS

Tropic of Cancer

M E X I C O

HONDURAS

CUBA

ANTIGUA & BARBUDA

MONTSERRAT (to UK)

BELIZE

JAMAICA

GUADELOUPE (to France)

*Hawaii
(part of US)*

NAVASSA I.
(to US)

HAITI

DOMINICA

MARSHALL
ISLANDS

GUATEMALA

NETH. ANT.
(to Neth.)

MARTINIQUE (to France)

EL SALVADOR

ARUBA
(to Neth.)

ST LUCIA

3

WALLIS & FUTUNA
(to France)

KINGMAN REEF (to US)

NICARAGUA

BARBADOS

ST VINCENT & THE GRENADINES

PALMYRA ATOLL (to US)

COSTA RICA

VENEZUELA

GRENADA

NAURU

BAKER &
HOWLAND
ISLANDS
(to US)

JARVIS ISLAND
(to US)

PANAMA

TRINIDAD & TOBAGO

FRENCH GUIANA
(to France)

COLOMBIA

K I R I B A T I

Equator

ECUADOR

GUYANA

Equator

TUVALU

SURINAM

SOLOMON
ISLANDS

TOKELAU
(to NZ)

B R A Z I L

VANUATU

COOK
ISLANDS
(to NZ)

P E R U

NEW
CALEDONIA
(to France)

FRENCH POLYNESIA
(to France)

BOLIVIA

FIJI

PARAGUAY

Tropic of Capricorn

4

TONGA

NIUE (to NZ)

SAMOA

AMERICAN
SAMOA
(to US)

PITCAIRN
ISLANDS
(to UK)

CHILE

URUGUAY

A R G E N T I N A

NEW
ZEALAND

*P A C I F I C

O C E A N*

FALKLAND ISLANDS
(to UK)

CHILE

5

Antarctic Circle

A N T A R C T I C A

45

GOVERNMENTS OF THE WORLD

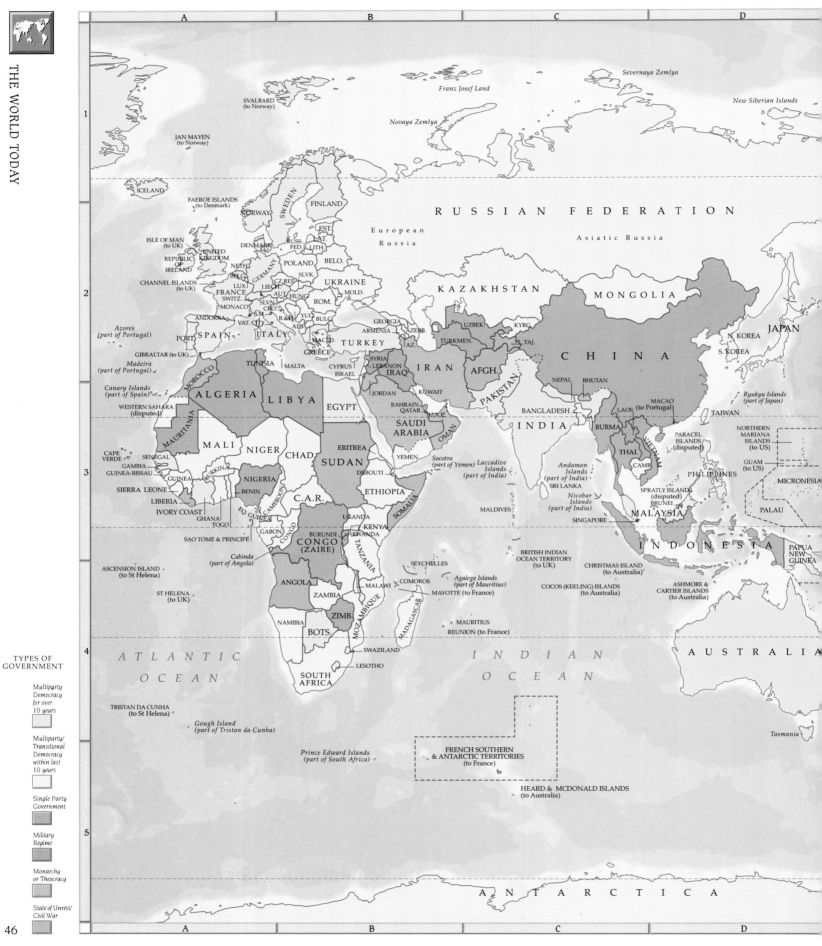

TYPES OF GOVERNMENT

Multiparty Democracy for over 10 years

Multiparty/ Transitional Democracy within last 10 years

Single Party Government

Military Regime

Monarchy or Theocracy

State of Unrest/ Civil War

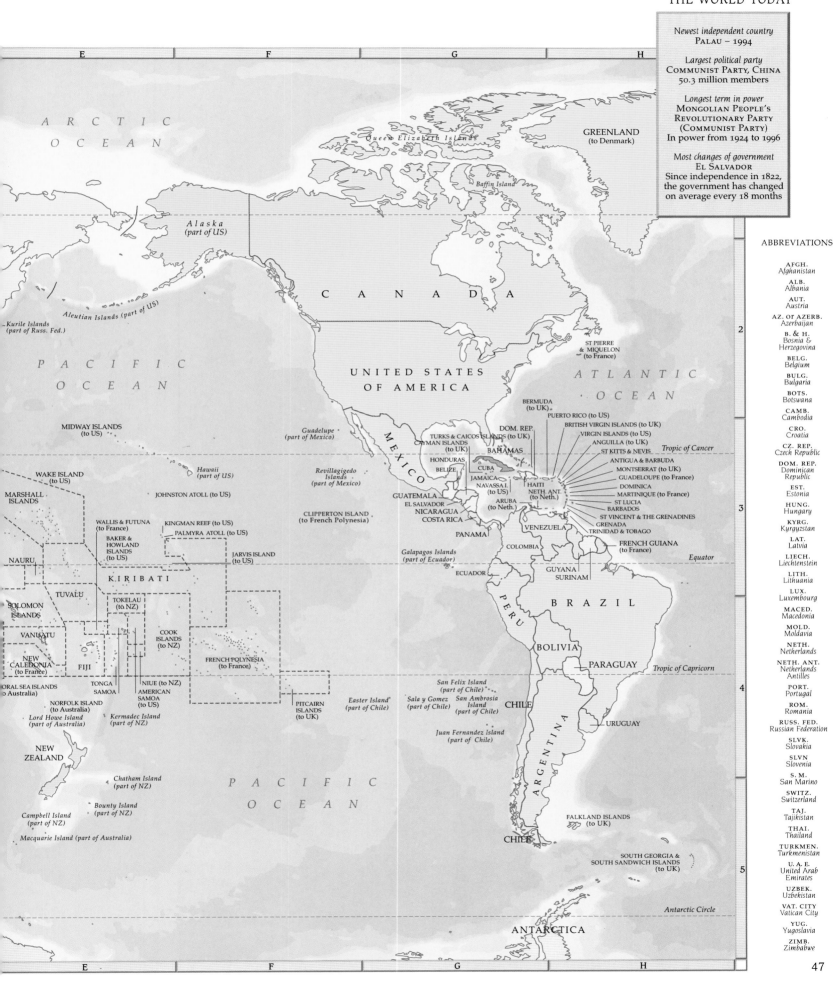

THE WORLD TODAY

Newest independent country
PALAU – 1994

Largest political party
COMMUNIST PARTY, CHINA
50.3 million members

Longest term in power
MONGOLIAN PEOPLE'S
REVOLUTIONARY PARTY
(COMMUNIST PARTY)
In power from 1924 to 1996

Most changes of government
EL SALVADOR
Since independence in 1822,
the government has changed
on average every 18 months

ARCTIC OCEAN

GREENLAND (to Denmark)

Queen Elizabeth Islands

Baffin Island

Alaska (part of US)

Aleutian Islands (part of US)

Kurile Islands (part of Russ. Fed.)

PACIFIC OCEAN

CANADA

UNITED STATES OF AMERICA

ATLANTIC OCEAN

ST PIERRE & MIQUELON (to France)

MIDWAY ISLANDS (to US)

Guadelupe (part of Mexico)

BERMUDA (to UK)

PUERTO RICO (to US)

BRITISH VIRGIN ISLANDS (to UK)

VIRGIN ISLANDS (to US)

ANGUILLA (to UK)

ST KITTS & NEVIS

Tropic of Cancer

DOM. REP.

TURKS & CAICOS ISLANDS (to UK)

CAYMAN ISLANDS (to UK)

BAHAMAS

MEXICO

WAKE ISLAND (to US)

Hawaii (part of US)

Revillagigedo Islands (part of Mexico)

HONDURAS

BELIZE

CUBA

ANTIGUA & BARBUDA

MONTSERRAT (to UK)

GUADELOUPE (to France)

DOMINICA

MARTINIQUE (to France)

ST LUCIA

BARBADOS

ST VINCENT & THE GRENADINES

GRENADA

TRINIDAD & TOBAGO

MARSHALL ISLANDS

JOHNSTON ATOLL (to US)

JAMAICA

NAVASSA I. (to US)

HAITI

NETH. ANT. (to Neth.)

GUATEMALA

EL SALVADOR

NICARAGUA

COSTA RICA

ARUBA (to Neth.)

WALLIS & FUTUNA (to France)

KINGMAN REEF (to US)

PALMYRA ATOLL (to US)

CLIPPERTON ISLAND (to French Polynesia)

PANAMA

VENEZUELA

FRENCH GUIANA (to France)

BAKER & HOWLAND ISLANDS (to US)

JARVIS ISLAND (to US)

COLOMBIA

Galapagos Islands (part of Ecuador)

Equator

NAURU

KIRIBATI

ECUADOR

GUYANA

SURINAM

TUVALU

PERU

BRAZIL

SOLOMON ISLANDS

TOKELAU (to NZ)

COOK ISLANDS (to NZ)

BOLIVIA

VANUATU

NEW CALEDONIA (to France)

FIJI

NIUE (to NZ)

TONGA

SAMOA

AMERICAN SAMOA (to US)

FRENCH POLYNESIA (to France)

San Felix Island (part of Chile)

Sala y Gomez (part of Chile)

San Ambrosia Island (part of Chile)

PARAGUAY

Tropic of Capricorn

CHILE

CORAL SEA ISLANDS (to Australia)

NORFOLK ISLAND (to Australia)

Lord Howe Island (part of Australia)

Kermadec Island (part of NZ)

PITCAIRN ISLANDS (to UK)

Easter Island (part of Chile)

Juan Fernandez Island (part of Chile)

URUGUAY

ARGENTINA

NEW ZEALAND

Chatham Island (part of NZ)

PACIFIC OCEAN

Bounty Island (part of NZ)

Campbell Island (part of NZ)

Macquarie Island (part of Australia)

FALKLAND ISLANDS (to UK)

CHILE

SOUTH GEORGIA & SOUTH SANDWICH ISLANDS (to UK)

Antarctic Circle

ANTARCTICA

ABBREVIATIONS

AFGH. *Afghanistan*
ALB. *Albania*
AUT. *Austria*
AZ. or AZERB. *Azerbaijan*
B. & H. *Bosnia & Herzegovina*
BELG. *Belgium*
BULG. *Bulgaria*
BOTS. *Botswana*
CAMB. *Cambodia*
CRO. *Croatia*
CZ. REP. *Czech Republic*
DOM. REP. *Dominican Republic*
EST. *Estonia*
HUNG. *Hungary*
KYRG. *Kyrgyzstan*
LAT. *Latvia*
LIECH. *Liechtenstein*
LITH. *Lithuania*
LUX. *Luxembourg*
MACED. *Macedonia*
MOLD. *Moldavia*
NETH. *Netherlands*
NETH. ANT. *Netherlands Antilles*
PORT. *Portugal*
ROM. *Romania*
RUSS. FED. *Russian Federation*
SLVK. *Slovakia*
SLVN. *Slovenia*
S. M. *San Marino*
SWITZ. *Switzerland*
TAJ. *Tajikistan*
THAI. *Thailand*
TURKMEN. *Turkmenistan*
U. A. E. *United Arab Emirates*
UZBEK. *Uzbekistan*
VAT. CITY *Vatican City*
YUG. *Yugoslavia*
ZIMB. *Zimbabwe*

47

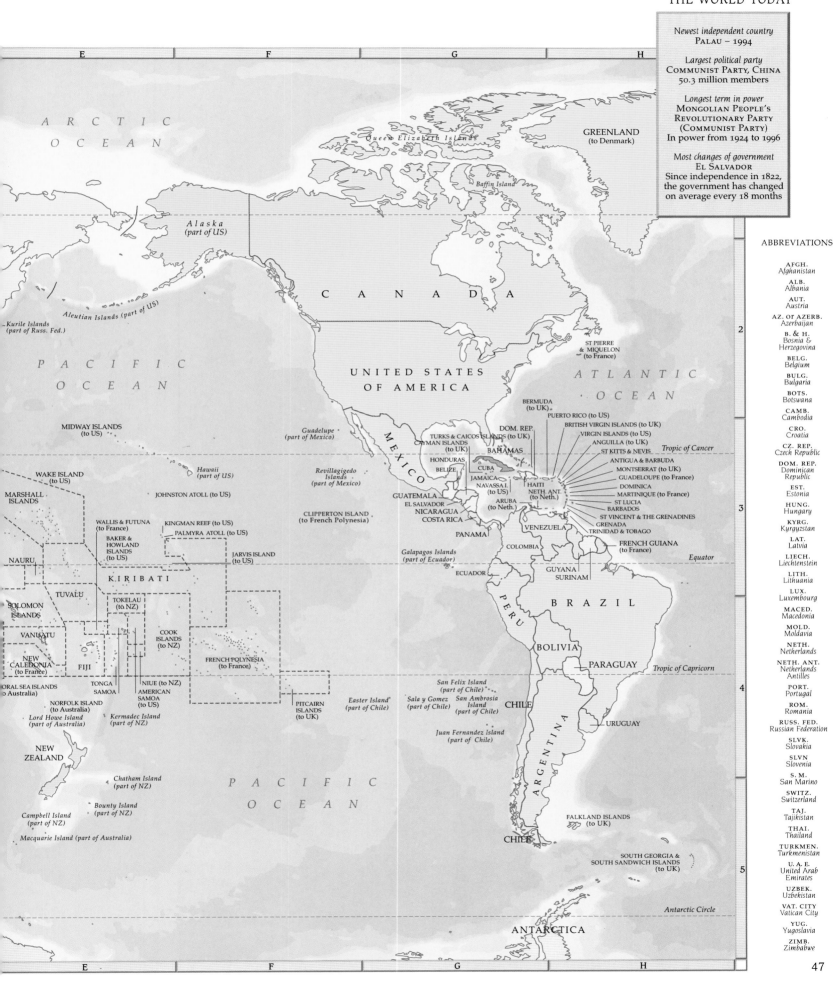

THE WORLD TODAY

Newest independent country
PALAU – 1994

Largest political party
COMMUNIST PARTY, CHINA
50.3 million members

Longest term in power
MONGOLIAN PEOPLE'S
REVOLUTIONARY PARTY
(COMMUNIST PARTY)
In power from 1924 to 1996

Most changes of government
EL SALVADOR
Since independence in 1822,
the government has changed
on average every 18 months

ABBREVIATIONS

AFGH. *Afghanistan*
ALB. *Albania*
AUT. *Austria*
AZ. or AZERB. *Azerbaijan*
B. & H. *Bosnia & Herzegovina*
BELG. *Belgium*
BULG. *Bulgaria*
BOTS. *Botswana*
CAMB. *Cambodia*
CRO. *Croatia*
CZ. REP. *Czech Republic*
DOM. REP. *Dominican Republic*
EST. *Estonia*
HUNG. *Hungary*
KYRG. *Kyrgyzstan*
LAT. *Latvia*
LIECH. *Liechtenstein*
LITH. *Lithuania*
LUX. *Luxembourg*
MACED. *Macedonia*
MOLD. *Moldavia*
NETH. *Netherlands*
NETH. ANT. *Netherlands Antilles*
PORT. *Portugal*
ROM. *Romania*
RUSS. FED. *Russian Federation*
SLVK. *Slovakia*
SLVN. *Slovenia*
S. M. *San Marino*
SWITZ. *Switzerland*
TAJ. *Tajikistan*
THAI. *Thailand*
TURKMEN. *Turkmenistan*
U. A. E. *United Arab Emirates*
UZBEK. *Uzbekistan*
VAT. CITY *Vatican City*
YUG. *Yugoslavia*
ZIMB. *Zimbabwe*

WORLD TOURISM

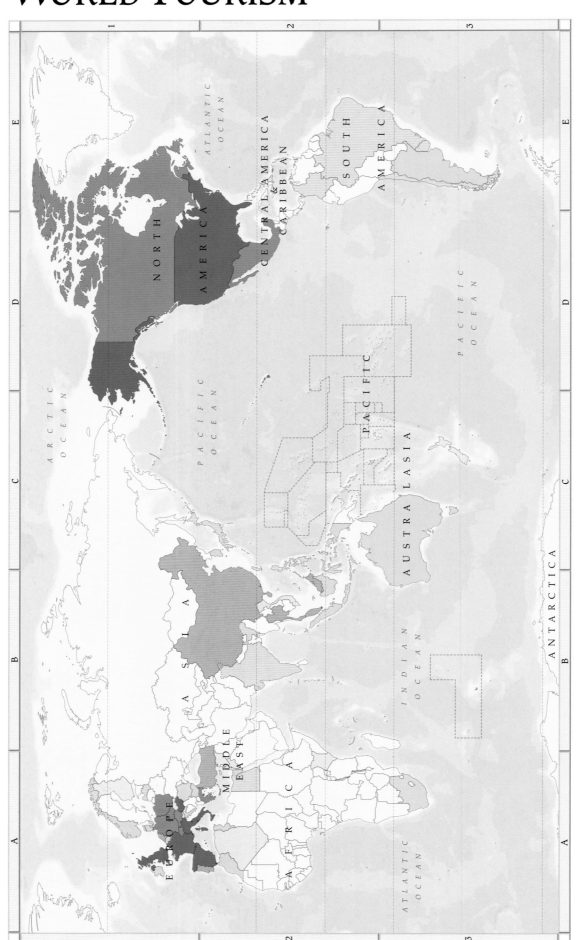

ATLANTIC OCEAN

NORTH AMERICA

CENTRAL AMERICA & CARIBBEAN

SOUTH AMERICA

ARCTIC OCEAN

PACIFIC OCEAN

PACIFIC OCEAN

PACIFIC

AUSTRALASIA

ASIA

INDIAN OCEAN

MIDDLE EAST

EUROPE

AFRICA

ATLANTIC OCEAN

ANTARCTICA

*Most popular
tourist destinations*
FRANCE, SPAIN,
UNITED STATES OF
AMERICA, ITALY,
UNITED KINGDOM,
HUNGARY, MEXICO,
POLAND, AUSTRIA,
CANADA

Tourists visiting France, 1995
61 MILLION

*Number of tourists
worldwide, 1995*
567 MILLION

*Estimated number
of tourists, 2010*
937 MILLION

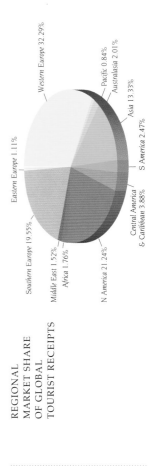

REGIONAL
MARKET SHARE
OF GLOBAL
TOURIST RECEIPTS

Western Europe 32.29%
Pacific 0.84%
Australasia 2.01%
Asia 13.33%
S America 2.47%
Central America & Caribbean 3.88%
N America 21.24%
Africa 1.76%
Middle East 1.52%
Southern Europe 19.55%
Eastern Europe 1.11%

TOURIST ARRIVALS

more than 20 million	10 million – 20 million	5 million – 10 million
2.5 million – 5 million	1 million – 2.5 million	700,000 – 999,000
		less than 700,000

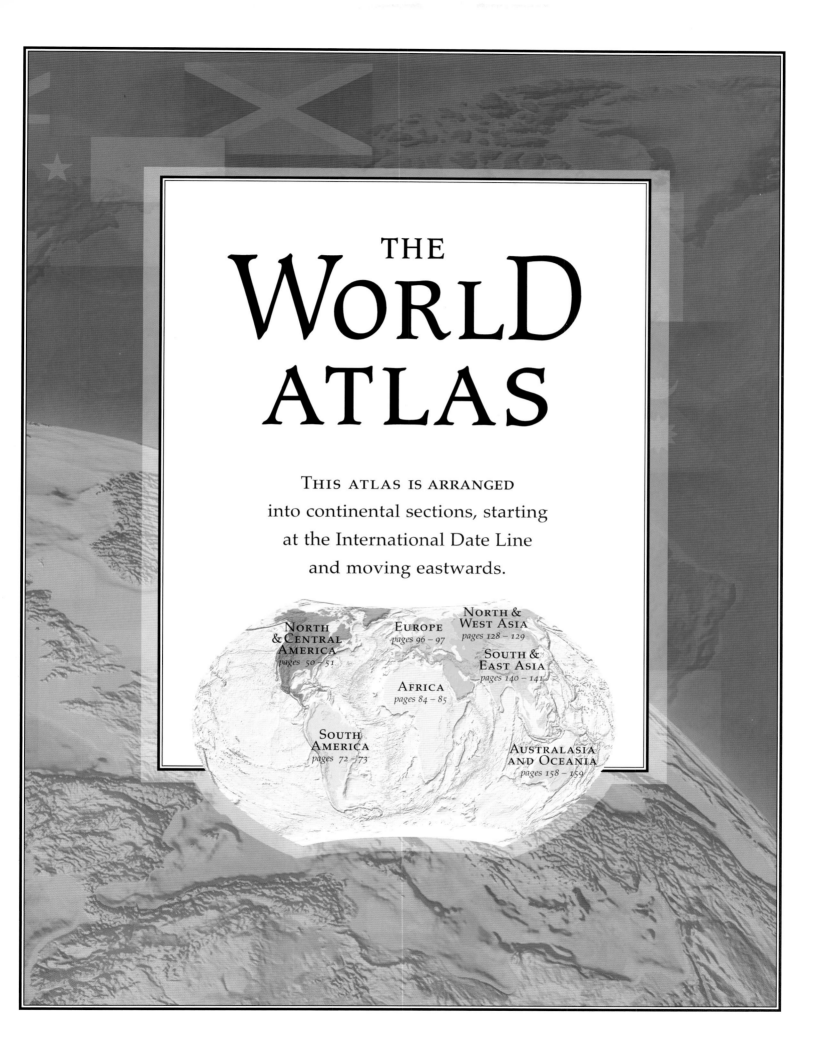

THE
WORLD
ATLAS

THIS ATLAS IS ARRANGED
into continental sections, starting
at the International Date Line
and moving eastwards.

NORTH
& CENTRAL
AMERICA
pages 50 – 51

EUROPE
pages 96 – 97

NORTH &
WEST ASIA
pages 128 – 129

SOUTH &
EAST ASIA
pages 140 – 141

AFRICA
pages 84 – 85

SOUTH
AMERICA
pages 72 –73

AUSTRALASIA
AND OCEANIA
pages 158 – 159

NORTH & CENTRAL AMERICA

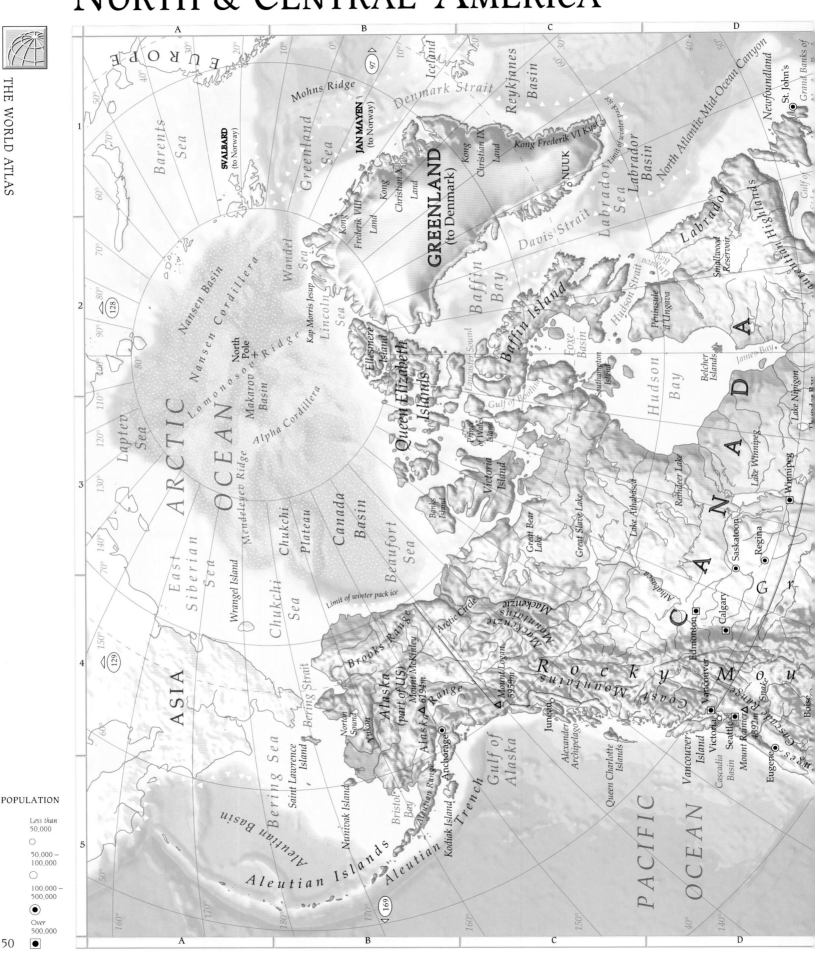

POPULATION

Less than
50,000
○

50,000 –
100,000
○

100,000 –
500,000
◉

Over
500,000
◼

ATLANTIC

OCEAN

MIQUELON
(to France)

Halifax

Sargasso Sea

Bermuda Rise

Nares Plain

Tropic of Cancer

VIRGIN ISLANDS (to US)
BRITISH VIRGIN ISLANDS (to UK)
ANGUILLA (to UK)
ANTIGUA & BARBUDA
GUADELOUPE
(to France)
DOMINICA
Lesser
MARTINIQUE (to France)
Antilles
ST LUCIA
ST VINCENT &
THE GRENADINES
BARBADOS
GRENADA
PORT-OF-SPAIN
TRINIDAD & TOBAGO

ST KITTS & NEVIS
MONTSERRAT (to UK)

Quebec
Montréal
Scotia
Newfoundland

Georges
Bank
Boston
Cape Cod
New York
Philadelphia
Baltimore
WASHINGTON DC
Richmond

OTTAWA
Lake Ontario
Albany
Niagara
Falls
Lake Erie
Toronto

Raleigh

Appalachian Mountains

Columbia

BERMUDA
(to UK)

Hatteras Plain

TURKS & CAICOS
ISLANDS
(to UK)

Greater Antilles

PUERTO
RICO
(to US)

NETHERLANDS
ANTILLES
(to Neth.)

ARUBA
(to Neth.)

SOUTH
AMERICA

Andes

Equator

Jacksonville

Blake
Plateau

BAHAMAS
NASSAU

Straits of Florida

DOMINICAN
REPUBLIC
SANTO
DOMINGO

HAITI
PORT-AU-PRINCE
KINGSTON
JAMAICA

Caribbean Sea

Colombian
Basin

Detroit
Cleveland
Columbus

Nashville

Atlanta
Montgomery

Memphis

Jackson

Baton Rouge
New Orleans

Miami
Tampa

HAVANA

CUBA

CAYMAN
ISLANDS
(to UK)

PANAMA CITY
PANAMA

Panama
Basin

ELEVATION

Milwaukee
Madison
Chicago
Indianapolis

Springfield

Little Rock

Arkansas
Red River

Houston

Gulf of Mexico

Yucatan
Peninsula

BELMOPAN
BELIZE
TEGUCIGALPA
HONDURAS

NICARAGUA
Lake Nicaragua
MANAGUA

COSTA RICA
SAN JOSÉ

Cocos Ridge

Galapagos Islands
(part of Ecuador)

PACIFIC

4 000 m
13 124 ft

2 000 m
6 562 ft

Des Moines
Lincoln

Topeka
Oklahoma City

Dallas

Austin

San Antonio
Rio Grande

Monterrey

Mississippi
Delta

MEXICO CITY
Volcán
Pico de Orizaba
5700m

GUATEMALA CITY
GUATEMALA
SAN SALVADOR
EL SALVADOR

Guatemala Basin

Colón Ridge

1 000 m
3 281 ft

500 m
1 640 ft

250 m
820 ft

UNITED STATES
OF AMERICA

Denver

El Paso

Phoenix

Sierra Madre Oriental

MEXICO

Acapulco

Middle America Trench

East Pacific Rise

100 m
328 ft

Sea
Level

Sea
Level

Mount Whitney
4418m

Grand
Canyon
Colorado

Guadalajara

Sierra Madre Occidental

Gulf of California

Lower California

Recillagigedo
Islands
(part of Mexico)

-250 m
-820 ft

San Francisco
San Jose
Los Angeles
San Diego

Coast

Tropic of Cancer

Clarion Fracture Zone

CLIPPERTON ISLAND
(to French Polynesia)

0 km
0 miles

1000

1000

N

Gallego
Rise

Equator

-500 m
-1 640 ft

-1 000 m
-3 281 ft

-2 000 m
-6 562 ft

-3 000 m
-9 843 ft

-4 000 m
-13 124 ft

WESTERN CANADA & ALASKA

RUSSIAN FEDERATION

Poluostrov Kamchatka

Arctic Circle

Ostrov Vrangelya

ARCTIC

Chukchi Sea

Near Islands

Attu Island

Bering Sea

Wevok
Point Lay
Barrow
Kivalina

Bering Strait

Gambell
Wales
Saint Lawrence Island
Deering
Umiat
Prudhoe Bay
Kaktovik

Rat Islands

Colville River
Brooks Range

Amchitka Island

Norton Sound

Alakanuk

Nunivak Island

Grayling
Yukon River
Kokrines
Fort Yukon
Aklavik

Andreanof Islands

Pribilof Islands

Kwigillingok

ALASKA (part of US)

Fort McPherson

Aleutian Islands

Atka

Platinum

Kuskokwim Mts

Fairbanks

Yukon River

Umnak Island
Dutch Harbor
Unalaska Island
Unimak Island
Belkofski

Bristol Bay

Iliamna Lake

Alaska Range
Mount McKinley 6194m
McKinley Park

Susitna
Anchorage

YUKON

Mackenzie

Kodiak
Shumagin Islands
Kodiak Island

Alaska Peninsula

Hope
Valdez
Cordova
Katalla

Gulkana
Chitina

TERRITORY

Mount Logan 5959m

Yakutat

Whitehorse

Gulf of Alaska

Haines
Gustavus
Atlin

BRITISH

Juneau
Kake

Alexander Archipelago

Port Alexander

PACIFIC

Ketchikan

Prince Rupert

Coast Mountains

OCEAN

Queen Charlotte Islands

Kitimat

Ocean Falls

Queen Charlotte Sound

Mount Waddington 4016m

Port Hardy
Campbell River

Vancouver Island

Nanaimo
Victoria

POPULATION

Less than 50,000

50,000 – 100,000

100,000 – 500,000

Over 500,000

52

0 km   400

0 miles   400

O C E A N

Beaufort
Sea

Alert

Ellesmere Island

Axel Heiberg
Island

Ellef Ringnes
Island
Isachsen

Amund
Ringnes
Island

Knud Rasmussen Land

GREENLAND
(Danish external
territory)

Prince Patrick
Island

Mould Bay

Queen Elizabeth Islands

Bathurst
Island   Cornwallis
Island

Devon Island

Baffin
Bay

Melville
Island

Resolute

Viscount Melville
Sound

Lancaster Sound

Davis Strait

Sachs Harbour

Banks
Island

Somerset
Island

Prince of
Wales Island

Broderi
Peninsula

Baffin Island

Tuktoyaktuk   Amundsen
Gulf

Holman

Victoria
Island

Boothia
Peninsula

Igloolik

Cumberland Sound

Nettilling
Lake

nuvik
Paulatuk

Fort
Good Hope

Coppermine

Great
Bear
Lake   Echo Bay

Burnside

Cambridge Bay

King William
Island

Pelly Bay

Gjoa Haven

Melville
Peninsula

Foxe
Basin

Iqaluit

Amadjuak
Lake

Repulse Bay

Southampton
Island

Hudson Strait

Back

Garry Lake

Baker Lake

Coral
Harbour

Péninsule
d' Ungava

N O R T H W E S T   T E R R I T O R I E S

Dubawnt

Rankin Inlet

Coats
Island

Mansel
Island

ungsten

Rae-Edzo

Yellowknife   Reliance

Whale Cove

Q U É B E C

Fort Simpson

Lutselk'e

Fort Providence

Great Slave
Lake

Arviat

Hudson

Fort Liard

Hay River

Bay

Fort Nelson

Fort Smith

Lake Athabasca

Churchill

James
Bay

OLUMBIA

Vare

Fort Vermilion

Wollaston Lake

Reindeer Lake

Southern
Indian Lake

Belcher
Islands

C
Fort St.John   A

Fort
McMurray   N   Fox Mine

Nelson

A

D

A

ALBERTA

Grande Prairie

Buffalo
Narrows

Thompson

O N T A R I O

Prince George

Athabasca

Athabasca

SASKATCHEWAN

Flin Flon

The Pas

Lake
Winnipeg

Edmonton

North Saskatchewan

Saskatchewan

M A N I T O B A

Mount Robson
3954m

Leduc

Prince Albert

Red Deer

Saskatoon

Kamloops

Calgary

Kindersley   Yorkton

Lake
Manitoba

Kelowna

Medicine Hat

Regina   Qu' Appelle

Lake
of the Woods

Winnipeg

ancouver

Cranbrook

Lethbridge

Brandon
Weyburn

Melita

Milk River

Estevan

Lake Superior

Lake
Michigan

Lake Huron

U N I T E D   S T A T E S   O F   A M E R I C A

ELEVATION

4 000 m	13 124 ft
2 000 m	6 562 ft
1 000 m	3 281 ft
500 m	1 640 ft
250 m	820 ft
100 m	328 ft
Sea Level	Sea Level
-250 m	-820 ft
-500 m	-1 640 ft
-1 000 m	-3 281 ft
-2 000 m	-6 562 ft
-3 000 m	-9 843 ft
-4 000 m	-13 124 ft

EASTERN CANADA

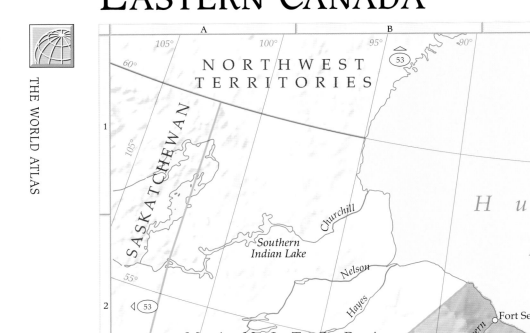

NORTHWEST TERRITORIES

SASKATCHEWAN

Churchill

Southern Indian Lake

Nelson

Hayes

MANITOBA

Cedar Lake

Lake Winnipeg

Lake Winnipegosis

Lake Manitoba

C

Sandy Lake

ONTARIO

Attawapiskat

Attawapiskat

Albany

Fort Albany

Moosonee

A

N

Coats Island

Mansel Island

Ivujivik

Charles Island

Hudson

Péninsule d' Ungava

Inukjuak

Koksoak

H U D S O N

B A Y

Ottawa Islands

Belcher Islands

James Bay

Akimiski Island

Lac Minto

Lac Bienville

QUÉ

A

Eastmain

Rivière de Rupert

Lac Mistassini

Chibougamau

Réservoir Gouin

Fort Severn

Winisk

Winisk

Severn

Red River

Kenora

Dryden

Armstrong

Lac Seul

Longlac

Lake of the Woods

Fort Frances

Lake Nipigon

Nipigon

Atikokan

Rainy Lake

Thunder Bay

Hearst

Kapuskasing

Cochrane

Moose

Harricana

Amos

Rouyn-Noranda

Val-d'Or

Marathon
Tip Top Mountain 640m

Timmins

Wawa

Foleyet

Kirkland Lake

NORTH DAKOTA

MINNESOTA

Lake Superior

Sault Ste.Marie

Sudbury

North Bay

Pembroke

Gatineau

Lav

Hull

OTTAWA

SOUTH DAKOTA

M I C H I G A N

Manitoulin Island

Georgian Bay

Midland

Lake Huron

Peterborough

Kingston

Lake Ontario

UNITED STATES

WISCONSIN

OF AMERICA

IOWA

NEBRASKA

Lake Michigan

Brampton

Kitchener

Hamilton

Sarnia

London

Windsor

Toronto

Oshawa

St. Catharines

Niagara Falls

NEW YORK

Leamington

Lake Erie

Mississippi River

ILLINOIS

INDIANA

OHIO

PENNSYLVANIA

POPULATION

Less than 50,000
○

50,000 – 100,000
○

100,000 – 500,000
◉

Over 500,000
◉

Baffin
Island

Strait

Resolution
Island

Button Islands

Akpatok
Island

*Ungava
Bay*

Kuujjuaq

Rivière à la Baleine

Caniapiscau

Nain

Hopedale

Makkovik

Cape Harrison

Scheffervile

NEWFOUNDLAND

Cartwright

*Smallwood
Reservoir*

Lake Melville

Churchill

L a b r a d o r   S e a

98

82

ELEVATION

St.Anthony

B E C

D

A

*Réservoir de
Caniapiscau*

& LABRADOR

4 000 *m*
13 124 *ft*

2 000 *m*
6 562 *ft*

*Réservoir
Manicouagan*

Laurentian Highlands

Havre-St-Pierre

Gander

Grand Falls

St.John's

1 000 *m*
3 281 *ft*

Corner Brook

Newfoundland

500 *m*
1 640 *ft*

Sept-Îles

Strait of Belle Isle

Île d'Anticosti

*Lac
St-Jean*

Baie-Comeau

St.Lawrence

Gaspé

*Péninsule de
Gaspé*

*Gulf of
St. Lawrence*

Chicoutimi

Matane

Rimouski

Rivière-du-Loup

*Îles de la
Madeleine*

Bathurst

Channel-Port
aux Basques

Cape Race

250 *m*
820 *ft*

onquière

La Tuque

Edmundston

NEW

PRINCE
EDWARD
ISLAND

Glace Bay

**ST PIERRE
& MIQUELON**
(French territorial
collectivity)

100 *m*
328 *ft*

Charlesbourg

BRUNSWICK

Moncton

Charlottetown

Sydney

*Cape Breton
Island*

82

Sea
Level

Sea
Level

Québec

Amherst

New Glasgow

Oromocto

Trois-
Rivières

St-Georges

Fredericton

Truro

NOVA SCOTIA

-250 *m*
-820 *ft*

Drummondville

St.John

Montréal

MAINE

Bay of Fundy

Dartmouth

Sherbrooke

Halifax

Sable Island

-500 *m*
-1 640 *ft*

Liverpool

Yarmouth

VERMONT

NEW
HAMPSHIRE

A T L A N T I C

-1 000 *m*
-3 281 *ft*

-2 000 *m*
-6 562 *ft*

MASSACHUSETTS

Cape Cod

O C E A N

N

-3 000 *m*
-9 843 *ft*

CONNECTICUT

RHODE ISLAND

0 km   400

82

0 miles   400

-4 000 *m*
-13 124 *ft*

POPULATION

Less than
50,000

50,000 –
100,000

100,000 –
500,000

Over
500,000

MINNESOTA

Upper Red Lake
Lower Red Lake
Namakan Lake

Isle Royale

Lake Superior

Keweenaw Peninsula

Apostle Islands

Superior
Ashland
Ironwood
Houghton
Marquette
Saint Ignace

Gogebic Range
Sault Sainte Marie

Mille Lacs Lake

Rice Lake
Woodruff
Rhinelander
Iron Mountain
Escanabar
Cheboygan

WISCONSIN

MICHIGAN

Beaver Island
Petoskey
Alpena

Lake Huron

Georgian Bay

River Falls
Eau Claire
Wausau
Stevens Point
Green Bay
Traverse City
Beulah
Roscommon

Wisconsin Rapids
Appleton
Cadillac

Tomah
Oshkosh
Lake Winnebago
Ludington

La Crosse
Fond du Lac
Midland
Bay City

Sheboygan
Mount Pleasant
Muskegon
Saginaw

West Bend
Grand Rapids
Flint

Madison
Milwaukee
Wyoming
Lansing
Pontiac
Port Huron

Waukesha
Racine
Kalamazoo
Livonia
Warren

Janesville
Kenosha
Ann Arbor
Detroit

Rockford
Waukegan
Adrian
Toledo

Elgin
Evanston
South Bend
Cleveland
Euclid
Warre

Sterling
Chicago
Gary
Elkhart
Akron

Aurora
Joliet
Valparaiso
Bowling Green
Sandusky
Youngstown

Rock Island
Ottawa
Findlay
Mansfield
Canton

Galesburg
Kankakee
Fort Wayne
Van Wert
Aliquip

Peoria
Wabash
Marion
Wheeling

Macomb
Bloomington
Lafayette
Kokomo
Sidney
Delaware
Cambridge

Pekin
Champaign
Anderson
Muncie
Springfield
Zanesville

Quincy
Carmel
Columbus
Athens
Clarksbur

Springfield
Decatur
Indianapolis
Dayton
Kettering
Wilmington

Jacksonville
Terre Haute
Chillicothe
Parkersburg

ILLINOIS
Columbus
Cincinnati
WEST

Alton
Effingham
Bloomington
Newport
Portsmouth
VIRGINIA

East Saint Louis
Vincennes
Huntington
Charleston

Belleville
Mount Vernon
New Albany
Louisville
Lexington
Saint Albans

MISSOURI
Carbondale
Henderson
Frankfort
Richmond
Beckley

Owensboro
Elizabethtown

Alton
Paducah
KENTUCKY
Pikeville
Bluefie

Lake of the Ozarks
Bowling Green
Somerset
London
Pulas

Hopkinsville
Green River
Middlesboro
Bristol

Ozark Plateau
Kentucky Lake

ARKANSAS
TENNESSEE

IOWA

INDIANA
OHIO

Missouri River
Mississippi River
Wabash River
Ohio River
Illinois River
Wisconsin River
Saint Croix River

Lake Michigan
Green Bay
Door Peninsula
Saginaw Bay
Lake Saint Clair
Lake Erie

Appalachians

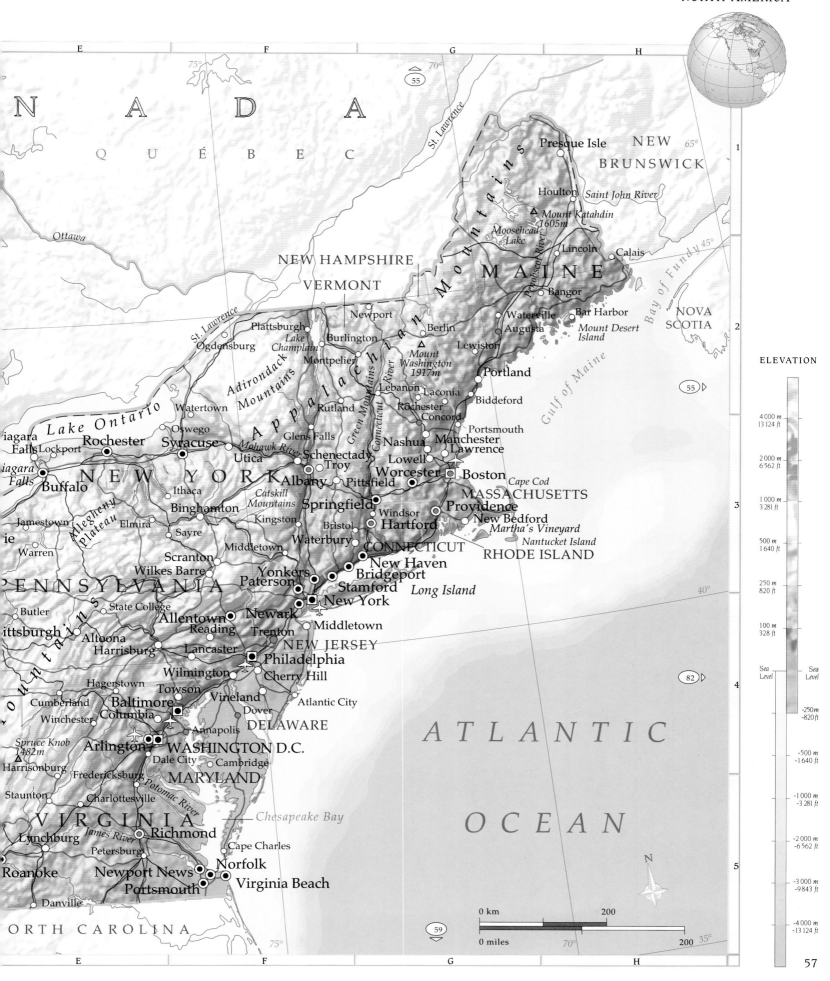

CANADA

QUÉBEC

Ottawa

St. Lawrence

NEW
BRUNSWICK

Presque Isle

Houlton · Saint John River

Mount Katahdin
1605m

MAINE

Moosehead
Lake

Lincoln · Calais

Penobscot River

Bangor

NOVA
SCOTIA

Bay of Fundy 45°

NEW HAMPSHIRE

VERMONT

Newport

Berlin

Waterville

Bar Harbor

Mount Desert
Island

Plattsburgh

Burlington

Augusta

Lewiston

Gulf of Maine

Ogdensburg

Lake
Champlain

Montpelier

Mount
Washington
1917m

Portland

St. Lawrence

Watertown

Adirondack
Mountains

Rutland

Lebanon

Biddeford

Laconia

Rochester

Concord

Portsmouth

Oswego

Glens Falls

Nashua

Manchester

Niagara
Falls · Lockport

Rochester

Syracuse

Utica

Schenectady

Lowell

Lawrence

Mohawk River

Troy

Worcester

Boston

Cape Cod

Niagara
Falls

Buffalo

NEW YORK

Albany

Pittsfield

MASSACHUSETTS

Ithaca

Springfield

Providence

Binghamton

Catskill
Mountains

Windsor

New Bedford

Jamestown

Allegheny
Plateau

Elmira

Kingston

Bristol

Hartford

Martha's Vineyard

Nantucket Island

Warren

Sayre

Middletown

Waterbury

CONNECTICUT

RHODE ISLAND

ie

PENNSYLVANIA

Scranton

New Haven

Wilkes Barre

Yonkers

Bridgeport

Paterson

Stamford

Long Island

Butler

State College

New York

Pittsburgh

Allentown

Newark

Altoona

Reading

Middletown

Harrisburg

Lancaster

Trenton

NEW JERSEY

Wilmington

Philadelphia

Cherry Hill

Hagerstown

Towson

Vineland

Atlantic City

Cumberland

Baltimore

Dover

Winchester

Columbia

Annapolis

DELAWARE

Spruce Knob
1482m

Arlington

WASHINGTON D.C.

Harrisonburg

Dale City

Cambridge

MARYLAND

Fredericksburg

Potomac River

Chesapeake Bay

ATLANTIC

Staunton

Charlottesville

VIRGINIA

James River

Richmond

OCEAN

Lynchburg

Petersburg

Cape Charles

Roanoke

Newport News

Norfolk

Portsmouth

Virginia Beach

Danville

NORTH CAROLINA

N

0 km   200

0 miles   200

35°

4 000 m
13 124 ft

2 000 m
6 562 ft

1 000 m
3 281 ft

500 m
1 640 ft

250 m
820 ft

100 m
328 ft

Sea
Level

Sea
Level

-250 m
-820 ft

-500 m
-1 640 ft

-1 000 m
-3 281 ft

-2 000 m
-6 562 ft

-3 000 m
-9 843 ft

-4 000 m
-13 124 ft

SOUTHEAST USA

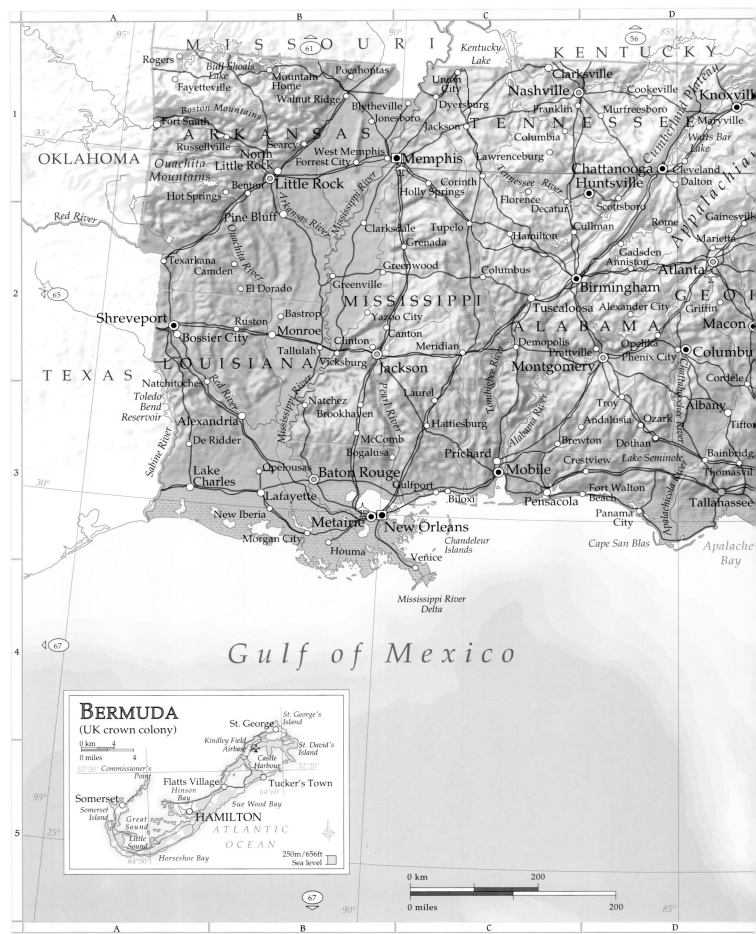

MISSOURI

Rogers
Bull Shoals Lake
Fayetteville
Mountain Home
Walnut Ridge
Pocahontas
Boston Mountains
Blytheville
Jonesboro
Union City
Dyersburg
Jackson
KENTUCKY
Kentucky Lake
Clarksville
Cookeville
Knoxville
Nashville
Franklin
Murfreesboro
Maryville
Watts Bar Lake

Fort Smith
ARKANSAS
Russellville
Searcy
West Memphis
Forrest City
Memphis
Corinth
Columbia
Lawrenceburg
TENNESSEE
Chattanooga
Cleveland
Little Rock
North Little Rock
Holly Springs
Florence
Huntsville
Dalton
OKLAHOMA
Ouachita Mountains
Benton
Little Rock
Decatur
Scottsboro
Hot Springs
Pine Bluff
Hamilton
Cullman
Rome
Gainesville
Ouachita River
Clarksdale
Tupelo
Marietta
Texarkana
Grenada
Columbus
Gadsden
Anniston
Atlanta
Camden
Greenwood
Birmingham
El Dorado
Greenville
MISSISSIPPI
Tuscaloosa
Alexander City
Griffin
GEORGIA
Macon
Shreveport
Bastrop
Yazoo City
Canton
ALABAMA
Ruston
Bossier City
Monroe
Clinton
Meridian
Demopolis
Prattville
Opelika
Phenix City
Columbus
Tallulah
Vicksburg
Jackson
Montgomery
Cordele
LOUISIANA
Natchitoches
Natchez
Brookhaven
Laurel
Troy
Albany
Toledo Bend Reservoir
Alexandria
Andalusia
Ozark
Tifton
De Ridder
McComb
Hattiesburg
Brewton
Dothan
Bainbridge
Bogalusa
Crestview
Thomasville
Lake Charles
Opelousas
Baton Rouge
Prichard
Mobile
Fort Walton Beach
Lake Seminole
Lafayette
Gulfport
Pensacola
Panama City
Tallahassee
New Iberia
Metairie
New Orleans
Biloxi
Cape San Blas
Apalachee Bay
Morgan City
Houma
Chandeleur Islands
Venice

Mississippi River Delta

Gulf of Mexico

Red River
Arkansas River
Mississippi River
Tennessee River
Cumberland Plateau
Appalachian
Red River
Sabine River
Pearl River
Tombigbee River
Alabama River
Chattahoochee River
Apalachicola River

BERMUDA
(UK crown colony)

0 km 4
0 miles 4

Commissioner's Point
Somerset
Somerset Island
Great Sound
Little Sound
Horseshoe Bay
Flatts Village
Hinson Bay
HAMILTON
St. George
Kindley Field Airbase
Castle Harbour
Sue Wood Bay
Tucker's Town
St. George's Island
St. David's Island

ATLANTIC OCEAN

250m/656ft
Sea level

0 km 200
0 miles 200

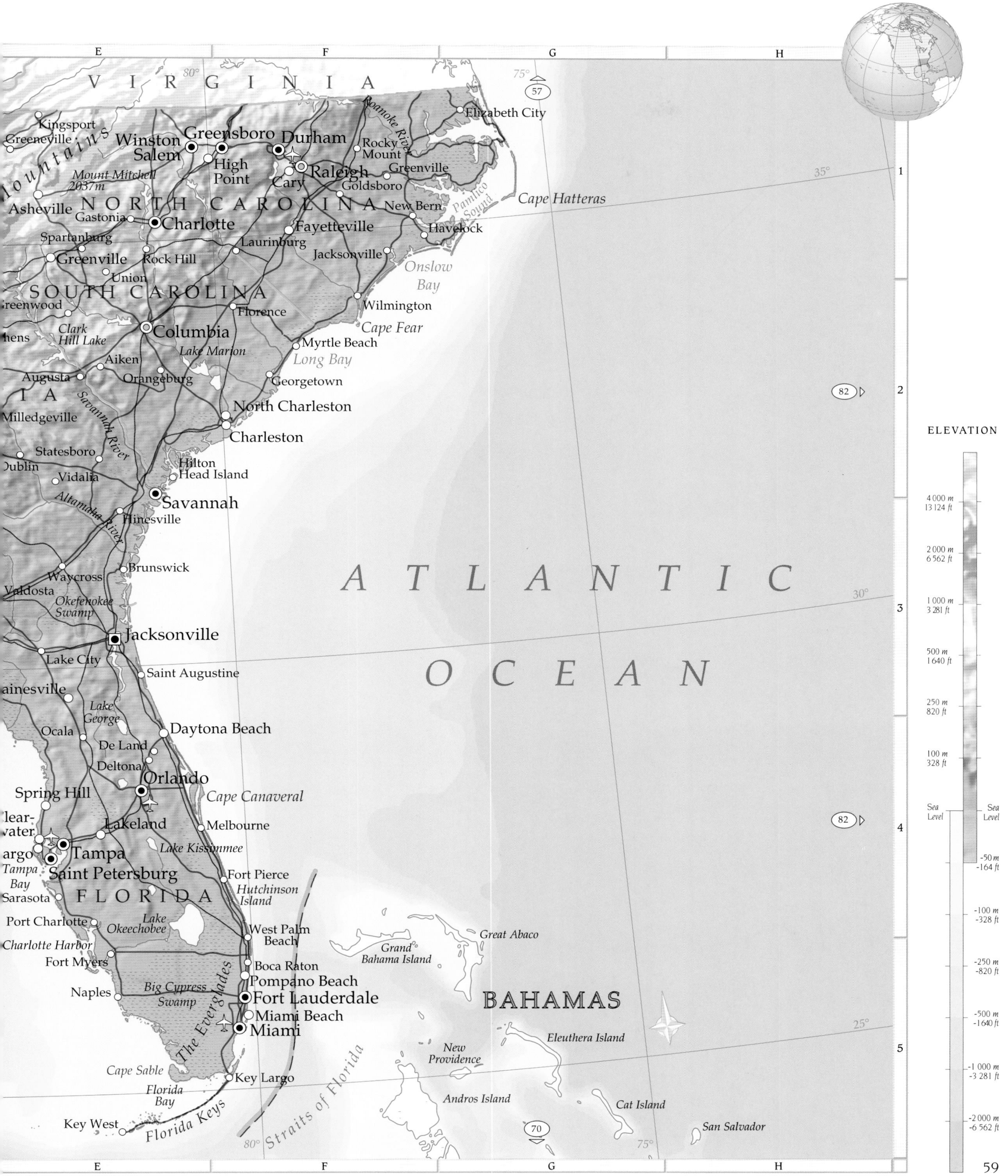

E
F
G
H
1
2
3
4
5
VIRGINIA
NORTH CAROLINA
SOUTH CAROLINA
FLORIDA
BAHAMAS
ATLANTIC
OCEAN
80°
75°
35°
30°
25°
57
82
70
Kingsport
Greeneville
Mountains
Winston Salem
Greensboro
Durham
High Point
Rocky Mount
Roanoke River
Elizabeth City
Mount Mitchell 2037m
Raleigh
Cary
Greenville
Goldsboro
Pamlico Sound
Cape Hatteras
Asheville
New Bern
Gastonia
Charlotte
Fayetteville
Havelock
Spartanburg
Laurinburg
Greenville
Rock Hill
Jacksonville
Union
Onslow Bay
reenwood
Florence
Wilmington
Clark Hill Lake
Columbia
Cape Fear
hens
Lake Marion
Myrtle Beach
Aiken
Long Bay
Augusta
Orangeburg
Georgetown
IA
Savannah River
North Charleston
Milledgeville
Charleston
Statesboro
Dublin
Hilton Head Island
Vidalia
Savannah
Altamaha River
Hinesville
Brunswick
Waycross
Valdosta
Okefenokee Swamp
Jacksonville
Lake City
Saint Augustine
ainesville
Lake George
Ocala
Daytona Beach
De Land
Deltona
Orlando
Spring Hill
Cape Canaveral
lear-vater
Lakeland
Melbourne
argo
Tampa
Lake Kissimmee
Tampa Bay
Saint Petersburg
Fort Pierce
Hutchinson Island
Sarasota
Port Charlotte
Lake Okeechobee
West Palm Beach
Great Abaco
Charlotte Harbor
Grand Bahama Island
Fort Myers
Boca Raton
Pompano Beach
Naples
Big Cypress Swamp
Fort Lauderdale
Miami Beach
Miami
The Everglades
Eleuthera Island
New Providence
Cape Sable
Key Largo
Straits of Florida
Florida Bay
Andros Island
Cat Island
Key West
Florida Keys
San Salvador
ELEVATION
4 000 m
13 124 ft
2 000 m
6 562 ft
1 000 m
3 281 ft
500 m
1 640 ft
250 m
820 ft
100 m
328 ft
Sea Level
Sea Level
-50 m
-164 ft
-100 m
-328 ft
-250 m
-820 ft
-500 m
-1 640 ft
-1 000 m
-3 281 ft
-2 000 m
-6 562 ft

CENTRAL USA

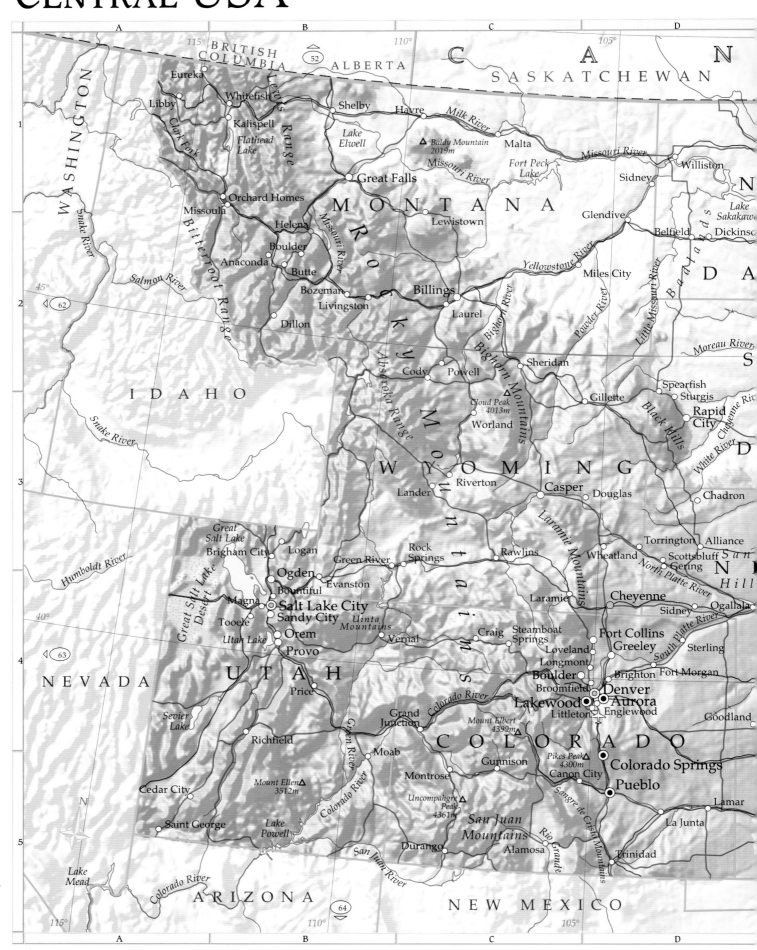

POPULATION

Less than
50,000
○

50,000 –
100,000
○

100,000 –
500,000
◉

Over
500,000
◼

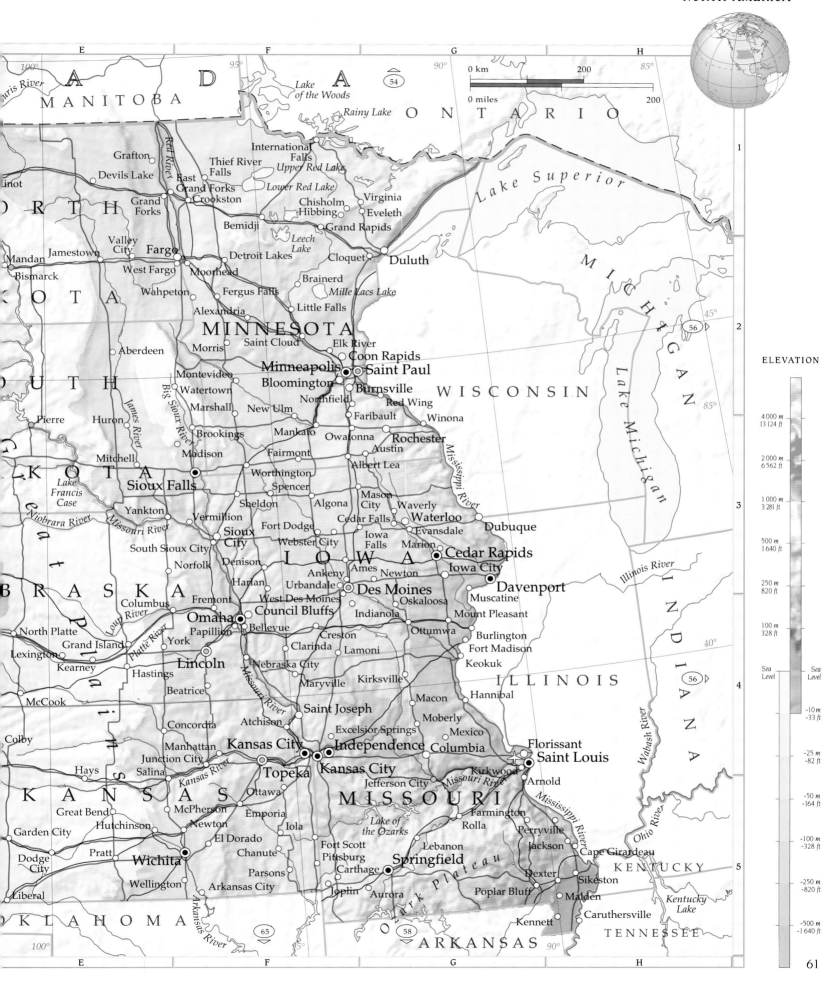

MANITOBA

CANADA

ONTARIO

Souris River

Lake of the Woods

Rainy Lake

Lake Superior

54

0 km   200

0 miles   200

MICHIGAN

100°   95°   90°   85°

Grafton

Devils Lake

Minot

East Grand Forks

Grand Forks

Crookston

Red River

Thief River Falls

International Falls

Upper Red Lake

Lower Red Lake

Virginia

Chisholm

Hibbing

Eveleth

Grand Rapids

Bemidji

Leech Lake

NORTH

Valley City

Jamestown

Fargo

West Fargo

Moorhead

Detroit Lakes

Cloquet

Duluth

Brainerd

Lake Michigan

85°

Mandan

Bismarck

Wahpeton

Fergus Falls

Mille Lacs Lake

1

DAKOTA

Alexandria

Little Falls

MINNESOTA

Aberdeen

Morris

Saint Cloud

Elk River

Coon Rapids

Minneapolis

Saint Paul

WISCONSIN

2

SOUTH

Montevideo

Watertown

Bloomington

Burnsville

Northfield

Red Wing

Pierre

Huron

Marshall

New Ulm

Faribault

Winona

45°

DAKOTA

Big Sioux River

Brookings

Mankato

Owatonna

Rochester

Austin

Mississippi River

Mitchell

Madison

Fairmont

Albert Lea

Lake Francis Case

Sioux Falls

Worthington

Spencer

Mason City

Waverly

Dubuque

3

Niobrara River

Yankton

Vermillion

Sheldon

Algona

Cedar Falls

Waterloo

Evansdale

Missouri River

Sioux City

Fort Dodge

Iowa Falls

Marion

Cedar Rapids

South Sioux City

Webster City

IOWA

Iowa City

Davenport

Norfolk

Denison

Ankeny

Ames

Newton

Muscatine

N E B R A S K A

Harlan

Urbandale

Des Moines

Oskaloosa

Mount Pleasant

Illinois River

Columbus

Loup River

Fremont

West Des Moines

Council Bluffs

Indianola

Ottumwa

Burlington

Omaha

Papillion

Bellevue

Creston

Fort Madison

North Platte

Platte River

York

Clarinda

Lamoni

Keokuk

Grand Island

Lincoln

Nebraska City

4

I N D I A N A

Lexington

Kearney

Hastings

Maryville

Kirksville

ILLINOIS

40°

McCook

Beatrice

Macon

Hannibal

Saint Joseph

Wabash River

Colby

Concordia

Atchison

Excelsior Springs

Moberly

Mexico

Kansas City

Independence

Columbia

Florissant

Saint Louis

Manhattan

Junction City

Kansas City

Kirkwood

Arnold

Hays

Salina

Kansas River

Topeka

Jefferson City

Missouri River

K A N S A S

Ottawa

MISSOURI

Farmington

Mississippi River

Ohio River

Great Bend

McPherson

Emporia

Lake of the Ozarks

Rolla

Perryville

Garden City

Hutchinson

Newton

Iola

Lebanon

Jackson

Cape Girardeau

KENTUCKY

Dodge City

Pratt

El Dorado

Chanute

Fort Scott

Pittsburg

Springfield

Ozark Plateau

Dexter

Sikeston

Wichita

Parsons

Carthage

Malden

Kentucky Lake

Liberal

Wellington

Arkansas City

Joplin

Aurora

Poplar Bluff

Caruthersville

TENNESSEE

Arkansas River

65

58

Kennett

OKLAHOMA

ARKANSAS

100°   95°   90°

5

E   F   G   H

ELEVATION

| 4 000 m / 13 124 ft |
| 2 000 m / 6 562 ft |
| 1 000 m / 3 281 ft |
| 500 m / 1 640 ft |
| 250 m / 820 ft |
| 100 m / 328 ft |
| Sea Level |
| −10 m / −33 ft |
| −25 m / −82 ft |
| −50 m / −164 ft |
| −100 m / −328 ft |
| −250 m / −820 ft |
| −500 m / −1 640 ft |

Sea Level

WEST USA

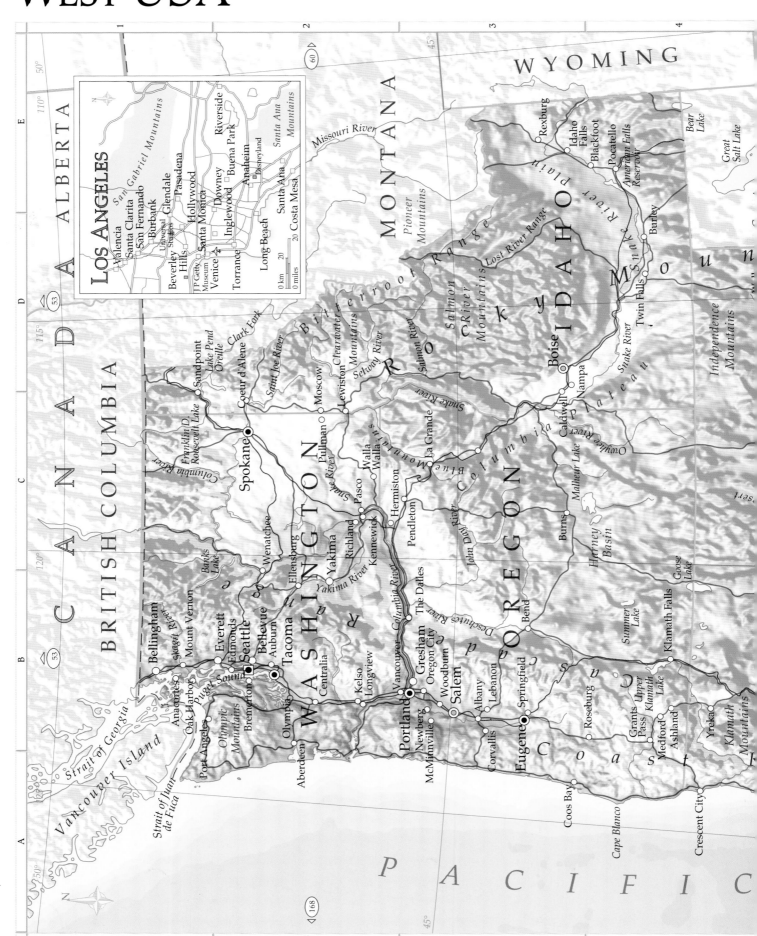

LOS ANGELES

Valencia · Santa Clarita · San Gabriel Mountains · San Fernando · Burbank · Universal Studios · Glendale · Pasadena · Beverley Hills · Hollywood · Santa Monica · JP Getty Museum · Venice · Inglewood · Downey · Buena Park · Anaheim · Disneyland · Santa Ana Mountains · Torrance · Long Beach · Costa Mesa · Santa Ana

0 km 20
0 miles

CANADA · ALBERTA · BRITISH COLUMBIA

MONTANA · WYOMING

IDAHO

Rexburg · Idaho Falls · Blackfoot · Pocatello · American Falls Reservoir · Bear Lake · Great Salt Lake

Missouri River

Pioneer Mountains · Lost River Range · Salmon River Mountains · Independence Mountains

Bitterroot Mountains · Clearwater Mountains · Selway River · Salmon River · Rocky Range · ROCKY Mountains

Sandpoint · Lake Pend Oreille · Clark Fork · Saint Joe River · Coeur d'Alene · Moscow · Lewiston · Pullman

Franklin D. Roosevelt Lake · Columbia River

Spokane

WASHINGTON

Wenatchee · Banks Lake · Ellensburg · Yakima · Yakima River · Richland · Pasco · Kennewick · Walla Walla · Hermiston · Pendleton · La Grande · Boise · Caldwell · Nampa · Snake River · Twin Falls · Burley · Snake River Plain · Columbia Plateau · Owyhee River

Blue Mountains · Columbia River

Bellingham · Skagit River · Mount Vernon · Everett · Edmonds · Seattle · Bellevue · Auburn · Tacoma · Puget Sound · Bremerton · Olympia · Centralia · Kelso · Longview · Vancouver · Gresham · Oregon City · Woodburn · Salem · Portland · Newberg · McMinnville · Albany · Lebanon · Springfield · Eugene · Corvallis

Anacortes · Oak Harbor · Port Angeles · Olympic Mountains · Aberdeen · Strait of Juan de Fuca · Vancouver Island · Strait of Georgia

OREGON

The Dalles · Deschutes River · Bend · John Day River · Burns · Harney Basin · Malheur Lake · Desert · Summer Lake · Goose Lake · Klamath Falls · Roseburg · Grants Pass · Upper Klamath Lake · Medford · Ashland · Yreka · Klamath Mountains · Crescent City · Coos Bay · Cape Blanco · Coast

Cascades

PACIFIC

POPULATION

Less than 50,000 ○

50,000 – 100,000 ○

100,000 – 500,000 ◉

Over 500,000 ◉

UTAH

ARIZONA

MEXICO

NEVADA

CALIFORNIA

Great Basin

Sierra Nevada

Central Valley

San Joaquin Valley

Sacramento Valley

Schell Creek Range

Ruby Mountains

Reese River

Humboldt River

Pyramid Lake

Black Roc

Honey Lake

Walker Lake

Mono Lake

Carson Sink

Death Valley

Mojave Desert

Chocolate Mountains

San Rafael Mountains

Santa Lucia Range

Colorado River

Gila River

Grand Canyon

Lake Powell

Lake Mead

Lake Mohave

Salton Sea

Great Salt Lake Desert

Mount Whitney 4418m

Tulare Lake Bed

Monterey Bay

Channel Islands

Santa Rosa Island

Santa Catalina Island

San Clemente Island

PACIFIC OCEAN

Eureka
Redanges
Redding
Susanville
Chico
Ukiah
Santa Rosa
Napa
Vallejo
Berkeley
San Francisco
Palo Alto
Sunnyvale
San Jose
Santa Cruz
Monterey
Salinas
Gilroy
Woodland
Sacramento
Fairfield
Stockton
Oakland
Yuba City
Citrus Heights
Manteca
Modesto
Turlock
Madera
Fresno
Hanford
Visalia
Selma
Porterville
Delano
Atascadero
San Luis Obispo
Santa Maria
Lompoc
Santa Barbara
Oxnard
Bakersfield
Ridgecrest
Lancaster
Barstow
Victorville
Los Angeles
Pasadena
San Bernardino
Riverside
Santa Ana
Long Beach
Huntington Beach
Oceanside
Escondido
Encinitas
Fallbrook
Palm Springs
El Cajon
San Diego
Lakeside
Chula Vista
Brawley
El Centro
Blythe
Henderson
Las Vegas
Alamo
Ely
Tonopah
Hawthorne
Sparks
Reno
Carson City
South Lake Tahoe
Lake Tahoe

HAWAII

Niihau
Kauai
Lihue
Wahiawa
Honolulu
Oahu
Kaneohe
Molokai
Maui
Wailuku
Hawaii
Hilo
Mauna Kea 4205m

PACIFIC OCEAN

ELEVATION

4 000 m
13 124 ft

2 000 m
6 562 ft

1 000 m
3 281 ft

500 m
1 640 ft

250 m
820 ft

100 m
328 ft

Sea Level

Sea Level

-250 m
-820 ft

-500 m
-1 640 ft

-1 000 m
-3 281 ft

-2 000 m
-6 562 ft

-3 000 m
-9 843 ft

-4 000 m
-13 124 ft

63

SOUTHWEST USA

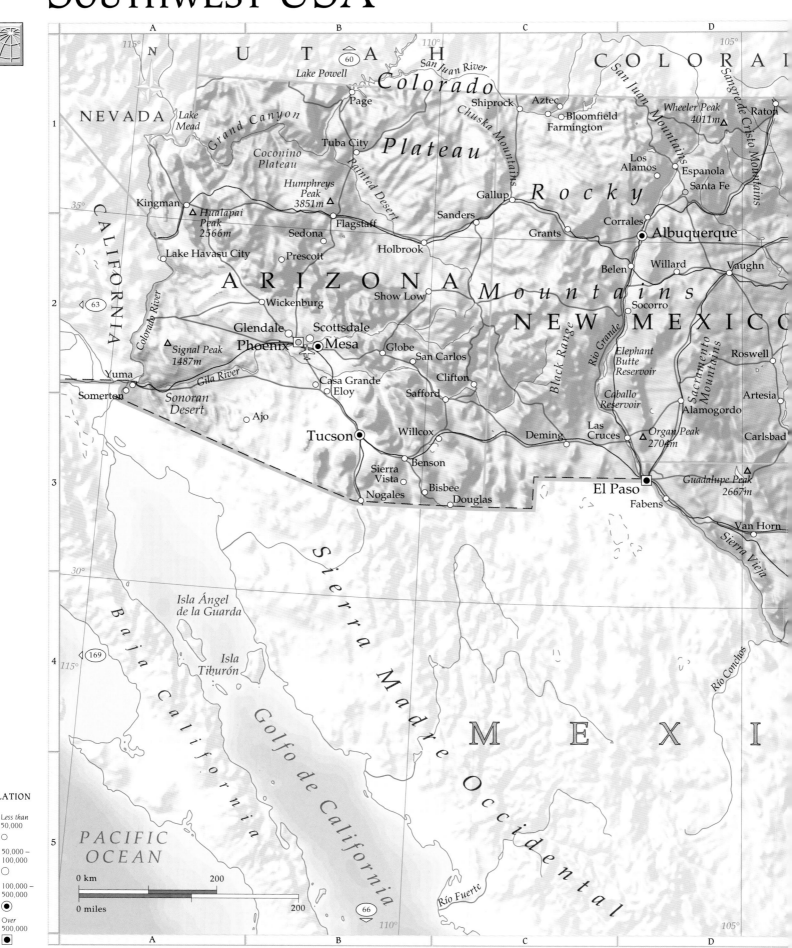

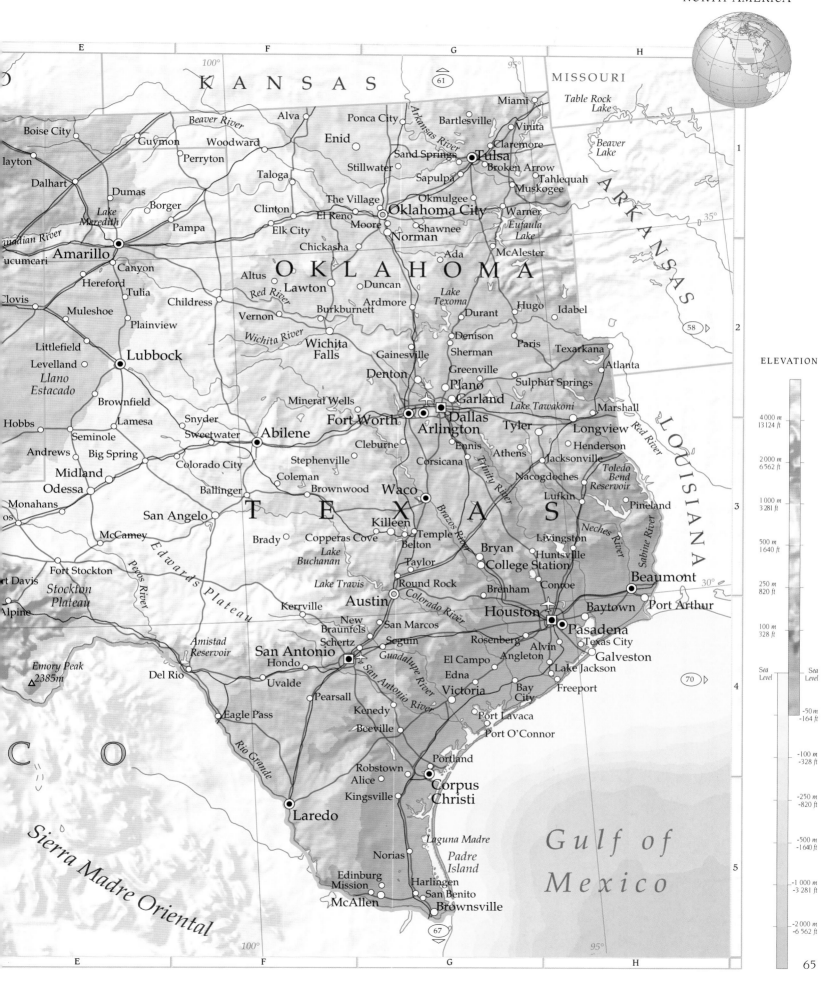

KANSAS

MISSOURI

ARKANSAS

OKLAHOMA

TEXAS

LOUISIANA

C O

Sierra Madre Oriental

Gulf of Mexico

Boise City
layton
Dalhart
ucumcari
Amarillo
Canyon
Hereford
Tulia
Clovis
Muleshoe
Plainview
Littlefield
Levelland
Lubbock
Llano
Estacado
Brownfield
Hobbs
Lamesa
Andrews
Seminole
Big Spring
Midland
Odessa
Monahans
os
San Angelo
McCamey
t Davis
Fort Stockton
Stockton
Plateau
Alpine
Emory Peak
2385m
Del Rio
Eagle Pass
Guymon
Woodward
Perryton
Dumas
Borger
Pampa
Lake
Meredith
adian River
Clinton
Elk City
Altus
Lawton
Childress
Vernon
Wichita River
Snyder
Sweetwater
Abilene
Colorado City
Coleman
Ballinger
Brownwood
Brady
Copperas Cove
Lake
Buchanan
Edwards Plateau
Pecos River
Kerrville
Uvalde
Pearsall
Kenedy
Beeville
Rio Grande
Norias
Edinburg
Mission
McAllen
Laredo
Alva
Ponca City
Enid
Stillwater
Taloga
The Village
El Reno
Moore
Oklahoma City
Norman
Chickasha
Duncan
Burkburnett
Wichita
Falls
Gainesville
Denton
Mineral Wells
Fort Worth
Arlington
Cleburne
Stephenville
Waco
Killeen
Temple
Belton
Taylor
Round Rock
Austin
San Marcos
New
Braunfels
Schertz
Seguin
San Antonio
Hondo
San Antonio River
Guadalupe River
Robstown
Alice
Kingsville
Harlingen
San Benito
Brownsville
Beaver River
Arkansas River
61
Sand Springs
Tulsa
Sapulpa
Okmulgee
Shawnee
Ada
Ardmore
Red River
Lake
Texoma
Denison
Sherman
Greenville
Plano
Garland
Dallas
Ennis
Corsicana
Trinity River
Brazos River
Bryan
College Station
Brenham
Conroe
Rosenberg
Victoria
Edna
El Campo
Bay
City
Port Lavaca
Port O'Connor
Portland
Corpus
Christi
Laguna Madre
Padre
Island
Miami
Bartlesville
Vinita
Claremore
Broken Arrow
Tahlequah
Muskogee
Warner
Eufaula
Lake
McAlester
Hugo
Idabel
Paris
Texarkana
Atlanta
Sulphur Springs
Lake Tawakoni
Marshall
Tyler
Longview
Athens
Henderson
Jacksonville
Nacogdoches
Toledo
Bend
Reservoir
Lufkin
Pineland
Neches River
Sabine River
Livingston
Huntsville
Red River
Table Rock
Lake
Beaver
Lake
Amistad
Reservoir
Lake Travis
Colorado River
Houston
Pasadena
Baytown
Texas City
Galveston
Lake Jackson
Freeport
Angleton
Alvin
Beaumont
Port Arthur
Bay
City
58
70
67

100°

95°

35°

30°

1

2

3

4

5

E

F

G

H

ELEVATION

4 000 m
13 124 ft

2 000 m
6 562 ft

1 000 m
3 281 ft

500 m
1 640 ft

250 m
820 ft

100 m
328 ft

Sea
Level

Sea
Level

-50 m
-164 ft

-100 m
-328 ft

-250 m
-820 ft

-500 m
-1 640 ft

-1 000 m
-3 281 ft

-2 000 m
-6 562 ft

MEXICO

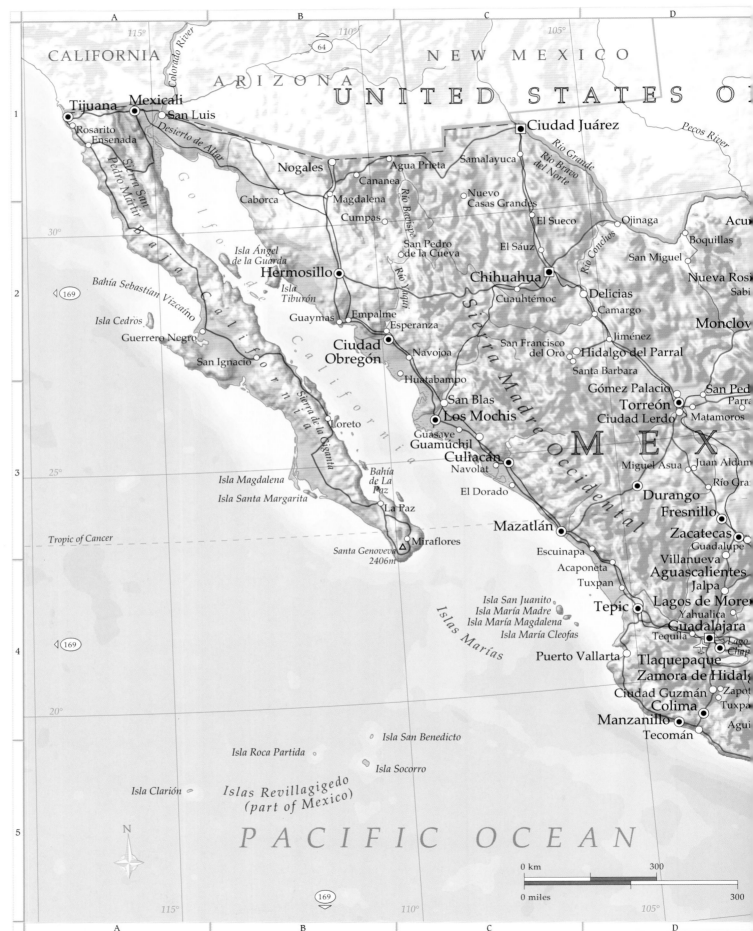

CALIFORNIA

NEW MEXICO

ARIZONA

UNITED STATES OF

Tijuana
Mexicali
San Luis
Rosarito
Ensenada

Ciudad Juárez

Colorado River

Desierto de Altar

Nogales
Agua Prieta
Samalayuca
Pecos River

Cananea
Río Grande
Río Bravo del Norte

Caborca
Magdalena
Nuevo
Casas Grandes

Cumpas
El Sueco
Ojinaga
Acu

Golfo

Bahía Sebastián Vizcaíno
Isla Ángel de la Guarda
San Pedro
de la Cueva
El Sáuz
Boquillas

Hermosillo
Chihuahua
San Miguel
Nueva Rosi

Isla Tiburón
Cuauhtémoc
Delicias
Sabi

Isla Cedros
Guaymas
Empalme
Camargo

Guerrero Negro
Esperanza
San Francisco
del Oro
Jiménez
Monclov

San Ignacio
Navojoa
Hidalgo del Parral

Sierra de la Giganta
Huatabampo
Santa Barbara

San Blas
Gómez Palacio
San Ped

Loreto
Los Mochis
Torreón
Parra

Guasave
Ciudad Lerdo
Matamoros

Guamúchil
MEX

Bahía de La Paz
Culiacán
Miguel Asua
Juan Aldam

Isla Magdalena
Navolat

Isla Santa Margarita
El Dorado
Durango
Río Gra

La Paz
Fresnillo

Tropic of Cancer
Mazatlán
Zacatecas

Miraflores
Escuinapa
Guadalupe

Santa Genoveva
2406m
Acaponeta
Villanueva
Aguascalientes

Tuxpan
Jalpa

Isla San Juanito
Isla María Madre
Tepic
Lagos de More

Isla María Magdalena
Yahualica

Isla María Cleofas
Guadalajara

Islas Marías
Tequila

Puerto Vallarta
Tlaquepaque
Zamora de Hidal

Ciudad Guzmán
Zapot

Colima
Tuxpa

Manzanillo
Agui

Tecomán

Isla San Benedicto

Isla Roca Partida

Isla Socorro

Isla Clarión
*Islas Revillagigedo
(part of Mexico)*

PACIFIC OCEAN

N

0 km   300

0 miles   300

AMERICA

E X A S

TEXAS

Brazos River

Red River

Sabine River

Mississippi River

ALABAMA
FLORIDA

MISSISSIPPI

LOUISIANA

Mississippi River Delta

Colorado River

1

Piedras Negras

Río Grande

Nuevo Laredo

Padre Island

2

Sabinas
Hidalgo

Ciudad
Miguel Alemán

G u l f   o f

Reynosa

Río
Bravo

Matamoros

M e x i c o

Monterrey

Saltillo

Montemorelos
Linares

Laguna Madre

Tropic of Cancer

C O

Sierra Madre Oriental

Ciudad Victoria

Yucatan Channel

3

Ciudad
Mante

Rio Lagartos
Tizimín

Cancún

Isla Cozumel

Progreso
Motul

San Luis
Potosí

Ciudad Madero

Mérida

Pánuco

Tampico

Umán

Ticul

Valladolid

Río Verde

Ciudad Valles

Tekax
Peto

Dolores
Hidalgo

Tamazunchale

Laguna de Tamiahua

Oxkutzcab

Yucatan Peninsula

Félipe Carrillo
Puerto

León

Tuxpán

Bahía de Campeche

Campeche

Guanajuato

Poza Rica

Champotón

Chetumal

Irapuato

Querétaro

Papantla

Tulancingo

Pachuca

Teziutlán

Xalapa

Laguna de Términos

4

Morelia

MÉXICO

Tlaxcala

Perote

Veracruz

Frontera

Fransisco Escárcega

68

(MEXICO CITY)

Alvarado

Comalcaleo

Carmen

Toluca

Puebla

Córdoba

Coatzacoalcos

Villahermosa

BELIZE

Uruapan

Cuernavaca

Popocatépetl 5452m

Tehuacán

San
Andrés
Tuxtla

Macuspana

Río Usumacinta

Gulf of Honduras

Zacatepec
Taxco

Cuautla

Tuxtepec

Minatitlán

Teapa

Presa del Infiernillo

Río Balsas

Iguala

Istmo de Tehuantepec

Tuxtla

San Cristóbal
de Las Casas

Sierra

Huajuapan

Ocozocuautla
Matías Romero

Chiapa de
Cerzo

Comitán

Lázaro Cárdenas

Chilpancingo

Oaxaca

Ixtepec

Presa de la Angostura

Ixtapa

Tecpan

Madre del Sur

Tehuantepec

Juchitán

Arriaga

Acapulco

Pinotepa
Nacional

Miahuatlán

Salina Cruz

Pijijiapán

GUATEMALA

HONDURAS

5

Golfo de Tehuantepec

Escuintla

Puerto
Escondido

Puerto
Angel

Huixtla

Tapachula

Ciudad Hidalgo

EL SALVADOR

169

ELEVATION

4 000 m
13 124 ft

2 000 m
6 562 ft

1 000 m
3 281 ft

500 m
1 640 ft

250 m
820 ft

100 m
328 ft

Sea
Level

Sea
Level

-250 m
-820 ft

-500 m
-1 640 ft

-1 000 m
-3 281 ft

-2 000 m
-6 562 ft

-3 000 m
-9 843 ft

-4 000 m
-13 124 ft

67

CENTRAL AMERICA

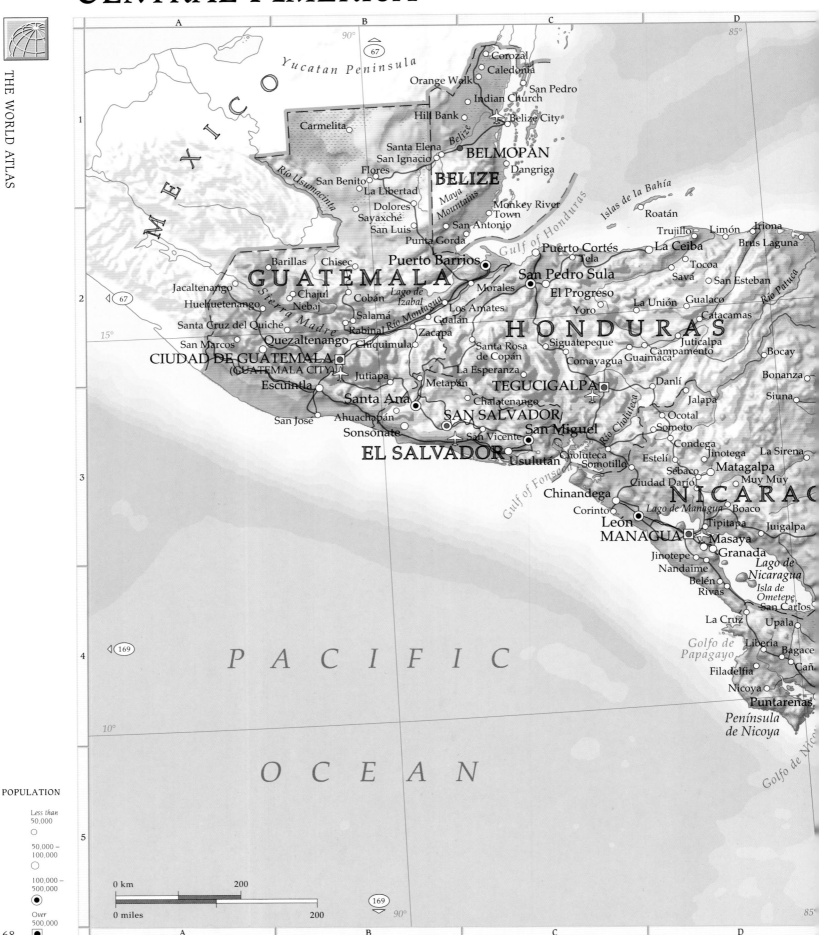

Yucatan Peninsula

MEXICO

Corozal
Caledonia
Orange Walk
San Pedro
Indian Church
Hill Bank
Belize City
Carmelita
Santa Elena
San Ignacio
BELMOPAN
Río Usumacinta
Flores
San Benito
BELIZE
La Libertad
Dangriga
Dolores
Maya Mountains
Sayaxché
Monkey River Town
San Luis
San Antonio
Punta Gorda
Islas de la Bahía
Roatán
Barillas Chisec
Puerto Barrios
Gulf of Honduras
Puerto Cortés
Trujillo Limón Iriona
Brus Laguna
GUATEMALA
Tela
La Ceiba
Jacaltenango
Lago de Izabal
Morales
San Pedro Sula
Tocoa
Savá
San Esteban
Huehuetenango
Chajul
Cobán
Los Amates
El Progreso
La Unión Gualaco
Río Patuca
Nebaj
Salamá
Gualán
Yoro
Catacamas
Santa Cruz del Quiché
Rabinal Río Motagua
Zacapa
HONDURAS
Sierra Madre
San Marcos
Quezaltenango
Chiquimula
Santa Rosa de Copán
Siguatepeque
Juticalpa
Bocay
CIUDAD DE GUATEMALA
(GUATEMALA CITY)
Comayagua Guaimaca
Campamento
Bonanza
Jutiapa
La Esperanza
TEGUCIGALPA
Danlí
Escuintla
Metapán
Jalapa
Siuna
Santa Ana
Chalatenango
Ocotal
San José
Ahuachapán
SAN SALVADOR
San Miguel
Somoto
Condega
Sonsonate
San Vicente
Río Choluteca
La Sirena
EL SALVADOR
Usulután
Choluteca
Estelí Jinotega
Somotillo
Sébaco Matagalpa
Gulf of Fonseca
Ciudad Darío Muy Muy
Chinandega
NICARAGUA
Corinto
Lago de Managua Boaco
Juigalpa
León
Tipitapa
MANAGUA Masaya
Jinotepe Granada
Nandaime
Lago de Nicaragua
Belén
Isla de Ometepe
Rivas
San Carlos
La Cruz
Upala
Golfo de Papagayo
Liberia
Bagace
Filadelfia
Cañ
Nicoya
Puntarenas
Península de Nicoya
Golfo de Nico

PACIFIC

OCEAN

POPULATION

Less than 50,000

50,000 – 100,000

100,000 – 500,000

Over 500,000

0 km   200

0 miles   200

E   F   G   H

80°   75°

⬡ 70

N

1

*Islas Santanilla
(part of Honduras)*

*Bajo Nuevo
(part of Colombia)*

15°

*Cayo de Serranilla
(part of Colombia)*

Laguna de Caratasca

○ Puerto Lempira

⬡ 71 ▷   2

*Cayo de Serrana
(part of Colombia)*

Río Coco

○ Waspam

Cayos Miskitos

○ Yablis

○ Tuapi

C   a   r   i   b   b   e   a   n

○ Puerto Cabezas

*Isla de Providencia
(part of Colombia)*

○ Prinzapolka

S   e   a

75°

○ Barra de Río Grande

Mosquito Coast

3

Laguna de Perlas

UA

*Isla de San Andrés
(part of Colombia)*

○ El Rama

Islas del Maíz

○ Bluefields

○ Punta Gorda

10°

○ San Juan del Norte

Río San Juan

○ Puerto
Viejo

⬡ 74 ▷   4

○ Quesada

Istmo de Panamá

COSTA RICA

○ El Porvenir

ajuela

○ Siquirres

Portobelo ○

Gulf of

○ Heredia

Colón ●

Ailigandí ○

◉ SAN JOSÉ ● Limón

Cristóbal ○

Cordillera de San Blas

Darien

○ Cartago

○ Guabito

Panama Canal

Lago Bayano

*Cerro Chirripó
Grande
3819m*

○ Almirante

*Golfo de los
Mosquitos*

Lago Gatún

✈ ● San Miguelito

Puerto Obaldía ○

*Cordillera de
Talamanca*

○ Laguna
de Chiriquí

Balboa ○

PANAMÁ
(PANAMA CITY)

uepos

○ Buenos Aires

Capira ○

Chimán ○

Serranía del Darién

○ Cortés

△ *Volcán Barú 3475m*

Penonomé ○

La Palma ○

○ Palmar Sur

○ Boquete

Cordillera Central

*Archipiélago
de las Perlas*

*Isla
del Rey*

Yaviza ○

*Bahía
de Coronado*

Aguadulce ○

El Real ○

◉ David

P   A   N   A   M   A

Garachiné ○

Península de Osa

*Golfo
Dulce*

○ La Concepción

Santiago ○

Chitré ○

COLOMBIA

*Golfo
de Chiriquí*

Guarumal ○

Ocú ○

Las Tablas ○

Golfo

*Península de
Azuere*

de Panamá

Jaqué ○

5

Isla de Coiba

*Isla
Cébaco*

80°

⬡ 74

E   F   G   H

69

THE CARIBBEAN

UNITED STATES OF AMERICA

Gulf of Mexico

The Everglades

Florida Keys

Straits of Florida

Tropic of Cancer

Grand Bahama Island
Freeport
Marsh Harbour
Great Abaco

Bimini Islands
Berry Islands
Northwest Providence Channel

Nicholls Town
NASSAU
New Providence
Eleuthera Island
Rock Sound
Cat Island

Andros Town
Exuma Cays
Andros Island

BAHAMAS
San Salvador
Rum Cay

George Town
Great Exuma Island
Long Island
Clarence Town
Crooked Island

Archipiélago de Camagüey
Crooked Island Passage
Acklins Island
Mayaguana Passage
Mayaguana
Caicos Passage

Ragged Island Range
Little Inagua

Cay Sal
Anguilla Cays

LA HABANA (HAVANA)
Guanabacoa
Cárdenas
Artemisa
Matanzas
Sagua la Grande
Pinar del Río
Consolación del Sur
Santa Clara
La Fé
Placetas
Cienfuegos
Nueva Gerona
Golfo de Batabanó
Isla de la Juventud
Archipiélago de los Canarreos
Cayo Largo
Bahía de Cochinos
Sancti Spíritus
Morón
Ciego de Ávila
CUBA
Camagüey
Nuevitas

Archipiélago de los Jardines de la Reina
Las Tunas
Holguín
Manzanillo
Bayamo
Palma Soriano
Guantánamo
Santiago de Cuba

Lake Rosa
Matthew Town
Great Inagua

Cap-Haïtien
Gonaïves
HAITI
Jérémie
PORT-AU-PRINCE
Windward Passage

Yucatan Channel

Little Cayman
Cayman Brac

GEORGE TOWN
Grand Cayman
CAYMAN ISLANDS
(UK dependent territory)

NAVASSA ISLAND
(US unincorporated territory)

Cayes
Jacmel

Montego Bay
Spanish Town
Portmore
KINGSTON
JAMAICA
Pedro Cays

Jamaica Channel

HONDURAS

NICARAGUA

COSTA RICA

COLOMBIA

Caribbean Sea

JAMAICA

Montego Bay
Lucea
Falmouth
Runaway Bay
St Ann's Bay
Ocho Rios
Caribbean Sea

Cambridge
The Cockpit Country
Annotto Bay
Buff Bay
Port Antonio

Christiana
Ewarton
Savanna-La-Mar
Blue Mountain Peak 2258m

Mandeville
Spanish Town
KINGSTON
Black River
May Pen
Portmore
Old Harbour
Morant Bay
Portland Bight

Caribbean Sea

0 km 20
0 miles 20

2000m/6562ft
1000m/3281ft
500m/1640ft
200m/656ft
Sea level

0 km 200
0 miles 200

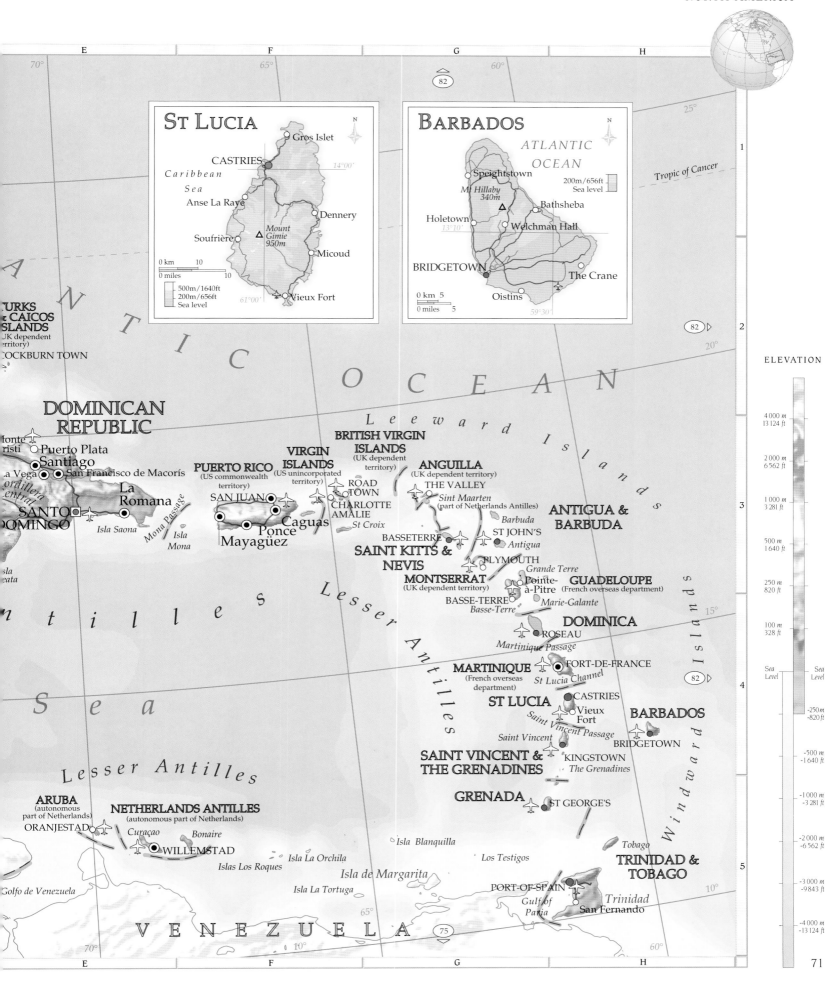

St Lucia

Gros Islet

CASTRIES

Caribbean Sea

14°00'

Anse La Raye

Dennery

Soufrière

△ *Mount Gimie 950m*

Micoud

0 km   10

0 miles   10

500m/1640ft
200m/656ft
Sea level

61°00'

Vieux Fort

Barbados

ATLANTIC OCEAN

Speightstown

Mt Hillaby 340m △

Bathsheba

200m/656ft
Sea level

Holetown

13°10'

Welchman Hall

BRIDGETOWN

The Crane

0 km   5

0 miles   5

Oistins

59°30'

Tropic of Cancer

25°

82

20°

TURKS & CAICOS ISLANDS
(UK dependent territory)
COCKBURN TOWN

A T L A N T I C   O C E A N

L e e w a r d

DOMINICAN REPUBLIC

Monte Cristi

Puerto Plata

Santiago

a Vega

San Francisco de Macorís

I s l a n d s

BRITISH VIRGIN ISLANDS
(UK dependent territory)

VIRGIN ISLANDS
(US unincorporated territory)

ANGUILLA
(UK dependent territory)

PUERTO RICO
(US commonwealth territory)

THE VALLEY

La Romana

ROAD TOWN

Sint Maarten
(part of Netherlands Antilles)

ANTIGUA & BARBUDA

SANTO DOMINGO

SAN JUAN

CHARLOTTE AMALIE

Barbuda

Isla Saona

Mona Passage

Isla Mona

Caguas

St Croix

BASSETERRE

ST JOHN'S

Ponce

Antigua

sla ata

Mayagüez

SAINT KITTS & NEVIS

PLYMOUTH

Grande Terre

GUADELOUPE
(French overseas department)

A n t i l l e s

L e s s e r   A n t i l l e s

MONTSERRAT
(UK dependent territory)

Pointe-à-Pitre

BASSE-TERRE
Basse-Terre

Marie-Galante

DOMINICA

S e a

ROSEAU

15°

Martinique Passage

W i n d w a r d   I s l a n d s

MARTINIQUE
(French overseas department)

FORT-DE-FRANCE

St Lucia Channel

82

ST LUCIA

CASTRIES

Vieux Fort

Saint Vincent Passage

BARBADOS

Saint Vincent

BRIDGETOWN

Lesser Antilles

SAINT VINCENT & THE GRENADINES

KINGSTOWN

The Grenadines

ARUBA
(autonomous part of Netherlands)

NETHERLANDS ANTILLES
(autonomous part of Netherlands)

GRENADA

ST GEORGE'S

ORANJESTAD

Curaçao

Bonaire

WILLEMSTAD

Isla La Orchila

Isla Blanquilla

Los Testigos

Tobago

Islas Los Roques

Isla de Margarita

TRINIDAD & TOBAGO

Golfo de Venezuela

Isla La Tortuga

Isla Saona

PORT-OF-SPAIN

Trinidad

Gulf of Paria

San Fernando

V E N E Z U E L A

75

70°   65°   10°   60°

E   F   G   H

4000 m
13 124 ft

2000 m
6 562 ft

1000 m
3 281 ft

500 m
1 640 ft

250 m
820 ft

100 m
328 ft

Sea Level   Sea Level

-250m
-820 ft

-500 m
-1 640 ft

-1 000 m
-3 281 ft

-2 000 m
-6 562 ft

-3 000 m
-9 843 ft

-4 000 m
-13 124 ft

SOUTH AMERICA

ATLANTIC OCEAN

Mid-Atlantic Ridge

Demerara Plain

Ceará Plain

Natal
João Pessoa
Recife
Maceió
Mossoró
Aracaju
Fortaleza
Planalto da Borborema
Salvador
São Francisco
Serra do Espinhaço
Abrolhos Bank

Teresina

Amazon Fan

São Luís

Belém
BRASÍLIA
Brazilian Highlands
Tocantins
Goiânia

CAYENNE
PARAMARIBO
FRENCH GUIANA
(to France)
SURINAM
GEORGETOWN
Linden
GUYANA
(claimed by Venezuela)
Tumuc-Humac Mountains
(claimed by Surinam)
Essequibo

B R A Z I L

Guiana Highlands

Santarém
Amazon
Xingu
Tapajós
Serra do Cachimbo
Cuiabá
Planalto de Mato Grosso
Serra Formosa
Serra do Roncador
Araguaia
Santa Cruz

Cumaná
Trinidad

Puerto Rico Trench
Lesser Antilles
Greater Antilles
Venezuelan Basin
Puerto Rico
Caribbean Sea
Jamaica
Hispaniola

VENEZUELA
CARACAS
Maracay
Valencia
Maracaibo
Barquisimeto
Barinas
San Cristóbal
Orinoco
Meta
Caroní

Amazon Basin
Manaus
Represa Balbina
Rio Negro
Branco
Madeira
Purus
Juruá
Porto Velho
Rio Branco
Madre de Dios
Chapada dos Parecis
Beni

BOLIVIA
LA PAZ
Cochabamba
Oruro
SUCRE
Altiplano
Lake Titicaca

COLOMBIA
BOGOTÁ
Cúcuta
Bucaramanga
Ibagué
Medellín
Manizales
Pereira
Cali
Montería
Santa Marta
Barranquilla
Cartagena
Magdalena
Cauca
Colombian Basin

Pasto
Guaviare
Caquetá
Putumayo
Napo
(claimed by Ecuador)
Içá
Marañón
Ucayali

ECUADOR
QUITO
Portoviejo
Chimborazo 6310m
Guayaquil
Riobamba
Cuenca
Machala
Esmeraldas
Gulf of Guayaquil
(claimed by Ecuador)
Piura
Chiclayo
Trujillo
Equator

PERU
LIMA
Callao
Cusco
Arequipa
Tacna
Arica
Iquitos

A n d e s
Peru-Chile Trench
Peru Basin
Panama Basin
Isthmus of Panama

Tropic of Capricorn

30°

Rio Grande Rise

Santos Plateau

Jboz de Fora
Nova Iguaçu
Rio de Janeiro
São Paulo
Santos
Campinas
Curitiba
Florianópolis

Londrina

Serra Geral

Porto Alegre

Lagoa dos Patos

Mirim Lagoon

ATLANTIC
OCEAN

*Argentine
Basin*

83

South Sandwich Trench

SOUTH GEORGIA
(to UK)

SOUTH SANDWICH
ISLANDS
(to UK)

South Orkney Islands

170

ELEVATION

PARAGUAY
ASUNCIÓN
Ciudad del Este
Posadas
Santa María

Formosa
Resistencia
Corrientes

Paraguay

Pilcomayo

Paraná

Mesopotamia

Paraná

URUGUAY
BUENOS AIRES
MONTEVIDEO
Rosario
La Plata
Santa Fe

Negro

Río de la Plata

Mar del Plata

FALKLAND ISLANDS
(to UK)
STANLEY
East Falkland

Falkland Plateau

Scotia Sea

Summer limit of pack ice

ANTARCTICA

4 000 m
13 124 ft

2 000 m
6 562 ft

1 000 m
3 281 ft

Chaco

Gran Chaco

San Salvador
de Jujuy
Salta
San Miguel
de Tucumán
Santiago
del Estero
La Rioja

ARGENTINA

Cerro Ojos
del Salado
6880m

San Juan
Cerro Aconcagua
6960m
Mendoza

Córdoba

Pampas

Bahía Blanca

Bahía Blanca

Golfo San Matías

Rawson

Gulf of San Jorge

Bahía Grande
West Falkland

Strait of Magellan

Tierra del Fuego

Cape Horn

Drake Passage

South Shetland Islands

Winter limit of pack ice

500 m
1 640 ft

250 m
820 ft

100 m
328 ft

Sea
Level

Sea
Level

Tocopilla
Antofagasta

Atacama Desert

Andes

Colorado

Río Negro

Neuquén

Chubut

Chico

Desado

Chico

Patagonia

Punta Arenas

-250m
-820 ft

La Serena
Coquimbo
Viña del Mar
Valparaíso
SANTIAGO

San Juan

Concepción
Temuco
Valdivia
Puerto Montt
Isla de Chiloé

-500 m
-1 640 ft

Chile Basin

Isla San Ambrosio
(part of Chile)
Isla San Félix
(part of Chile)
Islas Juan Fernández
(part of Chile)

PACIFIC
OCEAN

Chile Rise

30°

40°

50°

80°

90°

169

N

0 km   500

0 miles   500

-1 000 m
-3 281 ft

-2 000 m
-6 562 ft

-3 000 m
-9 843 ft

-4 000 m
-13 124 ft

NORTHERN SOUTH AMERICA

Caribbean Sea

Lesser Ant

ARUBA
(autonomous part
of Netherlands)

Curaçao

Bonaire

**NETHERLANDS
ANTILLES**
(autonomous part
of Netherlands)

Islas
Los Roques

Isla
La Orchil

Península
de la
Guajira

Puerto López

Punto Fijo

Ríohacha

Maicao

Golfo de
Venezuela

Coro

Puerto
Cumarebo

Sabaneta

Puerto
Cabello

CARACAS

Santa Marta

Ciénaga

Dabajuro

Barranquilla

Soledad

Pico Cristóbal Colón
5775m

La Concepción

Maracaibo

Cabimas

San Felipe

Valencia

Maracay

Cartagena

Sabanalarga

Valledupar

Ciudad Ojeda

Carora

Barquisimeto

San Juan
de los Morro

El Carmen
de Bolívar

Machiques

Lago de
Maracaibo

Acarigua

Sincelejo

Magangué

San Carlos
del Zulia

Valera

Guanare

Calabozo

Valle de
la Pascu

Montería

Cereté

Mérida

Barinas

Río Guanare

Planeta Rica

Aguachica

El Vigía

△ Pico Bolívar
5007m

Caucasia

Ocaña

San Fernando

Dabeiba

Río Cauca

Cúcuta

San Cristóbal

Río Apure

Yarumal

Pamplona

Bucaramanga

Río Arauca

VENE

Bello

Barrancabermeja

Arauca

L L a n

Medellín

Puerto Berrío

Río Meta

Itagüí

Sogamoso

Puerto Carreño

Nuquí

Quibdó

Tunja

Puerto Ayacucho

Manizales

Zipaquira

Yopal

Pereira

Río Meta

Armenia

BOGOTÁ

Tuluá

Ibagué

Girardot

Villavicencio

Río Guaviare

Buenaventura

Buga

Espinal

Puerto Inírida

Palmira

Río Putumayo

C O L O M B I A

Cali

Neiva

Popayán

Garzón

San José del Guaviare

Tumaco

Pitalito

Mitú

Pasto

Mocoa

Florencia

Río Vaupés

Nevada de Cumbal
4764m

Ipiales

Orito

Río Apaporis

Equator

(claimed by
Ecuador)

Río Caquetá

E C U A D O R

Río Putumayo

Río Napo

Río Japurá

P E R U

Río Içá

Amazon

Río Juruá

Panama
Canal

PANAMA

Golfo de
Panamá

*PACIFIC
OCEAN*

Gulf of
Darien

Cordillera Occidental

Cordillera Central

Cordillera Oriental

A n d e s

ATLANTIC

OCEAN

SAINT VINCENT &
THE GRENADINES

BARBADOS

GRENADA

Isla Blanquilla

*Isla de
Margarita*

Tortuga

La Asunción
Porlamar

Carúpano

Tobago

Islas Los Testigos

TRINIDAD &
TOBAGO

umaná

Cariaco

Güiria

*Gulf of
Paria*

Trinidad

Puerto La Cruz

The Serpent's Mouth

Barcelona

San Mateo
Anaco

Maturín

araza

Cantaura

El Tigre

Tucupita

Río Orinoco

Ciudad Guayana

Upata

Ciudad
Bolívar

ZUELA

Embalse de Guri

El Callao

Matthews
Ridge

Charity

Spring Garden

Parika

GEORGETOWN

Río Paragua

El Dorado

Cuyuni River

Aurora

New
Amsterdam

Río Caura

*Salto
Ángel*

Peters Mine

Bartica

Rockstone

Totness

PARAMARIBO
Nieuw Amsterdam

St-Laurent-
du-Maroni

Sinnamary
Kourou

Río Caroní

Kamarang

Linden

GUYANA

Nieuw
Nickerie

Apoera

Kaaimanston

Maroni River

Mount Roraima △
2810m

Orealla

5°

Pakaraima Mountains

Kurupukari

W. J. van
Blommesteinmeer

SURINAM

△ *Juliana Top*
1230m

*Montagnes
de la Trinité*

CAYENNE

Grand-
Santi

Mouragne
Tortue

Ouanary

FRENCH
GUIANA
(French
overseas
department)

St-Georges

(Venezuela claims all
of Guyana west of
Essequibo River)

Lethem

Essequibo River

Courantyne River

Camopi

Guiana

Río Orinoco

H i g h l a n d s

Tumuc Humac Mountains

(claimed by
Surinam)

Acarai Mountains

(claimed by
Surinam)

Equator

Rio Negro

B R A Z I L

z o n   B a s i n

Amazon

Rio Purus

Rio Tapajós

ELEVATION

4 000 m
13 124 ft

2 000 m
6 562 ft

1 000 m
3 281 ft

500 m
1 640 ft

250 m
820 ft

100 m
328 ft

Sea
Level

Sea
Level

-250 m
-820 ft

-500 m
-1 640 ft

-1 000 m
-3 281 ft

-2 000 m
-6 562 ft

-3 000 m
-9 843 ft

-4 000 m
-13 124 ft

0 km   200

0 miles   200

WESTERN SOUTH AMERICA

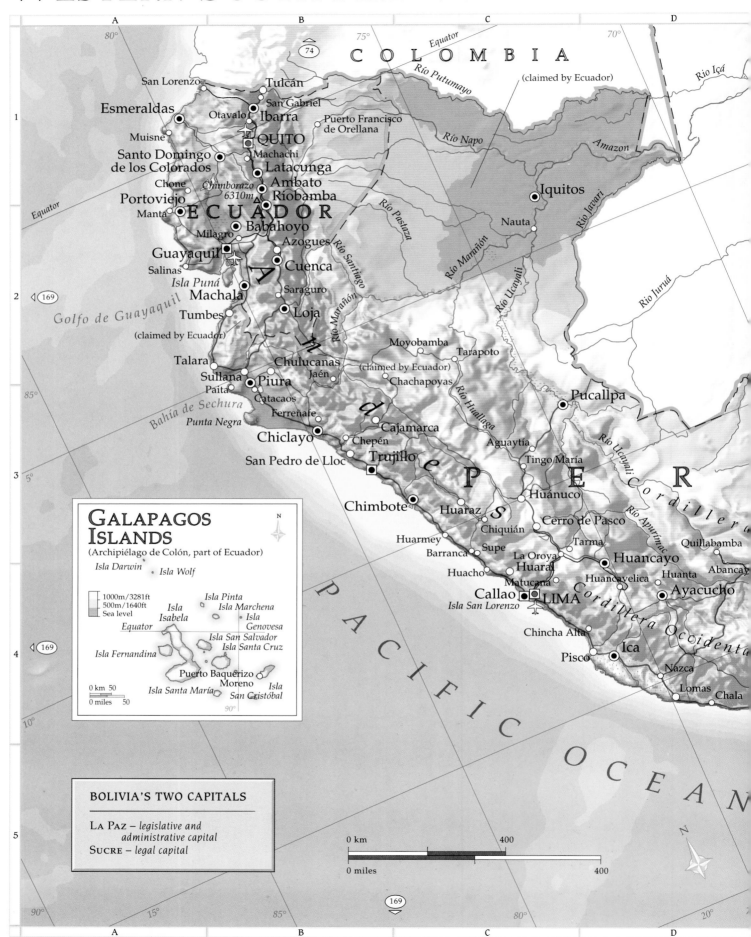

C O L O M B I A

Río Putumayo
Río Içá

Equator

80° 75° 70°

△ 74

San Lorenzo
Tulcán
Esmeraldas
San Gabriel
Otavalo · Ibarra
Muisne
★ QUITO
Puerto Francisco
de Orellana
Machachi
1

Río Napo

(claimed by Ecuador)

Santo Domingo
de los Colorados
Latacunga
Chone
Ambato
Portoviejo
Chimborazo
6310m Riobamba
Manta E C U A D O R
Babahoyo
Milagro
Azogues
Guayaquil
Salinas
Cuenca
Isla Puná
Saraguro
Machala
Loja
Tumbes
2

Iquitos
Nauta

Río Pastaza
Río Santiago
Río Marañón
Río Ucayali
Río Juruá
Río Jıcari

Equator
A
m
Talara
(claimed by Ecuador)
Chulucanas
Jaén
Sullana Piura
Paita
Catacaos
Chachapoyas
Ferreñafe
Moyobamba
Tarapoto
(claimed by Ecuador)

Río Huallaga

Pucallpa

85°

Bahía de Sechura
Punta Negra
Chiclayo
Chepén
Cajamarca
San Pedro de Lloc
Trujillo
Aguaytía
Tingo María
3

d
e
s
P E R
Chimbote
Huaraz
Huánuco
Chiquián
Cerro de Pasco
Tarma
Quillabamba

Río Apurímac
Río Ucayali

Cordillera

5°

GALAPAGOS ISLANDS

(Archipiélago de Colón, part of Ecuador)

N

Isla Darwin   · *Isla Wolf*

| 1000m/3281ft
| 500m/1640ft
| Sea level

Isla Pinta
Isla Marchena
Isla
Genovesa
Isla
Isabela
Equator
Isla San Salvador
Isla Santa Cruz
Isla Fernandina
Puerto Baquerizo
Moreno
Isla
Isla Santa María
San Cristóbal

0 km 50
0 miles 50

90°

Huarmey
Barranca
Supe
Huacho
Matucana
Callao ◻ LIMA
Isla San Lorenzo

La Oroya
Huaral
Huancavelica
Huancayo
Huanta
Ayacucho
Abancay

Chincha Alta

Cordillera Occidental

Pisco
Ica
Nazca
Lomas
Chala

P A C I F I C   O C E A N

4

N

POPULATION

Less than
50,000
○

50,000 –
100,000
○

100,000 –
500,000
◉

Over
500,000
◼

BOLIVIA'S TWO CAPITALS

LA PAZ – *legislative and*
administrative capital
SUCRE – *legal capital*

0 km   400

0 miles   400

△ 169

90° 85° 80°

15°

10°

5

E   F   G   H

Amazon

65°

A m a z o n   B a s i n

60°

Rio Madeira

5°

78

Serra do Cachimbo

Rio São Manuel

55°

1

10°

Rio Purus

B   R   A   Z   I   L

Rio Iuruena

79

2

ELEVATION

Rio Abunã Fortaleza

Villa Bella

Chapada dos Parecis

Rio Madre de Dios Riberalta

Rio Guaporé

15°

4000 m
13 124 ft

Cobija

Rio Beni

Porvenir

Magdalena

55°

San Matías

3

2000 m
6 562 ft

U

Puerto
Maldonado

Santa Ana

Rio Mamoré

Reyes

San Ignacio

Trinidad

Rio San Miguel

Concepción

1000 m
3 281 ft

Pantanal

500 m
1 640 ft

O r i e n t a l

B O L I V I A

usco

Sicuani

Nevado Pupuya
△ 5818m

Montero
Warnes

San José

Puerto
Suárez

250 m
820 ft

Ayaviri

Moho

Puerto Acosta

Portachuelo

Buena Vista

Santa Cruz

20°

C h a c o

Paraguay

100 m
328 ft

4

79

A

Juliaca

*Lake
Titicaca*

Achacachi

Copacabana

Cochabamba

Comarapa

Puno

LA PAZ

Aiquile

Sea
Level

Sea
Level

Nevado Ampato
6310m
△

Ilave

Viacha

Corocoro

Oruro

Huanuni

Uncía

C o r d i l l e r a

A l t i p l a n o

SUCRE

Lagunillas

Monteagudo

-250 m
-820 ft

Volcán Misti
5822m
△

Challapata

Potosí

O r i e n t a l

Arequipa

Nevado
Sajama
6520m △

*Lago
Poopó*

P A R A G U A Y

Moquegua

amaná

Tacna

C o r d i l l e r a

d e l

-500 m
-1 640 ft

Mollendo

Ilo

La Yarada

Sabaya

Uyuni

Cotagaita

San Lorenzo

Tropic of Capricorn

-1000 m
-3 281 ft

O c c i d e n t a l   C H I L E

Villa Martín

Tupiza

Tarija

G r a n

Pilcomayo

D e s i e r t o   d e   A t a c a m a

San Pablo

Villazón

-2000 m
-6 562 ft

5

25°

A R G E N T I N A

-3 000 m
-9 843 ft

70°

Tropic of Capricorn

65°

80

25°

60°

-4 000 m
-13 124 ft

E   F   G   H

BRAZIL

VENEZUELA

COLOMBIA

GUYANA

Uraricoera
Boa Vista

Caracaraí

Guiana Highland

Roraima

Pico da Neblina
3014m

Rio Negro

Represa Balbin

ECUADOR

Rio Putumayo

Rio Japurá

Rio Napo

Rio Içá

Rio Juruá

Tefé

Amazon

Manaus

Coari

Rio Madeira

Galapagos Islands
(Archipiélago de Colón)
(part of Ecuador)

Rio Marañón

Rio Javari

Amazon

B a s

Humaitá

Rio Ucayali

Rio Javari

Japiim

Feijó

Rio Purus

B Porto Velho R

Rondônia

Rio Juruen

Equator

Río Napo

A c r e

Rio Abunã

Chapada dos Parecis

Guaporé

Vilher

PERU

*A
n
d
e
s*

Cordillera

Rio Mamoré

Lake
Titicaca

Cordillera Occidental

BOLIVIA

Cordillera Oriental

Lago
Poopó

PACIFIC

Desierto de Atacama

PAR

Pilcomayo

Río Bermejo

OCEAN

CHILE

*A
n
d
e
s*

Tropic of Capricorn

Río Salado

Paraguay

Paraná

N

0 km   600

0 miles   600

ATLANTIC OCEAN

SURINAM

FRENCH GUIANA
(French overseas department)

Tumuc Humac Mountains

Amapá

Mouths of the Amazon

Ilha Caviana de Fora

Macapá

Ilha de Marajó

Baía de Marajó

Belém

Baía de São Marco

Alenquer

Santarém

Amazon

São Luís

Parnaíba

Camocim

Altamira

Represa de Tucuruí

Bacabal

Piripiri

Fortaleza

Atol das Rocas

San Fernando de Noronha (part of Brazil)

Itaituba

Rio Tapajós

Marabá

Rio Xingu

Imperatriz

Teresina

Mossoró

Açu

Cabo de São Roque

P a r á

Maranhão

Ceará

Rio Grande do Norte

Natal

Serra do Cachimbo

Carolina

Floriano

Juazeiro do Norte

João Pessoa

B R A Z I L

Balsas

Picos

Piauí

Paraíba

Campina Grande

Serra dos Gradaús

Serra Formosa

Rio Tocantins

Represa de Sobradinho

Pernambuco

Alagoas

Recife

Rio São Manuel

Juazeiro

Maceió

Rio Tocantins

Tocantins

Rio São Fransisco

Chapada Diamantina

Aracaju

Estância

Taguatinga

Feira de Santana

B a h i a

Salvador

Cuiabá

Planalto

Central

Anápolis

BRASÍLIA

Janaúba

Baía de Todos os Santos

Itabuna

Vitória da Conquista

Rondonópolis

G o i á s

M i n a s

Canavieiras

Jataí

Goiânia

Montes Claros

Araguari

Araçuaí

G e r a i s

Governador Valadares

Rio Araguaia

Uberlândia

Uberaba

Espírito Santo

Campo Grande

Belo Horizonte

Vitória

Aquidauana

Ribeirão Preto

Divinópolis

Pantanal

Presidente Epitácio

Marília

Juiz de Fora

Campos

Mato Grosso do Sul

Campinas

Nova

Londrina

S ã o P a u l o

Iguaçu

Rio de Janeiro

Maringá

São Paulo

P a r a n á

Santos

Represa de Itaipú

Ponta Grossa

Tropic of Capricorn

Salto do Iguaçu

Rio Iguaçu

Curitiba

Paraná

Joinville

Blumenau

Santa Catarina

Florianópolis

Passo Fundo

Rio Grande

nta Maria

Canoas

do Sul

Rio Negro

Porto Alegre

URUGUAY

Bagé

Lagoa dos Patos

Rio Grande

Mirim Lagoon

ATLANTIC OCEAN

ELEVATION

4 000 m
13 124 ft

2 000 m
6 562 ft

1 000 m
3 281 ft

500 m
1 640 ft

250 m
820 ft

100 m
328 ft

Sea Level

Sea Level

-250 m
-820 ft

-500 m
-1 640 ft

-1 000 m
-3 281 ft

-2 000 m
-6 562 ft

-3 000 m
-9 843 ft

-4 000 m
-13 124 ft

79

SOUTHERN SOUTH AMERICA

Planalto de Mato Grosso

B R A Z I L

Tropic of Capricorn

Represa de Itaipú

Pedro Juan Caballero

Ciudad del Este

Coronel Oviedo

Eldorado

Posadas

Encarnación

Concepción

Paraguay

P A R A G U A Y

Rosario

ASUNCIÓN

Villarrica

Caazapá

Yuty

San Juan Bautista

Pilar

Corrientes

Goya

Santo Tomé

Mercedes

B O L I V I A

Cordillera Oriental

Lago Poopó

Cordillera Occidental

Capitán Pablo Lagerenza

Fuerte Olimpo

General Eugenio A.Garay

Mariscal Estigarribia

Pantanal

P E R U

Arica

Iquique

Lagunas

Tocopilla

Mejillones

Antofagasta

Taltal

Chañaral

Caldera

Copiapó

Vallenar

Domeyko

La Serena

Coquimbo

Ovalle

Illapel

Salamanca

Calama

Chuquicamata

Quiaca

La Quiaca

San Ramón de la Nueva Orán

San Salvador de Jujuy

Salta

Metán

Cafayate

Cerro Galán 6600m

San Fernando del Valle de Catamarca

La Rioja

San Juan

Mendoza

Godoy Cruz

San Rafael

General Alvear

Monte Patria

Cerro Aconcagua 6959m

La Ligua

La Calera

Viña del Mar

Valparaíso

San Antonio

SANTIAGO

Rancagua

Pichilemu

Curicó

Talca

C H I L E

A R G E N T I N A

A N D E S

Desierto de Atacama

Cerro Ojos del Salado 6880m

Nevado de Chañi 6200m

Rosario de la Frontera

San Miguel de Tucumán

Formosa

Resistencia

Santiago del Estero

Frías

Añatuya

Reconquista

Vera

Río Salado

Laguna Mar Chiquita

Rafaela

Santa Fe

Paraná

Rosario

Deán Funes

Jesús María

Villa María

Río Cuarto

San Luis

Mercedes

Rufino

Realicó

Córdoba

San Juan

Pilcomayo

Río Bermejo

Las Lomitas

Río Salado

Monte Caseros

Paraná

Concordia

Gualeguaychú

Dolores

Zárate

Pergamino

Junín

Trenque Lauquen

U R U G U A Y

Rivera

Artigas

Salto

Paysandú

Tacuarembó

Río Negro

Mercedes

Trinidad

Florida

Melo

Chuy

Mirim Lagoon

Lagoa dos Patos

BUENOS AIRES

La Plata

Lomas de Zamora

MONTEVIDEO

Río de la Plata

Uruguay

P A C I F I C   O C E A N

Tropic of Capricorn

POPULATION

Less than 50,000 ○

50,000 – 100,000 ○

100,000 – 500,000 ◉

Over 500,000 ◼

ATLANTIC OCEAN

PACIFIC

ARGENTINA

CHILE

Mar del Plata
Tandil
Balcarce
Necochea
Coronel Dorrego
Tres Arroyos
Bahía Blanca
Bahía Blanca
Punta Alta
Choele Choel
Río Negro
San Antonio Oeste
Viedma
Golfo San Matías
Península Valdés
Golfo Nuevo
Rawson
Trelew
Río Chubut
Comodoro Rivadavia
Golfo San Jorge
Caleta Olivia
Puerto Deseado
Río Deseado
Puerto San Julián
Río Chico
Bahía Grande
Río Gallegos
Río Santa Cruz
El Calafate
Puerto Natales
Punta Arenas
Strait of Magellan
Tierra del Fuego
Porvenir
Ushuaia
Beagle Channel
Cabo de Hornos (Cape Horn)
Isla de los Estados
Drake Passage

FALKLAND ISLANDS
(UK dependent territory)
STANLEY
East Falkland
West Falkland
Goose Green

Concepción
Los Ángeles
Lebu
Río Bío Bío
Temuco
Loncoche
Valdivia
Osorno
Puerto Varas
Puerto Montt
Ancud
Castro
Isla de Chiloé
Archipiélago de los Chonos
Golfo de Penas
Isla Wellington
Puerto Aisén
Coihaique
Chile Chico
Cochrane
Cerro San Valentín 4058m
Cerro Melizo Sur 3050m
Golfo Corcovado

Cipolletti
Neuquén
Zapata
Río Colorado
San Carlos de Bariloche
Lago Nahuel Huapi
Esquel
Paso de Indios
Lago Musters
Lago Buenos Aires
Sarmiento
Perito Moreno
Lago Buenos Aires

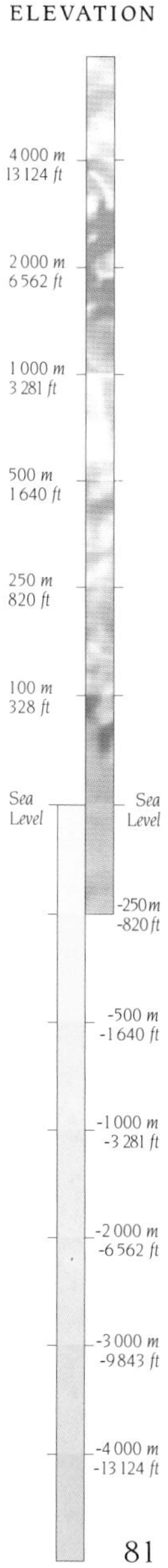

ELEVATION

4 000 m / 13 124 ft
2 000 m / 6 562 ft
1 000 m / 3 281 ft
500 m / 1 640 ft
250 m / 820 ft
100 m / 328 ft
Sea Level / Sea Level
-250 m / -820 ft
-500 m / -1 640 ft
-1 000 m / -3 281 ft
-2 000 m / -6 562 ft
-3 000 m / -9 843 ft
-4 000 m / -13 124 ft

0 km   200
0 miles   200

THE ATLANTIC OCEAN

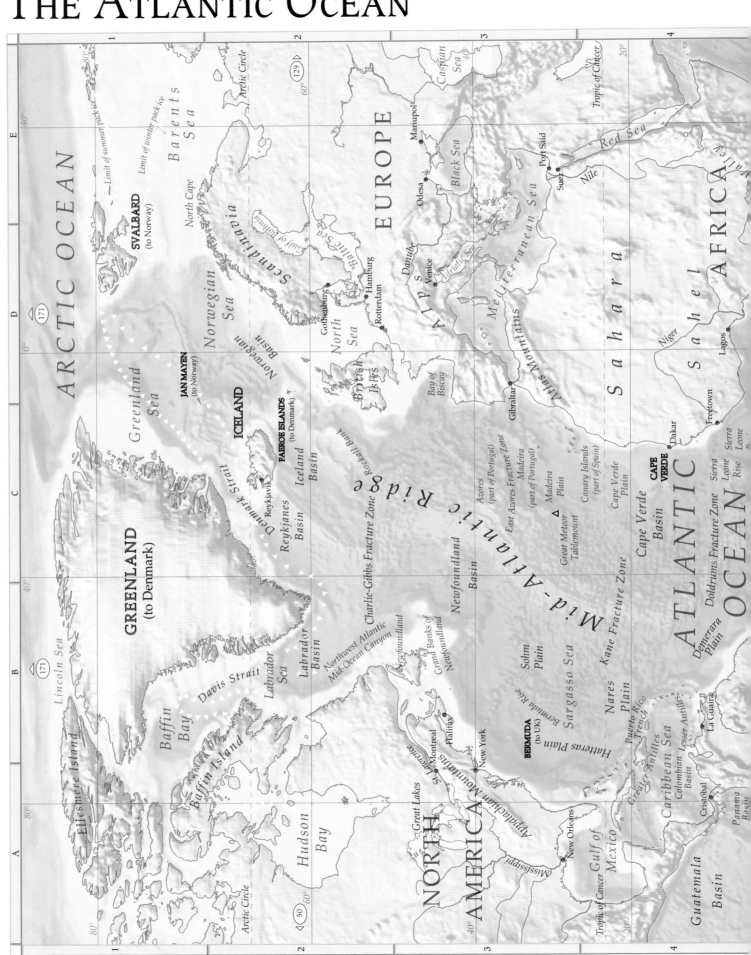

ARCTIC OCEAN

Ellesmere Island

Lincoln Sea

SVALBARD
(to Norway)

Limit of summer pack ice

Limit of winter pack ice

*Barents
Sea*

North Cape

Scandinavia

Gulf of Bothnia

EUROPE

Mariupol'

*Caspian
Sea*

Black Sea

Odesa

Port Said

Red Sea

Suez

Nile

Tropic of Cancer

AFRICA

Baltic Sea

*Norwegian
Sea*

Gothenburg

Hamburg

Rotterdam

*North
Sea*

Danube

Venice

Alps

Adriatic Sea

Mediterranean Sea

Atlas Mountains

S a h a r a

*Norwegian
Basin*

JAN MAYEN
(to Norway)

ICELAND

FAEROE ISLANDS
(to Denmark)

Denmark Strait

Reykjavík

*Reykjanes
Basin*

*Iceland
Basin*

*British
Isles*

*Bay of
Biscay*

Gibraltar

S a h e l

Saharah

Niger

Lagos

Freetown

Dakar

Greenland
Sea

GREENLAND
(to Denmark)

Rockall Bank

Charlie-Gibbs Fracture Zone

Azores
(part of Portugal)

East Azores Fracture Zone

Madeira
(part of Portugal)

Canary Islands
(part of Spain)

*Cape Verde
Plain*

**CAPE
VERDE**

*Cape Verde
Basin*

*Great Meteor
Tablemount*

*Madeira
Plain*

Sierra
Leone
Rise

*Newfoundland
Basin*

*Northwest Atlantic
Mid-Ocean Canyon*

Newfoundland

*Grand Banks of
Newfoundland*

M i d - A t l a n t i c   R i d g e

Kane Fracture Zone

ATLANTIC

OCEAN

Doldrums Fracture Zone

*Demerara
Plain*

Baffin
Bay

Davis Strait

*Labrador
Sea*

*Labrador
Basin*

Baffin Island

Hudson
Bay

Great Lakes

St. Lawrence

Montreal

Halifax

New York

New Orleans

Gulf of
Mexico

Mississippi

Appalachian Mountains

*Sohm
Plain*

Bermuda Rise

BERMUDA
(to UK)

Hatteras Plain

Sargasso Sea

*Nares
Plain*

Puerto Rico
Trench

Greater Antilles

Lesser Antilles

Caribbean Sea

*Colombian
Basin*

Cristóbal

La Guaira

*Panama
Basin*

*Demerara
Plain*

NORTH

AMERICA

Tropic of Cancer

*Guatemala
Basin*

Arctic Circle

Arctic Circle

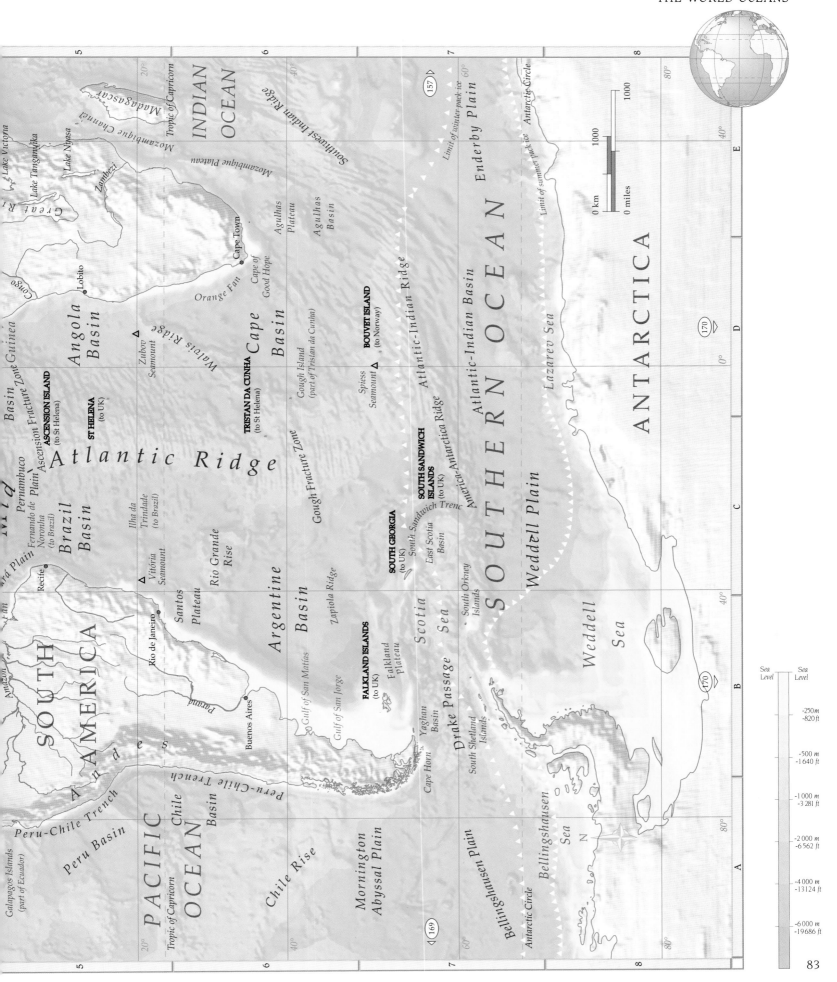

INDIAN OCEAN

Madagascar

Mozambique Channel

Lake Victoria

Lake Tanganyika

Lake Nyasa

Zambezi

Great Ri

Congo

Tropic of Capricorn

Mozambique Plateau

Southwest Indian Ridge

Agulhas Plateau

Agulhas Basin

Cape Town

Cape of Good Hope

Orange Fan

Lobito

Angola Basin

Walvis Ridge

Zubov Seamount

ASCENSION ISLAND

ST HELENA (to UK)

Basin Guinea

Pernambuco

Ascension Fracture Zone

Cape Basin

TRISTAN DA CUNHA (to St Helena)

Gough Island (part of Tristan da Cunha)

BOUVET ISLAND (to Norway)

Spiess Seamount

Atlantic-Indian Ridge

Enderby Plain

Antarctic Circle

Limit of winter pack ice

Limit of summer pack ice

157

Atlantic-Indian Basin

Lazarev Sea

170

ANTARCTICA

SOUTHERN OCEAN

Mid-

Atlantic Ridge

Pernambuco Plain

Brazil Basin

Ilha da Trindade (to Brazil)

Fernando de Noronha (to Brazil)

Gough Fracture Zone

America-Antarctica Ridge

SOUTH SANDWICH ISLANDS (to UK)

South Sandwich Trench

Weddell Plain

ard Plain

Recife

Vitória Seamount

Rio Grande Rise

Zapiola Ridge

SOUTH GEORGIA (to UK)

East Scotia Basin

South Orkney Islands

SOUTH AMERICA

Andes

Rio de Janeiro

Santos Plateau

Argentine Basin

Gulf of San Matias

Gulf of San Jorge

FALKLAND ISLANDS (to UK)

Falkland Plateau

Scotia Sea

Weddell Sea

Amazon

Paraná

Buenos Aires

Yaghan Basin

Drake Passage

Cape Horn

South Shetland Islands

PACIFIC OCEAN

Galápagos Islands (part of Ecuador)

Tropic of Capricorn

Peru-Chile Trench

Peru Basin

Chile Basin

Chile Rise

Mornington Abyssal Plain

Peru-Chile Trench

Bellingshausen Plain

Bellingshausen Sea

Antarctic Circle

N

20°

40°

40°

60°

80°

80°

40°

20°

40°

0°

80°

5

6

7

8

E

D

C

B

A

1000

1000

0 km

0 miles

Sea Level

Sea Level

-250 m
-820 ft

-500 m
-1 640 ft

-1 000 m
-3 281 ft

-2 000 m
-6 562 ft

-4 000 m
-13 124 ft

-6 000 m
-19 686 ft

169

170

AFRICA

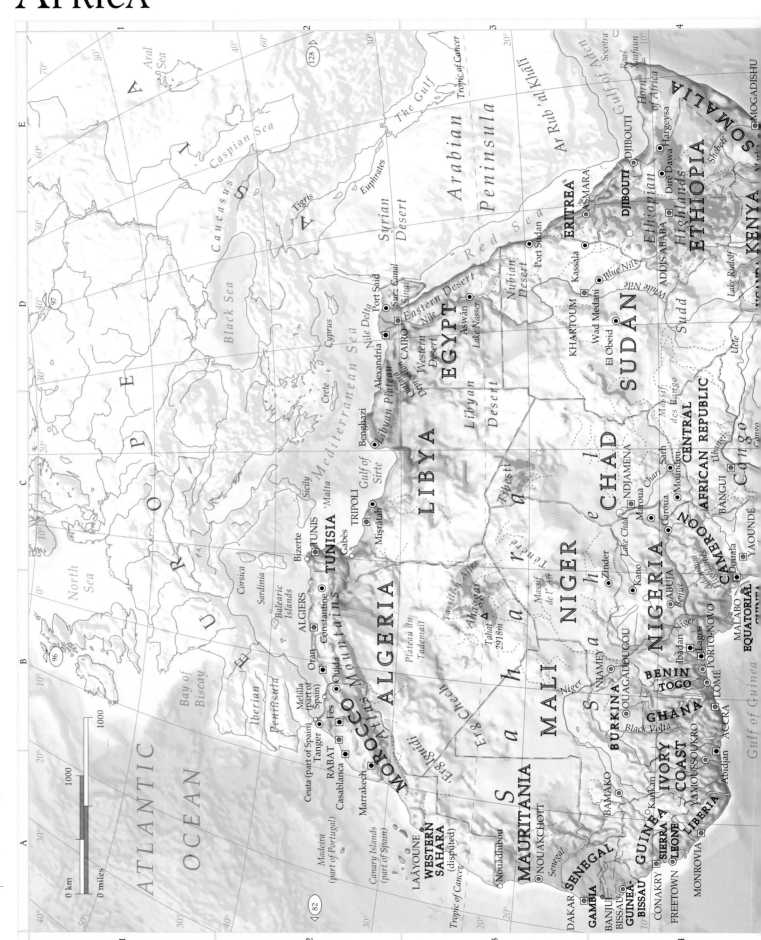

Aral Sea

Caspian Sea

E U R O P E

Black Sea

Caucasus

Mediterranean Sea

Tigris

Euphrates

Syrian Desert

Arabian Peninsula

The Gulf

Ar Rub 'al Khāli

Tropic of Cancer

Gulf of Aden

Horn of Africa

Ras Xaafuun

Socotra

MOGADISHU

SOMALIA

KENYA

ETHIOPIA

Ethiopian Highlands

ADDIS ABABA

Dire Dawa

Hargeysa

DJIBOUTI

Lake Rudolf

ASMARA

ERITREA

Red Sea

Kassala

Blue Nile

White Nile

KHARTOUM

Wad Medani

El Obeid

Port Sudan

Nubian Desert

SUDAN

Sudd

Uele

Ubangi

Massif des Bongo

CENTRAL AFRICAN REPUBLIC

BANGUI

Congo

Aswān

Lake Nasser

CAIRO

Alexandria

Port Said

Suez Canal

Sinai

Nile Delta

EGYPT

Eastern Desert

Western Desert

Qattara Depression

Libyan Plateau

Benghazi

Gulf of Sirte

Libyan Desert

Tibesti

LIBYA

Tripoli

Misrātah

Gabes

TUNISIA

TUNIS

Bizerte

Sicily

Malta

Sardinia

Corsica

Balearic Islands

ALGIERS

Constantine

Ahaggar

Tahat 2918m

Tassili-n-Ajjer

Plateau du Tademaït

ALGERIA

Oran

Oujda

Fès

MOROCCO

Atlas Mountains

Tanger

Ceuta (part of Spain)

Melilla (part of Spain)

RABAT

Casablanca

Marrakech

Iberian Peninsula

Madeira (part of Portugal)

Bay of Biscay

North Sea

ATLANTIC OCEAN

Canary Islands (part of Spain)

LAÂYOUNE

WESTERN SAHARA (disputed)

Nouâdhibou

NOUAKCHOTT

MAURITANIA

Senegal

DAKAR

SENEGAL

GAMBIA

BANJUL

BISSAU

GUINEA-BISSAU

CONAKRY

GUINEA

FREETOWN

SIERRA LEONE

MONROVIA

LIBERIA

Kankan

BAMAKO

MALI

IVORY COAST

YAMOUSSOUKRO

Abidjan

GHANA

ACCRA

Black Volta

BURKINA

OUAGADOUGOU

Niger

NIAMEY

NIGER

Zinder

Kano

BENIN

TOGO

LOMÉ

PORTO-NOVO

Lagos

Ibadan

ABUJA

NIGERIA

Benue

MALABO

EQUATORIAL GUINEA

YAOUNDÉ

Douala

CAMEROON

Garoua

Maroua

Moundou

Sarh

NDJAMENA

CHAD

Lake Chad

Chari

Massif de l'Aïr

S a h e l

S a h a r a

Erg Chech

Erg Iguidi

Ténéré

Niger

Gulf of Guinea

Tropic of Cancer

POPULATION

Less than
50,000

50,000 –
100,000

100,000 –
500,000

Over
500,000

84

1000

1000

0 km

0 miles

96

97

128

82

A B C D E

Equator

5

6

7

8

Equator

Somali Basin

Kismaayo

Mombasa
Tanga
Pemba
Zanzibar
Dar es Salaam

ANTANANARIVO
ANTANANARIVO

MAYOTTE
(to France)

COMOROS
MORONI

Aldabra Group

Mahajanga
Nacala
Nampula
Toliara

Tropic of Capricorn

Madagascar Basin

MADAGASCAR

Fianarantsoa

156

Prince Edward Islands
(part of South Africa)

Crozet Plateau

E

NAIROBI
Kilimanjaro
5895m
5200m
KIGALI
RWANDA
BUJUMBURA
BURUNDI
Kisumu
Lake Victoria
Lake Tanganyika
Bukavu

Masai Steppe
DODOMA
TANZANIA

MALAWI
Ruvuma
Lake Nyasa
LILONGWE
Blantyre
Lake Rukwa

Lutio

Mozambique Channel

Madagascar Plateau

INDIAN

OCEAN

Southwest Indian Ridge

D

Beira

MOZAMBIQUE

Mozambique Plateau

Great Rift Valley

Lake Mweru
Ndola
Kitwe
Lubumbashi
Kananga
Ilebo
Kasai
KINSHASA
Cuango

CONGO (ZAIRE)

Congo Basin

ZAMBIA
LUSAKA
Lake Kariba
HARARE
ZIMBABWE
Bulawayo
Victoria Falls
Zambezi

Kalemie
Luvua
Luena
Lake Mweru

Limpopo
PRETORIA
MAPUTO
MBABANE
SWAZILAND
GABORONE
Johannesburg
Vaal
Francistown
Okavango Delta
Cuando
Cubango
Kalahari
BOTSWANA
WINDHOEK
Nossob
Desert
Orange River
BLOEMFONTEIN
LESOTHO
MASERU
Durban
Drakensberg
East London
Port Elizabeth

SOUTH AFRICA

Great Karoo

Agulhas Plateau

Agulhas Basin

C

ANGOLA
Huambo
Móco 2619m
Lubango
Namibe
LUANDA
Cuanza

NAMIBIA
Namib Desert
Etosha Pan
Cunene

CAPE TOWN
Cape of Good Hope

Orange Fan

Cape Basin

Winter limit of pack ice
Summer limit of pack ice

170

GABON
BRAZZAVILLE
POINTE-NOIRE
Matadi
Cabinda
(part of Angola)

SÃO TOMÉ
Port-Gentil

& PRÍNCIPE

Angola Basin

B

Guinea Basin

Ascension Fracture Zone

ASCENSION ISLAND
(to Saint Helena)

SAINT HELENA
(to UK)

ATLANTIC

OCEAN

Walvis Ridge

Tropic of Capricorn

TRISTAN DA CUNHA
(to Saint Helena)

Gough Island
(part of Tristan da Cunha)

Atlantic-Indian Ridge

170

A

Mid - Atlantic Ridge

83

Z

ELEVATION

| 4000 m |
| 13 124 ft |

| 2000 m |
| 6562 ft |

| 1000 m |
| 3281 ft |

| 500 m |
| 1640 ft |

| 250 m |
| 820 ft |

| 100 m |
| 328 ft |

| Sea Level | Sea Level |

| -250 m |
| -820 ft |

| -500 m |
| -1640 ft |

| -1000 m |
| -3281 ft |

| -2000 m |
| -6562 ft |

| -3000 m |
| -9843 ft |

| -4000 m |
| -13 124 ft |

NORTHWEST AFRICA

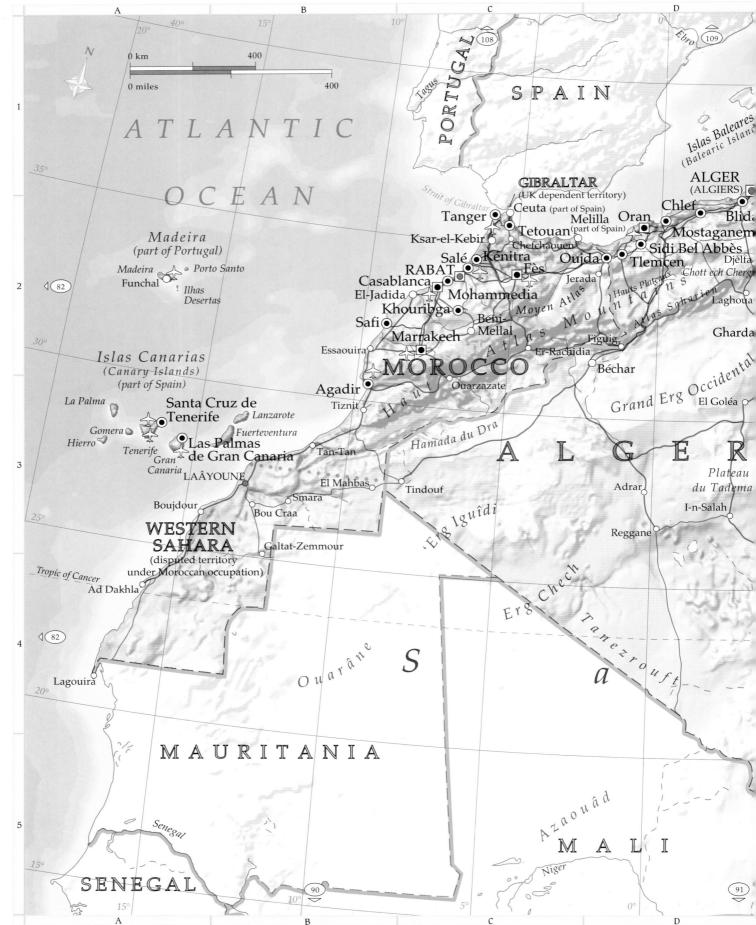

ATLANTIC

OCEAN

SPAIN

PORTUGAL

Tagus

108

Ebro 109

Islas Baleares
(Balearic Islands)

GIBRALTAR
(UK dependent territory)

ALGER
(ALGIERS)

Strait of Gibraltar

Ceuta (part of Spain)

Tanger

Chlef

Blida

Tetouan

Melilla
(part of Spain)

Oran

Mostaganem

Ksar-el-Kebir

Chefchaouen

Salé

Kénitra

Oujda

Sidi Bel Abbès

RABAT

Fès

Tlemcen

Djelfa

Casablanca

Jerada

Hauts Plateaux

Chott ech Chergui

Mohammedia

El-Jadida

Moyen Atlas

Laghoua

Khouribga

Beni-
Mellal

Safi

Figuig

Gharda

Marrakech

Er-Rachidia

MOROCCO

Essaouira

Béchar

Ouarzazate

Agadir

Madeira
(part of Portugal)

Madeira   *Porto Santo*

Funchal

*Ilhas
Desertas*

82

Islas Canarias
(Canary Islands)
(part of Spain)

La Palma

Santa Cruz de
Tenerife

Lanzarote

Tiznit

Haut

Atlas

Mountains

Atlas Saharien

Grand Erg Occidental

El Goléa

Gomera

Fuerteventura

Hierro

Tenerife

Las Palmas
de Gran Canaria

*Gran
Canaria*

LAÂYOUNE

Tan-Tan

Hamada du Dra

ALGER

*Plateau
du Tadema*

Adrar

I-n-Salah

Boujdour

El Mahbas

Tindouf

Bou Craa

Smara

Reggane

**WESTERN
SAHARA**
(disputed territory
under Moroccan occupation)

Galtat-Zemmour

'Erg Iguîdi

Erg Chech

Tanezrouft

Tropic of Cancer

Ad Dakhla

82

Ouarâne

S

Lagouira

MAURITANIA

Azaouâd

MALI

Senegal

Niger

SENEGAL

90

91

POPULATION

○ Less than
50,000

○ 50,000 –
100,000

◉ 100,000 –
500,000

◉ Over
500,000

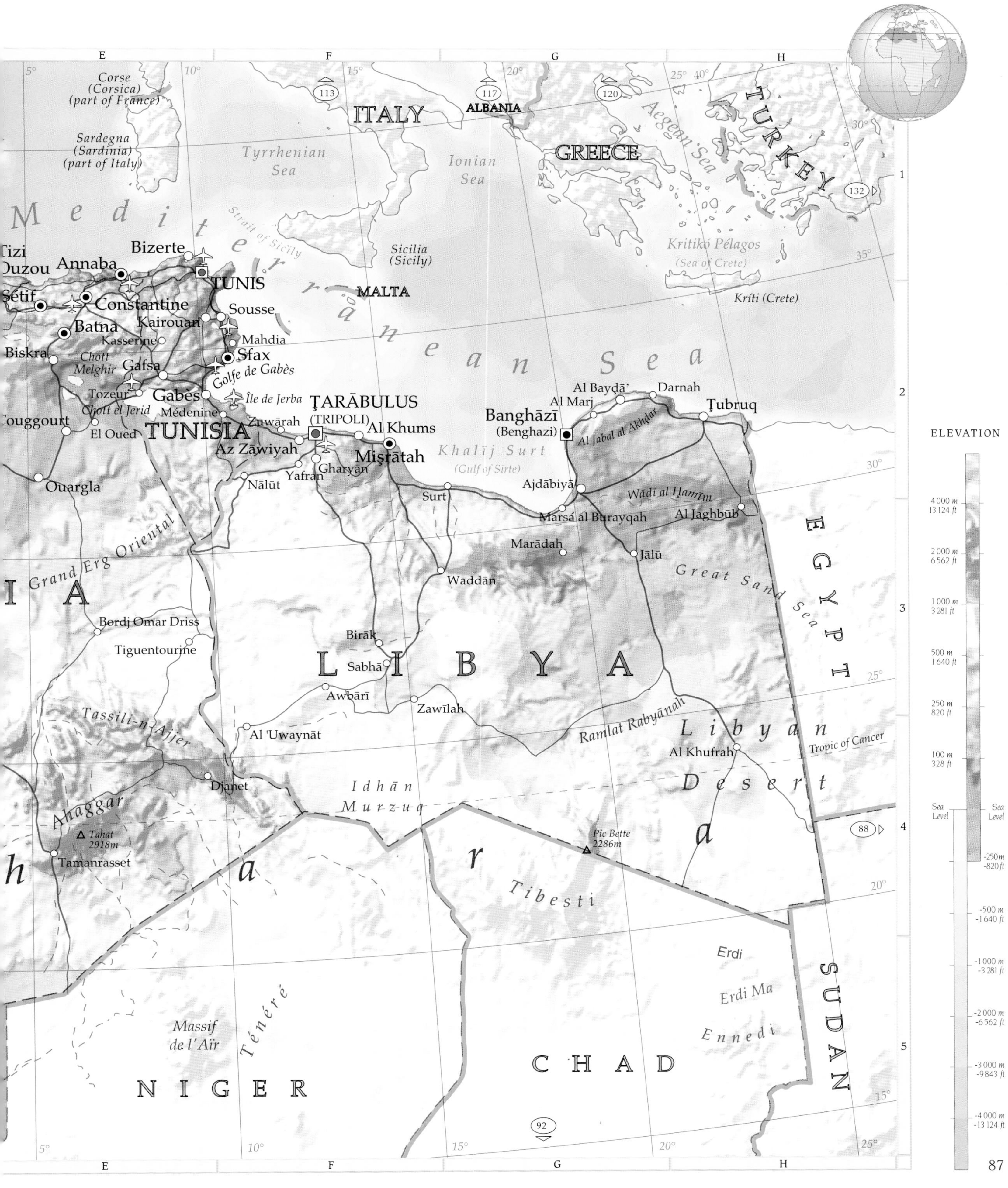

E · 5° · 10° · F · 15° · G · 20° · 25° · 40° · H · 30°

Corse
(Corsica)
(part of France)

Sardegna
(Sardinia)
(part of Italy)

ITALY

Tyrrhenian
Sea

Ionian
Sea

ALBANIA

GREECE

Aegean Sea

TURKEY

113

117

120

132

1

35°

Kritikó Pélagos
(Sea of Crete)

M e d i t e r r a n e a n   S e a

Strait of Sicily

Sicilia
(Sicily)

Kríti (Crete)

Tizi
Ouzou

Annaba

Bizerte

TUNIS

Sétif

Constantine

Sousse

Kairouan

Batna

Kasserine

Mahdia

Biskra

Chott
Melghir

Gafsa

Sfax

Golfe de Gabès

MALTA

Al Baydā'

Darnah

Al Marj

Ţubruq

Banghāzī
(Benghazi)

2

Tozeur

Gabes

Île de Jerba

ŢARĀBULUS

Al Jabal al Akhḑar

Touggourt

Chott el Jerid

Médenine

Zuwārah

(TRIPOLI)

Al Khums

El Oued

TUNISIA

Az Zāwiyah

Miṣrātah

Khalīj Surt
(Gulf of Sirte)

Ajdābiyā

Wādī al Ḩamīm

Al Jaghbūb

E
G
Y
P
T

Ouargla

Nālūt

Yafran

Gharyān

Surt

30°

Marsá al Burayqah

Marādah

Jālū

Great Sand Sea

Waddān

Grand Erg Oriental

I
A

Bordj Omar Driss

Birāk

L   I   B   Y   A

Tiguentourine

Sabhā

25°

Tassili-n-Ajjer

Awbārī

Zawīlah

L i b y a n

Al 'Uwaynāt

Ramlat Rabyānah

Tropic of Cancer

Al Khufrah

D e s e r t

88

Djanet

I d h ā n

Ahaggar

Tahat
2918m

M u r z u q

Pic Bette
2286m

4

20°

Tamanrasset

a

r

Tibesti

Erdi

S
U
D
A
N

Erdi Ma

Massif
de l'Aïr

Ténéré

Ennedi

5

15°

N   I   G   E   R

C   H   A   D

92

5° · 10° · F · 15° · G · 20° · 25° · H

E

ELEVATION

4 000 m
13 124 ft

2 000 m
6 562 ft

1 000 m
3 281 ft

500 m
1 640 ft

250 m
820 ft

100 m
328 ft

Sea
Level

Sea
Level

-250 m
-820 ft

-500 m
-1 640 ft

-1 000 m
-3 281 ft

-2 000 m
-6 562 ft

-3 000 m
-9 843 ft

-4 000 m
-13 124 ft

NORTHEAST AFRICA

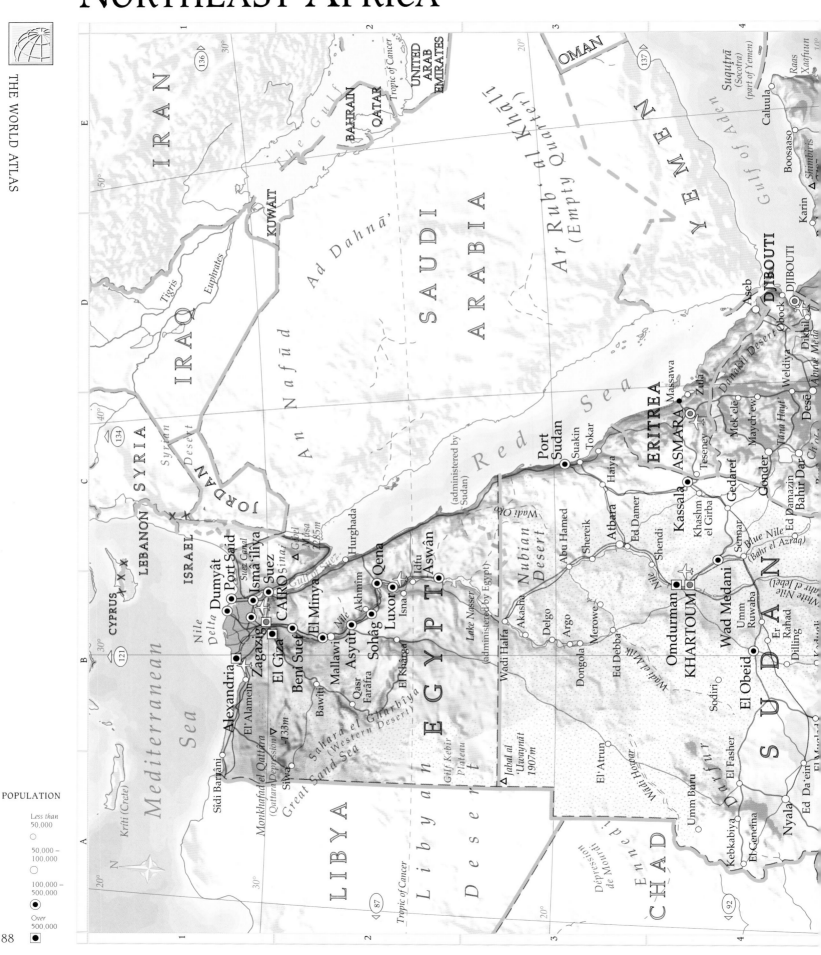

IRAN

IRAQ

SYRIA

LEBANON

ISRAEL

JORDAN

CYPRUS

Kríti (Crete)

Mediterranean Sea

KUWAIT

BAHRAIN

QATAR

UNITED ARAB EMIRATES

OMAN

SAUDI ARABIA

Ad Dahnā'

An Nafūd

Syrian Desert

Tigris

Euphrates

The Gulf

Ar Rub' al Khālī

Ar Rub' al Khālī (Empty Quarter)

Y E M E N

Gulf of Aden

Suqutrā (Socotra) (part of Yemen)

Raas Xaafuun

Caluula

Boosaaso

Shimbiris

Karin

Red Sea

Tropic of Cancer

DJIBOUTI

DJIBOUTI

Aseb

Obock

Dikhil

Weldiya

Danakil Desert

Abuē Mēda

ERITREA

ASMARA

Massawa

Zula

Mek'elē

Maych'ew

Tana Hayk'

Desē

Port Sudan

Suakin

Tokar

Haiya

Teseney

Kassala

Khashm el Girba

Gedaref

Gonder

Ed Damazin

Bahir Dar

(administered by Sudan)

Wadi Oko

Nubian Desert

Abu Hamed

Shereik

Atbara

Ed Damer

Shendi

Semna

Blue Nile (Bahr el Azraq)

SUDAN

KHARTOUM

Omdurman

Wad Medani

White Nile (Bahr el Jebel)

Akasha

Delgo

Argo

Dongola

Ed Debba

Merowe

Wadi el Milk

Umm Ruwaba

Er Rahad

El Obeid

Sodiri

Dilling

Port Said

Dumyât

Ismâ'iliya

Suez

Suez Canal

Zagazig

Gebel Mūsa 2285m

Gulf of Suez

Sinai

Hurghada

El Gîza

CAIRO

Beni Suef

Mallawi

El Minya

Asyût

Akhmīm

Sohâg

Qena

Luxor

Isna

Idfu

Aswân

Qasr Farâfra

El Khârga

Lake Nasser

Wadi Halfa

(administered by Egypt)

E G Y P T

Alexandria

El 'Alamein

Nile Delta

Zagazig

Monkhafad el Qattâra (Qattara Depression) -133m

Siwa

Sîdi Barâni

Bawiti

Sahara el Gharbîya (Western Desert)

Great Sand Sea

L I B Y A

Gulf Kebir Plateau

Libyan Desert

Jabal al 'Uwaynāt 1907m

Tropic of Cancer

El 'Atrun

Wâdi Howar

Umm Buru

Darfur

Kebkabiya

El Geneina

Nyala

El Fasher

Ed Da'ein

Dilling

C H A D

Ennedi

Dépression de Mourdi

Wâdi el Milk

POPULATION

Less than 50,000

50,000 – 100,000

100,000 – 500,000

Over 500,000

N

CENTRAL
AFRICAN
REPUBLIC

Massif
des
Bongo

Bahr Aouk

Kotto

Uele

Bomu

Congo

Lualaba

Congo
Basin

Sankuru

Kasai

CONGO
(ZAIRE)

Sudd

Raga

Wau

Tonj

Tambura

Rumbek

Yambio

Amadi

Maridi

Juba

Bor

White Nile (Bahr el Jebel)

Kapoeta

Lokitaung

Lodwar

Kongor

Duk Faiwil

Elemi Triangle
(administered
by Kenya)

3187 m

Kapoeta

Sobat

Gore

Agaro

Jima

Awash

Mi'eso

Nazrēt

ADIS ABEBA
(ADDIS ABABA)

ETHIOPIA

Highlands

Abaya Hāyk'

Negēlē

Yabēlo

Great Rift Valley

Hargeysa

SOMALIA

Daaxo Nugaaleed

Sinujiif

Garoowe

Gaalkacyo

Dhuusa Mareeb

Gellinsoor

Shilabo

Ogaden

Xuddur

Doolow

Luuq

Baydhabo

Beledweyne

Buulobarde

Jawhar

MUQDISHO
(MOGADISHU)

Marka

Baraawe

Shabeeli

Wanlaweyn

Baardheere

Jamaame

Kismaayo

Buur Gaabo

Afmadow

Garissa

Garsen

KENYA

Marsabit

Lake
Rudolf

Meru

Nyeri

NAIROBI

Kirinyaga
5200m

Malindi

Mombasa

Pemba

Tanga

Zanzibar

Zanzibar

Dar es Salaam

Mafia

Mohoro

Kilwa Kivinje

Lindi

Mtwara

Masasi

Newala

Tunduru

Songea

MOZAMBIQUE

Rio Lúrio

Rio de Lugenda

Lake Nyasa

MALAWI

INDIAN

OCEAN

SEYCHELLES

COMOROS

MAYOTTE
(French territorial collectivity)

MADAGASCAR

Equator

UGANDA

Arua

Gulu

Lira

Masindi

KAMPALA

Jinja

Entebbe

Mbale

Eldoret

Kisumu

Nakuru

Kitale

Lake
Victoria

Bukoba

Mwanza

Musoma

Nyantakara

Shinyanga

Nzega

Singida

Tabora

DODOMA

Morogoro

Kilimanjaro
5895m

Moshi

Arusha

Masai
Steppe

TANZANIA

Iringa

Njombe

Mbeya

Sumbawanga

Kasulu

Kigoma

Malagarasi

Lake
Tanganyika

Kipili

Lake
Rukwa

Sao Hill

Great Ruaha

Rufiji

Nyamtumbo

Mbarara

Kabale

RWANDA

KIGALI

Lake Kivu

BUJUMBURA

BURUNDI

Bukavu

Lake Edward

Lake
Albert

Lualaba

Lukuga

Luvua

Lake Mweru

Lufira

Lufira

ZAMBIA

ANGOLA

Zambezi

Kafue

Lake
Bangweulu

Lake
Mweru
Wantipa

Great Rift Valley

ELEVATION

4 000 m
13 124 ft

2 000 m
6 562 ft

1 000 m
3 281 ft

500 m
1 640 ft

250 m
820 ft

100 m
328 ft

Sea
Level

Sea
Level

-250 m
-820 ft

-500 m
-1 640 ft

-1 000 m
-3 281 ft

-2 000 m
-6 562 ft

-3 000 m
-9 843 ft

-4 000 m
-13 124 ft

400

400

0 km

0 miles

WEST AFRICA

WESTERN SAHARA
(disputed territory under Moroccan occupation)

'Aïn Ben Tili

Bîr Mogreïn

Fdérik   Zouérat
          Touâjîl

Choûm

MAURITANIA

Nouâdhibou

Akchâr   Atâr   Chinguetti
Akjoujt   Oujeft

El Mreyyé

NOUAKCHOTT   Idîni
          Boutilimit   Magta   Tidjikja   Tîchît
          Rkîz   Lahjar
Rosso   Aleg   Boûmdeïd   Oualâta
Richard Toll   Dagana   Senegal   Kaédi   Kiffa   Tâmchekket
Saint Louis   'Ayoûn el 'Atroûs   Néma
          Louga   Matam   Timbedgha   Amourj
Mékhé   SENEGAL   Sélibabi   Bassikouno
DAKAR   Thiès   Mbaké   Nioro
          Diourbel   Kayes
Mbour   Kaolack   Ténenkou
Sokone   Koulikani   Niger
          Tambacounda   Kayes   Ségou
BANJUL   GAMBIA   Toukoto   Kolokani   Bani
Bignona   Kolda   Gambia   Kita   Koulikoro   San
Ziguinchor   Sédhiou   BAMAKO
          Bafata   Koutiala
BISSAU   Gaoual   Sikass
GUINEA-   Labé   Dinguiraye   Niger   Siguiri   Bougouni
BISSAU   Boké   Pita   Bougouni
          Kindia   Mamou   GUINEA   Kankan   Tengréla
          Faranah   Odienné   Ferkessédougo
CONAKRY   Tokounou   Boundiali   Korhog
          Makeni   Kissidougou   IVORY
SIERRA   Beyla   Katiola   COAST
FREETOWN   LEONE   Bo   Kenema   Nzérékoré
          Gbanga   Danané   Kossi
Tubmanburg   YAMOUSSOUKRO   Gagnoa
MONROVIA   Harbel   Zwedru   Divo
Buchanan   LIBERIA   Sassandra
          Harper   San-Pédro

ATLANTIC

CAPE
VERDE

Ilhas de Barlavento
Santo
Antão   Mindelo
São   Pedra Lume
Vicente   São   Sal
Nicolau   Boa Vista

Santiago   Maio
Fogo   PRAIA
Ilhas de Sotavento

OCEAN

Tropic of Cancer

POPULATION

Less than
50,000
○

50,000 –
100,000
○

100,000 –
500,000
◉

Over
500,000
◉

0 km   400

0 miles   400

E · F · G · H

10° · 15°

ⓧ 87

Tassili-n-Ajjer

L I B Y A

A L G E R I A

25° · 1

'Erg echech

Tanezrouft

Ahaggar

Tropic of Cancer

Tibesti

Taoudenni

a h a r a a

Ténéré du Tafassâsset

Séguédine

20° · 2

'Erg I-n-Sâkâne

Tessalit

Assamakka

Iferouâne

ⓧ 92 ▷

Araouane

Adrar des Ifôghas

Massif de l'Aïr

Ténéré

M A L I

Azaouâd

Monts Bagzane △ 2022m

ac guibine

Tombouctou

Agadez

Grand Erg de Bilma

Ngourti

Goundam

Gao

N I G E R

C H A D

Lac Niangay

Ansongo

Ménaka

15° · 3

Mopti

Hombori

Ayorou

Tahoua

Keïta

Dilia

Nguigmi

h

Tillabéri

Dakoro

Lake Chad

e

Dogondoutchi

Birnin Konni

Tessaoua

Zinder

Gouré

l

Ouahigouya

NIAMEY ✈

Maradi

Guidimouni

Hadejia

Kaya

Sokoto

Nguru

oudougou

OUAGADOUGOU ✈

Fada-Ngourma

Sokoto

Sokoto

Katsina

Hadejia

Maiduguri

BURKINA

Jega

Gusau

Kano ✈

obo-Dioulasso

Tenkodogo

Bawku

Koko

Zaria

Gongola

Biu

Bolgatanga

Sansanné-Mango

Kandi

Yelwa

Kaduna

Bauchi

Kumo

Wa

Oti

Natitingou

Kainji Reservoir

Gombi

10° · 4

Yendi

BENIN

N I G E R I A

Jos

Jos Plateau

Yola

Tamale

Parakou

Minna

Benue

Shebshi Mountains

T O G O

Sokodé

Jebba

Niger

ABUJA ✈

Lafia

Wukari

Adamawa Highlands

Ilorin

Oyo

Ogbomosho

Lokoja

Makurdi

Goter Mountains

GHANA

Ede

Owo

C A M E R O O N

Wenchi

Lake Volta

Ibadan

Benin City

Enugu

Djèrem

Sunyani

Abomey

PORTO-NOVO

Onitsha

C.A.R.

bengourou

Kumasi

Kpalimé

Sapele

Aba

Calabar

5° · 5

Nsawam

LOMÉ

Cotonou

Lagos

Warri

Owerri

Asamankese

ACCRA

Port Harcourt

Uyo

bidjan

Cape Coast

Bight of Benin

Mouths of the Niger

Sanaga

Sekondi-Takoradi

ⓧ 93 ▽

Isla de Bioco

EQUATORIAL GUINEA

Gulf of Guinea

0° · 5° · 10° · 15°

E · F · G · H

ELEVATION

4000 m / 13 124 ft

2000 m / 6562 ft

1000 m / 3281 ft

500 m / 1640 ft

250 m / 820 ft

100 m / 328 ft

Sea Level / Sea Level

-250 m / -820 ft

-500 m / -1640 ft

-1000 m / -3281 ft

-2000 m / -6562 ft

-3000 m / -9843 ft

-4000 m / -13 124 ft

91

CENTRAL AFRICA

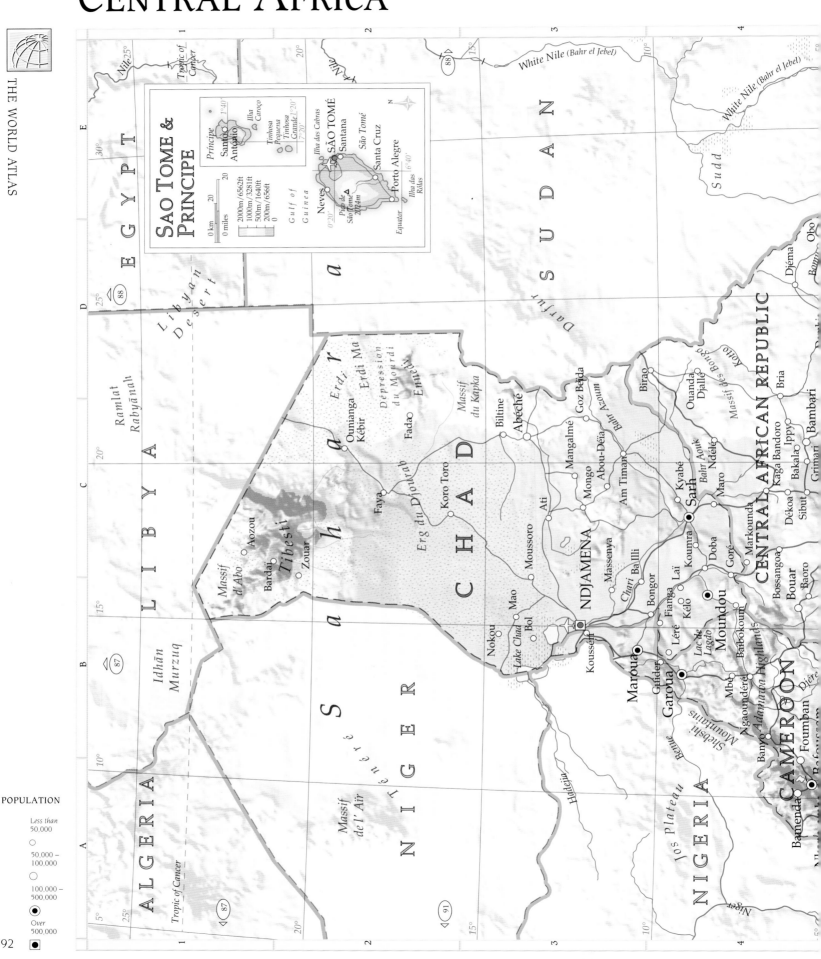

SAO TOME & PRINCIPE

Príncipe

Santo
António

Ilha
Caroço

Tinhosa
Pequena
Tinhosa
Grande

Neves

SÃO TOMÉ
Santana

São Tomé

Santa Cruz

Ilha das Cabras

São Tomé

Forto Alegre

Pico de
São Tomé
2024m

Ilha das
Rôlas

Equator

Gulf of
Guinea

2000m/6562ft
1000m/3281ft
500m/1640ft
200m/656ft

0 km   20
0 miles   20

EGYPT

Tropic of Cancer

Nile

Libyan Desert

Ramlat
Rabyānah

LIBYA

Idhān
Murzuq

ALGERIA

Tropic of Cancer

NIGER

Massif
de l'Aïr

Ténéré

S a h a r a

Massif
d'Abo

Aozou

Bardaï

Tibesti

Zouar

Erdi Ma

Ennedi

Erdi

Ounianga
Kébir

Fada

Dépression
du Mourdi

Massif
du Kapka

Faya

Koro Toro

Erg du Djourab

CHAD

Moussoro

Ati

Mongo

Mangalmé

Abou-Déïa

Am Timan

Biltine

Abéché

Goz Beïda

Birao

Ouanda
Djallé

Ndélé

Bahr Aouk

Kyabé

Sarh

Maro

Bahr Azoum

Darfur

SUDAN

White Nile (Bahr el Jebel)

White Nile (Bahr el Jebel)

Sudd

CENTRAL AFRICAN REPUBLIC

Djéma

Bria

Kaga Bandoro

Ippy

Bakala

Bambari

Grimari

Massif des Bongo

Kotto

Sibut

Dékoa

Markounda

Bossangoa

Bouar

Baoro

Doba

Gore

Koumra

Kélo

Moundou

Baïbokoum

Lac de
Lagdo

Mbé

Ngaoundéré

Adamawa Highlands

CAMEROON

Shebshi
Mountains

Garoua

Guider

Maroua

Mora

Kousséri

NDJAMENA

Massenya

Chari Baïlli

Bongor

Fianga

Léré

Lai

Bol

Mao

Nokou

Lake Chad

NIGERIA

Jos Plateau

Benue

Hadejia

Niger

Bamenda

Foumban

Banyo

Massif
du Mayo

POPULATION

Less than
50,000

50,000 –
100,000

100,000 –
500,000

Over
500,000

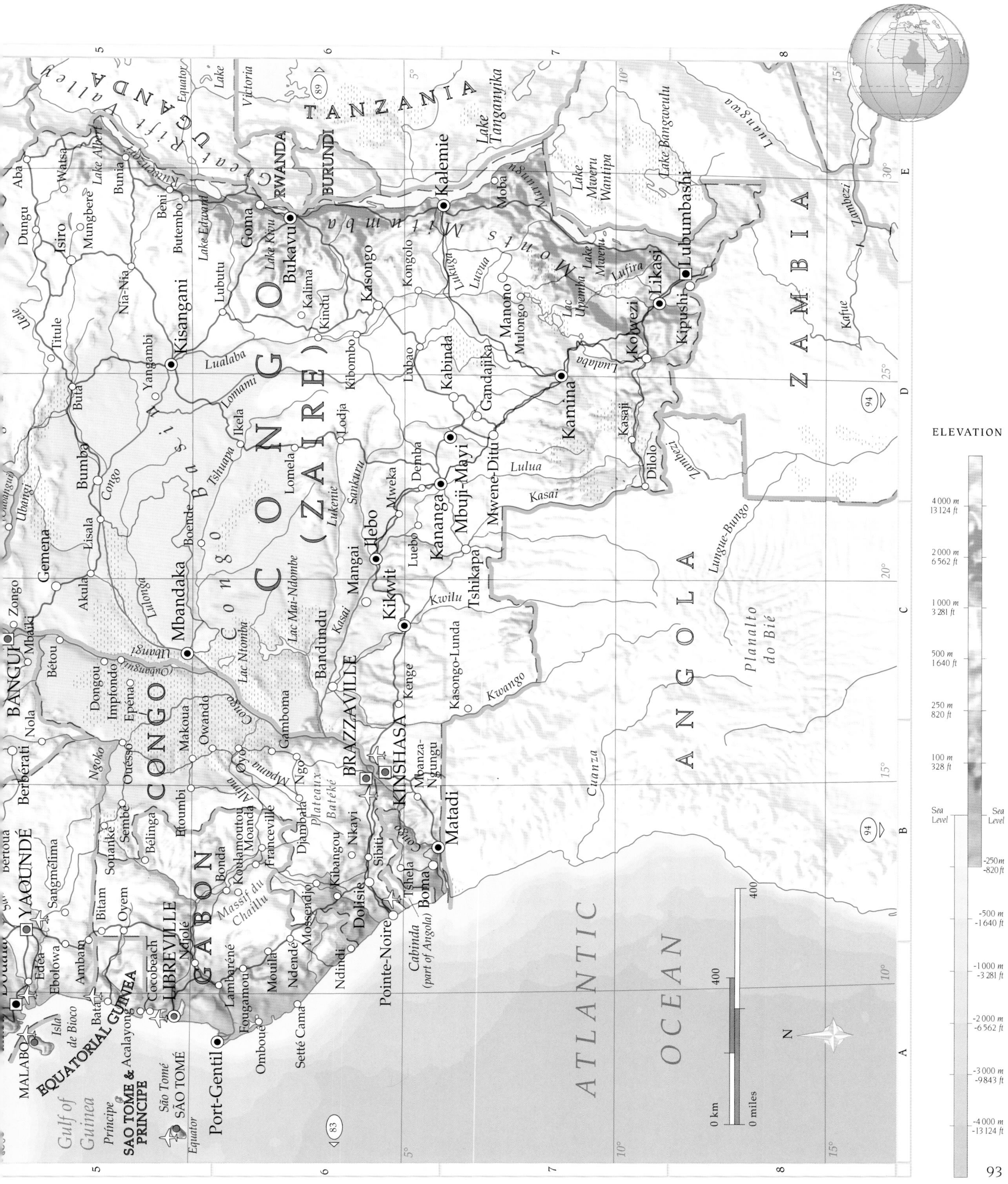

ELEVATION

	4 000 m 13 124 ft
	2 000 m 6 562 ft
	1 000 m 3 281 ft
	500 m 1 640 ft
	250 m 820 ft
	100 m 328 ft
Sea Level	Sea Level
	-250 m -820 ft
	-500 m -1 640 ft
	-1 000 m -3 281 ft
	-2 000 m -6 562 ft
	-3 000 m -9 843 ft
	-4 000 m -13 124 ft

TANZANIA

RWANDA

BURUNDI

ZAMBIA

CONGO (ZAIRE)

ANGOLA

CONGO

GABON

EQUATORIAL GUINEA

SAO TOME & PRINCIPE

Great Rift Valley

UGANDA

Lake Victoria

Lake Tanganyika

Lake Bangweulu

Kalemie
Lubumbashi
Likasi
Kipushi
Kolwezi
Kamina
Mbuji-Mayi
Kananga
Kananga
Mwene-Ditu
Kikwit
Kenge
KINSHASA
BRAZZAVILLE
Matadi
Boma
Pointe-Noire
Kisangani
Bukavu
Goma
Mbandaka
BANGUI
YAOUNDÉ
LIBREVILLE
MALABO
Port-Gentil

ATLANTIC OCEAN

Gulf of Guinea

Cabinda
(part of Angola)

N

0 km   400
0 miles   400

SOUTHERN AFRICA

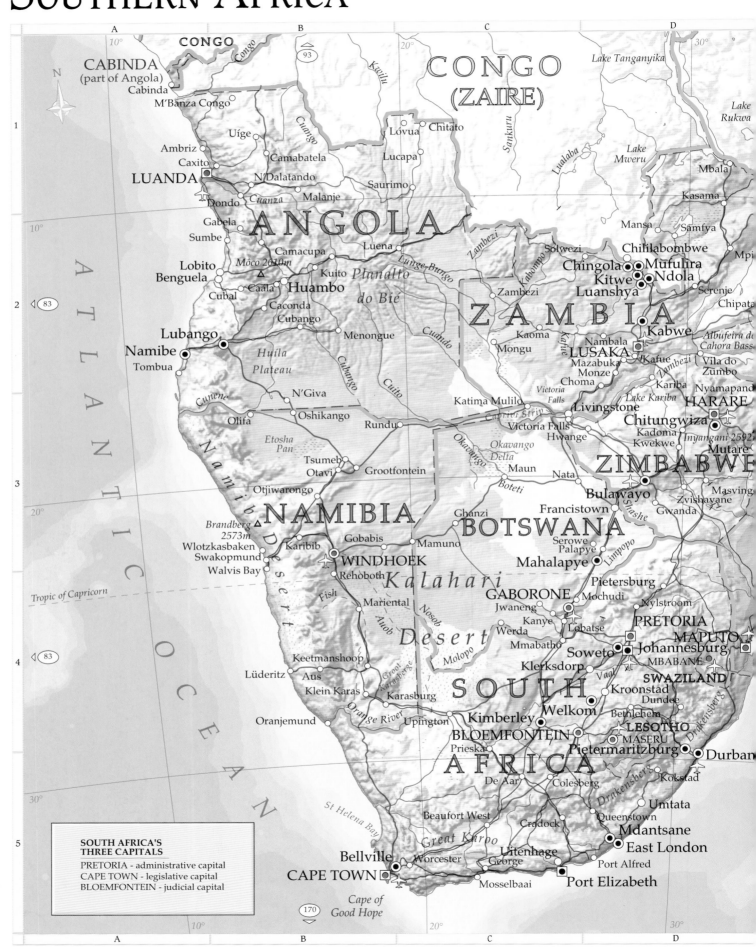

CONGO

CABINDA
(part of Angola)
Cabinda
M'Banza Congo
Uíge
Ambriz
Caxito
LUANDA
Dondo
Camabatela
N'Dalatando
Gabela
Sumbe
Camacupa
Lobito
Benguela
Môco 2610m
Cubal
Caala
Kuito
Huambo
Caconda
Cubango
Lubango
Menongue
Namibe
Tombua
Huíla
Plateau
N'Giva
Olifa
Oshikango

ANGOLA

CONGO
(ZAIRE)

Lake Tanganyika
Lake Rukwa
Lake Mweru
Mbala
Kasama
Mansa
Samfya
Mpi
Chililabombwe
Chingola
Mufulira
Kitwe
Ndola
Luanshya
Serenje
Chipata
Lóvua
Chitato
Lucapa
Saurimo
Luena
Lunge-Bungo
Zambezi
Solwezi
Planalto
do Bié
Cuanza
Cuando
Cuito
Kaoma
Mongu
Zambezi
Mazabuka
Monze
Choma
LUSAKA
Nambala
Kafue
Kabwe
Albufeira de
Cahora Bass
Vila do
Zumbo

ZAMBIA

Katima Mulilo
Victoria
Falls
Rundu
Victoria Falls
Hwange
Livingstone
Kariba
Lake Kariba
Nyamapand
Kadoma
Kwekwe
HARARE
Chitungwiza
Inyangani 2592
Mutare
Etosha
Pan
Tsumeb
Otavi
Grootfontein
Okavango
Delta
Okavango
Maun
Nata
Boteti
ZIMBABWE
Masving
Zvishavane
Otjiwarongo
Bulawayo
Gwanda
Brandberg
2573m
NAMIBIA
Ghanzi
Francistown
Serowe
BOTSWANA
Shashe
Gobabis
Mamuno
Palapye
Wlotzkasbaken
Karibib
Swakopmund
Walvis Bay
WINDHOEK
Rehoboth
Kalahari
Mahalapye
Limpopo
Pietersburg
Nylstroom
Fish
Mariental
Desert
GABORONE
Mochudi
Jwaneng
Kanye
Werda
Lobatse
PRETORIA
Namib
Desert
Nosob
Auob
Mmabatho
MAPUTO
Keetmanshoop
Mmabatho
Soweto
Johannesburg
MBABANE
Lüderitz
Aus
Klein Karas
Karasburg
Molopo
SOUTH
Klerksdorp
SWAZILAND
Kroonstad
Dundee
Oranjemund
Upington
Kimberley
Welkom
Bethlehem
LESOTHO
Orange River
Groot
Karasberge
BLOEMFONTEIN
MASERU
Drakensberg
Pietermaritzburg
Durban
Prieska
AFRICA
De Aar
Colesberg
Kokstad
Drakensberg
Umtata
Beaufort West
Cradock
Queenstown
Mdantsane
East London
St Helena Bay
Great Karoo
Uitenhage
Port Alfred
Bellville
Worcester
George
CAPE TOWN
Mosselbaai
Port Elizabeth
Cape of
Good Hope

SOUTH AFRICA'S
THREE CAPITALS
PRETORIA - administrative capital
CAPE TOWN - legislative capital
BLOEMFONTEIN - judicial capital

Tropic of Capricorn

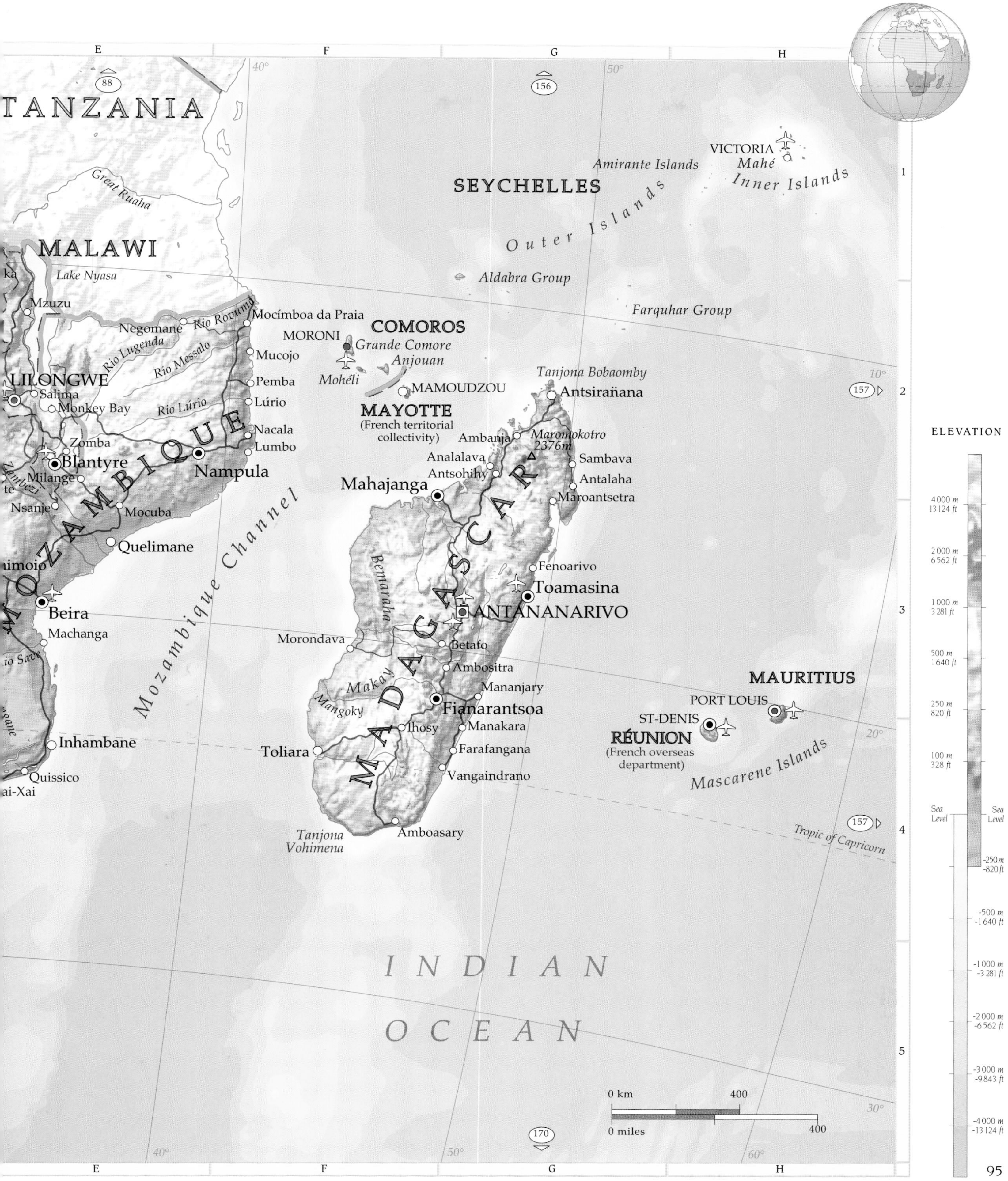

TANZANIA

MALAWI

Great Ruaha

Lake Nyasa

ka

Mzuzu

Negomane   Rio Rovuma   Mocímboa da Praia

Rio Lugenda

Mucojo

Rio Messalo

LILONGWE   Pemba

Salima   Rio Lúrio   Lúrio

Monkey Bay   Nacala

Zomba   Lumbo

Blantyre   Nampula

Milange

te

Nsanje   Mocuba

Quelimane

imoio

Beira

Machanga

io Save

Inhambane

Quissico

ai-Xai

SEYCHELLES

Amirante Islands   VICTORIA
                     Mahé
Outer Islands   *Inner Islands*

Aldabra Group

Farquhar Group

COMOROS

MORONI   *Grande Comore*
         Anjouan
Mohéli

MAMOUDZOU

MAYOTTE
(French territorial
collectivity)

Ambanja

Analalava

Antsohihy

Mahajanga

Tanjona Bobaomby

Antsiranana

Maromokotro
2376m

Sambava

Antalaha

Maroantsetra

Fenoarivo

Toamasina

ANTANANARIVO

Betafo

Morondava

Ambositra

Mananjary

Fianarantsoa

Ihosy   Manakara

Toliara   Farafangana

Vangaindrano

Tanjona   Amboasary
Vohimena

MAURITIUS

PORT LOUIS

ST-DENIS

RÉUNION
(French overseas
department)

Mascarene Islands

Tropic of Capricorn

M A D A G A S C A R

Bemaraha

Makay

Mangoky

Mozambique Channel

M O Z A M B I Q U E

I N D I A N

O C E A N

ELEVATION

4 000 m / 13 124 ft
2 000 m / 6 562 ft
1 000 m / 3 281 ft
500 m / 1 640 ft
250 m / 820 ft
100 m / 328 ft
Sea Level / Sea Level
-250 m / -820 ft
-500 m / -1 640 ft
-1 000 m / -3 281 ft
-2 000 m / -6 562 ft
-3 000 m / -9 843 ft
-4 000 m / -13 124 ft

0 km   400

0 miles   400

EUROPE

Reykjanes Basin

171

Limit of winter pack ice

Charlie-Gibbs Fracture Zone

Reykjanes Ridge

REYKJAVÍK

ICELAND

Vatnajökull

Norwegian Basin

Iceland Basin

Lofot

82

Hatton Ridge

Faeroe-Iceland Ridge

Norwegian Sea

NORW

FAEROE ISLANDS
(to Denmark)

Trondheim

Rockall Bank

Outer Hebrides

Shetland Islands

Faeroe-Shetland Trough

Bergen

NO

Rockall Trough

Orkney Islands

Stavanger

OSLO

SW

British Isles

North Sea

Glasgow   Edinburgh

Gothenburg

Vä

Mid-Atlantic Ridge

Ireland

Belfast

Jönköping

REPUBLIC OF IRELAND

DUBLIN   ISLE OF MAN
(to UK)

UNITED KINGDOM

Ålborg

Jylland

Porcupine Plain

Liverpool   Manchester

DENMARK   COPENHA

Celtic Sea

Britain

Birmingham

Odense   Malmö

ATLANTIC

Cardiff   LONDON

Hamburg

OCEAN

Celtic Shelf

English Channel

NETHERLANDS

THE HAGUE   AMSTERDAM   Hannover

N O

Channel Islands
(to UK)

Rotterdam

Elbe

Porcupine Plain

le Havre

BELGIUM   BRUSSELS

BERLIN

Pozn

Biscay Plain

Seine

Liège   Bonn

Azores-Biscay Rise

Charcot Seamounts

Rennes

LUXEMBOURG

GERMANY

Wrocław

Od

PARIS

LUXEMBOURG

Frankfurt am Main

PRAG

Iberian Plain

Nantes   Orléans

Rhine

CZECH

Bay of Biscay

Loire

Strasbourg   Stuttgart

REPUBLIC

A Coruña

FRANCE

Munich

BRATISL

Galicia Bank

Zürich

Salzburg

Bordeaux

LIECH.   VIENNA

Cordillera Cantábrica

Bilbao

Lyon   BERN

Innsbruck   AUSTRIA

Iberian Plain

Porto

Garonne

SWITZERLAND

Mont Blanc
4807m

SLOVENIA

Duero

Massif Central

Milan   Venice   LJUBLJANA

PORTUGAL

Iberian

Zaragoza   Ebro

Toulouse

Rhône

Po   ZAG

Peninsula

Tagus

Pyrenees

ANDORRA

Nice   Turin

Bologna   CROAT

Tagus Plain

MADRID

Marseille

MONACO

SAN MARINO

BOS & HE

LISBON

SPAIN

Barcelona

Pisa

Apennines

SARAJE

Horseshoe Seamounts

Peninsula

Guadalquivir

Valencia

Corsica

VATICAN CITY

ITALY

Mostar

Madeira
(part of Portugal)

Seville

Sardinia

ROME

Adriatic Sea

Palma

Naples   Bari

Málaga

Balearic Islands

Algerian Basin

Tyrrhenian Sea

GIBRALTAR
(to UK)

Ceuta
(part of Spain)

Mediterranean

Cagliari

Cosenza

Canary Islands
(part of Spain)

Melilla
(part of Spain)

Palermo

Mount Etna
3340m

Sicily

Catania

Ionian Basi

Atlas   Mountains

AFRICA

84

MALTA
VALLETTA

POPULATION

Less than
50,000

50,000 –
100,000

100,000 –
500,000

Over
500,000

96

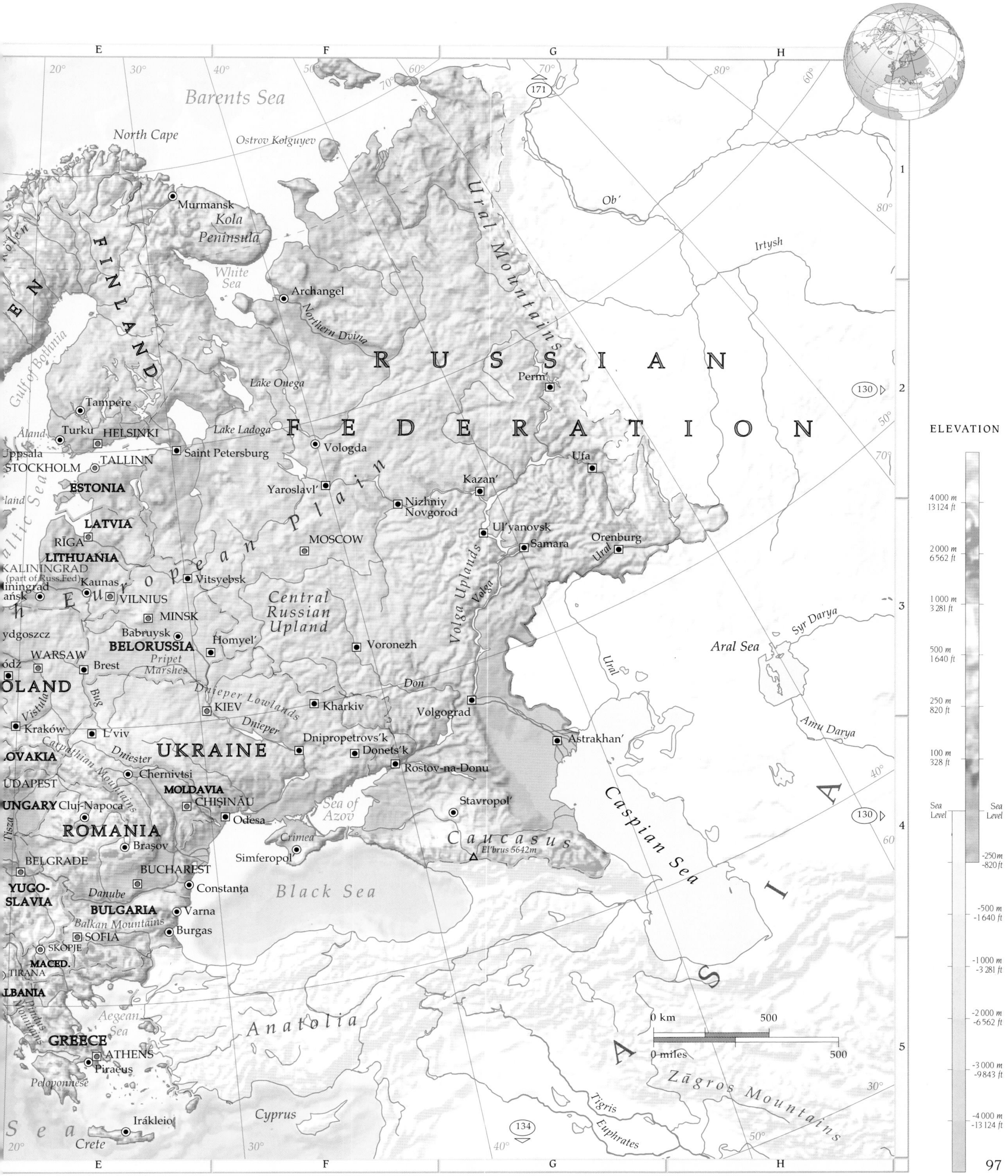

Barents Sea

North Cape

Ostrov Kolguyev

Ural Mountains

171

1

Ob'

Irtysh

Murmansk

Kola Peninsula

White Sea

Archangel

Northern Dvina

FINLAND

R U S S I A N

Perm

130

2

Lake Onega

Ufa

Tampere

Lake Ladoga

F E D E R A T I O N

Turku   HELSINKI

Vologda

Kazan'

Uppsala

Saint Petersburg

Yaroslavl'

STOCKHOLM   TALLINN

Ul'yanovsk

ESTONIA

Nizhniy Novgorod

Samara   Orenburg

LATVIA

MOSCOW

Volga Uplands

Ural

3

RĪGA

Volga

LITHUANIA

Syr Darya

KALININGRAD (part of Russ.Fed)

Central Russian Upland

Aral Sea

Kaunas   Vitsyebsk

iningrad   VILNIUS

ańsk

MINSK

Amu Darya

ydgoszcz

Babruysk

Homyel'

WARSAW

BELORUSSIA

Voronezh

Brest

Pripet Marshes

Ural

ódź

Dnieper Lowlands

Don

OLAND

KIEV   Kharkiv

Volgograd

Kraków   L'viv

Dnieper

Astrakhan'

OVAKIA

Dniester

UKRAINE

Dnipropetrovs'k

Chernivtsi

Donets'k

Rostov-na-Donu

Caspian Sea

UDAPEST

MOLDAVIA

UNGARY   Cluj-Napoca

CHIŞINĂU

Stavropol'

130

4

Odesa

Sea of Azov

ROMANIA

Braşov

Crimea

Caucasus

Tisza

BELGRADE

Simferopol'

El'brus 5642m

YUGO-SLAVIA

Constanţa

Danube

Black Sea

BULGARIA   Varna

Balkan Mountains

SOFIA   Burgas

SKOPJE

MACED.

TIRANA

LBANIA

Aegean Sea

Anatolia

GREECE

0 km   500

ATHENS

Piraeus

0 miles   500

5

Peloponnese

Zāgros Mountains

Irákleio

134

Sea

Cyprus

Tigris   Euphrates

Crete

ELEVATION

4 000 m
13 124 ft

2 000 m
6 562 ft

1 000 m
3 281 ft

500 m
1 640 ft

250 m
820 ft

100 m
328 ft

Sea Level   Sea Level

-250 m
-820 ft

-500 m
-1 640 ft

-1 000 m
-3 281 ft

-2 000 m
-6 562 ft

-3 000 m
-9 843 ft

-4 000 m
-13 124 ft

THE NORTH ATLANTIC

NORTHWEST TERRITORIES

Devon Island

Ellesmere Island

Gulf of Boothia

Nares Strait

Qaanaaq

Knud Rasmussen Land

Innaanganeq

Savissivik

Qimusseriarsuaq

Hudson Bay

Southampton Island

Foxe Basin

CANADA

Baffin Island

Baffin Bay

Kullorsuaq

Upernavik

Limit of summer pack ice

Péninsule d'Ungava

Hudson Strait

Cumberland Sound

Uummannaq

Qeqertarsuaq

Qeqertarsuaq

QUÉBEC

Arnaud

Frobisher Bay

Davis Strait

Qeqertarsuup Tunua

Qasigiannguit

Sisimiut

Kong Frederik IX Land

GREENLAND

(Danish external territory)

Ungava Bay

Maniitsoq

George

NUUK

Kong Christian IX Land

Gunnbjørn Fje

Mont Forel 3360m

3700

Aputiteeq

Paamiut

Ammassalik

Ivittuut

Kong Frederik VI Kyst

Denmark

Labrador Sea

Qaqortoq

Nanortalik

Limit of winter pack ice

Reykjanes Basin

Uummannarsuaq

NEWFOUNDLAND & LABRADOR

Arctic Circle

ATLANTIC OCEAN

0 km   400

0 miles   400

ARCTIC
OCEAN

Lincoln Sea

Kap Morris Jesup

Wandel Sea

Independence Fjord

Nord

SVALBARD
(Norwegian dependency)

Zemlya Frantsa-Iosifa

Kvitøya

Nordaustlandet

Kong Karls Land

Novaya Zemlya

Spitsbergen

Barentsøya

Edgeøya

LONGYEARBYEN

Barentsberg

Storfjorden

Barents Sea

Greenland Sea

Limit of winter pack ice

Kong Frederik VIII Land

Kong Christian X Land

Limit of summer pack ice

Daneborg

△ *Petermann Bjerg*
2940m

Bjørnøya
(part of Norway)

Nordkapp
(North Cape)

FINLAND

Kong Oscar Fjord

Mohns Ridge

Ittoqqortoormiit

Kangertittivaq

Kangikajik

JAN MAYEN
(Norwegian dependency)

Arctic Circle

1000 000

Norwegian

Sea

Vestfjorden

S

W

E

D

E

N

*Gulf
of
Bothnia*

ICELAND

Bolungarvík

Siglufjördhur

Raufarhöfn

safjördhur

Húsavík

Akureyri

Stykkishólmur

Seydhisfjördhur

REYKJAVÍK

Neskaupstadhur

Vatnajökull

Selfoss

Djúpivogur

Norwegian Basin

Thorlákshöfn

△ *Hvannadalshnúkur*
2119m

Surtsey

Vestmannaeyjar

FAEROE ISLANDS
(Danish external territory)

N

TÓRSHAVN

*Shetland
Islands*
(part of UK)

NORWAY

kaflói

ELEVATION

4 000 m	13 124 ft
2 000 m	6 562 ft
1 000 m	3 281 ft
500 m	1 640 ft
250 m	820 ft
100 m	328 ft
Sea Level	Sea Level
-250 m	-820 ft
-500 m	-1 640 ft
-1 000 m	-3 281 ft
-2 000 m	-6 562 ft
-3 000 m	-9 843 ft
-4 000 m	-13 124 ft

SCANDINAVIA & FINLAND

RUSSIAN FEDERATION

FINLAND

SWEDEN

A R C T I C   O C E A N

Barents Sea

Norwegian Sea

Lapland

Gulf of Bothnia

POPULATION

Less than
50,000

○

50,000 –
100,000

○

100,000 –
500,000

◉

Over
500,000

◉

200

200

0 km

0 miles

Nordkapp
(North Cape)

Mageroya

Soroya

Ringvassoy

Kvaloya

Tromsø

Senja

Andoya

Vesterålen

Lofoten

Hitra

Froya

Vega

Varangerhalvoya

Varangerfjorden

Kirkenes

Tana

Tana

Vadso

Karasjok

Karigasniemi

Inarijärvi

Kaamanen

Ivalo

Saariselkä

Laksely

Lakselv

Alta

Talvik

Finnmarksvidda

Kautokeino

Kaaresuvanto

Torneträsk

Kiruna

Kebnekaise
2117m

Muonioälv

Muonio

Kolari

Sattanen

Sodankylä

Kittilä

Ounasjoki

Rovaniemi

Kemijärvi

Kuusamo

Pudasjärvi

Kuhmo

Sotkamo

Kajaani

Nurmes

Pielinen

Iisalmi

Oulujärvi

Oulujoki

Oulu

Kempele

Haukipudas

Kemi

Tornio

Kalixälven

Kalix

Haparanda

Luleå

Piteå

Skelleftea

Umeå

Jakobstad

Kokkola
(Karleby)

Raahe

Hailuoto

Suomussalmi

Pyhäjoki

Kiiminki

Tornionjoki

Kemijoki

Boden

Luleälven

Jokkmokk

Luleälven

Gällivare

Malmberget

Skalka

Arvidsjaur

Storuman

Storuman

Skellefteälven

Umeälven

Lycksele

Vilhelmina

Dorotea

Hoting

Strömsund

Ångermanälven

Borgafjäll

Borgefjell

Mosjøen

Mo i Rana

Fauske

Bodø

Narvik

Hamaroy

Harstad

Vestfjorden

Saltfjellet

Svartisen

Kvarnbergsvattnet

Strömsund

Levanger

Verdalsøra

Steinkjer

Namsos

Fosdalen

Trondheimsfjorden

(North)

100,000

171

171

126

99

70°

35°

30°

25°

20°

15°

10°

5°

0°

70°

65°

Arctic Circle

Arctic Circle

35°

65°

N

RUSS. FED.

BELORUSSIA

LATVIA

ESTONIA

LITHUANIA

KALININGRAD
(part of Russian
Federation)

POLAND

GERMANY

NORWAY

DENMARK

(claimed by Estonia)

(claimed by Estonia)

Lake Peipus

Gulf of Finland

Gulf of Riga

Baltic Sea

Courland Lagoon

Gulf of
Danzig

Hiiumaa

Saaremaa

Gotland

Öland

Bornholm

Western Dvina

Neman

Wisła

Oder

Elbe

Weser

Ems

North Sea

Skagerrak

Kattegat

Ålands hav

Åland

HELSINKI
Espoo
Vantaa
Porvoo
Kotka
Kouvola
Lahti
Lappeenranta
Tampere
Nokia
Hämeenlinna
Riihimäki
Hyvinkää
Salo
Turku (Åbo)
Hanko (Hangö)
Pori
Rauma
Kankaanpää
Närpes (Närpiö)
Kaskö
Seinäjoki
Lapua
Äänekoski
Jyväskylä
Keuruu
Joutseno
Imatra
Savonlinna
arkaus
Kaltávesi

Ladozhskoye Ozero

STOCKHOLM
Uppsala
Täby
Sollentuna
Södertälje
Norrtälje
Enköping
Nyköping
Norrköping
Linköping
Västerås
Sala
Avesta
Falun
Örebro
Karlstad
Filipstad
Ludvika
Borlänge
Mora
Malung
Leksand
Rättvik
Bollnäs
Söderhamn
Gävle
Sandviken
Tierp
Hudiksvall
Sundsvall
Härnösand
Timrå
Kramfors
Ånge
Sveg
Idre
Östersund
Storsjön
Ratan
Svenstavik

Jönköping
Borås
Mölndal
Kungsbacka
Varberg
Halmstad
Laholm
Ljungby
Växjö
Kalmar
Borgholm
Oskarshamn
Visby
Karlskrona
Kristianstad
Helsingborg
Lund
Malmö
Ronne
Göteborg (Gothenburg)
Trollhättan
Uddevalla
Lidköping
Mariestad
Säffle
Åmål
Grums
Mellerud
Strömstad

OSLO
Lillestrøm
Ski
Moss
Sandvika
Drammen
Sarpsborg
Fredrikstad
Halden
Hamar
Mjøsa
Lillehammer
Gjøvik
Gol
Geilo
Eidfjord
Kongsberg
Horten
Porsgrunn
Skien
Arendal
Kristiansand
Mandal
Liknes
Moi
Evje
Stavanger
Sandnes
Haugesund
Leirvik
Bergen
Ålesund
Åndalsnes
Molde
Dombås
Ringebu
Røros

KØBENHAVN (Copenhagen)
Ålborg
Århus
Randers
Hjørring
Hobro
Viborg
Holstebro
Herning
Esbjerg
Varde
Kolding
Odense
Slagelse
Nykøbing
Vejle
Silkeborg
Svendborg

Sjælland
Fyn
Lolland
Falster
Møn

Jylland

Ringkøbing Fjord

Storebælt

Hanöbukten

ELEVATION

Sea Level

4 000 m / 13 124 ft
2 000 m / 6 562 ft
1 000 m / 3 281 ft
500 m / 1 640 ft
250 m / 820 ft
100 m / 328 ft
Sea Level
−50 m / −164 ft
−100 m / −328 ft
−250 m / −820 ft
−500 m / −1 640 ft
−1 000 m / −3 281 ft
−2 000 m / −6 562 ft

101

THE LOW COUNTRIES

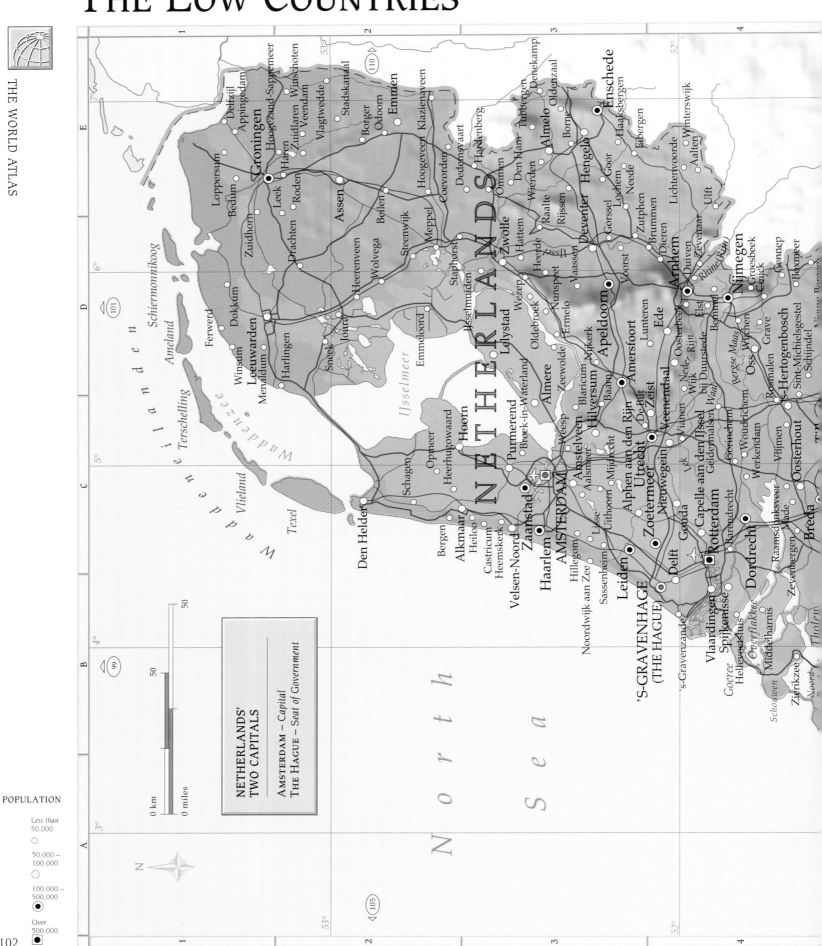

NETHERLANDS'
TWO CAPITALS

AMSTERDAM – *Capital*
THE HAGUE – *Seat of Government*

50

50

50

0 km

0 miles

POPULATION

Less than
50,000
○

50,000 –
100,000
○

100,000 –
500,000
◉

Over
500,000
●

102

Map labels

North Sea

Waddenzee

IJsselmeer

Wadden eilanden

Schiermonnikoog

Ameland

Terschelling

Vlieland

Texel

NETHERLANDS

Delfzijl
Appingedam
Hoogezand-Sappemeer
Winschoten
Vlagtwedde
Stadskanaal
Groningen
Haren
Leek
Roden
Zuidlaren
Veendam
Hoogeveen
Klazienaveen
Emmen
Odoorn
Borger
Coevorden
Dedemsvaart
Hardenberg
Denekamp
Oldenzaal
Enschede
Haaksbergen
Winterswijk
Aalten
Ulft
Lichtenvoorde
Eibergen
Neede
Borne
Almelo
Den Ham
Tubbergen
Wierden
Rijssen
Raalte
Goor
Lochem
Gorssel
Hengelo
Deventer
Zutphen
Brummen
Dieren
Zevenaar
Duiven
Arnhem
Rhine (Rijn)
Nijmegen
Groesbeek
Gennep
Cuijk
Boxmeer
's-Hertogenbosch
Sint-Michielsgestel
Schijndel
Oss
Grave
Wijchen
Rosmalen
Bergse Maas
Waal
Woudrichem
Gorinchem
Werkendam
Vlijmen
Oosterhout
Breda
Zevenbergen
Made
Raamsdonksveer
Dordrecht
Barendrecht
Capelle aan den IJssel
Rotterdam
Spijkenisse
Vlaardingen
'S-GRAVENHAGE (THE HAGUE)
's-Gravenzande
Goeree
Hellevoetsluis
Middelharnis
Overflakkee
Zierikzee
Schouwen
Tholen
Noord
Leiden
Delft
Gouda
Alphen aan den Rijn
Zoetermeer
Nieuwegein
Utrecht
Vianen
Wijk bij Duurstede
Geldermalsen
Culemborg
Bennekom
Elst
Oosterbeek
Bemmel
Lunteren
Ede
Veenendaal
De Bilt
Zeist
Amersfoort
Baarn
Hilversum
Blaricum
Nijkerk
Weesp
Mijdrecht
Uithoorn
Aalsmeer
Amstelveen
AMSTERDAM
Zaanstad
Haarlem
Velsen-Noord
Heemskerk
Castricum
Heiloo
Alkmaar
Bergen
Den Helder
Schagen
Opmeer
Heerhugowaard
Hoorn
Purmerend
Broek-in-Waterland
Almere
Zeewolde
Lelystad
Nunspeet
Ermelo
Harderwijk
Nijkerk
Voorst
Apeldoorn
Vaassen
Epe
Heerde
Hattem
Wezep
Oldebroek
Elburg
Zwolle
Meppel
Staphorst
IJsselmuiden
Steenwijk
Wolvega
Heerenveen
Joure
Sneek
Emmeloord
Bolsward
Harlingen
Leeuwarden
Menaldum
Dokkum
Ferwerd
Winsum
Bedum
Loppersum
Zuidhorn
Drachten
Bellen
Assen
Noordwijk aan Zee
Sassenheim
Hillegom
Lisse
Noordwijk
Nieuw
Wageningen

Rhine (Rijn)
Neder-Rijn
IJssel
Lek

110
101
99
105

N

GERMANY

FRANCE

BELGIUM

LUXEMBOURG

Rhine (Rhein)

Mosel

Horst
Venlo
Deurne
Reuver
Beesel
Roermond
Posterholt
Eindhoven
Someren
Tegelen
Weert
Nederweert
Echt
Susteren
Sittard
Geleen
Heerlen
Kerkrade
Simpelveld
Maastricht
Eijsden
Vaals
Valkenswaard
Veldhoven
Eersel
Bergeyk
Baarle-Hertog
Neerpelt
Kinrooi
Bree
Maaseik
Meerssen
Visé
Herstal
Riemst
Our
Eupen
Verviers
Hautes Fagnes
Malmédy
Weiswampach
Hosingen
Diekirch
Ettelbrück
Grevenmacher
LUXEMBOURG
Moselle
Alzette
Pétange
Differdange
Dudelange
Esch-sur-Alzette
Aubange
Virton
Arlon
Etalle
Neufchâteau
Bastogne
Recogne
Rochefort
Marche-en-Famenne
Ourthe
Ciney
Dinant
Andenne
Huy
Amay
Seraing
Liège
Waremme
Tongeren
Landen
Hasselt
Genk
Bilzen
Diepenbeek
Beringen
Zonhoven
Herk-de-Stad
Tienen
Leuven
Louvain-la-Neuve
Wavre
Gembloux
Éghezée
Namur
Meuse
Semois Ardenne
Couvin
Walcourt
Thuin
Anderlues
Binche
Erquelinnes
Jeumont
Jemappes
Mons
Leuze-en-Hainaut
Ath
Dender
Enghien
Braine-le-Comte
La Louvière
Châtelet
Gerpinnes
Charleroi
Chimay
Fagne
Oise
Somme
Sambre
Tournai
Pecq
Péruwelz
Mouscron
Kortrijk
Zwevegem
Izegem
Harelbeke
Deinze
Gent (Ghent)
Eeklo
Beernem
Aalter
Brugge (Bruges)
Zeebrugge
Blankenberge
Knokke-Heist
Oostende (Ostend)
Middelkerke
Koksijde
Veurne
Ieper
Poperinge
Roeselare
Torhout
Diksmuide
Flanders
Vlaanderen
Westerschelde
Zuid-Beveland
Vlissingen
Terneuzen
Axel
Hulst
Sint-Niklaas
Beveren
Temse
Mechelen
Schelde
Rupel
Antwerpen (Antwerp)
Wijnegem
Schoten
Brecht
Essen
Kalmthout
Turnhout
Mol
Geel
Herentals
Lier
Duffel
BRUSSEL/BRUXELLES (BRUSSELS)
Schaerbeek
Vilvoorde
Halle
Aalst
Zele
Dendermonde
Lokeren
Melle
Gavere
Oudenaarde

ELEVATION

4 000 m / 13 124 ft
2 000 m / 6 562 ft
1 000 m / 3 281 ft
500 m / 1 640 ft
250 m / 820 ft
100 m / 328 ft
Sea Level
Sea Level
-10 m / -33 ft
-25 m / -82 ft
-50 m / -164 ft
-100 m / -328 ft
-250 m / -820 ft
-500 m / -1 640 ft

Botrange 694 m

Lorraine

THE BRITISH ISLES

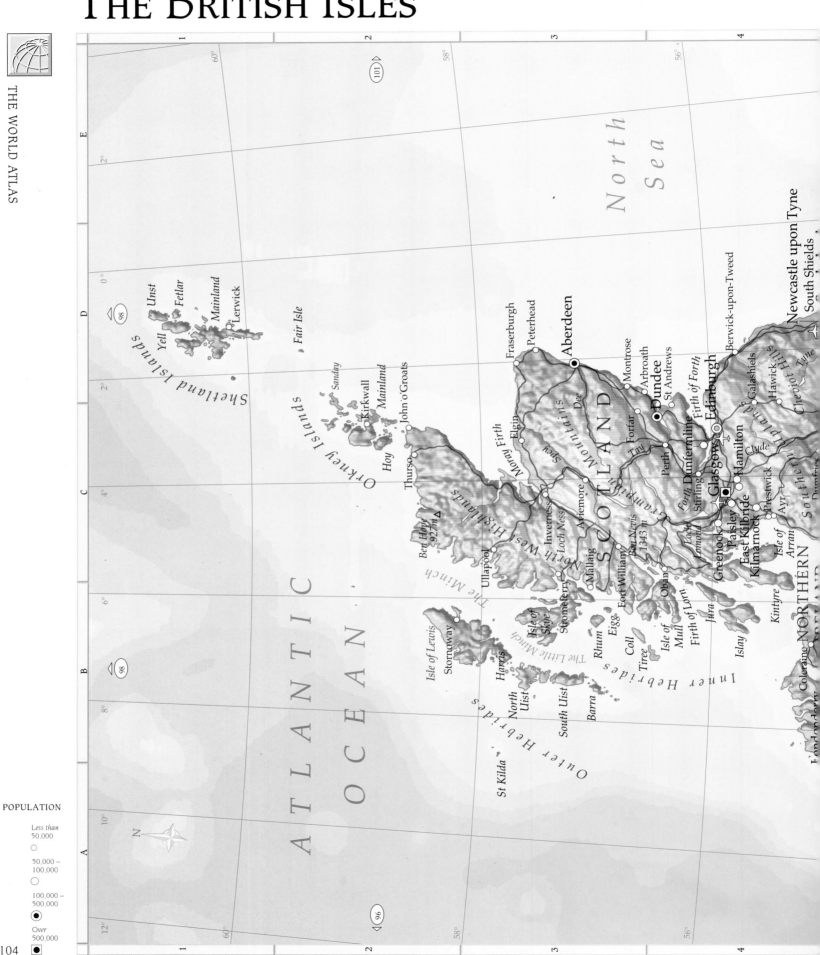

North Sea

ATLANTIC OCEAN

Shetland Islands

Unst
Yell
Fetlar
Mainland
Lerwick

Fair Isle

Orkney Islands

Sanday
Kirkwall
Mainland
Hoy
John o'Groats

Thurso

Ben Hope
927 m △

Ullapool

The Minch

Isle of Lewis
Stornoway

Harris

North Uist

South Uist

Barra

St Kilda

Outer Hebrides

The Little Minch

Isle of Skye
Stromeferry
Mallaig
Eigg
Rhum
Coll
Tiree
Isle of Mull
Firth of Lorn

Moray Firth
Elgin
Spey

Fraserburgh
Peterhead

Aberdeen

Dee

Grampian Mountains

Aviemore
Inverness
Loch Ness

North West Highlands

Fort William
Ben Nevis
1343 m

Oban

Jura
Islay

Isle of Arran
Kintyre

Inner Hebrides

SCOTLAND

Montrose
Arbroath
Dundee
St Andrews
Firth of Tay
Tay
Forfar
Perth

Firth of Forth
Dunfermline
Stirling
Loch Lomond
Forth

Glasgow
Greenock
Paisley
East Kilbride
Kilmarnock
Hamilton
Clyde

Prestwick
Ayr

Southern Uplands

Edinburgh

Berwick-upon-Tweed
Galashiels
Hawick
Cheviot Hills

Newcastle upon Tyne
South Shields

Tyne

NORTHERN

Coleraine
Londonderry

POPULATION

Less than
50,000

50,000 –
100,000

100,000 –
500,000

Over
500,000

FRANCE

UNITED KINGDOM

ENGLAND

WALES

ISLE OF MAN
(UK crown dependency)

REPUBLIC OF IRELAND

Channel Islands
GUERNSEY (UK crown dependency)
JERSEY (UK crown dependency)

English Channel

Irish Sea

Celtic Sea

St George's Channel

Cardigan Bay

Bristol Channel

Seine

ELEVATION

4 000 m / 13 124 ft	
2 000 m / 6 562 ft	
1 000 m / 3 281 ft	
500 m / 1 640 ft	
250 m / 820 ft	
100 m / 328 ft	
Sea Level	Sea Level
-50 m / -164 ft	
-100 m / -328 ft	
-250 m / -820 ft	
-500 m / -1640 ft	
-1 000 m / -3 281 ft	
-2 000 m / -6 562 ft	

Hartlepool, Middlesbrough, Whitby, Northallerton, Scarborough, Bridlington, Beverley, Kingston upon Hull, Grimsby, Skegness, Louth, Lincoln, The Wash, King's Lynn, Great Yarmouth, Lowestoft, Norwich, Felixstowe, Harwich, Ipswich, Colchester, Newmarket, Peterborough, Cambridge, Bedford, Milton Keynes, Stevenage, Harlow, Southend-on-Sea, Margate, Canterbury, Dover, Channel Tunnel, Maidstone, Folkestone, Hastings, Eastbourne, Brighton, Hove, Crawley, Guildford, Croydon, London, Watford, Windsor, Reading, St Albans, Luton, Oxford, Swindon, Cheltenham, Gloucester, Worcester, Kidderminster, Birmingham, Coventry, Nuneaton, Leicester, Derby, Nottingham, Boston, Sheffield, Doncaster, Castleford, Leeds, Bradford, Huddersfield, York, Harrogate, Manchester, Bolton, Preston, Blackpool, Liverpool, Birkenhead, Chester, Stoke-on-Trent, Crewe, Shrewsbury, Stafford, Wolverhampton, Cambrian Mountains, Snowdonia, Bangor, Holyhead, Anglesey, Barmouth, Tywyn, Aberystwyth, Fishguard, Haverfordwest, Milford Haven, Carmarthen, Llanelli, Swansea, Port Talbot, Cardiff, Newport, Brecon Beacons, Wye, Weston-super-Mare, Bristol, Bath, Salisbury, Andover, Basingstoke, Winchester, Southampton, Eastleigh, Havant, Portsmouth, Isle of Wight, Newport, Bournemouth, Poole, Dorchester, Weymouth, Bridport, Lyme Bay, Exeter, Exmoor, Tiverton, Taunton, Yeovil, Dartmoor, Torquay, Plymouth, Saltash, Tamar, Bideford, Barnstaple, Ilfracombe, Bodmin, Newquay, St Austell, Truro, Falmouth, Penzance, Land's End, Isles of Scilly

Workington, Whitehaven, Barrow-in-Furness, Lancaster, Kendal, Lake District, Darlington, Durham, Newcastle, Carlisle

Douglas, Isle of Man

Belfast, Bangor, Newtownabbey, Downpatrick, Newry, Armagh, Portadown, Lurgan, Omagh, Enniskillen, Lough Neagh, Upper Lough Erne, Lower Lough Erne, Donegal, Donegal Bay, Sligo, Castlebar, Lough Conn, Galway, Galway Bay, Connaught, Longford, Athlone, Shannon, Lough Derg, Ennis, Limerick, Tralee, Dingle Bay, Killarney, Bantry Bay, Cork, Munster, Clonmel, Waterford, Wexford, Kilkenny, Carlow, Port Laoise, Newbridge, Leinster, Wicklow Mts, Lucan, DUBLIN, Dún Laoghaire, Drogheda, Dundalk, Barrow, Blackwater, Liffey

Republic of Ireland, Ireland

LONDON

N

M25, M1, Watford, Edgware, Wembley, Heathrow, M40, M4, M3, A3, Kingston upon Thames, Epsom, Wimbledon, Richmond, Buckingham Palace, Wandsworth, Croydon, A23, M23, Bromley, Orpington, M25, M26, M20, Bexley, Dartford, Greenwich, City, St Paul's Cathedral, Houses of Parliament, Trafalgar Square, Hampstead, Finchley, Barnet, Enfield, Walthamstow, Dagenham, A12, M11, A10, A41, A21, Thames

□ Places of interest
□ Regions/suburbs

0 km 10
0 miles 10

FRANCE, ANDORRA & MONACO

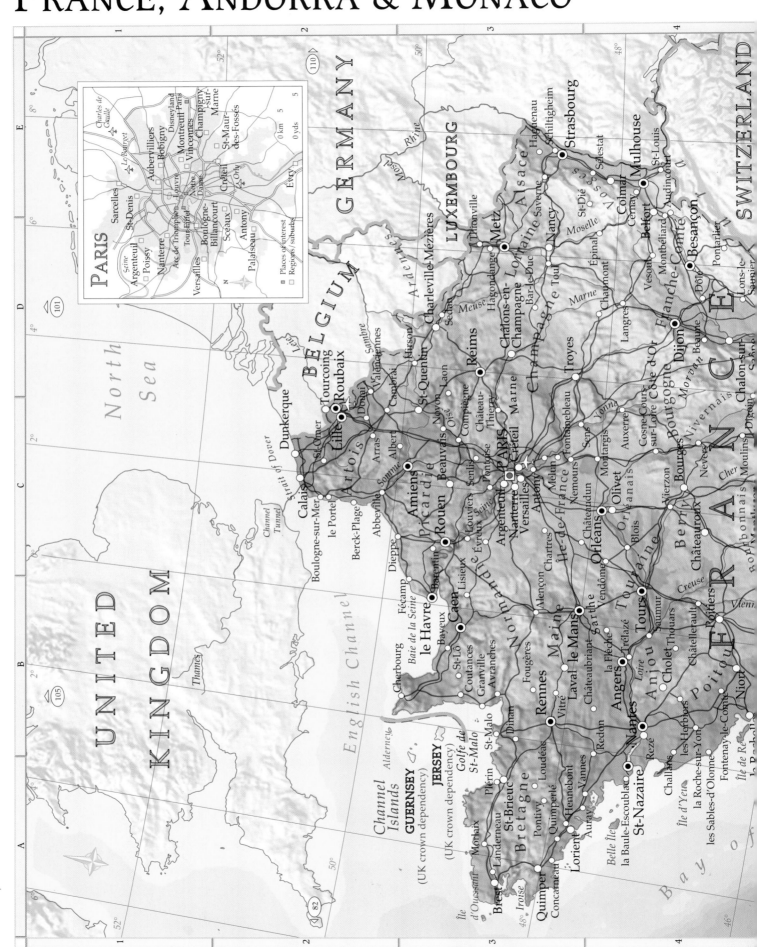

POPULATION

Less than
50,000

50,000 –
100,000

100,000 –
500,000

Over
500,000

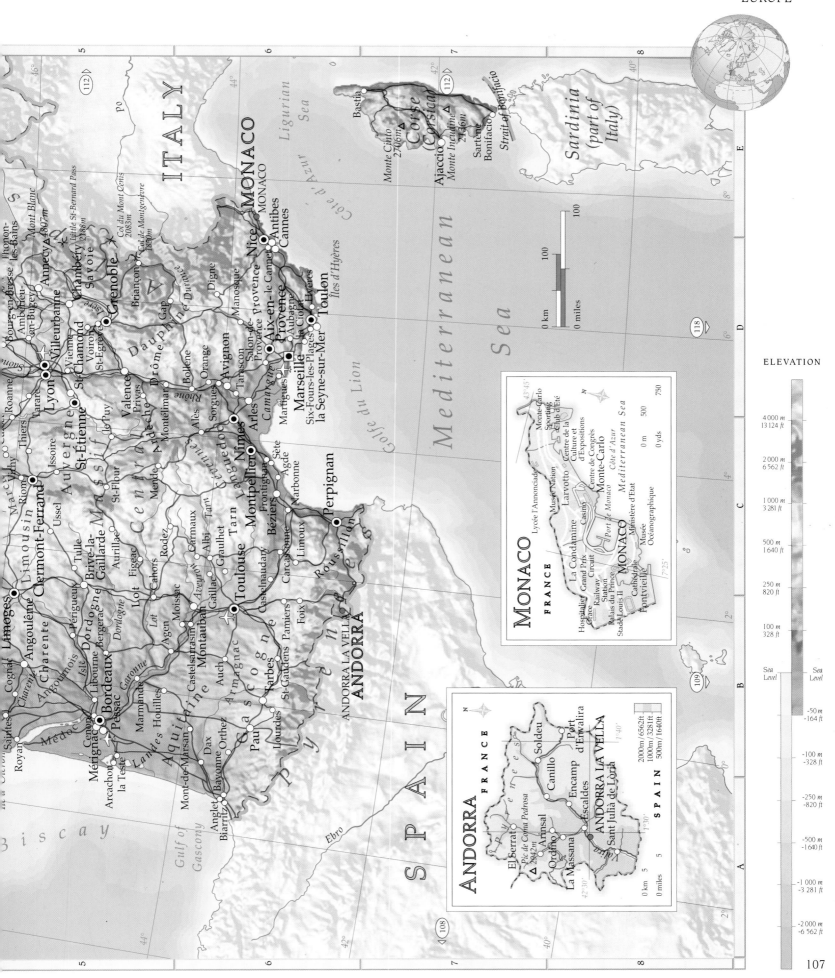

ELEVATION

4 000 m	13 124 ft
2 000 m	6 562 ft
1 000 m	3 281 ft
500 m	1 640 ft
250 m	820 ft
100 m	328 ft
Sea Level	Sea Level
-50 m	-164 ft
-100 m	-328 ft
-250 m	-820 ft
-500 m	-1 640 ft
-1 000 m	-3 281 ft
-2 000 m	-6 562 ft

SPAIN & PORTUGAL

ATLANTIC OCEAN

Bay of Biscay
Costa Verde

Spain cities & towns:
Ferrol, A Coruña, Betanzos, Laracha, Luarca, Avilés, Gijón, Villaviciosa, Santander, Pravia, Tineo, Oviedo, Mieres, Torrelavega, Llanes, Cantabria, Santa Comba, Galicia, Lugo, Pola de Lena, Cabañaquinta, Reinosa, Cabo Fisterra, Outes, Santiago, Chantada, Ponferrada, León, Muros, Lalin, Carballiño, Monforte, Astorga, Ribeira, Pontevedra, Castilla-León, Burgos, Marín, Ourense, Benavente, Palencia, Vigo, Ponteareas, Xinzo de Limia, Lerma, Aranda de Duero

Viana do Castelo, Ponte da Barca, Bragança, Embalse de Ricobayo, Valladolid, Braga, Guimarães, Chaves, Zamora, Toro, Duero, Medina del Campo, Póvoa de Varzim, Vila do Conde, Vila Real, Segovia, Matosinhos, Porto (Oporto), Lamego, Embalse de Almendra, Salamanca, Vila Nova de Gaia, Douro, Ovar, São João da Madeira, S P... Ávila, Albergaria-a-Velha, Aveiro, Viseu, Sistema Central, Ílhavo, Ciudad-Rodrigo, MADRID, Getafe, Alto da Torre 1993m, Guarda, Béjar, Sierra de Gredos, Coimbra, Covilhã, Plasencia, Talavera de la Reina, Aranjuez, Figueira da Foz, Serra da Estrela, Coria, Toledo, Ocañ, Leiria, PORTUGAL, Castelo Branco, Tagus, Embalse de Alcántara, Cáceres, Embalse de Valdecañas, Tomar, Entroncamento, Trujillo, Daimie, Abrantes, Portalegre, Extremadura, Herrera del Duque, Santarém, Coruche, Estremoz, Elvas, Mérida, Villanueva de la Serena, Ciudad Real, Torres Vedras, Sintra, Estremoz, Serra d'Ossa, Badajoz, Don Benito, Castuera, Puertollano, Cascais, LISBOA (LISBON), Évora, Castuera, Almada, Barreiro, Guadiana, Almendralejo, Villafranca de los Barros, Setúbal, Zafra, Pozoblanco, Alcácer do Sal, Azuaga, La Carolina, Baía de Setúbal, Jérez de los Caballeros, Bailén, Sines, Beja, Sierra Morena, Montoro, Córdoba, Bujalance, Linares, Jaén, Cortegana, Guadalquivir, Palma del Río, Martos, Alcaudete, Ourique, Nerva, Carmona, Ecija, Andalucía, Algarve, Valverde del Camino, La Algaba, Sevilla (Seville), Osuna, Sistema, Portimão, Ayamonte, Lepe, Dos Hermanas, Granada, Lagos, Faro, Tavira, Isla Cristina, Huelva, Antequera, Archidona, Olhão, Las Cabezas de San Juan, Olvera, Álora, Sierra, Cabo de São Vicente, Golfo de Cádiz, Lebrija, Motr, Sanlúcar de Barrameda, Ubrique, Ronda, El Puerto de Santa María, Jérez de la Frontera, Coín, Málaga, Cádiz, Fuengirola, San Fernando, Vejer de la Frontera, Estepona, Marbella, Costa del Sol, Barbate de Franco, Costa de la Luz, Algeciras, GIBRALTAR (UK dependent territory), Strait of Gibraltar, Ceuta (part of Spain), MOROCCO

AZORES (part of Portugal)
Corvo, Flores, São Jorge, Graciosa, Faial, Pico, Terceira, São Miguel, Ponta Delgada, Santa Maria

0 km 84
0 miles 84

200m/656ft
Sea level

FRANCE

Golfe du Lion

redo
Bermeo
Zarautz
Donostia-San Sebastián
Irún
Eibar
Tolosa
ilbao
Bergara
País Vasco
Pamplona
Vitoria-Gasteiz
Miranda
de Ebro
Estella
Navarra
Jaca
Monte Perdido
3348m
La See d'Urgel
ANDORRA
Logroño
Ripoll
Figueres
Banyoles
Arnedo
Calahorra
Berga
Manlleu
Girona
La Rioja
Ejea de
los Caballeros
Huesca
Barbastro
Cataluña
Vic
Palafrugell
Tudela
Monzón
Palamós
Sistema Ibérico
Tarazona
Soria
Balaguer
Cervera
Blanes
Sabadell
Arenys de Mar
El Burgo
de Osma
Zaragoza
Lleida
(Lérida)
Tàrrega
Terrassa
Mataró
Costa Brava
Fraga
Barcelona
Calatayud
Aragón
Vilafranca del Penedès
L'Hospitalet de Llobregat
Sierra de
Guadarrama
Daroca
Valls
Sitges
Medinaceli
Alcañiz
Reus
El Vendrell
Tortosa
Tarragona
Guadalajara
Amposta
Alcalá de Henares
Sant Carles de la Ràpita
rrejón de Ardoz
Teruel
Vinaròs
Tagus
Javalambre
2020m
Menorca
(Minorca)
Ciutadella de Menorca
Cuenca
País Valenciano
Onda
Castelló de la Plana
Mahón
Tarancón
Burriana
Pollença
Sa Pobla
Castilla-La Mancha
Vall d' Uxó
Sagunto
Palma
Manacor
Mota del Cuervo
Burjassot
Valencia
Lluemajor
Felanitx
Campo de Criptana
Torrente
Catarroja
Mallorca
(Majorca)
Socuéllamos
Júcar
Sueca
Cabrera
La Roda
Algemesí
Cullera
Tomelloso
Xàtiva
Gandía
Islas Baleares
Manzanares
Oliva
Eivissa
(Ibiza)
(Balearic Islands)
La Solana
Almansa
Onthyent
Alcoy
Denia
Eivissa
depeñas
Villanueva de los Infantes
Villena
Benidorm
Formentera
Hellín
Jumilla
Elda
Villajoyosa
Beas de Segura
Segura
Monóvar
San Juan de Alicante
Moratalla
Elche
Alicante
Villacarrillo
Cieza
Callosa de Segura
beda
Mula
Orihuela
Cazorla
Murcia
Murcia
Mediterranean Sea
Huéscar
Totana
La Unión
Baza
Lorca
Cartagena
Aguilas
Guadix
Mulhacén
3481m
Mojácar
Nevada
Berja
Almería
Adra

ALGERIA

0 km   100
0 miles   100

ELEVATION

4 000 m
13 124 ft

2 000 m
6 562 ft

1 000 m
3 281 ft

500 m
1 640 ft

250 m
820 ft

100 m
328 ft

Sea
Level

Sea
Level

-250 m
-820 ft

-500 m
-1 640 ft

-1 000 m
-3 281 ft

-2 000 m
-6 562 ft

-3 000 m
-9 843 ft

-4 000 m
-13 124 ft

GERMANY & THE ALPINE STATES

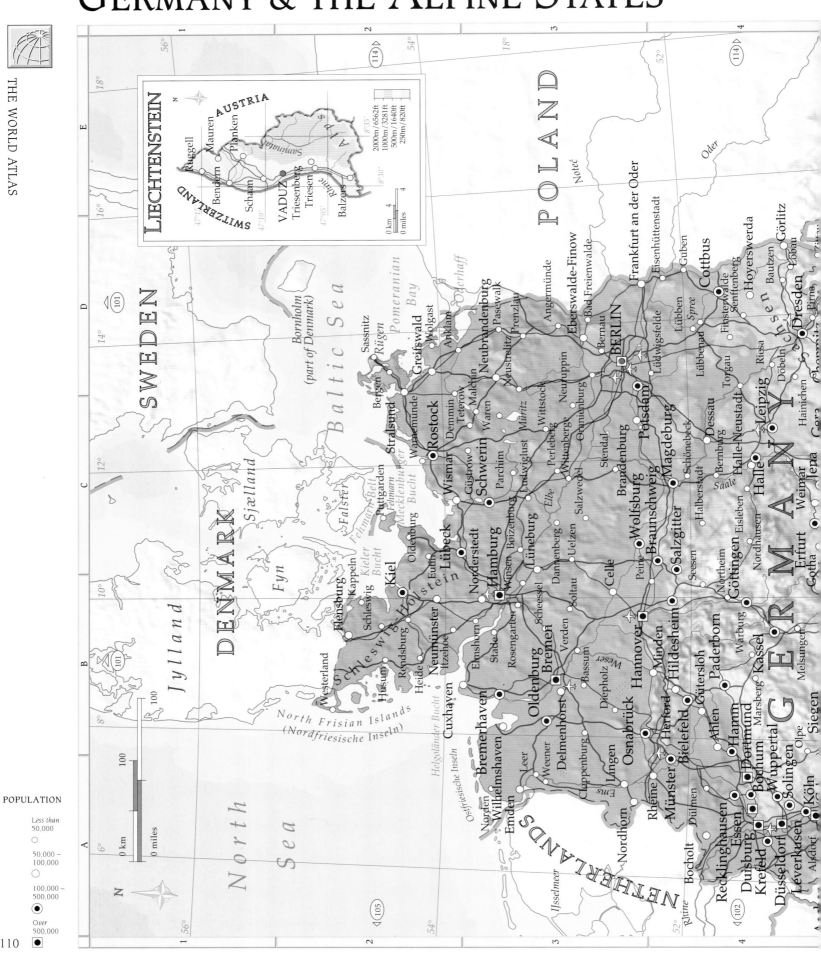

LIECHTENSTEIN

AUSTRIA

SWITZERLAND

Ruggell · Mauren · Planken
Bendern · Schaan · Triesenberg
VADUZ · Triesen
Triesenberg
Balzers

Alps

Samtnaat

Rhine

2000m/6562ft
1000m/3281ft
500m/1640ft
250m/820ft

POLAND

SWEDEN

DENMARK

Baltic Sea

Jylland

Sjælland

Fyn

Falster

Bornholm
(part of Denmark)

North Frisian Islands
(Nordfriesische Inseln)

North Sea

NETHERLANDS

GERMANY

Oder

Noteć

Rügen

Pomeranian Bay

Oderhaff

Greifswald · Wolgast
Sassnitz · Bergen · Anklam · Pasewalk
Stralsund · Prenzlau
Warnemünde · Demmin · Neubrandenburg
Rostock · Teterow · Neustrelitz · Angermünde
Wismar · Güstrow · Waren · Eberswalde-Finow
Schwerin · Parchim · Müritz · Neuruppin · Bernau · Bad Freienwalde
Ludwigslust · Wittstock · Oranienburg · BERLIN
Boizenburg · Perleberg · Potsdam
Frankfurt an der Oder
Eisenhüttenstadt
Guben · Cottbus
Finsterwalde · Senftenberg · Hoyerswerda
Lübben · Spree · Bautzen · Görlitz
Lübbenau · Löbau
Torgau · Riesa · Döbeln
Leipzig · Dresden · Pirna
Halle · Weimar · Gotha · Erfurt

Kiel · Lübeck · Hamburg
Flensburg · Schleswig · Eutin · Norderstedt · Winsen
Kappeln · Rendsburg · Heide · Itzehoe · Lüneburg
Husum · Neumünster · Stade · Danneberg · Uelzen
Westerland · Elmshorn · Rosengarten · Soltau · Celle
Cuxhaven · Bremen · Verden · Bassum · Peine
Bremerhaven · Oldenburg · Diepholz · Hannover · Minden · Hildesheim
Wilhelmshaven · Delmenhorst · Osnabrück · Herford · Bielefeld
Norden · Emden · Leer · Weener · Cloppenburg · Lingen · Rheine · Münster
Nordhorn · Hamm · Dortmund
Recklinghausen · Bochum · Essen
Duisburg · Krefeld · Wuppertal · Solingen
Düsseldorf · Leverkusen · Köln

Wolfsburg · Magdeburg · Brandenburg · Halle-Neustadt · Dessau
Braunschweig · Salzgitter · Schöningen · Schönebeck
Halberstadt · Bernburg · Eisleben · Nordhausen
Seesen · Northeim · Göttingen · Warburg · Kassel · Melsungen
Paderborn · Ahlen · Gütersloh · Marsberg
Bocholt · Olpe · Siegen · Alsdorf

POPULATION

Less than 50,000 ○

50,000 – 100,000 ○

100,000 – 500,000 ●

Over 500,000 ■

BELGIUM

CZECH REPUBLIC

SLOVAKIA

HUNGARY

CROATIA

AUSTRIA

SLOVENIA

ITALY

FRANCE

SWITZERLAND

LIECHTENSTEIN

LUX.

Bohemian Forest

Erzgebirge

Rhenisches Schiefergebirge

Eifel

Hessen

Bayern

Schwäbische Alb

Fränkische Alb

Pfälzerwald

Vosges

Jura

Tirol

Bavarian Alps

Kitzbühler Alpen

Hohe Tauern

Niedere Tauern

Gurktaler Alpen

Berner Alpen

Pennine Alps

Istra

Gulf of Venice

Po Valley

Cities and towns

Plauen, Hof, Suhl, Fulda, Gießen, Wetzlar, Coburg, Kronach, Lichtenfels, Münchberg, Marktredwitz, Bayreuth, Forchheim, Bamberg, Schweinfurt, Würzburg, Erlangen, Fürth, Nürnberg (Nuremberg), Neumarkt, Regensburg, Schwandorf, Deggendorf, Straubing, Ingolstadt, Landshut, Passau, Pocking, Ried im Innkreis

Neuwied, Koblenz, Boppard, Bad Homburg vor der Höhe, Frankfurt am Main, Offenbach, Darmstadt, Aschaffenburg, Heilbronn, Ludwigsburg, Stuttgart, Göppingen, Aalen, Weissenburg, Heidenheim an der Brenz, Donauwörth, Augsburg, München (Munich), Rosenheim

Mainz, Wiesbaden, Worms, Mannheim, Ludwigshafen, Heidelberg, Neustadt an der Weinstrasse, Karlsruhe, Pforzheim, Sindelfingen, Reutlingen, Tübingen, Ulm, Neu-Ulm, Memmingen, Mindelheim, Kaufbeuren, Kempten, Füssen

Saarbrücken, Neunkirchen, Kaiserslautern, Merzig, Trier, Bitburg, Wittlich, Birkenfeld, Blankenheim

Baden-Baden, Kehl, Offenburg, Lahr, Emmendingen, Freiburg im Breisgau, Bad Krozingen, Müllheim, Lörrach, Basel, Bad Säckingen, Waldshut

Schaffhausen, Singen, Konstanz, Friedrichshafen, Sankt Gallen, Winterthur, Zürich, Zug, Luzern, Schwyz, Chur, Klosters, St.Moritz, Bellinzona, Locarno, Lugano

Bern, Biel, Thun, Interlaken, Brig, Sion, Monthey, Genève (Geneva), Lausanne, Neuchâtel, La Chaux-de-Fonds

Linz, Wels, Vöcklabruck, Steyr, Salzburg, Bad Ischl, Ebensee, Liezen, Schwaz, Innsbruck, Hohenems, Villach, Lienz, Spittal

Sankt Pölten, Tulln, Hollabrunn, Mistelbach an der Zaya, WIEN (VIENNA), Traiskirchen, Perchtoldsdorf, Bad Vöslau, Eisenstadt, Wiener Neustadt, Mürzzuschlag, Leoben, Judenburg, Wolfsberg, Klagenfurt, Graz, Maribor

LJUBLJANA, Jesenice, Kranj, Tolmin, Celje, Velenje, Trbovlje, Krško, Novo Mesto, Kočevje, Postojna, Nova Gorica, Koper, Ptuj, Murska Sobota

Zwettl

Neusiedler See

Rivers / features

Elbe, Main, Neckar, Rhine (Rhein), Danube (Donau), Inn, Enns, Mur, Drava, Sava, Rhône, Po, Mosel

Lake Constance, Zürichsee, Thuner See, Lake Geneva (Lac de Neuchâtel), Lake Maggiore

Passes / peaks

Zugspitze 2962m, Grossglockner 3798m, Plöcken Pass 1357m, Loibl Pass 1367m, Brenner Pass 1374m, Simplon Pass 2005m, Matterhorn 4478m, Grand Saint Bernard Pass 2469m, 3970m, Col 2 962m

ELEVATION

4 000 m	13 124 ft
2 000 m	6 562 ft
1 000 m	3 281 ft
500 m	1 640 ft
250 m	820 ft
100 m	328 ft
Sea Level	Sea Level
-10 m	-33 ft
-25 m	-82 ft
-50 m	-164 ft
-100 m	-328 ft
-250 m	-820 ft
-500 m	-1 640 ft

ITALY

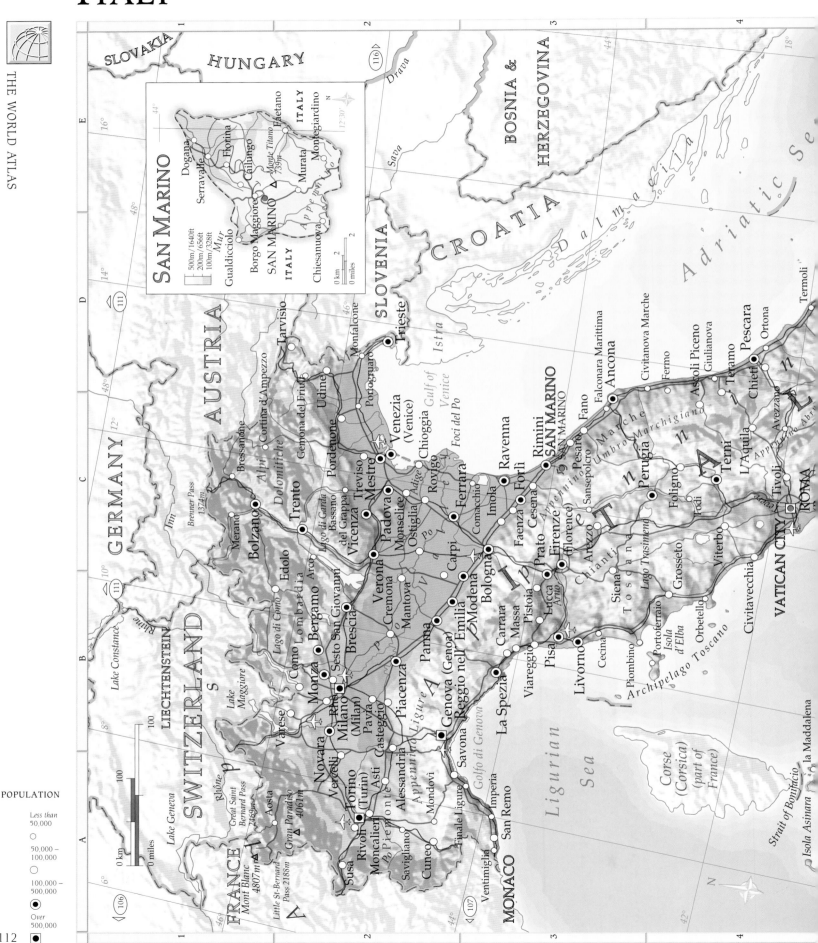

SLOVAKIA

HUNGARY

116

Drava

BOSNIA & HERZEGOVINA

Sava

CROATIA

D a l m a c i j a

Adriatic Sea

GERMANY

AUSTRIA

SLOVENIA

Tarvisio

Trieste

Istra

Termoli

111

Cortina d'Ampezzo

Montfalcone

Gulf of Venice

Pescara

Ortona

Gemona del Friuli

Portogruaro

Civitanova Marche

Teramo

Chieti

Bressanône

Udine

Venezia (Venice)

Chioggia

Foci del Po

Falconara Marittima

Fermo

Ascoli Piceno

Giulianova

L'Aquila

111

Alpi

Dolomitiche

Pordenone

Treviso

Mestre

Rovigo

Ravenna

Rimini

SAN MARINO

Fano

Ancona

Marche

Umbro Marchigiano

Avezzano

Appennino Abru

Merano

Trento

Lago di Garda

Bassano del Grappa

Vicenza

Padova

Monselice

Adige

Ferrara

Comacchio

Forlì

Cesena

Pesaro

Sansepolcro

Perugia

Foligno

Terni

Tivoli

ROMA

Bolzano

Arco

Po

Ostiglia

Po

Imola

Faenza

Prato

Arezzo

Lago Trasimeno

Todi

Edolo

Bergamo

Verona

Cremona

Mantova

Modena

Carpi

Bologna

Pistoia

Firenze (Florence)

Chianti

Siena

Viterbo

VATICAN CITY

Civitavecchia

Inn

Brenner Pass
1374m

Como

Brescia

P o

Parma

Reggio nell' Emilia

Lucca

Lucca

Arno

Toscana

Grosseto

Orbetello

Lago di Como

Monza

Sesto San Giovanni

Piacenza

Carrara

Massa

Pisa

Cecina

Archipelago Toscano

Lago Maggiore

Varese

Rho

Milano (Milan)

Pavia

Casteggio

Appennino Ligure

Genova (Genoa)

Savona

La Spezia

Viareggio

Livorno

Piombino

Isola d'Elba

Portoferraio

Novara

Vercelli

Alessandria

Asti

Golfo di Genova

Imperia

Ligurian Sea

Corse (Corsica) (part of France)

Torino (Turin)

Moncalieri

Savigliano

Po Piemonte

Appennino Piemonte

Mondovì

Finale Ligure

San Remo

Strait of Bonifacio

Isola Asinara

La Maddalena

SWITZERLAND

LIECHTENSTEIN

Lake Constance

Rhine

Rhône

Lake Geneva

Great Saint Bernard Pass

Little St-Bernard Pass 2469m

Aosta

Gran Paradiso 4061m

Rivoli

Susa

Cuneo

Ventimiglia

MONACO

FRANCE

Mont Blanc 4807m

106

107

GERMANY

SLOVENIA

SAN MARINO

Dogana

Serravalle

Gualdicciolo

Mar

Borgo Maggiore

SAN MARINO

Fiorina

Cailungo

Murata

Monte Titano 739m

Faetano

Montegiardino

ITALY

ITALY

Chiesanuova

Appennino

500m/1640ft
200m/656ft
100m/328ft

0 km   2
0 miles   2

POPULATION

Less than
50,000

○

50,000 –
100,000

○

100,000 –
500,000

◉

Over
500,000

◉

0 km   100

0 miles   100

Maglie
Lecce
Brindisi
Strait of Otranto
Taranto
Manduria
Gallipoli
Bari
Bitonto
Molfetta
Barletta
Andria
Altamura
Matera
Puglia
Golfo di Taranto
Ciró Marina
Crotone
Catanzaro
La Sila
Rossano
Manfredonia
Foggia
Cerignola
Beneventó
Avellino
Campania
Potenza
San Consilina Lucano
Castrovillari
Apennino Lucano
Sapri
Lauria
Cosenza
Amantea
Lamezia
Siderno
Reggio di Calabria
Palmi
Campobasso
Volturno
Vesuvio 1277 m
Caserta
Napoli (Naples)
Torre del Greco
Battipaglia
Agropoli
Golfo di Salerno
Salerno
Isola di Capri
Isole Eolie
Isola Stromboli
Isola Lipari
Isola Vulcano
Stretto di Messina
Messina
Monte Etna 3340m
Simeto
Catania
Siracusa
Medica
Ragusa
Pozzallo
Cefalú
Sicilia (Sicily)
Caltanissetta
Caltagirone
Gela
Vittoria
Palermo
Alcamo
Agrigento
Trapani
Marsala
Castelvetrano
Isole Egadi
Strait of Sicily
Isola d'Ustica
Isola di Pantelleria
Isole Pelagie
Malta Channel
Gozo
MALTA
VALLETTA
Malta
Ionian Sea
Tyrrhenian Sea
Mediterranean Sea
Gaeta
Golfo di Gaeta
Terracina
Isole Ponziane
Laura
Sardegna (Sardinia)
Siniscola
Ozieri
Nuoro
Macomer
Oristano
Punta La Marmora 1834 m
Villacidro
Iglesias
Carbonia
Cagliari
Quartu Sant' Elena
Alghero
Quola
TUNISIA

117
121
87
87
87

117

ELEVATION

4000 m	13 124 ft
2000 m	6 562 ft
1000 m	3 281 ft
500 m	1 640 ft
250 m	820 ft
100 m	328 ft
Sea Level	Sea Level
-50 m	-164 ft
-100 m	-328 ft
-250 m	-820 ft
-500 m	-1 640 ft
-1 000 m	-3 281 ft
-2 000 m	-6 562 ft

VATICAN CITY

N
Main Entrance
Pigna Courtyard
Vatican Museums
Vatican Gardens
Raphael Stanza
Papal Apartments
Sistine Chapel
Saint Peter's Basilica
St Peter's Square
Radio Vatican
Monte Vaticano
Vatican Railway Station
Papal Heliport
ROME
ROME

0 m 200
0 yds 250

CENTRAL EUROPE

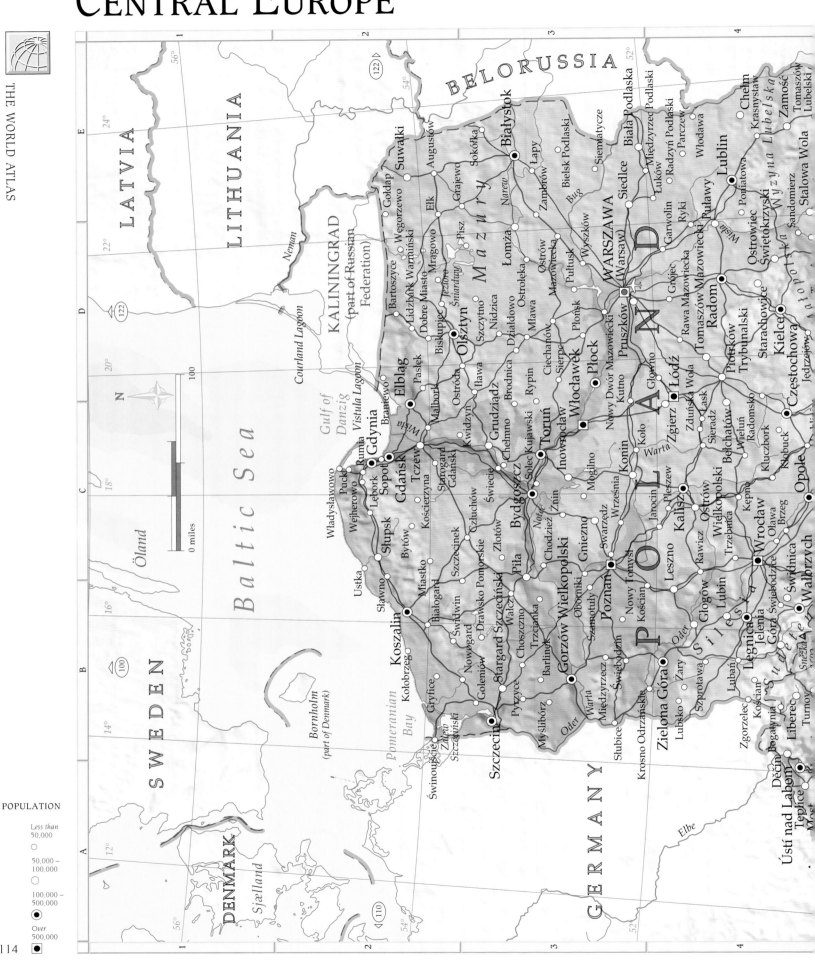

SWEDEN

DENMARK

Siælland

Öland

Bornholm
(part of Denmark)

Baltic Sea

LATVIA

LITHUANIA

Neman

KALININGRAD
*(part of Russian
Federation)*

Courland Lagoon

*Gulf of
Danzig*

Vistula Lagoon

BELORUSSIA

P O L A N D

N

100

0 miles

POPULATION

Less than
50,000
○

50,000 –
100,000
○

100,000 –
500,000
◉

Over
500,000
◼

114

Cities and towns

Świnoujście · Szczecin · Koszalin · Kołobrzeg · Gryfice · Goleniów · Nowogard · Stargard Szczeciński · Pyrzyce · Myślibórz · Ustka · Sławno · Białogard · Świdwin · Drawsko Pomorskie · Wałcz · Choszczno · Barlinek · Gorzów Wielkopolski · Międzyrzecz · Świebodzin · Sulechów · Krosno Odrzańskie · Zielona Góra · Lubsko · Żary · Szprotawa · Lubań · Głogów · Leszno

Władysławowo · Puck · Rumia · Gdynia · Sopot · Gdańsk · Wejherowo · Lębork · Bytów · Kościerzyna · Słupsk · Miastko · Szczecinek · Złotów · Piła · Oborniki · Szamotuły · Nowy Tomyśl · Poznań · Września · Swarzędz · Jarocin · Pleszew · Kalisz · Ostrów Wielkopolski · Rawicz · Kościan · Nowy Tomyśl

Człuchów · Chojnice · Świecie · Żnin · Mogilno · Gniezno · Konin · Koło · Turek · Sieradz · Łask · Zduńska Wola · Zgierz · Łódź · Pabianice · Bełchatów · Wieluń · Wieruszów · Kępno · Kluczbork · Olesno · Ostrzeszów

Braniewo · Elbląg · Malbork · Kwidzyn · Grudziądz · Chełmno · Toruń · Bydgoszcz · Inowrocław · Włocławek · Kutno · Łowicz

Pasłęk · Sztum · Ostróda · Iława · Brodnica · Rypin · Sierpc · Płock · Gostynin · Kutno · Głowno

Gołdap · Węgorzewo · Giżycko · Mrągowo · Biskupiec · Olsztyn · Szczytno · Nidzica · Działdowo · Mława · Ciechanów · Płońsk · Raciąż

Suwałki · Augustów · Ełk · Pisz · Łomża · Ostrołęka · Ostrów Mazowiecka · Pułtusk · Wyszków · Nowy Dwór Mazowiecki · Warszawa (Warsaw) · Pruszków

Sokółka · Białystok · Łapy · Bielsk Podlaski · Siemiatycze · Zambrów · Siedlce · Garwolin · Grójec · Rawa Mazowiecka

Biała Podlaska · Międzyrzec Podlaski · Radzyń Podlaski · Łuków · Parczew · Włodawa · Chełm · Krasnystaw

Lublin · Puławy · Ryki · Dęblin · Radom · Tomaszów Mazowiecki · Piotrków Trybunalski · Radomsko · Częstochowa · Opole · Brzeg · Oława · Wrocław · Świdnica · Wałbrzych · Legnica · Jelenia Góra · Świebodzice · Kłodzko · Ząbkowice

Ostrowiec Świętokrzyski · Starachowice · Skarżysko · Kielce · Jędrzejów · Sandomierz · Stalowa Wola · Tarnobrzeg · Zamość · Tomaszów Lubelski

GERMANY

Silesia

Oder

Warta

Noteć

Wisła

Elbe

Ústí nad Labem · Děčín · Teplice · Most · Liberec · Turnov · Zgorzelec

*Pomeranian
Bay*

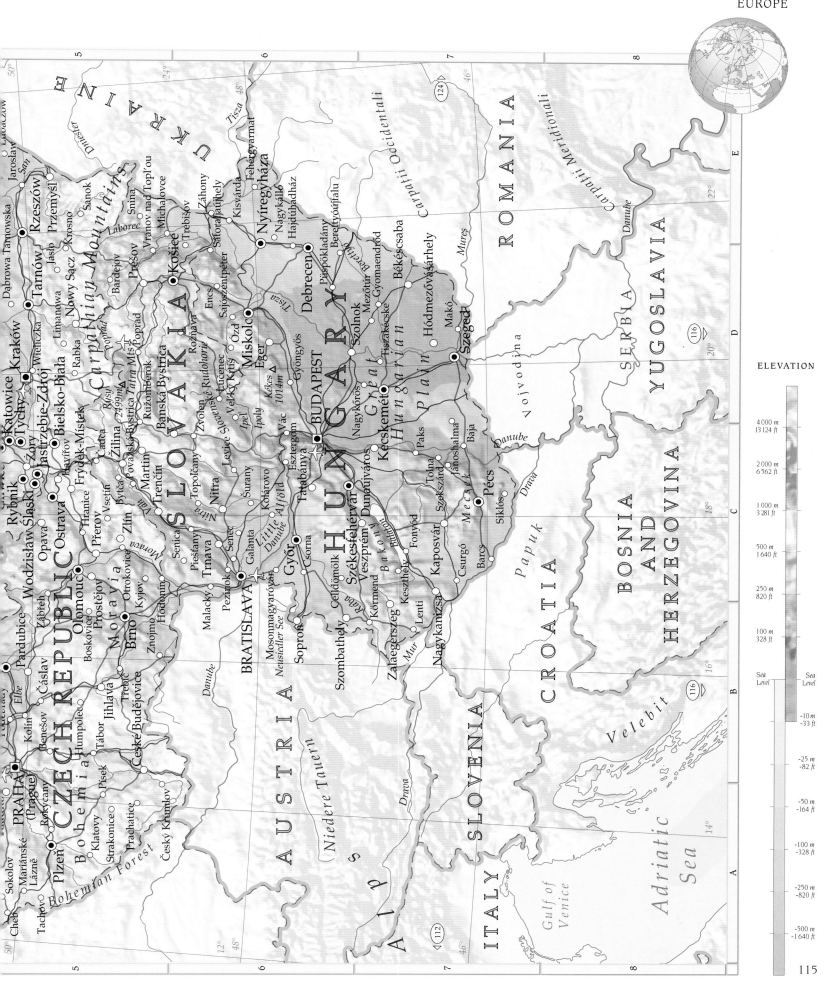

ELEVATION

4 000 *m* 13 124 *ft*	
2 000 *m* 6 562 *ft*	
1 000 *m* 3 281 *ft*	
500 *m* 1 640 *ft*	
250 *m* 820 *ft*	
100 *m* 328 *ft*	
Sea Level	Sea Level
-10 *m* -33 *ft*	
-25 *m* -82 *ft*	
-50 *m* -164 *ft*	
-100 *m* -328 *ft*	
-250 *m* -820 *ft*	
-500 *m* -1 640 *ft*	

WESTERN BALKANS

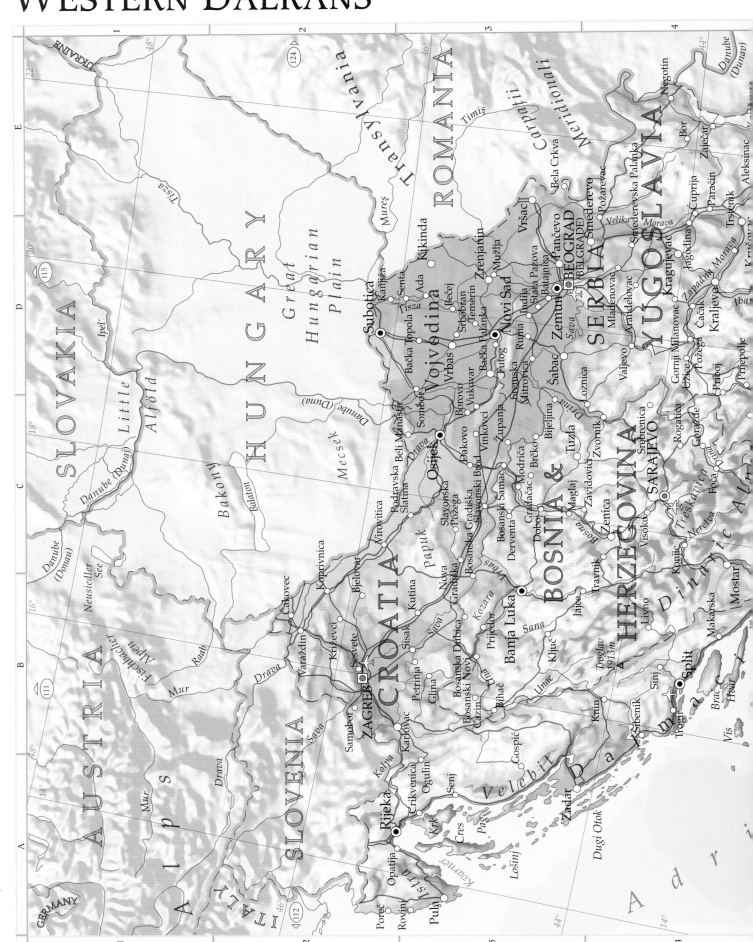

POPULATION

Less than
50,000

○

50,000 –
100,000

○

100,000 –
500,000

◉

Over
500,000

◉

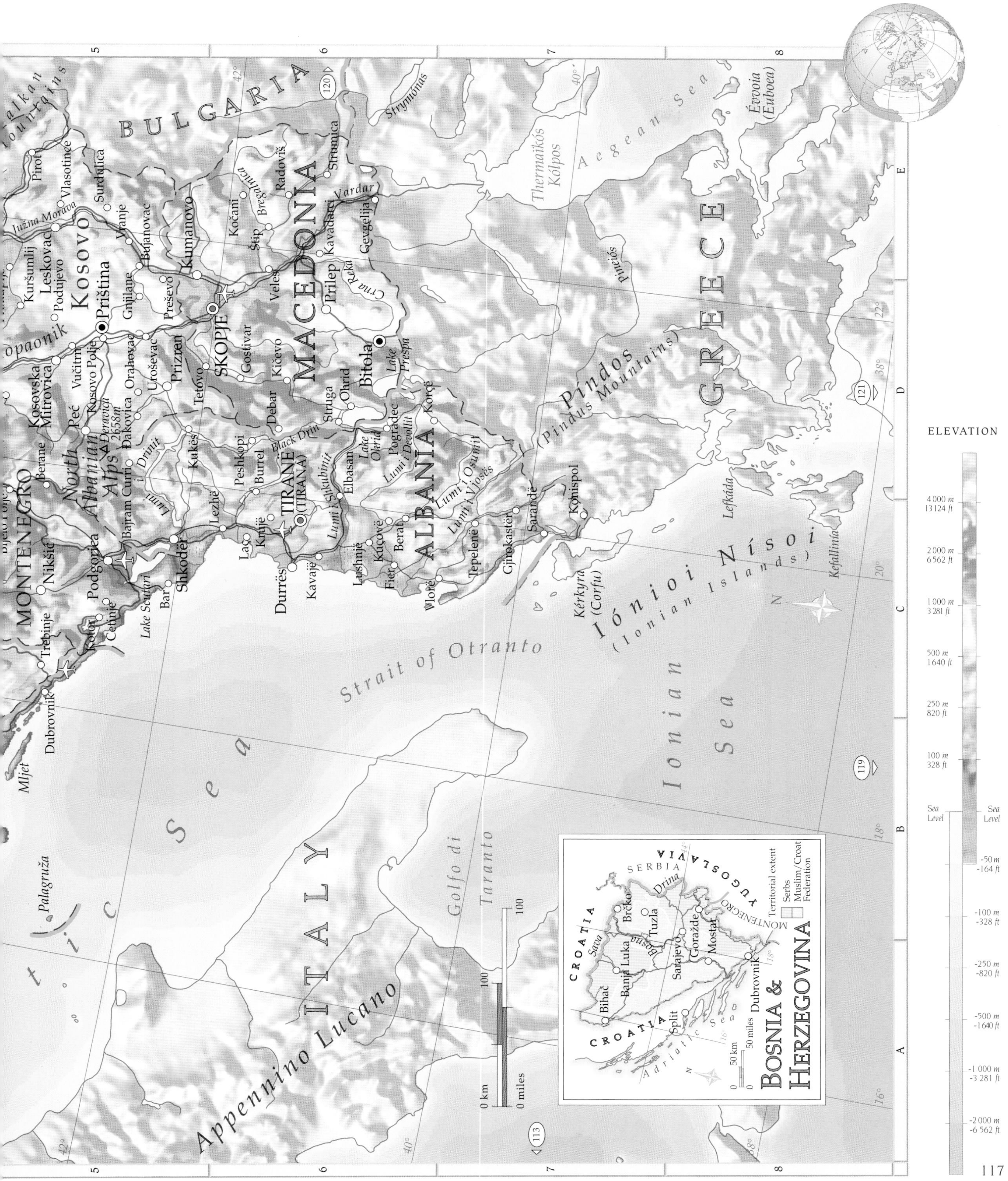

BULGARIA

MACEDONIA

GREECE

KOSOVO

ALBANIA

MONTENEGRO

ITALY

Priština
Skopje
TIRANE (TIRANA)

Balkan Mountains

Strymónas

Thermaïkós Kólpos

Aegean Sea

Évvoia (Euboea)

Pindos (Pindus Mountains)

Piniós

Kefallinía

Lefkáda

Kérkyra (Corfu)

Iónioi Nísoi (Ionian Islands)

Ionian Sea

Strait of Otranto

Golfo di Taranto

Appennino Lucano

Adriatic Sea

Palagruža

Mljet

Pirot
Vlasotince
Surdulica
Kuršumlij
Leskovac
Podujevo
Vranje
Bujanovac
Preševo
Gnjilane
Kumanovo
Kočani
Radoviš
Štip
Bregalnica
Strumica
Vardar
Gevgelija
Kavadarci
Prilep
Veles
Bitola
Lake Prespa
Crna Reka
Ohrid
Struga
Kičevo
Gostivar
Tetovo
Uroševac
Prizren
Debar
Lake Ohrid
Pogradec
Korçë
Peshkopi
Burrel
Burrel
Elbasan
Lumi i Devollit
Lumi i Osumit
Berat
Gjirokastër
Tepelenë
Lumi i Vjosës
Sarandë
Konispol
Vlorë
Fier
Kuçovë
Lushnjë
Kavajë
Durrës
Krujë
Laç
Lezhë
Lumi i Shkumbinit
Black Drin
Kukës
Bajram Curri
Lumi i Drinit
Shkodër
Lake Scutari
Bar
Kotor
Cetinje
Ulcinj
Podgorica
Nikšić
Trebinje
Dubrovnik
Bijelo Polje
Berane
North Albanian Alps
Đeravica 2655m
Dakovica
Orahovac
Kosovo Polje
Vučitrn
Peć
Kosovska Mitrovica
Kopaonik
Južna Morava
Topaonik

Južna Morava

ELEVATION

4000 m	13 124 ft
2000 m	6562 ft
1000 m	3281 ft
500 m	1640 ft
250 m	820 ft
100 m	328 ft
Sea Level	Sea Level
-50 m	-164 ft
-100 m	-328 ft
-250 m	-820 ft
-500 m	-1640 ft
-1000 m	-3281 ft
-2000 m	-6562 ft

BOSNIA & HERZEGOVINA

CROATIA
SERBIA
YUGOSLAVIA
MONTENEGRO
Sava
Brčko
Bihać
Banja Luka
Bosna
Tuzla
Sarajevo
Goražde
Mostar
Drina
Split
Dubrovnik
Adriatic Sea

Territorial extent
Serbs
Muslim/Croat Federation

0 km 100
0 miles 100

50 km
50 miles

THE MEDITERRANEAN

ATLANTIC OCEAN

Bay of Biscay

Quimper
106
St-Nazaire
Île d'Yeu
Nantes
Tours
Loire

FRANCE

Dijon
Zürich
Innsbruck
München (Munich)
LIECH.
VADUZ

BERN
SWITZ.
Milano (Milan)
Alpi Dolomitiche
Venezia (Venice)
Gulf of Venic

Limoges
Clermont-Ferrand
Lyon
Lake Geneva
Mont Blanc
4807m
Torino (Turin)

Dordogne
Massif
Central
Bordeaux
Garonne
Genova (Genoa)
Po
Bologna

A Coruña
Santander
Bilbao
Toulouse
Montpellier
Nîmes
MONACO
Marseille
Nice
Côte d'Azur
Ligurian Sea
Golfo di Genova
Pisa
SAN MARINO

Vigo
82
Cordillera Cantábrica
Sistema Ibérico
PYRENEES
ANDORRA
Perpignan
Golfe du Lion
Corse (Corsica)
Isola d'Elba
ROMA (ROME)

Porto
Duero
Valladolid
Ebro
Zaragoza
Barcelona
Costa Brava
Tarragona
Ajaccio
VATICAN CITY

PORTUGAL
Sistema Central
Tagus
MADRID
SPAIN
Castelló de la Plana
Mallorca (Majorca)
Palma
Menorca (Minorca)
Isola Asinara
Sassari
Sardegna (Sardinia)
Tyrrhenian Sea

LISBOA (LISBON)
Valencia
Golfo de Valencia
Islas Baleares (Balearic Islands)
Cagliari

Sierra Morena
Guadalquivir
Sistemas Béticos
Alicante
Costa Blanca
Eivissa (Ibiza)
Formentera
M e d i t e r
Sicilia (Sicily)
Palermo

Sevilla (Seville)
Murcia
Cartagena
Golfe de Tunis
Cap Bon
Isola di Pantelle

Golfo de Cádiz
Málaga
Almería
Cap Bougaroun
Annaba
TUNIS

Cádiz
Costa del Sol
ALGER (ALGIERS)
Tizi Ouzou
Constantine
Sétif
Sousse
Golfe de Hammamet
Isole Pelag

GIBRALTAR (to UK)
Ceuta (part of Spain)
Tangier
Tétouan
Oran
Mostaganem
Atlas Tellien
Massif de l'Aurès

Strait of Gibraltar
Melilla (part of Spain)
Tlemcen
Chott el Hodna
Sfax
Îles de Kerkenah

RABAT
Fes
Oujda
Chott ech Chergui
Chott el Jerid
Golfe de Gabès

Casablanca
MOROCCO
Moyen Atlas
Haut Plateaux
Chott Melghir
Gabès
Île de Jerba

Safi
Haut Atlas
Atlas Mountains
ALGERIA
TUNISIA
ȚARĂBULUS (TRIPOLI)

Gharyān

MALTA

Victoria
Nadur
Comino (Kemmuna)
Gozo
Mgarr
Mellieħa
St Julian's
Sliema
Mosta
VALLETTA
Ħamrun
Paola
Rabat
Birżebbuġa
Malta

250m/820ft
100m/328ft
Sea Level
0 km 10
0 miles 10

CYPRUS

Agialoúsa (Yenierenköy)
Lápithos (Lapta)
Kerýneia (Girne)
TURKISH REPUBLIC OF NORTHERN CYPRUS
(recognized only by Turkey)
Mórfou (Güzelyurt)
Kólpos Ammóchostos (Gazimağusa Körfezi)
Pólis
NICOSIA
Ammóchostos (Gazimağusa/Famagusta)
Dekéleia
Tróodos
Lárnaka
Páfos
Sovereign Base Area (to UK)
Sovereign Base Area (to UK)
Akrotírion
Lemesós (Limassol)

1000m/3281ft
500m/1640ft
250m/820ft
Sea Level
0 km 25
0 miles 25

Mediterranean Sea

S a h a r a
86

POPULATION

Less than 50,000

50,000 – 100,000

100,000 – 500,000

Over 500,000

118

SLOVAKIA
WIEN (VIENNA)
Danube
BUDAPEST
Satu Mare
Tisza
Carpathian Mountains
Bâlti
UKRAINE
MOLD.
CHIŞINĂU
Dniester
Kakhovs'ka Vodoskhovyshche

HUNGARY
Great Hungarian Plain
Târgu Mures
ROMANIA
Dnieper
Odesa
Berdyans'k

LJUBLJANA
VN.
ZAGREB
CROATIA
Novi Sad
Carpaţii Meridonali
Galaţi
Sea of Azov
Kryms'kyy Pivostrov
Kerch
RUSS. FED.
1

Rijeka
Sava
BOSNIA & HERZ.
BEOGRAD (BELGRADE)
BUCUREŞTI (BUCHAREST)
Danube
Constanţa
Sevastopol'
Novorossiysk

scara
Adriatic Sea
Dalmatia
SARAJEVO
YUGOSLAVIA
BULGARIA
Balkan Mountains
Varna
Black Sea

Pristina
SOFIYA (SOFIA)
Burgas
İstanbul Boğazı (Bosporus)
133
2

Bari
TIRANË (TIRANA)
ALBANIA
SKOPJE
MACED.
Rhodope Mountains
Edirne
İstanbul
Zonguldak
Küre Dağları
Samsun

Y
Vesuvio 1277m
Lecce
Strait of Otranto
Thessaloniki (Salonica)
Marmara Denizi
Bursa
Kızıl Irmak
Ordu

Napoli (Naples)
Golfo di Taranto
Pindos (Pindus) Mts.
Límnos
ANKARA
TURKEY

Cosenza
Kérkyra (Corfu)
Lárisa
Aegean Sea
Balıkesir
40°

Catanzaro
Ionian
GREECE
Tuz Gölü
Kayseri

Kefallinía
Chíos
İzmir
3

Monte Etna 3340m
Catania
Sea
ATHÍNA (ATHENS)
Sámos
Dodekánisos (Dodecanese)
Gaziantep

Siracusa
Zákynthos
Mirtóo Pelagos
Kykládes (Cyclades)
Antalya
Toros Dağları
Adana
Euphrates

Kýthira
Kritikó Pélagos (Sea of Crete)
Ródos (Rhodes)
Antalya Körfezi
İskenderun Körfezi
Halab (Aleppo)

VALLETTA
MALTA
Irákleio
Kárpathos
NICOSIA
CYPRUS
Lárnaka
SYRIA

Kríti (Crete)
Lemesós (Limassol)
LEBANON
35°

BEYROUTH (BEIRUT)

DIMASHQ (DAMASCUS)
Hefa
4

Mişrātah
Darnah
Banghāzī (Benghazi)
Libyan Plateau
ISRAEL
'AMMĀN
135

Surt
Khalīj Surt (Gulf of Sirte)
Ţubruq
Tel Aviv-Yafo
JERUSALEM
Gaza
Dead Sea

Ajdābiyā
Libyan Plateau
Alexandria
Nile Delta
Port Said
JORDAN

Great Sand Sea
Monkhafad al Qattâra (Qattara Depression)
CAIRO
Suez Canal
30°

Waddān
El Giza
Suez
Elat
Al 'Aqabah

LIBYA
Libyan Desert
EGYPT
Nile
Sahara el Sharqīya (Eastern Desert)
Sinai
Gulf of Suez
SAUDI ARABIA
5

Red Sea

0 km 400
0 miles 400
87
88

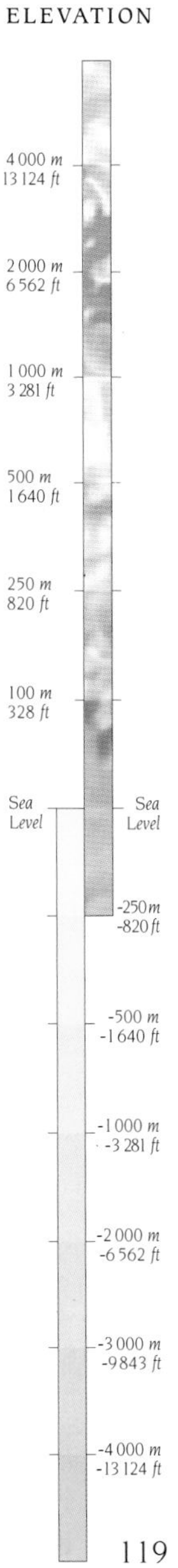

ELEVATION

4 000 m / 13 124 ft
2 000 m / 6 562 ft
1 000 m / 3 281 ft
500 m / 1 640 ft
250 m / 820 ft
100 m / 328 ft
Sea Level / Sea Level
-250 m / -820 ft
-500 m / -1 640 ft
-1 000 m / -3 281 ft
-2 000 m / -6 562 ft
-3 000 m / -9 843 ft
-4 000 m / -13 124 ft

BULGARIA & GREECE

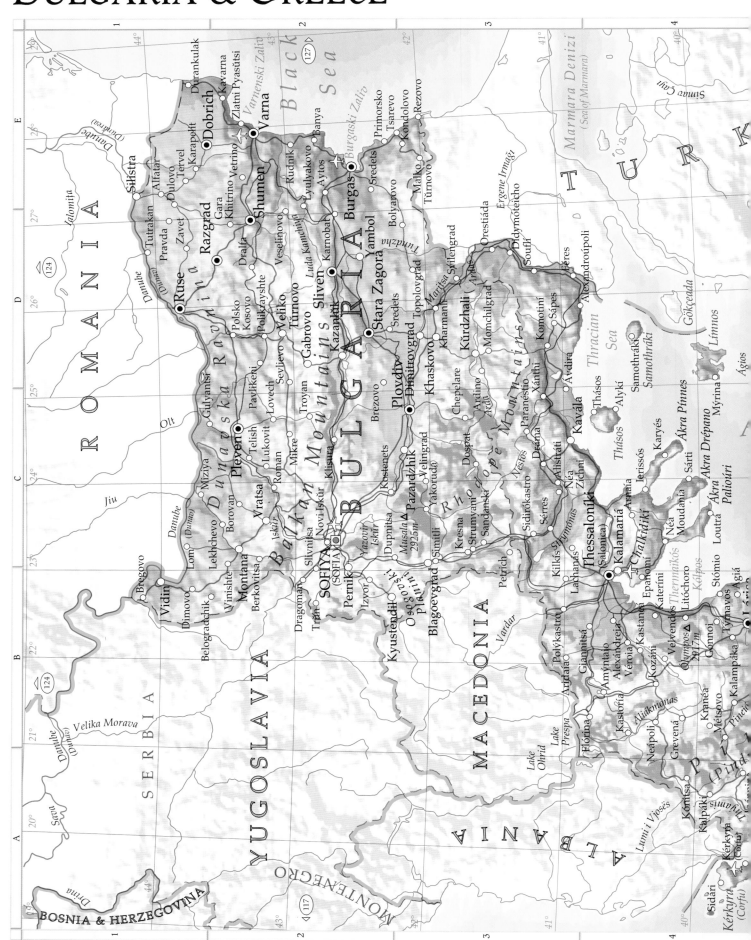

POPULATION

Less than
50,000

50,000 –
100,000

100,000 –
500,000

Over
500,000

Gediz

Büyükmenderes Nehri

E Y

Mytilíni
Plomári
Antíssa
Lésvos
(Lesbos)
Chíos
Psará
Antípsara
Chíos
(Lesbos)

Aegean Sea

Sámos
Sámos
Ikaría
Karlovási
Thérma

Arkoí
Lipsoí
Patmos
Léros
Kálimnos
Agía
Marína
Kos
Kos
Nísyros
Tílos

Ródos
(Rhodes)
Lindos

132

Chálki

Saría
Kattaviá
Kárpathos
Kárpathos

Dodekánisos (Dodecanese)

Amorgós
Amorgós
Akra Floúda
Astypálaia

Syrna
Anáfi

Ródos
(Rhodes)

119

Kásos

Sporades
Alónnisos
Skíathos
Skópelos
Strofyliá
Skýros
Vóreioi Sporádes

Skýros

Évvoia
(Euboea)

Mýkonos
Tínos
Kéa
Sýros
Ermoúpoli
Kykládes (Cyclades)
Páros
Náxos
Náxos
Kástro
Íos
Íos
Thíra
Thíra
Anáfi

Kritikó Pélagos
(Sea of Crete)

Neápoli
Siteía
Ágios Nikólaos
Ierápetra
Myrtós

Kými
Álónnisos

Kárystos
Ándros
Ándros

Kéa
Lávrio
Kythnos
Kýthnos
Sérifos
Sífnos
Mílos
Folégandros

Miríóo Pélagos

Kriti (Crete)
Chaniá
Lefká Óri
Panórmos
Zarós
Irákleio
Díkti

Kastélli
Kántanos
Spíli
Sfákia
Tympáki
Gávdos

Mediterranean Sea

ATHÍNA
(ATHENS)
Peiraiás
(Piraeus)

Marathónas
Kálamos
Vília
Mándra
Aígina
Póros
Pataiá Epídavros
Ýdra
Ermióni

Kéa

Karavás
Neápoli
Daimoniá
Léonidi
Geráki
Gýtheio
Monemvasía
Kýthira
Kýthira

Antikýthira
Potamós
Antikýthira

Livanátes
Malesína
Chalkída
Alivéri
Théva
Aliartos

Korinthiakós
Kólpos
Kiáto
Xylókastro
Kórinthos
(Corinth)
Némea
Árgos
Trípoli
Náfplio

Spárti
Kalámata

Koróni
Gerolimenas
Areópoli

Peloponnísos
(Peloponnese)

Pátra

Aígio
Achaía
Lechainá
Gastoúni
Pýrgos
Alfeiós
Zácharo
Kyparissía
Pýlos
Messíni
Lámpeia
Keri

Árta
Rentína
Karpenísi
Lamía
Domokós
Agrínio
Amfilochía
Náfpaktos
Thérmo

Kardítsa
Kalambáka

Préveza
Lefkáda
Vasilikí
Argostóli
Kefallinía
Zákynthos
Kéri

Paxoí
Antípaxoi

Iónioi Nísoi
(Ionian Islands)

Ionian Sea

GREECE

Mountains

100
0 km
100
0 miles

N

THE BALTIC STATES & BELORUSSIA

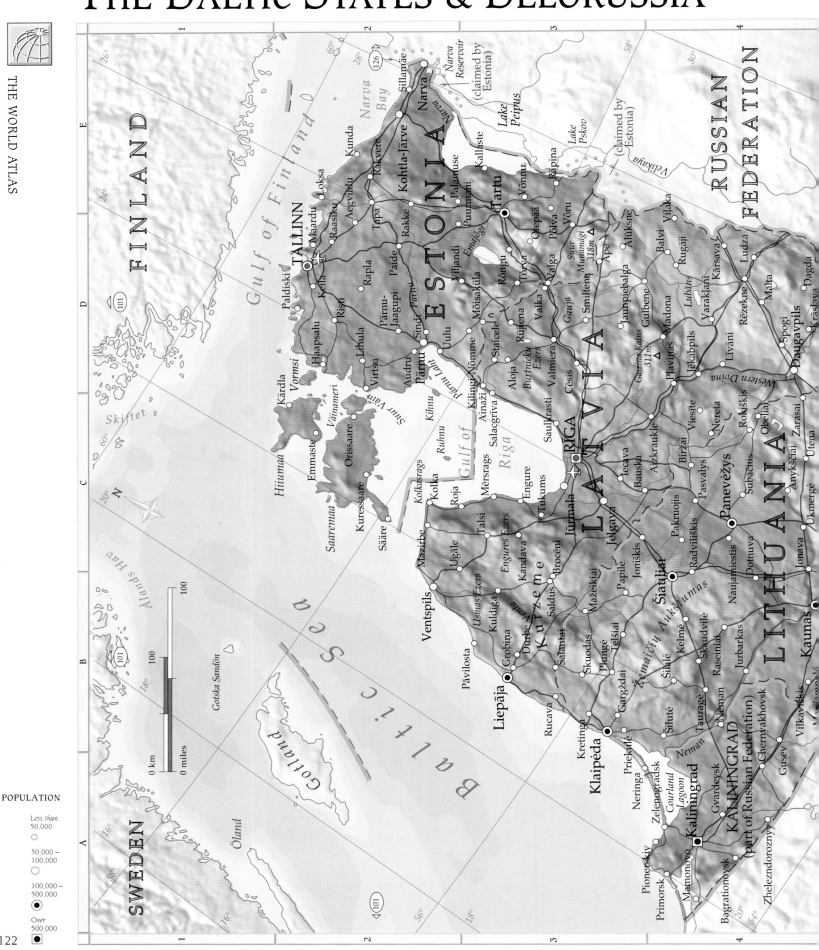

SWEDEN

FINLAND

Gulf of Finland

Skiftet

Ålands Hav

Gotska Sandön

Gotland

Öland

Baltic Sea

Narva Bay

Narva Reservoir (claimed by Estonia)

Sillamäe
Narva
Kunda
Loksa
Aegviidu
Rakvere
Kohtla-Järve
Kallaste
Lake Peipus
Viru-Nigula
Tapa
Rakke
Lake Pskov (claimed by Estonia)
Velikaja

RUSSIAN FEDERATION

Paldiski
TALLINN
Keila
Maardu
Raasiku
Paide
Palamuse
Puurmani
Tartu
Võnnu
Otepää
Põlva
Võru

ESTONIA

Rapla
Rapla
Viljandi
Emajõgi
Rõngu
Torva
Valga
Suur Munamägi 318m △
Ape
Alūksne
Balvi
Vilaka

Risti
Haapsalu
Lihula
Pärnu-Jaagupi
Sindi
Pärnu
Uulu
Mõisaküla
Karksi-Nuia
Valka
Smilteņe
Jaunpiebalga
Gulbene
Rugāji

Kärdla
Vormsi
Emmaste
Väinameri
Orissaare
Kuressaare

Hiiumaa

Saaremaa

Säare

Audru
Virtsu
Pärnu Laht
Kihnu
Killingi-Nõmme
Ainaži
Staicele
Aloja
Rūjiena
Valmiera
Cēsis
Gauja
Gaiziņa Kalns 311m △
Madona
Lubāns
Jēkabpils
Varakļāni
Rēzekne
Balvi
Ludza
Kārsava
Spogi
Daugavpils
Krāslava
Dagda

Suur Väin
Ruhnu
Gulf of Riga
Mērsrags
Salacgrīva
Saulkrasti
RĪGA

LATVIA

Viesīte
Līvāni
Malta
Jūrmala
Bauska

Kolkasrags
Kolka
Roja
Mazirbe
Talsi
Engures Ezers
Engure
Tukums
Jelgava
Iecava
Aizkraukle
Plaviņas
Biržai
Pasvalys
Subačius
Rokiškis
Obeliai
Zarasai
Utena

Ventspils

Ugāle
Usmas Ezers
Kuldīga
Kandava
Saldus
Brocēni
Pakruojis
Radviliškis
Panevėžys
Naujamiestis
Anykščiai
Ukmergė

Kurzeme

Drube
Venta
Mažeikiai
Papilė
Joniškis
Šiauliai
Žemaičiu Aukštumas
Dotnuva

Pāvilosta
Grobiņa
Skuodas
Plungė
Telšiai
Kelmė
Skaudvilė
Raseiniai
Jurbarkas

Liepāja

Rucava
Salantai
Gargždai
Šilalė
Taurage
Neman

LITHUANIA

Kretinga
Silutė
Neman
Jonava
Vilkaviškis
Kaunas

Klaipėda

Neringa
Priekulė
Neman
Gvardeysk
Chernyakhovsk
Gusev

Courland Lagoon

Zelenogradsk
Gvardeysk
KALININGRAD (part of Russian Federation)

Pionerskiy
Primorsk
Mamonovo
Bagrationovsk
Bratrionovsk
Zheleznodorozhny

POPULATION

Less than 50,000 ○

50,000 – 100,000 ○

100,000 – 500,000 ◉

Over 500,000 ◉

BELORUSSIA

POLAND

RUSSIAN FEDERATION

UKRAINE

Cities and towns:

Haradok, Yezyaryshcha, Surazh, Vitsyebsk, Navapolatsk, Polatsk, Harany, Obal', Vyetryna, Drysa, Vyerkhnyadzvinsk, Vidzy, Pastavy, Hlybokaye, Shumilina, Bacheykava, Sarodyna, Lyepyel', Chashniki, Plyeshchanitsy, Byahoml', Myadzyel, Vilyeyka, Smarhon, Ashmyany, Maladzyechna, Krasnaye, Barysaw, Zhodzina, Zhodzina, Byalynichy, Talachyn, Krupki, Orsha, Shklow, Horki, Dnieper, Sava, Lyozna, Bahushewsk, Mahilyow, Harbavichy, Khodasy, Krychaw, Cherykaw, Klimavichy, Kastsyukovichy, Baron'ki, Dobrush, Tsyerakhowka

MINSK

Vilnius, Neris, Viliya, Trakai, Salcininkai, Voranava, Lida, Orlya, Navahrudak, Valozhyn, Stowbtsy, Rudzyensk, Mar'ina Horka, Pukhavichy, Chervyen, Yalizava, Chachevichy, Babruysk, Abidavichy, Rahachow, Zhlobin, Buda-Kashalyova, Uvaravichy, Bal'shavik, Kastsyukowka, Homyel', Khoyniki, Loyew, Byval'ki, Narowlya, Mazyr, Svyetlahorsk, Shyichy, Rechytsa, Kalinkavichy, Yel'sk, Dabryn, Milashavichy, Lyel'chytsy, Simanichy, Pripet, Pyetrykaw, Kaptsevichy, Zhytkavichy, Tonyezh, Luninyets, Pinsk, Lyusina, Hantsavichy, Drahichyn, Ivanava, Ivatsevichy, Lyakhavichy, Baranavichy, Nyasvizh, Kapyl', Slutsk, Starobyn, Salihorsk, Staryya Darohi, Shyshchytsy, Asipovichy, Bastyn', Mikashevichy

Slonim, Zel'va, Ruzhany, Pruzhany, Kobryn, Zhabinka, Damachava, Makrany, Brest, Novy Dvor, Haradzyets, Drahichyn

Hrodna, Masty, Shchuchyn, Skidal', Vawkavysk, Vasilishki, Parechcha, Skabin, Merkine, Varena, Rudiskes, Kalvarija, Veisiejai, Druskininkai, Hrandzichy, Alytus, Trakai

Pripet Marshes, Byelaruskaya Hrada, Minskaya Wzvyshsha, Byerezino, P'tsich, Dnieper Lowland, Kyyivs'ke Vodoskhovyshche, Horyn', Styr, Yasyel'da, Bug, Wyzyna Lubelska, Wysoczyzna, Neman, Mazury, Western Dvina

127, 125, 124, 114

ELEVATION

4 000 m	13 124 ft
2 000 m	6 562 ft
1 000 m	3 281 ft
500 m	1 640 ft
250 m	820 ft
100 m	328 ft
Sea Level	Sea Level
-10 m	-33 ft
-25 m	-82 ft
-50 m	-164 ft
-100 m	-328 ft
-250 m	-820 ft
-500 m	-1 640 ft

UKRAINE, MOLDAVIA & ROMANIA

BELORUSSIA

POLAND

Małopolska

Wyżyna Lubelska

Wisła

Carpathian Mountains

Tatra Mountains

SLOVAKIA

Slovenské Rudohorie

HUNGARY

Tisza

Great Hungarian Plain

Pripet
Pripet
Pripet Marshes
Styr
Sluch
Kovel'
Sarny
Olevs'k
Ovruch
Volodymyr-Volyns'kyy
Kivertsi
Korosten'
Novovolyns'k
Luts'k
Rivne
Malyn
Radomyshl'
Sokal'
Dubno
Novohrad-Volyns'kyy
Chervonohrad
Slavuta
Shepetivka
Zhytomyr
Zhovkva
Kremenets'
Polonne
Berdychiv
Yavoriv
L'viv
Zolochiv
Izyaslav
Starokostyantyniv
Horodok
Zbarazh
Kozyat
Sambir
Khodoriv
Ternopil'
Khmel'nyts'kyy
Drohobych
Berezhany
Vinnytsya
Boryslav
Zhydachiv
Lypovets'
Stryy
Chortkiv
Kalush
Haysyn
UKR
Dolyna
Ivano-Frankivs'k
Kam'yanets'-Podil's'kyy
Zhmerynka
Tul'chyn
Uzhhorod
Nadvirna
Mukacheve
Kolomyya
Chernivtsi
Mohyliv-Podil's'kyy
Berehove
Podil's'ka Vysochyna
Vynohradiv
△ Hora Hoverla 2061m
Darabani
Khust
Soroca
Negreşti-Oaş
Rădăuţi
Dorohoi
Dniester
Satu Mare
Balta
Carei
Baia Mare
Solca
Botoşani
Bălţi
Ribniţa
Marghita
Baia Sprie
Borşa
Suceava
Kotovs'
Someş
Fălticeni
MOLDAVIA
Oradea
Zalău
Năsăud
Paşcani
Călăraşi
Aleşd
Dej
Bistriţa
Târgu-Neamţ
Ungheni
Orhei
Dubăsa
Salonta
Beiuş
Reghin
Bicaz
Roman
Iaşi
Străşeni
Curtici
Transylvania
Cluj-Napoca
Topliţa
Piatra-Neamţ
CHIŞINĂU
Ineu
Turda
Ludus
Gheorgheni
Bacău
Hînceşti
Tighina
Arad
Abrud
Aiud
Medias
Târgu Mureş
Miercuea-Ciuc
Vaslui
Tiraspol
Sânnicolau Mare
Lipova
Cristuru Secuiesc
Bârlad
Comrat
Mureş
Alba Iulia
Deva
Rupea
Târgu Ocna
Basarabeasca
Jimbolia
Timiş
Timişoara
ROMANIA
Făgăraş
Târgu Secuiesc
Adjud
Ciadîr-Lunga
Lugoj
Hunedoara
Sibiu
Codlea
Stânta Gheorghe
Taraclia
Oţelu Roşu
Haţeg
Cisnădie
Vârful Moldoveanu 2544m
Câmpulung
Braşov
Focşani
Cahul
Artsyz
Bocşa
Câmpulung
Râşnov
Bolhrad
Reşiţa
Petroşani
Carpaţii Meridionali
Râmnicu Sărat
Galaţi
Reni
Kiliya
Oraviţa
Anina
Târgu Jiu
Călimăneşti
Sinaia
Ozero Yalpuh
Moldova Nouă
Curtea de Argeş
Câmpina
Buzău
Braila
Izmayil
Orşova
Motru
Moreni
Brăila
Drobeta-Turnu Severin
Strehaia
Râmnicu Vâlcea
Mizil
Măcin
Tulcea
Danube
Filiaşi
Piteşti
Titu
Târgovişte
Ploieşti
Urziceni
Isaccea
Drăgăşani
Babadag
Wallachia
Buftea
Ialomiţa
Ţăndărei
Hârşova
Lacul Razim
YUGOSLAVIA
Craiova
Slatina
BUCUREŞTI (BUCHAREST)
Slobozia
Lacul Sinoie
Balş
Caracal
Olteniţa
Feteşti
Medgidia
Băileşti
Calafat
Roşiori de Vede
Alexandria
Călăraşi
Constanţa
Velika Morava
Jiu
Corabia
Turnu Măgurele
Zimnicea
Giurgiu
Oll
Techirghiol
Eforie Sud
SERBIA
Danube (Dunărea)
Dunavska Ravnina
Mangalia
BULGARIA

RUSSIAN FEDERATION

Srednerusskaya Vozvyshennost'

Don

52°
40°
50°
48°
46°
44°

30° 32° 34° 36° 38° 40°

E F G H

Dnieper (Dnyapro)

Horodnya
Shchors
Shostka
Hlukhiv
Krolevets'
Chernihiv
Konotop
Bakhmach
Nizhyn
Romny
Sumy
Nosivka
Oster
Desna
Brovary
Kyyivs'ke Vodoskhovyshche
KYYIV (KIEV)
Boyarka
Vasyl'kiv
Pryluky
Yahotyn
Pyryatyn
Lebedyn
Okhtyrka
Zolochiv
Derhachi
Fastiv
Hrebinka
Lubny
Myrhorod
Lyubotyn
Kharkiv
Kaniv
Kaniv's'ke Vodoskhovyshche
Bila Tserkva
Merefa
Oskil
Kup''yans'k
Bohuslav
Zolotonosha
Hlobyne
Poltava
Horodyshche
Cherkasy
Starobil's'k
Zvenyhorodka
Smila
Kremenchuts'ke Vodoskhovyshche
Sivers'kyy Donets
Izyum
Shpola
Chyhyryn
Kreminna
Rubizhne
Tal'ne
Oleksandrivka
Svitlovods'k
Kremenchuk
Dniprodzerzhyns'ke Vodoskhovyshche
Slov''yans'k
Syeverodonets'k
Znam''yanka
Oleksandriya
Kramators'k
Lysychans'k
Uman'
Mala Vyska
Novomoskovs'k
Zolote
Iolovanivs'k
Dniprodzerzhyns'k
Pavlohrad
Kostyantynivka
Luhans'k
Kirovohrad
Zhovti Vody
Dnipropetrovs'k
Horlivka
Stakhanov
Ulyanivka
P''yatykhatky
Krasnodon
Vil'shanka
Synel'nykove
Yenakiyeve
Pervomays'k
Dolyns'ka
Krasnyy Luch
Kryve Ozero
Arbyzynka
Bobrynets'
Kryvyy Rih
Pokrovs'ke
Donets'k
Makiyivka
Torez
Novyy Buh
Inhulets'
Prydniprovs'ka Vysochyna
Voznesens'k
Ordzhonikidze
Nikopol
Zaporizhzhya
Orikhiv
Amvrosiyivka
Kam''yanka-Dniprovs'ka
Marhanets'
Dokuchayevs'k
Volnovakha
Dniprorudne
Polohy
Don
Black Sea
Prydennyy Buh
Kakhovs'ka Vodoskhovyshche
Tokmak
Novoazovs'k
Mariupol'
Mykolayiv
Dnieper (Dnipro)
Molochans'k
Gulf of Taganrog
Zhovtneve
Kakhovka
Melitopol'
Yeya
Kherson
Akinovka
Prymors'k
Berdyans'k
Ochakiv
Tsyurupyns'k
Odesa
Hola Prystan'
Chaplynka
Novotroyits'ke
Illichivs'k
Kalanchak
Heniches'k
Armyans'k
Sea of Azov
RUSSIAN FEDERATION
Karkinits'ka Zatoka
Krasnoperekops'k
Rozdol'ne
Dzhankoy
Kerch Strait
Krasnohvardiys'ke
Zatoka Syvash
Kerch
Chornomors'ke
Nyzhn'ohirs'kyy
Kuban'
Yevpatoriya
Kryms'kyy Pivostriv
Lenine
Saky
Simferopol'
Feodosiya
Bakhchysaray
Kryms'ki Hory
Sevastopol'
Alushta
Yalta
Alupka

Black Sea

0 km 100
0 miles 100

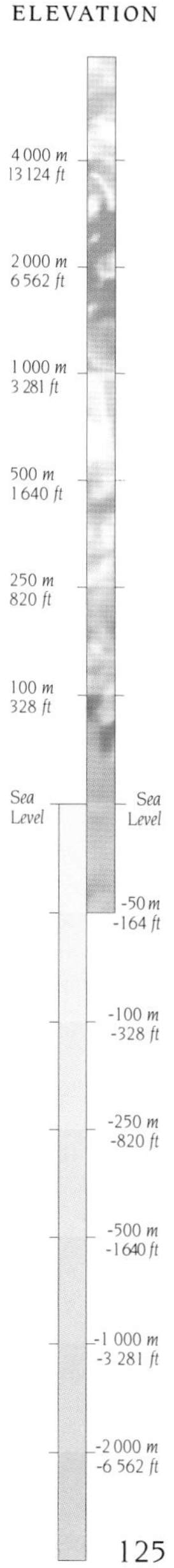

ELEVATION

4 000 m
13 124 ft

2 000 m
6 562 ft

1 000 m
3 281 ft

500 m
1 640 ft

250 m
820 ft

100 m
328 ft

Sea Level — Sea Level

-50 m
-164 ft

-100 m
-328 ft

-250 m
-820 ft

-500 m
-1640 ft

-1 000 m
-3 281 ft

-2 000 m
-6 562 ft

123
127
127
127
127
132

EUROPEAN RUSSIA

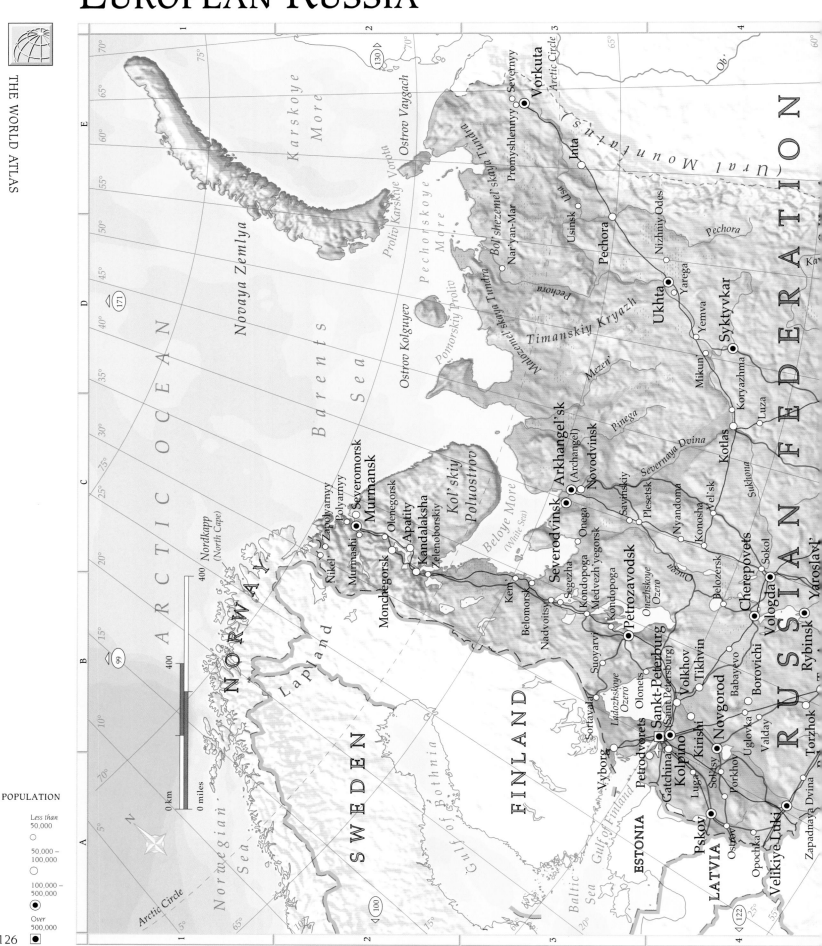

POPULATION

Less than
50,000
○

50,000 –
100,000
○

100,000 –
500,000
◉

Over
500,000
◉

126
◉

5 55° 6 50° 7 130 45° 8

E

Ural'skiye Gory

Kyzyl Kum

Syr Darya

65°

KAZAKHSTAN

UZBEKISTAN

60°

Aral Sea

Amu Darya

Berezniki
Chusovoy
Perm'
Kungur
Krasnokamsk
Glazov
Zuyevka
Izhevsk
Chaykovskiy
Beloretsk
Sibay
Baymak
Orsk
Neftekamsk
Naberezhnyye Chelny
Birsk
Ufa
Oktyabr'skiy
Salavat
Kumertau
Novotroitsk
Sterlitamak
Al'met'yevsk
Saraktash
Orenburg
Sol'-Iletsk

D

138

Kirghiz Steppe

TURKMEN.

Ustyurt Plateau

55°

TURKMEN.

Vyatka
Yoshkar-Ola
Novocheboksarsk
Kazan'
Kuybyshevskoye Vodokhranilishche
Nizhnekamsk
Al'met'yevsk
Bugurulan
Buzuluk
Ural

C

Caspian Sea

50°

Uren'
Nolinsk
Yaransk
Cheboksary
Kanash
Samara
Tol'yatti
Chapayevsk

Urzhum
Dzerzhinsk
Nizhniy Novgorod
Saransk
Ul'yanovsk
Dimitrovgrad
Syzran'
Balakovo
Krasnyy Kut

Ivanovo
Vladimir
Murom
Penza
Kuznetsk
Vol'sk
Saratov
Kamyshin

Elektrostal'
Kolomna
Ryazan'
Sasovo
Tambov
Borisoglebsk
Balashov
Volzhskiy

Akhtubinsk

B

Caspian Depression

Kuma

AZERB.

45°

Zelenograd
MOSKVA (MOSCOW)
Podol'sk
Serpukhov
Aleksin
Tula
Shchëkino
Michurinsk
Gryazi
Voronezh
Liski
Rossosh'
Kantemirovka
Millerovo
Don
Ilovlya
Volgograd
Volga
Astrakhan'
Elista
Zimovniki
Sal'sk
Volgodonsk
Elbrus 5642m

Georgia

Pochinok
Roslavl'
Kaluga
Oryol
Yelets
Lipetsk
Staryy Oskol
Gubkin
Belgorod
Shebekino
Rossosh'

Svetlograd
Stavropol'
Cherkessk
Nevinnomyssk
Pyatigorsk
Prokhladnyy
Nal'chik
Grozny
Khasavyurt
Makhachkala
Kaspiysk
Derbent

Smolensk
BELORUSSIA
Klintsy
Bryansk
Zheleznogorsk
Kursk

Kamensk-Shakhtinskiy
Novoshakhtinsk
Novocherkassk
Rostov-na-Donu
Kropotkin
Krasnodar
Maykop
Kislovodsk
Vladikavkaz

GEORGIA

ARM.

AZERB.

40°

A

Dnieper
Desna

UKRAINE

Donets

Sea of Azov
Starominskaya
Taganrog
Tuapse
Sochi
Novorossiysk
Tikhoretsk

Black Sea

Doğu Karadeniz Dağları

TURKEY

Euphrates

125

35° 6 40° 7 8

ELEVATION

4 000 m / 13 124 ft
2 000 m / 6 562 ft
1 000 m / 3 281 ft
500 m / 1 640 ft
250 m / 820 ft
100 m / 328 ft
Sea Level / Sea Level
-50 m / -164 ft
-100 m / -328 ft
-250 m / -820 ft
-500 m / -1 640 ft
-1 000 m / -3 281 ft
-2 000 m / -6 562 ft

North & West Asia

POPULATION

Less than 50,000
○

50,000 – 100,000
○

100,000 – 500,000
◉

Over 500,000
◉

128 ◉

A
20°
40°
B
60°
C
80°
D
100°

Summer limit of pack ice

Winter limit of pack ice

A R C T I C

Franz Josef Land

Severnaya Zem

Ostrov Komsomolets

Ostrov Oktyabr'skoy Revolyutsii
Ostrov Bol'shevik

Novaya Zemlya

East Novaya Zemlya Trench

Kara Sea

Poluostrov Taymyr

North Siberia

Kheta

Ozero Tayn

Norwegian Sea

North Cape

Barents Sea

Ostrov Kolguyev

Poluostrov Yamal

Gulf of Ob

● Noril'sk

Central Siberian Plateau

● Murmansk

Kola Peninsula

White Sea

● Archangel

R U S S I A N   F E

West Siberian Plain

Ob'

Kureyka

Lower Tunguska

Gulf of Bothnia

Lake Onega

Northern Dvina

Ob'

Stony Tunguska

S i

● Vologda

Perm ●

● Yekaterinburg

Irtysh

● Tomsk

Chulym

● Krasnoyarsk

Angara

■ Saint Petersburg
● Yaroslavl'

Lake Ladoga

MOSCOW

Volga

Nizhniy Novgorod

● Kazan'

Ufa ●

● Chelyabinsk

Ishim

● Omsk

Irtysh

● Novosibirsk

● Novokuznetsk

● Irku

■ Kaliningrad

Baltic Sea

Central Russian Upland

Ul'yanovsk ●

● Samara

● Orenburg

Kirghiz Steppe

● Akmola

● Karaganda

● Semipalatinsk

Sayanskiy Khrebet

A

S

KALININGRAD
(part of Russ. Fed.)

Voronezh ●

Saratov ●

Volga

Ural'sk ●

Ural

KAZAKHSTAN

Kazakh Uplands

Altai Mountains

● Irk

E U R O P E

Rostov-na-Donu ●

Don

Volgograd ●

Astrakhan ●

Aral'sk ●

Aral Sea

Syr Darya

Lake Balkhash

Ozera Zaysan

G

Danube

Black Sea

Stavropol' ●

El'brus 5642m△

Caucasus

Aktau ●

Ustyurt Plateau

Aral Sea

Kyzyl Kum

Kzyl-Orda ●

Zhambyl ●

Ili

ALMA-ATA ◉

Tien Shan

Istanbul ■

GEORGIA
T'BILISI ●

ARMENIA
AZERB.

Kara Kum

BAKU ●

UZBEKISTAN

BISHKEK ●

KYRGYZSTAN

Küre Dağları

ANKARA ■

YEREVAN ●

Lake Van

Dashkhovuz ●

Amu Darya

TASHKENT ●

TURKMENISTAN

DUSHANBE ●

Anatolia

TURKEY

Gaziantep ●

Tabriz ●

ASHGABAT ●

TAJIKISTAN

Adana ●

Aleppo ●

Mosul ●

TEHRAN ■

Qom ●

KABUL ●

Hindu Kush

Jalalabad ●

Kunlun Mountains

Tripoli ●

SYRIA   **IRAQ**

DAMASCUS ●

Isfahan ●

Iranian Plateau

● Herat

AFGHANISTAN

Khyber Pass

H i m a l a y a s

BEIRUT ●

LEBANON

BAGHDAD ●

Syrian Desert

Tigris

Zagros Mountains

ISRAEL

AMMAN ●

Basra ●

IRAN

Zahedan ●

JERUSALEM ●

JORDAN

An Nafud

KUWAIT
KUWAIT ●

Shiraz ●

Bandar-e 'Abbas ●

Thar Desert

Indus Fan

Euphrates

Mediterranean Sea

Tropic of Cancer

Nile

MANAMA ●

BAHRAIN

RIYADH ●

The Gulf

Dubai ●

DOHA ●

QATAR

ABU DHABI ●

U.A.E.

MUSCAT ●

Sur ●

Gulf of Oman

Murray Ridge

Ganges

Ganges Fan

SAUDI ARABIA

Arabian Peninsula

Red Sea

At Ta'if ●

Ar Rub' al Khali

OMAN

Bay of Bengal

Mek

A F R I C A

SANA ●

YEMEN

Ta'iz ●

Aden ●

Gulf of Aden

Socotra (part of Yemen)

Arabian Sea

20°
40°
B
60°
C
80°
D
100°

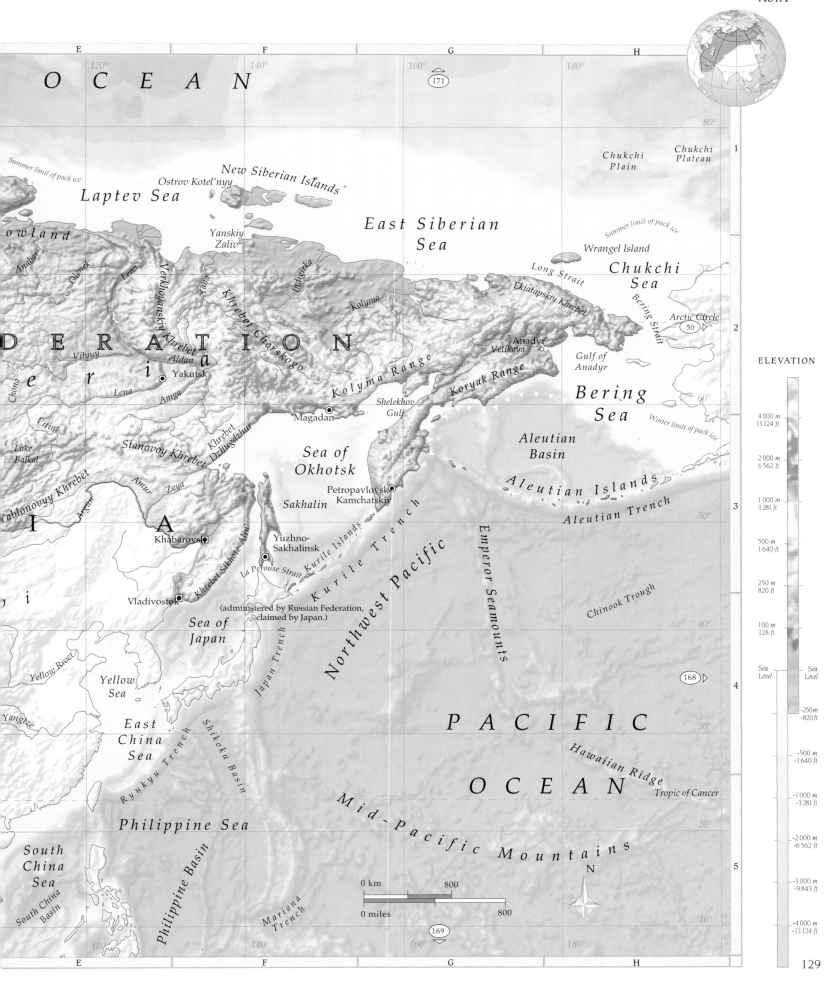

O C E A N

120°   140°   160°   180°

171

80°

1

*Chukchi
Plain*   *Chukchi
Plateau*

Summer limit of pack ice

New Siberian Islands

Ostrov Kotel'nyy

Laptev Sea

*East Siberian
Sea*

Summer limit of pack ice

Wrangel Island

owland

Anabar

*Yanskiy
Zaliv*

Long Strait   *Chukchi
Sea*   70°

Olenek   *Lena*   *Yana*   *Indigirka*   *Kolyma*   *Ekiatapskiy Khrebet*   *Bering Strait*

Verkhoyanskiy Khrebet   *Khrebet Cherskogo*   *Arctic Circle*
50   ▷

2

DERATION   *Vilyuy*   *Aldan*   *Anadyr'*
Velikaya

*Gulf of
Anadyr*

eri   *a*   ⊙ *Yakutsk*   *Kolyma Range*   *Koryak Range*   *Bering
Sea*   60°

Lena   *Amga*   *Shelekhov
Gulf*

Vitim   ◉ *Magadan*

Winter limit of pack ice

Lake
Baikal   *Stanovoy Khrebet*   *Khrebet
Dzhugdzhur*   *Sea of
Okhotsk*   *Aleutian
Basin*

Kablonovyy Khrebet   *Amur*   *Zeya*   ◉ *Petropavlovsk-
Kamchatskiy*   *Aleutian Islands*

Aleutian Trench   50°   3

I   A   *Khabarovsk* ▣   *Sakhalin*   *Kurile Islands*

*Yuzhno-
Sakhalinsk*   *Emperor Seamounts*

Khrebet Sikhote Alin   *Kurile Trench*   *Northwest Pacific*

La Perouse Strait   *Chinook Trough*

Vladivostok ◉   (administered by Russian Federation,
claimed by Japan.)   40°

*Sea of
Japan*   *Japan Trench*

PACIFIC   30°

*East
China
Sea*   *Hawaiian Ridge*

Shikoku Basin

Ryukyu Trench   OCEAN

*Yellow
Sea*   *Tropic of Cancer*

168   ▷

Philippine Sea   *Mid-Pacific Mountains*   20°

*South
China
Sea*   N   5

Philippine Basin   0 km   800

0 miles   800

*Mariana
Trench*   10°

169

120°   140°   160°   180°

E   F   G   H

ELEVATION

4 000 m
13 124 ft

2 000 m
6 562 ft

1 000 m
3 281 ft

500 m
1 640 ft

250 m
820 ft

100 m
328 ft

Sea
Level   Sea
Level

-250 m
-820 ft

-500 m
-1 640 ft

-1 000 m
-3 281 ft

-2 000 m
-6 562 ft

-3 000 m
-9 843 ft

-4 000 m
-13 124 ft

129

RUSSIA & KAZAKHSTAN

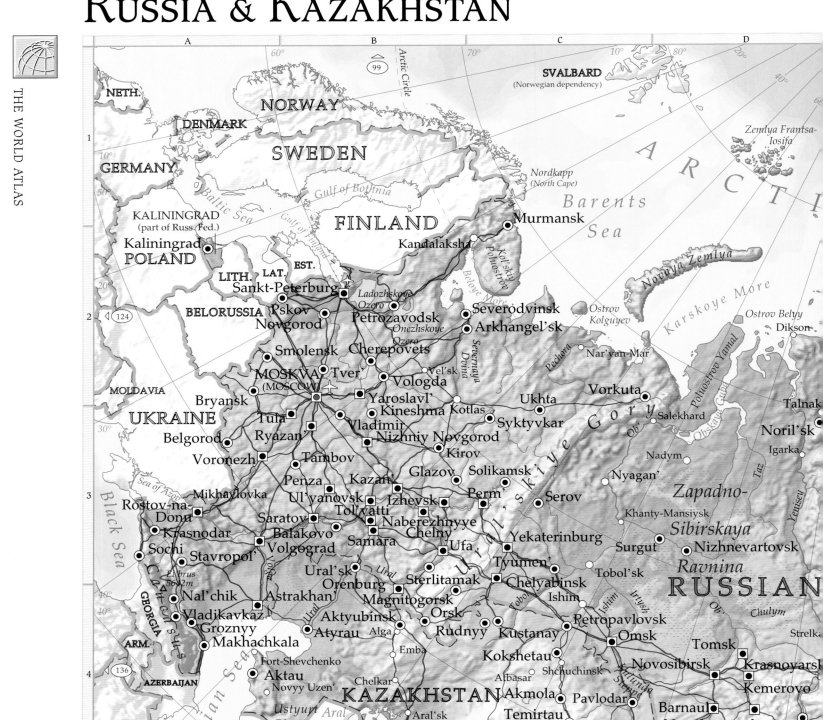

SVALBARD
(Norwegian dependency)

NORWAY

DENMARK

SWEDEN

GERMANY

FINLAND

Zemlya Frantsa-
Iosifa

Murmansk

Barents
Sea

ARCTI

Kandalaksha

Nordkapp
(North Cape)

Novaya Zemlya

KALININGRAD
(part of Russ. Fed.)

Kaliningrad
POLAND

Ostrov
Kolguyev

Karskoye More

LITH. LAT. EST.
Sankt-Peterburg
Ladozhskoye
Ozero

Severodvinsk
Arkhangel'sk

Ostrov Belyy

Dikson

BELORUSSIA
Pskov
Novgorod

Petrozavodsk
Onezhskoye
Ozero

Beloye More

Severnaya Dvina

Nar'yan-Mar

Poluostrov Yamal

Smolensk
Cherepovets
Vel'sk
Vologda

Ukhta

Vorkuta

Talnak

MOSKVA
(MOSCOW) Tver'

Yaroslavl'
Kineshma
Kotlas

Syktyvkar

Salekhard

Obskaya Guba

Noril'sk

MOLDAVIA
Bryansk
Belgorod

Tula
Ryazan'

Vladimir
Nizhniy Novgorod

Kirov
Glazov

Solikamsk

Igarka

UKRAINE

Voronezh

Tambov

Penza

Kazan'

Izhevsk
Perm'

Serov

Nadym

Nyagan'

Zapadno-

Sibirskaya

Sea of Azov
Mikhaylovka
Rostov-na-
Donu

Ul'yanovsk
Tol'yatti
Saratov
Naberezhnyye
Chelny

Khanty-Mansiysk

Krasnodar
Balakovo
Volgograd
Samara

Ufa
Chelyabinsk

Yekaterinburg
Tyumen'

Surgut

Nizhnevartovsk

Ravnina

Sochi
Stavropol'

Ural'sk

Sterlitamak

Tobol'sk

RUSSIAN

El'brus
5642m

Nal'chik

Astrakhan'
Orenburg
Magnitogorsk

Ishim
Chulym

GEORGIA
Vladikavkaz
Grozny
Makhachkala

Aktyubinsk
Orsk

Alga
Emba

Rudnyy

Petropavlovsk

Kustanay
Omsk

Tomsk

Strelk

Black
Sea

Caspian Sea

ARM.

AZERBAIJAN

Fort-Shevchenko
Aktau
Novyy Uzen'

Chelkar

Kokshetau
Shchuchinsk

Albasar

KAZAKHSTAN

Akmola
Pavlodar

Novosibirsk
Krasnoyars

Barnaul
Kemerovo

Novokuznetsk
Abaka

Ustyurt
Plateau

Aral
Sea

Aral'sk
Novokazalinsk

Syr Darya

Temirtau
Saran'
Karaganda

Kazakhskiy
Melkosopochnik

Semipalatinsk

Leninogorsk
Zyryanovsk

Kyzy

Zhezkazgan
Dzhusaly

Charsk

Ust'-Kamenogorsk

Gora Belukha
4506m

Kzyl-Orda

Balkhash

Ayaguz
Ozero
Zaysan

TURKMENISTAN

UZBEKISTAN

Kyzyl Kum

Turkestan
Kentau

Ozero
Balkhash

Altai
Mountains

Amu Darya

Shymkent
Arys'

Karatau
Shu

Taldykorgan
Tekeli

IRAN

Zhambyl

Kirghiz Range

ALMATY
(ALMA-ATA)

Zapadnyy

TAJIKISTAN
KYRGYZSTAN

CHINA

AFGHANISTAN

Tien Shan

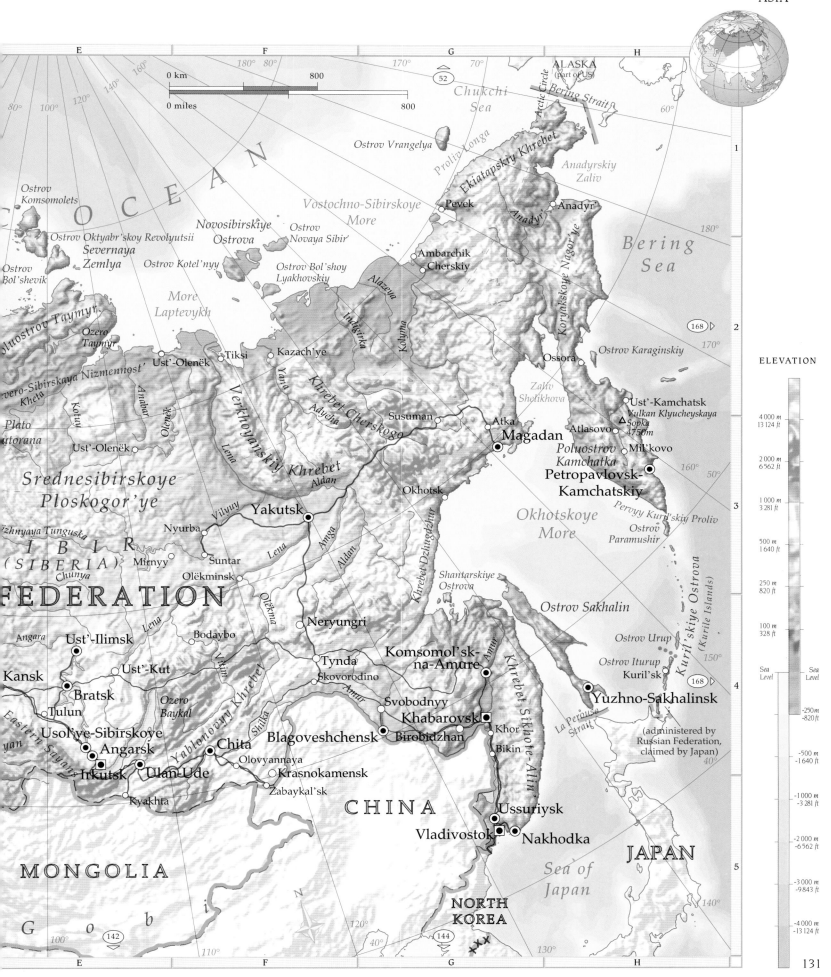

ALASKA
(part of US)

*Chukchi
Sea*

Bering Strait

Arctic Circle

70°

60°

180°

Ostrov Vrangelya

Proliv Longa

Ekiatapskiy Khrebet

*Anadyrskiy
Zaliv*

Pevek

Anadyr

*Vostochno-Sibirskoye
More*

Anadyr'

*Bering
Sea*

Ambarchik
Cherskiy

Alazeya

Kolyma

Koryakskoye Nagor'ye

168

170°

Ossora

Ostrov Karaginskiy

*Zaliv
Shelikhova*

Susuman

Ust'-Kamchatsk
*Vulkan Klyucheyskaya
Sopka
4750m*

△

Kazach'ye

Indigirka

Yana

Adycha

Khrebet Cherskogo

Atka

Magadan

Atlasovo

Mil'kovo

*Poluostrov
Kamchatka*

OCEAN

*Ostrov
Komsomolets*

Ostrov Oktyabr'skoy Revolyutsii
*Severnaya
Zemlya*

*Ostrov
Bol'shevik*

*Novosibirskiye
Ostrova*

*Ostrov
Novaya Sibir'*

Ostrov Kotel'nyy

*Ostrov Bol'shoy
Lyakhovskiy*

*More
Laptevykh*

oluostrov Taymyr

*Ozero
Taymyr*

vero-Sibirskaya Nizmennost'

Kheta

Kotuy

Anabar

Olenëk

Ust'-Olenëk

Tiksi

Lena

Verkhoyanskiy Khrebet

Aldan

Okhotsk

Petropavlovsk-
Kamchatskiy

160°

50°

*Okhotskoye
More*

Pervyy Kuril'skiy Proliv

*Ostrov
Paramushir*

*Plato
utorana*

Ust'-Olenëk

*Srednesibirskoye
Ploskogor'ye*

Yakutsk

Vilyuy

Nyurba

Lena

Amga

Aldan

Khrebet Dzhugdzhur

3

izhnyaya Tunguska

*I B I R
(S I B E R I A)*

Chunya

Mirnyy

Suntar

Olëkminsk

Shantarskiye
Ostrova

Ostrov Sakhalin

*Kuril'skiye Ostrova
(Kurile Islands)*

FEDERATION

Angara

Ust'-Ilimsk

Bodaybo

Neryungri

Ostrov Urup

Ostrov Iturup

Kuril'sk

150°

168

Kansk

Bratsk

Ust'-Kut

Olëkma

Vitim

Tynda

Skovorodino

Amur

Komsomol'sk-
na-Amure

Amur

Khrebet Sikhote-Alin'

Yuzhno-Sakhalinsk

4

Tulun

*Ozero
Baykal*

Yablonovyy Khrebet

Shilka

Svobodnyy

Khabarovsk

La Perouse
Strait

(administered by
Russian Federation,
claimed by Japan)

Usol'ye-Sibirskoye
Angarsk

Chita

Blagoveshchensk

Birobidzhan

Khor

yan

Eastern Sayans

Irkutsk

Ulan-Ude

Olovyannaya

Bikin

Krasnokamensk

Kyakhta

Zabaykal'sk

CHINA

Ussuriysk

40°

MONGOLIA

Vladivostok

Nakhodka

JAPAN

*Sea of
Japan*

**NORTH
KOREA**

G

o

b

i

N

142

100°

110°

144

40°

130°

120°

5

ELEVATION

4 000 m
13 124 ft

2 000 m
6 562 ft

1 000 m
3 281 ft

500 m
1 640 ft

250 m
820 ft

100 m
328 ft

Sea
Level

Sea
Level

-250 m
-820 ft

-500 m
-1 640 ft

-1 000 m
-3 281 ft

-2 000 m
-6 562 ft

-3 000 m
-9 843 ft

-4 000 m
-13 124 ft

0 km   800

0 miles   800

E   F   G   H

TURKEY & THE CAUCASUS

ROMANIA

UKRAINE

Lacul Razim
Lacul Sinoie

Kryms'kyy
Pivostriv

Danube

BULGARIA

Black Sea

Varnenski
Zaliv

Burgaski
Zaliv

Maritsa

Kırklareli
İnebolu · Sinop
· Gerze

Cide
Edirne · Bartın · *Küre Dağları* · Bafra
Çorlu · Zonguldak · Kastamonu · Samsun
Tekirdağ · İstanbul · Karabük · Kargı · Ünye
Karlışla Devrek · Çerkeş · *Anik Dağları* · Ordu

Ersene Nehri

İstanbul Boğazı
(Bosporus)

Bandırma · Yalova · İzmit · Adapazarı · Merzifon
Marmara Denizi · Bolu · Gerede · Çankırı
(Sea of Marmara) · *İznik Gölü* · *Kızıl Irmak* · Çorum

Çanakkale · Bursa · Bilecik · ANKARA · Kalecik · Tokat · Alaca · Yıldızeli
Çanakkale · Bozüyük · Eskişehir · Kırıkkale · Sorgun · Zara
Boğazı · Balıkesir · Polatlı · *T* · *U* · *R* · Şarkışla · Sivas
(Dardanelles) · Edremit · Kütahya · *Hirfanlı* · Boğazlıyan
Ayvalık · Simav · *Barajı*
Lésvos · Akhisar · Gediz · Kulu · *Tuz Gölü* · Bünyan
Chios · Manisa · Uşak · Afyon · Cihanbeyli · İncesu · Gürün
Menemen · *Gediz Nehri* · Nevşehir · Kayseri
İzmir · Akşehir · Aksaray · *Gün*
Sámos · Ödemiş · Alaşehir · *A* · Göksun
Aydın · Nazilli · Dinar · *n* · *a* · *t* · Niğde
Söke · *Büyükmenderes Nehri* · Denizli · *Beyşehir* · Konya · Kahramanmaraş
Milas · Tavas · Burdur · *Gölü* · İsparta · Ereğli
Bodrum · Muğla · *Burdur* · *Suğla Gölü* · Karaman · Ceyhan · Gaziantep
Gölü · *T* · Tarsus · Adana · Osmaniye
Marmaris · Dalaman · Antalya · Manavgat · *o* · *r* · Mersin · İskenderun · Kilis
Fethiye · Alanya · Mut · *o* · *s* · Antakya · Kırıkhan
Kaş · Finike · *Antalya* · *Dağları*
Körfezi · Silifke
Anamur

Dodecánese

Ródos
(Rhodes)

Kárpathos

CYPRUS

TURKISH REPUBLIC OF
NORTHERN CYPRUS
(recognised only by Turkey)

Orantes

Mediterranean
Sea

LEBANON

POPULATION

Less than
50,000
○

50,000 –
100,000
○

100,000 –
500,000
●

Over
500,000
◉

0 km   200

0 miles   200

RUSSIAN

FEDERATION

Caspian

Sea

Gagra
Gudaut'a
Sokhumi
Och'amch'ire

Abkhazia

Enguri
Mestia

Kazbek
5047m

Caucasus

Greater Caucasus

Xaçmaz

Quba
Siyäzän

K'ut'aisi
Samtredia
P'ot'i
K'obulet'i
Bat'umi
Hopa
Ajaria
Pazar
Rize
Of

South
Ossetia

GEORGIA

Lesser Caucasus

Gori
Tsalka
Akhalts'ikhe
Artvin

T'BILISI
Rust'avi

Zaqatala
Şäki

Şamaxı

Sumqayıt
BAKI
(BAKU)

Trabzon
Giresun
Gümüşhane

Doğu Karadeniz Dağları

Çoruh Nehri

İspir

Gyumri

Kars

Artik

Vanadzor

Sevan

ARMENIA

Sevana Lich

Gäncä
Mingäçevir
Yevlax

AZERBAIJAN

Nagornyy
Karabakh

Kura

Imişli

Qazimämmäd
Äli-Bayramı

Biläsuvar

Länkäran

Sarıkamış
Aşkale
Pasinler

Horasan

YEREVAN

Aras
Büyükağrı Dağı
(Mount Ararat)
5137 m

Artashat

AZERBAIJAN

Xankändi

Goris

Aras

Erzincan
Erzurum
Tercan

Ağrı

Doğubayazıt

Patnos

Naxçıvan

Kemah

Muradiye

Bingöl

Muş
Tatvan

Erciş

Van Gölü

Van

Daryācheh-ye Orūmīyeh

Reshteh-ye Kūhhā-ye Alborz
(Elburz Mountains)

Elazığ
Malatya

Doğu

Silvan

Bitlis

Gevaş

Siirt

IRAN

Adıyaman
Silverek
Diyarbakır

Toroslar

Batman

Mardin

Kurdistan

Şırnak

Viranşehir
Şanlıurfa
Ceylanpınar

Nusaybin

Ataturk Baraji

Tigris

Al Jazīrah

Euphrates

Jabal Bishrī

IRAQ

Buḥayrat ath Tharthār

Kūhhā-ye Zagros
(Zagros Mountains)

Keban Baraji

Buḥayrat al Asad

Euphrates (Fırat Nehri)

SYRIA

127
138
136
134
136

ELEVATION

4 000 m / 13 124 ft
2 000 m / 6 562 ft
1 000 m / 3 281 ft
500 m / 1 640 ft
250 m / 820 ft
100 m / 328 ft
Sea Level / Sea Level
-50 m / -164 ft
-100 m / -328 ft
-250 m / -820 ft
-500 m / -1 640 ft
-1 000 m / -3 281 ft
-2 000 m / -6 562 ft

THE NEAR EAST

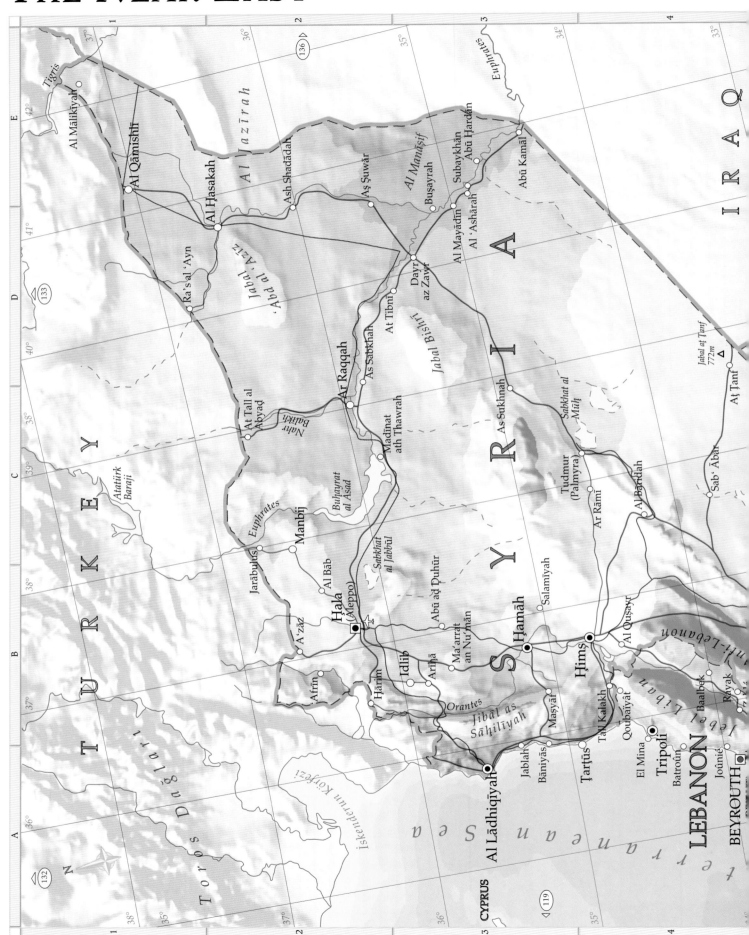

POPULATION

Less than
50,000
○

50,000 –
100,000
○

100,000 –
500,000
◉

Over
500,000
▣

134 ▣

E

D

C

B

A

T U R K E Y

S Y R I A

I R A Q

LEBANON

CYPRUS

Tigris

Al Mālikīyah

Al Qāmishlī

Al Ḥasakah

Ra's al 'Ayn

At Tall al Abyaḍ

Manbij

Jarābulus

A'zāz

Afrīn

Ḥārim

Idlib

Arīḥā

Ḥalab
(Aleppo)

Al Bāb

Abū aḍ Ḍuhūr

Ma'arrat an Nu'mān

Al Jazīrah

Ash Shadādah

Aṣ Şuwār

Al Manājif

Busayrah

Subaykhān

Abū Ḥardān

Abū Kamāl

Al Mayādīn

Al 'Ashārah

Dayr az Zawr

At Tibnī

Ar Raqqah

As Sabkhah

Madīnat ath Thawrah

Jabal 'Abd al 'Azīz

Jabal Bishrī

Nahr Balīkh

Euphrates

Euphrates

Buḥayrat al Asad

Sabkhat al Jabbūl

Atatürk Barajı

As Sukhnah

Tudmur
(Palmyra)

Ar Rāmī

Al Bardah

Sabkhat al Māḥ

Sab' Ābār

Jabal aṭ Ṭanf
772m

Aṭ Ṭanf

Salamīyah

Ḥamāh

Ḥimṣ

Al Quṣayr

Masyāf

Orantes

Jibāl as Sāḥilīyah

Al Lādhiqīyah

Jablah

Bāniyās

Ṭarṭūs

Tall Kalakh

Qoubaïyât

El Mina

Tripoli

Batroûn

Baalbek

Râyak

Joûnié

BEYROUTH

Anti-Lebanon

Jebel Liban

Toros Dağları

İskenderun Körfezi

M e d i t e r r a n e a n   S e a

42°

41°

40°

39°

38°

37°

36°

37°

36°

35°

34°

33°

135°

1

2

3

4

N

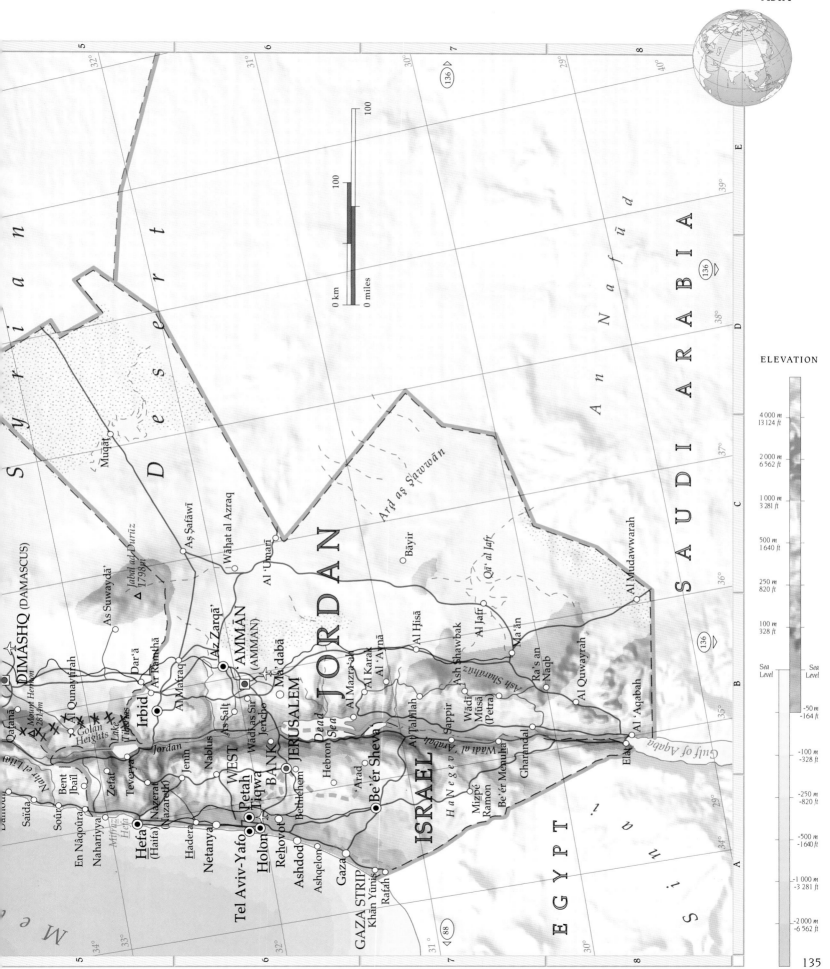

ELEVATION

4 000 m	13 124 ft
2 000 m	6 562 ft
1 000 m	3 281 ft
500 m	1 640 ft
250 m	820 ft
100 m	328 ft
Sea Level	Sea Level
-50 m	-164 ft
-100 m	-328 ft
-250 m	-820 ft
-500 m	-1640 ft
-1 000 m	-3 281 ft
-2 000 m	-6 562 ft

S y r i a n   D e s e r t

SAUDI ARABIA

A n   N a f ū d

Ard aş Şawwān

JORDAN

DIMASHQ (DAMASCUS)

As Suwaydā'

△ Jabal ad Durūz
1798 m

Muqāt

Aş Şafāwī

Wāhat al Azraq

Al 'Umarī

Bāyir

Qā' al Jafr

Al Mudawwarah

Dar'ā
Ar Ramthā
Al Mafraq
Az Zarqā'
ʻAMMAN (AMMAN)
Maʻdabā

Al Quwayfirah

Irbid

As Salt
Wādi as Sir
Jericho

Al Karak
Al Mazra'al
Al 'Aynā

Al Ḥşā

Ash Shawbak
Wādi Mūsā (Petra)

Al Jafr

Ma'ān

Ra's an Naqb

Al Quwayrah

Al Jafr

Mount Hermon

Qafana

Al Qunayfirah

Golan Heights
Lake Tiberias

Teverya

Zefat
Nazerat (Nazareth)

Jordan

Nablus

Jenin

WEST BANK

Petah Tiqwa

JERUSALEM
Bethlehem

Hebron

Arad

Be'ér Sheva

Dead Sea

At Tafīlah

Sappir

Aţ Ţalḩah

Gharandal

Be'ér Menuha

Mizpé Ramon

Elat
Al 'Aqabah

ISRAEL

H a N e g e v

Wādi al 'Arabā

Ash Sharāhtuz

Gulf of Aqaba

Saïda

Soûr

En Nâqoûra

Nahariyya

Hefa (Haifa)

Hadera

Netanya

Tel Aviv-Yafo
Holon
Rehovot

Ashdod

Ashqelon

Gaza

GAZA STRIP
Khān Yūnis
Rafah

EGYPT

Bent Jbaïl

Zefat

Nahr el Lītāni

Damoûr

M e   d   i   t   e   r   r   a   n   e   a   n

136 ▷

88 ◁

135

THE MIDDLE EAST

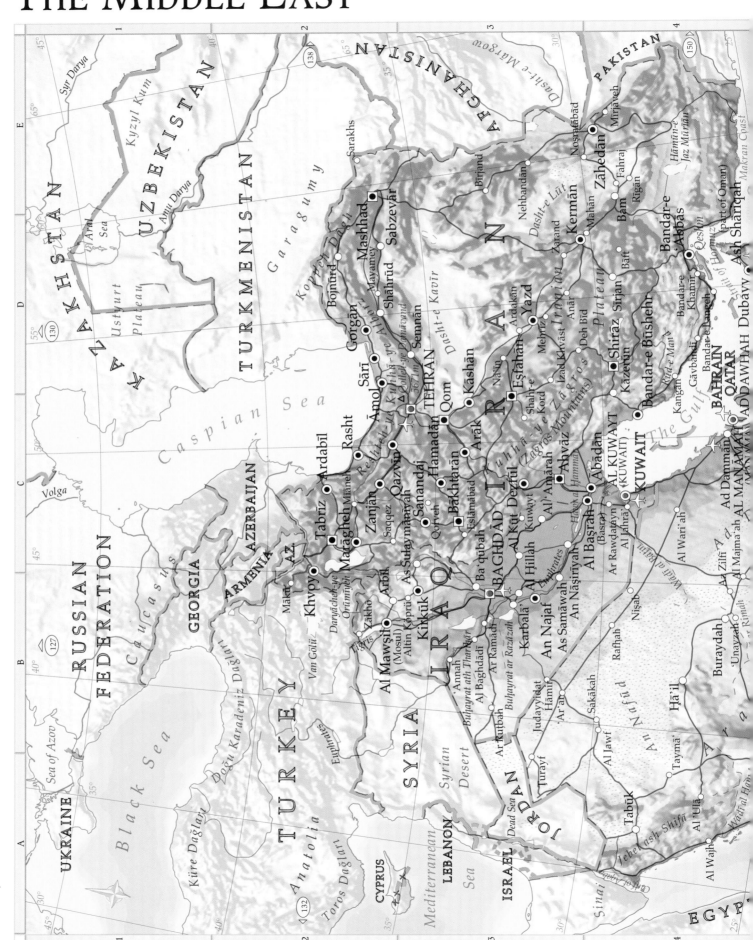

UKRAINE

RUSSIAN FEDERATION

KAZAKHSTAN

UZBEKISTAN

TURKMENISTAN

Kyzyl Kum

Syr Darya

Amu Darya

Aral Sea

Ustyurt Plateau

Garagumy

Koppeh Dāgh

AFGHANISTAN

PAKISTAN

Dasht-e Margow

Sarakhs

Sabzevār

Mashhad

Bojnūrd

Shāhrūd

Semnān

Gorgān

Mayāmey

Dasht-e Kavīr

Birjand

Nehbandān

Nosratābād

Mīrjāveh

Zāhedān

Fahraj

Rīgān

Bam

Mahān

Kermān

Zarand

Anār

Dasht-e Lūt

Bandar-e Abbās

Qeshm

Hāmūn-e Jāz Mūrīān

Makran Coast

Sārī

Āmol

Rasht

Ardabīl

Tabrīz

Maku

Khvoy

Zākho

Arbīl

Al Mawşil (Mosul)

Ardakān

Yazd

Naīn

Izad Khvāst

Deh Bid

Anār

Sīrjān

Bāft

Kermān

Bandar-e Lengeh

Khamīr

Gāvbandī

Kangān

Bandar-e Būshehr

Kāzerūn

Shīrāz

Shahr-e Kord

Eşfahān

Mehrīz

Iranian Plateau

Kūhhā-ye Zagros (Zagros Mountains)

Kūhhā-ye Hamma

Kūhhā-ye Kuhhā-ye

Qolleh-ye Damāvand 5671 m

TEHRAN

Qom

Kāshān

Hamadān

Arāk

Bākhtarān

Eslāmābād

Qorveh

Sanandaj

As Sulaymānīyah

Saqqez

Zanjān

Mīāneh

Marāgheh

Qazvīn

Daryācheh-ye Orūmīyeh

Altin Köprü

Kirkūk

Ba'qūbah

BAGHDĀD

Al Kūt

Al 'Amārah

Ahvāz

Dezfūl

Shūsh

Ābādān

AL KUWAYT (KUWAIT)

KUWAIT

Al Jahrā

Ar Rawdatayn

Ad Dammām

AL MANĀMAH

BAHRAIN

QATAR

AD DAWHAH

Dubayy

Ash Shāriqah

(part of Oman)

Strait of Hormuz

The Gulf

Rūd-e Mand

Al Wari'ah

Al Majma'ah

Al Majma'ah

Az Zilfī

Nişāb

Būraydah

'Unayzah

Ar Rimāh

Ḩā'il

An Nafūd

Ar Razāzah

Buḩayrat ar Razāzah

Buḩayrat ath Tharthār

Ar Ramādī

Ar Rutbah

Al Baghdādī

'Annah

Amrah

Al Ḩillah

Karbalā'

An Najaf

As Samāwah

An Nāşirīyah

Al Başrah (Basra)

Euphrates

Tigris

Euphrates

Sakākah

Hamīr

Judayyidat Ḩamīr

Ar'ar

Rafḩah

Al Jawf

Turayf

Ḩamī

Al Wajh

Al 'Ulā

Taymā'

Tabūk

Jebel ash Shifā

Sinai

Gulf of Aqaba

Dead Sea

Wadi al Bāṭin

Wādī al Ḩamḍ

JORDAN

ISRAEL

LEBANON

CYPRUS

SYRIA

Syrian Desert

IRAQ

TURKEY

Anatolia

Toros Dağları

Küre Dağları

Doğu Karadeniz Dağları

Van Gölü

Tigris

Euphrates

Doğu Karadeniz Dağları

Mediterranean Sea

Black Sea

Sea of Azov

Volga

Caucasus

GEORGIA

ARMENIA

AZERBAIJAN

AZ.

Caspian Sea

EGYPT

IRAN

45°

65°

60°

55°

50°

45°

40°

35°

30°

25°

35°

30°

40°

65°

35°

30°

(138)

(130)

(127)

(132)

(150)

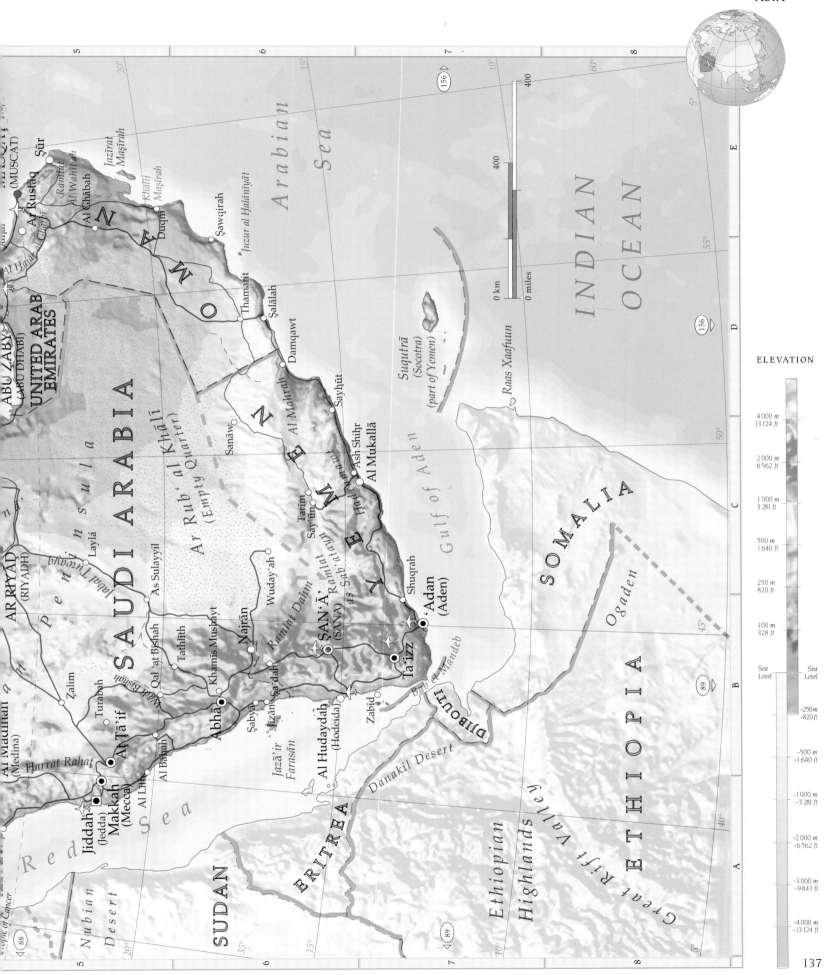

Arabian Sea

INDIAN OCEAN

5

6

7

8

MUSCAT

(MUSCAT) Şūr

Ar Rustāq

Ramlat
Al Wahībah

Jazīrat
Maşīrah

Al Ghābah

Khalīj
Maşīrah

Duqm

Şawqirah

Juzur al Halānīyāt

O M A N

Thamarīt

Şalālah

Damqawt

Sayḥūt

Suquṭrā
(Socotra)
(part of Yemen)

Raas Xaafuun

UNITED ARAB
EMIRATES

ABU ZABY
(ABU DHABI)

Al Hajar al Gharbī

Al Hajar al Gharbī

Sanāw

Al Mahrah

Ash Shiḥr
Al Mukallā

Ḥaḍ Mawt

S A U D I   A R A B I A

P e n i n s u l a

Ar Rub' al Khālī
(Empty Quarter)

Laylá

As Sulayyil

Wuday'ah

Ramlat Dahm

Tarīm
Sayʾūn

Y E M E N

SOMALIA

Gulf of Aden

Ar Rub' al Khālī

Jabal Tuwayq

Ogaden

AR RIYAD
(RIYADH)

Tathlīth

Najrān

Şa'dah

SAN'Ā'
(SANA)

Ramlat
as Sab'atayn

Shuqrah

Adan
(Aden)

Al Maḥālī

Khamīs Mushayt

Wadi Bīshah

Qal'at Bīshah

Abhā

Ta'izz

Bāb el Mandeb

DJIBOUTI

Al Madīnah
(Medina)

Zalim

Turabah

Aṭ Ṭā'if

Harrat Rahat

Şabyāʾ
Jīzān

Al Hudaydah
(Hodeida)

Zabīd

Bāb el Mandeb

ETHIOPIA

Great Rift Valley

Jiddah
(Jedda)

Makkah
(Mecca)

Al Lītḥ

Al Bāḥah

Jazāʾir
Farasān

ERITREA

Danakil Desert

Ethiopian
Highlands

Red   Sea

Nubian
Desert

SUDAN

Tropic of Cancer

88

89

156

156

89

ELEVATION

ELEVATION
4 000 m 13 124 ft
2 000 m 6 562 ft
1 000 m 3 281 ft
500 m 1 640 ft
250 m 820 ft
100 m 328 ft
Sea Level · Sea Level
-250 m -820 ft
-500 m -1 640 ft
-1 000 m -3 281 ft
-2 000 m -6 562 ft
-3 000 m -9 843 ft
-4 000 m -13 124 ft

0 km   400

0 miles   400

CENTRAL ASIA

RUSSIAN
FEDERATION

GEORGIA

AZERBAIJAN

*Caspian
Sea*

*Ustyurt
Plateau*

*Aral
Sea*

Müynoq

Chimboy
Takhtakŭpir

Kĕneurgench
Nukus
Takhiatosh
Gubadag
Il'yaly
Urganch
Dashkhovuz
Türtkŭl
Khiwa
Gaz-Achak
Lebap
Zarafshon

Uchquduq

UZBEKIS

Turan   Lowland

Kyzyl

Amu Darya

Turkmenbashi

*Krasnovodskiy
Zaliv*
Cheleken

Nebitdag

Gazandzhyk

*Turkmenskiy
Zaliv*

*Zaunguzskiye
Garagumy*

Darvaza

Gazli

Ghijduwon
Bukhoro

Seydi
Deynau
Kogon

Chardzhev

Plato Kaplangky
Peski Uchtagan

TURKMENISTAN

Gyzylarbat
Kara-Kala
Bakharden

Kopetdag Gershi

Byuzmeyin
Geok-Tepe
*Gora Chapan
2889m*
△ **ASHGABAT**

Kaakhka
Tedzhen
Mary
Bayramaly
Sayat

Garagumy

*Kelifskiy
Garagumskiy Kana*
Uzboy

Murgab
Serakhs

Murgab

Andkhvo

*Vozvyshennost'
Karabil'*

Reshteh-ye Kūhhā-ye Alborz

Bālā Morghāb
Gushgy
Towraghoudī

Daryā-ye Morghāb

Meymaneh

Selseleh-ye Safid Kūh

Ghūriān

Herāt

AFGHAN

Shīndand

IRAN

*Iranian

Plateau*

Kūhhā-ye Zāgros

Farāh Rūd

Farāh
Delārām

Gereshk

Dasht-e Khāsh

*Hāmūn-e
Şāberī*
Chakhānsūr
Zaranj

Lashkar Gāh

Kūchnay
Darweyshā

Dasht-e Mārgow

Deh Shū

Daryā-ye Helmand

Rigestān

Chāgai Hills

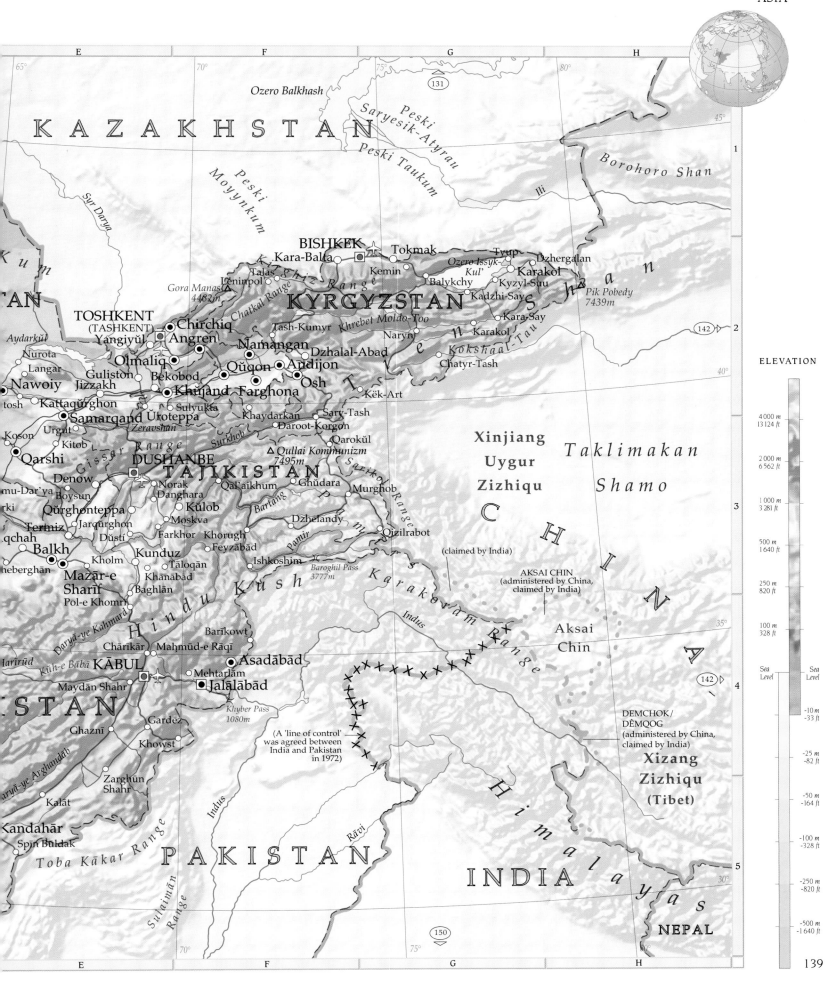

KAZAKHSTAN

Ozero Balkhash

Peski Saryesik-Atyrau

Peski Taukum

131

Peski Moyynkum

Ili

Borohoro Shan

Syr Darya

Peski Moyynkum

BISHKEK
Kara-Balta
Tokmak
Tyup
Dzhergalan

Talas
Kemin
Ozero Issyk-Kul'
Karakol

Leninpol
Balykchy
Kyzyl-Suu

Gora Manas 4482m
Kadzhi-Say
Kara-Say

KYRGYZSTAN
Naryn
Karakol
Pik Pobedy 7439m

TOSHKENT
(TASHKENT)
Chirchiq
Tash-Kumyr
Khrebet Moldo-Too
Chatyr-Tash
Kokshaal-Tau

Yangiyŭl
Angren
Namangan
Dzhalal-Abad

Nurota
Olmaliq
Qŭqon
Andijon

Langar
Guliston
Bekobod
Osh

Nawoiy
Jizzakh
Khŭjand
Farghona

tosh
Kattaqŭrghon
Sulyukta
Kĕk-Art

Samarqand
Ŭroteppa
Khaydarkan
Sary-Tash

Urgut
Zeravshan
Daroot-Korgon

Koson
Kitob
Qarokŭl

Gissar Range
Surkhob
Xinjiang Uygur Zizhiqu
Taklimakan Shamo

Qarshi
Range
△ *Qullai Kommunizm 7495m*

Denow
DUSHANBE
Norak
Qal'aikhum
Ghŭdara
Murghob
C
H

mu-Dar'ya
Boysun
TAJIKISTAN
Sarikol Range

rki
Qŭrghonteppa
Danghara
Bartang
I

qchah
Jarqŭrghon
Kŭlob
Dzhelandy
Pamir
Qizilrabot
N

Termiz
Dŭstí
Moskva
(claimed by India)

Balkh
Farkhor
Khorugh
A

heberghan
Kholm
Kunduz
Tāloqān
Feyzābād
AKSAI CHIN (administered by China, claimed by India)

Mazār-e Sharīf
Khānābād
Ishkoshim
Baroghil Pass 3777m
Karakoram Range
Aksai Chin

Pol-e Khomrí
Baghlān
Hindu Kush
Indus

Daryā-ye Kahmard
X
Aksai Chin

Chārīkār
Mahmūd-e Rāqí
Barīkowt
A

larīrūd
Kūh-e Bābā
KĀBUL
Asadābād
142

Maydān Shahr
Mehtarlām
142

Jalālābād
DEMCHOK/DÊMQOG (administered by China, claimed by India)

Ghaznī
Gardēz
Khyber Pass 1080m
Xizang Zizhiqu (Tibet)

Khowst
(A 'line of control' was agreed between India and Pakistan in 1972)

Zarghūn Shahr

Kalāt

Kandahār
Spīn Būldak
Indus
Ravi
Himalayas

Toba Kākar Range
PAKISTAN
INDIA

Sulaimān Range
150
NEPAL

ELEVATION

4000 m	13 124 ft
2000 m	6 562 ft
1000 m	3 281 ft
500 m	1 640 ft
250 m	820 ft
100 m	328 ft
Sea Level	Sea Level
-10 m	-33 ft
-25 m	-82 ft
-50 m	-164 ft
-100 m	-328 ft
-250 m	-820 ft
-500 m	-1 640 ft

SOUTH & EAST ASIA

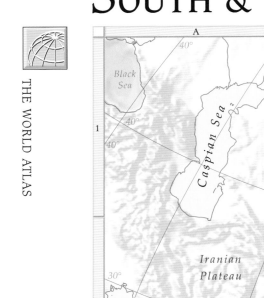

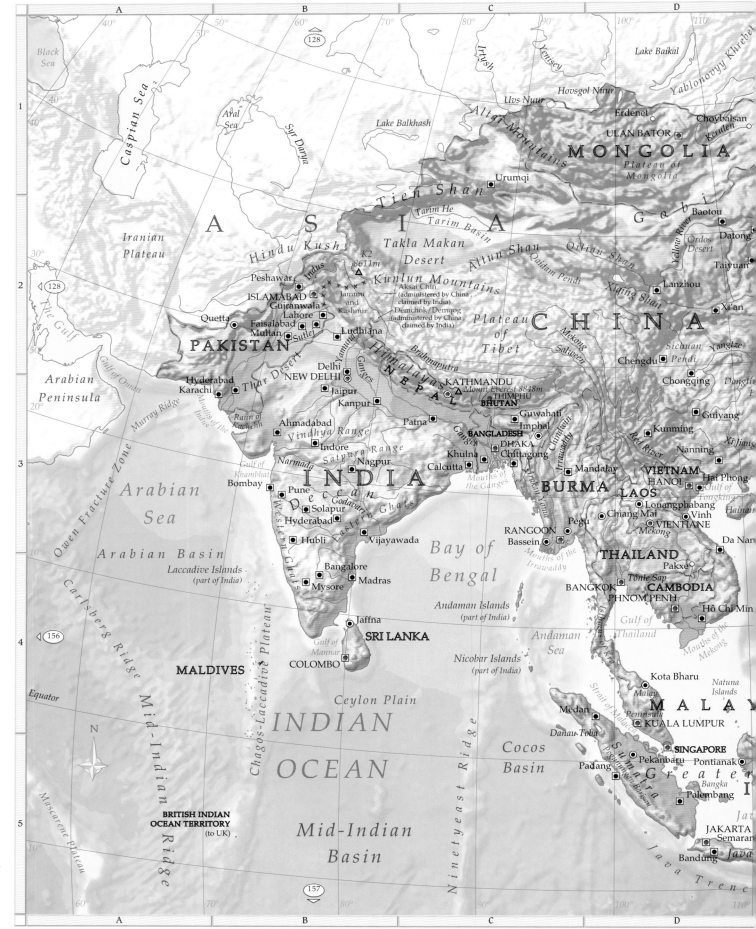

Black Sea

Caspian Sea

Aral Sea

Lake Balkhash

Lake Baikal

Irtysh

Yenisey

Hovsgol Nuur

Uvs Nuur

Altai Mountains

Erdenet

Choybalsan

ULAN BATOR

Kerulen

Yablonovyy Khrebet

MONGOLIA

Plateau of Mongolia

Urumqi

Gobi

Baotou

Datong

Ordos Desert

Taiyuan

Yellow River

Tien Shan

Tarim He

Tarim Basin

Takla Makan Desert

K2 8611m

Kunlun Mountains

Altun Shan

Qilian Shan

Xiqing Shan

Lanzhou

Xi'an

Qaidam Pendi

Plateau of Tibet

CHINA

Chengdu

Sichuan Pendi

Yangtze

Mekong

Salween

Chongqing

Dongting

Guiyang

A S I A

Iranian Plateau

Hindu Kush

Indus

Peshawar

ISLAMABAD

Jammu and Kashmir

Aksai Chin (administered by China, claimed by India)

Demchok/Demqog (administered by China, claimed by India)

Gujranwala

Lahore

Quetta

Faisalabad

Multan

Sutlej

Ludhiana

PAKISTAN

The Gulf

Gulf of Oman

Arabian Peninsula

Hyderabad

Karachi

Thar Desert

Murray Ridge

Mouths of the Indus

Rann of Kachchh

Delhi

NEW DELHI

Jaipur

Kanpur

Yamuna

Ganges

NEPAL

Himalayas

KATHMANDU

Mount Everest 8848m

THIMPHU

BHUTAN

Brahmaputra

Guwahati

Imphal

Kunming

Nanning

Xijiang

Guiyang

Ahmadabad

Vindhya Range

Patna

Ganges

BANGLADESH

DHAKA

Chittagong

Khulna

Chindwin

Mandalay

Irrawaddy

Red River

Owen Fracture Zone

Arabian Sea

Arabian Basin

Laccadive Islands (part of India)

Carlsberg Ridge

Mid-Indian Ridge

Mascarene Plateau

Indore

Satpura Range

Nagpur

Narmada

Godavari

Calcutta

Mouths of the Ganges

INDIA

Bombay

Pune

Deccan

Solapur

Hyderabad

Hubli

Western Ghats

Eastern Ghats

Vijayawada

Arakan Yoma

BURMA

Pegu

RANGOON

Bassein

Mouths of the Irrawaddy

VIETNAM

HANOI

Hai Phong

Gulf of Tongking

Hainan

LAOS

Louangphabang

Chiang Mai

Vinh

VIENTIANE

Mekong

Da Nang

THAILAND

Pakxe

Tônlé Sap

BANGKOK

CAMBODIA

PHNOM PENH

Hô Chi Minh

Gulf of Thailand

Mouths of the Mekong

Bay of Bengal

Andaman Islands (part of India)

Andaman Sea

Isthmus of Kra

Strait of Kra

Bangalore

Madras

Mysore

Jaffna

SRI LANKA

Gulf of Mannar

COLOMBO

MALDIVES

Nicobar Islands (part of India)

Ceylon Plain

INDIAN

OCEAN

Equator

N

Chagos-Laccadive Plateau

Ninetyeast Ridge

Cocos Basin

Mid-Indian Basin

BRITISH INDIAN OCEAN TERRITORY (to UK)

Kota Bharu

Natuna Islands

Malay Peninsula

Medan

Danau Toba

Strait of Malacca

M A L A Y

KUALA LUMPUR

SINGAPORE

Pekanbaru

Pontianak

Padang

Sumatra

Pegunungan Barisan

Greater

Bangka

Palembang

Java

JAKARTA

Semarang

Bandung

Java Trench

Java Sea

POPULATION

Less than 50,000 ○

50,000 – 100,000 ○

100,000 – 500,000 ◉

Over 500,000 ●

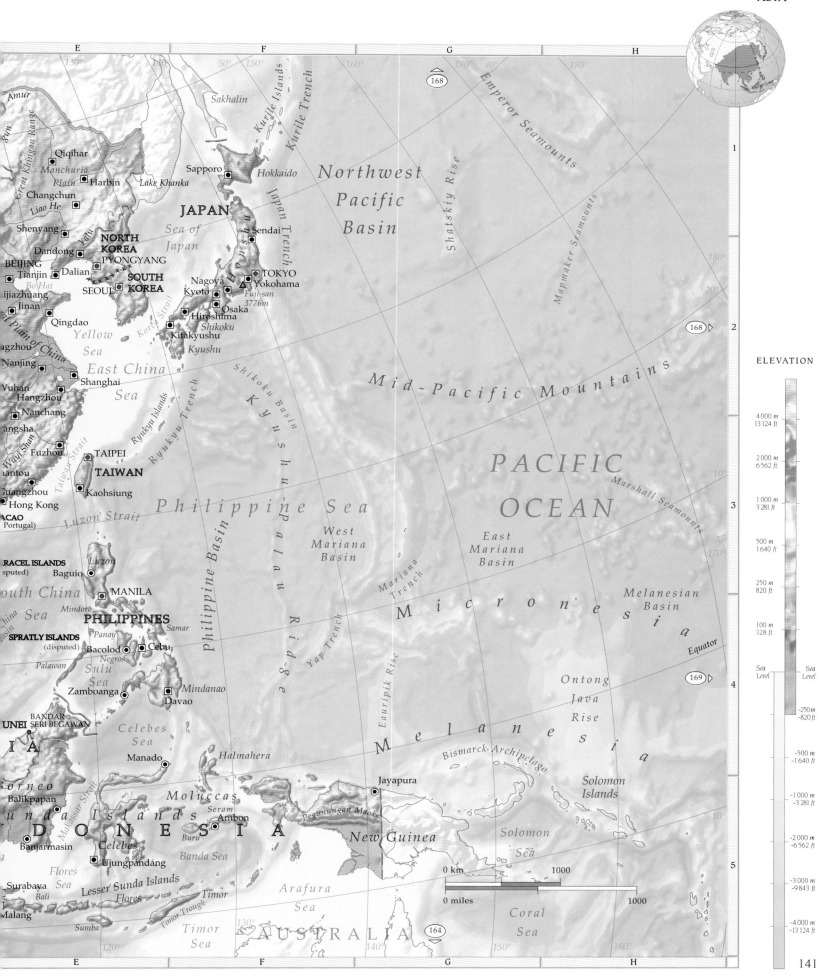

E   F   50°   150°   G   40°   180°   H   30°   1

Amur   Qiqihar   *Sakhalin*   Kurile Islands   Kurile Trench   168

Great Khingan Range   *Manchuria Plain*   Harbin   Sapporo   *Hokkaido*   *Northwest Pacific Basin*   *Shatskiy Rise*   *Emperor Seamounts*

Changchun   *Lake Khanka*
Liao He

Shenyang   **JAPAN**   *Sea of Japan*

NORTH KOREA   Sendai   *Honshū*   *Japan Trench*   180°
Dandong   **PYONGYANG**

BEIJING   **SOUTH KOREA**   Nagoya   Yokohama   20°
Tianjin   Dalian   Kyoto   TOKYO   168
ijiazhuang   **SEOUL**   Osaka   *Fuji-san 3776m*
Jinan   *Bo Hai*   Hiroshima   *Shikoku*
Qingdao   *Yellow Sea*   Kitakyushu   *Kyushu*   2

Plain of China   *Kōra Strait*   *East China Sea*   *Shikoku Basin*   *Mid-Pacific Mountains*
agzhou
Nanjing   Shanghai
Vuhan   Hangzhou   *Ryukyu Islands*   *Kyushu-Palau Ridge*
Nanchang   *Ryukyu Trench*
angsha   *Wuyi Shan*   **PACIFIC**   *Marshall Seamounts*   10°
Fuzhou   **TAIPEI**   **OCEAN**
antou   *Taiwan Strait*   **TAIWAN**   3
Guangzhou   Kaohsiung   *Philippine Sea*
Hong Kong   *Luzon Strait*   *West Mariana Basin*   *East Mariana Basin*   170°
ACAO (Portugal)

RACEL ISLANDS (sputed)   Baguio   *Luzon*   *Mariana Trench*   *Melanesian Basin*   250°
uth China   MANILA   **M i c r o n e s i a**   Equator
Sea   *Mindoro*   **PHILIPPINES**   *Samar*
SPRATLY ISLANDS (disputed)   *Panay*   Bacolod   Cebu   *Philippine Basin*   *Yap Trench*   169   4
hina   *Negros*   *Eauripik Rise*   *Ontong Java Rise*
Palawan   *Sulu Sea*   Zamboanga   *Mindanao*   Davao   **M e l a n e s i a**

UNEI   **BANDAR SERI BEGAWAN**   *Celebes Sea*   Manado   *Halmahera*   *Bismarck Archipelago*   *Solomon Islands*
IA   Jayapura

orneo   Balikpapan   *Moluccas*   *Seram*   *Solomon Sea*
unda Islands   *Makassar Strait*   Ambon   *Pegunungan Maoke*
N D O N E S I A   *Burú*   *New Guinea*   5
Banjarmasin   *Celebes*   *Banda Sea*
Surabaya   Ujungpandang   *Flores Sea*   *Lesser Sunda Islands*   *Flores*   *Timor*   *Arafura Sea*   0 km   1000
Bali   *Sumba*   *Timor Trough*   0 miles   1000
Malang   *Timor Sea*   **AUSTRALIA**   164   *Coral Sea*

E   120°   F   130°   140°   G   150°   H   160°

ELEVATION

4000 m / 13124 ft
2000 m / 6562 ft
1000 m / 3281 ft
500 m / 1640 ft
250 m / 820 ft
100 m / 328 ft
Sea Level / Sea Level
-250 m / -820 ft
-500 m / -1640 ft
-1000 m / -3281 ft
-2000 m / -6562 ft
-3000 m / -9843 ft
-4000 m / -13124 ft

RUSSIAN FED

Yenisey

Kulunda Steppe

Zapadnyy Sayan

Hövsgöl Nuur

KAZAKHSTAN

Kazakhskiy

Melkosopochnik

Ozero Zaysan

Uvs Nuur

Ulaangom

Ölgiy • Mörön

Altay

Ozero Balkhash

Hyargas Nuur

Charus Nuur

Hovd • *Har Nuur*

Tsetserleg

Hangayn Nuruu

MONGO

Karamay

Ullungur Hu

Gurbantünggüt Shamo

Altay • Bayanhongor

Kuytun

Yining Shihezi Fukang Jimsar

Ürümqi Qitai

△ Aj Bogd Uul 3802m

Atas Bogd △ 2702m **G**

KYRGYZSTAN

Ozero Issyk-Kul'

Tien Shan Turpan

Turpan Pendi Hami

△ Pik Pobedy 7439m

Korla *Bosten Hu* Xingxingxia Ejin Qi

Kuruktag

TAJIKISTAN

Kashi *Tarim He Tarim Basin*

Lop Nur **GANSU**

Yengisar **XINJIANG UYGUR** *Qilian Shan*

AFGH. Shache **ZIZHIQU**

Yecheng (claimed by India) Ruoqiang

Pishan *Taklimakan* *Altun Shan Danghe Nanshan Qinghai Hu*

Moyu *Shamo*

Hotan *Qaidam Pendi*

PAKISTAN Qira △ K2 8611m *Kunlun Shan*

Karakoram Range Golmud *Burhan Budai Shan* Dulan

AKSAI CHIN *Anyemaqen Sha*

Kashmir AKSAI CHIN (administered by China, claimed by India) **C**

Indus **QINGHAI**

JAMMU AND KASHMIR *Qingzang Gaoyuan* (Plateau of Tibet) *Tongtian He* *Bayan Har Shan*

Rutog

DEMCHOK/ DÊMQOG (administered by China, claimed by India) Yushu

Gar **XIZANG** *Tanggula Shan* *Mekong*

Zanda Nyima Amdo

ZIZHIQU *Siling Co* Qamdo

Tangra Yumco *Gyaring Co* Nagqu *Salween*

(**Tibet**) *Ngangzê Co* *Nam Co* Damxung *Jinsha Jiang*

NEPAL *Brahmaputra* *Nyainqêntanglha Shan* *Hengduan Shan*

Yamuna *Ganges* Lhazê Xigazê Maizhokunggar **ARUNACHAL PRADESH** (claimed by China)

Lhasa

Gonggar Gyangzê

△ Mount Everest 8848m

INDIA **BHUTAN** **INDIA** **BURMA**

POPULATION

Less than 50,000 ○

50,000 – 100,000 ○

100,000 – 500,000 ◉

Over 500,000 ◼

0 km 400

0 miles 400

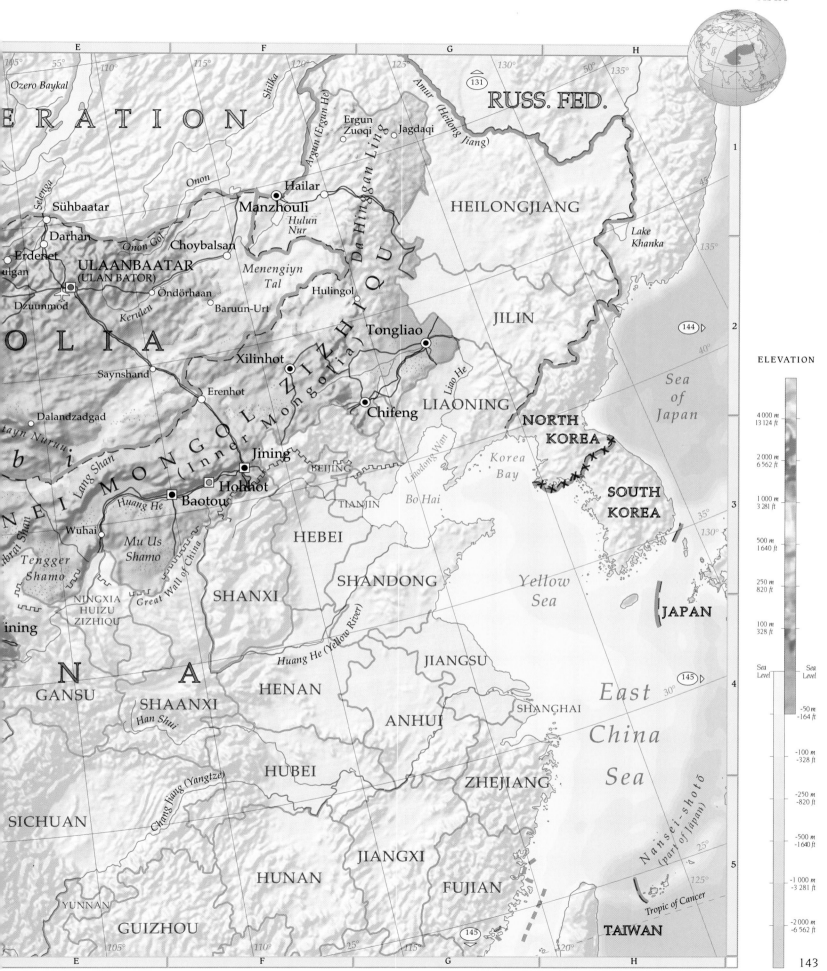

RUSS. FED.

E   55°   110°   115°   F   120°   125°   G   130°   50°   135°   H

105°

Ozero Baykal

ERATION

Shilka

131

Amur (Heilong Jiang)

1

Onon

Ergun Zuoqi

Jagdaqi

Selenga

Argun (Ergun He)

45°

Sühbaatar

Hailar

Manzhouli

HEILONGJIANG

Darhan

Onon Gol

Choybalsan

Hulun Nur

Da Hinggan Ling

135°

Erdenet

ULAANBAATAR (ULAN BATOR)

Lake Khanka

ulgan

Menengiyn Tal

JILIN

Dzuunmod

Öndörhaan

Kerulen

Hulingol

144

OLIA

Baruun-Urt

Tongliao

40°

Xilinhot

Saynshand

(Inner Mongolia)

Erenhot

Chifeng

LIAONING

NEI MONGOL ZIZHIQU

Sea of Japan

Dalandzadgad

NORTH KOREA

tayn Nuruu

Liao He

Lang Shan

Jining

Liaodong Wan

Korea Bay

SOUTH KOREA

b i

Hohhot

BEIJING

Huang He

Baotou

35°

Wuhai

TIANJIN

Bo Hai

3

130°

ibrai Shan

Mu Us Shamo

HEBEI

Tengger Shamo

Great Wall of China

JAPAN

NINGXIA HUIZU ZIZHIQU

SHANDONG

ining

SHANXI

N   A

Huang He (Yellow River)

GANSU

HENAN

JIANGSU

145

East

30°

SHAANXI

4

Han Shui

ANHUI

SHANGHAI

China

HUBEI

Chang Jiang (Yangtze)

ZHEJIANG

Sea

SICHUAN

JIANGXI

25°

Nansei-shotō (part of Japan)

5

HUNAN

FUJIAN

125°

YUNNAN

105°

110°

Tropic of Cancer

115°

25°

120°

GUIZHOU

145

TAIWAN

E   F   G   H

ELEVATION

4 000 m	
13 124 ft	
2 000 m	
6 562 ft	
1 000 m	
3 281 ft	
500 m	
1 640 ft	
250 m	
820 ft	
100 m	
328 ft	
Sea Level	Sea Level
-50 m	
-164 ft	
-100 m	
-328 ft	
-250 m	
-820 ft	
-500 m	
-1 640 ft	
-1 000 m	
-3 281 ft	
-2 000 m	
-6 562 ft	

EASTERN CHINA & KOREA

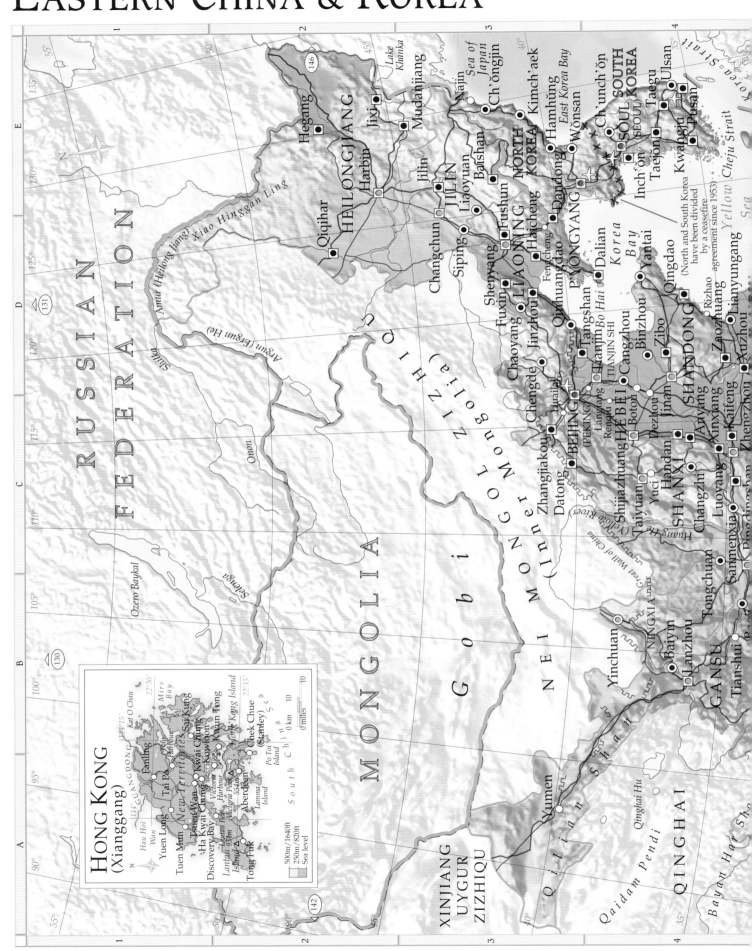

POPULATION

Less than
50,000

50,000 –
100,000

100,000 –
500,000

Over
500,000

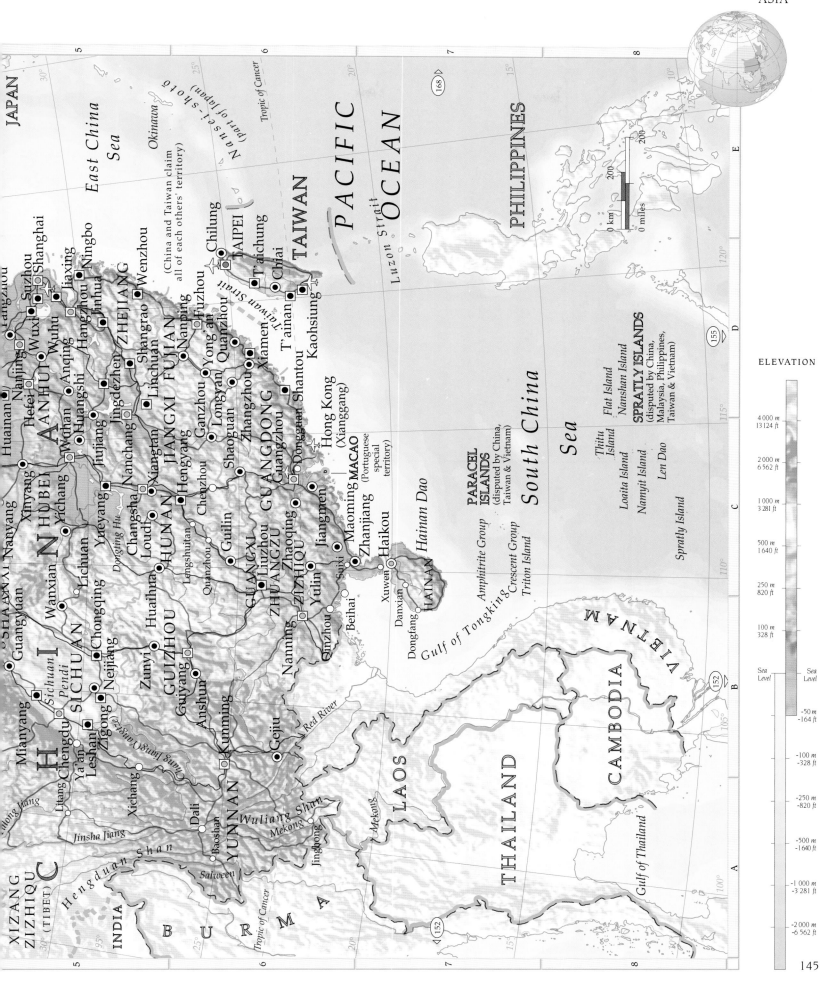

JAPAN

East China Sea

Okinawa

Nansei-shoto (part of Japan)

Tropic of Cancer

(China and Taiwan claim all of each others' territory)

Chilung
TAIPEI
T'aichung
Chiai
T'ainan
Kaohsiung

TAIWAN

Taiwan Strait

PACIFIC

OCEAN

Luzon Strait

PHILIPPINES

Huainan
Nanjing
Hefei
Xinyang
Wuxi (Wuhu)
Suzhou
Wuhu
Shanghai
Jiaxing
Hangzhou
Jinhua
Ningbo
Wenzhou
Shangrao

SHAANXI
Nanyang
HUBEI
ANHUI
Yichang
Wuhan
Huangshi
Anqing
Jingdezhen
ZHEJIANG

Shashi
Lichuan
Jiujiang
Nanchang
JIANGXI
FUJIAN
Fuzhou
Yong'an
Quanzhou

Wanxian
SICHUAN
Chongqing
Neijiang
HUNAN
Changsha
Xiangtan
Hengyang
Shaoguan
Ganzhou
Longyan
Xiamen

Mianyang
Chengdu
Zigong
Zunyi
GUIZHOU
Guiyang
Anshun
Kunming
GUANGDONG
Guangzhou
Dongguan
Shantou

Litang
Ya'an
Leshan
Xichang
Dali
Baoshan
YUNNAN
Gejiu
Jinghong

Zhangzhou

Hong Kong (Xianggang)
MACAO (Portuguese special territory)

Maoming
Zhanjiang
Haikou
Hainan Dao
HAINAN

South China Sea

PARACEL ISLANDS
(disputed by China, Taiwan & Vietnam)
Amphitrite Group
Crescent Group
Triton Island

Thitu Island
Flat Island
Nanshan Island
SPRATLY ISLANDS
(disputed by China, Malaysia, Philippines, Taiwan & Vietnam)
Loaita Island
Namyit Island
Len Dao
Spratly Island

Gulf of Tongking

Xuwen
Dongfang
Danxian

VIETNAM

LAOS

THAILAND

CAMBODIA

Gulf of Thailand

Red River

Mekong

Wuliang Shan

Hengduan Shan

Salween

Jinsha Jiang

Nu Jiang

Chang Jiang (Yangtze)

Dongting Hu

Lengshuitan
Quanzhou
Huaihua
Guilin
GUANGXI
Liuzhou
ZHUANGZU
Yulin
Nanning
Qinzhou
Beihai
Suixi

ZIZHIQU
Zhaoqing
Jiangmen

XIZANG ZIZHIQU (TIBET)

INDIA

BURMA

Tropic of Cancer

ELEVATION

4 000 m	13 124 ft
2 000 m	6 562 ft
1 000 m	3 281 ft
500 m	1 640 ft
250 m	820 ft
100 m	328 ft
Sea Level	Sea Level
-50 m	-164 ft
-100 m	-328 ft
-250 m	-820 ft
-500 m	-1 640 ft
-1 000 m	-3 281 ft
-2 000 m	-6 562 ft

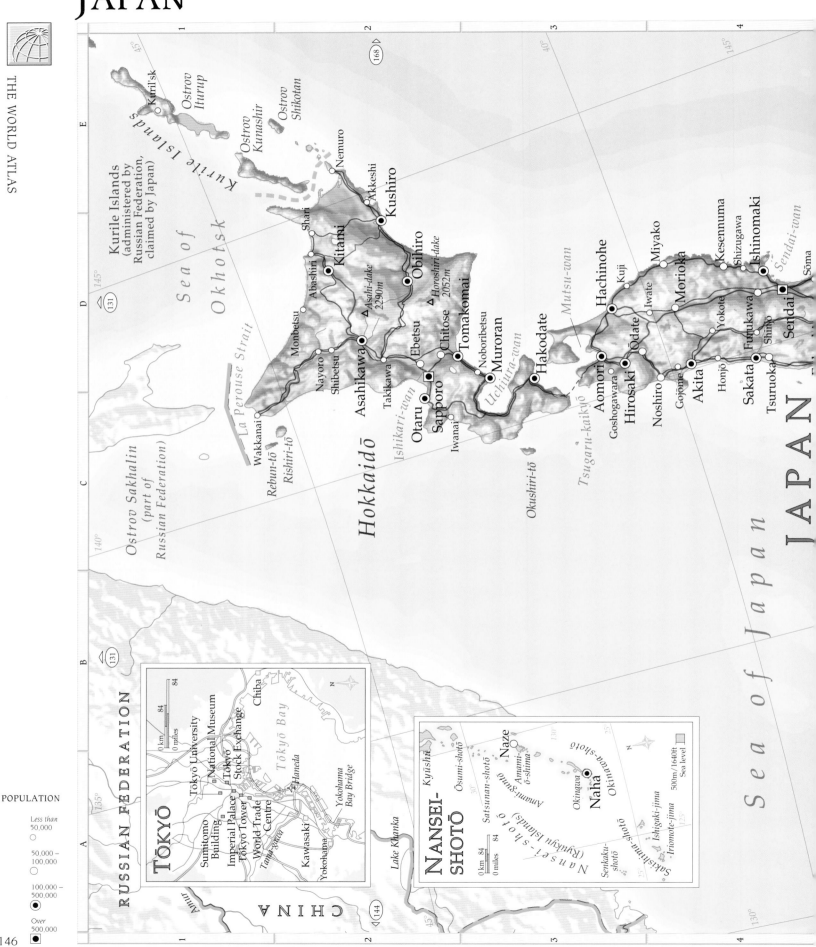

Kuril'sk

Ostrov
Iturup

Kurile Islands

Ostrov
Shikotan

Ostrov
Kunashir

Kurile Islands
(administered by
Russian Federation,
claimed by Japan)

Sea of
Okhotsk

Nemuro

Akkeshi

Shari

Kushiro

Kitami

Abashiri

Obihiro

△ Asahi-dake
2290m

△ Horoshiri-dake
2052m

Monbetsu

Nayoro

Shibetsu

Ebetsu

Chitose

Tomakomai

Noboribetsu

Muroran

Hakodate

Mutsu-wan

Kesennuma

Shizugawa

Ishinomaki

Sendai-wan

Sōma

Miyako

Hachinohe

Kuji

Morioka

Iwate

Yokote

Takikawa

Asahikawa

Otaru

Sapporo

Iwanai

Wakkanai

Rebun-tō

Rishiri-tō

La Perouse Strait

Ostrov Sakhalin
(part of
Russian Federation)

Ishikari-wan

Hokkaidō

Okushiri-tō

Uchiura-wan

Tsugaru-kaikyō

Aomori

Goshogawara

Hirosaki

Noshiro

Gojome

Akita

Odate

Honjō

Sakata

Tsuruoka

Shinjō

Sendai

Futukawa

JAPAN

Sea of Japan

TŌKYŌ

Chiba

N

Tokyo University

National Museum

Tōkyō
Stock Exchange

Sumitomo
Building

Imperial Palace

Tōkyō Tower

World Trade
Centre

Haneda

Tōkyō Bay

*Yokohama
Bay Bridge*

Kawasaki

Yokohama

Tama-gawa

0 km   84
0 miles

Lake Khanka

CHINA

Amur

NANSEI-
SHOTŌ

Kyūshū

Ōsumi-shotō

Satsunan-shotō

Naze

Amami-
ō-shima

Amami-guntō

Okinawa

Naha

Okinawa-shotō

*Nansei-shotō
(Ryūkyū Islands)*

Senkaku-
shotō

Sakishima-shotō

Ishigaki-jima

Iriomote-jima

500m/1640ft

Sea level

N

0 km   84
0 miles

POPULATION

Less than
50,000

○

50,000 –
100,000

◎

100,000 –
500,000

◉

Over
500,000

◼

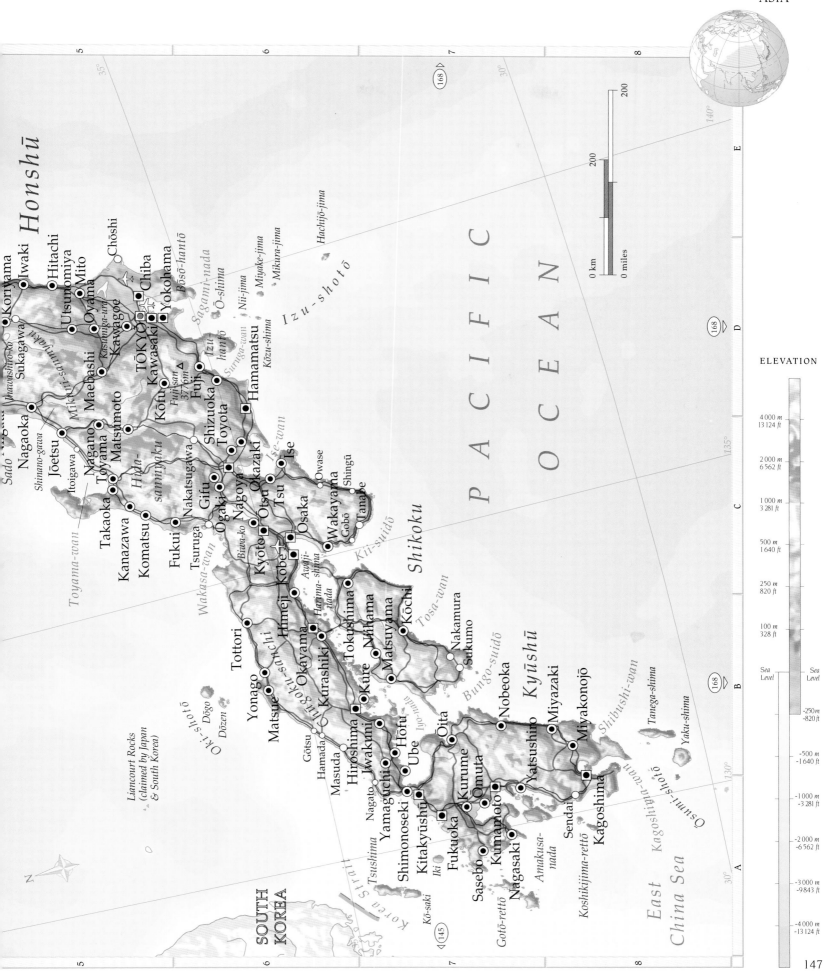

Honshū

Koriyama
Iwaki
Hitachi
Sukagawa
Utsunomiya
Mito
Oyama
Chōshi
Ibaraki-ko
Kasumiga-ura
Maebashi
Kawagoe
Chiba
TOKYO
Yokohama
Nagaoka
Kawasaki
Bōsō-hantō
Jōetsu
Nagano
Matsumoto
Kōfu
Fuji
Sagami-nada
Sado
Shinano-gawa
Itoigawa
Toyama
Fujisan △ 3776 m
Shizuoka
Hamamatsu
Izu
Izu hantō
Ō-shima
Nii-jima
Miyake-jima
Mikura-jima
Hachijō-jima
Izu-shotō
Takaoka
Kanazawa
Komatsu
Nagano
Hida-sanmyaku
Gifu
Nakatsugawa
Toyota
Suruga-wan
Kōzu-shima
Toyama-wan
Fukui
Tsuruga
Ogaki
Nagoya
Okazaki
Ōtsu
Tsu
Ise
Ise-wan
Owase
Shingū
Wakasa-wan
Biwa-ko
Kyōto
Kōbe
Wakayama
Gobō
Tanabe
Kii-suidō
San'in-sanchi
Awaji-shima
Ōsaka
Harima-nada
Shikoku
Tottori
Himeji
Chūgoku-sanchi
Okayama
Kurashiki
Tokushima
Niihama
Kōchi
Tosa-wan
Yonago
Matsue
Kure
Matsuyama
Nakamura
Sukumo
Kyūshū
Nobeoka
Miyazaki
Miyakonojō
Hiroshima
Iwakuni
Hōfu
Ōita
Bungo-suidō
Iyo-nada
Gōtsu
Hamada
Masuda
Yamaguchi
Ube
Kurume
Ōmuta
Yatsushiro
Sendai
Kagoshima
Tanega-shima
Shibushi-wan
Yaku-shima
Nagato
Shimonoseki
Kitakyūshū
Fukuoka
Kumamoto
Amakusa-nada
Sasebo
Nagasaki
Koshikijima-rettō
Gotō-rettō
Ōsumi-shotō
Kagoshima-wan
Tsushima
Iki
Kō-saki

SOUTH KOREA

Korea Strait

Liancourt Rocks
(claimed by Japan
& South Korea)

Oki-shotō
Dōgo
Dōzen

P A C I F I C

O C E A N

East China Sea

ELEVATION

4000 m 13 124 ft	
2000 m 6562 ft	
1000 m 3281 ft	
500 m 1640 ft	
250 m 820 ft	
100 m 328 ft	
Sea Level	Sea Level
-250 m -820 ft	
-500 m -1640 ft	
-1000 m -3281 ft	
-2000 m -6562 ft	
-3000 m -9843 ft	
-4000 m -13 124 ft	

200
0 km
0 miles

SOUTH INDIA & SRI LANKA

A

B

C

D

70°

(150)

N

25°

Godavari

80°

1

Kalyān

Bombay (Mumbai)

Pune

Ahmadnagar

Nānded

Jagdalpur

Bārāmati

Nizāmābād

Andhra Pradesh

Karīmnagar

Vizianagaram

Solāpur

I N D I A

Secunderābād

Visākhapatna

Sāngli

Gulbarga

Hyderābād

Rājahmundry

Kolhāpur

Deccan

Kākināda

Karnātaka

Rāichūr

Krishna

Vijayawāda

Belgaum

Kurnool

Machilīpatnam

15°

Panaji (Goa)

Gadag

Chīrāla

Hublī

Nandyāl

Ongole

Tungabhadra Reservoir

Tādpatri

Kāvali

A r a b i a n

Dāvangere

Anantapur

Nellore

S e a

Shimoga

Cuddapah

Bhadrāvati

Udupi

Tumkūr

Mangalore

Bangalore

Vellore

Madras

2

Kāsaragod

Mandya

Kānchīpuram

Cannanore

Krishnagiri

Tiruppattūr

Mysore

Coromandel Coast

Calicut

Erode

Salem

Pondicherry

Amīndīvi Islands

Neyveli

Coimbatore

Tamil Nādu

Kavaratti Island

Trichūr

Tiruchchirāppalli

Lakshadweep

Ernākulam

Dindigul

(Laccadive Islands)

Cochin

Madurai

Palk Strait

(part of India)

Kalpeni Island

Jaffna

SRI LANKA

Alleppey

Rājapālaiyam

Mannar

Nine Degree Channel

Quilon

Vavuniya

Malabar Coast

Trivandrum

Tuticorin

Trincomalee

3

Minicoy Island

Nāgercoil

Puttalam

Anurādhapura

Eight Degree Channel

Gulf of Mannar

Batticaloa

Matale

Negombo

Kandy

Ihavandippolhu Atoll

Sri Jayawardanapura

MALDIVES

COLOMBO

Kalutara

Ratnapura

Faadhippolhu Atoll

Galle

Horsburgh Atoll

Matara

4

(89)

Male' Atoll

Ari Atoll

MALE'

Felidhu Atoll

Mulaku Atoll

Kolhumadulu Atoll

I N D I A N

Hadhdhunmathi Atoll

North Huvadhu Atoll

5

Equator

South Huvadhu Atoll

Addu Atoll ○ Gan

(156)

70°

75°

80°

A

B

C

D

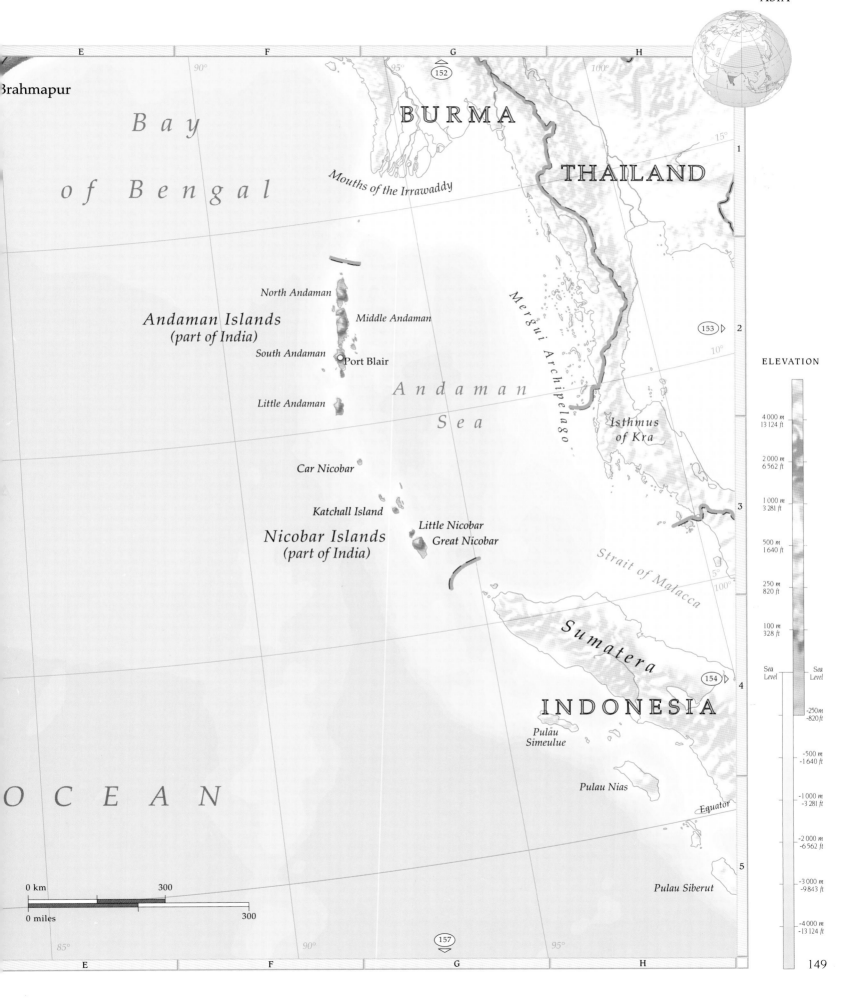

Brahmapur

Bay

of Bengal

BURMA

Mouths of the Irrawaddy

THAILAND

North Andaman

Andaman Islands
(part of India)

Middle Andaman

South Andaman

Port Blair

Mergui Archipelago

A n d a m a n

Little Andaman

S e a

Isthmus
of Kra

Car Nicobar

Katchall Island

Nicobar Islands
(part of India)

Little Nicobar
Great Nicobar

Strait of Malacca

S u m a t e r a

INDONESIA

Pulau
Simeulue

Pulau Nias

Equator

Pulau Siberut

O C E A N

ELEVATION

4 000 *m*
13 124 *ft*

2 000 *m*
6 562 *ft*

1 000 *m*
3 281 *ft*

500 *m*
1 640 *ft*

250 *m*
820 *ft*

100 *m*
328 *ft*

Sea
Level

Sea
Level

-250 *m*
-820 *ft*

-500 *m*
-1 640 *ft*

-1 000 *m*
-3 281 *ft*

-2 000 *m*
-6 562 *ft*

-3 000 *m*
-9 843 *ft*

-4 000 *m*
-13 124 *ft*

0 km   300

0 miles   300

152

153

154

157

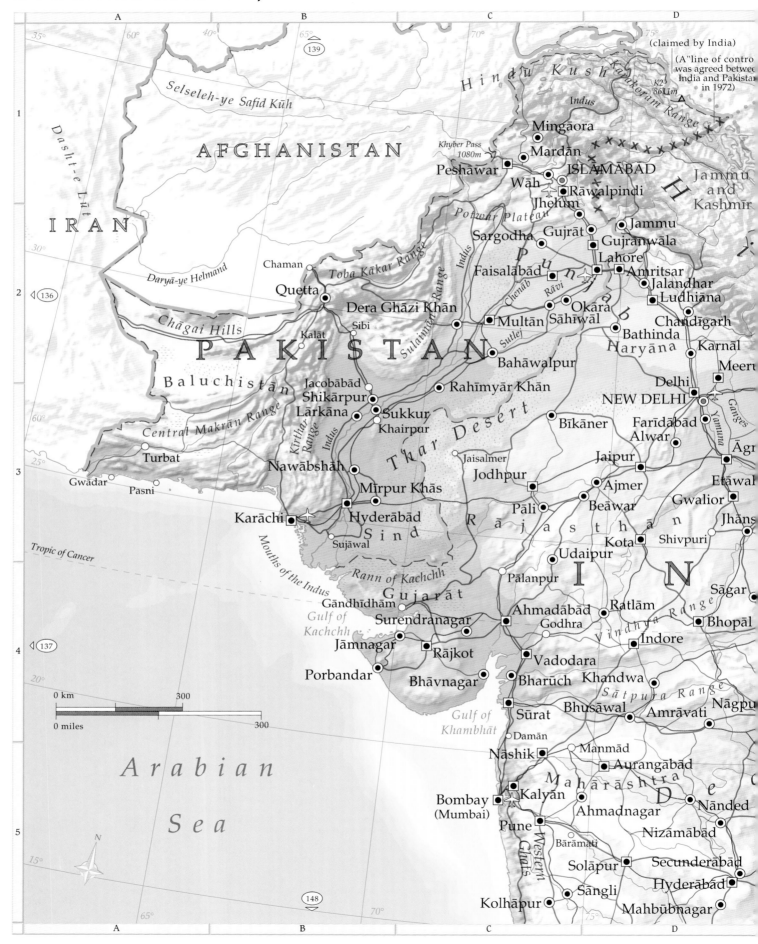

(claimed by India)

(A "line of contro
was agreed betwee
India and Pakistan
in 1972)

AFGHANISTAN

Selseleh-ye Safid Kūh

Hindū Kush

Karakoram Range

K2
8611m

Indus

Mingāora

Khyber Pass
1080m

Mardān

**Jammu
and
Kashmīr**

IRAN

Peshāwar

Wāh

ISLĀMĀBĀD

Rāwalpindi

Dasht-e Lūt

Jhelum

Potwar Plateau

Jammu

Daryā-ye Helmand

Chaman

Toba Kākar Range

Sargodha

Gujrāt

Gujrānwāla

Indus

Quetta

Dera Ghāzi Khān

Faisalābād

Chenāb

Lahore

Amritsar

Jalandhar

Chāgai Hills

Kalāt

Sibi

Sulaimān Range

Multān

Rāvi

Sāhīwāl

Okāra

Ludhiāna

Chandīgarh

PAKISTAN

Baluchistān

Sutlej

Bahāwalpur

Bathinda

Haryāna

Karnāl

Meer

Jacobābād

Rahīmyār Khān

Bīkāner

Delhi

Central Makrān Range

Shikārpur

Lārkāna

Sukkur

NEW DELHI

Farīdābād

Alwar

Āg

Khairpur

Indus

Thar Desert

Turbat

Jaisalmer

Jaipur

Etāwa

Gwādar

Pasni

Nawābshāh

Jodhpur

Ajmer

Gwalior

Jhāns

Mīrpur Khās

R

a

Pāli

Beāwar

Karāchi

Hyderābād

Sind

j

a

s

t

h

a

n

Kota

Shivpuri

Tropic of Cancer

Sujāwal

Udaipur

I

N

Mouths of the Indus

Rann of Kachchh

Pālanpur

Sāgar

Gāndhīdhām

Gujarāt

Ahmadābād

Ratlām

Vindhya Range

Bhopāl

*Gulf of
Kachchh*

Surendranagar

Godhra

Indore

Jāmnagar

Rājkot

Vadodara

Khandwa

Sātpura Range

Nāgpu

Porbandar

Bhāvnagar

Bharūch

*Gulf of
Khambhāt*

Sūrat

Bhusāwal

Amrāvati

Damān

Manmād

Nāshik

Aurangābād

*Arabian

Sea*

Mahārāshtra

D

e

Bombay
(Mumbai)

Kalyān

Ahmadnagar

Nānded

Pune

Nizāmābad

Bārāmati

Western Ghats

Solāpur

Secunderābād

Hyderābad

Kolhāpur

Sāngli

Mahbūbnagar

Scale:

0 km   300

0 miles   300

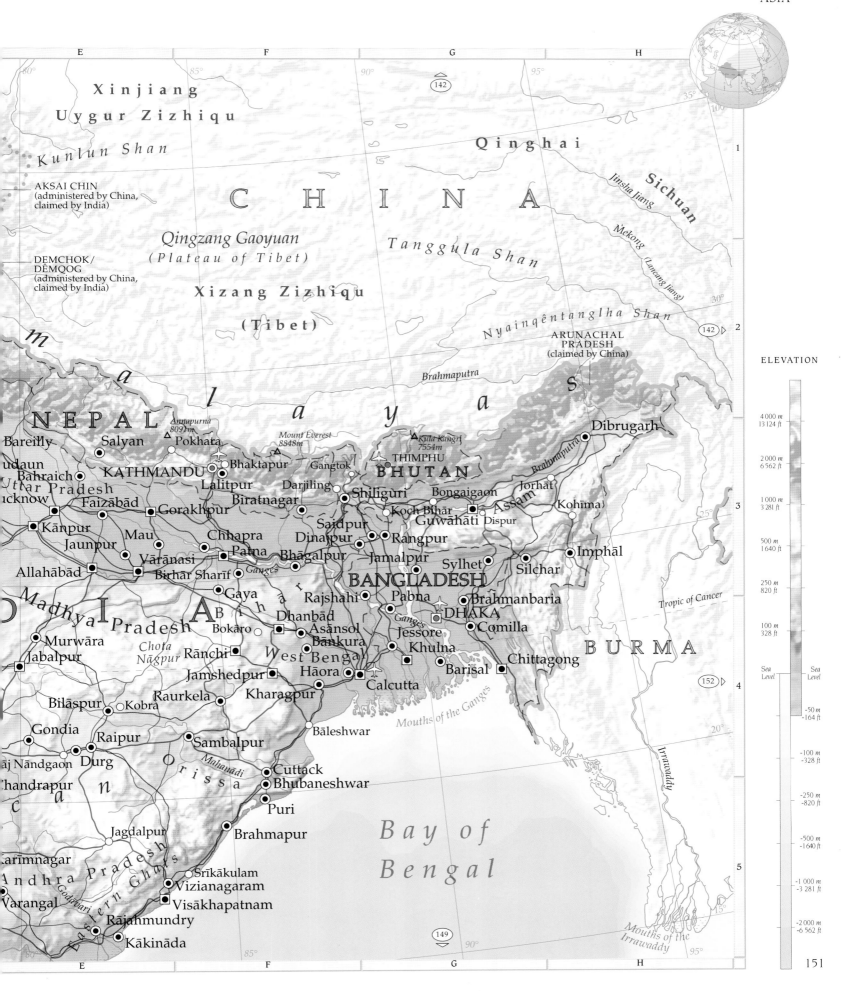

Xinjiang

Uygur Zizhiqu

Kunlun Shan

AKSAI CHIN
(administered by China,
claimed by India)

DEMCHOK/
DÊMQOG
(administered by China,
claimed by India)

C H I N A

Qingzang Gaoyuan
(Plateau of Tibet)

Xizang Zizhiqu

(Tibet)

Qinghai

Sichuan

Jinsha Jiang

Mekong (Lancang Jiang)

Tanggula Shan

Nyainqêntanglha Shan

ARUNACHAL
PRADESH
(claimed by China)

142

Brahmaputra

m *a* *l* *a* *y* *a* *s*

N E P A L

Bareilly   Salyan   △ *Annapurna*   *Mount Everest*   △ *Kula Kangri*   Dibrugarh
                                   8091m   Pokhata   *8848m*   *7554m*
udaun   Jorhat
Bahraich   ✈ Bhaktapur   Gangtok   THIMPHU   *Brahmaputra*
        Uttar Pradesh KATHMANDU   **BHUTAN**   Bongaigaon
icknow   Faizābād Lalitpur Darjiling Shiligŭri   Assam   Kohīma
        Gorakhpur   Biratnagar   Koch Bihār   Guwāhati Dispur
Kānpur   Saidpur   Rangpur   Imphāl
Jaunpur   Mau   Chhapra   Dinajpur
        Vārānasi Patna Bhāgalpur   Jamalpur   Sylhet   Silchar
Allahābād   Birhar Sharīf *Ganges*   **B A N G L A D E S H**
        I N D I A Gaya   Rajshahi   Pabna   Brahmanbaria   Tropic of Cancer
Madhya Pradesh   Bokāro   Dhanbād   *Ganges* **DHAKA**
Murwāra   Rānchi   Asānsol   Jessore Comilla   **B U R M A**
Jabalpur   Chota   *West Bengal* Bankura   Khulna
                Nāgpur   Chittagong
        Jamshedpur   Hāora   Barisal
Bilāspur   Kobra Raurkela Kharagpur Calcutta
Gondia   Raipur   *Mouths of the Ganges*   *Irrawaddy*
āj Nāndgaon Durg   Sambalpur Bāleshwar
        Mahanadi
Chandrapur   *Orissa* Cuttack
        n   Bhubaneshwar
        a   Jagdalpur   Puri
            c *a*   **Bay of**
Karimnagar   Brahmapur   **Bengal**
Andhra Pradesh   Srīkākulam
Warangal   *Godāvari* Vizianagaram
        Rājahmundry Visākhapatnam
            Kākināda   *Mouths of the*
                                              Irrawaddy

142

152

149

ELEVATION

4 000 m
13 124 ft

2 000 m
6 562 ft

1 000 m
3 281 ft

500 m
1 640 ft

250 m
820 ft

100 m
328 ft

Sea   Sea
Level   Level

−50 m
−164 ft

−100 m
−328 ft

−250 m
−820 ft

−500 m
−1 640 ft

−1 000 m
−3 281 ft

−2 000 m
−6 562 ft

MAINLAND SOUTHEAST ASIA

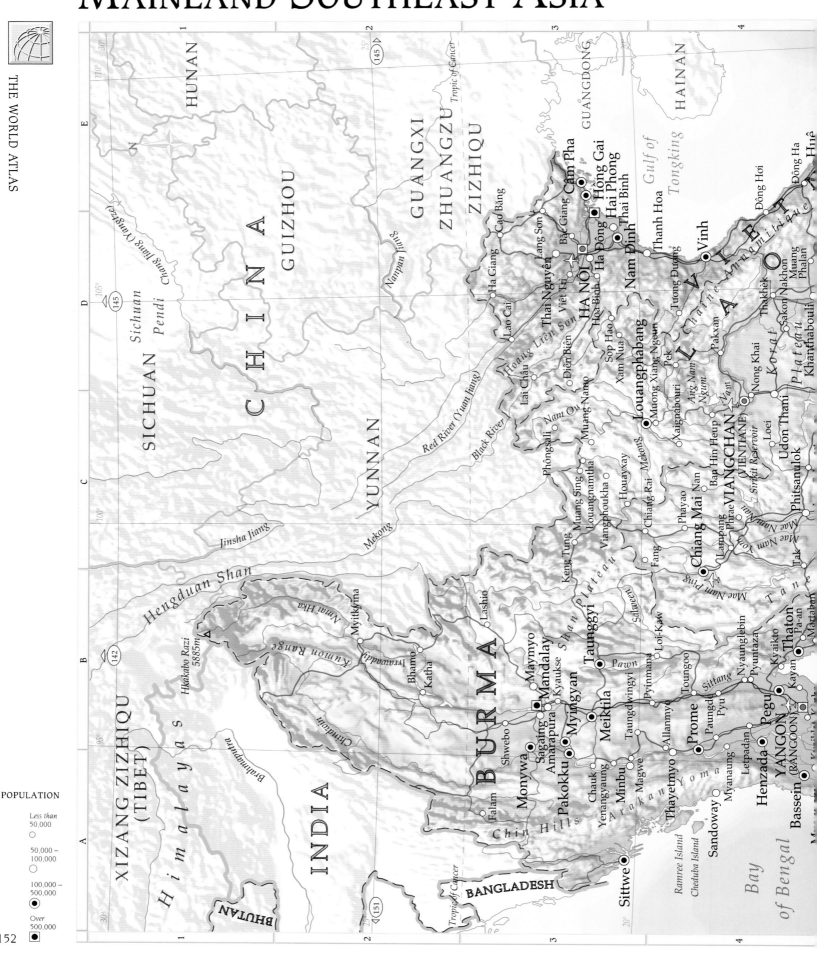

POPULATION

Less than
50,000
○

50,000 –
100,000
○

100,000 –
500,000
◉

Over
500,000
◼

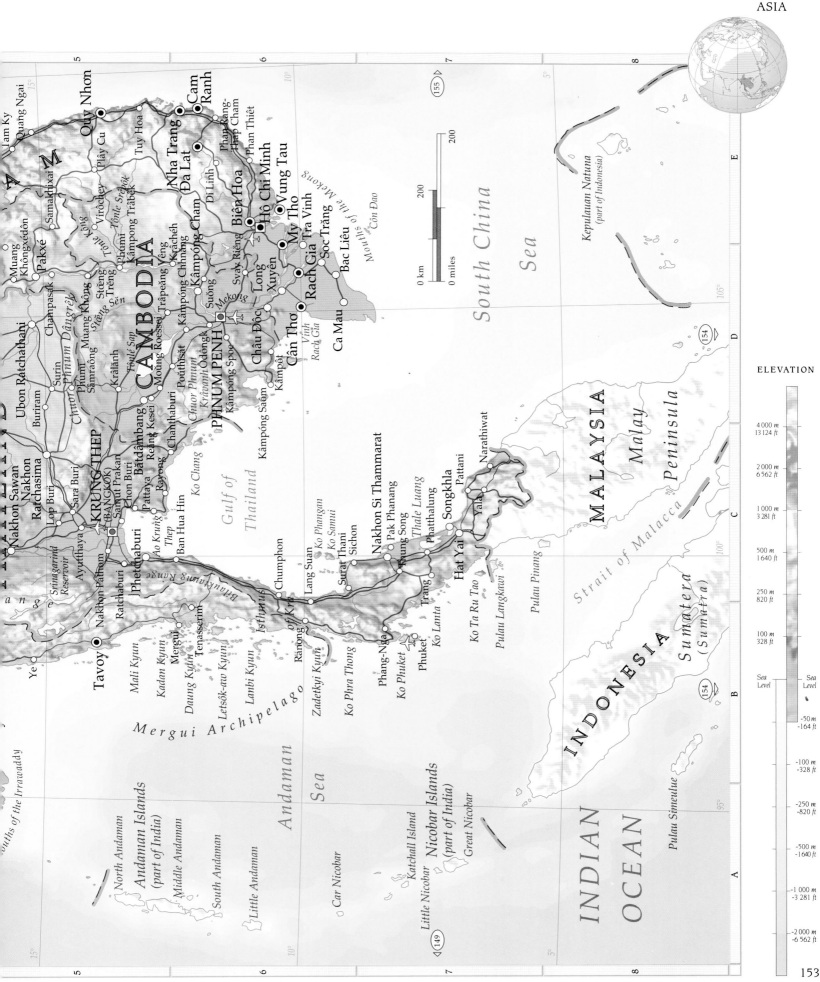

South China

Sea

Kepulauan Natuna
(part of Indonesia)

200

200

km

0 miles

Mouths of the Mekong

Côn Đao

Phan Rang-
Tháp Chàm

Phan Thiết

Cam
Ranh

Ouy Nhon

Quang Ngai
Nam Ky

Play Cu
Tuy Hoa

Nha Trang
Đà Lat

Di Linh

Biên Hoa
Hồ Chi Minh
Vung Tau

My Tho
Trà Vinh

Samakhixai
Virochey
Tônle Srêpôk

Muang
Khôngxedôn
Pakxé

Champasak

Tônle San
Stoeng Trêng
Lumphat
Kâmpong Trâbêk

Phumi
Stoeng Trêng

Krâchéh

Kâmpóng Cham

Suông

Long
Xuyên
Svay Riêng

Rach Gia
Sóc Trăng

Bac Liêu

Ca Mau

CAMBODIA

Muang Roessei
Trâpeăng Veng
Kâmpóng Chhnang

Vinh
Rach Gia

Muang Không

Muang
Khôngxedôn

Phumi Sâmrâong
Kralănh

Chhlong

Kâmpóng Thum
Trâpeăng

Châu Đôc
Cân Thơ

Mekong

Ubon Ratchathani
Buriram
Surin

Phnum Dângrêk

Chumphon
Chhtor

PHNUM PENH

Kâmpóng Spoe

Nakhon
Ratchasima

Nakhon
Sawan

Sara Buri
Lop Buri

KRUNG THEP
(BANGKOK)

Samut Prakan

Potthisăt

Bătdâmbang
Reăng Kesei

Chanthaburi

Kâmpông Saôm

Kâmpôt

Chuor Phnum
Krâvanh
Krâsomh Odâng

Pattaya
Rayong

Chon Buri

Ko Chang

Gulf of
Thailand

Ye

Tavoy

Ao Krung
Thep

Ban Hua Hin

Nakhon Pathom
Ratchaburi
Phetchaburi

Srinagarind
Reservoir

Ayutthaya

Bilauktaung Range

Isthmus
of Kra

Ranong

Chumphon

Lang Suan

Surat Thani

Sichon

Nakhon Si Thammarat

Ko Phangan
Ko Samui

Pak Phanang

Chung Song

Phatthalung

Thale Luang

Songkhla

Pattani

Narathiwat

Yala

Hat Yai

Trang

Ko Lanta

Ko Ta Ru Tao

Pulau Langkawi

Pulau Pinang

MALAYSIA

Malay

Peninsula

Strait of Malacca

Phang-Nga

Ko Phuket
Phuket

Tenasserim

Mergui

Mali Kyun

Kadan Kyun

Daung Kyun

Letsók-aw Kyun

Lanbi Kyun

Zadetkyi Kyun

Mergui Archipelago

Ko Phra Thong

Andaman

Sea

North Andaman

Andaman Islands
(part of India)

Middle Andaman

South Andaman

Little Andaman

Car Nicobar

Nicobar Islands
(part of India)

Katchall Island

Little Nicobar

Great Nicobar

Pulau Simeulue

INDONESIA

Sumatra
(Sumatera)

INDIAN

OCEAN

Mouths of the Irrawaddy

4 000 m 13 124 ft
2 000 m 6 562 ft
1 000 m 3 281 ft
500 m 1 640 ft
250 m 820 ft
100 m 328 ft
Sea Level
-50 m -164 ft
-100 m -328 ft
-250 m -820 ft
-500 m -1 640 ft
-1 000 m -3 281 ft
-2 000 m -6 562 ft

15°

10°

10°

5°

105°

100°

95°

5

6

7

8

E

D

C

B

A

MARITIME SOUTHEAST ASIA

SINGAPORE

0 km 10
0 miles 10

MALAYSIA

Johore Strait
Causeway
Lim Chu Kang
Bukit Panjang New Town
Hougang
Pulau Ubin
Pulau Tekong
Choa Chu Kang
Changi
Queenstown
Bukit Timah 176m
City
Bedok New Town
Jurong Industrial Estate
Telok Blangah
Sentosa
Selat Pandan
Pulau Sudong
Pulau Pawai
Strait of Singapore

Urban areas
Open areas
Nature reserves

BURMA

LAOS

Gulf of Tongking

Hainan Dao (part of China)

VIETNAM

THAILAND

PARACEL ISLANDS
(disputed by China, Taiwan and Vietnam)

South China

Mekong

CAMBODIA

Sea

SPRATLY ISLANDS
(disputed by China, Malaysia, Philippines, Taiwan and Vietnam)

Andaman Sea

Gulf of Thailand

Mouths of the Mekong

Nicobar Islands (part of India)

Isthmus of Kra

Balabac Strait

Bandaaceh
Sigli
George Town
Kota Bharu
Gunung Kinabalu 4101m
Kota Kinabalu
BANDAR SERI BEGAWAN
Butterworth
Kuala Terengganu
Pulau Pinang
Taiping
Meulaboh
Langsa
Dungun
Ipoh
BRUNEI
Miri
Tawa
Cukai
Pulau Simeulue
Medan
Tebingtinggi
Kuantan
Kepulauan Natuna
Bintulu
Pematangsiantar
Klang
KUALA LUMPUR
MALAYSIA
Seremban
Kepulauan Banyak
Melaka
Keluang
Sibu
Batang Raja
Danau Toba
Muar
Johor Bahru
Sarawak
Sungai Kayan
Sibolga
Batu Pahat
SINGAPORE
Kuching
Selat Serasan
Sri Aman
Pulau Nias
Pekanbaru
Singkawang
Sidas
Banjaran Tapadoh
Solok
Rengat
Kepulauan Lingga
Pontianak
Sungai Kapuas
Borneo
Padang
Sungai Mahakam
Pulau Siberut
Batang Hari
Kualatungkal
Samarinda
Balikpapan
Sungaipenuh
Jambi
Bangka
Pegunungan Muller
Kepulauan Mentawai
Pangkalpinang
Selat Karimata
Kalimantan
Palembang
Sampit
Amuntai
Kandangan
Lahat
Sungai Barito
Bengkulu
Pulau Belitung
Pulau Laut
Banjarmasin
Kotabumi
Java Sea
Makass
Cirebon
Tegal
Bandarlampung
Pekalongan
Pulau Madura
Sumatera (Sumatra)
Serang
JAKARTA
Semarang
Kudus
Bogor
Surabaya
Sukabumi
Probolinggo
Bandung
Jember
Mataram
Tasikmalaya
Malang
Jawa (Java)
Cilacap
Kediri
Denpasar
Magelang
Madiun
Bali
Pulau Lombok
Yogyakarta
Surakarta

INDIAN

OCEAN

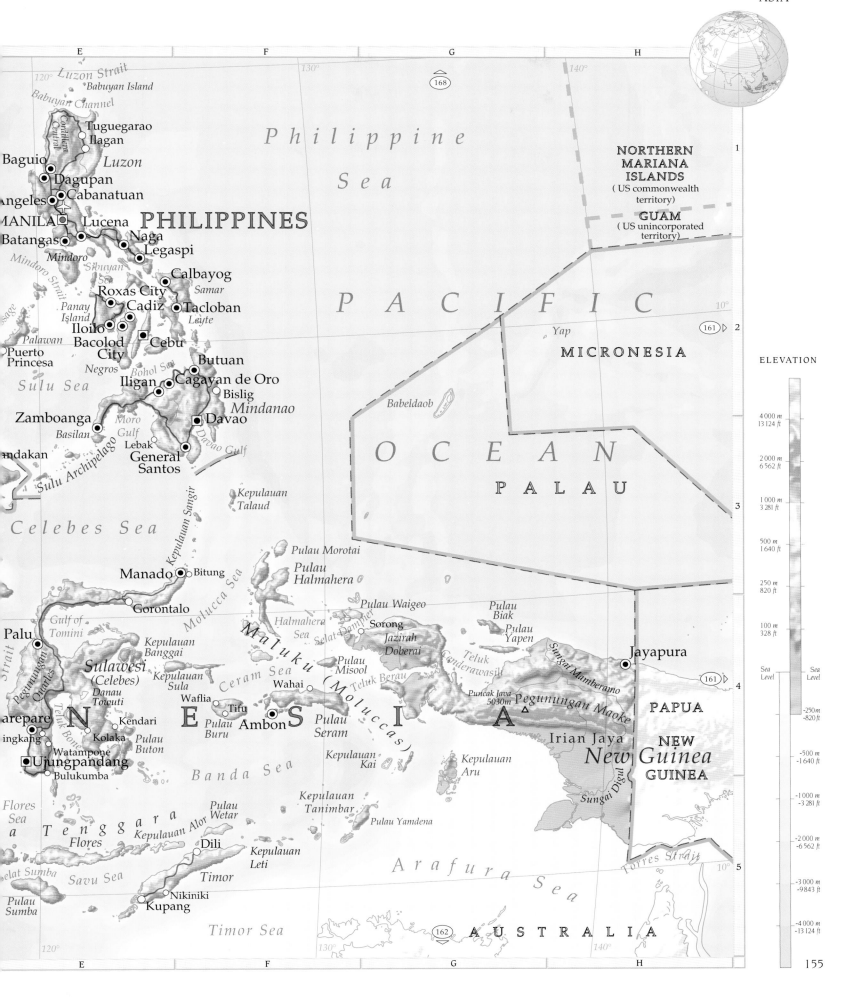

Luzon Strait

120°

Babuyan Island

Babuyan Channel

Philippine

Sea

130°

168

140°

1

NORTHERN
MARIANA
ISLANDS
(US commonwealth
territory)

Tuguegarao
Ilagan

Baguio

Luzon

Dagupan

Cabanatuan

Angeles

MANILA

Lucena

PHILIPPINES

Batangas

Mindoro

Naga

Legaspi

GUAM
(US unincorporated
territory)

Mindoro Strait

Sibuyan
Sea

Calbayog

Samar

161

2

PACIFIC

Roxas City

Cadiz

Tacloban

Panay
Island

Leyte

MICRONESIA

10°

Yap

Iloilo

Palawan

Bacolod
City

Cebu

Puerto
Princesa

Negros

Bohol Sea

Butuan

OCEAN

Babeldaob

Sulu Sea

Iligan

Cagayan de Oro

Bislig

PALAU

Zamboanga

Basilan

Moro
Gulf

Mindanao

Davao

andakan

Lebak

Davao Gulf

Sulu Archipelago

General
Santos

Kepulauan
Talaud

3

Celebes Sea

Kepulauan Sangir

Pulau Morotai

Pulau
Halmahera

Manado

Bitung

Pulau Waigeo

Pulau
Biak

Gorontalo

Molucca Sea

Halmahera
Sea

Sorong

Jazirah
Doberai

Pulau
Yapen

Jayapura

Gulf of
Tomini

Kepulauan
Banggai

Maluku

Selat Dampier

Pulau
Misool

Teluk Berau

Teluk
Cenderawasih

Sungai Mamberamo

161

4

Palu

Pegunungan Quarles

Sulawesi
(Celebes)

Kepulauan
Sula

Ceram Sea

Wahai

(Moluccas)

Puncak Jaya
5030m

Pegunungan Maoke

PAPUA

Danau
Towuti

Waflia

Tifu

Pulau
Seram

I

A

Irian Jaya

NEW

arepare

N

E

S

New Guinea

ingkang

Kendari

Pulau
Buru

Ambon

GUINEA

Teluk Bone

Kolaka

Kepulauan
Kai

Kepulauan
Aru

Watampone

Pulau
Buton

Ujungpandang

Bulukumba

Banda Sea

Kepulauan
Tanimbar

Sungai Digul

Flores
Sea

a

Tenggara

Pulau
Wetar

Kepulauan Alor

Kepulauan
Leti

Pulau Yamdena

Flores

Selat Sumba

Savu Sea

Dili

Kepulauan
Leti

Timor

Arafura Sea

Torres Strait

10°

5

Pulau
Sumba

Nikiniki

Kupang

Timor Sea

162

AUSTRALIA

120°

130°

140°

ELEVATION

4 000 m
13 124 ft

2 000 m
6 562 ft

1 000 m
3 281 ft

500 m
1 640 ft

250 m
820 ft

100 m
328 ft

Sea
Level

Sea
Level

-250 m
-820 ft

-500 m
-1 640 ft

-1 000 m
-3 281 ft

-2 000 m
-6 562 ft

-3 000 m
-9 843 ft

-4 000 m
-13 124 ft

THE INDIAN OCEAN

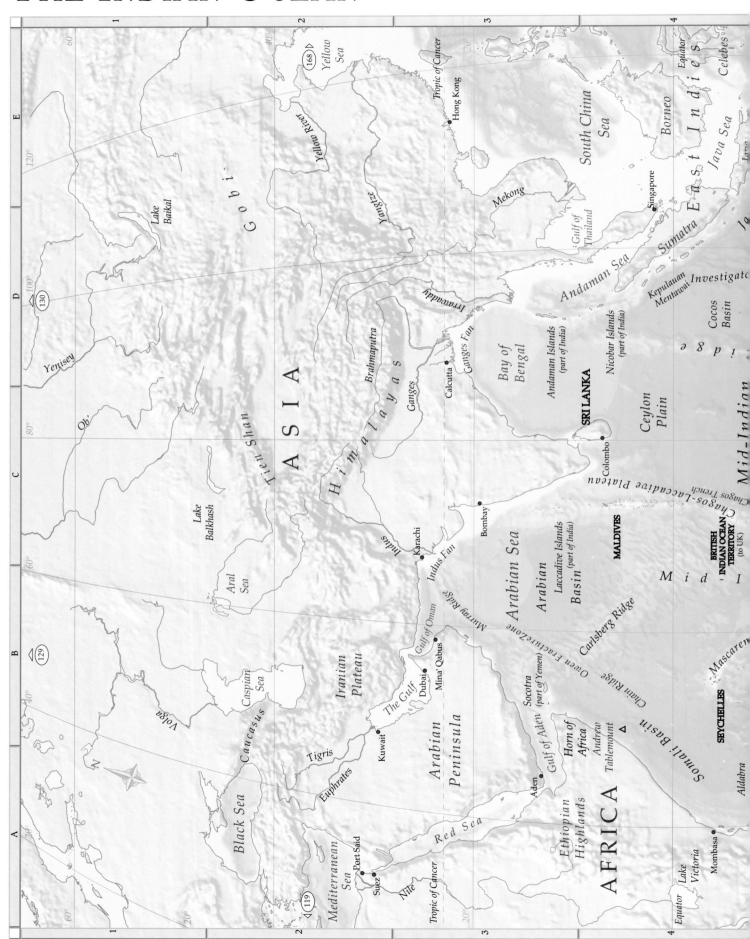

AUSTRALIA

Fremantle

Tropic of Capricorn

North Australian Basin

Exmouth Plateau

Cuvier Plateau

Perth Basin

Naturaliste Plateau

Diamantina Fracture Zone

CHRISTMAS ISLAND (to Australia)

COCOS ISLANDS (to Australia)

Ridge

Wharton Basin

East Indiaman Ridge

Broken Ridge

Osborn Plateau

Ninetyeast Ridge

INDIAN

OCEAN

Amsterdam Island

Île St-Paul

Southeast Indian Ridge

South Indian Basin

SOUTHERN OCEAN

ANTARCTICA

Limit of winter pack ice

Limit of summer pack ice

Antarctic Circle

Mascarene Basin

Plateau

MAURITIUS
RÉUNION (to France)

Argo Fracture Zone

Egeria Fracture Zone

Central Indian Ridge

Madagascar Basin

Mascarene Plain

Farafangana

MADAGASCAR

MAYOTTE (to France)

COMOROS

Davie Ridge

Lake Nyasa

Zambezi

Durban

Tropic of Capricorn

Africana Seamount

Agulhas Plateau

Agulhas Basin

Natal Basin

Madagascar Plateau

Mozambique Plateau

Mozambique Channel

Prince Edward Islands (part of South Africa)

Crozet Basin

Southwest Indian Ridge

Indomed Fracture Zone

Crozet Islands

Crozet Plateau

FRENCH SOUTHERN & ANTARCTIC TERRITORIES (to France)

Kerguelen Plateau

Kerguelen

HEARD & McDONALD ISLANDS (to Australia)

Ob' Tablemount

Lena Tablemount

Banzare Seamounts

Enderby Plain

Atlantic-Indian Basin

Antarctic Circle

Sea Level

-250 m / -820 ft
-500 m / -1 640 ft
-1 000 m / -3 281 ft
-2 000 m / -6 562 ft
-3 000 m / -9 843 ft
-4 000 m / -13 124 ft

1500

0 km

0 miles

157

AUSTRALASIA & OCEANIA

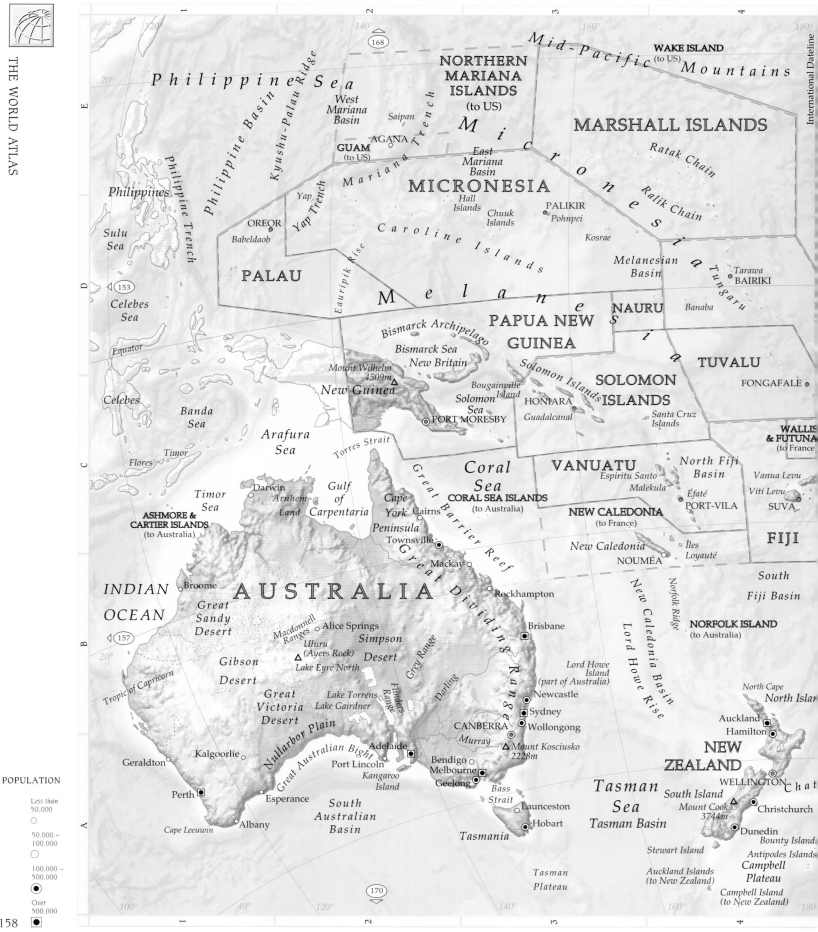

POPULATION

Less than
50,000
○

50,000 –
100,000
○

100,000 –
500,000
◉

Over
500,000
◉

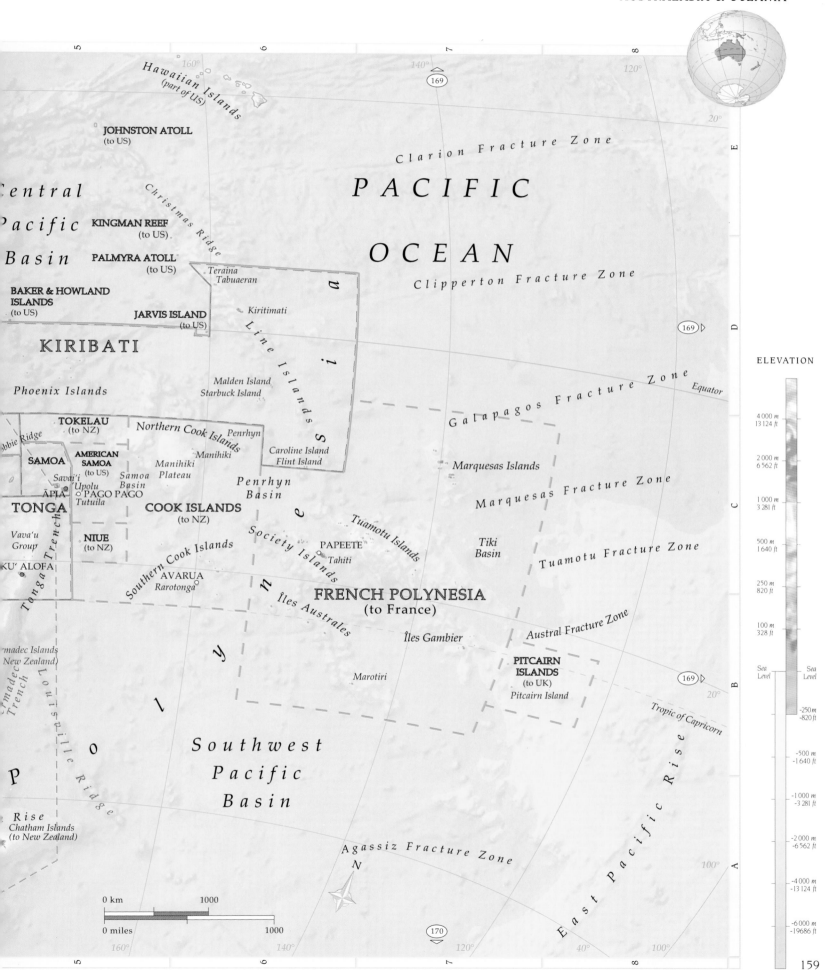

Central

Pacific

Basin

JOHNSTON ATOLL
(to US)

KINGMAN REEF
(to US)

PALMYRA ATOLL
(to US)

BAKER & HOWLAND
ISLANDS
(to US)

JARVIS ISLAND (to US)

KIRIBATI

Phoenix Islands

TOKELAU
(to NZ)

SAMOA

Savai'i
Upolu
ÁPIA

AMERICAN
SAMOA
(to US)

TONGA

Vava'u
Group

KU' ALOFA

NIUE
(to NZ)

Samoa
Basin

PAGO PAGO
Tutuila

Manihiki
Plateau

Northern Cook Islands

Manihiki

Penrhyn

Teraina
Tabuaeran

Kiritimati

Malden Island
Starbuck Island

Caroline Island
Flint Island

Christmas Ridge

Line Islands

Penrhyn
Basin

COOK ISLANDS
(to NZ)

Southern Cook Islands

AVARUA
Rarotonga

Society Islands

PAPEETE
Tahiti

Îles Australes

FRENCH POLYNESIA
(to France)

Îles Gambier

Marotiri

Tuamotu Islands

Marquesas Islands

Tiki
Basin

PITCAIRN
ISLANDS
(to UK)

Pitcairn Island

Clarion Fracture Zone

PACIFIC

OCEAN

Clipperton Fracture Zone

Galapagos Fracture Zone

Equator

Marquesas Fracture Zone

Tuamotu Fracture Zone

Austral Fracture Zone

Tropic of Capricorn

Southwest
Pacific
Basin

Kermadec Islands
(to New Zealand)

Tonga Trench

Louisville Ridge

Kermadec Trench

Rise
Chatham Islands
(to New Zealand)

P

o

l

y

n

e

s

i

a

Agassiz Fracture Zone

N

East Pacific Rise

ELEVATION

4 000 m 13 124 ft	
2 000 m 6 562 ft	
1 000 m 3 281 ft	
500 m 1 640 ft	
250 m 820 ft	
100 m 328 ft	
Sea Level	Sea Level
-250 m -820 ft	
-500 m -1 640 ft	
-1 000 m -3 281 ft	
-2 000 m -6 562 ft	
-4 000 m -13 124 ft	
-6 000 m -19 686 ft	

0 km   1000

0 miles   1000

THE SOUTHWEST PACIFIC

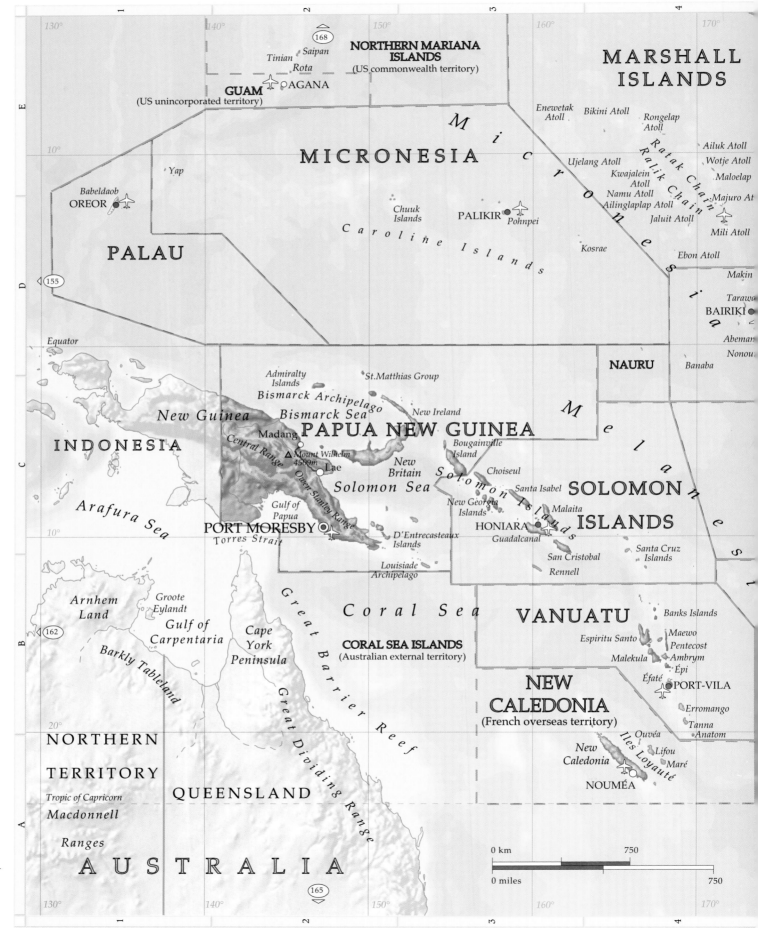

130° 140° 150° 160° 170°

168

NORTHERN MARIANA ISLANDS
(US commonwealth territory)

Tinian *Saipan*
Rota

GUAM
(US unincorporated territory)

AGANA

MARSHALL ISLANDS

Enewetak Atoll *Bikini Atoll* *Rongelap Atoll*

10°

MICRONESIA

Ujelang Atoll *Kwajalein Atoll* *Namu Atoll* *Ailinglaplap Atoll* *Jaluit Atoll*

Ailuk Atoll
Wotje Atoll
Maloelap

Majuro At

Mili Atoll

Yap

155

Babeldaob
OREOR

PALAU

Chuuk Islands

PALIKIR
Pohnpei

Caroline Islands

Kosrae

Ebon Atoll

Makin

Tarawa
BAIRIKI

Abeman
Nonou

Equator

Admiralty Islands *St.Matthias Group*

NAURU

Banaba

Bismarck Archipelago

INDONESIA

New Guinea

Bismarck Sea
Madang

Central Range △Mount Wilhelm 4509m Lae

PAPUA NEW GUINEA

New Ireland

Bougainville Island

New Britain

New Georgia Islands

Choiseul

Santa Isabel

Malaita

HONIARA
Guadalcanal

SOLOMON ISLANDS

Arafura Sea

Owen Stanley Range

Solomon Sea

10°

PORT MORESBY

Gulf of Papua

Torres Strait

D'Entrecasteaux Islands

San Cristobal

Rennell

Santa Cruz Islands

Louisiade Archipelago

Arnhem Land *Groote Eylandt*

162

Gulf of Carpentaria

Barkly Tableland

Cape York Peninsula

Coral Sea

CORAL SEA ISLANDS
(Australian external territory)

VANUATU

Banks Islands

Espiritu Santo

Maewo
Pentecost

Malekula *Ambrym*
Épi

Éfaté PORT-VILA

20°

NORTHERN TERRITORY

Great Barrier Reef

Great Dividing Range

NEW CALEDONIA
(French overseas territory)

Erromango

Tanna
Anatom

Ouvéa
Lifou

New Caledonia

Iles Loyauté

Maré

Tropic of Capricorn

Macdonnell

QUEENSLAND

NOUMÉA

Ranges

AUSTRALIA

165

130° 140° 150° 160° 170°

POPULATION

Less than 50,000
○

50,000 – 100,000
○

100,000 – 500,000
◉

Over 500,000
◉

0 km   750

0 miles   750

160

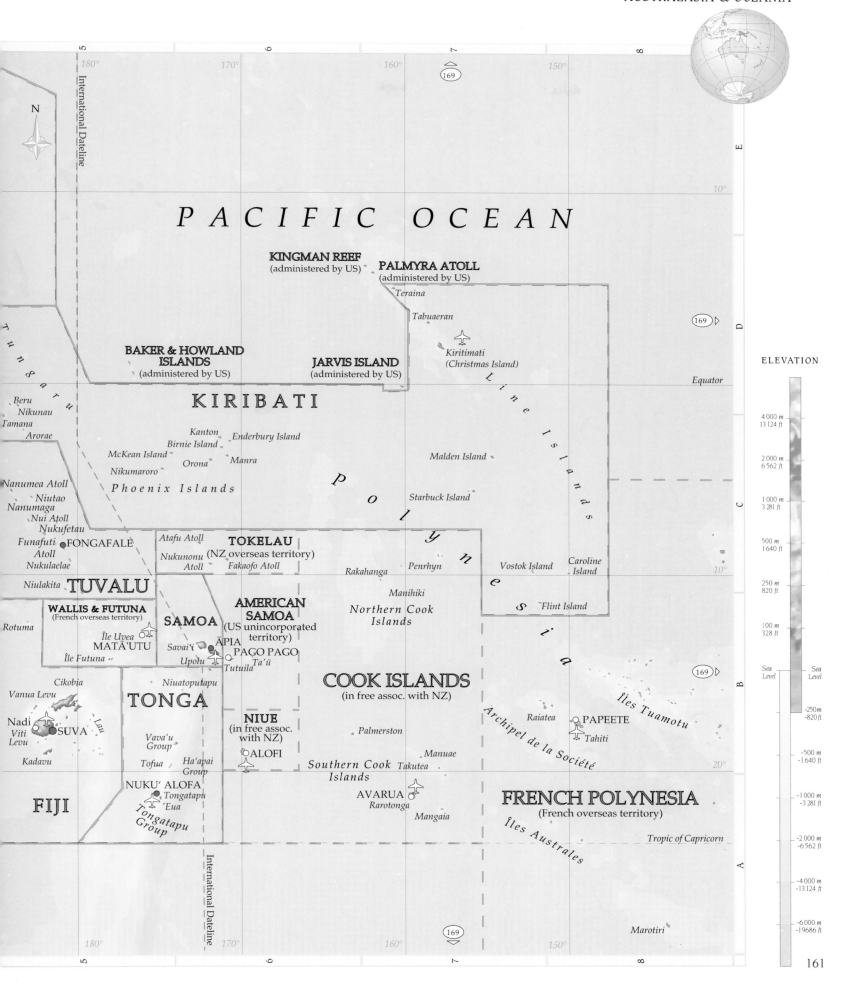

N

180°   170°   160°   150°

⌂ 169

PACIFIC OCEAN

KINGMAN REEF
(administered by US)

PALMYRA ATOLL
(administered by US)

Teraina

Tabuaeran

**BAKER & HOWLAND
ISLANDS**
(administered by US)

JARVIS ISLAND
(administered by US)

Kiritimati
(Christmas Island)

Equator

169 ▷

ELEVATION

Tungaru

Beru
Nikunau
Tamana
Arorae

KIRIBATI

Kanton
Birnie Island
McKean Island
Nikumaroro   Orona
Manra

Enderbury Island

Malden Island

Nanumea Atoll
Niutao
Nanumaga
Nui Atoll
Nukufetau
Funafuti
Atoll ●FONGAFALE
Nukulaelae

Phoenix Islands

P
o
l
y
n

Starbuck Island

4 000 m
13 124 ft

2 000 m
6 562 ft

1 000 m
3 281 ft

Atafu Atoll

Nukunonu
Atoll
Fakaofo Atoll

TOKELAU
(NZ overseas territory)

Rakahanga

Penrhyn

Vostok Island

Caroline
Island

500 m
1 640 ft

Niulakita **TUVALU**

WALLIS & FUTUNA
(French overseas territory)

Rotuma

Île Uvea
MATA'UTU
Île Futuna

SAMOA

Savai'i
Upolu

**AMERICAN
SAMOA**
(US unincorporated
territory)

ĀPIA
PAGO PAGO
Ta'ū
Tutuila

Manihiki

e
s

*Northern Cook
Islands*

Flint Island

i
a

250 m
820 ft

100 m
328 ft

Cikobia
Vanua Levu

Nadi
Viti
Levu

●SUVA

Lau

Niuatoputapu

TONGA

Vava'u
Group

COOK ISLANDS
(in free assoc. with NZ)

NIUE
(in free assoc.
with NZ)

Palmerston

Raiatea

Î
l
e
s

PAPEETE

Tahiti

T
u
a
m
o
t
u

Sea
Level

Sea
Level

-250 m
-820 ft

Kadavu

Tofua

Ha'apai
Group

◉ALOFI

Manuae

Southern Cook
Islands Takutea

A
r
c
h
i
p
e
l

d
e

l
a

S
o
c
i
é
t
é

-500 m
-1 640 ft

FIJI

NUKU'ALOFA
Tongatapu
'Eua

Tongatapu
Group

AVARUA
Rarotonga

Mangaia

FRENCH POLYNESIA
(French overseas territory)

Î
l
e
s

A
u
s
t
r
a
l
e
s

-1 000 m
-3 281 ft

-2 000 m
-6 562 ft

Tropic of Capricorn

180°   170°   160°   150°

⌂ 169

Marotiri

-4 000 m
-13 124 ft

-6 000 m
-19 686 ft

Arafura Sea

Croker Island
South Goulburn Island

164 ▷

Arnhem Land

Tanimbar Kepulauan

Katherine

Daly Waters

Top Springs Roadhouse

Tennant Creek

NORTHERN

Melville Island

Van Diemen Gulf

Pine Creek

Tanami Desert

TERRITORY

Macdonnell Ranges

Tropic of Capricorn

Bathurst Island

Darwin

Victoria River

Wyndham

Kununurra

Lake Mackay

I N D O N E S I A

Timor

Joseph Bonaparte Gulf

Halls Creek

Cape Londonderry

Kimberley Plateau

T i m o r S e a

Fitzroy Crossing

Great Sandy Desert

155

Bonaparte
Bigge Island
Archipelago

Heywood Islands

Fitzroy River

Percival Lakes

Flores

King Sound

Lake Disappointment

Pulau Sumba

Broome

WESTERN

154

Pulau Wetar

I N D I A N

Marble Bar

Newman

Pulau Lombok

Port Hedland

Hamersley Range

Fortescue River

O C E A N

Ashburton River

Barlee River

Bali

Barrow Island

Dampier

Onslow

Java

157

Exmouth Gulf

Exmouth

Tropic of Capricorn

Eighty Mile Beach

POPULATION

Less than
50,000
○

50,000 –
100,000
○

100,000 –
500,000
◉

Over
500,000
▣

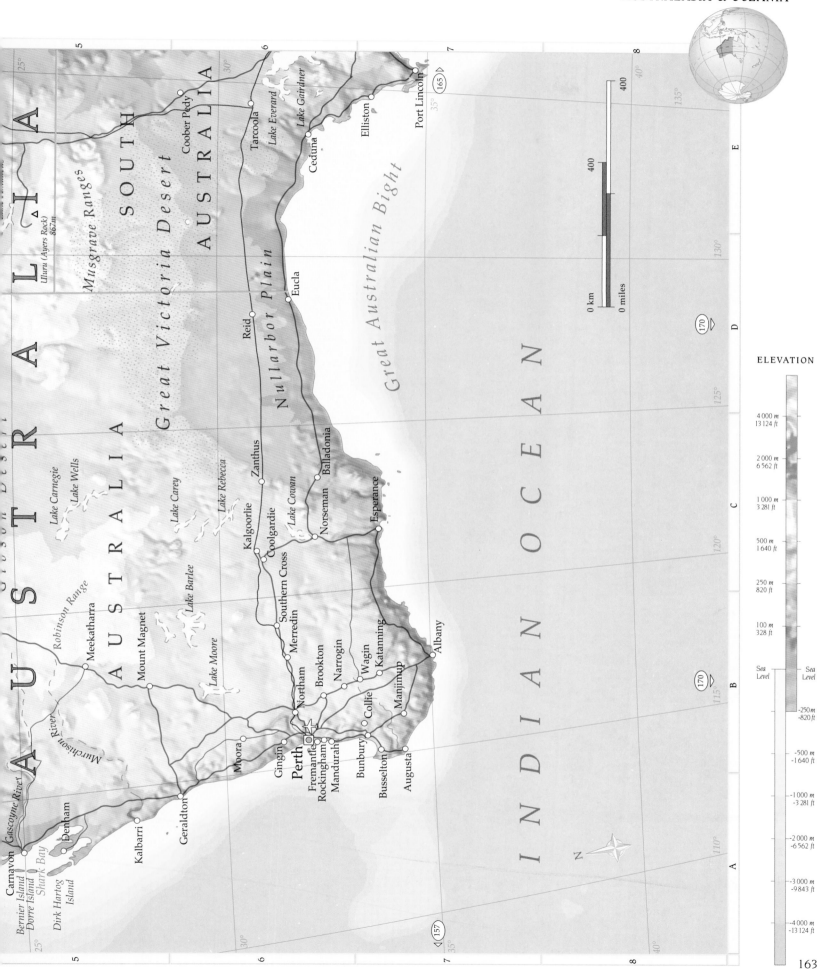

ELEVATION

4 000 m	13 124 ft
2 000 m	6 562 ft
1 000 m	3 281 ft
500 m	1 640 ft
250 m	820 ft
100 m	328 ft
Sea Level	Sea Level
-250 m	-820 ft
-500 m	-1 640 ft
-1 000 m	-3 281 ft
-2 000 m	-6 562 ft
-3 000 m	-9 843 ft
-4 000 m	-13 124 ft

A U S T R A L I A

SOUTH AUSTRALIA

AUSTRALIA

Great Victoria Desert

Nullarbor Plain

Great Australian Bight

INDIAN OCEAN

Musgrave Ranges

Uluru (Ayers Rock) 867m

Gibson Desert

Lake Carnegie

Lake Wells

Lake Carey

Lake Rebecca

Lake Cowan

Lake Barlee

Lake Moore

Robinson Range

Murchison River

Gascoyne River

Shark Bay

Bernier Island

Dorre Island

Dirk Hartog Island

Carnavon

Denham

Kalbarri

Geraldton

Moora

Gingin

Perth

Fremantle

Rockingham

Mandurah

Bunbury

Busselton

Augusta

Collie

Manjimup

Katanning

Wagin

Narrogin

Brookton

Northam

Merredin

Southern Cross

Kalgoorlie

Coolgardie

Zanthus

Reid

Eucla

Balladonia

Norseman

Esperance

Albany

Meekatharra

Mount Magnet

Coober Pedy

Tarcoola

Lake Everard

Lake Gairdner

Ceduna

Elliston

Port Lincoln

400

400

0 km

0 miles

165

N

EASTERN AUSTRALIA

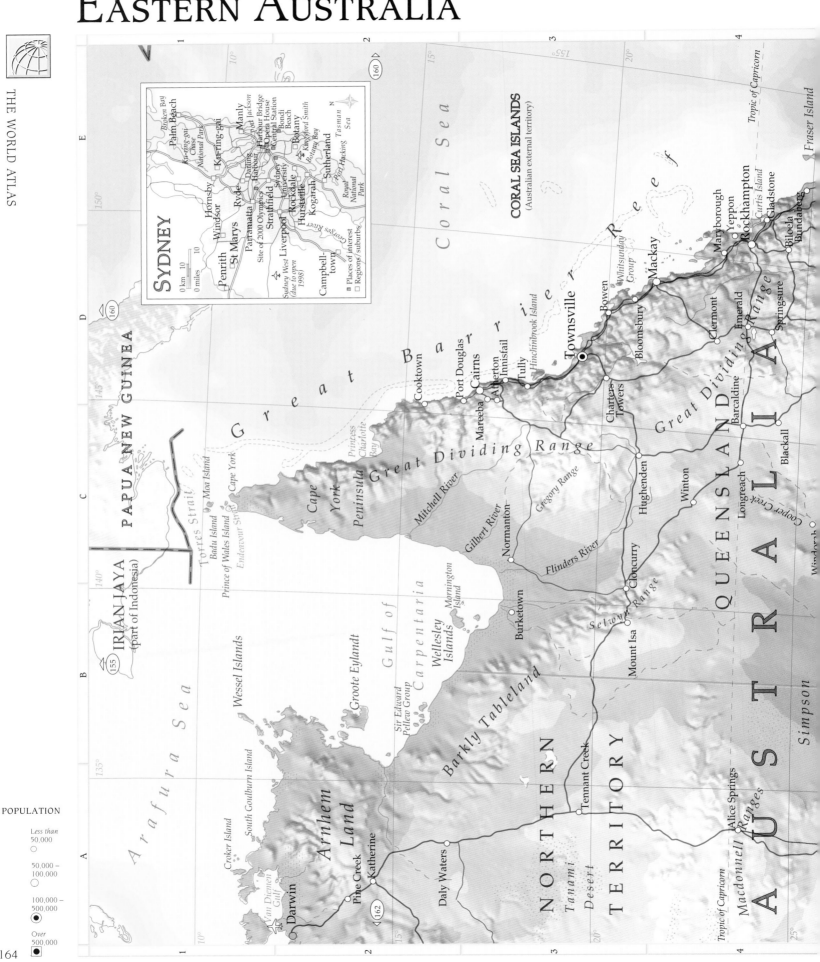

SYDNEY

Broken Bay
Palm Beach
Ku-ring-gai Chase National Park
Ku-ring-gai
Manly
Port Jackson
Harbour Bridge
Opera House
Central Station
Bondi
Bondi Beach
Botany
Kingsford Smith
Botany Bay
Sutherland
Port Hacking
Tasman Sea
N
Hornsby
Windsor
Ryde
Darling Harbour
Sydney University
Sydney
Strathfield
Rockdale
Hurstville
Kogarah
Penrith
St Marys
Parramatta
Site of 2000 Olympics
Liverpool
Sydney West (due to open 1998)
Georges River
Royal National Park
Campbell-town

0 km 10
0 miles 10

■ Places of interest
□ Regions/suburbs

CORAL SEA ISLANDS
(Australian external territory)

Coral Sea

Great Barrier Reef

Tropic of Capricorn

PAPUA NEW GUINEA

IRIAN JAYA
(part of Indonesia)

155

160

Torres Strait
Moa Island
Badu Island
Prince of Wales Island
Cape York
Endeavour Strait

Princess Charlotte Bay

Cape York Peninsula

Great Dividing Range

Mitchell River

Gilbert River

Normanton

Flinders River

Arafura Sea

Croker Island
South Goulburn Island
Wessel Islands
Groote Eylandt
Sir Edward Pellew Group
Mornington Island
Wellesley Islands

Gulf of Carpentaria

Burketown

Carpentaria

Van Diemen Gulf
Darwin
Pine Creek
Katherine

162

Daly Waters

Tanami Desert

NORTHERN TERRITORY

Tennant Creek

Barkly Tableland

Mount Isa
Cloncurry
Selwyn Range

Gregory Range

Hughenden
Winton
Longreach

Cooktown
Port Douglas
Cairns
Mareeba
Atherton
Innisfail
Tully
Hinchinbrook Island
Townsville
Bowen
Bloomsbury
Mackay
Whitsunday Group
Maryborough
Yeppon
Rockhampton
Curtis Island
Gladstone
Biloela
Bundaberg
Fraser Island

Charters Towers

Clermont
Emerald
Springsure

Great Dividing Range

Barcaldine
Blackall
Windorah

QUEENSLAND

AUSTRALIA

Simpson Desert

Alice Springs
Macdonnell Ranges

Tropic of Capricorn

POPULATION

○ Less than 50,000

○ 50,000 – 100,000

◉ 100,000 – 500,000

■ Over 500,000

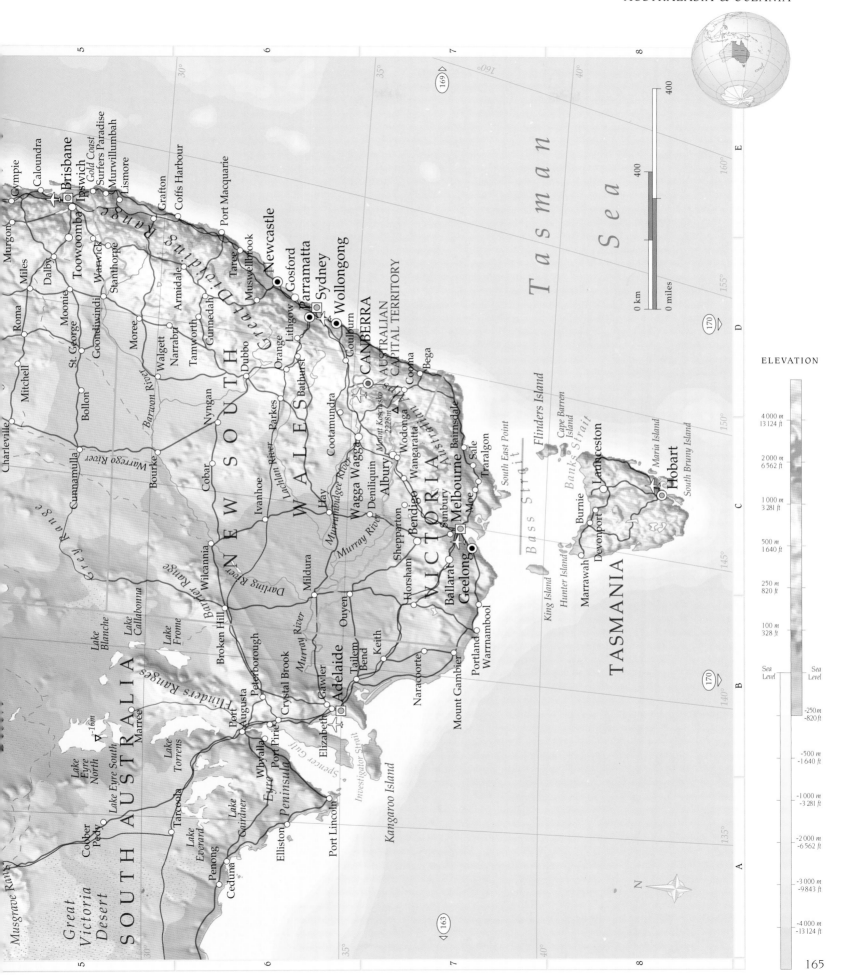

ELEVATION

4 000 m	13 124 ft
2 000 m	6 562 ft
1 000 m	3 281 ft
500 m	1 640 ft
250 m	820 ft
100 m	328 ft
Sea Level	Sea Level
-250 m	-820 ft
-500 m	-1 640 ft
-1 000 m	-3 281 ft
-2 000 m	-6 562 ft
-3 000 m	-9 843 ft
-4 000 m	-13 124 ft

165

NEW ZEALAND

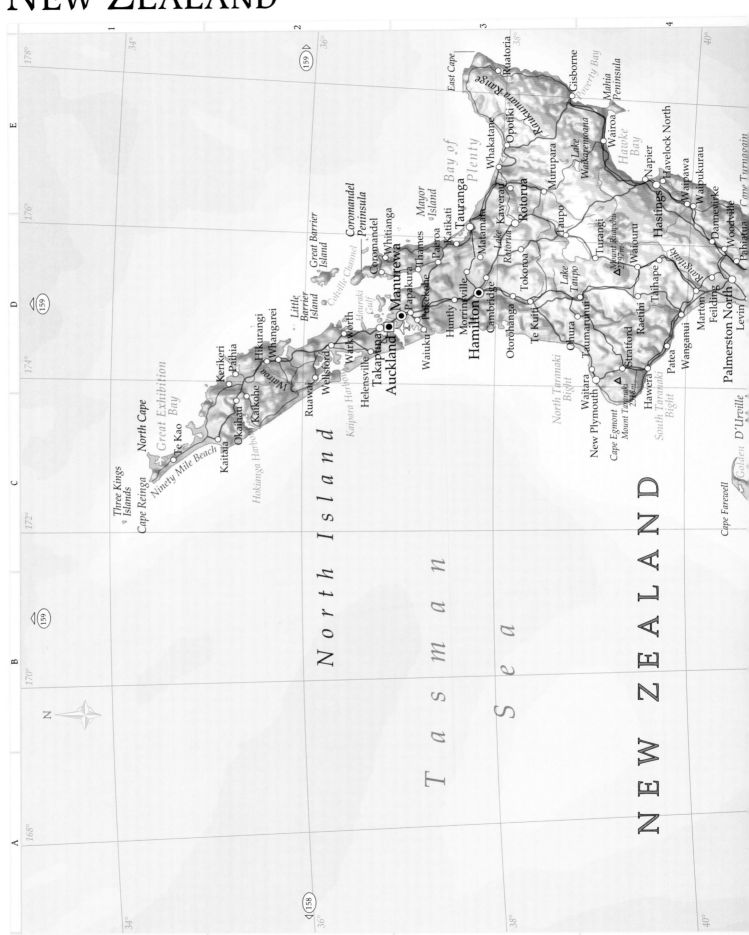

Three Kings Islands

Cape Reinga
North Cape
Te Kao
Kaitaia
Okaihau
Kaikohe
Kerikeri
Paihia
Hikurangi
Whangarei
Warkworth
Helensville
Wellsford
Ruawai
Takapuna
Auckland
Manurewa
Papakura
Pukekohe
Waiuka
Huntly
Morrinsville
Hamilton
Cambridge
Otorohanga
Te Kuiti
Taumarunui
Ohura
Stratford
New Plymouth
Waitara
Hawera
Patea
Wanganui
Marton
Feilding
Palmerston North
Levin

Coromandel
Whitianga
Thames
Paeroa
Katikati
Tauranga
Matamata
Kawerau
Rotorua
Taupo
Turangi
Waiouru
Taihape
Raetihi

Whakatane
Opotiki
Murupara
Wairoa
Napier
Hastings
Havelock North
Waipawa
Waipukurau
Dannevirke
Woodville
Pahiatua

Ruatoria
Gisborne

Mangaweka

North Island

North Cape
Great Exhibition Bay
Ninety Mile Beach
Hokianga Harbour
Wairoa
Kaipara Harbour
Coville Channel
Great Barrier Island
Little Barrier Island
Coromandel Peninsula
Mayor Island
Bay of Plenty
East Cape
Poverty Bay
Mahia Peninsula
Hawke Bay
Lake Waikaremoana
Raukumara Range
Lake Rotorua
Lake Taupo
Mount Ruapehu 2797m
Ruahine Range
North Taranaki Bight
South Taranaki Bight
Cape Egmont
Mount Taranaki 2518m
Cape Farewell
Golden D'Urville
Cape Turnagain

N E W   Z E A L A N D

T a s m a n   S e a

N

POPULATION

Less than
50,000
○

50,000 –
100,000
○

100,000 –
500,000
◉

Over
500,000
▣

166

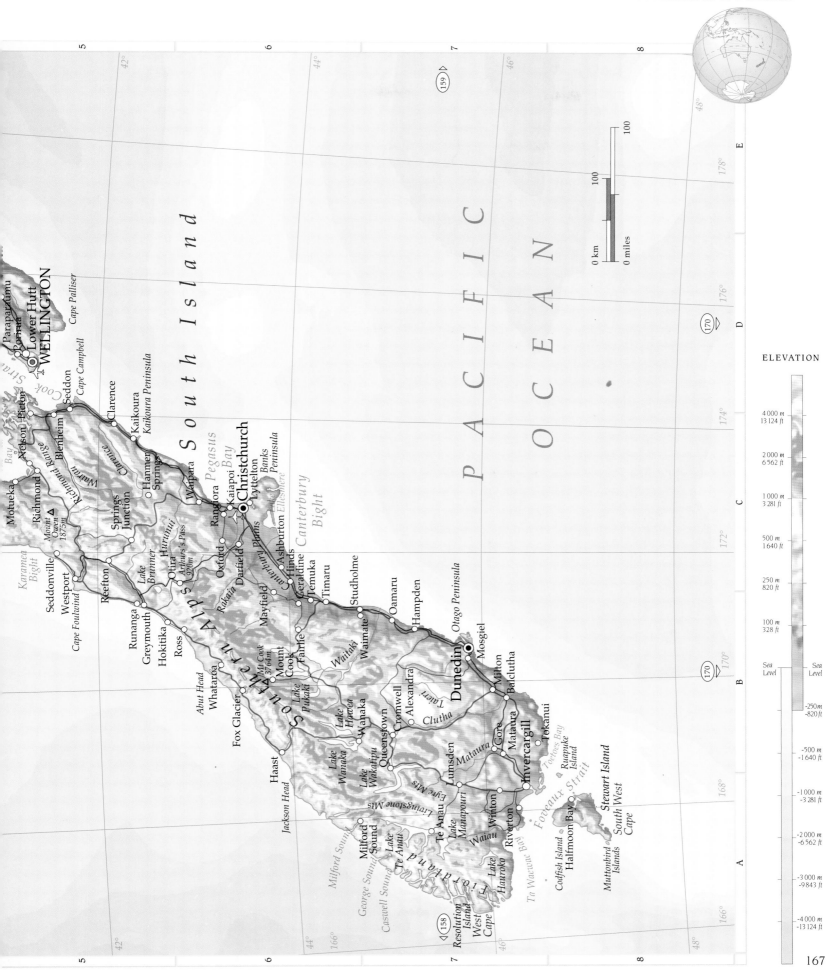

PACIFIC OCEAN

South Island

Southern Alps

Fiordland

Stewart Island

WELLINGTON
Lower Hutt
Paraparaumu
Porirua
Cook Strait
Cape Palliser
Cape Campbell
Seddon
Picton
Nelson
Blenheim
Clarence
Kaikoura
Kaikoura Peninsula
Cloudy Bay
Motueka
Richmond
Richmond Range
Mount Owen 1875m
Springs Junction
Hanmer Springs
Hurunui
Arthur's Pass 920m
Rangiora
Waipara
Pegasus Bay
Kaiapoi Bay
Christchurch
Lyttelton
Banks Peninsula
Lake Ellesmere
Canterbury Bight
Seddonville
Westport
Cape Foulwind
Reefton
Lake Brunner
Otira
Oxford
Darfield
Ashburton
Canterbury Plains
Hinds
Geraldine
Temuka
Timaru
Studholme
Runanga
Greymouth
Hokitika
Ross
Mayfield
Rakaia
Mount Cook
Mt Cook 3764m
Fairlie
Waitaki
Waimate
Oamaru
Hampden
Abut Head
Whataroa
Fox Glacier
Lake Pukaki
Otago Peninsula
Mosgiel
Dunedin
Haast
Lake Wanaka
Lake Hawea
Wanaka
Cromwell
Alexandra
L. Aviemore
Clutha
Milton
Balclutha
Jackson Head
Lake Wakatipu
Queenstown
Lumsden
Mataura
Gore
Mataura
Tokanui
Milford Sound
George Sound
Caswell Sound
Te Anau
Lake Te Anau
Lake Manapouri
Eyre Mts
Livingstone Mts
Waiau
Winton
Riverton
Invercargill
Foveaux Strait
Ruapuke Island
Te Waewae Bay
Lake Hauroka
Resolution Island
West Cape
Codfish Island
Halfmoon Bay
Muttonbird Islands
Stewart Island
South West Cape
Oreti Bay

ELEVATION

4 000 m	13 124 ft
2 000 m	6 562 ft
1 000 m	3 281 ft
500 m	1 640 ft
250 m	820 ft
100 m	328 ft
Sea Level	Sea Level
-250 m	-820 ft
-500 m	-1 640 ft
-1 000 m	-3 281 ft
-2 000 m	-6 562 ft
-3 000 m	-9 843 ft
-4 000 m	-13 124 ft

100 km
0 km

100 miles
0 miles

159
170
170
158

THE PACIFIC OCEAN

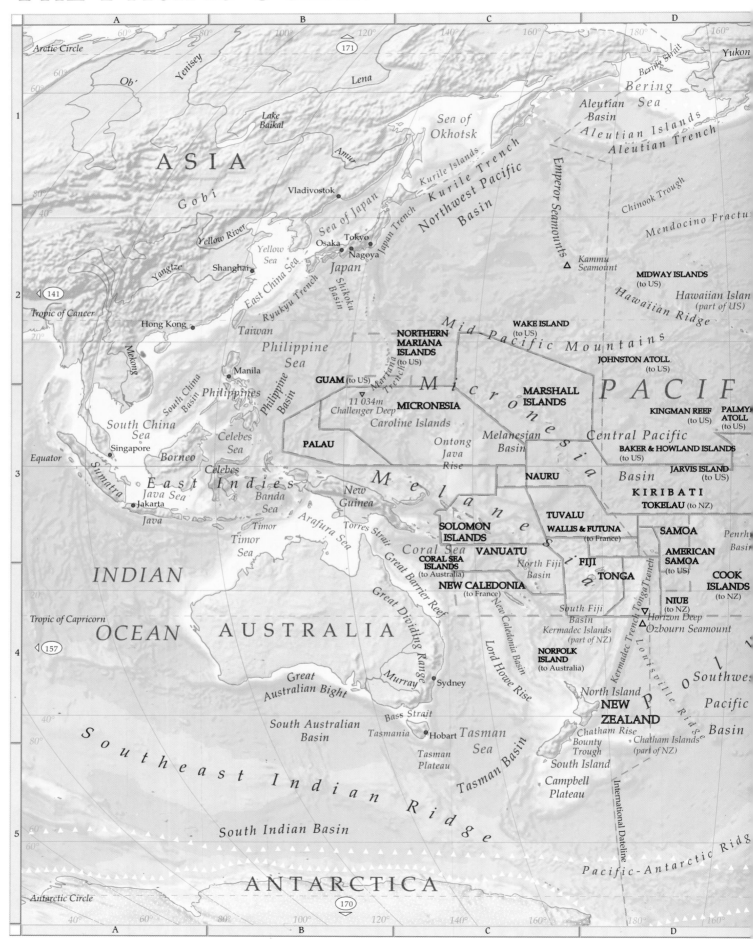

Arctic Circle

Yenisey
Ob'
Lena

171

Bering Strait
Yukon

Lake
Baikal

Sea of
Okhotsk

Bering
Sea

Aleutian
Basin

Aleutian Islands

Aleutian Trench

ASIA

Gobi

Amur

Kurile Islands

Kurile Trench

Emperor Seamounts

Chinook Trough

Vladivostok

Sea of Japan

Japan Trench

Northwest Pacific
Basin

Mendocino Fracture

Yellow River

Osaka
Tokyo
Nagoya

△ Kammu
Seamount

MIDWAY ISLANDS
(to US)

Yangtze

Shanghai

Yellow
Sea

Japan

Shikoku
Basin

Hawaiian Islan
(part of US)

141

East China Sea

Ryukyu Trench

Tropic of Cancer

Hong Kong

Taiwan

Mid Pacific Mountains

Hawaiian Ridge

WAKE ISLAND
(to US)

**NORTHERN
MARIANA
ISLANDS**
(to US)

JOHNSTON ATOLL
(to US)

Philippine
Sea

Mekong

Mi

PACIF

Manila

GUAM (to US)

▽
11 034m
Challenger Deep

MICRONESIA

**MARSHALL
ISLANDS**

KINGMAN REEF
(to US)

**PALMY
ATOLL**
(to US)

Philippines

South China
Basin

Philippine
Basin

Caroline Islands

Central Pacific

c

South China
Sea

Celebes
Sea

PALAU

Ontong
Java
Rise

Melanesian
Basin

r

o

n

e

BAKER & HOWLAND ISLANDS
(to US)

Singapore

Borneo

Equator

Celebes

s

Basin

JARVIS ISLAND
(to US)

Sumatra

East Indies

M

NAURU

i

a

KIRIBATI

Java Sea

Banda
Sea

New
Guinea

e

l

TOKELAU (to NZ)

Jakarta

Java

Timor

a

Torres Strait

Great Barrier Reef

n

TUVALU

WALLIS & FUTUNA
(to France)

SAMOA

Timor
Sea

Arafura Sea

e

**SOLOMON
ISLANDS**

Coral Sea

North Fiji
Basin

s

FIJI

**AMERICAN
SAMOA**
(to US)

Penrh
Basin

INDIAN

VANUATU

i

a

**CORAL SEA
ISLANDS**
(to Australia)

New Caledonia Basin

TONGA

**COOK
ISLANDS**
(to NZ)

OCEAN

AUSTRALIA

Great Dividing Range

NEW CALEDONIA
(to France)

South Fiji
Basin

NIUE
(to NZ)

Tropic of Capricorn

157

Lord Howe Rise

Kermadec Islands
(part of NZ)

▽
△ Horizon Deep
Ozbourn Seamount

P

Great
Australian Bight

Murray

Sydney

**NORFOLK
ISLAND**
(to Australia)

o

Southwe

Bass Strait

North Island

Pacific
Basin

South Australian
Basin

Tasmania

Hobart

Tasman
Sea

**NEW
ZEALAND**

Chatham Rise

Chatham Islands
(part of NZ)

Tasman
Plateau

Tasman Basin

Bounty
Trough

South Island

Campbell
Plateau

South Indian Basin

Southeast Indian Ridge

International Dateline

Pacific-Antarctic Ridg

ANTARCTICA

170

Antarctic Circle

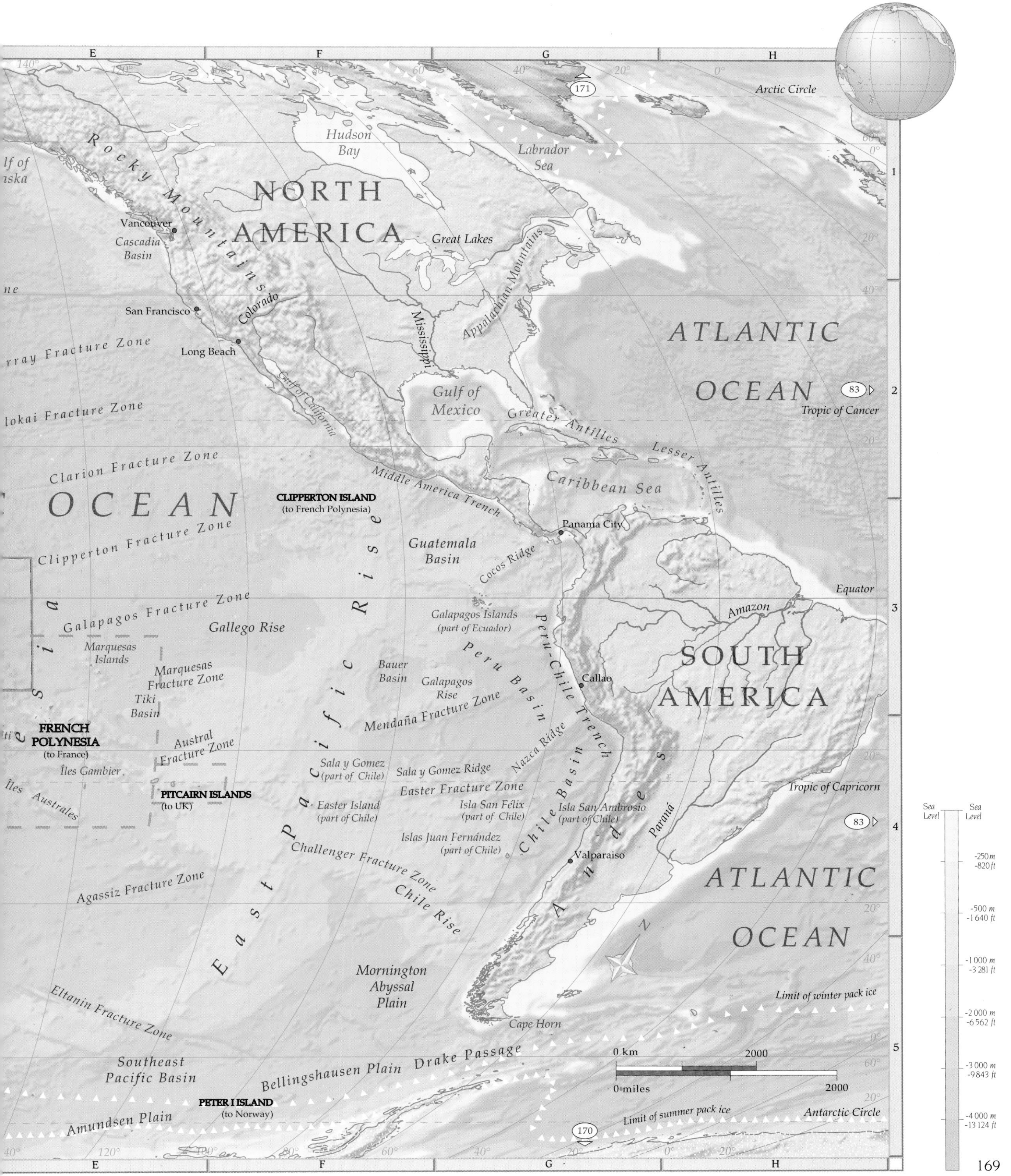

E   F   G   H

140°   120°   100°   80°   60°   40°   20°   0°

Arctic Circle

171

60°   1

lf of
ıska

Rocky Mountains

Hudson
Bay

Labrador
Sea

NORTH
AMERICA

Vancouver
*Cascadia
Basin*

Great Lakes

ne

San Francisco   *Colorado*

ATLANTIC

40°   2

rray Fracture Zone

Long Beach

Mississippi

Appalachian Mountains

OCEAN   83 ▷

lokai Fracture Zone

Gulf of California

Gulf of
Mexico

Greater Antilles

Tropic of Cancer

20°

Clarion Fracture Zone

Lesser Antilles

OCEAN

Middle America Trench

Caribbean Sea

CLIPPERTON ISLAND
(to French Polynesia)

Clipperton Fracture Zone

Panama City

0°   3

East Pacific Rise

Guatemala
Basin

Cocos Ridge

Galapagos Fracture Zone

Gallego Rise

Galapagos Islands
(part of Ecuador)

Equator

Amazon

Peru-Chile Trench

*Marquesas
Islands*

*Bauer
Basin*

*Galapagos
Rise*

SOUTH
AMERICA

*Marquesas
Fracture Zone*

Peru Basin

*Tiki
Basin*

Callao

FRENCH
POLYNESIA
(to France)

Mendaña Fracture Zone

Nazca Ridge

*Austral
Fracture Zone*

Îles Gambier

Tropic of Capricorn   20°

Îles Australes

PITCAIRN ISLANDS
(to UK)

Sala y Gomez
(part of Chile)

Sala y Gomez Ridge

Easter Fracture Zone

Chile Basin

Paraná

83 ▷   4

Easter Island
(part of Chile)

Isla San Félix
(part of Chile)

Isla San Ambrosio
(part of Chile)

Andes

Islas Juan Fernández
(part of Chile)

ATLANTIC

Challenger Fracture Zone

Valparaiso

Agassiz Fracture Zone

Chile Rise

40°

OCEAN

Mornington
Abyssal
Plain

N

Eltanin Fracture Zone

Limit of winter pack ice   60°   5

*Southeast
Pacific Basin*

Bellingshausen Plain *Drake Passage*

0 km   2000

0 miles   2000

Cape Horn

PETER I ISLAND
(to Norway)

Limit of summer pack ice   Antarctic Circle

Amundsen Plain

170 ▽

40°   120°   100°   80°   60°   40°   20°   0°   20°

E   F   G   H

169

Sea
Level

Sea
Level

−250 m
−820 ft

−500 m
−1 640 ft

−1 000 m
−3 281 ft

−2 000 m
−6 562 ft

−3 000 m
−9 843 ft

−4 000 m
−13 124 ft

ANTARCTICA

ATLANTIC

OCEAN

83

South Sandwich Trench

America-Antarctica Ridge

SOUTH GEORGIA
(to UK)

SOUTH SANDWICH
ISLANDS
(to UK)

Atlantic-Indian Basin

INDIAN

OCEAN

*Scotia
Sea*

Antarctic Circle

Lazarev Sea

Enderby Plain

Orcadas
(Argentina)

*South Orkney
Islands*

Signy
(UK)

Weddell Plain

Sanae
(South Africa)

Georg von Neumayer
(Germany)

Novolazarevskaya
(Russian Federation)

Drake Passage

73

*South Shetland
Islands*

Esperanza
(Argentina)

Capitán Arturo Prat
(Chile)

Halley
(UK)

*Dronning Maud
Land*

*Lützow
Holmbukta*

Molodezhnaya
(Russian Federation)

Syowa
(Japan)

157

*Enderby
Land*

ELEVATION

Palmer
(US)

*Weddell
Sea*

*Coats
Land*

Mawson
(Australia)

Rothera
(UK)

San Martín
(Argentina)

Belgrano II
(Argentina)

*Berkner
Island*

Cape Darnley

4 000 m 13 124 ft	

Graham Land

Antarctic Peninsula

Palmer Land

*Ronne
Ice Shelf*

*Mackenzie
Bay*

Prydz Bay

*Alexander
Island*

ANTARCTICA

*Princess
Elizabeth
Land*

Davis
(Australia)

2 000 m
6 562 ft

*Bellingshausen
Sea*

Vinson Massif
4897m

Greater

*Davis
Sea*

PETER I ISLAND
(to Norway)

*Ellsworth
Land*

Lesser

Amundsen-Scott
(US)

South
Pole

Antarctica

Mirny
(Russian Federation)

1 000 m
3 281 ft

Limit of winter pack ice

Limit of summer pack ice

Antarctica

South
Geomagnetic
Pole

Vostok
(Russian Federation)

*Shackleton
Ice Shelf*

500 m
1 640 ft

Marie Byrd Land

Transantarctic Mountains

Mount Kirkpatrick
4528m

250 m
820 ft

*Amundsen
Sea*

Mount Sidley
4181m

Mount Markham
4351m

*Ross Ice
Shelf*

*Wilkes
Land*

Casey
(Australia)

100 m
328 ft

Mount Siple
3100m

*Roosevelt
Island*

Scott Base
(N.Z)

*Cape
Poinsett*

Sea
Level

Sea
Level

PACIFIC

McMurdo Base
(US)

Mount Erebus
3794m

Victoria Land

*Terre
Adélie*

South

-250 m
-820 ft

OCEAN

*Amundsen
Plain*

*Ross
Sea*

George V
Land

Dumont d'Urville
(France)

Indian

157

-500 m
-1640 ft

Cape Adare

Leningradskaya
(Russian Federation)

Basin

-1 000 m
-3 281 ft

Udintsev Fracture Zone

Scott Island

-2 000 m
-6 562 ft

Balleny Islands

*Macquarie
Ridge*

-3 000 m
-9843 ft

Eltanin Fracture Zone

Pacific-Antarctic Ridge

0 km   500
0 miles   500

169

-4 000 m
-13 124 ft

○ Antarctic Research Stations

169

ARCTIC OCEAN

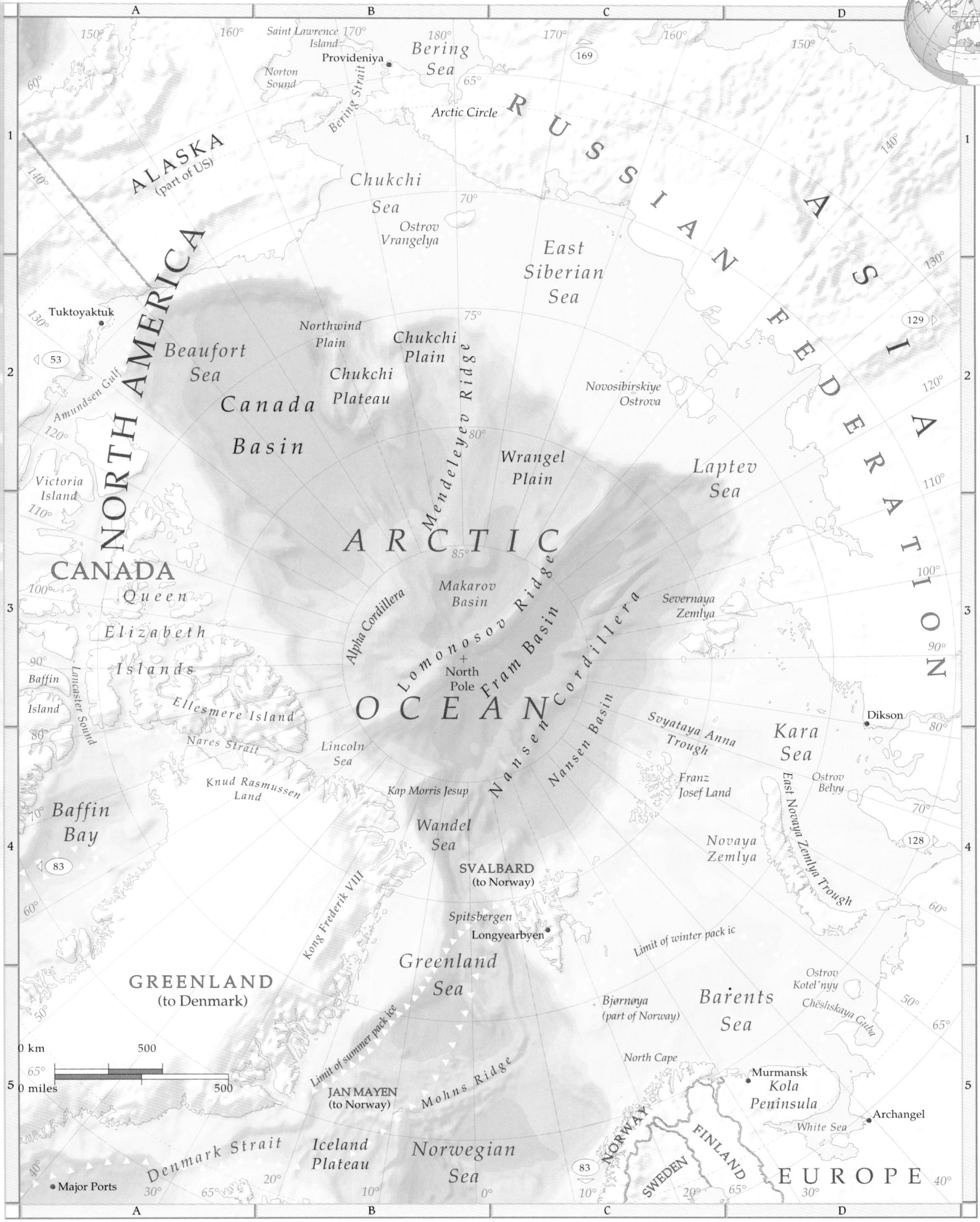

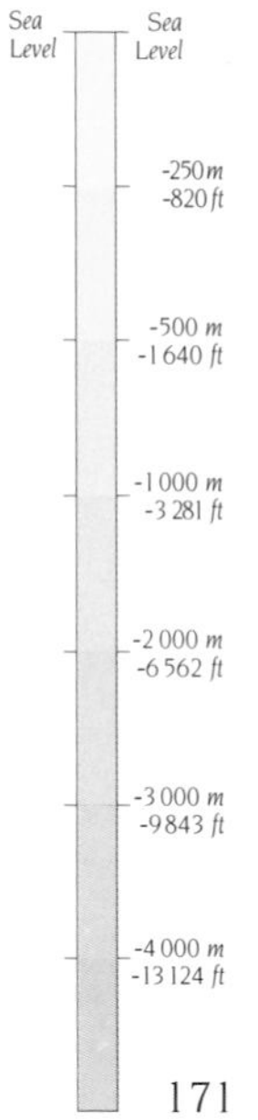

ALASKA
(part of US)

RUSSIAN FEDERATION

Saint Lawrence Island

Provid*eniya*

Bering Sea

169

Arctic Circle

Norton Sound

Bering Strait

Chukchi Sea

Ostrov Vrangelya

East Siberian Sea

NORTH AMERICA

Tuktoyaktuk

53

Beaufort Sea

Northwind Plain

Chukchi Plain

Novosibirskiye Ostrova

129

Amundsen Gulf

Canada Basin

Chukchi Plateau

Mendeleyev Ridge

Wrangel Plain

Laptev Sea

Victoria Island

CANADA

Queen

Elizabeth

Islands

ARCTIC

Alpha Cordillera

Makarov Basin

Lomonosov Ridge

Fram Basin

Severnaya Zemlya

Baffin Island

Lancaster Sound

Nansen Cordillera

North Pole

Nansen Basin

Dikson

Ellesmere Island

OCEAN

Svyataya Anna Trough

Kara Sea

Nares Strait

Lincoln Sea

Nansen Basin

Ostrov Belyy

Franz Josef Land

East Novaya Zemlya Trough

Knud Rasmussen Land

Kap Morris Jesup

128

Baffin Bay

83

Wandel Sea

Novaya Zemlya

Kong Frederik VIII

SVALBARD
(to Norway)

Limit of winter pack ic

Ostrov Kotel'nyy

Spitsbergen

Longyearbyen

Chëshskaya Guba

GREENLAND
(to Denmark)

Greenland Sea

Bjørnøya
(part of Norway)

Barents Sea

Limit of summer pack ice

North Cape

Mohns Ridge

Murmansk

Kola Peninsula

JAN MAYEN
(to Norway)

NORWAY

White Sea

Archangel

Denmark Strait

Iceland Plateau

Norwegian Sea

83

SWEDEN

FINLAND

EUROPE

0 km   500
0 miles   500

Major Ports

Sea Level	Sea Level
	-250 m / -820 ft
	-500 m / -1640 ft
	-1000 m / -3281 ft
	-2000 m / -6562 ft
	-3000 m / -9843 ft
	-4000 m / -13124 ft

171

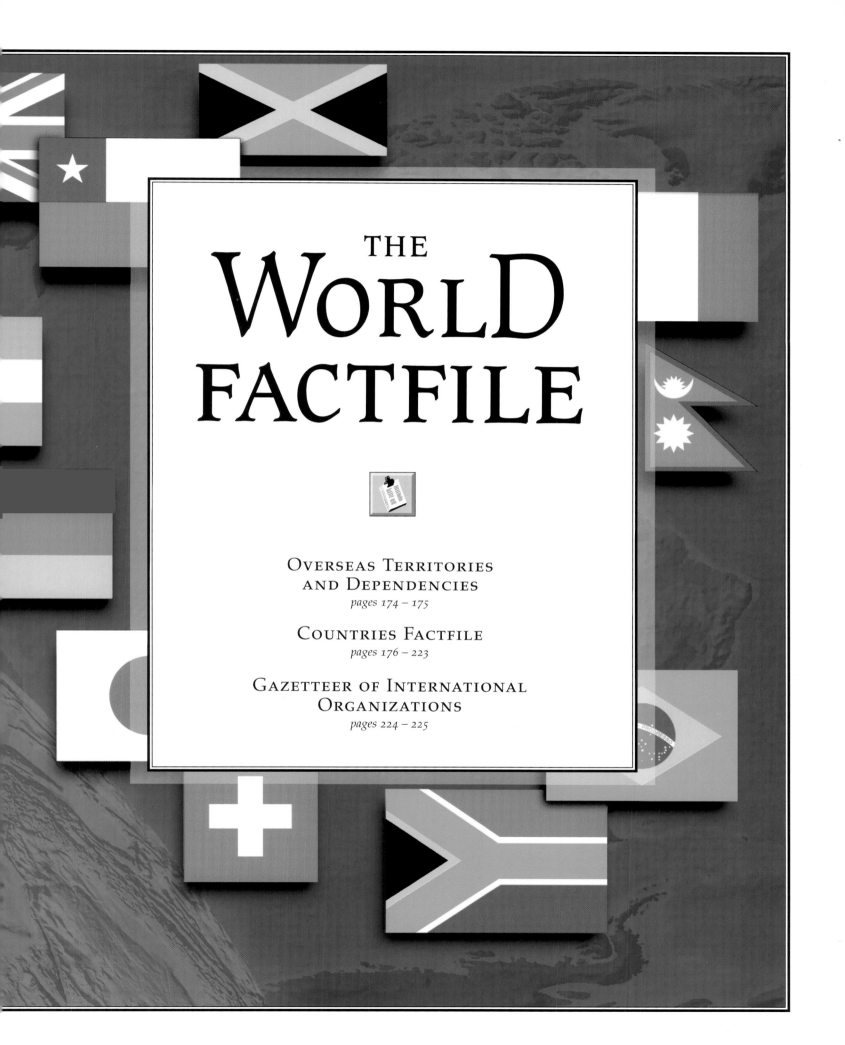

THE WORLD FACTFILE

OVERSEAS TERRITORIES AND DEPENDENCIES

DESPITE THE RAPID PROCESS of decolonization since the end of the Second World War, around 10 million people in over 50 territories around the world continue to live under the protection of France, Australia, the Netherlands, Denmark, Norway, Portugal, New Zealand, the United Kingdom, or the USA. These remnants of former colonial empires may have persisted for economic, strategic or political reasons, and are administered in a variety of ways.

AUSTRALIA

AUSTRALIA'S OVERSEAS territories have not been an issue since Papua New Guinea became independent in 1975. Consequently there is no overriding policy towards them. Some of Norfolk Island is inhabited by descendants of the HMS Bounty mutineers and more recent Australian migrants.

ASHMORE & CARTIER ISLANDS
INDIAN OCEAN

Status External territory
Claimed 1978
Capital not applicable
Population None
Area 5.2 sq km (2 sq miles)

CHRISTMAS ISLAND
INDIAN OCEAN

Status External territory
Claimed 1958
Capital Flying Fish Cove
Population 2,871
Area 134.6 sq km (52 sq miles)

COCOS ISLANDS
INDIAN OCEAN

Status External territory
Claimed 1955
Capital No official capital
Population 555
Area 14.24 sq km (5.5 sq miles)

CORAL SEA ISLANDS
SOUTH PACIFIC

Status External territory
Claimed 1969
Capital None
Population 8 (meteorologists)
Area Less than 3 sq km
(1.16 sq miles)

HEARD & McDONALD ISLANDS
INDIAN OCEAN

Status External territory
Claimed 1947
Capital not applicable
Population None
Area 417 sq km (161 sq miles)

NORFOLK ISLAND
SOUTH PACIFIC

Status External territory
Claimed 1913
Capital Kingston
Population 2,637
Area 34.4 sq km (13.3 sq miles)

DENMARK

THE FAEROE ISLANDS have been under Danish administration since Queen Margreth I of Denmark inherited Norway in 1380. The Home Rule Act of 1948 gave the Faeroese control over all their internal affairs. Greenland first came under Danish rule in 1380. Today, Denmark remains responsible for the island's foreign affairs and defence.

FAEROE ISLANDS
NORTH ATLANTIC

Status External territory
Claimed 1380
Capital Tórshavn
Population 47,310
Area 1,399 sq km (540 sq miles)

GREENLAND
NORTH ATLANTIC

Status External territory
Claimed 1380
Capital Nuuk
Population 55,385
Area 2,175,516 sq km (840,000 sq miles)

FRANCE

FRANCE HAS DEVELOPED economic ties with its overseas territories, thereby stressing interdependence over independence. Overseas *départements*, officially part of France, have their own governments. Territorial *collectivités* and overseas *territoires* have varying degrees of autonomy.

CLIPPERTON ISLAND
EAST PACIFIC

Status Dependency of French Polynesia
Claimed 1930
Capital not applicable
Population None
Area 7 sq km (2.7 sq miles)

FRENCH GUIANA
SOUTH AMERICA

Status Overseas department
Claimed 1817
Capital Cayenne
Population 135,000
Area 90,996 sq km (35,135 sq miles)

FRENCH POLYNESIA
SOUTH PACIFIC

Status Overseas territory
Claimed 1843
Capital Papeete
Population 211,000
Area 4,165 sq km (1,608 sq miles)

GUADELOUPE
WEST INDIES

Status Overseas department
Claimed 1635
Capital Basse-Terre
Population 413,000
Area 1,780 sq km (687 sq miles)

MARTINIQUE
WEST INDIES

Status Overseas department
Claimed 1635
Capital Fort-de-France
Population 371,000
Area 1,100 sq km (425 sq miles)

MAYOTTE
INDIAN OCEAN

Status Territorial collectivity
Claimed 1843
Capital Mamoudzou
Population 97,088
Area 374 sq km (144 sq miles)

NEW CALEDONIA
SOUTH PACIFIC

Status Overseas territory
Claimed 1853
Capital Noumeá
Population 179,000
Area 19,103 sq km (7,374 sq miles)

RÉUNION
INDIAN OCEAN

Status Overseas department
Claimed 1638
Capital Denis
Population 632,000
Area 2,512 sq km (970 sq miles)

ST PIERRE & MIQUELON
NORTH AMERICA

Status Territorial collectivity
Claimed 1604
Capital Saint-Pierre
Population 6,000
Area 242 sq km (93.4 sq miles)

WALLIS & FUTUNA
SOUTH PACIFIC

Status Overseas territory
Claimed 1842
Capital Matā'Utu
Population 14,000
Area 274 sq km (106 sq miles)

NETHERLANDS

THE COUNTRY'S TWO remaining overseas territories were formerly part of the Dutch West Indies. Both are now self-governing, but the Netherlands remains responsible for their defence.

ARUBA
WEST INDIES

Status Autonomous part of the Netherlands
Claimed 1643
Capital Oranjestad
Population 69,000
Area 194 sq km (75 sq miles)

NETHERLANDS ANTILLES
WEST INDIES

Status Autonomous part of the Netherlands
Claimed 1816
Capital Willemstad
Population 195,000
Area 800 sq km (308 sq miles)

NEW ZEALAND

NEW ZEALAND'S GOVERNMENT has no desire to retain any overseas territories. However, the economic weakness of its dependent territory, Tokelau and its freely associated states, Niue and the Cook Islands, has forced New Zealand to remain responsible for their foreign policy and defence.

COOK ISLANDS
SOUTH PACIFIC

Status Associated territory
Claimed 1901
Capital Avarua
Population 19,000
Area 293 sq km (113 sq miles)

NIUE
SOUTH PACIFIC

Status Associated territory
Claimed 1901
Capital Alofi
Population 2,000
Area 264 sq km (102 sq miles)

TOKELAU
SOUTH PACIFIC

Status Dependent territory
Claimed 1926
Capital not applicable
Population 2,000
Area 10.4 sq km (4 sq miles)

NORWAY

IN 1920, 41 nations signed the Spitsbergen treaty recognizing Norwegian sovereignty over Svalbard. There is a NATO base on Jan Mayen. Bouvet Island is a nature reserve.

BOUVET ISLAND
SOUTH ATLANTIC

Status Dependency
Claimed 1928
Capital not applicable
Population None
Area 58 sq km (22 sq miles)

JAN MAYEN
NORTH ATLANTIC
Status Dependency
Claimed 1929
Capital not applicable
Population None
Area 381 sq km (147 sq miles)

PETER I ISLAND
SOUTHERN OCEAN
Status Dependency
Claimed 1931
Capital not applicable
Population None
Area 180 sq km (69 sq miles)

SVALBARD
ARCTIC OCEAN
Status Dependency
Claimed 1920
Capital Longyearbyen
Population 3,431
Area 62,906 sq km (24,289 sq miles)

PORTUGAL

AFTER A COUP in 1974, Portugal's overseas possessions were rapidly granted sovereignty. Macao is the only one remaining and it is to become a Special Administrative Region of China in 1999.

MACAO
SOUTH CHINA
Status Special territory
Claimed 1557
Capital Macao
Population 388,000
Area 18 sq km (7 sq miles)

UNITED KINGDOM

THE UK STILL has the largest number of overseas territories. Locally-governed by a mixture of elected representatives and appointed officials, they all enjoy a large measure of internal self-government, but certain powers, such as foreign affairs and defence, are reserved for Governors of the British Crown.

ANGUILLA
WEST INDIES
Status Dependent territory
Claimed 1650
Capital The Valley
Population 8,960
Area 96 sq km (37 sq miles)

ASCENSION ISLAND
SOUTH ATLANTIC
Status Dependency of St Helena
Claimed 1673
Capital Georgetown
Population 1,099
Area 88 sq km (34 sq miles)

BERMUDA
NORTH ATLANTIC
Status Crown colony
Claimed 1612
Capital Hamilton
Population 60,686
Area 53 sq km (20.5 sq miles)

BRITISH INDIAN OCEAN TERRITORY
INDIAN OCEAN
Status Dependent territory
Claimed 1814
Capital No official capital
Population 3,400
Area 60 sq km (23 sq miles)

BRITISH VIRGIN ISLANDS
WEST INDIES
Status Dependent territory
Claimed 1672
Capital Road Town
Population 16,644
Area 153 sq km (59 sq miles)

CAYMAN ISLANDS
WEST INDIES
Status Dependent territory
Claimed 1670
Capital George Town
Population 25,355
Area 259 sq km (100 sq miles)

FALKLAND ISLANDS
SOUTH ATLANTIC
Status Dependent territory
Claimed 1832
Capital Stanley
Population 2,121
Area 12,173 sq km (4,699 sq miles)

GIBRALTAR
SOUTHWEST EUROPE
Status Crown colony
Claimed 1713
Capital Gibraltar
Population 28,074
Area 6.5 sq km (2.5 sq miles)

GUERNSEY
CHANNEL ISLANDS
Status Crown dependency
Claimed 1066
Capital St Peter Port
Population 58,000
Area 65 sq km (25 sq miles)

ISLE OF MAN
BRITISH ISLES
Status Crown dependency
Claimed 1765
Capital Douglas
Population 71,000
Area 572 sq km (221 sq miles)

JERSEY
CHANNEL ISLANDS
Status Crown dependency
Claimed 1066
Capital St Helier
Population 84,082
Area 116 sq km (45 sq miles)

MONTSERRAT
WEST INDIES
Status Dependent territory
Claimed 1632
Capital Plymouth (currently uninhabitable)
Population 11,000
Area 102 sq km (40 sq miles)

PITCAIRN ISLANDS
SOUTH PACIFIC
Status Dependent territory
Claimed 1887
Capital Adamstown
Population 66
Area 3.5 sq km (1.35 sq miles)

ST HELENA
SOUTH ATLANTIC
Status Dependent territory
Claimed 1673
Capital Jamestown
Population 6,000
Area 122 sq km (47 sq miles)

SOUTH GEORGIA & THE SOUTH SANDWICH ISLANDS
SOUTH ATLANTIC
Status Dependent territory
Claimed 1775
Population No permanent residents
Area 3,592 sq km (1,387 sq miles)

TRISTAN DA CUNHA
SOUTH ATLANTIC
Status Dependency of St Helena
Claimed 1612
Population 297
Area 98 sq km (38 sq miles)

TURKS & CAICOS ISLANDS
WEST INDIES
Status Dependent territory
Claimed 1766
Capital Cockburn Town
Population 13,000
Area 430 sq km (166 sq miles)

UNITED STATES OF AMERICA

AMERICA'S OVERSEAS TERRITORIES have been seen as strategically useful, if expensive, links with its 'backyards'. The US has, in most cases, given the local population a say in deciding their own status. A US Commonwealth territory, such as Puerto Rico has a greater level of independence than that of a US unincorporated or external territory.

AMERICAN SAMOA
SOUTH PACIFIC
Status Unincorporated territory
Claimed 1900
Capital Pago Pago
Population 51,000
Area 195 sq km (75 sq miles)

BAKER & HOWLAND ISLANDS
SOUTH PACIFIC
Status Unincorporated territory
Claimed 1856
Capital not applicable
Population None
Area 1.4 sq km (0.54 sq miles)

GUAM
WEST PACIFIC
Status Unincorporated territory
Claimed 1898
Capital Agaña
Population 144,000
Area 549 sq km (212 sq miles)

JARVIS ISLAND
SOUTH PACIFIC
Status Unincorporated territory
Claimed 1856
Capital not applicable
Population None
Area 4.5 sq km (1.7 sq miles)

JOHNSTON ATOLL
CENTRAL PACIFIC
Status Unincorporated territory
Claimed 1858
Capital not applicable
Population 327
Area 2.8 sq km (1 sq mile)

KINGMAN REEF
CENTRAL PACIFIC
Status Administered territory
Claimed 1856
Capital not applicable
Population None
Area 1 sq km (0.4 sq miles)

MIDWAY ISLANDS
CENTRAL PACIFIC
Status Administered territory
Claimed 1867
Capital not applicable
Population 453
Area 5.2 sq km (2 sq miles)

NAVASSA ISLAND
WEST INDIES
Status Unincorporated territory
Claimed 1856
Capital not applicable
Population None
Area 5.2 sq km (2 sq miles)

NORTHERN MARIANA ISLANDS
WEST PACIFIC
Status Commonwealth territory
Claimed 1947
Capital No official capital
Population 47,000
Area 457 sq km (177 sq miles)

PALMYRA ATOLL
CENTRAL PACIFIC
Status Unincorporated territory
Claimed 1898
Capital not applicable
Population None
Area 12 sq km (5 sq miles)

PUERTO RICO
WEST INDIES
Status Commonwealth territory
Claimed 1898
Capital San Juan
Population 3.6 million
Area 8,959 sq km (3,458 sq miles)

VIRGIN ISLANDS
WEST INDIES
Status Unincorporated territory
Claimed 1917
Capital Charlotte Amalie
Population 104,000
Area 355 sq km (137 sq miles)

WAKE ISLAND
CENTRAL PACIFIC
Status Unincorporated territory
Claimed 1898
Capital not applicable
Population 302
Area 6.5 sq km (2.5 sq miles)

CANADA

CANADA EXTENDS from its US border north to the Arctic Ocean. In recent years, French-speaking Québec has sought independence from the rest of the country.

GEOGRAPHY
Arctic tundra and islands give way to forests, interspersed with lakes and rivers, and then central plains, with vast prairies. Rocky Mountains in the west.

CLIMATE
Ranges from polar in the north, to cool in the south. Winters in the interior are colder than on the coast, with freezing temperatures and deep snow.

PEOPLE AND SOCIETY
Most people live along narrow strip near US border. Social issues include welfare provision and Commonwealth membership. Government welcomes ethnic diversity among immigrants. Land claims by indigenous peoples settled recently.

The Niagara Falls are situated on the Canada–US border.

THE ECONOMY
Wide-ranging resources, providing cheap energy and raw materials for manufactures, underpin high standard of living. Better productivity and rise of high-tech industries have increased unemployment. Concern over primary export prices.

FACTFILE
Official Name Canada
Date of Formation 1867/1949
Capital Ottawa
Population 27.8 million
Total Area
9,976,140 sq km (3,851,788 sq miles)
Density 3 people per sq km
Languages English*, French*, Chinese, Italian, German, Portuguese, Cree, Inuktitut
Religions Catholic 46%, Protestant 30%, other 24%
Ethnic Mix British origin 40%, French origin 27%, other European 20%, Indian and Inuit 2%, other 11%
Government Parliamentary state
Currency Canadian $ = 100 cents

UNITED STATES OF AMERICA

STRETCHING ACROSS the most temperate part of North America, and with many natural resources, the USA is the world's leading economic power.

GEOGRAPHY
Central plain, mountains in west, hills and low mountains in east. Forested north and east, south-western deserts.

CLIMATE
Continental in north, hot summers and mild winters in southeast, desert climate in southwest. Arctic climate in Alaska; Florida and Hawaii tropical.

PEOPLE AND SOCIETY
Multiracial population, established through immigration, initially from Europe and Africa, with more recent influxes from Latin America and Asia. Strong sense of nationhood.

THE ECONOMY
Innovation, skilled labour and venture capital help high-tech industries replace outdated manufacturing. Global dominance of US culture boosts services, manufactures. Vast agriculture, mining sectors.

FACTFILE
Official Name United States of America
Date of Formation 1787/1959
Capital Washington DC
Population 265.8 million
Total Area
9,372,610 sq km (3,681,760 sq miles)
Density
28 people per sq km
Languages
English*, Spanish, other
Religions Protestant 56%, Catholic 28%, Jewish 2%, other 14%
Ethnic Mix White (inc. Hispanic) 83%, Black 13%, other 4%
Government
Multiparty republic
Currency
US $ = 100 cents

MEXICO

LOCATED BETWEEN the United States of America and the Central American states, Mexico was a Spanish colony for 300 years until 1836.

GEOGRAPHY
Coastal plains along Pacific and Atlantic seaboards rise to a high arid central plateau. To the east and west are Sierra Madre mountain ranges. Limestone lowlands in the Yucatan peninsula.

CLIMATE
Plateau and high mountains are warm for much of year. Pacific coast is tropical: storms occur mostly March–December. Northwest is dry.

PEOPLE AND SOCIETY
Faster-growing population than any other large country – it doubled between 1960 and 1980. Most Mexicans are of mixed Spanish and Indian descent. Rural Indians largely segregated from Hispanic society and most live in poverty.

The cathedral of Santa Prisca at Taxco in Guerrero, Mexico.

THE ECONOMY
One of the world's largest oil producers. Tropical fruits, vegetables grown as cash crops. US companies poised to move into Mexico and enter competition with Mexican industry.

FACTFILE
Official Name United Mexican States
Date of Formation 1836/1867
Capital Mexico City
Population 95.5 million
Total Area
1,958,200 sq km (756,061 sq miles)
Density
49 people per sq km
Languages
Spanish*, Mayan dialects
Religions Roman Catholic 89%, Protestant 6%, other 5%
Ethnic Mix Mestizo 55%, Indian 30%, White 6%, other 9%
Government
Multiparty republic
Currency
Peso = 100 centavos

GUATEMALA

THE LARGEST state on the Central American isthmus, Guatemala returned to civilian rule in 1986, after 32 years of repressive military rule.

GEOGRAPHY
Narrow Pacific coastal plain. Central highlands with volcanoes. Short, swampy Caribbean coast. Tropical rainforests in the north.

CLIMATE
Tropical, hot and humid in coastal regions and north. More temperate in central highlands

PEOPLE AND SOCIETY
Indians form a majority, but power, wealth and land controlled by ladino elite. Highland Indians were main victims of the military's indiscriminate campaign against guerrilla groups 1978–84. Since civilian rule, the level of violence has diminished, but extreme poverty is still widespread.

THE ECONOMY
Agriculture is key sector. Sugar, coffee, beef, bananas and cardamom top exports. Political stability has revived tourism.

FACTFILE
Official Name Republic of Guatemala
Date of Formation 1838
Capital Guatemala City
Population 10.9 million
Total Area
108,890 sq km (42,043 sq miles)
Density
100 people per sq km
Languages Spanish*, Quiché, Mam, Kekchí, Cakchiquel
Religions
Christian 99%, other 1%
Ethnic Mix Maya Indian 55%, ladino (Euro-Indian, White) 45%
Government
Multiparty republic
Currency
Quetzal = 100 centavos

BELIZE

BELIZE LIES on the eastern shore of the Yucatan Peninsula in Central America. A former British colony, it became fully independent in 1981.

GEOGRAPHY
Almost half the land area is forested. Low mountains in south-east. Flat swampy coastal plains.

CLIMATE
Tropical. Very hot and humid, with May–December rainy season.

PEOPLE AND SOCIETY
Spanish-speaking mestizos now outnumber black Creoles for the first time. Huge influx of migrants from other states in the region in the past decade. This has caused some tension. Newcomers provide manpower for agriculture, but have put pressure on social services. Creoles have traditionally dominated society. Emigration to US has weakened their influence.

Fishermen near Belize City. More than 500 tonnes of Caribbean spiny lobster are caught annually.

THE ECONOMY
Agriculture, tourism and remittances from Belizeans living abroad are economic mainstays. Citrus fruit concentrates, lobsters, shrimps and textiles are exported.

FACTFILE
Official Name Belize
Date of Formation 1981
Capital Belmopan
Population 200,000
Total Area
22,960 sq km (8,865 sq miles)
Density
9 people per sq km
Languages English*, English Creole, Spanish, Maya, Garifuna
Religions
Christian 87%, other 13%
Ethnic Mix Mestizo 44%, Creole 30%, Indian 11%, Garifuna 8%, other 7%
Government
Parliamentary democracy
Currency Belizean $ = 100 cents

EL SALVADOR

EL SALVADOR is Central America's smallest state. A 12-year war between US-backed government troops and left-wing guerrillas ended in 1992.

GEOGRAPHY
Narrow coastal belt backed by mountain ranges with over 20 volcanic peaks. Central plateau.

CLIMATE
Tropical coastal belt is very hot, with seasonal rains. Cooler, temperate climate in highlands.

PEOPLE AND SOCIETY
Population is largely mestizo; ethnic tensions are few. The civil war was fought over economic disparities, which still exist, despite some reform. 75,000 people died during the war, many were unarmed civilians. Around 500,000 more were displaced – mainly rural peasant families. In 1992, left-wing movement gave up its arms and joined formal political process.

THE ECONOMY
Civil war caused $2 billion-worth of damage. Huge amounts of foreign aid needed for survival. Over-dependence on coffee, which accounts for 90% of exports.

FACTFILE
Official Name Republic of El Salvador
Date of Formation 1856/1838
Capital San Salvador
Population 5.9 million
Total Area
21,040 sq km (8,124 sq miles)
Density
280 people per sq km
Languages
Spanish*, Nahua
Religions Roman Catholic 75%, other (including Protestant) 25%
Ethnic Mix Mestizo (Euro-Indian) 89%, Indian 10%, White 1%
Government
Multiparty republic
Currency
Colón = 100 centavos

HONDURAS

STRADDLING THE Central American isthmus, Honduras returned to democratic civilian rule in 1981, after a succession of military regimes.

GEOGRAPHY
Narrow plains along both coasts. Mountainous interior, cut by river valleys. Tropical forests, swamps and lagoons in the east.

CLIMATE
Tropical coastal lowlands are hot and humid, with May–October rains. Interior is cooler and drier.

PEOPLE AND SOCIETY
Majority of population is mestizo. Garifunas on Caribbean coast maintain their own language and culture. Indians inhabit the east, and remote mountain areas; their land rights are often violated. Most of the rural population live in poverty. Land reform, and high unemployment are major issues facing the government.

Honduras' main cash crops are bananas and coffee, accounting for 60% of export revenue. Tobacco (above) accounts for 1%.

THE ECONOMY
Second poorest country in the region. Bananas are traditional cash crop – production dominated by two US companies. Coffee, timber and livestock also exported.

FACTFILE
Official Name Republic of Honduras
Date of Formation 1838
Capital Tegucigalpa
Population 5.8 million
Total Area
112,090 sq km (43,278 sq miles)
Density
52 people per sq km
Languages Spanish*, English Creole, Garifuna, Indian languages
Religions
Catholic 97%, other 3%
Ethnic Mix Mestizo 90%, Indian 7%, Garifuna (Black Carib) 2%, White 1%
Government
Multiparty republic
Currency Lempira = 100 centavos

NICARAGUA

NICARAGUA LIES at the heart of Central America. An 11-year war between left-wing Sandinistas and right-wing US-backed Contras ended in 1989.

GEOGRAPHY
Extensive forested plains in the east. Central mountain region with many active volcanoes. Pacific coastlands are dominated by lakes.

CLIMATE
Tropical. Hot all year round in the lowlands. Cooler in the mountains. Occasional hurricanes.

PEOPLE AND SOCIETY
The isolated Atlantic regions, populated by Miskito Indians and blacks, gained limited independence in 1987. Elections in 1990 brought a right-wing pro-US party to power, but the Sandinistas remain a major political force in a country where poverty and unrest are rising.

THE ECONOMY
Coffee, sugar and cotton are the main exports. All are affected by low world prices. Economy dependent on foreign aid; the US is the largest donor.

FACTFILE
Official Name Republic of Nicaragua
Date of Formation 1838
Capital Managua
Population 4.6 million
Total Area
130,000 sq km (50,193 sq miles)
Density
35 people per sq km
Languages
Spanish*, English Creole, Miskito
Religions
Catholic 95%, other 5%
Ethnic Mix Mestizo 69%, White 17%, Black 9%, Indian 5%
Government
Multiparty republic
Currency
Córdoba = 100 pence

COSTA RICA

COSTA RICA is the most stable country in Central America. Its neutrality in foreign affairs is long-standing, but it has very strong ties with the US.

GEOGRAPHY
Coastal plains of swamp and savannah rise to a fertile central plateau, which leads to a mountain range with active volcanic peaks.

CLIMATE
Hot and humid in coastal regions. Temperate uplands. High annual rainfall.

PEOPLE AND SOCIETY
Population has a mixture of Spanish, African and native Indian ancestry. Costa Rica's long democratic tradition, developed public health system and high literacy rates are unrivalled in the region. Plantation-owning families and the US are influential in politics.

The Pan-American Highway runs for 663 km through Costa Rica, at times as only a simple gravel road.

THE ECONOMY
Traditionally agricultural, but mining and manufacturing are developing rapidly. Bananas, beef and coffee are the leading exports. Tourist numbers have increased considerably in recent years.

FACTFILE
Official Name Republic of Costa Rica

Date of Formation 1821 / 1838

Capital San José

Population 3.5 million

Total Area
51,100 sq km (19,730 sq miles)

Density
68 people per sq km

Languages Spanish*, English Creole, Bribri, Cabecar

Religions
Catholic 95%, other 5%

Ethnic Mix White / mestizo (Euro-Indian) 96%, Black 2%, Indian 2%

Government
Multiparty republic

Currency
Colón = 100 centimos

JAMAICA

FIRST COLONIZED by the Spanish and then, from 1655, by the English, the Caribbean island of Jamaica achieved independence in 1962.

GEOGRAPHY
Mainly mountainous, with lush tropical vegetation. Inaccessible limestone area in the northwest. Low, irregular coastal plains are broken by hills and plateaux.

CLIMATE
Tropical. Hot and humid, with temperate interior. Hurricanes are likely June–November.

PEOPLE AND SOCIETY
Ethnically diverse, but tensions result from the gulf between rich and poor, rather than race. Economic and political life dominated by a few wealthy, long-established families. Armed crime, much of it drugs-related, is a problem. Large areas of Kingston are ruled by Dons, gang leaders who administer their own violent justice.

THE ECONOMY
Major producer of bauxite (aluminium ore). Tourism well developed. Light industry and data processing for US companies. Sugar, coffee and rum are exported.

FACTFILE
Official Name Jamaica

Date of Formation 1962

Capital Kingston

Population 2.5 million

Total Area
10,990 sq km (4,243 sq miles)

Density
227 people per sq km

Languages English*, English Creole, Hindi, Spanish, Chinese

Religions
Christian 60%, other 40%

Ethnic Mix Black 75%, mixed 15%, South Asian 5%, other 5%

Government
Parliamentary democracy

Currency
Jamaican $ = 100 cents

PANAMA

PANAMA IS the country southernmost in Central America. The Panama Canal (under US-control until 2000) links the Pacific and Atlantic oceans.

GEOGRAPHY
Lowlands along both coasts, with savannah-covered plains and rolling hills. Mountainous interior. Swamps and rainforests in the east.

CLIMATE
Hot and humid, with heavy rainfall in May–December wet season. Cooler at high altitudes.

PEOPLE AND SOCIETY
Multi-ethnic society, dominated by people of Spanish origin. Indians live in remote areas. The Canal, and US military bases, have given society a cosmopolitan outlook, but the Catholic extended family remains strong. In 1989, US troops invaded to arrest its dictator General Noriega, on drugs charges, and to restore civilian rule.

THE ECONOMY
Important banking sector, plus related financial and insurance services. Earnings from merchant ships sailing under Panamanian flag. Banana and shrimp exports.

FACTFILE
Official Name Republic of Panama

Date of Formation 1903 / 1914

Capital Panama City

Population 2.7 million

Total Area
77,080 sq km (29,761 sq miles)

Density
35 people per sq km

Languages Spanish*, English Creole, Indian languages

Religions
Catholic 93%, other 7%

Ethnic Mix Mestizo 70%, Black 14%, White 10%, Indian 6%

Government
Multiparty republic

Currency
Balboa = 100 centesimos

CUBA

CUBA IS the largest island in the Caribbean and the only Communist country in the Americas. It has been led by Fidel Castro since 1959.

GEOGRAPHY
Mostly fertile plains and basins. Three mountainous areas. Forests of pine and mahogany cover one quarter of the country.

CLIMATE
Subtropical. Hot all year round, and very hot in summer. Heaviest rainfall in the mountains. Hurricanes can strike in autumn.

Canefields near Pinar del Río, Cuba. The undulating countryside is ideal for sugarcane.

PEOPLE AND SOCIETY
Castro's regime has reduced once extreme wealth disparities, given education a high priority and established an efficient health service. Political dissent, however, is not tolerated. Dramatic fall in living standards in recent years has led 30,000 Cubans to flee by boat to the US, to seek asylum.

THE ECONOMY
Main product is sugar. Cuba's economy is in crisis following the loss of its patron and supplier, the former USSR. Recent reforms have allowed small-scale enterprise and use of US dollar. The 30-year-old US trade embargo continues.

FACTFILE
Official Name Republic of Cuba

Date of Formation 1902 / 1898

Capital Havana

Population 11.1 million

Total Area
110,860 sq km (42,803 sq miles)

Density
100 people per sq km

Languages Spanish*, English, French, Chinese

Religions
Roman Catholic 85%, other 15%

Ethnic Mix White 66%, Afro-European 22%, other 12%

Government
Socialist republic

Currency
Peso = 100 centavos

BAHAMAS

LOCATED IN the western Atlantic, off the Florida coast, the Bahamas comprise some 700 islands and 2,400 cays, 30 of which are inhabited.

GEOGRAPHY
Long, mainly flat coral formations with a few low hills. Some islands have pine forests, lagoons and mangrove swamps.

CLIMATE
Subtropical. Hot summers, and mild winters. Heavy rainfall, especially in summer. Hurricanes can strike from July–December.

PEOPLE AND SOCIETY
Over half the population live on New Providence. Tourist industry employs 40% of the work force. Remainder are engaged in traditional fishing and agriculture, or in administration. Close ties with US were strained in 1980s, with senior government members implicated in narcotics corruption. In 1993, tough policies instituted to deter settling of Haitian refugees.

Six tourists for every one of the Bahamas' inhabitants visit the islands every year.

THE ECONOMY
Tourism accounts for half of all revenues. Major international financial services sector, including banking and insurance.

FACTFILE
Official Name The Commonwealth of the Bahamas

Date of Formation 1973

Capital Nassau

Population 300,000

Total Area 13,880 sq km (5,359 sq miles)

Density 22 people per sq km

Languages English*, English Creole

Religions Protestant 76%, Roman Catholic 19%, other 5%

Ethnic Mix Black 85%, White 15%

Government Parliamentary democracy

Currency Bahamian $ = 100 cents

HAITI

SHARES THE Caribbean island of Hispaniola with the Dominican Republic. At independence in 1804, it became the world's first black republic.

GEOGRAPHY
Predominantly mountainous, with forests and fertile plains.

CLIMATE
Tropical, with rain throughout the year. Humid in coastal areas, much cooler in the mountains.

PEOPLE AND SOCIETY
Majority of population is of African descent. A few have European roots, primarily French. Rigid class structure maintains vast disparities of wealth. Most Haitians live in extreme poverty. In recent years, political oppression and a collapsing economy led thousands to seek asylum in the USA. In 1994, US-led troops reinstated the elected president, who was ousted by the military in 1991.

THE ECONOMY
Few natural resources. In 1994, after 3 years of UN sanctions, the country's economic links were restored and foreign aid resumed.

FACTFILE
Official Name Republic of Haiti

Date of Formation 1804

Capital Port-au-Prince

Population 7.3 million

Total Area 27,750 sq km (10,714 sq miles)

Density 263 people per sq km

Languages French*, French Creole*, English

Religions Roman Catholic 80%, Protestant 16%, Voodoo 4%

Ethnic Mix Black 95%, Afro-European 5%

Government Multiparty republic

Currency Gourde = 100 centimes

DOMINICAN REPUBLIC

OCCUPIES THE eastern two-thirds of the island of Hispaniola in the Caribbean. Frequent coups and a strong US influence mark its recent past.

GEOGRAPHY
Highlands and rainforested mountains – including highest peak in Caribbean, Pico Duarte – interspersed with fertile valleys. Extensive coastal plain in the east.

CLIMATE
Hot and humid close to sea level, cooler at altitude. Heavy rainfall, especially in the northeast.

View south from Pico Duarte, at 3,175 m, the highest point in the Dominican Republic.

PEOPLE AND SOCIETY
White landowners and the military hold political power. Mixed-race majority control commerce and form bulk of middle classes. Many of the poor are black. White and mixed-race women are starting to enter the professions. Widespread poverty and high unemployment have led some Dominicans to emigrate to the USA, or become drug-traffickers.

THE ECONOMY
Mining – mainly of nickel and gold – and sugar are major sectors. Hidden economy based on trans-shipment of narcotics to the US. Recent dramatic growth in tourism.

FACTFILE
Official Name Dominican Republic

Date of Formation 1865

Capital Santo Domingo

Population 8 million

Total Area 48,730 sq km (18,815 sq miles)

Density 164 people per sq km

Languages Spanish*, French Creole

Religions Roman Catholic 95%, other (Protestant, Jewish) 5%

Ethnic Mix Afro-European 73%, White 16%, Black 11%

Government Multiparty republic

Currency Peso = 100 centavos

ST KITTS & NEVIS

ST KITTS AND NEVIS lies in the northern part of the Leeward Islands chain in the Caribbean. Nevis is the less developed of the two islands.

GEOGRAPHY
Volcanic in origin, with forested, mountainous interiors. Nevis has hot and cold springs.

CLIMATE
Tropical, tempered by trade winds. Little seasonal variation in temperature. Moderate rainfall.

PEOPLE AND SOCIETY
Majority of the population is of African descent. Intermarriage has blurred other racial lines and eliminated ethnic tensions. For most people, the extended family is the norm. Wealth disparities are not great, but urban professionals enjoy a higher standard of living than rural sugar cane farmers. Politics is based on the British system; funds are provided by professionals and the trade unions. The proposed Leeward Islands' union is the main political issue.

THE ECONOMY
Sugar industry, currently UK-managed, has preferential access to EU and US markets. Successful and still expanding tourist industry.

FACTFILE
Official Name Federation of Saint Christopher and Nevis

Date of Formation 1983

Capital Basseterre

Population 41,000

Total Area 360 sq km (139 sq miles)

Density 114 people per sq km

Languages English*, English Creole

Religions Protestant 85%, Roman Catholic 10%, other Christian 5%

Ethnic Mix Black 95%, mixed 5%

Government Parliamentary democracy

Currency E. Caribbean $ = 100 cents

ANTIGUA & BARBUDA

LYING ON the Atlantic edge of the Leeward Islands, Antigua and Barbuda's area includes the uninhabited islet of Redonda.

GEOGRAPHY
Mainly low-lying limestone and coral islands with some higher volcanic areas. Antigua's coast is indented with bays and harbours.

CLIMATE
Tropical, moderated by trade winds and sea breezes. Humidity and rainfall are low for the region.

PEOPLE AND SOCIETY
Population almost entirely of African origin, with small groups of Europeans and South Asians. Women's status has risen as a result of greater access to education. Wealth disparities are small and unemployment is low. Politics dominated for past 30 years by the Bird family.

Inshore fishing boats, which mostly supply the domestic market, hauled up on a Dominican beach.

THE ECONOMY
Tourism is the main source of revenue and the biggest provider of jobs. Fishing and sea-island cotton industries are expanding.

FACTFILE
Official Name Antigua and Barbuda
Date of Formation 1981
Capital St John's
Population 65,000
Total Area
   440 sq km (170 sq miles)
Density
   148 people per sq km
Languages
   English*, English Creole
Religions Protestant 87%, Roman
   Catholic 10%, other 3%
Ethnic Mix
   Black 98%, other 2%
Government
   Parliamentary democracy
Currency
   E. Caribbean $ = 100 cents

DOMINICA

DOMINICA RESISTED European colonization until the 18th century, when it was controlled first by the French, and then, until 1978, by the British.

GEOGRAPHY
Mountainous and densely forested. Volcanic activity has given it very fertile soils, hot springs, geysers and black sand beaches.

CLIMATE
Tropical, cooled by constant trade winds. Heavy annual rainfall. Tropical depressions and hurricanes are likely June–November.

PEOPLE AND SOCIETY
Population mainly of African origin. Small community of Carib Indians – the last remaining in the Caribbean – on the east coast. Most people live in extended families. Electoral system based on British model; politicians tend to come from professional classes, usually doctors or lawyers. For 15 years until 1995, Dominica was governed by Eugenia Charles, the first female prime minister in the Caribbean.

THE ECONOMY
Bananas and tourism are the economic mainstays. Current preferential access to EU and US markets now threatened by moves to deregulate the banana trade.

FACTFILE
Official Name Commonwealth
   of Dominica
Date of Formation 1978
Capital Roseau
Population 71,000
Total Area
   750 sq km (290 sq miles)
Density
   95 people per sq km
Languages English*, French Creole,
   Carib, Cocoy
Religions Roman Catholic 77%,
   Protestant 15%, other 8%
Ethnic Mix
   Black 98%, Indian 2%
Government
   Multiparty republic
Currency E. Caribbean $ = 100 cents

ST LUCIA

AMONG THE most beautiful of the Caribbean Windward Islands, St Lucia retains both French and British influences from its colonial history.

GEOGRAPHY
Volcanic and mountainous, with some broad fertile valleys. The Pitons, ancient lava cones, rise from the sea on the forested west coast.

CLIMATE
Tropical, moderated by trade winds. May–October wet season brings daily warm showers. Rainfall is highest in the mountains.

PEOPLE AND SOCIETY
Population is a tension-free mixture of descendants of Africans, Europeans and South Asians. Family life and the Church are important to most St Lucians. In rural areas women often head the households, and run much of the farming. There is growing local resistance to over-development of the island by tourism. A proposed union with the other Windward Islands is the main political issue.

THE ECONOMY
Mainly agricultural, some light industry. Bananas are biggest export. Successful tourist industry, but most resorts are foreign-owned.

FACTFILE
Official Name Saint Lucia
Date of Formation 1979
Capital Castries
Population 141,000
Total Area
   620 sq km (239 sq miles)
Density
   227 people per sq km
Languages English*, French Creole,
   Hindi, Urdu
Religions
   Catholic 90%, other 10%
Ethnic Mix Black 90%, Afro-
   European 6%, South Asian 4%
Government
   Parliamentary democracy
Currency
   E. Caribbean $ = 100 cents

ST VINCENT & THE GRENADINES

INDEPENDENT FROM Britain in 1979, the volcanic islands of St Vincent and the Grenadines form part of the Windward Islands of the Caribbean.

GEOGRAPHY
St Vincent is mountainous and forested, with one of two active volcanoes in the Caribbean, La Soufrière. The Grenadines are 32 islands and cays fringed by beaches.

An aerial view of Union Island in the Grenadines chain. The government is developing the island as a yachting centre.

CLIMATE
Tropical, with constant trade winds. Hurricanes are likely during the July–November wet season.

PEOPLE AND SOCIETY
Population is racially diverse, but intermarriage has reduced tensions. Society is informal and relaxed, but family life is strongly influenced by the Anglican Church. Locals fear that their traditional lifestyle is being threatened by the expanding tourist industry.

THE ECONOMY
Dependent on agriculture and tourism. Bananas are the main cash crop. Tourism, targeted at the jet-set and cruise-ship markets, is concentrated on the Grenadines.

FACTFILE
Official Name St Vincent
   and the Grenadines
Date of Formation 1979
Capital Kingstown
Population 111,000
Total Area
   340 sq km (131 sq miles)
Density 326 people per sq km
Languages
   English*, English Creole
Religions Protestant 62% Roman
   Catholic 19%, other 19%
Ethnic Mix
   Black 82%, mixed 14%,
   White 3%, South Asian 1%
Government
   Parliamentary democracy
Currency E. Caribbean $ = 100 cents

BARBADOS

**BARBADOS IS the
most easterly of the
Caribbean Windward
Islands. Under British rule
for 339 years, it became
fully independent in 1966.**

GEOGRAPHY
Encircled by coral reefs.
Fertile and predominantly flat, with
a few gentle hills to the north.

CLIMATE
Moderate tropical climate.
Sunnier and drier than its more
mountainous neighbours

PEOPLE AND SOCIETY
Some latent tension between
white community, who control
politics and much of the economy,
and majority black
population, but
violence is rare.
Increasing social
mobility has
enabled black
Bajans to enter the
professions. Despite
political stability
and good welfare
and education
services, emigration
is high, notably to
the US and UK.

THE ECONOMY
Sugar is the traditional cash
crop. Well-developed tourist
industry employs almost 40% of
the work force. Financial services
and information processing are
important new growth sectors.

FACTFILE
Official Name Barbados

Date of Formation 1966

Capital Bridgetown

Population 300,000

Total Area
430 sq km (166 sq miles)

Density
698 people per sq km

Languages
English*, English Creole

Religions Protestant 94%, Roman
Catholic 5%, other 1%

Ethnic Mix Black 80%, mixed
15%, White 4%, other 1%

Government Parliamentary
democracy

Currency
Barbados $ = 100 cents

GRENADA

**THE WINDWARD island
of Grenada became a focus
of attention in 1983, when
the US mounted an invasion
to sever the growing links
with Cuba.**

GEOGRAPHY
Volcanic in origin, with
densely forested central mountains.
Its territory includes the islands of
Carriacou and Petite Martinique.

CLIMATE
Tropical, tempered by trade
winds. Hurricanes are a hazard in
the July–November wet season.

PEOPLE AND SOCIETY
Grenadians are mainly of
African origin; their traditions
remain strong,
especially on
Carriacou. Inter-
ethnic marriage has
reduced tensions
between the
groups. Extended
families, often
headed by women,
are the norm. The
invasion ousted
the Marxist regime
and restored
democracy.

THE ECONOMY
Nutmeg, the most
important crop, is currently
affected by low world prices. Mace,
cocoa, saffron and cloves are also
grown. Tourism has developed
in the past decade.

FACTFILE
Official Name Grenada

Date of Formation 1974

Capital St George's

Population 92,000

Total Area
340 sq km (131 sq miles)

Density
271 people per sq km

Languages
English*, English Creole

Religions Roman Catholic 68%,
Protestant 32%

Ethnic Mix Black 84%, Afro-
European 13%, South Asian 3%

Government Parliamentary
democracy

Currency
E. Caribbean $ = 100 cents

St George's harbour in
Grenada. Most tourist
developments are on the
beaches south of the capital.

TRINIDAD & TOBAGO

**THE FORMER British
colony of Trinidad and Tobago
is the most southerly of the
West Indies, lying just 15 km
(9 miles) off the coast
of Venezuela.**

GEOGRAPHY
Both islands are hilly and
wooded. Trinidad has a rugged
mountain range
in the north, and
swamps on its east
and west coasts

CLIMATE
Tropical,
with July–
December wet
season. Escapes
the region's
hurricanes, which
pass to the north.

Tobago's white sand beaches,
verdant landscape and natural
anchorages have encouraged
tourist development on the island.

PEOPLE AND SOCIETY
Blacks and South
Asians are the biggest groups.
Minorities of Chinese and
Europeans. Politics has recently
become fragmented, and
dominated by the race issue.
An attempted coup by a Muslim
sect in 1990 strengthened black
opposition to the possibility
of a South Asian prime minister.

THE ECONOMY
Oil accounts for 70%
of export earnings. Gas is
increasingly being exploited to
support new industries. Tourism,
particularly on Tobago,
is being developed.

FACTFILE
Official Name Republic of Trinidad
and Tobago

Date of Formation 1962

Capital Port-of-Spain

Population 1.3 million

Total Area
5,130 sq km (1,981 sq miles)

Density
253 people per sq km

Languages
English*, other

Religions Christian 58%, Hindu 30%,
Muslim 8%, other 4%

Ethnic Mix Black 43%, South Asian
40%, mixed 14%, other 3%

Government
Multiparty republic

Currency Trin. & Tob. $ = 100 cents

COLOMBIA

**LYING IN northwest
South America, Colombia
is one of the world's most
violent countries, with
powerful drugs cartels
and guerrilla activity.**

GEOGRAPHY
The densely forested and
almost uninhabited east is separated
from the western
coastal plains by
the Andes, which
divide into three
ranges with
intervening valleys.

CLIMATE
Coastal
plains are hot and
wet. The highlands
are cooler.
The equatorial
east has two wet seasons.

PEOPLE AND SOCIETY
Most Colombians are of
mixed blood. Native Indians are
concentrated in the southwest and
Amazonia. Recent constitutional
reform has given them a greater
political voice. Blacks are the
least represented group. The
government, with US help,
is engaged in an all-out war
against the drugs barons.

THE ECONOMY
Healthy and diversified export
sector – especially coffee and coal.
Considerable growth potential, but
drugs-related violence and
corruption deter foreign investors.

FACTFILE
Official Name Republic of Colombia

Date of Formation 1819/1922

Capital Bogotá

Population 35.7 million

Total Area
1,138,910 sq km (439,733 sq miles)

Density
31 people per sq km

Languages Spanish*, Indian
languages, English Creole

Religions
Catholic 95%, other 5%

Ethnic Mix Mestizo 58%, White 20%,
mixed 14%, other 8%

Government
Multiparty republic

Currency
Peso = 100 centavos

VENEZUELA

LOCATED ON the north coast of South America, Venezuela has the continent's most urbanized society. Most people live in the northern cities.

GEOGRAPHY
Andes mountains and the Maracaibo lowlands in the north-west. Central grassy plains drained by Orinoco river system. Forested Guiana Highlands in the southeast.

CLIMATE
Tropical. Hot and humid. Uplands are cooler. Orinoco plains are alternately parched or flooded.

PEOPLE AND SOCIETY
Latin America's 'melting pot' with immigrants from Europe and all over South America. The few indigenous Indians live in remote areas and maintain their traditional lifestyle. Oil wealth has brought prosperity, but many people still live in poverty – there were food riots in 1991. Corruption is a feature of Venezuelan political life.

THE ECONOMY
In addition to oil, Venezuela has vast reserves of coal, bauxite, iron and gold. Government revenues dented by over-manned and often inefficient state sector, plus widespread tax evasion.

FACTFILE
Official Name Republic of Venezuela

Date of Formation 1830/1929

Capital Caracas

Population 22.3 million

Total Area
912,050 sq km (352,143 sq miles)

Density
24 people per sq km

Languages
Spanish*, Indian languages

Religions Roman Catholic 96%,
Protestant 2%, other 2%

Ethnic Mix Mestizo 67%, White 21%,
Black 10%, Indian 2%

Government
Multiparty republic

Currency
Bolívar = 100 centimos

GUYANA

THE ONLY English-speaking country in South America, Guyana gained independence from Britain in 1966, and became a republic in 1970.

GEOGRAPHY
Mainly artificial coast, re-claimed by dykes and dams from swamps and tidal marshes. Forests cover 85% of the interior, rising to savannah uplands and mountains.

CLIMATE
Tropical. Coast cooled by sea breezes. Lowlands are hot, wet and humid. Highlands are a little cooler.

The Orinoco River, Venezuela. The huge llanos (plains) close to the river are grazed by five million cattle.

PEOPLE AND SOCIETY
Population largely descended from Africans brought over during slave trade, or from South Asian labourers who arrived after slavery was abolished. Racial rivalry exists between the two groups. Small numbers of Chinese and native Indians. Government was once characterized by favouritism towards Afro-Guyanese. This was reversed with the election in 1992 of a South Asian-dominated party.

THE ECONOMY
Free-market economics have improved prospects. Bauxite, gold, rice and diamonds are produced.

FACTFILE
Official Name Republic of Guyana

Date of Formation 1966

Capital Georgetown

Population 800,000

Total Area
214,970 sq km (83,000 sq miles)

Density
4 people per sq km

Languages English*, English Creole,
Hindi, Urdu, Indian languages

Religions Christian 57%, Hindu 33%,
Muslim 9%, other 1%

Ethnic Mix South Asian 51%, Black
and mixed 43%, other 6%

Government
Multiparty republic

Currency
Guyana $ =100 cents

SURINAM

A FORMER Dutch colony on the north coast of South America. Democracy was restored in 1991, after almost 11 years of military rule.

GEOGRAPHY
Mostly covered by tropical rainforest. Coastal plain, central plateaux and the Guiana Highlands.

CLIMATE
Tropical. Hot and humid, cooled by trade winds. High rainfall, especially in the interior.

PEOPLE AND SOCIETY
About 200,000 people have emigrated to the Netherlands since independence. Of those left, 90% live near the coast, the rest live in scattered rainforest communities. Around 7,000 are indigenous Indians. Also bosnegers – descendants of runaway African slaves. They fought the Creole-dominated government in the 1980s. Many South Asians and Javanese work in farming. Since return to civilian rule, each group has a political party representing its interests.

THE ECONOMY
Aluminium and bauxite are the leading exports. Rice and fruit are main cash crops. Oil reserves.

FACTFILE
Official Name Republic of Surinam

Date of Formation 1975

Capital Paramaribo

Population 400,000

Total Area
163,270 sq km (63,039 sq miles)

Density
2 people per sq km

Languages Dutch*, Pidgin English
(Taki-Taki), Hindi, Javanese,
Carib

Religions Christian 48%, Hindu 27%,
Muslim 20%, other 5%

Ethnic Mix South Asian 37%, Creole
31%, Javanese 15%, other 17%

Government
Multiparty republic

Currency Guilder = 100 cents

ECUADOR

ECUADOR SITS high on South America's western coast. Its territory includes the Galapagos Islands, 970 km (610 miles) to the west.

GEOGRAPHY
Broad coastal plain, inter-Andean central highlands, dense jungle in upper Amazon Basin.

CLIMATE
Hot and moist on the coast, cool in the Andes, and hot equatorial in the Amazon Basin.

PEOPLE AND SOCIETY
Most people live in coastal lowlands or Andean highlands. Many have migrated from over-farmed Andean valleys to main port and commercial centre, Guayaquil. Strong and unified Indian movement backed by Catholic Church. Amazonian Indians are successfully pressing for recognition of land rights.

Surinam's captial, Paramaribo has fine examples of Dutch 18th and 19th century architecture.

THE ECONOMY
World's biggest banana producer. Net oil exporter. Commercial agriculture is main employer. Fishing industry. Eco-tourism on Galapagos Islands.

FACTFILE
Official Name Republic of Ecuador

Date of Formation 1830/1942

Capital Quito

Population 11.7 million

Total Area
283,560 sq km (109,483 sq miles)

Density
41 people per sq km

Languages Spanish*, Quechua* and
eight other Indian languages

Religions
Catholic 95%, other 5%

Ethnic Mix Mestizo (Euro-Indian)
55%, Indian 25%, Black 10%,
White 10%

Government
Multiparty republic

Currency Sucre = 100 centavos

PERU

ONCE THE heart of the Inca empire, before the Spanish conquest in the 16th century, Peru lies on the Pacific coast of South America.

GEOGRAPHY

Coastal plain rises to Andes mountains. Uplands, dissected by fertile valleys, lie east of Andes. Tropical forest in extreme east.

CLIMATE

Coast is mainly arid. Middle slopes of Andes are temperate; higher peaks are snow-covered. East is hot, humid and very wet.

PEOPLE AND SOCIETY

Populated mainly by Indians or mixed-race mestizos, but society is dominated by a small group of Spanish descendants. Indians, together with the small black community, suffer discrimination in the towns. In 1980, Sendero Luminoso (Shining Path) guerrillas began armed struggle against the government. Since then, over 25,000 people have died as a result of guerrilla, and army, violence.

THE ECONOMY

Abundant mineral resources. Rich fish stocks. Illegal export of coca leaves for cocaine production.

FACTFILE

Official Name Republic of Peru

Date of Formation 1824 / 1942

Capital Lima

Population 24.2 million

Total Area
1,285,220 sq km (496,223 sq miles)

Density
19 people per sq km

Languages Spanish*, Quechua*, Aymará*, other Indian languages

Religions
Catholic 95%, other 5%

Ethnic Mix Indian 45%, mestizo 37%, White 15%, Black, Japanese, Chinese and other 3%

Government
Multiparty republic

Currency New sol = 100 centimos

BRAZIL

BRAZIL COVERS more than half of South America and is the site of the world's largest and most important rainforest. The country has immense natural resources

GEOGRAPHY

Vast, forested Amazon Basin in north. Semi-arid scrubland in northeast mountains, fertile highlands in the south. Coastal plain with swampy areas in the southeast. Atlantic coastline is 2,000 km (1,240 miles) long.

CLIMATE

Hot and humid in Amazon Basin. Frequent droughts in northeast. Range of temperature and rainfall on plateau. Hot summers and cool winters in south.

With a population of 11 million, the Rio de Janeiro conurbation is Brazil's largest urban area after São Paulo.

PEOPLE AND SOCIETY

Population includes native Indians, blacks, and people of mixed race. Shanty towns in the cities attract migrants from the northeast. Urban crime, land disputes and unchecked Amazonia development tarnish image. Catholicism and the family remain strong.

THE ECONOMY

Hyperinflation, poor planning and corruption frustrate efforts to harness mineral reserves, diverse industry and agriculture.

FACTFILE

Official Name Federative Republic of Brazil

Date of Formation 1822 / 1929

Capital Brasília

Population 164.4 million

Total Area 8,511,970 sq km (3,286,472 sq miles)

Density
19 people per sq km

Languages Portuguese*, German, Italian, English, Spanish, Polish, Japanese, Indian languages

Religions Catholic 90%, other 10%

Ethnic Mix White (Portuguese, Italian, German, Japanese) 55%, mixed 38%, Black 6%, other 1%

Government Multiparty republic

Currency Real = 100 centavos

CHILE

EXTENDS IN a ribbon down the west coast of South America. It returned to democracy in 1989 after a referendum rejected its military dictator.

GEOGRAPHY

Pampas (broad grassy plains) between coastal uplands and Andes. Atacama Desert in north. Deep sea channels, lakes and fiords in south.

CLIMATE

Arid in the north. Hot, dry summers and mild winters in the centre. Higher Andean peaks have glaciers and year-round snow. Very wet and stormy in the south.

PEOPLE AND SOCIETY

Most people are of European stock, and are highly urbanized. Indigenous Indians live almost exclusively in the south. Poor housing, water and air pollution are problems in Santiago. General Pinochet's dictatorship was brutally repressive, but the business and middle classes prospered. Growth has continued under civilian rule, but many Chileans live in poverty.

THE ECONOMY

World's biggest producer of copper. Growth in foreign investment due to political stability. Wine, fishmeal, fruits and salmon are exported.

FACTFILE

Official Name Republic of Chile

Date of Formation 1818 / 1929

Capital Santiago

Population 14.5 million

Total Area
756,950 sq km (292,258 sq miles)

Density
19 people per sq km

Languages
Spanish*, Indian languages

Religions Roman Catholic 89%, Protestant 11%

Ethnic Mix White and mestizo 92%, Indian 6%, other 2%

Government
Multiparty republic

Currency
Peso = 100 centavos

BOLIVIA

BOLIVIA LIES land-locked high in central South America. Mineral riches once made it the region's wealthiest state. Today, it is the poorest.

GEOGRAPHY

A high windswept plateau, the altiplano, lies between two Andean mountain ranges. Semi-arid grasslands to the southeast; dense tropical forests to the north.

Lake Titicaca lies on the border between Bolivia and Peru. It is the world's highest lake.

CLIMATE

Altiplano has extreme tropical climate, with night frost in winter. North and east are hot and humid.

PEOPLE AND SOCIETY

Indigenous majority is discriminated against at most levels of society. Political process and economy remain under the control of a few wealthy families of Spanish descent. Most Bolivians are poor subsistence farmers or miners. Women have low status.

THE ECONOMY

Gold, silver, zinc and tin are mined. Recently discovered oil and natural gas deposits. Overseas investors remain deterred by social problems of extreme poverty, and the influence of cocaine barons.

FACTFILE

Official Name Republic of Bolivia

Date of Formation 1825 / 1938

Capital La Paz

Population 7.6 million

Total Area
1,098,580 sq km (424,162 sq miles)

Density
7 people per sq km

Languages Spanish*, Quechua*, Aymará*, Tupi-Guaraní

Religions
Catholic 95%, other 5%

Ethnic Mix Indian 55%, mestizo 27%, White 10%, other 8%

Government
Multiparty republic

Currency
Boliviano = 100 centavos

PARAGUAY

LAND-LOCKED in central South America. Its post-independence history has included periods of military rule. Free elections were held in 1993.

GEOGRAPHY
The River Paraguay divides hilly and forested east from a flat alluvial plain with marsh and semi-desert scrubland in the west.

CLIMATE
Subtropical. Gran Chaco is generally hotter and drier. All areas experience floods and droughts.

PEOPLE AND SOCIETY
Population mainly of mixed Spanish and native Indian origin. Most are bilingual, but Guaraní is spoken by preference outside the capital. Gran Chaco is home to small groups of pure Guaraní Indians, cattle-ranchers and Mennonites, a sect of German origin, who live by a co-operative farming system.

The Iguazu Falls lie on the border between Brazil and Paraguay.

THE ECONOMY
Agriculture employs 45% of the work force. Soybeans and cotton are main exports. Electricity exporter – earnings cover oil imports. Growth is slow due to remote, land-locked position.

FACTFILE

Official Name Republic of Paraguay

Date of Formation 1811 / 1938

Capital Asunción

Population 5.1 million

Total Area
406,750 sq km (157,046 sq miles)

Density
13 people per sq km

Languages Spanish*, Guaraní*,
Plattdeutsch (Low German)

Religions
Catholic 90%, other 10%

Ethnic Mix Mestizo (Euro-Indian)
95%, White 3%, Indian 2%

Government
Multiparty republic

Currency
Guaraní = 100 centimos

URUGUAY

URUGUAY IS situated in southeastern South America. It returned to civilian government in 1985, after 12 years of military dictatorship.

GEOGRAPHY
Low, rolling grasslands cover 80% of the country. Narrow coastal plain. Alluvial flood plain in south-west. Five rivers flow westwards and drain into the River Uruguay.

CLIMATE
Temperate throughout the country. Warm summers, mild winters and moderate rainfall.

PEOPLE AND SOCIETY
Uruguayans are largely second or third generation Italians or Spaniards. Wealth derived from cattle ranching enabled the country to become the first welfare state in South America. Economic decline since 1960s, but a large, if less prosperous, middle class remains. Although a Roman Catholic country, Uruguay is liberal in its attitude to religion and all forms are tolerated. Divorce is legal.

THE ECONOMY
Most land given over to crops and livestock. Wool, meat and hides are exported. Earnings as offshore banking centre. Buoyant tourism.

FACTFILE

Official Name Republic of Uruguay

Date of Formation 1828 / 1909

Capital Montevideo

Population 3.2 million

Total Area
177,410 sq km (68,498 sq miles)

Density
18 people per sq km

Languages
Spanish*, other

Religions
Catholic 77%, Protestant 3%,
Jewish 2%, other 18%

Ethnic Mix White 88%, mestizo
(Euro-Indian) 8%, Black 4%

Government
Multiparty republic

Currency Peso = 100 centesimos

ARGENTINA

OCCUPYING MOST of the southern half of South America, Argentina extends 3,460 km (2,145 miles) from Bolivia to Tierra del Fuego.

GEOGRAPHY
Andes mountains in the west form a natural border with Chile. East of the Andes are heavily wooded plains in the north, treeless but fertile Pampas plains in the centre. Bleak, arid Patagonia in south.

CLIMATE
Northeast is sub-tropical. Andes are semi-arid in the north, snowy in the south. Western lowlands are arid. Pampas have mild climate.

Herding cattle in northeast Argentina, near Corrientes. Beef is still one of the country's major exports.

PEOPLE AND SOCIETY
People largely of European descent, mostly from 20th-century migrations from Italy and Germany. Indigenous peoples now in a minority, living mainly in Andean regions or the Gran Chaco. Over 85% of Argentinians are urban dwellers; 40% live in capital.

THE ECONOMY
Rich and varied agricultural base. Powerful agribusiness – leading exporter of beef, wheat and fruit. Important oil and gas reserves still under-exploited.

FACTFILE

Official Name Argentine Republic

Date of Formation 1816 / 1925

Capital Buenos Aires

Population 35 million

Total Area 2,766,890 sq km
(1,068,296 sq miles)

Density
13 people per sq km

Languages Spanish*, Italian,
English, German, French,
Indian languages

Religions
Catholic 90%, Jewish 2%, other 8%

Ethnic Mix White 85%,
other (including mestizo
and Indian) 15%

Government Multiparty republic

Currency Peso = 100 centavos

MOROCCO

A FORMER French colony in northwest Africa, independent in 1956. Morocco has occupied the disputed territory of Western Sahara since 1975.

GEOGRAPHY
Fertile coastal plain is interrupted in the east by the Rif mountains. Atlas Mountain ranges to the south. Beyond lies the outer fringe of the Sahara.

CLIMATE
Ranges from temperate and warm in the north, to semi-arid in the south. Cooler in the mountains.

PEOPLE AND SOCIETY
About 35% are descendants of original Berber inhabitants of northwest Africa, and live mainly in mountain villages. Arab majority inhabit lowlands. Large rural-urban gap in wealth. High birth rate. King Hassan heads a powerful monarchy. Government threatened by Islamic militants who fear country is losing its Islamic, Arab identity and becoming too influenced by Europe.

THE ECONOMY
World's main exporter of phosphates. Tourism and agriculture have great potential.

FACTFILE

Official Name Kingdom of Morocco

Date of Formation 1956

Capital Rabat

Population 27.6 million

Total Area
698,670 sq km (269,757 sq miles)

Density
40 people per sq km

Languages
Arabic*, Berber, French

Religions
Muslim 99%, other 1%

Ethnic Mix Arab and Berber 99%,
European 1%

Government
Constitutional monarchy

Currency
Dirham = 100 centimes

AFRICA

ALGERIA

ALGERIA ACHIEVED independence from France in 1962. Today, its military-dominated government faces a severe challenge from Islamic extremists.

GEOGRAPHY
85% of the country lies within the Sahara. Fertile coastal region with plains and hills rises in the southeast to the Atlas Mountains.

CLIMATE
Coastal areas are warm and temperate, with most rainfall during the mild winters. The south is very hot, with negligible rainfall.

PEOPLE AND SOCIETY
Algerians are predominantly Arab, under 30 years of age and urban. Most indigenous Berbers consider the mountainous Kabylia region in the northeast to be their homeland. The Sahara sustains just 500,000 people, mainly oil workers and Tuareg nomads with goat and camel herds, who move between the irrigated oases. In recent years, political violence has claimed the lives of 3,000 people.

A Saharan town showing the wide range of Algeria's scenery, from irrigated gardens to sandy dunes.

THE ECONOMY
Oil and gas exports. Political turmoil has led to exodus of skilled foreign labour. Limited agriculture.

FACTFILE
Official Name Democratic and Popular Republic of Algeria
Date of Formation 1962
Capital Algiers
Population 28.6 million
Total Area 2,381,740 sq km (919,590 sq miles)
Density 12 people per sq km
Languages Arabic*, Berber, French
Religions Muslim 99%, Christian and Jewish 1%
Ethnic Mix Arab and Berber 99% European 1%
Government Military regime
Currency Dinar = 100 centimes

AFRICA

TUNISIA

TUNISIA HAS traditionally been one of the more liberal Arab states, but its government is now facing a challenge from Islamic fundamentalists.

GEOGRAPHY
Mountains in the north are surrounded by plains. Vast, low-lying salt pans in the centre. To the south lies the Sahara.

CLIMATE
Summer temperatures are high. The north is often wet and windy in winter. Far south is arid.

PEOPLE AND SOCIETY
Population almost entirely of Arab-Berber descent, with Jewish and Christian minorities. Many still live in extended families. Women have better rights than in any other Arab country and make up 25% of the total work force. Politics, however, remains a male preserve. Low birth rate is a result of a long-standing family planning policy.

THE ECONOMY
Well-diversified, despite limited resources. Oil and gas are exported. Expanding manufacturing and tourist industries have been aided by European investment.

FACTFILE
Official Name Republic of Tunisia
Date of Formation 1956
Capital Tunis
Population 9.1 million
Total Area 163,610 sq km (63,170 sq miles)
Density 56 people per sq km
Languages Arabic*, French
Religions Muslim 98%, Christian 1%, other 1%
Ethnic Mix Arab and Berber 98%, European 1%, other 1%
Government Multiparty republic
Currency Dinar = 1,000 millimes

AFRICA

LIBYA

SITUATED ON the Mediterranean coast of North Africa, Libya is a Muslim dictatorship, politically marginalized by the West for its terrorist links.

GEOGRAPHY
Apart from the coastal strip and a mountain range in the south, Libya is desert or semi-desert. Oases provide agricultural land.

CLIMATE
Hot and arid. Coastal area has temperate climate, with mild, wet winters and hot, dry summers.

A Roman amphitheatre at Sabratah, Libya, reflects the country's strategic importance in classical times.

PEOPLE AND SOCIETY
Most Libyans are of Arab and Berber origin. 1969 revolution brought Colonel Gadaffi to power. He stands for Islamic faith, communal lifestyle and hatred of urban rich. Revolution wiped out private enterprise and middle classes. Jews and European settlers were banished. Libya has changed from being a nation of nomads and livestock herders to 70% city-dwellers.

THE ECONOMY
90% of export earnings come from oil. Subject to fluctuating world prices. Dates, olives, peaches and grapes are grown in the oases.

FACTFILE
Official Name The Great Socialist People's Libyan Arab Jamahiriya
Date of Formation 1951
Capital Tripoli
Population 5.6 million
Total Area 1,759,540 sq km (679,358 sq miles)
Density 3 people per sq km
Languages Arabic*, Tuareg
Religions Muslim 97%, other 3%
Ethnic Mix Arab and Berber 97%, other 3%
Government Socialist jamahiriya (state of the masses)
Currency Dinar = 1,000 dirhams

AFRICA

EGYPT

EGYPT OCCUPIES the northeast corner of Africa. Its essentially pro-Western, military-backed regime is being challenged by Islamic fundamentalists.

GEOGRAPHY
Fertile Nile valley separates arid Libyan Desert from smaller semiarid eastern desert. Sinai peninsula has mountains in south.

CLIMATE
Summers are very hot, but winters are cooler. Rainfall is negligible, except on the coast.

PEOPLE AND SOCIETY
Continuously inhabited for over 8,000 years, with a tradition of religious and ethnic tolerance. Egyptians are mostly Arabs, Bedouins, and Nubians. Women play full part in education system, politics, and economy. Government is fighting Islamic terrorist groups, whose acts of violence have included attacks on politicians, police, and tourists.

THE ECONOMY
Oil and gas are main sources of revenue. Tolls from the Suez Canal. Successful tourist industry is threatened by security fears.

FACTFILE
Official Name Arab Republic of Egypt
Date of Formation 1936/1982
Capital Cairo
Population 64.2 million
Total Area 1,001,450 sq km (386,660 sq miles)
Density 64 people per sq km
Languages Arabic*, French, English, Berber, Greek, Armenian
Religions Muslim 94%, other 6%
Ethnic Mix Eastern Hamitic 90%, other (inc. Greek, Armenian) 10%
Government Multiparty republic
Currency Pound = 100 piastres

SUDAN

THE LARGEST country in Africa, Sudan borders the Red Sea. In 1989, an army coup installed a military Islamic fundamentalist regime.

GEOGRAPHY
Lies within the upper Nile basin. Mostly arid plains, with marshes in the south. Highlands border the Red Sea in the northeast.

CLIMATE
North is hot, arid desert with constant dry winds. Rainy season ranging from two months in the centre, to eight in the south.

PEOPLE AND SOCIETY
Large number of ethnic and linguistic groups. Two million people are nomads, moving over ancient tribal areas in the south. Major social division is between Arabized Muslims in north, and mostly African, largely Christian or animist peoples in south. Attempts to impose Arab and Islamic values throughout Sudan have been the root cause of the civil war that has ravaged the south since 1983.

THE ECONOMY
Sudan is frequently affected by drought and food shortages. Sesame seeds, cotton, gum arabic are main cash crops.

FACTFILE
Official Name Republic of Sudan
Date of Formation 1956
Capital Khartoum
Population 28.9 million
Total Area 2,505,815 sq km (967,493 sq miles)
Density 12 people per sq km
Languages Arabic*, other
Religions Muslim 70%, traditional beliefs 20%, Christian 5%, other 5%
Ethnic Mix Arab 51%, Dinka 13%, Nuba 9%, Beja 7%, other 20%
Government Military regime
Currency Pound = 100 piastres

ERITREA

LYING ON the shores of the Red Sea, Eritrea effectively seceded from Ethiopia in 1993, following a 30-year war for independence.

GEOGRAPHY
Mostly rugged mountains, bush, and the Danakil Desert, which falls below sea level.

CLIMATE
Warm in the mountains; desert areas are hot. Droughts from July onwards are common.

PEOPLE AND SOCIETY
Nine main ethnic groups. Tigrinya-speakers are the largest in number. Strong sense of nationhood forged by the war. Women played important role in the war, fighting alongside men. Over 80% of people are subsistence farmers. Few live beyond the age of 45. Transitional government will hold multiparty elections in 1997.

THE ECONOMY
Legacy of disruption and destruction from war. Susceptible to drought and famine. Most of the population live at subsistence level. Potential for mining of gold, copper, silver and zinc. Possible foreign earnings from oil exports.

FACTFILE
Official Name State of Eritrea
Date of Formation 1993
Capital Asmara
Population 3.6 million
Total Area 93,680 sq km (36,170 sq miles)
Density 38 people per sq km
Languages Tigrinya*, Arabic*, Tigre, Afar, Bilen, Kunama, Nara
Religions Coptic Christian 45%, Muslim 45%, other 10%
Ethnic Mix Nine main ethnic groups
Government Provisional military government
Currency Birr = 100 cents

DJIBOUTI

A CITY STATE with a desert hinterland, Djibouti lies in northeast Africa. Once known as French Somaliland, it became independent in 1977.

GEOGRAPHY
Mainly low-lying desert and semi-desert, with a volcanic mountain range in the north.

CLIMATE
Hot all year round, with June–August temperatures reaching 45°C (109°F). Very low rainfall.

Lalibela in Ethiopia's central highlands is an important pilgrimage centre, famed for its ten 12th century Christian churches.

PEOPLE AND SOCIETY
Dominant ethnic groups are the Issas in the south, and the mainly nomadic Afars in the north. Tensions between them developed into a guerrilla war in 1991. Smaller tribal groups make up the rest of the population, together with French and other European expatriates, and Arabs. Population was swelled by 20,000 Somali refugees in 1992. France still exerts considerable influence in Djibouti, supporting it financially and maintaining a naval base and a military garrison.

THE ECONOMY
Djibouti's major asset is its port in a key Red Sea location.

FACTFILE
Official Name Republic of Djibouti
Date of Formation 1977
Capital Djibouti
Population 600,000
Total Area 23,200 sq km (8,958 sq miles)
Density 26 people per sq km
Languages Arabic*, French*, Somali, Afar, other
Religions Christian 87%, other 13%
Ethnic Mix Issa 35%, Afar 20%, Gadaboursis and Isaaks 28%, other (inc. Arab, European) 17%
Government Single-party republic
Currency Franc = 100 centimes

ETHIOPIA

LOCATED IN northeast Africa, Ethiopia was a Marxist regime from 1974–91. It has suffered a series of economic, civil and natural crises.

GEOGRAPHY
Great Rift Valley divides mountainous northwest region from desert lowlands in northeast and southeast. Ethiopian Highlands are drained mainly by the Blue Nile.

CLIMATE
Generally moderate with summer rains. Highlands are warm, with night frost and snowfalls on the mountains.

PEOPLE AND SOCIETY
76 Ethiopian nationalities speak 286 languages. Oromo are largest group. In 1995, the first multiparty elections were held, beginning a new nine-state federation.

THE ECONOMY
Most people are subsistence farmers. Despite war-damaged infrastructure and periodic serious droughts, agricultural and industrial output are growing as it moves towards a market economy.

FACTFILE
Official Name Undetermined
Date of Formation 1903/1993
Capital Addis Ababa
Population 56.7 million
Total Area 1,128,221 sq km (435,605 sq miles)
Density 50 people per sq km
Languages Amharic*, English, Arabic, Tigrinya, Orominga
Religions Muslim 43%, Christian 37%, traditional beliefs, other 20%
Ethnic Mix Oromo 40%, Amhara and Tigrean 32%, other 28%
Government Multiparty republic
Currency Birr = 100 cents

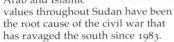

Camel caravans in Sudan. Periodic drought and war mean that Sudan requires food aid.

SOMALIA

A SEMI-ARID state occupying the horn of Africa. Italian Somaliland and British Somaliland were united in 1960 to form an independent Somalia.

GEOGRAPHY
Highlands in the north, flatter scrub-covered land to the south. Northern coastal areas are hot and humid and are more fertile.

CLIMATE
Very dry, except for the north coast, which is hot and humid. Interior has among world's highest average yearly temperatures.

PEOPLE AND SOCIETY
Clan system forms the basis of all commercial, political and social activities. Most people are herders (Samaal) while the rest are farmers (Sab). Years of clan-based civil war have resulted in collapse of central government. US-led UN peace keeping force was deployed to try and bring peace to the country, but it was withdrawn in 1994.

THE ECONOMY
Somalia is heavily reliant on foreign aid, since all commodities, except arms, are in short supply. Formal economy has collapsed due to civil war and drought.

FACTFILE
Official Name Somali Democratic Republic
Date of Formation 1960
Capital Mogadishu
Population 9.5 million
Total Area
   637,660 sq km (246,200 sq miles)
Density
   15 people per sq km
Languages
   Somali*, Arabic*, other
Religions Sunni Muslim 99%, other (inc. Christian) 1%
Ethnic Mix Somali 98%, Bantu, Arab 1.5%, European, other 0.5%
Government
   Transitional
Currency Shilling = 100 cents

UGANDA

UGANDA LIES land-locked in East Africa. It was ruled by one of Africa's more eccentric leaders, the dictator Idi Amin Dada, from 1971–1980.

GEOGRAPHY
A large plateau with Great Rift Valley and Ruwenzori mountain range in the west; Lake Victoria in the southeast. Vegetation is of savannah type.

CLIMATE
Altitude and the influence of the lakes modify the equatorial climate. Rain falls throughout the year; spring is the wettest period.

PEOPLE AND SOCIETY
Large rural population with 13 main ethnic groups. President Museveni allowed the restoration of Uganda's four historical monarchies in 1993 to help with the breakdown of traditional animosities. New constitution will use a federal system with boundaries based on those of the old kingdoms.

Kampala, the Ugandan capital lies in the country's most populous region, close to Lake Victoria.

THE ECONOMY
Coffee earns 93% of export income. Hydroelectric power planned to replace 50% of oil imports. Reopening of mines should improve the economy.

FACTFILE
Official Name Republic of Uganda
Date of Formation 1962
Capital Kampala
Population 22 million
Total Area 235,880 sq km (91,073 sq miles)
Density
   93 people per sq km
Languages English*, Luganda, Nkole, Chiga, Lango, Acholi, Teso
Religions Catholic/Protestant 66%, traditional beliefs 18%, Muslim 16%
Ethnic Mix Buganda 18%, Banyoro 14%, Teso 9%, other 59%
Government Multiparty republic
Currency Shilling = 100 cents

KENYA

KENYA STRADDLES the Equator on Africa's east coast. It became a multiparty democracy in 1992 and has been led by President Moi since 1978.

GEOGRAPHY
Central plateau divided by Great Rift Valley. North of the Equator is mainly semi-desert. To the east lies a fertile coastal belt.

CLIMATE
Coast and Great Rift Valley are hot and humid. Plateau interior is temperate. Northeastern desert is hot and dry. Rain generally falls April–May and October–November.

The Kenyan Conference Centre at Nairobi, the country's capital. The modern skyline contrasts sharply with the shacks on its outskirts.

PEOPLE AND SOCIETY
Kenya's 70 ethnic groups share about 40 languages. Rural majority has strong clan and family links. One of the world's highest population growth rates, together with poverty, has exacerbated the recent surge in ethnic violence.

THE ECONOMY
Tourism is the leading foreign exchange earner. Tea and coffee grown as cash crops. Large and diversified manufacturing sector.

FACTFILE
Official Name Republic of Kenya
Date of Formation 1963
Capital Nairobi
Population 29.1 million
Total Area 580,370 sq km (224,081 sq miles)
Density
   50 people per sq km
Languages Swahili*, English, Kikuyu, Luo, Kamba, other
Religions Catholic/Protestant 66%, animist 26%, Muslim 6%, other 2%
Ethnic Mix Kikuyu 21%, Luhya 14%, Kamba 11%, other 54%
Government
   Multiparty republic
Currency Shilling = 100 cents

RWANDA

RWANDA LIES just south of the Equator in east central Africa. Since independence from France in 1962, ethnic tensions have dominated politics.

GEOGRAPHY
Series of plateaux descend from ridge of volcanic peaks in the west to Akagera River on eastern border. Great Rift Valley also passes through this region.

CLIMATE
Tropical, tempered by the altitude. Two wet seasons are separated by a dry season, June–August. Heaviest rain in the west.

PEOPLE AND SOCIETY
Rwandans live a subsistence existence. Traditional family and clan structures are strong. For over 500 years Tutsi were politically dominant over the Hutu tribe. In 1959, violent revolt led to a reversal of the roles. In 1994 over 200,000 people died in tribal violence.

THE ECONOMY
Rwanda has few resources, but under peaceful conditions, it produces coffee. Possible oil and gas reserves.

FACTFILE
Official Name Rwandese Republic
Date of Formation 1962
Capital Kigali
Population 8.2 million
Total Area
   26,340 sq km (10,170 sq miles)
Density
   311 people per sq km
Languages Kinyarwanda*, French*, Kiswahili
Religions Catholic 65%, Protestant 7%, traditional beliefs 25%, other 1%
Ethnic Mix Hutu 90%, Tutsi 9%, Twa pygmy 1%
Government
   Multiparty republic
Currency Franc = 100 centimes

BURUNDI

SMALL, DENSELY populated and land-locked, Burundi lies just south of the Equator, on the Nile–Congo watershed in Central Africa.

GEOGRAPHY
Hilly with high plateaux in centre and savannah in the east. Great Rift Valley and Lake Tanganyika on western side.

CLIMATE
Temperate, with high humidity. Heavy and frequent rainfall, mostly October–May.

PEOPLE AND SOCIETY
Burundi's post-independence history has been dominated by ethnic conflict – with repeated large-scale massacres – between majority Hutu and the Tutsi, who control the army. Over 120,000 people, mostly Hutu, have been killed since 1992. Twa pygmies are not involved in the conflict. Most people are subsistence farmers. Majority of Burundians are Roman Catholics.

Pig farming and fish ponds in Burundi. Most of the country's population depends on agriculture.

THE ECONOMY
Overwhelmingly agricultural economy. Small quantities of gold and tungsten. Potential of oil in Lake Tanganyika. Burundi has 5% of the world's nickel reserves.

FACTFILE
Official Name Republic of Burundi

Date of Formation 1962

Capital Bujumbura

Population 6.6 million

Total Area
27,830 sq km (10,750 sq miles)

Density
237 people per sq km

Languages Kirundi*, French*, Swahili, other

Religions Catholic 62%, traditional beliefs 32%, Protestant 6%

Ethnic Mix Hutu 85%, Tutsi 13%, Twa pygmy 1%, other 1%

Government
Multiparty republic

Currency
Franc = 100 centimes

CENTRAL AFRICAN REPUBLIC

A LAND-LOCKED country lying between the basins of the Chad and Congo rivers. Its arid north sustains less than 2% of the population.

GEOGRAPHY
Comprises a low plateau, covered by scrub or savannah. Rainforests in the south. One of Africa's great rivers, the Ubangi, forms the border with Congo (Zaire).

CLIMATE
The south is equatorial; the north is hot and dry. Rain occurs all year round, with heaviest falls between July and October.

PEOPLE AND SOCIETY
Baya and Banda are largest ethnic groups, but Sangho, spoken by minority river peoples in the south, is the lingua franca. Most political leaders since independence have come from the south. Women, as in other non-Muslim African countries, have considerable power. Large number of ethnic groups helps limit disputes.

THE ECONOMY
Dominated by subsistence farming. Exports include gold, diamonds, cotton and timber. Country is self-sufficient in food production. Poor infrastructure.

FACTFILE
Official Name Central African Republic

Date of Formation 1960

Capital Bangui

Population 3.4 million

Total Area
622,980 sq km (240,530 sq miles)

Density
5 people per sq km

Languages French*, Sangho, Banda

Religions Christian 50%, traditional beliefs 27%, Muslim 15%, other 8%

Ethnic Mix Baya 34%, Banda 27%, Mandjia 21%, Sara 10%, other 8%

Government Multiparty republic

Currency CFA franc = 100 centimes

CONGO [ZAIRE]

STRADDLING THE Equator in east central Africa, Congo (Zaire) is one of Africa's largest countries. It achieved independence from Belgium in 1960.

GEOGRAPHY
Rainforested basin of River Congo occupies 60% of the land. High mountain ranges stretch down the eastern border.

CLIMATE
Tropical and humid. Distinct wet and dry seasons south of the Equator. The north is mainly wet.

The Congo River is navigable for 1,600 km and provides one of the most convenient ways of travelling in the country.

PEOPLE AND SOCIETY
12 main groups and around 190 smaller ones. Original inhabitants, Forest Pygmies, are now a marginalized group. Ethnic tensions inherited from colonial period were contained until 1990, since when outbreaks of ethnic violence have occurred. Despotic regime of President Mobutu overthrown by rebel forces in 1997.

THE ECONOMY
25 years of mismanagement have brought economy near to collapse. Hyperinflation. Minerals, including copper and diamonds, provide 85% of export earnings

FACTFILE
Official Name Democratic Republic of Congo

Date of Formation 1960

Capital Kinshasa

Population 45.3 million

Total Area 2,345,410 sq km (905,563 sq miles)

Density 19 people per sq km

Languages French*, Kiswahili, Tshiluba, Kikongo, Lingala

Religions Christian 70%, traditional beliefs 20%, Muslim 10%

Ethnic Mix Bantu 23%, Hamitic 23%, other (inc. Pygmy) 54%

Government
Single party republic

Currency
New zaire = 100 makuta

NIGER

NIGER LIES land-locked in West Africa, but it is linked to the sea by its one permanent river, the Niger. It became independent of France in 1960.

GEOGRAPHY
North and northeast regions are part of Sahara and Sahel. Aïr mountains in centre rise high above the desert. Savannah in the south.

CLIMATE
High temperatures for most of the year – around 35°C (95°F). The north is virtually rainless.

PEOPLE AND SOCIETY
A largely Islamic society. Women have limited rights, and restricted access to education. Considerable tensions exist between Tuareg nomads in the north and groups in the south. Tuaregs have felt alienated from mainstream politics. They mounted a low-key revolt in 1990. Sense of community and egalitarianism among southern peoples helps to combat economic difficulties.

THE ECONOMY
Vast uranium deposits. Frequent droughts and southwest expansion of Sahara are problems.

FACTFILE
Official Name Republic of Niger

Date of Formation 1960

Capital Niamey

Population 9.5 million

Total Area 1,267,000 sq km (489,188 sq miles)

Density
7 people per sq km

Languages French*, Hausa, Djerma, Fulani, Tuareg, Teda

Religions Muslim 85%, traditional beliefs 14%, Christian 1%

Ethnic Mix Hausa 56%, Djerma 22%, Fulani 9%, other 13%

Government
Multiparty republic

Currency
CFA franc = 100 centimes

CHAD

LAND-LOCKED in north central Africa, Chad has been torn by intermittent periods of civil war since independence from France in 1960.

GEOGRAPHY
Mostly plateaus sloping westwards to Lake Chad. Northern third is Sahara. Tibesti mountains in north rise to 3,300 m (10,826 ft).

CLIMATE
Three distinct zones: desert in north, semi-arid region in centre and tropics in south.

PEOPLE AND SOCIETY
Half the population live in southern fifth of the country. Northern third has only 100,000 people, mainly Muslim Toubeu nomads. Political strife between Muslims in north and Christians in south. Recent attempts to introduce multi-party system, after 30 years of military and one-party rule.

THE ECONOMY
One of Africa's poorest states. Arid lands not suitable for commercial agriculture. Vast majority of people involved in subsistence agriculture, notably cotton and cattle herding. Recent discovery of large oil deposits.

FACTFILE
Official Name Republic of Chad
Date of Formation 1960
Capital Ndjamena
Population 6.5 million
Total Area 1,284,000 sq km (495,752 sq miles)
Density 5 people per sq km
Languages French*, Sara, Maba
Religions Muslim 44%, Christian 33%, traditional beliefs 23%
Ethnic Mix Bagirmi, Sara and Kreish 31%, Sudanic Arab 26%, Teda 7%, other 36%
Government Transitional
Currency CFA franc = 100 centimes

MAURITANIA

SITUATED IN northwest Africa, two-thirds of Mauritania's territory is desert. A former French colony, it achieved independence in 1960.

GEOGRAPHY
The Sahara, barren with scattered oases, covers the north. Savannah lands to the south.

CLIMATE
Generally hot and dry, aggravated by dusty harmattan wind. Summer rain in the south, virtually none in the north.

PEOPLE AND SOCIETY
The Maures, who make up two-third of the population, control political life and dominate the minority black population. Ethnic tension centres on the oppression of blacks by Maures. Tens of thousands of blacks are estimated to be in slavery. Tensions came to a head in 1989 when over 200,000 Maures fled from Senegal. Family solidarity among nomadic peoples is particularly strong.

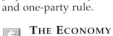
Only 1% of Mauritania's land is suitable for grain crops. Two-thirds of the country is Sahara desert.

THE ECONOMY
Agriculture and herding are main agricultural activities. Iron and copper mining. World's largest gypsum deposits. Rich fishing grounds. Large foreign debt.

FACTFILE
Official Name Islamic Republic of Mauritania
Date of Formation 1960
Capital Nouakchott
Population 2.3 million
Total Area 1,025,520 sq km (395,953 sq miles)
Density 2 people per sq km
Languages French*, Hassaniyah Arabic, Wolof
Religions Muslim 100%
Ethnic Mix Maure 80%, Wolof 7%, Tukulor 5%, other 8%
Government Multiparty republic
Currency Ouguiya = 5 khoums

MALI

LAND-LOCKED in the heart of West Africa, Mali held its first free elections in 1992, more than 30 years after it gained independence from France.

GEOGRAPHY
Land-locked nation. Northern half lies in the Sahara. Inland delta of River Niger flows through grassy savannah region in the south.

CLIMATE
In the south, intensely hot, dry weather precedes the westerly rains. The north is almost rainless.

A village near Bandiagara in eastern Mali. The low broken hills are typical of the region, the homeland of the Dogon people.

PEOPLE AND SOCIETY
Most people live in southern savannah region. Bambara are politically dominant. A few nomadic Fulani and Tuareg herders travel northern plains. Extended family provides social security. Tension between peoples of the south and Tuaregs in north. 80% of population are Muslim.

THE ECONOMY
One of the poorest countries in the world. Less than 2% of land can be cultivated. Most people are farmers, herders or river fishermen. Gold deposits now being mined.

FACTFILE
Official Name Republic of Mali
Date of Formation 1960
Capital Bamako
Population 11.1 million
Total Area 1,240,190 sq km (478,837 sq miles)
Density 9 people per sq km
Languages French*, Bambara, Fulani, Senufo, Soninké
Religions Muslim 80%, traditional beliefs 18%, Christian 2%
Ethnic Mix Bambara 31%, Fulani 13%, Senufo 12%, other 44%
Government Multiparty republic
Currency CFA franc = 100 centimes

SENEGAL

A FORMER French colony, Senegal achieved independence in 1960. Its capital, Dakar, stands on the westernmost cape of Africa.

GEOGRAPHY
Arid semi-desert in the north. The south is mainly savannah bushland. Plains in the southeast.

CLIMATE
Tropical, with humid rainy conditions June–October, and drier season December–May. Coast is cooled by northern trade winds.

PEOPLE AND SOCIETY
Little ethnic tension, due to significant intermarriage. Groups can be identified regionally. Dakar is a Wolof area, the Senegal River is dominated by the Toucouleur, and the Malinke mostly live in the east. The Diola in Casamance have felt politically excluded and this has led to unrest. French-influenced class system still exists and has become more obvious recently.

THE ECONOMY
70% of people are farmers – groundnuts are main export crop. Phosphate is mined. More industry than most West African countries.

FACTFILE
Official Name Republic of Senegal
Date of Formation 1960
Capital Dakar
Population 8.5 million
Total Area 196,720 sq km (75,950 sq miles)
Density 43 people per sq km
Languages French*, Wolof, Fulani, Serer, Diola, Malinke, Soninke
Religions Muslim 92%, traditional beliefs 6%, Christian 2%
Ethnic Mix Wolof 46%, Fulani 25%, Serer 16%, Diola 7%, Malinke 6%
Government Multiparty republic
Currency CFA franc = 100 centimes

THE GAMBIA

A NARROW state on
the west coast of Africa,
The Gambia was renowned
for its stability until its
government was overthrown
in a coup in 1994.

GEOGRAPHY
Narrow strip of land which
borders River Gambia. Long, sandy
beaches backed by mangrove
swamps along river. Savannah
and tropical forests higher up.

CLIMATE
Sub-tropical, with wet, humid
months July–October and warm,
dry season November–May

PEOPLE AND SOCIETY
Little tension between
various ethnic groups. Creole
community – the
Aku, is small but
socially prominent.
People leaving rural
areas for the towns,
where average
incomes are four
times higher. Each
year seasonal immi-
grants from
neighbouring states
come to farm groundnuts. Women
are active as traders.

A fish market in Gambia.

THE ECONOMY
80% of the labour force is
involved in agriculture. Groundnuts are the principal crop. The
fisheries sector is being improved.
Growth in tourism now halted by
political instability.

FACTFILE

Official Name Republic of
The Gambia

Date of Formation 1965

Capital Banjul

Population 1.2 million

Total Area 11,300 sq km
(4,363 sq miles)

Density
106 people per sq km

Languages
English*, other

Religions Muslim 85%, Christian
9%, traditional beliefs 6%

Ethnic Mix Mandinka 41%, Fulani
14%, Wolof 13%, other 32%

Government
Military regime

Currency Dalasi = 100 butut

CAPE VERDE

OFF THE west coast of
Africa, in the Atlantic
Ocean, lies the group
of islands that make up
Cape Verde, a Portuguese
colony until 1975.

GEOGRAPHY
Ten main islands and eight
smaller islets, all of volcanic origin.
Mostly mountainous, with steep
cliffs and rocky headlands.

CLIMATE
Warm, and very dry.
Subject to droughts that may
last for years at a time.

PEOPLE AND SOCIETY
Most people are of mixed
Portuguese-African origin; the rest
are largely African, descended from
slaves or from
more recent
immigrants from
the mainland. 50%
of the population
live on Santiago.
Strong Roman
Catholic influences.
Some ethnic
tension between
islands.
Peaceful transition to multiparty
democracy in 1991.

THE ECONOMY
Most people are subsistence
farmers. Fish is the main export.
Only minerals produced are salt,
and volcanic rock for cement.
Experiments with natural energy
taking place.

FACTFILE

Official Name Republic of
Cape Verde

Date of Formation 1975

Capital Praia

Population 400,000

Total Area 4,030 sq km
(1,556 sq miles)

Density
99 people per sq km

Languages
Portuguese*, Creole

Religions Roman Catholic 98%,
Protestant 2%

Ethnic Mix Creole (mestiço) 71%,
Black 28%, White 1%

Government
Multiparty republic

Currency Escudo = 100 centavos

GUINEA-BISSAU

KNOWN AS Portuguese
Guinea during its days
as a colony, Guinea-Bissau
is situated on Africa's
west coast, bordered by
Senegal and Guinea.

GEOGRAPHY
Low-lying, apart from
savannah highlands in northeast.
Rainforests and
swamps are
found along
coastal areas.

CLIMATE
Tropical,
with wet season
May–November
and dry season
December–April.
Hot harmattan
wind blows during
dry season

*Bafatá, in central Guinea-Bissau
lies on the Gêba River and is an
important inland port.*

PEOPLE AND SOCIETY
Largest ethnic group is
Balante, who live in the south.
Mixed Portuguese-African
mestiços dominate top ranks
of government and bureaucracy
but comprise less than 2% of
population. Most people live
on small family farms in self-
contained villages. First multiparty
elections held in 1994.

THE ECONOMY
Mostly subsistence farming –
maize, sweet potatoes, cassava.
Main cash crops are cashews,
groundnuts and palm kernels.
Offshore oil as yet untapped.

FACTFILE

Official Name Republic of
Guinea-Bissau

Date of Formation 1974

Capital Bissau

Population 1.1 million

Total Area
36,120 sq km (13,940 sq miles)

Density
30 people per sq km

Languages
Portuguese*, other

Religions Traditional beliefs 54%,
Muslim 38%, Christian 8%

Ethnic Mix Balante 27%, Fulani
22%, Malinke 12%, other 39%

Government
Multiparty republic

Currency Peso = 100 centavos

GUINEA

FACING THE Atlantic
Ocean, on the west coast
of Africa, Guinea became
the first French colony
in Africa to gain
independence, in 1958.

GEOGRAPHY
Coastal plains and mangrove
swamps in west rise to forested
or savannah
highlands
in the south.
Semi-desert
in the north.

CLIMATE
Tropical,
with wet season
April–October.
Heavy annual
rainfall. In
dry season,
hot harmattan
wind blows from the Sahara.

PEOPLE AND SOCIETY
Malinke and Fulani make
up most of the population, but
traditional rivalries between them
have allowed coastal peoples such
as the Susu to dominate politics.
Women gained influence under
Marxist party rule from 1958–84,
but Muslim revival since then has
reversed the trend. First multiparty
elections held in 1995.

THE ECONOMY
Two-thirds of people are
farmers. Cash crops are palm oil,
bananas, pineapples and rice. Gold,
diamond and bauxite reserves.

FACTFILE

Official Name Republic of Guinea

Date of Formation 1958

Capital Conakry

Population 6.9 million

Total Area 245,860 sq km
(94,926 sq miles)

Density
28 people per sq km

Languages French*, Fulani,
Malinke, Susu, Kissi, other

Religions Muslim 85%, Christian
8%, traditional beliefs 7%

Ethnic Mix Fulani 40%, Malinke
25%, Susu 12%, Kissi 7%,
other 16%

Government
Multiparty republic

Currency Franc = 100 centimes

SIERRA LEONE

THE WEST AFRICAN state of Sierra Leone achieved independence from the British in 1961. Today, it is one of the world's poorest nations.

🌐 GEOGRAPHY
Flat plain, running the length of the coast, stretches inland for 133 km (83 miles). Forests rise to highlands near neighbouring Guinea in the northeast.

☀ CLIMATE
Hot tropical weather, with very high rainfall and humidity. Dusty, northeastern harmattan wind blows November–April.

👥 PEOPLE AND SOCIETY
Mende and Temne are major ethnic groups. Freetown's citizens descended from slaves freed from Britain and the US, resulting in a strongly anglicized Creole culture. A military coup in 1992 halted plans to turn the government into a multiparty democracy. Rebel forces have been fighting the government since 1991; leading to a coup in 1997.

💲 THE ECONOMY
Vast majority of people are subsistence farmers. Cash crops include palm kernels, cocoa beans, and kola. Main export is diamonds.

FACTFILE

Official Name Republic of Sierra Leone

Date of Formation 1961

Capital Freetown

Population 4.6 million

Total Area 71,740 sq km (27,699 sq miles)

Density 64 people per sq km

Languages English*, Krio (Creole)

Religions Traditional beliefs 52%, Muslim 40%, Christian 8%

Ethnic Mix Mende 34%, Temne 31%, Limba 9%, Kono 5%, other 21%

Government Military regime

Currency Leone = 100 cents

LIBERIA

LIBERIA FACES the Atlantic Ocean in equatorial West Africa. Africa's oldest republic, it was established in 1847. Today it is torn by civil war.

🌐 GEOGRAPHY
Coastline of beaches and mangrove swamps rises to forested plateaux and highlands inland.

☀ CLIMATE
High temperatures. Except in extreme southeast, there is only one wet season, May–October.

👥 PEOPLE AND SOCIETY
Key social distinction has been between Americo-Liberians – descendants of freed slaves – and the indigenous tribal peoples.

A village near Gbanga, Liberia. The largest of Liberia's indigenous groups, the Kpelle, live in this area.

However, political assimilation and intermarriage have eased tensions. Inter-tribal tension is now a problem. A civil war has ravaged the country since 1990, with private armies competing for power.

💲 THE ECONOMY
Civil war has led to collapse of economy – little commercial activity. Only 1% of land is arable. Estimated one billion tonnes of iron-ore reserves at Mount Nimba, but current state of world demand does not justify their exploitation.

FACTFILE

Official Name Republic of Liberia

Date of Formation 1847/1907

Capital Monrovia

Population 3.1 million

Total Area 111,370 sq km (43,000 sq miles)

Density 28 people per sq km

Languages English*, Kpelle, Bassa Vai, Grebo, Kru, Kissi, Gola

Religions Traditional beliefs 70%, Muslim 20%, Christian 10%

Ethnic Mix Kpelle 20%, Bassa 14%, Americo-Liberians 5%, other 61%

Government Transitional

Currency Liberian $ = 100 cents

IVORY COAST

ONE OF the larger nations along the coast of West Africa, the Ivory Coast remains under the influence of its former colonial ruler, France.

🌐 GEOGRAPHY
Sandy coastal strip backed by a largely rainforested interior, and a savannah plateau in the north.

☀ CLIMATE
High temperatures all year round. South has two wet seasons; north has one, with lower rainfall.

👥 PEOPLE AND SOCIETY
More than 60 ethnic groups. President Houphouët-Boigny, who ruled from independence until 1993, promoted his own group, the Baoule. Succession of Konan Bedic, another Baoule, has annoyed other tribes. The extended family keeps labourers who migrate to the cities in contact with their villages. Improved education means that many women now hold top jobs.

💲 THE ECONOMY
Cash crops include cocoa, coffee, palm oil, bananas and rubber. Teak, mahogany and ebony in rainforests. Oil reserves.

FACTFILE

Official Name Republic of the Ivory Coast

Date of Formation 1960

Capital Yamoussoukro

Population 14.7 million

Total Area 322,463 sq km (124,503 sq miles)

Density 46 people per sq km

Languages French*, Akran, other

Religions Traditional beliefs 63%, Muslim 25%, Christian 12%

Ethnic Mix Baoule 23%, Bété 18%, Kru 17%, Malinke 15%, other 27%

Government Multiparty republic

Currency CFA franc = 100 centimes

BURKINA

KNOWN AS Upper Volta until 1984, the West African state of Burkina has been under military rule for most of its post-independence history.

🌐 GEOGRAPHY
North of country is covered by the Sahara. South is largely savannah. Three main rivers are Black, White and Red Voltas

☀ CLIMATE
Tropical. Dry, cool weather November-February. Erratic rain March-April, mostly in southeast.

A camel being used to plough fields in Burkina. The poor soil quality and frequent droughts leads to seasonal emigration.

👥 PEOPLE AND SOCIETY
No ethnic group is dominant, but the Mossi have always played an important part in government. Extreme poverty has led to a strong sense of egalitarianism. The extended family is important, and reaches from villages into towns and cities. Women wield considerable power and influence within this system, but most are still denied access to education

💲 THE ECONOMY
Based on agriculture – cotton is most valuable cash crop – but not self-sufficient in food. Gold is the leading non-agricultural export.

FACTFILE

Official Name Burkina

Date of Formation 1960

Capital Ouagadougou

Population 10.6 million

Total Area 274,200 sq km (105,870 sq miles)

Density 39 people per sq km

Languages French*, Mossi, Fulani, Tuareg, Dyula, Songhai

Religions Traditional beliefs 65%, Muslim 25%, Christian 10%

Ethnic Mix Mossi 45%, Mande 10%, Fulani 10%, others 35%

Government Multiparty republic

Currency CFA franc = 100 centimes

AFRICA

GHANA

ONCE KNOWN as the Gold Coast, Ghana in West Africa has experienced intermittent periods of military rule since independence in 1957.

GEOGRAPHY
Mostly low-lying. West is covered by rainforest. Lake Volta – the world's third largest artificial lake – was created by damming the White Volta River.

CLIMATE
Tropical. Two wet seasons in the south; one in the north.

PEOPLE AND SOCIETY
Around 75 ethnic groups of which the largest is the Akan. Over 100 languages and dialects are spoken. Southern peoples are richer and more urbanized than those of the north. In recent years, tension between groups in the north has erupted into violence. Multiparty elections in 1992 confirmed former military leader Jerry Rawlings in power.

Kabye cultivation near Kara, northern Togo. The main crops are cassava, yams and maize

THE ECONOMY
Ghana produces 15% of the world's cocoa. Good-quality hardwood trees such as maple and sapele are exploited for timber. Gold, diamonds, bauxite and manganese are major exports.

FACTFILE
Official Name Republic of Ghana

Date of Formation 1957

Capital Accra

Population 18 million

Total Area 238,540 sq km (92,100 sq miles)

Density 75 people per sq km

Languages English*, Akan, Mossi, Ewe, Ga, Twi, Fanti, Gurma, other

Religions Traditional beliefs 38%, Muslim 30%, Christian 24%, other 8%

Ethnic Mix Akan 52%, Mossi 15%, Ewe 12%, Ga 8%, other 13%

Government Multiparty republic

Currency Cedi = 100 pesewas

AFRICA

TOGO

TOGO LIES sandwiched between Ghana and Benin in West Africa. The 1993–94 elections were the first since its independence in 1960.

GEOGRAPHY
Central forested region bounded by savannah lands to the north and south. Mountain range stretches southwest to northeast.

CLIMATE
Coast hot and humid; drier inland. Rainy season March–July, with heaviest falls in the west.

PEOPLE AND SOCIETY
Harsh resentment between Ewe in the south and Kabye in the north. Kabye control military, but are far less developed than people of the south. Extended family is important. Tribalism and nepotism are key factors in everyday life. Some ethnic groups, such as the Mina, have matriarchal societies.

THE ECONOMY
Most people are farmers. Self-sufficient in basic foodstuffs. Main export crops are coffee, cocoa and cotton. Half of all export revenues come from phosphate deposits with the world's highest mineral content.

FACTFILE
Official Name Togolese Republic

Date of Formation 1960

Capital Lomé

Population 4.3 million

Total Area 56,790 sq km (21,927 sq miles)

Density 76 people per sq km

Languages French*, Ewe, Kabye, Gurma, other

Religions Traditional beliefs 70%, Christian 20%, Muslim 10%

Ethnic Mix Ewe 43%, Kabye 26%, Gurma 16%, other 15%

Government Multiparty republic

Currency CFA franc = 100 centimes

AFRICA

BENIN

STRETCHES NORTH from the West African coast. In 1990, it became one of the pioneers of African democratization, ending years of military rule.

GEOGRAPHY
Long, sandy coastal region. Numerous lagoons lie just behind the shoreline. Forested plateaux inland. Mountains in the northwest.

CLIMATE
Hot and humid in the south. Two rainy seasons. Hot, dusty harmattan winds blow during December-February dry season.

Fishing boats near Cotonou, on the Benin coast. There are numerous small lagoons clustered behind the short (100-km) coastline.

PEOPLE AND SOCIETY
Around 50 ethnic groups. Fon people in the south dominate politics. Other major groups are Adja and Yoruba. In the far north, Fulani are nomadic. Tension between north and south, partly reflects Muslim–Christian divide, and greater development of south. Women hold positions of power in retail trade.

THE ECONOMY
Mostly subsistence farming. Cash crops include cotton, cocoa beans and coffee. Some oil and limestone are produced. France is the main aid donor.

FACTFILE
Official Name Republic of Benin

Date of Formation 1960

Capital Porto-Novo

Population 5.6 million

Total Area 112,620 sq km (43,480 sq miles)

Density 50 people per sq km

Languages French*, Fon, Bariba, Yoruba, Adja, Houeda, Fulani

Religions Traditional beliefs 70%, Muslim 15%, Christian 15%

Ethnic Mix Fon 39%, Yoruba 12%, Adja 10%, other 39%

Government Multiparty republic

Currency CFA franc = 100 centimes

AFRICA

NIGERIA

FOUR TIMES the size of the United Kingdom, from which it gained independence in 1960, Nigeria in West Africa is a federation of 30 states.

GEOGRAPHY
Coastal area of beaches, swamps and lagoons gives way to rainforest, and then to savannah on high plateaux. Semi-desert in north.

CLIMATE
South is hot, rainy and humid for most of the year. Arid north has one very humid wet season. Jos plateau and highlands are cooler.

PEOPLE AND SOCIETY
Some 250 ethnic groups: the largest are Hausa, Yoruba, Ibo and Fulani. Tensions between groups threaten national unity, although this has been largely contained in recent years. International condemnation over govenment treatment of dissidents. Except in the Islamic north, women are allowed economic independence.

THE ECONOMY
Oil has been the economic mainstay since 1970s, accounting for 90% of export earnings.

FACTFILE
Official Name Federal Republic of Nigeria

Date of Formation 1960

Capital Abuja

Population 115 million

Total Area 923,770 sq km (356,668 sq miles)

Density 124 people per sq km

Languages English*, Hausa, Yoruba

Religions Muslim 50%, Christian 40%, traditional beliefs 10%

Ethnic Mix Hausa 21%, Yoruba 20%, Ibo 17%, Fulani 9%, other 33%

Government Military regime

Currency Naira = 100 kobo

CAMEROON

SITUATED ON the central West African coast, Cameroon was effectively a one-party state for 30 years. Multiparty elections were held in 1992.

GEOGRAPHY
Over half the land is forested: equatorial rainforest in north, evergreen forest and wooded savannah in south. Mountains in the west.

CLIMATE
South is equatorial, with plentiful rainfall, declining inland. Far north is beset by drought.

PEOPLE AND SOCIETY
Around 230 ethnic groups; no single group is dominant. Bamileke is the largest, but it has never held political power. Some tension between more affluent south and poorer north, albeit diminished by the ethnic diversity. Also rivalry between majority French-speakers and minority English-speakers, with sections of the latter group demanding autonomy.

The steep slopes of Mindif Pic flatten out into a savannah landscape in Cameroon's far north.

THE ECONOMY
Moderate oil reserves. Very diversified agricultural economy – timber, cocoa, coffee, rubber. Self-sufficient in food. Growing national debt owing to failure to adjust to falling oil revenues.

FACTFILE
Official Name Republic of Cameroon
Date of Formation 1960
Capital Yaoundé
Population 13.6 million
Total Area 475,440 sq km (183,570 sq miles)
Density 29 people per sq km
Languages English*, French*, Fang, Bulu, Yaunde, Duala, Mbum
Religions Traditional beliefs 51%, Christian 33%, Muslim 16%
Ethnic Mix Bamileke and Manum 20%, Fang 19%, other 61%
Government Multiparty republic
Currency CFA franc = 100 centimes

EQUATORIAL GUINEA

COMPRISES THE mainland territory of Rio Muni and five islands on the west coast of central Africa. In 1993, the first free elections were held.

GEOGRAPHY
Islands are mountainous and volcanic. Mainland is lower, with mangrove swamps along coast.

CLIMATE
The Isla de Bioco is extremely wet and humid. The mainland is only marginally drier and cooler.

PEOPLE AND SOCIETY
The mainland is sparsely populated. Most people are Fang, the dominant group in politics. The ruling Mongomo clan hold most of the country's wealth. The Isla de Bioco is populated mostly by Bubi people and a minority of Creoles known as Fernandinos. Extended family ties have remained strong despite disruptive social pressure during the years of the Macías dictatorship.

THE ECONOMY
The Isla de Bioco generates the most income. Main exports are tropical timber and cocoa is the major cash crop. Oil and gas reserves are yet to be fully exploited.

FACTFILE
Official Name Republic of Equatorial Guinea
Date of Formation 1968
Capital Malabo
Population 400,000
Total Area 28,050 sq km (10,830 sq miles)
Density 14 people per sq km
Languages Spanish*, Fang, other
Religions Christian (mainly Roman Catholic) 89%, other 11%
Ethnic Mix Fang 72%, Bubi 14%, Duala 3%, Ibibio 2%, other 9%
Government Multiparty republic
Currency CFA franc = 100 centimes

SAO TOME & PRINCIPE

A FORMER Portuguese colony off Africa's west coast, comprising two main islands and smaller islets. 1991 elections ended 15 years of Marxism.

GEOGRAPHY
Islands are scattered across Equator. São Tomé and Príncipe are heavily forested and mountainous.

CLIMATE
Hot and humid, slightly cooled by Benguela Current. Plentiful rainfall, but dry July–August.

PEOPLE AND SOCIETY
Population is entirely descended from immigrants as islands were uninhabited when Portuguese arrived in 1470. People mostly black, although Portuguese culture predominates. Blacks run the political parties. Society is well integrated and free of racial prejudice. Growing business class. Extended family offers main form of social security. Príncipe assumed autonomous status in April 1995.

THE ECONOMY
Cocoa provides for 90% of export earnings. Palm oil, pepper and coffee are also farmed. One of Africa's highest aid-to-population ratios.

FACTFILE
Official Name Democratic Republic of Sao Tome and Principe
Date of Formation 1975
Capital São Tomé
Population 125,000
Total Area 964 sq km (372 sq miles)
Density 130 people per sq km
Languages Portuguese*, Portuguese Creole, other
Religions Roman Catholic 90%, other Christian 10%
Ethnic Mix Black 90%, Portuguese and Creole 10%
Government Multiparty republic
Currency Dobra = 100 centimos

GABON

A FORMER French colony straddling the Equator on Africa's west coast. It returned to multiparty politics in 1990, after 22 years of one-party rule.

GEOGRAPHY
Low plateaux and mountains lie beyond the coastal strip. Two-thirds of the land is rainforested.

CLIMATE
Hot and tropical, with little distinction between seasons. Cold Benguela Current cools the coast.

The Albert Schweitzer Hospital at Lambaréné, on the lower Ogooué River, Gabon. Schweitzer won a Nobel Prize for his work in Africa.

PEOPLE AND SOCIETY
Some 40 different languages are spoken. The Fang, who live mainly in the north, are the largest ethnic group, but have yet to gain control of the government. Oil wealth has led to growth of an affluent middle class. Menial jobs are done by immigrant workers. Education follows the French system. Gabon is one of Africa's most urbanized countries. The government is encouraging population growth.

THE ECONOMY
Oil is the main source of revenue. Tropical hardwoods are being exploited. Cocoa beans, coffee and rice grown for export.

FACTFILE
Official Name The Gabonese Republic
Date of Formation 1960
Capital Libreville
Population 1.4 million
Total Area 267,670 sq km (103,347 sq miles)
Density 5 people per sq km
Languages French*, Fang, other
Religions Catholic, other Christian 96%, Muslim 2%, other 2%
Ethnic Mix Fang 36%, Mpongwe 15%, Mbete 14%, other 35%
Government Multiparty republic
Currency CFA franc = 100 centimes

CONGO

ASTRIDE THE Equator in west central Africa, this former French colony emerged from 20 years of Marxist-Leninist rule in 1990.

GEOGRAPHY
Mostly forest- or savannah-covered plateaux, drained by Ubangi and Congo River systems. Narrow coastal plain is lined with sand dunes and lagoons.

CLIMATE
Hot, tropical. Temperatures rarely fall below 30°C (86°F). Two wet and two dry seasons. Rainfall is heaviest south of the Equator.

PEOPLE AND SOCIETY
One of the most tribally conscious nations in Africa. Four main ethnic groups Bakongo, Sangha, Teke and Mboshi. Main tensions between Bakongo in the north and Mboshi in the south. Middle class is sustained by oil wealth. Schools are run according to the French system and are still subject to inspection from Paris. Multiparty elections held in 1992.

THE ECONOMY
Oil is main source of revenue. Cash crops include sugar, coffee, cocoa and palm oil. Substantial industrial base. Large foreign debt.

FACTFILE
Official Name The Republic of the Congo

Date of Formation 1960

Capital Brazzaville

Population 2.7 million

Total Area 342,000 sq km (132,040 sq miles)

Density 8 people per sq km

Languages French*, Kongo, other

Religions Catholic 50%, traditional beliefs 48%, other (inc. Muslim) 2%

Ethnic Mix Bakongo 48%, Teke 17%, Mboshi 17%, Sangha 5%, other 13%

Government Multiparty republic

Currency CFA franc = 100 centimes

ANGOLA

LOCATED IN southwest Africa, Angola was in an almost continuous state of civil war from 1975–94, following independence from Portugal.

GEOGRAPHY
Most of the land is hilly and grass-covered. Desert in the south. Mountains in the centre and north.

CLIMATE
Varies from temperate to tropical. Rainfall decreases north to south. Coast is cooler and dry.

PEOPLE AND SOCIETY
Civil war was fought by two groups. UNITA cast itself as sole representative of the Ovimbundu, in order to attack ruling Kimbundu-dominated MPLA. In 1991–92, MPLA abandoned Marxist rule and held free elections. UNITA lost, and resumed civil war. Up to 500,000 people died as a result. In 1995, UN troops were deployed to begin a phased de-militarization operation.

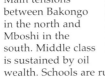

Luanda, the Angolan capital, was founded in 1573 by Portuguese colonists.

THE ECONOMY
Rich mineral resources give Angola the potential to be one of Africa's richest countries, but civil war has severely hampered economic development. Oil and diamonds are exported.

FACTFILE
Official Name Republic of Angola

Date of Formation 1975

Capital Luanda

Population 11.5 million

Total Area 1,246,700 sq km (481,551 sq miles)

Density 9 people per sq km

Languages Portuguese*, other

Religions Catholic/Protestant 64%, traditional beliefs 34%, other 2%

Ethnic Mix Ovimbundu 37%, Kimbundu 25%, Bakongo 13%, mixed 1%, other 24%

Government Multiparty republic

Currency Kwanza = 100 lwei

ZAMBIA

ZAMBIA LIES land-locked at the heart of southern Africa. In 1991, it made a peaceful transition from single-party rule to multiparty democracy.

GEOGRAPHY
A high savannah plateau, broken by mountains in northeast. Vegetation mainly trees and scrub

CLIMATE
Tropical, with three seasons cool and dry, hot and dry, and wet. Southwest is prone to drought.

PEOPLE AND SOCIETY
One of the continent's most urbanized countries. Although there are more than 70 different ethnic groups, Zambia has been less affected by ethnic tensions than many African states. Largest group is Bemba in northeast. Other major groups are Tonga in the south, and Lozi in the west. Women still have subordinate role in the family and politics. Rural population live by subsistence farming.

THE ECONOMY
Copper mining is the main industry – exports bring in 80% of foreign income. However, domestic reserves are declining rapidly.

FACTFILE
Official Name Republic of Zambia

Date of Formation 1964

Capital Lusaka

Population 9.7 million

Total Area 752,610 sq km (290,563 sq miles)

Density 13 people per sq km

Languages English*, Bemba, Tonga, Nyanja, Lozi, Lunda

Religions Christian 63%, traditional beliefs 35%, other 2%

Ethnic Mix Bemba 36%, Maravi 18%, Tonga 15%, other 31%

Government Multiparty republic

Currency Kwacha = 100 ngwee

TANZANIA

THE EAST African state of Tanzania was formed in 1964 by the union of Tanganyika and Zanzibar. A third of its area is game reserve or national park.

GEOGRAPHY
Mainland is mostly a high plateau lying to the east of the Great Rift Valley. Forested coastal plain. Highlands in the north and south.

Tanzania's Arusha National Park lies in the Ngurdoto volcanic crater. Herds of buffalo, rhino, elephant and giraffe live in the park.

CLIMATE
Tropical on the coast and Zanzibar. Semi-arid on central plateau, semi-temperate in the highlands. March-May rains.

PEOPLE AND SOCIETY
99% of people belong to one of 120 small ethnic Bantu groups. Arabs, Asians and Europeans make up remaining population. Use of Swahili as lingua franca has eliminated ethnic rivalries. Family is still the focus of traditional rural life. Politics is moving towards democracy, though separatists in Zanzibar are a growing force.

THE ECONOMY
Reliant on agriculture, including forestry and livestock. Cotton, coffee, tea and cloves are cash crops. Diamonds are mined.

FACTFILE
Official Name United Republic of Tanzania

Date of Formation 1964

Capital Dodoma

Population 30.5 million

Total Area 945,090 sq km (364,900 sq miles)

Density 32 people per sq km

Languages English*, Swahili*

Religions Traditional beliefs 42%, Muslim 31%, Christian 27%

Ethnic Mix 120 ethnic Bantu groups 99%, other 1%

Government Single-party republic

Currency Shilling = 100 cents

MALAWI

A FORMER British colony, Malawi lies land-locked in southeast Africa. Its name means 'the land where the sun is reflected in the water like fire'.

GEOGRAPHY
Lake Nyasa takes up one fifth of the country. Highlands lie west of the lake. Much of the land is covered by forests and savannah.

CLIMATE
Mainly sub-tropical. South is hot and humid. Highlands are cooler. May–October dry season.

PEOPLE AND SOCIETY
Few ethnic tensions as most people share common Bantu origin. However, tensions between north and south have arisen in recent years. Northerners are increasingly disaffected by their lack of political representation but the new government has strived to reduce tensions. Many Asians are involved in the retail trade. Multi-party politics introduced in 1993.

THE ECONOMY
Tobacco accounts for 76% of export earnings. Tea and sugar production. Coal, bauxite reserves. Fishing takes place on Lake Nyasa.

FACTFILE
Official Name Republic of Malawi

Date of Formation 1964

Capital Lilongwe

Population 11.4 million

Total Area
118,480 sq km (45,745 sq miles)

Density
96 people per sq km

Languages
English*, Chewa*, other

Religions Protestant/Catholic 66%, traditional beliefs 18%, other 16%

Ethnic Mix Maravi 55%, Lomwe 17%, Yao 13%, Ngoni 7%, other (including Asian) 8%

Government Multiparty republic

Currency Kwacha = 100 tambala

ZIMBABWE

THE FORMER British colony of Southern Rhodesia became fully independent as Zimbabwe in 1980, after 15 years of troubled white minority rule.

GEOGRAPHY
High plateaux in centre bordered by Zambezi River in the north and Limpopo in the south. Rivers criss-cross central area.

CLIMATE
Tropical, though moderated by the altitude. Wet season November–March. Drought is common in eastern highlands.

PEOPLE AND SOCIETY
Two main ethnic groups, Ndebele in the north, and Shona in the south. Shona outnumber Ndebele by four to one. Whites make up just 1% of the population, but are generally far more affluent than blacks. Recent government policies aim at increasing black education and employment. Families are large and 45% of people are under 15.

The building of the Kariba Dam, created the vast Lake Kariba on the Zambezi River.

THE ECONOMY
Most broadly based African economy after South Africa. Virtually self-sufficient in food and energy. Tobacco is main cash crop.

FACTFILE
Official Name Republic of Zimbabwe

Date of Formation 1980

Capital Harare

Population 11.5 million

Total Area
390,580 sq km (150,800 sq miles)

Density
29 people per sq km

Languages
English*, Shona, Ndebele

Religions Syncretic (Christian and traditional beliefs) 50%, Christian 26%, traditional beliefs 24%

Ethnic Mix Shona 71%, Ndebele 16%, other 11%, White, Asian 2%

Government Multiparty republic

Currency Zimbabwe $ = 100 cents

MOZAMBIQUE

MOZAMBIQUE LIES on the southeast African coast. It was torn by a civil war between the Marxist government and a rebel group from 1977–1992.

GEOGRAPHY
Largely a savannah-covered plateau. Coast is fringed by coral reefs and lagoons. Zambezi River bisects country from east to west.

CLIMATE
Tropical. Hottest along the coast. Wet season usually March–October, but rains frequently fail.

PEOPLE AND SOCIETY
Racially diverse, but tensions in society are between northerners and southerners, rather than ethnic groups. Life is based around the extended family, which in some regions is matriarchal. Polygamy is fairly common. Government has faced huge task of re-settling the one million refugees from civil war. 90% of the population live in severe poverty.

Tea is an important cash crop in Mozambique. Other cash crops include cashew nuts, cotton, sugar, copra and citrus fruits.

THE ECONOMY
The country is almost entirely dependent on foreign aid. 85% of the population is engaged in agriculture.

FACTFILE
Official Name Republic of Mozambique

Date of Formation 1975

Capital Maputo

Population 16.5 million

Total Area
801,590 sq km (309,493 sq miles)

Density
21 people per sq km

Languages
Portuguese*, other

Religions Traditional beliefs 60%, Christian 30%, Muslim 10%

Ethnic Mix Makua-Lomwe 47%, Tsonga 23%, Malawi 12%, other 18%

Government Multiparty republic

Currency Metical = 100 centavos

NAMIBIA

LOCATED IN southwestern Africa, Namibia became free of South African control in 1990, after years of uncertainty and guerrilla activity.

GEOGRAPHY
Namib Desert stretches along coastal strip. Inland, a ridge of mountains rises to 2,500 m (8,200 ft). Kalahari Desert lies in the east.

CLIMATE
Almost rainless. Coast usually shrouded in thick fog, unless hot dry berg wind blows.

PEOPLE AND SOCIETY
Largest ethnic group, the Ovambo, live mainly in the north. Whites, including a large German community, are centred around Windhoek. Ethnic strife predicted at time of independence has not materialized. High illiteracy among blacks due to legacy of apartheid. Whites still control the economy.

THE ECONOMY
Third wealthiest country in sub-Saharan Africa. Varied mineral resources, including uranium and diamonds. Rich offshore fishing grounds. Lack of skilled labour inhibits economic development.

FACTFILE
Official Name Republic of Namibia

Date of Formation 1990/1994

Capital Windhoek

Population 1.6 million

Total Area
824,290 sq km (318,260 sq miles)

Density
2 people per sq km

Languages English*, Afrikaans, Ovambo, Kavango, German, other

Religions
Christian 90%, other 10%

Ethnic Mix Ovambo 50%, Kavango 9%, Herero 7%, Damara 7%, White 6%, other 21%

Government Multiparty republic

Currency Rand = 100 cents

BOTSWANA

ONCE THE British protectorate of Bechuanaland, Botswana lies land-locked in southern Africa. Diamonds provide it with a prosperous economy.

GEOGRAPHY
Lies on vast plateau, high above sea-level. Hills in the east. Kalahari Desert in centre and southwest. Swamps and salt-pans elsewhere and in Okavango basin.

CLIMATE
Dry and prone to drought. Summer wet season, April–October. Winters are warm, with cold nights.

PEOPLE AND SOCIETY
Tswana make up 75% of the population. San, or Kalahari Bushmen, the first inhabitants, have been marginalized. 72% of people live in rural areas. Traditional forms of authority such as the village kgotla, or parliament, remain important.

Botswana's Okavango Delta is home to a vast range of wildlife and rare plant species.

THE ECONOMY
Diamonds are the leading export and contribute by a 50% state-owned company. Deposits of copper, nickel, coal, salt and soda ash are also exported. Beef is exported to Europe. Tourism aimed at wealthy wildlife enthusiasts.

FACTFILE
Official Name Republic of Botswana

Date of Formation 1966

Capital Gaborone

Population 1.5 million

Total Area 581,730 sq km (224,600 sq miles)

Density 3 people per sq km

Languages Tswana, Shona, San, Khoikhoi, Ndebele

Religions Traditional beliefs 50%, Christian (mostly Anglican) 50%

Ethnic Mix Tswana 75%, Shona 12%, San 3%, White 1%, other 9%

Government Multiparty republic

Currency Pula = 100 thebe

LESOTHO

THE LAND-LOCKED kingdom of Lesotho is entirely surrounded by South Africa, which provides all its land transport links with the outside world.

GEOGRAPHY
High mountainous plateau, cut by valleys and ravines. Maluti range in centre. Drakensberg range in the east. Lowlands in the west.

CLIMATE
Temperate. Summers are hot and wet. Snow is frequent in the mountains in winter.

PEOPLE AND SOCIETY
Almost everyone is Basotho, although there are some Europeans, South Asians and Taiwanese. Strong sense of national identity has tended to minimize ethnic tensions. Many men work as migrant labourers in South Africa, leaving 72% of households, and most of the farms, run by women.

THE ECONOMY
Few natural resources and so is heavily reliant on the incomes of its migrant workers. Subsistence farming is the main activity. Exports include livestock, wool, mohair from goat herds.

FACTFILE
Official Name Kingdom of Lesotho

Date of Formation 1966

Capital Maseru

Population 2.1 million

Total Area 30,350 sq km (11,718 sq miles)

Density 69 people per sq km

Languages English*, Sesotho*, Zulu

Religions Roman Catholic and other Christian 93%, other 7%

Ethnic Mix Basotho 99%, other 1%

Government Constitutional monarchy

Currency Loti = 100 lisente

SWAZILAND

THE SOUTHERN African kingdom of Swaziland gained independence from Britain in 1968. It is economically dependent on South Africa.

GEOGRAPHY
Mainly high plateaux and mountains. Rolling grasslands and low scrub plains to the east. Pine forests on western border.

CLIMATE
Temperatures rise and rainfall declines as land descends eastward, from high to low veld.

The town of Mbabane lies on the high veld of Swaziland, where traditional cattle farming has led to soil erosion through overgrazing.

PEOPLE AND SOCIETY
One of Africa's most homogenous states. Also among its most conservative, although it is now coming under pressure from urban-based modernizers. Political system promotes Swazi tradition and is dominated by a powerful monarchy. Society is patriarchal and focused around various clans and chiefs.

THE ECONOMY
Sugarcane is the main cash crop. Others are pineapples, cotton, rice and tobacco. Asbestos, coal and wood pulp are also exported.

FACTFILE
Official Name Kingdom of Swaziland

Date of Formation 1968

Capital Mbabane

Population 900,000

Total Area 17,360 sq km (6,703 sq miles)

Density 52 people per sq km

Languages Siswati*, English*, Zulu

Religions Protestant and other Christian 60%, traditional beliefs 40%

Ethnic Mix Swazi 95%, other 5%

Government Executive monarchy

Currency Lilangeni = 100 cents

SOUTH AFRICA

SOUTH AFRICA is the most southerly nation on the African continent. The multiracial, multiparty elections of 1994 overturned 80 years of minority rule.

GEOGRAPHY
Large grassland plateaus, drained by the Orange and Limpopo rivers. Drakensberg mountains overshadow eastern coastal lowlands.

CLIMATE
Warm, temperate and dry. Interior of country gets most rain in summer. Coast around Cape Town has mediterranean climate.

PEOPLE AND SOCIETY
Dismantling of apartheid in early 1990s ended racial segregation. Some Zulus and whites have made demands for independent homelands. Racial imbalance to be addressed by focus on education, housing, land reform.

THE ECONOMY
Highly diversified economy with modern infrastructure. Growing manufacturing sector. Diamonds, gold, platinum, coal, silver, uranium, copper and asbestos mined.

FACTFILE
Official Name Republic of South Africa

Date of Formation 1910/1934

Capital Pretoria, Cape Town, Bloemfontein

Population 42.4 million

Total Area 1,221,040 sq km (471,443 sq miles)

Density 35 people per sq km

Languages Afrikaans*, English, 9 African languages

Religions Protestant 55%, Catholic 9%, Hindu 1%, Muslim 1%, other 34%

Ethnic Mix Black 75%, White 14%, mixed 9%, South Asian 2%

Government Multiparty republic

Currency Rand = 100 cents

COMOROS

IN THE Indian Ocean between Mozambique and Madagascar lie the Comoros, comprising three main islands and a number of smaller islets.

GEOGRAPHY
Main islands are of volcanic origin and are heavily forested. The remainder are coral atolls

CLIMATE
Hot and humid all year round. November–May is hottest and wettest period.

PEOPLE AND SOCIETY
Country has absorbed a diversity of people over the years Africans, Arabs, Polynesians and Persians. Also Portuguese, Dutch, French and Indian immigrants. Ethnic tension is rare. Wealth concentrated among political and business elite. Schools equipped to teach only basic literacy, hygiene and agricultural skills. Politically unstable – frequent coup attempts have been made during 1990s

Moroni, the Comoros capital, lies on the island of Grande Comore. The islands are fertile and forested.

THE ECONOMY
One of the world's poorest countries. 80% of people are farmers Vanilla and cloves are main cash crops. Lack of basic infrastructure.

FACTFILE
Official Name Federal Islamic Republic of the Comoros

Date of Formation 1975

Capital Moroni

Population 700,000

Total Area
2,230 sq km (861 sq miles)

Density
314 people per sq km

Languages
Arabic*, French*, other

Religions Muslim 86%, Roman Catholic 14%

Ethnic Mix Comorian 96%, Makua 2%, other (inc. French) 2%

Government Islamic republic

Currency Franc = 100 centimes

MADAGASCAR

LYING IN THE Indian Ocean, Madagascar is the world's fourth largest island. Free elections in 1993 ended 18 years of socialist government.

GEOGRAPHY
Two thirds of country is a savannah-covered plateau, which drops sharply to narrow coastal belt in the east.

CLIMATE
Tropical, often hit by cyclones. East coast affected by monsoons. Southwest is drier.

PEOPLE AND SOCIETY
People are Malay-Indonesian in origin, intermixed with later migrants from African mainland. Main ethnic division is between Merina of the central plateau and the poorer côtier (coastal) peoples. Merina were the country's historic rulers. They remain the social elite, and largely run the government

THE ECONOMY
80% of the people are farmers. Coffee is the most important cash crop. World's largest producer of vanilla. Prawns are a valuable export commodity.

FACTFILE
Official Name Democratic Republic of Madagascar

Date of Formation 1960

Capital Antananarivo

Population 15.2 million

Total Area 587,040 sq km (226,660 sq miles)

Density
26 people per sq km

Languages Malagasy*, French*

Religions Traditional beliefs 52%, Catholic/Protestant 41%, Muslim 7%

Ethnic Mix Merina 26%, Betsimisaraka 15%, Betsileo 12%, other 47%

Government Multiparty republic

Currency Franc = 100 centimes

SEYCHELLES

A FORMER British colony, comprising 115 islands in the Indian Ocean. Under one-party rule for 16 years, it became a multiparty democracy in 1993.

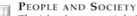

GEOGRAPHY
Mostly low-lying coral atolls, but 40 islands, including the largest, Mahé, are mountainous and are the only granitic islands in the world.

CLIMATE
Tropical oceanic climate. Hot and humid all year round. Rainy season December–May.

The Seychelles, like many islands in the Indian Ocean are threatened by rising sea levels.

PEOPLE AND SOCIETY
The islands were uninhabited when French settlers arrived in the 18th century. Today, the population is homogeneous – a result of inter-marriage between ethnic groups. Almost 90% of people live on Mahé. Living standards are among Africa's highest. Poverty is rare and the welfare system caters for all.

THE ECONOMY
Tourism is main source of income, based on appeal of beaches and exotic plants and animals. Tuna fished and canned for export. Virtually no mineral resources. All domestic requirements imported.

FACTFILE
Official Name Republic of the Seychelles

Date of Formation 1976

Capital Victoria

Population 74,000

Total Area
280 sq km (108 sq miles)

Density
264 people per sq km

Languages
Creole*, French, English

Religions Catholic 90%, other 10%

Ethnic Mix Seychellois (mixed African, South Asian and European) 95%, Chinese and South Asian 5%

Government Multiparty republic

Currency Rupee = 100 cents

MAURITIUS

LOCATED TO the east of Madagascar in the Indian Ocean. Independent in 1968, as part of the Commonwealth, it became a republic in 1993.

GEOGRAPHY
Main island, of volcanic origin, is ringed by coral reefs. Rises from coast to fertile central plateau. Outer islands lie some 500 km (311 miles) to the north

CLIMATE
Warm and humid. March–December are hottest and wettest months, with tropical storms.

PEOPLE AND SOCIETY
Most people are descendants of labourers brought over from India in the 19th century. Small minority of French descent are the wealthiest group. Literacy rate for under-30s is 95%. Crime rates on main island are fairly low; outer islands are virtually crime free.

THE ECONOMY
Sugar, tourism and clothing manufacture are main sources of income. Sugar accounts for 30% of exports. Potential as offshore financial centre is being developed.

FACTFILE
Official Name Mauritius

Date of Formation 1968

Capital Port Louis

Population 1.1 million

Total Area
1,860 sq km (718 sq miles)

Density
591 people per sq km

Languages English*, French Creole, Hindi, Bhojpuri, Chinese

Religions Hindu 52%, Catholic 26%, Muslim 17%, other 5%

Ethnic Mix Creole 55%, South Asian 40%, Chinese 3%, other 2%

Government
Multiparty republic

Currency
Rupee = 100 cents

ICELAND

EUROPE'S WESTERNMOST country, Iceland lies in the north Atlantic, straddling the Mid-Atlantic ridge. Its spectacular landscape is largely uninhabited.

GEOGRAPHY
Grassy coastal lowlands, with fiords in the north. Central plateau of cold lava desert, glaciers and geothermal springs. Around 200 volcanoes.

CLIMATE
Location in middle of Gulf Stream moderates climate. Mild winters and brief, cool summers.

PEOPLE AND SOCIETY
Prosperous and homogeneous society includes only 4,000 foreign residents. High social mobility, free health care and heating (using geothermal power). Longevity rates are among the highest in the world. Equivocal attitude towards Europe accompanies increasing US influence. Strong emphasis on education and reading. Low crime rate, but concerns about alcohol abuse.

THE ECONOMY
Fish products make up 80% of exports. Light industries produce knitwear, textiles, paint. Eco-tourism potential.

FACTFILE
Official Name Republic of Iceland
Date of Formation 1944
Capital Reykjavík
Population 300,000
Total Area
103,000 sq km (39,770 sq miles)
Density
3 people per sq km
Languages
Icelandic*, other
Religions Evangelical Lutheran 96%, other Christian 3%, other 1%
Ethnic Mix Icelandic (Norwegian-Celtic descent) 98%, other 2%
Government
Constitutional republic
Currency
Krona = 100 aurar

NORWAY

THE KINGDOM of Norway traces the rugged western coast of Scandinavia. Settlements are largely restricted to southern and coastal areas.

GEOGRAPHY
Highly indented Atlantic coast with fiords and tens of thousands of islands. Rugged mountains and plateaux cover most of the country.

CLIMATE
Mild coastal climate. Inland east is more extreme, with warm summers, and cold, snowy winters.

PEOPLE AND SOCIETY
Homogeneous, with some recent refugees from Bosnian conflict. Strong family tradition despite high divorce rate. Fair-minded consensus promotes female equality, boosted by generous childcare provision. Wealth more evenly distributed than in most developed countries. Most people have high standard of living.

The village of Reine on Moskenesøya, in Norway's Lofoten islands is a popular holiday resort.

THE ECONOMY
Europe's largest producer and exporter of oil and gas. Engineering, chemical and metal industries. Fishing and forestry are also significant industries.

FACTFILE
Official Name Kingdom of Norway
Date of Formation 1905/1930
Capital Oslo
Population 4.4 million
Total Area
323,900 sq km (125,060 sq miles)
Density
14 people per sq km
Languages Norwegian*
(Bokmal and Nynorsk), Lappish
Religions Evangelical Lutheran 88%, other Christian 12%
Ethnic Mix Norwegian 95%, Lapp 1%, other 4%
Government
Constitutional monarchy
Currency
Krone = 100 øre

DENMARK

OCCUPIES THE Jutland peninsula and over 400 islands in Scandinavia. Greenland and the Faeroe Islands are self-governing associated territories.

GEOGRAPHY
Fertile farmland covers two-thirds of the terrain, which is among the flattest in the world. About 100 islands are inhabited.

CLIMATE
Damp, temperate climate with mild summers and cold, wet winters. Rainfall is moderate.

The island of Fyn, like most of Denmark, is flat – lying barely above sea level. Coastal defences are needed to prevent flooding.

PEOPLE AND SOCIETY
Prosperous population maintains traditions of tolerance and welfare provision. High rates of divorce and cohabiting mean that almost 40% of children are brought up by unmarried couples or single parents. Over 75% of women work, due to generous state-funded childcare.

THE ECONOMY
Few natural resources but a diverse manufacturing base. The skilled work force is the key to high-tech industrial success. Bacon, ham and dairy products are major agricultural exports.

FACTFILE
Official Name Kingdom of Denmark
Date of Formation AD 960/1953
Capital Copenhagen
Population 5.2 million
Total Area
43,069 sq km (16,629 sq miles)
Density
121 people per sq km
Languages
Danish*, other
Religions Evangelical Lutheran 91% other Protestant and Catholic 9%
Ethnic Mix Danish 96%, Faeroese and Inuit 1%, other 3%
Government
Constitutional monarchy
Currency
Krone = 100 øre

SWEDEN

THE LARGEST Scandinavian country in both population and area, Sweden's strong industrial base helps to fund its extensive welfare system.

GEOGRAPHY
Heavily forested, with many lakes. Northern plateau extends beyond the Arctic Circle. Southern lowlands are widely cultivated.

CLIMATE
Southern coasts warmed by Gulf Stream. North has more extreme continental climate.

PEOPLE AND SOCIETY
Traditions of hard work and economic success are balanced by permissiveness and egalitarianism. High taxes pay for extensive child-care provision, medical protection and state education. Bulk of population and industry based in and around the southern cities. A 15,000-strong minority of Sami (Lapps) live in the north.

THE ECONOMY
Global companies, including Volvo, Saab, SFK, Ericsson. Highly developed infrastructure. Up-to-date technology Skilled labour force.

FACTFILE
Official Name Kingdom of Sweden
Date of Formation 1809/1905
Capital Stockholm
Population 8.8 million
Total Area
449,960 sq km (173,730 sq miles)
Density
20 people per sq km
Languages Swedish*, Finnish, Lappish, other
Religions Evangelical Lutheran 94%, Catholic 2%, other 4%
Ethnic Mix Swedish 87%, Finnish and Lapp 1%, other European 12%
Government
Constitutional monarchy
Currency Krona = 100 öre

FINLAND

FINLAND'S DISTINCTIVE language and national identity have been influenced by both its Scandinavian and its Russian neighbours.

GEOGRAPHY
South and centre are flat, with low hills and many lakes. Uplands and low mountains in the north. 60% of the land area is forested.

CLIMATE
Long, harsh winters with frequent snowfalls. Short, warmer summers. Rainfall is low, and decreases northwards.

PEOPLE AND SOCIETY
More than half the population live in the five districts around Helsinki. The Swedish minority live mainly in the Åland Islands in the southwest. The Sami (Lapps) lead a semi-nomadic existence in the north. Over 50% of women go out to work, continuing a tradition of equality between the sexes.

Kilpisjarvi – 'The Way of the Four Winds', where the borders of Finland, Sweden and Norway meet.

THE ECONOMY
Wood-based industries account for 40% of exports. Strong engineering and electronics sectors.

FACTFILE
Official Name Republic of Finland

Date of Formation 1917/1920

Capital Helsinki

Population 5.1 million

Total Area 338,130 sq km (130,552 sq miles)

Density 15 people per sq km

Languages Finnish*, Swedish, Lappish

Religions Evangelical Lutheran 89%, Greek Orthodox 1%, other 10%

Ethnic Mix Finnish 93%, Swedish 6%, other (inc. Sami) 1%

Government Multiparty republic

Currency Markka = 100 pennia

ESTONIA

ESTONIA IS the smallest and most developed of the three Baltic states and has the highest standard of living of any former Soviet republic.

GEOGRAPHY
Flat, boggy and partly forested, with over 1,500 islands. Lake Peipus forms much of the eastern border with Russia.

CLIMATE
Maritime, with some continental extremes. Harsh winters, cool summers and damp springs.

PEOPLE AND SOCIETY
The Estonians are related linguistically and ethnically to the Finns. Friction between ethnic Estonians and the large Russian minority has led to reassertion of Estonian culture and language, as well as job discrimination. Some post-independence political upheaval reflects disenchantment with free-market economics. Families are small; divorce rates are high.

THE ECONOMY
Agricultural machinery, electric motors and ships are the leading manufactures. Strong timber industry. Increased trade links with Finland and Germany.

FACTFILE
Official Name Republic of Estonia

Date of Formation 1991

Capital Tallinn

Population 1.5 million

Total Area 45,125 sq km (17,423 sq miles)

Density 33 people per sq km

Languages Estonian*, Russian

Religions Evangelical Lutheran 98%, Eastern Orthodox, Baptist 2%

Ethnic Mix Estonian 62%, Russian 30%, Ukrainian 3%, other 5%

Government Multiparty republic

Currency Kroon = 100 cents

LATVIA

SITUATED ON the east coast of the Baltic Sea. Like its Baltic neighbours, it became independent in 1991. It retains a large Russian population.

GEOGRAPHY
Flat coastal plain deeply indented by the Gulf of Riga. Poor drainage creates many bogs and swamps in the forested interior.

CLIMATE
Temperate warm summers and cold winters. Steady rainfall throughout the year.

PEOPLE AND SOCIETY
Latvia is the most urbanized of the three Baltic states, with more than 70% of the population living in cities and towns. Delicate relations with Russia are dictated by a large Russian minority, and energy and infrastructure investment dating from the Soviet period. The status of women is on a par with that in western Europe. The divorce rate is high.

The Russian Orthodox cathedral in Riga, the Latvian capital, was used as a planetarium during the Soviet era, but is now being restored.

THE ECONOMY
Transport and defence equipment lead strong industrial sector. Developed paper-making industry. Good ports. Russia remains main trading partner.

FACTFILE
Official Name Republic of Latvia

Date of Formation 1991

Capital Riga

Population 2.5 million

Total Area 64,589 sq km (24,938 sq miles)

Density 39 people per sq km

Languages Latvian*, Russian

Religions Evangelical Lutheran 85%, other Christian 15%

Ethnic Mix Latvian 52%, Russian 34%, Belorussian 5%, Ukrainian 4%, Polish 3%, other 2%

Government Multiparty republic

Currency Lats = 100 santimi

LITHUANIA

THE LARGEST and most powerful of the Baltic states, Lithuania was the first Baltic country to declare independence from Moscow, in 1991.

GEOGRAPHY
Mostly flat with moors, bogs and an intensively farmed central lowland. Numerous lakes, and forested sandy ridges in the east.

CLIMATE
Coastal location moderates continental extremes. Cold winters, cool summers and steady rainfall.

PEOPLE AND SOCIETY
Homogeneous population, with Lithuanians forming a large majority. Strong Roman Catholic tradition and historical links with Poland. Better relations among ethnic groups than in other Baltic states and inter-ethnic marriages are fairly common. However, some ethnic Russians and Poles see a threat of 'Lithuanianization'. Russian army presence until 1993, when all troops were withdrawn.

THE ECONOMY
Wide range of high-tech and heavy industries, includes textiles, engineering, shipbuilding and food processing. Agricultural surpluses.

FACTFILE
Official Name Republic of Lithuania

Date of Formation 1991

Capital Vilnius

Population 3.7 million

Total Area 65,200 sq km (25,174 sq miles)

Density 57 people per sq km

Languages Lithuanian*, Russian

Religions Roman Catholic 87%, Russian Orthodox 10%, other 3%

Ethnic Mix Lithuanian 80%, Russian 9%, Polish 8%, other 3%

Government Multiparty republic

Currency Litas = 100 centas

EUROPE

POLAND

WITH ITS seven international borders and strategic location, Poland has always played an important role in European affairs.

GEOGRAPHY
Lowlands, part of the North European Plain, cover most of the country. Carpathian Mountains run along the southern borders.

CLIMATE
Peak rainfall during hot summers. Cold winters with snow, especially in mountains

PEOPLE AND SOCIETY
Ethnic homogeneity masks a number of tensions. Secular liberals criticize semi-official status of Catholic Church; emerging wealth disparities resented by those unaffected by free-market reforms. German minority presses for action on Green issues. Many women hold policy-making posts

Neuschwanstein Castle, built for the eccentric King Ludwig II of Bavaria.

THE ECONOMY
High growth, with foreign investment linked to government privatization programme. Heavy industries still dominate, but service sector is quickly emerging.

FACTFILE
Official Name Republic of Poland
Date of Formation 1918/1945
Capital Warsaw
Population 38.4 million
Total Area
   312,680 sq km (120,720 sq miles)
Density
   123 people per sq km
Languages
   Polish*, German, other
Religions Roman Catholic 95%,
   other (inc. Protestant and
   Eastern Orthodox) 5%
Ethnic Mix
   Polish 98%, other 2%
Government
   Multiparty republic
Currency Zloty = 100 groszy

EUROPE

GERMANY

EUROPE'S STRONGEST economic power, Germany's democratic west and communist east were re-unified in 1990, after the fall of the east's regime.

GEOGRAPHY
Coastal plains in the north, rising to rolling hills of central region. Alpine region in the south.

CLIMATE
Damp, temperate in northern and central regions. Continental extremes in mountainous south.

PEOPLE AND SOCIETY
Social and economic differences reflect former divisions. Some prosperous western Germans resent added taxes since re-unification. Far-right political groups have emerged. Immigrant 'guest workers' – mainly Turks – face citizenship problems and occasional racial attacks. Strong feminist and Green movements.

THE ECONOMY
Massive exports of cars, heavy engineering, electronics and chemi-cals. Post-war 'miracle' powered by efficiency and good labour relations.

FACTFILE
Official Name Federal Republic
   of Germany
Date of Formation 1871/1990
Capital Berlin
Population 81.8 million
Total Area
   356,910 sq km (137,800 sq miles)
Density
   229 people per sq km
Languages
   German*, Sorbian, other
Religions Protestant 45%,
   Roman Catholic 37%, other 18%
Ethnic Mix
   German 92%, other 8%
Government Multiparty republic
Currency
   Deutsche Mark = 100 pfennigs

EUROPE

NETHERLANDS

ASTRIDE THE delta of five major rivers in northwest Europe, the Netherlands has a long trading tradition. Rotterdam is the world's largest port.

GEOGRAPHY
Mainly flat, with 27% of the land below sea level and protected by dunes, dykes and canals. Low hills in the south and east.

CLIMATE
Mild, rainy winters and cool summers. Gales from the North Sea are common in autumn and winter.

A century ago there were more than 10,000 windmills in the Netherlands. Today, there are only about 100 left.

PEOPLE AND SOCIETY
The Dutch see their country as the most tolerant in Europe. This reflects a long history of welcoming refugees and immigrants. Large urban concentration (89%) accounts for high population density. Laws concerning issues such as sexuality, euthanasia, and drug-taking are among the world's most liberal.

THE ECONOMY
Diverse industrial sector exports metals, machinery, chemicals and electronics. Many high-profile multinationals.

FACTFILE
Official Name Kingdom
   of the Netherlands
Date of Formation 1815/1890
Capital Amsterdam, The Hague
Population 15.6 million
Total Area
   37,330 sq km (14,410 sq miles)
Density
   418 people per sq km
Languages
   Dutch*, Frisian, other
Religions Catholic 36%, Protestant
   27%, other (inc. unaffiliated) 37%
Ethnic Mix
   Dutch 96%, other 4%
Government
   Constitutional monarchy
Currency Guilder = 100 cents

EUROPE

BELGIUM

BELGIUM LIES in northwestern Europe. Its history has been marked by the division between its Flemish- and French-speaking communities.

GEOGRAPHY
Low-lying coastal plain covers two-thirds of the country. Land becomes hilly and forested in southeast (Ardennes) region.

CLIMATE
Maritime climate with Gulf Stream influences. Temperatures are mild, with heavy cloud cover and rain. More rainfall and weather fluctuations on coast.

PEOPLE AND SOCIETY
Since 1970, Flemish-speaking regions have become more prosperous than those of the minority French-speakers (Walloons), overturning the traditional roles and increasing friction. In order to contain tensions, Belgium began to move towards federalism in 1980. Both groups now have their own governments and control most of their own affairs

THE ECONOMY
Variety of industrial exports, including steel, glassware, cut diamonds and textiles. Many foreign multinationals.

FACTFILE
Official Name Kingdom of Belgium
Date of Formation 1830
Capital Brussels
Population 10.1 million
Total Area
   33,100 sq km (12,780 sq miles)
Density
   305 people per sq km
Languages
   French*, Dutch*, Flemish
Religions
   Catholic 75%, other 25%
Ethnic Mix Flemish 58%, Walloon
   32%, other European 6%,
   other 4%
Government
   Constitutional monarchy
Currency Franc = 100 centimes

IRELAND

THE REPUBLIC of Ireland occupies 85% of the island of Ireland, with the remainder (Northern Ireland) being part of the United Kingdom.

GEOGRAPHY
Low mountain ranges along an irregular coastline surround an inland plain punctuated by lakes, undulating hills and peat bogs.

CLIMATE
The Gulf Stream accounts for the mild and wet climate. Snow is rare, except in the mountains.

PEOPLE AND SOCIETY
Although homogeneous in ethnicity and Catholic religion, the population shows signs of change. Younger Irish question Vatican teachings on birth control, divorce, abortion. Many people still emigrate to find jobs. 1994 terrorist ceasefire in Northern Ireland tempered the traditional aim of reunification.

Clew Bay in County Mayo on the western coast of Ireland.

THE ECONOMY
High unemployment tarnishes high-tech export successes and trade surplus. Highly educated work force. Efficient agriculture and food-processing industries.

FACTFILE

Official Name Republic of Ireland

Date of Formation 1921/1922

Capital Dublin

Population 3.6 million

Total Area
70,280 sq km (27,155 sq miles)

Density
51 people per sq km

Languages
English*, Irish Gaelic*

Religions Catholic 93%, Protestant (mainly Anglican) 5%, other 2%

Ethnic Mix Irish 95%, other (mainly British) 5%

Government
Multiparty republic

Currency
Irish pound = 100 pence

FRANCE

STRADDLING WESTERN Europe from the English Channel to the Mediterranean Sea, France is one of the world's leading industrial powers.

GEOGRAPHY
Broad plain covers northern half of the country. Tall mountain ranges in the east and southwest. Mountainous plateau in the centre.

CLIMATE
Three main climates temperate and damp northwest; continental east; and Mediterranean south.

PEOPLE AND SOCIETY
Strong French national identity co-exists with pronounced regional differences, including local languages. Long tradition of absorbing immigrants (European Jews, North African Muslims, economic migrants from Southern Europe). Catholic Church is no longer central to daily life.

THE ECONOMY
Steel, chemicals, electronics, heavy engineering, wine and aircraft typify a strong and diversified export sector.

FACTFILE

Official Name The French Republic

Date of Formation 1685/1920

Capital Paris

Population 58.2 million

Total Area
551,500 sq km (212,930 sq miles)

Density
106 people per sq km

Languages French*, Provençal, German, Breton, Catalan, Basque

Religions Catholic 90%, Protestant 2%, Jewish 1%, Muslim 1%, other 6%

Ethnic Mix French 92%, North African 3%, German 2%, other 3%

Government Multiparty republic

Currency Franc = 100 centimes

UNITED KINGDOM

SEPARATED FROM continental Europe by the North Sea and the English Channel, the UK comprises England, Wales, Scotland and Northern Ireland.

GEOGRAPHY
Mountainous in the north and west, undulating hills and lowlands in the south and east.

CLIMATE
Generally mild and temperate. Rainfall is heaviest in the west. Winter snow in mountainous areas.

PEOPLE AND SOCIETY
Although of mixed stock themselves, the British have an insular and ambivalent attitude towards Europe. The Welsh and Scottish are ethnically and culturally distinct. Asian and West Indian minorities in most cities. Class, the traditional source of division, is fading in the face of popular culture.

Black Mount at Rannoch Moor in the Scottish Highlands – one of the UK's wildest regions.

THE ECONOMY
World leader in financial services, pharmaceuticals and defence industries. Exports of steel, vehicles, aircraft, high-tech goods.

FACTFILE

Official Name United Kingdom of Great Britain and Northern Ireland

Date of Formation 1801/1922

Capital London

Population 58.4 million

Total Area
244,880 sq km (94,550 sq miles)

Density 238 people per sq km

Languages English*, other

Religions Protestant 52%, Catholic 9%, Muslim 3%, other 36%

Ethnic Mix English 81%, Scottish 10%, Welsh 2%, other 7%

Government
Constitutional monarchy

Currency
Pound sterling = 100 pence

LUXEMBOURG

MAKING UP part of the plateau of the Ardennes in Western Europe, Luxembourg is Europe's last independent duchy and one of its richest states.

GEOGRAPHY
Dense Ardennes forests in the north, low, open southern plateau. Undulating terrain throughout.

CLIMATE
Moist climate with warm summers and mild winters. Snow is common only in the Ardennes.

PEOPLE AND SOCIETY
Society is peaceable, despite large proportion of foreigners (half the work force and one third of the residents). Integration has been straightforward; most are fellow Western Europeans and Catholics, mainly from Italy and Portugal. High salaries and very low unemployment promote stability.

THE ECONOMY
Traditional industries such as steel-making have given way in recent years to a thriving banking and service sector. Tax-haven status attracts foreign companies.

FACTFILE

Official Name Grand Duchy of Luxembourg

Date of Formation 1890

Capital Luxembourg

Population 400,000

Total Area
2,586 sq km (998 sq miles)

Density 155 people per sq km

Languages Letzeburgish*, French*, German*, Italian, Portuguese, other

Religions Catholic 97%, other 3%

Ethnic Mix Luxemburger 72%, Portuguese 9%, Italian 5%, other 14%

Government
Constitutional monarchy

Currency Franc = 100 centimes

MONACO

A JET-SET image and a thriving service sector define the modern identity of this tiny enclave on the Côte d'Azur in southeastern France.

GEOGRAPHY
A rocky promontory over-looking a narrow coastal strip that has been enlarged through land reclamation.

CLIMATE
Mediterranean. Summers are hot and dry; days with 12 hours of sunshine are not uncommon. Winters are mild and sunny.

PEOPLE AND SOCIETY
Less than 20% of residents are Monégasques. The rest are Europeans – mainly French – attracted by the tax-haven, up-market lifestyle. Nationals enjoy considerable privileges, including housing benefits to protect them from high housing prices, and the right of first refusal before foreigners can take a job. Women have equal status but only acquired the vote in 1962.

Monte-Carlo is one of the world's most densely populated places.

THE ECONOMY
Tourism and gambling are the mainstays. Banking secrecy laws and tax-haven conditions attract foreign investment. Almost totally dependent on imports due to lack of natural resources.

FACTFILE
Official Name Principality of Monaco
Date of Formation 1861
Capital Monaco
Population 31,000
Total Area
1.95 sq km (0.75 sq miles)
Density
15897 people per sq km
Languages
French*, Italian, other
Religions Catholic 95%, other 5%
Ethnic Mix French 47%,
Monégasque 17%, Italian 16%,
other 20%
Government
Constitutional monarchy
Currency
French franc = 100 centimes

ANDORRA

A TINY land-locked principality, Andorra lies high in the eastern Pyrenees between France and Spain. It held its first full elections in 1993.

GEOGRAPHY
High mountains, and six deep, glaciated valleys that drain into the River Valira as it flows into Spain.

CLIMATE
Cool, wet springs followed by dry, warm summers. Mountain snows linger until March.

PEOPLE AND SOCIETY
Immigration is strictly monitored and restricted by quota to French and Spanish nationals seeking employment. A referendum in 1993 ended 715 years of semi-feudal status but society remains conservative. Divorce is illegal.

THE ECONOMY
Tourism and duty-free sales dominate the economy. Banking secrecy laws and low consumer taxes promote investment and commerce. Dependence on imported food and raw materials.

FACTFILE
Official Name Principality of Andorra
Date of Formation 1278
Capital Andorra la Vella
Population 65,000
Total Area
468 sq km (181 sq miles)
Density
139 people per sq km
Languages
Catalan*, Spanish, other
Religions Catholic 86%, other 14%
Ethnic Mix Catalan 61%, Spanish Castilian 30%, other 9%
Government
Parliamentary democracy
Currency French franc,
Spanish peseta

PORTUGAL

FACING THE Atlantic on the western side of the Iberian Peninsula, Portugal is the most westerly country on the European mainland.

GEOGRAPHY
The River Tagus runs through the country roughly east to west, dividing mountainous north from lower and more undulating south.

CLIMATE
North is cool and moist. South is warmer with dry, mild winters.

PEOPLE AND SOCIETY
Homogeneous and stable society, losing some of its conservative traditions. Small, well-assimilated immigrant population, mainly from former colonies. Urban areas and south are more socially progressive. North is more responsive to traditional Catholic values. Family ties remain all-important.

THE ECONOMY
Agricultural exports include grain, vegetables, fruits and wine, but farming methods are outdated. Strong banking and tourism sectors.

FACTFILE
Official Name Republic of Portugal
Date of Formation 1140/1640
Capital Lisbon
Population 9.8 million
Total Area
92,390 sq km (35,670 sq miles)
Density
106 people per sq km
Languages
Portuguese*
Religions Catholic 97%,
Protestant 1%, other 2%
Ethnic Mix Portuguese 98%,
African 1%, other 1%
Government
Multiparty republic
Currency
Escudo = 100 centavos

SPAIN

LODGED BETWEEN Europe and Africa, the Atlantic and the Mediterranean, Spain has occupied a pivotal position since it was united in 1492.

GEOGRAPHY
Mountain ranges in north, centre and south. Huge central plateau. Verdant valleys in north-west, Mediterranean lowlands

A ruined Moorish castle at Alcaudete, in Spain's Andalucían mountains between Granada and the River Guadalquivir.

CLIMATE
Maritime in north. Hotter and drier in south. Central plateau has an extreme climate.

PEOPLE AND SOCIETY
Ethnic regionalism, suppressed under General Franco's regime (1936–75), is increasing. 17 regions are now autonomous. People remain church-going, although Catholic teachings on social issues are often flouted. Status of women rising quickly, with strong political representation.

THE ECONOMY
Outdated labour practices and low investment hinder growth. Heavy industry, textiles and food-processing lead exports. Tourism and agriculture are important.

FACTFILE
Official Name Kingdom of Spain
Date of Formation 1492/1713
Capital Madrid
Population 39.7 million
Total Area
504,780 sq km (194,900 sq miles)
Density
79 people per sq km
Languages Castilian Spanish*,
Catalan*, Galician*,
Basque*, other
Religions Catholic 99%, other 1%
Ethnic Mix Castilian Spanish 72%,
Catalan 16%, Galician 7%,
Basque 2%, Gypsy 1%, other 2%
Government
Constitutional monarchy
Currency Peseta = 100 céntimos

EUROPE
ITALY

PROJECTING INTO the Mediterranean Sea in Southern Europe, Italy is an ancient land but also one of the continent's newest unified states.

GEOGRAPHY
Appennino form the backbone of a rugged peninsula, extending from the Alps into the Mediterranean Sea. Alluvial plain in the north.

CLIMATE
Mediterranean in the south. Seasonal extremes in mountains and on northern plain.

PEOPLE AND SOCIETY
Ethnically homogeneous, but gulf between prosperous, industrial north and poorer, agricultural south. Strong regional identities, especially on islands of Sicily and Sardinia. State institutions viewed as inefficient and corrupt. Allegiance to the family survives lessened influence of the Church.

The church of Santa Maria della Salute marks the entrance to the historic city of Venice.

THE ECONOMY
World leader in industrial and product design and textiles. Strong tourism and agriculture sectors. Weak currency. Large public sector debt.

FACTFILE
Official Name Italian Republic
Date of Formation 1871/1954
Capital Rome
Population 57.2 million
Total Area
  301,270 sq km (116,320 sq miles)
Density
  190 people per sq km
Languages Italian*, German, French, Rhaeto-Romanic, Sardinian
Religions
  Catholic 99%, other 1%
Ethnic Mix Italian 98%, other (inc. German, French, Greek, Slovenian, Albanian) 2%
Government Multiparty republic
Currency Lira = 100 centesimi

EUROPE
MALTA

THE MALTESE archipelago lies off southern Sicily, midway between Europe and Africa. The only inhabited islands are Malta, Gozo and Kemmuna.

GEOGRAPHY
The main island of Malta has low hills and a ragged coastline with numerous harbours, bays, sandy beaches and rocky coves. Gozo is more densely vegetated.

CLIMATE
Mediterranean climate. Many hours of sunshine throughout the year but very low rainfall.

PEOPLE AND SOCIETY
Over the centuries, the Maltese have been subject to Arab, Sicilian, Spanish, French and English influences. Today, the population is socially conservative and devoutly Roman Catholic. Divorce is illegal. Many young Maltese go abroad to find work – notably to the US and Australia – as opportunities for them on the islands are few.

THE ECONOMY
Tourism is the chief source of income. Offshore banking potential. Schemes to attract foreign high-tech industry. Almost all requirements have to be imported.

FACTFILE
Official Name Republic of Malta
Date of Formation 1964
Capital Valletta
Population 400,000
Total Area
  320 sq km (124 sq miles)
Density
  1250 people per sq km
Languages
  Maltese*, English
Religions Catholic 98%, other (mostly Anglican) 2%
Ethnic Mix Maltese (mixed Arab, Sicilian, Norman, Spanish, Italian, English) 98%, other 2%
Government
  Multiparty republic
Currency Lira = 100 cents

EUROPE
VATICAN CITY

THE VATICAN City, the seat of the Roman Catholic Church, is a walled enclave in the city of Rome. It is the world's smallest fully independent state.

GEOGRAPHY
Territory includes ten other buildings in Rome, plus the papal residence. The Vatican Gardens cover half the City's area.

CLIMATE
Mild winters with regular rainfall. Hot, dry summers with occasional thunderstorms.

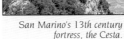

San Marino's 13th century fortress, the Cesta.

PEOPLE AND SOCIETY
The Vatican has about 1,000 permanent inhabitants, including several hundred lay persons, and employs a further 3,400 lay staff. Citizenship can be acquired through stable residence and holding an office or job within the City. Reigning Pope has supreme legislative and judicial powers, and holds office for life. State maintains a neutral stance in world affairs and has observer status in many international organizations.

THE ECONOMY
Investments and voluntary contributions by Catholics worldwide (known as Peter's Pence), backed up by tourist revenue and issue of Vatican stamps and coins.

FACTFILE
Official Name State of the Vatican City
Date of Formation 1929
Capital Not applicable
Population 1,000
Total Area
  0.44 sq km (0.17 sq miles)
Density
  2273 people per sq km
Languages
  Italian*, Latin*, other
Religions Catholic 100%
Ethnic Mix Italian 90%, Swiss 10% (including the Swiss Guard, which is responsible for papal security)
Government Papal Commission
Currency Italian lira = 100 centesimi

EUROPE
SAN MARINO

PERCHED ON the slopes of Monte Titano in the Italian Appennino, San Marino has maintained its independence since the 4th century AD.

GEOGRAPHY
Distinctive limestone outcrop of Monte Titano dominates wooded hills and pastures near Italy's Adriatic coast.

CLIMATE
Altitude and sea breezes moderate Mediterranean climate. Hot summers and cool, wet winters.

PEOPLE AND SOCIETY
Territory is divided into nine 'castles', or districts. Tightly knit society, with 16 centuries of tradition. Strict immigration rules require 30-year residence before applying for citizenship. Catholic Church remains a more powerful influence than in neighbouring Italy. Living standards are similar to those in northern Italy.

THE ECONOMY
Tourism provides 60% of government income. Light industries – led by mechanical engineering and high-quality clothing – generate export revenue. Italian infrastructure is a boon.

FACTFILE
Official Name Republic of San Marino
Date of Formation AD 301/1862
Capital San Marino
Population 25,000
Total Area
  61 sq km (24 sq miles)
Density
  410 people per sq km
Languages
  Italian*, other
Religions Catholic 96%, Protestant 2%, other 2%
Ethnic Mix Sammarinese 95%, Italian 4%, other 1%
Government
  Multiparty republic
Currency Italian lira = 100 centesimi

203

SWITZERLAND

ONE OF the world's most prosperous countries, with a long tradition of neutrality in foreign affairs, it lies at the centre of Western Europe.

GEOGRAPHY
Mostly mountainous, with river valleys. Alps cover 60% of its area; Jura in west cover 10%. Lowlands lie along east-west axis.

CLIMATE
Most rain falls in the warm summer months. Snowy winters, but milder and foggy away from the mountains.

PEOPLE AND SOCIETY
Composed of distinct Swiss-German, Swiss-French and Swiss-Italian linguistic groups, but national identity is strong. Country divided into 26 autonomous cantons (states), each with control over housing and economic policy. Tensions over membership of EU, drug abuse, and role of guest workers in economy. Some young see society as regimented and conformist.

THE ECONOMY
Diversified economy relies on services – with strong tourism and banking sectors – and specialized industries (engineering, watches).

FACTFILE
Official Name Swiss Confederation
Date of Formation 1815
Capital Bern
Population 7.3 million
Total Area
   41,290 sq km (15,940 sq miles)
Density
   177 people per sq km
Languages German*, French*, Italian*, Romansch*, other
Religions Catholic 48%, Protestant 44%, other 8%
Ethnic Mix German 65%, French 18%, Italian 10%, other 7%
Government
   Federal republic
Currency
   Franc = 100 centimes

LIECHTENSTEIN

TUCKED IN the Alps between Switzerland and Austria, Liechtenstein became an independent principality of the Holy Roman Empire in 1719.

GEOGRAPHY
Upper Rhine valley covers western third. Mountains and narrow valleys of the eastern Alps make up the remainder.

CLIMATE
Warm, dry summers. Cold winters, with heavy snow in mountains December–March.

PEOPLE AND SOCIETY
Country's role as a financial centre accounts for its many foreign residents (over 35% of the population), of whom half are Swiss and the rest mostly German. High standard of living results in few social tensions. Sovereignty cherished, despite close alliance with Switzerland, which handles its foreign relations and defence.

Liechtenstein allocates 2% of its state budget to restoring mountain vegetation and coordinating land use.

THE ECONOMY
Banking secrecy and low taxes attract foreign investment. Well-diversified exports include dental products, furniture and chemicals.

FACTFILE
Official Name Principality of Liechtenstein
Date of Formation 1719
Capital Vaduz
Population 31,000
Total Area
   160 sq km (62 sq miles)
Density 194 people per sq km
Languages German*, Alemannish
Religions Catholic 87%, Protestant 8%, other 5%
Ethnic Mix Liechtensteiner 63%, Swiss 15%, German 9%, other 13%
Government
   Constitutional monarchy
Currency
   Swiss franc = 100 centimes

AUSTRIA

BORDERING EIGHT countries in the heart of Europe, Austria was created in 1920 after the collapse of the Austro-Hungarian Empire the previous year.

GEOGRAPHY
Mainly mountainous. Alps and foothills cover the west and south. Lowlands in the east are part of the Danube River basin.

CLIMATE
Temperate continental climate. Western Alpine regions have colder winters and more rainfall.

The Hungarian capital, Budapest is actually two cities, Buda and Pest which lie on opposing banks of the River Danube.

PEOPLE AND SOCIETY
Although all are German-speaking, Austrians consider themselves ethnically distinct from Germans. Minorities are few; there are a small number of Hungarians, Slovenes and Croats, plus refugees from conflict in former Yugoslavia. Some Austrians are beginning to challenge patriarchal and class-conscious social values. Legislation reflects strong environmental concerns.

THE ECONOMY
Large manufacturing base, despite lack of energy resources. Skilled labour force the key to high-tech exports. Strong tourism sector.

FACTFILE
Official Name Republic of Austria
Date of Formation 1918/1945
Capital Vienna
Population 8 million
Total Area
   83,850 sq km (32,375 sq miles)
Density
   95 people per sq km
Languages German*, Croatian, Slovene, Hungarian (Magyar)
Religions Catholic 85%, Protestant 6%, other 9%
Ethnic Mix German 99%, other (inc. Hungarian, Slovene, Croat) 1%
Government
   Multiparty republic
Currency
   Schilling = 100 groschen

HUNGARY

HUNGARY IS bordered by seven states in Central Europe. It has changed its economic and political policies to develop closer ties with the EU.

GEOGRAPHY
Fertile plains in east and northwest; west and north are hilly. River Danube bisects the country from north to south.

CLIMATE
Continental. Wet springs; late, but very hot summers, and cold, cloudy winters.

PEOPLE AND SOCIETY
Ethnically homogenous and stable society, showing signs of stress since change to market economy. Most homes are overcrowded, due to a severe housing shortage. Since 1989, a middle class has emerged, but life for the unemployed and unskilled is harder than under communism. Concern over treatment of Hungarian nationals in neighbouring states.

THE ECONOMY
Weak banking sector and unemployment hamper moves to open economy. Heavy industries and agriculture remain strong. Growing tourism and services.

FACTFILE
Official Name Republic of Hungary
Date of Formation 1918/1945
Capital Budapest
Population 10.1 million
Total Area
   93,030 sq km (35,919 sq miles)
Density
   109 people per sq km
Languages Hungarian (Magyar)*, German, Slovak, other
Religions Catholic 68%, Protestant 25%, other 7%
Ethnic Mix Hungarian (Magyar) 90%, German 2%, other 8%
Government
   Multiparty republic
Currency
   Forint = 100 filler.

CZECH REPUBLIC

ONCE PART of Czechoslovakia in Central Europe, it became independent in 1993, after peacefully dissolving its federal union with Slovakia.

GEOGRAPHY
Western territory of Bohemia is a plateau surrounded by mountains. Moravia, in the east, has hills and lowlands.

CLIMATE
Cool, sometimes cold winters, and warm summer months, which bring most of the annual rainfall.

PEOPLE AND SOCIETY
Secular and urban society, with high divorce rates. Czechs make up the vast majority of the population. The 300,000 Slovaks left after partition now form largest ethnic minority. Ethnic tensions are few, but there is some hostility towards the Gypsy community. A new commercial elite is emerging alongside ex-communist entrepreneurs.

The Vltava River in Prague. Millions of tourists, mainly from Europe and the USA visit each year.

THE ECONOMY
Traditional heavy industries (machinery, iron, car-making) have been successfully privatized. Large tourism revenues. Skilled labour force. Rising unemployment.

FACTFILE
Official Name: Czech Republic
Date of Formation: 1993
Capital: Prague
Population: 10.3 million
Total Area:
78,370 sq km (30,260 sq miles)
Density:
131 people per sq km
Languages:
Czech*, Slovak, Romany, other
Religions: Catholic 44%, Protestant 6%, other Christian 12%, other 38%
Ethnic Mix: Czech 85%, Moravian 13%, other (inc. Slovak, Gypsy) 2%
Government: Multiparty republic
Currency: Koruna = 100 halura

SLOVAKIA

LAND-LOCKED in Central Europe, Slovakia has been independent since 1993. It is the less-developed half of the former Czechoslovakia.

GEOGRAPHY
Carpathian Mountains stretch along northern border with Poland. Southern lowlands include the fertile Danube plain.

CLIMATE
Continental. Moderately warm summers and steady rainfall. Cold winters with heavy snowfalls.

PEOPLE AND SOCIETY
Slovaks are largest and most dominant group. Tension between them and the Hungarian minority has increased, particularly over directive that Hungarians should adopt Slovak name endings. Before partition, many skilled Slovaks took jobs in Prague, but few have returned to help structure the new Slovakia. Catholic Church remains influential.

THE ECONOMY
Narrow emphasis on heavy industry, with poor record on innovation and capital investment. High inflation and unemployment. Growing tourism sector.

FACTFILE
Official Name: Slovak Republic
Date of Formation: 1993
Capital: Bratislava
Population: 5.4 million
Total Area:
49,500 sq km (19,100 sq miles)
Density:
109 people per sq km
Languages: Slovak*, Hungarian (Magyar), Romany, Czech, other
Religions: Catholic 80%, Protestant 12%, other 8%
Ethnic Mix: Slovak 85%, Hungarian 9%, Czech 1%, other (inc. Gypsy) 5%
Government:
Multiparty republic
Currency: Koruna = 100 halura

SLOVENIA

NORTHERNMOST of the former Yugoslav republics, Slovenia has the closest links with Western Europe. In 1991, it gained independence with little violence.

GEOGRAPHY
Alpine terrain with hills and mountains. Forests cover almost half the country's area. Short Adriatic coastline.

CLIMATE
Mediterranean climate on small coastal strip. Alpine interior has continental extremes.

PEOPLE AND SOCIETY
Homogeneous population accounts for relatively peaceful transition to independence. Traditional links with Austria and Italy, each with Slovene populations, account for the 'Alpine' rather than 'Balkan' outlook. Wages are the highest in Central Europe, but unemployment is rising. Institutional change is proceeding slowly.

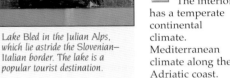

Lake Bled in the Julian Alps, which lie astride the Slovenian–Italian border. The lake is a popular tourist destination.

THE ECONOMY
Competitive manufacturing industry. Prospects for growth in electronics industry. Well-developed tourist sector. Czech demand for Slovenia's consumer goods exports.

FACTFILE
Official Name: Republic of Slovenia
Date of Formation: 1991
Capital: Ljubljana
Population: 1.9 million
Total Area:
20,250 sq km (7,820 sq miles)
Density:
94 people per sq km
Languages:
Slovene*, Serbo-Croatian
Religions: Roman Catholic 96%, Muslim 1%, other 3%
Ethnic Mix: Slovene 92%, Croat 3%, Serb 1%, other 4%
Government:
Multiparty republic
Currency:
Tolar = 100 stotins

CROATIA

A FORMER Yugoslav republic. Post-independence fighting thwarted its plans to capitalize on its prime location along the east Adriatic coast.

GEOGRAPHY
Rocky, mountainous Adriatic coastline is dotted with islands. Interior is a mixture of wooded mountains and broad valleys.

CLIMATE
The interior has a temperate continental climate. Mediterranean climate along the Adriatic coast.

PEOPLE AND SOCIETY
Turbulence was triggered by long-held ethnic hostilities. Open warfare between Croats and Serbs began in 1990. Some areas with local Serb majorities achieved *de facto* autonomy, after fierce fighting in 1992. Destruction was widespread; thousands of people were made homeless.

THE ECONOMY
Economy was severely strained by fighting and influx of refugees. Potential for renewed success in manufacturing, tourism. Exports to the West have grown, despite conflict.

FACTFILE
Official Name: Republic of Croatia
Date of Formation: 1991
Capital: Zagreb
Population: 4.5 million
Total Area:
56,540 sq km (21,830 sq miles)
Density:
80 people per sq km
Languages:
Croatian*, Serbian
Religions: Roman Catholic 77%, Orthodox Catholic 11%, Protestant 1%, Muslim 1%, other 10%
Ethnic Mix: Croat 80%, Serb 12%, Hungarian, Slovenian, other 8%
Government: Multiparty republic
Currency: Kuna = 100 para

BOSNIA & HERZEGOVINA

DOMINATING THE western Balkans, Bosnia and Herzegovina was the focus of the bitter conflict surrounding the break-up of former Yugoslavia.

GEOGRAPHY
Hills and mountains, with narrow river valleys. Lowlands in the north. Mainly deciduous forest covers about half of the total area.

CLIMATE
Continental. Hot summers and cold, often snowy winters.

PEOPLE AND SOCIETY
Civil war between rival ethnic groups. Ethnic Bosnians (mainly Muslim) form the largest group, with large minorities of Serbs and Croats. Communities have been destroyed or uprooted ('ethnic cleansing') as Serbs and Croats established separate ethnic areas. The UN and NATO have been involved as peacekeepers.

Prior to 1991, the glorious scenery of Serbia and Montenegro attracted over five million tourists annually.

THE ECONOMY
Before 1991, Bosnia was home to five of former Yugoslavia's largest companies. It has the potential to become a thriving market economy with a strong manufacturing base.

FACTFILE
Official Name: The Republic of Bosnia and Herzegovina

Date of Formation: 1992

Capital: Sarajevo

Population: 3.5 million

Total Area:
51,130 sq km (19,741 sq miles)

Density:
68 people per sq km

Languages:
Serbo-Croatian*, other

Religions: Muslim 40%, Orthodox Catholic 31%, other 29%

Ethnic Mix: Bosnian 44%, Serb 31%, Croat 17%, other 8%

Government:
Multiparty republic

Currency: Dinar = 100 para

YUGOSLAVIA
[SERBIA & MONTENEGRO]

THE FEDERAL Republic of Yugoslavia, comprising Serbia and Montenegro, is the successor state to the former Yugoslavia.

GEOGRAPHY
Fertile Danube plain in north, rolling uplands in centre. Mountains in south, and behind narrow Adriatic coastal plain.

CLIMATE
Mediterranean along coast, continental inland. Hot summers and cold winters, with heavy snow.

PEOPLE AND SOCIETY
Social order has disintegrated since dissolution of the former Yugoslavia. Serbia was vilified in the international community for its role in the conflict in the region. Serbian concerns over Bosnia and Croatia have masked domestic tensions, particularly unrest among the Albanian population in the southern region of Kosovo.

THE ECONOMY
Bosnian war and UN trade sanctions crippled the economy. Fuel and food shortages. Hyper-inflation created a barter economy.

FACTFILE
Official Name: Federal Republic of Yugoslavia

Date of Formation: 1992

Capital: Belgrade

Population: 10.9 million

Total Area:
25,715 sq km (9,929 sq miles)

Density:
424 people per sq km

Languages:
Serbo-Croatian*, other

Religions: Orthodox Catholic 65%, Muslim 19%, other 16%

Ethnic Mix: Serb 63%, Albanian 14%, Montenegrin 6%, other 17%

Government:
Multiparty republic

Currency: Dinar = 100 para

ALBANIA

LYING AT the southeastern end of the Adriatic Sea, Albania held its first multiparty elections in 1991, after nearly five decades of communism.

GEOGRAPHY
Narrow coastal plain. Interior is mostly hills and mountains. Forest and scrub cover over 40% of the land. Large lakes in the east.

CLIMATE
Mediterranean coastal climate, with warm summers and cool winters. Mountains receive heavy rains or snows in winter.

PEOPLE AND SOCIETY
Last eastern European country to move towards Western economic liberalism – pace of change remains a sensitive issue. Mosques and churches have reopened in what was once the world's only officially atheist state. Greek minority in the south suffers much discrimination.

Berat, in Albania, the 'city of a thousand windows' was preserved as a museum city while a new town was built further down the valley.

THE ECONOMY
Oil and gas reserves plus high growth rate have potential to offset rudimentary infrastructure and lack of foreign investment.

FACTFILE
Official Name: Republic of Albania

Date of Formation: 1912/1913

Capital: Tirana

Population: 3.5 million

Total Area:
28,750 sq km (11,100 sq miles)

Density:
122 people per sq km

Languages:
Albanian*, Greek

Religions: Muslim 70%, Greek Orthodox 20%, Roman Catholic 10%

Ethnic Mix: Albanian 96%, Greek 2%, other (inc. Macedonian) 2%

Government:
Multiparty republic

Currency: Lek = 100 qindars

MACEDONIA

LAND-LOCKED in the southern Balkans, Macedonia is affected by sanctions imposed on its northern trading partners and by Greek antagonism.

GEOGRAPHY
Mainly mountainous or hilly, with deep river basins in centre. Plains in northeast and southwest.

CLIMATE
Continental climate with wet springs and dry autumns. Heavy snowfalls in northern mountains.

PEOPLE AND SOCIETY
Slav Macedonians comprise two-thirds of the population. Officially 20% are Albanian, although Albanians claim they account for 40%. Tensions between the two groups have so far been restrained. Greek government is hostile towards the state because it suspects it may try to absorb northern Greece – also called Macedonia – in a 'Greater Macedonia'. Social structures remain essentially socialist.

THE ECONOMY
Serbian sanctions paralyse exports, but foreign aid and grants boost foreign exchange reserves. Growing private sector. Thriving black market in the capital.

FACTFILE
Official Name: Former Yugoslav Republic of Macedonia

Date of Formation: 1991

Capital: Skopje

Population: 2.2 million

Total Area:
25,715 sq km (9,929 sq miles)

Density:
86 people per sq km

Languages: Macedonian, Serbo-Croatian (no official language)

Religions: Christian 80%, Muslim 20%

Ethnic Mix: Macedonian 67%, Albanian 20%, Turkish 4%, other 9%

Government: Multiparty republic

Currency: Denar = 100 deni

EUROPE

BULGARIA

LOCATED IN southeastern Europe, Bulgaria has made slow progress towards democracy since the fall of its communist regime in 1990.

GEOGRAPHY
Mountains run east–west across centre and along southern border. Danube plain in north, Thracian plain in southeast.

CLIMATE
Warm summers and snowy winters, especially in mountains. East winds bring seasonal extremes.

PEOPLE AND SOCIETY
Government has sought to assimilate separate ethnic groups, thereby suppressing cultural identities. Large exodus of Bulgarian Turks in 1989. Recent privatization programme has left many Turks landless and prompted further emigration. Gypsies suffer much discrimination. Female equality exists only in theory. Ruling party, mainly ex-communists, have resisted change.

Rila monastery in Bulgaria's Rila Mountains is famous for its 1200 frescoes dating from the 19th century.

THE ECONOMY
Political and technical delays hinder privatization programme. Good agricultural production, including grapes for well-developed wine industry, and tobacco.

FACTFILE
Official Name Republic of Bulgaria

Date of Formation 1908/1923

Capital Sofia

Population 8.7 million

Total Area
110,910 sq km (42,822 sq miles)

Density
78 people per sq km

Languages Bulgarian*, Turkish, Macedonian, Romany, Armenian

Religions Christian 85%, Muslim 13%, Jewish 1%, other 1%

Ethnic Mix Bulgarian 85%, Turkish 9%, Macedonian 3%, Gypsy 3%

Government
Multiparty republic

Currency
Lev = 100 stotinki

EUROPE

GREECE

GREECE IS the southernmost Balkan nation. Surrounded by the Mediterranean, Aegean and Ionian seas, it has a strong seafaring tradition.

GEOGRAPHY
Mountainous peninsula with over 2,000 islands. Large central plain along the Aegean coast.

CLIMATE
Mainly Mediterranean with dry, hot summers. Alpine climate in northern mountain areas.

PEOPLE AND SOCIETY
Post-war industrial development altered the dominance of agriculture and seafaring. Rural exodus to industrial cities has been stemmed, but over half the population now live in the two largest cities. Age-old culture and Greek Orthodox Church balance social mobility.

THE ECONOMY
High inflation and poor investment work against strong economic sectors: tourism, shipping, agriculture. Thriving black economy.

FACTFILE
Official Name Hellenic Republic

Date of Formation 1830/1947

Capital Athens

Population 10.5 million

Total Area
131,990 sq km (50,961 sq miles)

Density
80 people per sq km

Languages Greek*, Turkish, Albanian, Macedonian

Religions Greek Orthodox 98%, Muslim 1%, other (mainly Roman Catholic and Jewish) 1%

Ethnic Mix
Greek 98%, other 2%

Government
Multiparty republic

Currency Drachma = 100 lepta

EUROPE

ROMANIA

ROMANIA LIES on the Black Sea coast. Since the overthrow of its communist regime in 1989, it has been slowly converting to a free-market economy.

GEOGRAPHY
Carpathian Mountains encircle Transylvanian plateau. Wide plains to the south and east. River Danube on southern border.

CLIMATE
Continental. Hot, humid summers and cold, snowy winters. Very heavy spring rains.

Moldavia's warm summers and even rainfall are ideal for growing a wide range of crops.

PEOPLE AND SOCIETY
Since 1989, there has been a rise in Romanian nationalism, aggravated by the hardships brought by economic reform. Incidence of ethnic violence has also risen, particularly towards Hungarians and Gypsies. Decrease in population in recent years due to emigration and falling birth rate.

THE ECONOMY
Outdated, polluting heavy industries and unmechanized agricultural sector. Wages have fallen since demise of communism. High number of small-scale foreign joint ventures. Tourism potential.

FACTFILE
Official Name Romania

Date of Formation 1947

Capital Bucharest

Population 22.8 million

Total Area
237,500 sq km (91,700 sq miles)

Density
96 people per sq km

Languages Romanian*, Hungarian

Religions Romanian Orthodox 70%, Roman Catholic 6%, Protestant 6%, Greek Catholic 3%, other 15%

Ethnic Mix Romanian 89%, Hungarian 8%, other (inc. Gypsy) 3%

Government Multiparty republic

Currency Leu = 100 bani

EUROPE

MOLDAVIA
[MOLDOVA]

THE SMALLEST AND most densely populated of the ex-Soviet republics, Moldavia has strong linguistic and cultural links with Romania to the west.

GEOGRAPHY
Steppes and hilly plains, drained by Dniester and Prut rivers.

CLIMATE
Warm summers and relatively mild winters. Moderate rainfall, evenly spread throughout the year.

PEOPLE AND SOCIETY
Shared heritage with Romania defines national identity, although in 1994 Moldavians voted against possible unification with Romania. Most of the population is engaged in intensive agriculture. The 1994 constitution granted special auto-nomous status to the Gagauz people in the south (Orthodox Christian Turks), and to the Slav peoples on the east bank of the River Dniester.

THE ECONOMY
Well-developed agricultural sector: wine, tobacco, cotton, food processing. Light manufacturing. Progress in establishing markets for exports. High unemployment.

FACTFILE
Official Name Republic of Moldova

Date of Formation 1991

Capital Chişinău

Population 4.4 million

Total Area
33,700 sq km (13,000 sq miles)

Density
131 people per sq km

Languages
Moldavian*, Russian

Religions Romanian Orthodox 98%, Jewish 1%, other 1%

Ethnic Mix Moldavian (Romanian) 65%, Ukrainian 14%, Russian 13%, Gagauz 4%, other 4%

Government
Multiparty republic

Currency Leu = 100 bani

BELORUSSIA
[BELARUS]

FORMERLY KNOWN as
White Russia, Belorussia
lies land-locked in eastern
Europe. It reluctantly
became independent
of the USSR in 1991.

GEOGRAPHY
Mainly plains and low hills.
Dnieper and Dvina rivers drain
eastern lowlands. Vast Pripet
Marshes in the southwest.

CLIMATE
Extreme continental climate.
Long, sub-freezing, but mainly dry
winters, and hot summers.

PEOPLE AND SOCIETY
Only 2% of people are non-
Slav, ethnic tension is minimal.
Entire population have right
to Belorussian
citizenship,
although only
11% are fluent in
Belorussian. Post-
Soviet constitution
was not adopted
until 1994. Wealth
is held by a small
ex-communist elite.
Fallout from 1986
Chornobyl' nuclear disaster in
Ukraine affected Belorussians'
health and environment.

*Much of southern Belorussia is
marshy and sparsely populated. It
includes the vast Pripet Marshes.*

THE ECONOMY
Food processing and heavy
industries stagnate while
politicians argue over market
reforms. Low unemployment but
high inflation.

FACTFILE
Official Name Republic of Belarus

Date of Formation 1991

Capital Minsk

Population 10.1 million

Total Area
207,600 sq km (80,154 sq miles)

Density
49 people per sq km

Languages Belorussian*, Russian

Religions Russian Orthodox 60%,
Catholic 8%, other (including
Uniate, Protestant, Muslim,
Jewish) 32%

Ethnic Mix Belorussian 78%,
Russian 13%, Polish 4%,
other 5%

Government Multiparty republic

Currency Rouble = 100 kopeks

UKRAINE

THE FORMER 'breadbasket
of the Soviet Union',
Ukraine balances assertive
nationalism with concerns
over its relations
with Russia.

GEOGRAPHY
Mainly fertile steppes and
forests. Carpathian Mountains in
southwest, Crimean chain in south.
Pripet Marshes in northwest.

CLIMATE
Mainly continental climate,
with distinct seasons. Southern
Crimea has Mediterranean climate.

PEOPLE AND SOCIETY
Over 90% of the population
in western Ukraine is Ukrainian.
However, in several cities in the
east and south,
Russians form
a majority. In
the Crimea, the
Tartars comprise
around 10% of
the population.
At independence
in 1991, most
Russians accepted
Ukrainian
sovereignty. However, tensions are
now rising as both groups adopt
more extremist nationalist policies.

THE ECONOMY
Hyperinflation, corruption,
and hostility from economic elite
stifle any reforms. Heavy industries
and agriculture largely unchanged
since independence.

FACTFILE
Official Name Ukraine

Date of Formation 1991

Capital Kiev

Population 51.3 million

Total Area
603,700 sq km (223,090 sq miles)

Density
85 people per sq km

Languages Ukrainian*,
Russian, Tartar

Religions Mostly Ukrainian
Orthodox, with Roman Catholic,
Protestant and Jewish minorities

Ethnic Mix Ukrainian 73%, Russian
22%, other (inc. Tartar) 5%

Government
Multiparty republic

Currency Karbovanets (coupons)

RUSSIAN
FEDERATION

STILL THE world's largest
state, despite the break-up
of the USSR in 1991,
the Russian Federation
is struggling to capitalize
on its diversity.

GEOGRAPHY
Ural Mountains divide
European steppes and forests from
tundra and forests
of Siberia. South-
central deserts and
mountains.

CLIMATE
Continental
in European Russia.
Elsewhere from
sub-arctic to
Mediterranean
and hot desert.

*The Kremlin, in Moscow is the
home of the Russian parliament. It
is enclosed by walls 2.5 km long.*

PEOPLE AND
SOCIETY
Ethnic Russians make up 80% of
the population, but many
minorities. 57 nationalities have
territorial status, a further 95 lack
their own territory. 1994 war with
Chechnya indicated potential for
ethnic crisis. Wealth disparities,
rising crime and black market
activity have accompanied reform.
Recent return to religious practice.

THE ECONOMY
Inefficiencies since transition
to market economy. Natural
resources, include oil and gas,
precious metals, timber and
hydrocarbons. Enormous
engineering and scientific base.

FACTFILE
Official Name Russian Federation

Date of Formation 1991

Capital Moscow

Population 146.7 million

Total Area 17,075,400 sq km
(6,592,800 sq miles)

Density
9 people per sq km

Languages
Russian*, other

Religions Russian Orthodox 80%,
other (inc. Jewish, Muslim) 20%

Ethnic Mix Russian 80%, Tatar 4%,
Ukrainian 3%, other 13%

Government
Multiparty republic

Currency
Rouble = 100 kopeks

AZERBAIJAN

SITUATED ON the western
coast of the Caspian Sea,
Azerbaijan was the first
Soviet republic to declare
independence from
Moscow in 1991.

GEOGRAPHY
Caucasus mountains in north
and Naxçivan enclave to south of
Armenia. Flat,
low-lying terrain
on the coast of
the Caspian Sea.

CLIMATE
Continental
with pronounced
seasonal
extremes. Low
rainfall, with
peak months
during summer.

PEOPLE AND SOCIETY
Azerbaijanis now form a large
majority. Thousands of Armenians,
Russians and Jews have left as a
result of rising nationalism among
Azerbaijanis. Racial hostility against
those who remain is increasing.
Influx of half a million Azerbaijani
refugees fleeing war with Armenia
over the disputed enclave of
Nagornoyy Karabakh. Once effective
social security system has collapsed.

THE ECONOMY
Oil and gas have considerable
potential. War is a major drain on
state resources. Market reforms
attract foreign interest.

FACTFILE
Official Name Republic of Azerbaijan

Date of Formation 1991

Capital Baku

Population 7.6 million

Total Area
86,600 sq km (33,436 sq miles)

Density
88 people per sq km

Languages Azerbaijani*, Russian,
Armenian, other

Religions Muslim 83%,
Armenian Apostolic,
Russian Orthodox 17%

Ethnic Mix Azerbaijani 83%,
Russian 6%, Armenian 6%,
other 5%

Government Multiparty republic

Currency Manat = 100 gopik

ASIA
ARMENIA

SMALLEST OF the former USSR's republics, Armenia lies in the Lesser Caucasus mountains. Since 1988, it has been at war with Azerbaijan.

GEOGRAPHY
Rugged and mountainous, with expanses of semi-desert and a large lake in the east, Sevana Lich.

CLIMATE
Continental climate, little rainfall in the lowlands. Winters are often bitterly cold.

PEOPLE AND SOCIETY
Strong commitment to Christianity, and to Armenian culture. Minority groups are well integrated. War with Azerbaijan over the enclave of Nagornyy Karabakh has meant 100,000 Armenians living in Azerbaijan forced to return home to live in poverty. In 1988, 25,000 people died in an earthquake in the west.

The island of Akdamar, in eastern Anatolia, surrounded by Lake Van is the site of the 10th-century Church of the Holy Cross.

THE ECONOMY
Few natural resources, though lead, copper and zinc are mined. Main agricultural products are wine, tobacco, olives and rice. Well-developed machine-building and manufacturing – includes textiles, and bottling of mineral water.

FACTFILE
Official Name Republic of Armenia

Date of Formation 1991

Capital Yerevan

Population 3.6 million

Total Area
  29,000 sq km (11,505 sq miles)

Density
  124 people per sq km

Languages Armenian*, Azerbaijani, Russian, Kurdish

Religions Armenian Apostolic 90%, other Christian and Muslim 10%

Ethnic Mix Armenian 93%, Azerbaijani 3%, Russian, Kurdish 4%

Government
  Multiparty republic

Currency Dram = 100 louma

ASIA
TURKEY

LYING PARTLY in Europe, but mostly in Asia, Turkey's position gives it significant influence in the Mediterranean, Black Sea and Middle East.

GEOGRAPHY
Asian Turkey (Anatolia) is dominated by two mountain ranges, separated by a high, semi-desert plateau. Coastal regions are fertile.

CLIMATE
Coast has a Mediterranean climate. Interior has cold, snowy winters and hot, dry summers.

PEOPLE AND SOCIETY
The Turks are racially diverse. Many are refugees or descendants of refugees, often from the Balkans or other territories once under Russian rule. However, the sense of national identity is strong. Since 1984, southeastern region has been the scene of a civil war waged by the Kurdish minority, demanding their rights within the country.

THE ECONOMY
Since the early 1980s, textiles, manufacturing and construction sectors all booming. Tourism is also a major foreign currency earner.

FACTFILE
Official Name Republic of Turkey

Date of Formation 1923/1939

Capital Ankara

Population 63.1 million

Total Area
  779,450 sq km (300,950 sq miles)

Density
  81 people per sq km

Languages Turkish*, Kurdish, Arabic, Circassian, Armenian

Religions
  Muslim 99%, other 1%

Ethnic Mix Turkish 80%, Kurdish 17%, other 3%

Government
  Multiparty republic

Currency
  Turkish lira = 100 krural

ASIA
GEORGIA

LOCATED ON the eastern shore of the Black Sea, Georgia has been torn by civil war since achieving independence from the USSR in 1991.

GEOGRAPHY
Kura valley lies between Caucasus mountains in the north and Lesser Caucasus range in south. Lowlands along the Black Sea coast.

CLIMATE
Sub-tropical along the coast, changing to continental extremes at high altitudes. Rainfall is moderate.

Beirut's seafront, the Corniche, damaged in the civil war, is due to be rebuilt by US engineers and architects

PEOPLE AND SOCIETY
Paternalistic society, with strong family, cultural and literary traditions. One in five live in poverty. Georgians majority group. An uneasy truce has followed the 1990–93 civil war, and the political scene remains volatile. In 1994, another civil war was fought, as ethnic Abkhazians attempted to secede from Georgia.

THE ECONOMY
Food processing and wine production are main industries. Economy has broken down due to war and severance of links with other former Soviet republics.

FACTFILE
Official Name Republic of Georgia

Date of Formation 1991

Capital Tbilisi

Population 5.5 million

Total Area
  69,700 sq km (26,911 sq miles)

Density
  79 people per sq km

Languages Georgian*, Russian, other

Religions Georgian Orthodox 70%, Russian Orthodox 10%, other 20%

Ethnic Mix Georgian 69%, Armenian 9%, Russian 6%, Azerbaijani 5%, other 11%

Government Republic

Currency Coupons

ASIA
LEBANON

LEBANON IS dwarfed by its two powerful neighbours, Syria and Israel. The state is rebuilding after 14 years of civil war.

GEOGRAPHY
Behind a narrow coastal plain, two parallel mountain ranges run the length of the country, separated by the fertile El Beqaa valley.

CLIMATE
Hot summers, with high humidity on the coast. Mild winters.

PEOPLE AND SOCIETY
Population is split between Christians and Muslims. Although in the minority, Christians have been the traditional rulers. In 1975, civil war broke out between the two groups. A settlement, which gave the Muslims more power, was reached in 1989. Elections in 1992 brought hope of greater stability. A huge gulf exists between the poor and a small, immensely rich elite.

THE ECONOMY
Infrastructure wrecked by civil war. Post-war opportunity to regain position as Arab centre for banking and services. Potentially a major producer of wine and fruit.

FACTFILE
Official Name Republic of Lebanon

Date of Formation 1944

Capital Beirut

Population 3.1 million

Total Area
  10,400 sq km (4,015 sq miles)

Density
  298 people per sq km

Languages Arabic*, French, Armenian, English

Religions Muslim (mainly Shi'a) 57%, Christian (mainly Maronite) 43%

Ethnic Mix Arab 93% (Lebanese 83%, Palestinian 10%), other 7%

Government
  Multiparty republic

Currency Pound = 100 piastres

SYRIA

STRETCHING FROM the eastern Mediterranean to the River Tigris, Syria's borders were created on its independence from France in 1946.

GEOGRAPHY
Northern coastal plain is backed by a low range of hills. The River Euphrates cuts through a vast interior desert plateau.

CLIMATE
Mediterranean coastal climate. Inland areas are arid. In winter, snow is common on the mountains.

PEOPLE AND SOCIETY
Most Syrians live near the coast, where the biggest cities are sited. 90% are Muslim, including the politically dominant Alawis. In the north and west are groups of Kurds, Armenians and Turkish-speaking peoples. Some 300,000 Palestinian refugees have also settled in Syria. They, together with the urban unemployed, make up the poorest groups in a growing gulf between rich and poor.

The city of Palmyra, in central Syria, possesses some of the Middle East's finest classical monuments.

THE ECONOMY
High defence spending is major drain on economy. Exporter of crude oil. Agriculture is thriving: crops include cotton, wheat, olives.

FACTFILE
Official Name Syrian Arab Republic
Date of Formation 1946
Capital Damascus
Population 15.2 million
Total Area
185,180 sq km (71,500 sq miles)
Density
82 people per sq km
Languages Arabic*, French, Kurdish, Armenian, Circassian, Aramaic
Religions Sunni Muslim 74%, other Muslim 16%, Christian 10%
Ethnic Mix
Arab 90%, other 10%
Government
Single-party republic
Currency Pound = 100 piastres

CYPRUS

CYPRUS LIES in the eastern Mediterranean. Since 1974, it has been partitioned between the Turkish-occupied north and the Greek south.

GEOGRAPHY
Mountains in the centre-west give way to a fertile plain in the east, flanked by hills to the northeast.

CLIMATE
Mediterranean. Summers are hot and dry. Winters are mild, with snow in the mountains.

PEOPLE AND SOCIETY
Majority of the population is Greek Christian. Since the 16th century, a minority community of Turkish Muslims has lived in the north of the island. In 1974 Turkish troops occupied the north, which was proclaimed the Turkish Republic of Northern Cyprus, but is recognized only by Turkey. The north remains poor, while the south, where the tourist industry is booming, is richer.

THE ECONOMY
In the south, tourism is the key industry. Shipping and light manufacturing also important. In the north, the main exports are citrus fruits and live animals.

FACTFILE
Official Name Republic of Cyprus
Date of Formation 1960/1983
Capital Nicosia
Population 800,000
Total Area
9,251 sq km (3,572 sq miles)
Density
86 people per sq km
Languages
Greek*, Turkish, other
Religions Greek Orthodox 77%, Muslim 18%, other 5%
Ethnic Mix Greek 77%, Turkish 18%, other (mainly British) 5%
Government
Multiparty republic
Currency
Cypriot £/Turkish lira

ISRAEL

CREATED AS a new state in 1948, on the east coast of the Mediterranean. Following wars with its Arab neighbours, it has extended its boundaries.

GEOGRAPHY
Coastal plain. Desert in the south. In the east lie the Great Rift Valley and the Dead Sea – the lowest point on the Earth's surface.

CLIMATE
Summers are hot and dry. Wet season, March–November, is mild.

PEOPLE AND SOCIETY
Large numbers of Jews settled in Palestine before Israel was founded. After World War II there was a huge increase in immigration. Sephardi Jews from the Middle East and Mediterranean are now in the majority, but Ashkenazi Jews from Central Europe still dominate business and politics. Palestinians in Gaza and Jericho gained limited autonomy in 1994.

THE ECONOMY
Huge potential of industrial, agricultural and manufacturing products. Major exporter of mineral salts. Important banking sector.

FACTFILE
Official Name State of Israel
Date of Formation 1948/1982
Capital Jerusalem
Population 5.8 million
Total Area
20,700 sq km (7,992 sq miles)
Density
280 people per sq km
Languages Hebrew*, Arabic, Yiddish, German, Russian, Polish, Romanian, Persian, English
Religions Jewish 83%, Muslim 13%, Christian 2%, other 2%
Ethnic Mix
Jewish 83%, Arab 17%
Government Multiparty republic
Currency New shekel = 100 agorot

JORDAN

THE KINGDOM of Jordan lies east of Israel. In 1993, King Hussein responded to calls for greater democracy by agreeing to multiparty elections.

GEOGRAPHY
Mostly desert plateaux, with occasional salt pans. Lowest parts lie along eastern shore of Dead Sea and east bank of the River Jordan.

Jordan's King's Highway, seen from the castle at Al Karak. This strategic fortress was built by Crusader knights in the 12th century.

CLIMATE
Hot, dry summers. Cool, wet winters. Areas below sea level very hot in summer, and warm in winter.

PEOPLE AND SOCIETY
A predominantly Muslim country with a strong national identity, Jordan's population has Bedouin roots. There is a Christian minority and a large Palestinian population who have moved to Jordan from Israeli-occupied territory. Jordan gave up its claim to the West Bank to the PLO in 1988. The monarchy's power base lies among the rural tribes, which also provide the backbone of the military.

THE ECONOMY
Phosphates, chemicals and fertilizers are principal exports. Skilled, educated workforce.

FACTFILE
Official Name Hashemite Kingdom of Jordan
Date of Formation 1946/1976
Capital Amman
Population 5.7 million
Total Area
89,210 sq km (34,440 sq miles)
Density
64 people per sq km
Languages
Arabic*, other
Religions Muslim 95%, Christian 5%
Ethnic Mix Arab 98% (Palestinian 49%), Armenian 1%, Circassian 1%
Government
Constitutional monarchy
Currency Dinar = 1,000 fils

SAUDI ARABIA

OCCUPYING MOST of the Arabian Peninsula, the oil- and gas-rich kingdom of Saudi Arabia covers an area the size of Western Europe.

GEOGRAPHY
Mostly desert or semi-desert plateau. Mountain ranges in the west run parallel to the Red Sea and drop steeply to a coastal plain.

CLIMATE
In summer, temperatures often soar above 48°C (118°F), but in winter they may fall below freezing. Rainfall is rare.

PEOPLE AND SOCIETY
Most Saudis are Sunni Muslims who follow the strictly orthodox *wahabi* interpretation of Islam and embrace *sharia* (Islamic law) in their daily lives. Women are obliged to wear the veil, cannot hold driving licences, and have no role in public life. The Al-Saud family have been absolutist rulers since 1932. With the support of the religious establishment, they control all political life.

THE ECONOMY
Vast oil and gas reserves. Other minerals include coal, iron and gold. Most food is imported.

FACTFILE

Official Name Kingdom of Saudi Arabia

Date of Formation 1932/1981

Capital Riyadh

Population 18.4 million

Total Area 2,149,690 sq km (829,995 sq miles)

Density 9 people per sq km

Languages Arabic*, other

Religions Sunni Muslim 85%, Shi'a Muslim 14%, Christian 1%

Ethnic Mix Arab 90%, Yemeni 8%, other Arab 1%, other 1%

Government Absolute monarchy

Currency Riyal = 100 malalah

YEMEN

LOCATED IN southern Arabia, Yemen was formerly two countries – a socialist regime in the south, and a republic in the north, which united in 1990.

GEOGRAPHY
Mountainous north with fertile strip along the Red Sea. Arid desert and mountains in south and east.

CLIMATE
Desert climate, modified by altitude, which affects temperatures by as much as 12°C (54°F).

PEOPLE AND SOCIETY
Yemenis are almost entirely of Arab and Bedouin descent. The majority are Sunni Muslims, of the Shafi sect. In rural areas and in the north, Islamic orthodoxy is strong and most women wear the veil. Tension continues to exist between the south, led by the cosmopolitan city of Aden, and the more conservative

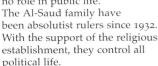

Hilltop village in northern Yemen, showing traditionally decorated, multi-storey houses built from mud bricks.

north. Clashes between their former armies escalated into a brief civil war in 1994.

THE ECONOMY
Poor economic development due to political instability. Large oil and gas reserves were discovered in 1984. Agriculture is the largest employer.

FACTFILE

Official Name Republic of Yemen

Date of Formation 1990

Capital Sana

Population 15.1 million

Total Area 527,970 sq km (203,849 sq miles)

Density 29 people per sq km

Languages Arabic*, other

Religions Sunni Muslim 55%, Shi'a Muslim 42%, other 3%

Ethnic Mix Arab 95%, Afro-Arab 3%, South Asian, African, European 2%

Government Multiparty republic

Currency Rial (North), Dinar (South) – both are legal currency

---

OMAN

SITUATED ON the eastern coast of the Arabian Peninsula, Oman is the least developed of the Gulf states, despite modest oil exports.

GEOGRAPHY
Mostly gravelly desert, with mountains in the north and south. Some narrow fertile coastal strips.

CLIMATE
Blistering heat in the north. Summer temperatures often climb above 45°C (113°F). Southern uplands receive rains June–September.

PEOPLE AND SOCIETY
Most Omanis still live on the land, especially in the south. The majority are Ibadi Muslims who follow an appointed leader, the Imam. Ibadism is not opposed to freedom for women, and a few women hold positions of authority. Baluchis from Pakistan are the largest group of foreign workers.

An oasis village near Al Fujayrah in the northeast UAE is now accessible through a network of new roads.

THE ECONOMY
Oil accounts for most export revenue. Gas is set to eventually supplant oil. Other exports include fish, dates, limes and coconuts.

FACTFILE

Official Name Sultanate of Oman

Date of Formation 1650

Capital Muscat

Population 1.7 million

Total Area 212,460 sq km (82,030 sq miles)

Density 8 people per sq km

Languages Arabic*, Baluchi, other

Religions Ibadi Muslim 75%, other Muslim 11% Hindu 14%

Ethnic Mix Arab 75%, Baluchi 15%, other (mainly South Asian) 10%

Government Monarchy with Consulative Council

Currency Rial = 1,000 baizas

UNITED ARAB EMIRATES

BORDERING THE GULF on the northern coast of the Arabian Peninsula is the United Arab Emirates, a federation of seven states.

GEOGRAPHY
Mostly flat, semi-arid desert with sand dunes, salt pans and occasional oases. Cities are watered by extensive irrigation systems.

CLIMATE
Summers are humid, despite minimal rainfall. Sand-laden *shamal* winds blow in winter and spring.

PEOPLE AND SOCIETY
People are mostly Sunni Muslims of Bedouin descent, and largely city-dwellers. In theory, women enjoy equal rights with men. Emirians make up one-fifth of the population. They are outnumbered by immigrants who arrived during the 1970s oil boom. Western expatriates are permitted a virtually unrestricted lifestyle. Islamic fundamentalism is growing among the young.

THE ECONOMY
Major exported of oil and natural gas. Fish and shellfish are caught in the Gulf, as well as oysters for pearls.

FACTFILE

Official Name United Arab Emirates

Date of Formation 1971

Capital Abu Dhabi

Population 1.9 million

Total Area 83,600 sq km (32,278 sq miles)

Density 23 people per sq km

Languages Arabic*, Farsi (Persian), Urdu, Hindi, English

Religions Sunni Muslim 77%, Shi'a Muslim 19% other 4%

Ethnic Mix South Asian 50%, Emirian 19%, other Arab 23%, other 8%

Government Federation of monarchs

Currency Dirham = 100 fils

QATAR

PROJECTING NORTH from the Arabian Peninsula into The Gulf, Qatar's reserves of oil and gas make it one of the region's wealthiest states.

GEOGRAPHY
Flat, semi-arid desert with sand dunes and salt pans. Vegetation limited to small patches of scrub.

CLIMATE
Hot and humid. Summer temperatures soar to over 40°C (104°F). Rainfall is rare.

PEOPLE AND SOCIETY
Only one in five Qataris is native-born. Most of the population are guest workers from the Indian subcontinent, Iran and North Africa. Qataris were once nomadic Bedouins, but since advent of oil wealth, have become city-dwellers. As a result, the north is dotted with abandoned villages. Political and religious life is dominated by the ruling Al-Thani family

THE ECONOMY
Steady supply of crude oil and huge gas reserves, plus related industries. Economy is heavily dependent on foreign work force. All raw materials and most foods, except vegetables, are imported.

FACTFILE

Official Name State of Qatar

Date of Formation 1971

Capital Doha

Population 600,000

Total Area
11,000 sq km (4,247 sq miles)

Density
55 people per sq km

Languages Arabic*, Farsi (Persian), Urdu, Hindi, English

Religions Sunni Muslim 86%, Hindu 10%, Christian 4%

Ethnic Mix Arab 40%, South Asian 35%, Persian 12%, other 13%

Government
Absolute monarchy

Currency
Riyal = 100 dirhams

BAHRAIN

BAHRAIN IS an archipelago of 33 islands between the Qatar peninsula and the Saudi Arabian mainland. Only three islands are inhabited.

GEOGRAPHY
All islands are low-lying. The largest, Bahrain island, is mainly sandy plains and salt marshes.

CLIMATE
Summers are hot and humid. Winters are mild. Low rainfall.

PEOPLE AND SOCIETY
Largely Muslim population is divided between Shi'a majority and Sunni minority. Tensions between the two groups. Ruling Sunni class hold the best jobs in bureaucracy and business. Shi'ites tend to do menial work. Al-Khalifa family has ruled since 1783. Regime is autocratic and political dissent is not tolerated. Bahrain is the most liberal of the Gulf states. Women have access to education and jobs.

The Grand Mosque, Manama, is the largest building in Bahrain.

THE ECONOMY
Main exports are refined petroleum and aluminium products. As oil reserves run out, gas is of increasing importance. Bahrain is also the Arab world's major offshore banking centre.

FACTFILE

Official Name State of Bahrain

Date of Formation 1971

Capital Manama

Population 600,000

Total Area
680 sq km (263 sq miles)

Density
882 people per sq km

Languages
Arabic*, English, Urdu

Religions Muslim (Shi'a majority) 85%, Christian 7%, other 8%

Ethnic Mix Arab 73%, South Asian 14%, Persian 8%, other 5%

Government Absolute monarchy (emirate)

Currency
Dinar = 1,000 fils

KUWAIT

KUWAIT LIES on the north of The Gulf. The state was a British protectorate from 1914 until 1961, when full independence was granted.

GEOGRAPHY
Low-lying desert. Lowest land in the north. Cultivation is only possible along the coast.

CLIMATE
Summers are very hot and dry. Winters are cooler, with some rain and occasional frost.

PEOPLE AND SOCIETY
Oil-rich monarchy, ruled by the Al-Sabah family. Oil wealth attracted workers from India, Pakistan and other Arab states. Iraqi invasion of 1990 overcome with aid of US-led alliance with UN backing following a short war in 1991. Many foreign workers expelled after the war, in attempt to ensure Kuwaiti majority.

Saffar Towers in the business centre of Kuwait. The country is re-building its economy following the 1991 Gulf War.

THE ECONOMY
Oil and gas production restored to pre-invasion levels. Skilled labour, raw materials and food have to be imported. Vulnerability to Iraqi attack deters Western industrial investment.

FACTFILE

Official Name State of Kuwait

Date of Formation 1961/1981

Capital Kuwait

Population 1.5 million

Total Area
17,820 sq km (6,880 sq miles)

Density
84 people per sq km

Languages
Arabic*, English, other

Religions Muslim 92%, Christian 6%, other 2%

Ethnic Mix Arab 85%, South Asian 9%, Persian 4%, other 2%

Government
Constitutional monarchy

Currency
Dinar = 1,000 fils

IRAQ

IRAQ IS situated in the central Middle East. Since the removal of the monarchy in 1958, it has experienced considerable political turmoil.

GEOGRAPHY
Mainly desert. Rivers Tigris and Euphrates water fertile regions and create southern marshland. Mountains along northeast border.

CLIMATE
South has hot, dry summers and mild winters. North has dry summers, but winters can be harsh in the mountains. Rainfall is low.

PEOPLE AND SOCIETY
Population mainly Arab and Kurdish. Small minorities of Turks and Persians. President Saddam Hussein has led the country into an inconclusive war with Iran (1980–88) and 1990 invasion of Kuwait precipitated the Gulf War against UN forces. Drainage schemes in the southern marshlands threaten unique lifestyle of the Marsh Arabs.

THE ECONOMY
Gulf War and resulting UN sanctions mean Iraq cannot sell its oil on the international market.

FACTFILE

Official Name Republic of Iraq

Date of Formation 1932/1981

Capital Baghdad

Population 21 million

Total Area
438,320 sq km (169,235 sq miles)

Density
48 people per sq km

Languages Arabic*, Kurdish, Turkish, Farsi (Persian)

Religions Shi'a Muslim 63%, Sunni Muslim 34%, other 3%

Ethnic Mix Arab 79%, Kurdish 16%, Persian 3%, Turkish 2%

Government
Single-party republic

Currency
Dinar = 1,000 fils

IRAN

SINCE THE 1979 revolution led by Ayatollah Khomeini, the Middle Eastern country of Iran has become the world's largest theocracy.

GEOGRAPHY
High desert plateau with large salt pans in the east. West and north are mountainous. Fertile coastal land borders Caspian Sea.

CLIMATE
Mostly desert climate. Hot summers, and bitterly cold winters. Area around the Caspian Sea is more temperate.

PEOPLE AND SOCIETY
Many ethnic groups, including Persians, Azerbaijanis and Kurds. Large number of refugees, mainly from Afghanistan. Since 1979 Islamic revolution, political life has been dominated by militant Islamic idealism. Mullahs' belief that adherence to religious values is more important than economic welfare has resulted in declining living standards. The role of women in public life is restricted.

THE ECONOMY
One of the world's biggest oil producers. Government restricts contact with the West, blocking acquisition of vital technology. High unemployment and inflation.

FACTFILE
Official Name Islamic Republic of Iran

Date of Formation 1906

Capital Tehran

Population 68.7 million

Total Area 1,648,000 sq km (636,293 sq miles)

Density 42 people per sq km

Languages Farsi (Persian)*, other

Religions Shi'a Muslim 95%, Sunni Muslim 4%, other 1%

Ethnic Mix Persian 52%, Azerbaijani 24%, Kurdish 9%, other 15%

Government Islamic republic

Currency Rial = 100 dinars

TURKMENISTAN

STRETCHING FROM the Caspian Sea into the deserts of Central Asia, the ex-Soviet state of Turkmenistan has adjusted better than most to independence.

GEOGRAPHY
Low Kara Kum desert covers 80% of the country. Mountains on southern border with Iran. Fertile Amu Darya valley in north.

CLIMATE
Arid desert climate with extreme summer heat, but sub-freezing winter temperatures.

PEOPLE AND SOCIETY
Before Tsarist Russia annexed the country in 1884, the Turkmen were a largely nomadic tribal people. Today, the tribal unit remains strong, with most of the population clustered around desert oases. Generally peaceful relations between Turkmen and Uzbek and Russian

Salt flats near the Kara Kum Canal zone in the Kara Kum desert in Turkmenistan.

minorities. Resurgence of Islam fosters ties with its Muslim neighbours to the south.

THE ECONOMY
Abundant reserves of natural gas. Least industrialized of the ex-Soviet states. Large cotton crop, but most food has to be imported.

FACTFILE
Official Name Republic of Turkmenistan

Date of Formation 1991

Capital Ashgabat

Population 4.2 million

Total Area 488,100 sq km (188,455 sq miles)

Density 9 people per sq km

Languages Turkmen*, Uzbek, other

Religions Muslim 85%, Eastern Orthodox 10%, other 5%

Ethnic Mix Turkmen 72%, Russian 9%, Uzbek 9%, other 10%

Government Single-party republic

Currency Manat = 100 tenge

UZBEKISTAN

SHARING THE Aral Sea coastline with its northern neighbour, Kazakhstan, Uzbekistan lies on the ancient Silk Road between Asia and Europe.

GEOGRAPHY
Arid and semi-arid plains in much of the west. Fertile, irrigated eastern farmland below peaks of the western Pamirs.

CLIMATE
Harsh continental climate. Summers can be extremely hot and dry; winters are cold.

PEOPLE AND SOCIETY
Complex ethnic make-up, with potential for racial and regional conflict. Ex-communists are in firm control, but traditional social patterns based on family, religion, clan and region have re-emerged. Population is concentrated in the fertile east. High birth rates, continued low status of women. Constitutional measures aim to control influence of Islam.

THE ECONOMY
Strong agricultural sector, led by widespread cotton production. Large unexploited deposits of oil and natural gas, gold and uranium. Very limited economic reform.

FACTFILE
Official Name Republic of Uzbekistan

Date of Formation 1991

Capital Tashkent

Population 23.3 million

Total Area 1,138,910 sq km (439,733 sq miles)

Density 20 people per sq km

Languages Uzbek*, Russian, other

Religions Muslim 88%, other (mostly Eastern Orthodox) 12%

Ethnic Mix Uzbek 71%, Russian 8%, Tajik 5%, Kazakh 4%, other 12%

Government Single-party republic

Currency Sum = 100 teen

KAZAKHSTAN

LARGEST OF the former Soviet republics, mineral-rich Kazakhstan has the potential to become the major Central Asian economic power.

GEOGRAPHY
Mainly steppe. Caspian Sea in the west. Central plateau. Mountains in the east. Semi-desert in the south.

The Altai Mountains in eastern Kazakhstan are cold and inhospitable. Rivers carry melt-water down onto the vast steppe.

CLIMATE
Dry continental. Hottest summers in desert south, coldest winters in northern steppes.

PEOPLE AND SOCIETY
Kazakhs only just outnumber Russians in a multi-ethnic society. Stable relations with Russia, plus increased international profile, preserve relative harmony. Few Kazakhs maintain a nomadic lifestyle, but Islam and loyalty to the three Hordes (clan federations) remain strong. Wealth is concentrated among former communists in the capital.

THE ECONOMY
Vast mineral resources, notably gas, oil, coal, uranium and gold. Increasing foreign investment, but living standards have fallen with market reforms to date.

FACTFILE
Official Name Republic of Kazakhstan

Date of Formation 1991

Capital Astana

Population 17.2 million

Total Area 2,717,300 sq km (1,049,150 sq miles)

Density 6 people per sq km

Languages Kazakh*, Russian, other

Religions Muslim 47%, other 53% (mostly Russian Orthodox, Lutheran)

Ethnic Mix Kazakh 40%, Russian 38%, Ukrainian 6%, other 16%

Government Multiparty republic

Currency Tenge = 100 tein

MONGOLIA

LYING BETWEEN **Russia and China, Mongolia is a vast and isolated country with a tiny population. Over two-thirds of the country is desert.**

GEOGRAPHY
High steppe plateau, with mountains in the north. Lakes in the north and west. Desert region of the Gobi dominates the south.

CLIMATE
Continental. Mild summers, and long, dry, very cold winters, with heavy snowfall. Temperatures can drop to –30°C (–22°F).

PEOPLE AND SOCIETY
Mongolia was unified by Genghis Khan in 1206 and was later absorbed into Manchu China. It became a communist People's Republic in 1924, and after 66 years of Soviet-style communist rule, introduced democracy in 1990. Most Mongolians still follow a traditional nomadic way of life, living in circular felt tents called gers. Others live on state-run farms.

The Naryn valley in eastern Kyrgyzstan.

THE ECONOMY
Rich in oil, coal, copper and other minerals, which were barely exploited under communism. In 1990s, some shift in agriculture away from traditional herding and towards a market economy.

FACTFILE

Official Name Mongolia

Date of Formation 1924

Capital Ulan Bator

Population 2.5 million

Total Area 1,565,000 sq km (604,247 sq miles)

Density 2 people per sq km

Languages Khalkha Mongol*, Turkic, Russian, Chinese

Religions Predominantly Tibetan Buddhist, with a Muslim minority

Ethnic Mix Khalkha Mongol 90%, Kazakh 4%, Chinese 2%, other 4%

Government Multiparty republic

Currency Tughrik = 100 möngös

KYRGYZSTAN

A MOUNTAINOUS, **land-locked state in Central Asia. The most rural of the ex-Soviet republics, it only gradually developed its own cultural nationalism.**

GEOGRAPHY
Mountainous spurs of Tien Shan range have glaciers, alpine meadows, forests and narrow valleys. Semi-desert in the west.

CLIMATE
Varies from permanent snow and cold deserts at altitude, to hot deserts in low regions.

PEOPLE AND SOCIETY
Ethnic Kyrgyz majority status dates only from the late 1980s, and is due to their higher birth rate. Considerable tension between Kyrgyz and other groups, particularly Uzbeks. Large Russian community no longer wields power, but is seen as necessary for transfer of skills. Concerns over rising crime rate and opium poppy cultivation accompany political reforms.

THE ECONOMY
Still dominated by the state, and tradition of collective farming. Small quantities of commercially exploitable coal, oil and gas. Great hydroelectric power potential.

FACTFILE

Official Name Kyrgyz Republic

Date of Formation 1991

Capital Bishkek

Population 4.8 million

Total Area 198,500 sq km (76,640 sq miles)

Density 24 people per sq km

Languages Kyrgyz*, Russian, Uzbek

Religions Muslim 65%, other (mostly Russian Orthodox) 35%

Ethnic Mix Kyrgyz 52%, Russian 21%, Uzbek 13%, other (mostly Kazakh and Tajik) 14%

Government Mutiparty republic

Currency Som = 100 teen

TAJIKISTAN

LIES LAND-LOCKED **on the western slopes of the Pamirs in Central Asia. The Tajiks' language and traditions are similiar to those of Iran.**

GEOGRAPHY
Mainly mountainous: bare slopes of Pamir ranges cover most of the country. Small, but fertile Fergana Valley in northwest.

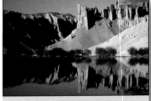

CLIMATE
Continental extremes in valleys. Bitterly cold winters in mountains. Low rainfall.

The Band-i-Amir River in the Hindu Kush. Afghanistan is mountainous and arid. Many Afghans are nomadic sheep farmers.

PEOPLE AND SOCIETY
Conflict between Tajiks, a Persian people, and minority Uzbeks (of Turkic origin), coupled with civil war between supporters of the government and Tajik Islamic rebels. Despite a ceasefire in late 1994, clashes continued in 1995. Already low living standards have been worsened by the conflict. Many Russians have left, to escape discrimination.

THE ECONOMY
Formal economy crippled by conflict. All sectors in decline, barter economy is widespread. Uranium potential and hydro-electric schemes depend on peace.

FACTFILE

Official Name Republic of Tajikistan

Date of Formation 1991

Capital Dushanbe

Population 6.3 million

Total Area 143,100 sq km (55,251 sq miles)

Density 44 people per sq km

Languages Tajik*, Uzbek, Russian

Religions Sunni Muslim 85%, Shi'a Muslim 5%, other 10%

Ethnic Mix Tajik 62%, Uzbek 24%, Russian 4%, Tatar 2%, other 8%

Government Single-party republic

Currency Tajik rouble = 100 kopeks

AFGHANISTAN

LAND-LOCKED **in southwestern Asia, about three-quarters of Afghanistan is inaccessible. Civil war means the country effectively has no government.**

GEOGRAPHY
Predominantly mountainous. Highest range is the Hindu Kush. Mountains are bordered by fertile plains. Desert plateau in the south.

CLIMATE
Harsh continental. Hot, dry summers. Cold winters with heavy snow, especially in Hindu Kush.

PEOPLE AND SOCIETY
In 1979, Soviet forces invaded to support communist government against Islamic guerrillas. Last Soviet troops pulled out in 1989. Civil war continues between Pashtuns, the country's traditional rulers, and minority groups of Tajiks, Hazaras and Uzbeks. Health and education systems have collapsed. Many Afghans are nomadic sheep farmers and live in extreme poverty

THE ECONOMY
Economy has collapsed. The largest sector, agriculture, has been damaged. Illicit opium trade is the main currency earner.

FACTFILE

Official Name Islamic State of Afghanistan

Date of Formation 1919

Capital Kabul

Population 21.5 million

Total Area 652,090 sq km (251,770 sq miles)

Density 33 people per sq km

Languages Persian*, Pashtu*, other

Religions Sunni Muslim 84%, Shi'a Muslim 15%, other 1%

Ethnic Mix Pashtun 38%, Tajik 25%, Hazara 19%, Uzbek 6%, other 12%

Government Mujahideen coalition

Currency Afghani = 100 puls

PAKISTAN

ONCE A part of British India, Pakistan was created in 1947 as an independent Muslim state. Today, it is divided into four provinces.

🌐 GEOGRAPHY
East and south is great flood plain drained by River Indus. Hindu Kush range in north. West is semi-desert plateau and mountains.

☀ CLIMATE
Temperatures can soar to 50°C (122°F) in south and west, and fall to –20°C (–4°F) in the Hindu Kush.

👥 PEOPLE AND SOCIETY
Majority Punjabis control bureaucracy and the army. Many tensions with minority groups. Vast gap between rich and poor. Bonded labourers, often recent converts to Islam, or Christians, form the underclass. Strong family ties, reflected in dynastic and nepotistic political system.

Collecting the harvest in a Nepalese village. Around 90% of Nepalis are farmers.

💲 THE ECONOMY
Leading producer of cotton and rice, but unpredictable weather conditions often affect the crop. Oil, gas reserves. Inefficient, haphazard government economic policies.

FACTFILE
Official Name Islamic Republic of Pakistan
Date of Formation 1947 / 1972
Capital Islamabad
Population 144.5 million
Total Area
796,100 sq km (307,374 sq miles)
Density 182 people per sq km
Languages Urdu*, Punjabi, other
Religions Sunni Muslim 77%, Shi'a Muslim 20%, Hindu 2%, Christian 1%
Ethnic Mix Punjabi 56%, Sindhi 13%, Pashtun 8%, other 23%
Government
Multiparty republic
Currency
Rupee = 100 paisa

NEPAL

NEPAL LIES between India and China, on the shoulder of the southern Himalayan mountains. It is one of the world's poorest countries.

🌐 GEOGRAPHY
Mainly mountainous. Includes some of the highest mountains in the world, such as Everest. Flat, fertile river plains in the south.

☀ CLIMATE
July–October warm monsoon. Rest of year dry, sunny, mild. Valley temperatures in Himalayas may average –10°C (14°F).

👥 PEOPLE AND SOCIETY
Few ethnic tensions, despite the variety of ethnic groups, including the Sherpas in the north, Terai peoples in the south, and the Newars, found mostly in the Kathmandu valley. Women's subordinate position enshrined in law. Hindu women are the most restricted. In 1991, first democratic elections for over 30 years ended period of absolute rule by the king.

💲 THE ECONOMY
90% of the people work on the land. Crops include rice, maize and millet. Dependent on foreign aid. Tourism is growing. Great potential for hydroelectric power.

FACTFILE
Official Name Kingdom of Nepal
Date of Formation 1769
Capital Kathmandu
Population 22.5 million
Total Area
140,800 sq km (54,363 sq miles)
Density
160 people per sq km
Languages
Nepali*, Maithili, other
Religions Hindu 90%, Buddhist 5%, Muslim 3%, other 2%
Ethnic Mix Nepalese 58%, Bihari 19%, Tamang 6%, other 17%
Government
Constitutional monarchy
Currency
Rupee = 100 paisa

BHUTAN

PERCHED IN the eastern Himalayas between India and China, the land-locked kingdom of Bhutan is largely closed to the outside world.

🌐 GEOGRAPHY
Low, tropical southern strip rising through fertile central valleys to high Himalayas in the north. Two-thirds of the land is forested.

☀ CLIMATE
South is tropical, north is alpine, cold and harsh. Central valleys warmer in east than west.

A Hindu festival in India. Festivals take place frequently and are an important part of the Hindu culture.

👥 PEOPLE AND SOCIETY
The king is absolute monarch, head of both state and government. Most people devoutly Buddhist. 24% Hindu Nepalese, who settled in the south. Twenty languages. In 1988, Dzongkha (a Tibetan dialect) was made the official language and Nepali was banned. Many southerners deported as illegal immigrants, creating fierce ethnic tensions.

💲 THE ECONOMY
80% of people farm their own plots of land and herd cattle and yaks. Development of cash crops for Asian markets.

FACTFILE
Official Name Kingdom of Bhutan
Date of Formation 1949 / 1865
Capital Thimphu
Population 1.7 million
Total Area
47,000 sq km (18,147 sq miles)
Density
36 people per sq km
Languages Dzongkha*, Nepali, other
Religions Mahayana Buddhist 70%, Hindu 24%, Muslim 5%, other 1%
Ethnic Mix Bhutia 61%, Gurung 15%, Assamese 13%, other 11%
Government
Constitutional monarchy
Currency
Ngultrum = 100 chetrum

INDIA

SEPARATED FROM the rest of Asia by the Himalayan mountain range, India forms a subcontinent. It is the world's second most populous country.

🌐 GEOGRAPHY
Three main regions Himalayan mountains; northern plain between Himalayas and Vindhya Range; southern Deccan plateau.

☀ CLIMATE
Most of India has three seasons: hot, wet and cool. In summer, the north is usually hotter than the south, with temperatures often over 40°C (104°F).

👥 PEOPLE AND SOCIETY
Most Indians are Hindu, born into one of thousands of castes and sub-castes, which determine their future status and occupation. Middle class enjoy comfortable lifestyle, but at least 30% of Indians live in extreme poverty.

💲 THE ECONOMY
Protectionist mixed economy moving to free market. Foreign investment. High-tech industries. Exports are clothing, jewellery, gems and engineering products.

FACTFILE
Official Name Republic of India
Date of Formation 1947 / 1961
Capital New Delhi
Population 953 million
Total Area 3,287,590 sq km (1,269,338 sq miles)
Density
290 people per sq km
Languages
Hindi*, English*, other
Religions Hindu 83%, Muslim 11%, Christian 2%, Sikh 2%, other 2%
Ethnic Mix Indo-Aryan 72%, Dravidian 25%, Mongoloid and other 3%
Government
Multiparty republic
Currency Rupee = 100 paisa

MALDIVES

THE MALDIVES is an archipelago of 1,190 small coral islands set in the Indian Ocean, southwest of Sri Lanka. Only 202 islands are inhabited.

GEOGRAPHY
Low-lying islands and coral atolls. The larger ones are covered in lush, tropical vegetation.

CLIMATE
Tropical. Rain in all months, but heaviest June–November, during monsoon. Violent storms occasionally hit northern islands.

PEOPLE AND SOCIETY
Maldivians are descended from Sinhalese, Dravidian, Arab and black ancestors. About 25% of the population, who are all Sunni Muslim, live on Male'. Tourism has grown in recent years, but resort islands are separate from settler islands. Politics is restricted to a small group of influential families, and is based around family and clan loyalties rather than formal parties. New young elite is pressing for a liberal political system.

THE ECONOMY
Too dependent on fluctuating tourist industry, which is the economic mainstay. Fish, especially bonita and tuna, are the leading exports.

FACTFILE
Official Name Republic of Maldives
Date of Formation 1965
Capital Male'
Population 300,000
Total Area
  300 sq km (116 sq miles)
Density
  1000 people per sq km
Languages Dhivehi (Maldivian)*, Sinhala, Tamil
Religions
  Sunni Muslim 100%
Ethnic Mix Maldivian 99%, Sinhalese and other South Asian 1%
Government
  Republic
Currency Rufiyaa = 100 laari

ASIA

SRI LANKA

SEPARATED FROM India by the narrow Palk Strait, Sri Lanka comprises one large island and several coral islets to the northwest.

GEOGRAPHY
Main island is dominated by rugged central highlands. Fertile northern plains dissected by rivers. Much of the land is tropical jungle.

CLIMATE
Tropical, with breezes on the coast and cooler air in highlands. Northeast is driest and hottest.

PEOPLE AND SOCIETY
Majority Sinhalese are mostly Buddhist, minority Tamils are mostly Muslim or Hindu. Since independence from Britain in 1948, Tamils have felt sidelined, and support for secession has grown. Long-standing tensions between the groups erupted into civil war in 1983. Tamils demand an independent state in the north and east.

A hilltop village in central Sri Lanka, close to Pidurutalagala, the country's highest peak.

THE ECONOMY
World's largest tea exporter. Manufacturing now accounts for 60% of export earnings. Civil war is a drain on government funds and deters investors and tourists.

FACTFILE
Official Name Democratic Socialist Republic of Sri Lanka
Date of Formation 1948
Capital Colombo
Population 18.6 million
Total Area
  65,610 sq km (25,332 sq miles)
Density
  283 people per sq km
Languages
  Sinhala*, Tamil, English
Religions Buddhist 70%, Hindu 15%, Christian 8%, Muslim 7%
Ethnic Mix Sinhalese 74%, Tamil 18%, Sri Lankan Moor 7%, other 1%
Government Multiparty republic
Currency Rupee = 100 cents

ASIA

BANGLADESH

BANGLADESH LIES at the north of the Bay of Bengal. It seceded from Pakistan in 1971 and, after much political instability, returned to democracy in 1991.

GEOGRAPHY
Mostly flat alluvial plains and deltas of the Brahmaputra and Ganges rivers. Southeast coasts are fringed with mangrove forests.

CLIMATE
Hot and humid. During the monsoon, water level can rise six metres (20 feet) above sea level, flooding two-thirds of the country.

Traders on the Meghna River, which flows from the Padma. Bangladesh's flood plains are among the world's most fertile.

PEOPLE AND SOCIETY
Bangladesh has suffered from a cycle of floods, cyclones, famine, political corruption and military coups. Although 55% of people still live below the poverty line, living standards have improved in past decade. By providing independent income, textile trade is a factor in growing emancipation of women.

THE ECONOMY
Heavily dependent on foreign aid. Agriculture is vulnerable to unpredictable climate. Bangladesh accounts for 80% of world jute fibre exports. Expanding textile industry.

FACTFILE
Official Name People's Republic of Bangladesh
Date of Formation 1971
Capital Dhaka
Population 123.1 million
Total Area
  143,998 sq km (55,598 sq miles)
Density
  855 people per sq km
Languages Bangla*, Urdu, Chakma, Marma (Margh), other
Religions Muslim 83%, Hindu 16%, other (Buddhist, Christian) 1%
Ethnic Mix
  Bengali 98%, other 2%
Government
  Multiparty republic
Currency Taka = 100 paisa

ASIA

BURMA
[MYANMAR]

BURMA FORMS the eastern shores of the Bay of Bengal and the Andaman Sea in Southeast Asia. It gained independence from Britain in 1948.

GEOGRAPHY
Fertile Irrawaddy basin in the centre. Mountains to the west, Shan plateau to the east. Tropical rainforest covers much of the land.

CLIMATE
Tropical. Hot summers, with high humidity, and warm winters.

PEOPLE AND SOCIETY
Under socialist military rule since 1962, Burma has suffered widespread political repression and ethnic conflict. Minority groups maintain low-level guerrilla activity against the state. 1990 election was won by opposition democratic party. Its leader, Aung San Suu Kyi, was placed under house arrest. She was released in 1995.

THE ECONOMY
Under socialism, Burma has plunged from prosperity to poverty. Nationwide black market, on which prices are soaring. Main products are teak, rice and gems.

FACTFILE
Official Name Union of Myanmar
Date of Formation 1948
Capital Rangoon (Yangon)
Population 47.5 million
Total Area
  676,550 sq km (261,200 sq miles)
Density
  70 people per sq km
Languages Burmese*, Karen, Shan, Chin, Kachin, Mon, Palaung, Wa
Religions Buddhist 89%, Muslim 4%, Baptist 3%, other 4%
Ethnic Mix Burman 68%, Shan 9%, Karen 6%, Rakhine 4%, other 13%
Government
  Military regime
Currency Kyat = 100 pyas

216

THAILAND

THAILAND LIES at the heart of mainland Southeast Asia. Continuing rapid industrialization has resulted in massive congestion in the capital.

GEOGRAPHY
One third is occupied by a low plateau, drained by tributaries of the Mekong River. Fertile central plain. Mountains in the north.

CLIMATE
Tropical. Hot, humid March–May, monsoon rains May–October, cooler season November–March.

PEOPLE AND SOCIETY
The king is head of state. Criticism of him is not tolerated. Buddhism is national binding force. North and northeast are home to about 600,000 hill tribespeople, with their own languages and culture. Sex tourism is a problem. Women from the poor northeast enter prostitution in Bangkok and Pattaya.

A farm in northeastern Laos. Three-quarters of Laotians are subsistence farmers.

THE ECONOMY
Rapid economic growth. Rise in manufacturing. Chief world exporter of rice and rubber. Gas reserves. Successful tourist industry.

FACTFILE
Official Name Kingdom of Thailand

Date of Formation 1822 / 1887

Capital Bangkok

Population 59.4 million

Total Area
513,120 sq km (198,116 sq miles)

Density 116 people per sq km

Languages Thai*, Chinese, Malay, Khmer, Mon, Karen, Miao, English

Religions Buddhist 95%, Muslim 4%, other (inc. Hindu, Christian) 1%

Ethnic Mix Thai 75%, Chinese 14%, Malay 4%, Khmer 3%, other 4%

Government
Constitutional monarchy

Currency Baht = 100 stangs

LAOS

A FORMER French colony, independent in 1953, Laos lies land-locked in Southeast Asia. It has been under communist rule since 1975.

GEOGRAPHY
Largely forested mountains, broadening in the north to a plateau. Lowlands along Mekong valley.

CLIMATE
Monsoon rains September–May. Rest of the year is hot and dry.

PEOPLE AND SOCIETY
Over 60 ethnic groups. Lowland Laotians (Lao Loum), live along Mekong River and are wet-rice farmers. Upland Laotians (Lao Theung) and mountain-top Laotians (Lao Soung) practise slash-and-burn farming. Government efforts to halt this traditional farming method, which can destroy forests and watersheds, have been resisted.

THE ECONOMY
One of the world's 20 least-developed nations. Government began to introduce market-oriented reforms in 1986. Potential for timber, mining, garment manufacturing.

FACTFILE
Official Name Lao People's Democratic Republic

Date of Formation 1953

Capital Vientiane

Population 5 million

Total Area
236,800 sq km (91,428 sq miles)

Density
21 people per sq km

Languages
Lao*, Miao, Yao, other

Religions Buddhist 85%, Christian 2%, Muslim 1%, other 12%

Ethnic Mix Lao Loum 56%, Lao Theung 34%, Lao Soung 10%

Government
Single-party republic

Currency Kip = 100 cents

CAMBODIA

LOCATED in mainland Southeast Asia, Cambodia has emerged from two decades of civil war and invasion from Vietnam.

GEOGRAPHY
Mostly low-lying basin. Tonle Sap (Great Lake) drains into the Mekong River. Forested mountains and plateau east of the Mekong.

CLIMATE
Tropical. High temperatures throughout the year. Heavy rainfall during May–October monsoon.

PEOPLE AND SOCIETY
Under Pol Pot's Marxist Khmer Rouge regime between 1975 and 1979, over one million Cambodians died. Half a million more went into exile in Thailand. Effects of revolution and civil war are still felt and are reflected in the world's highest rate of orphans and widows. Free elections held under UN supervision in 1993 brought fragile stability, although the Khmer Rouge, still led by Pol Pot, continues its armed struggle.

Angkor Wat stands in the ruins of the ancient city of Angkor, once the capital of the Khmer empire.

THE ECONOMY
Economy is still recovering from civil war. Loss of skilled workers as result of Khmer Rouge anti-bourgeois atrocities in 1970s. Modest trade in rubber and timber.

FACTFILE
Official Name State of Cambodia

Date of Formation 1953

Capital Phnom Penh

Population 10.5 million

Total Area
181,040 sq km (69,000 sq miles)

Density
58 people per sq km

Languages
Khmer*, French, other

Religions Buddhist 88%, Muslim 2%, Christian 1%, other 9%

Ethnic Mix Khmer 94%, Chinese 4%, Vietnamese 1%, other 1%

Government
Constitutional monarchy

Currency
Riel = 100 sen

VIETNAM

SITUATED IN the far east of mainland Southeast Asia, the country is still rebuilding after the devastating 1962–1975 Vietnam War.

GEOGRAPHY
Heavily forested mountain range separates northern Red River delta lowlands from southern Mekong delta in the south.

CLIMATE

Cool winters in north; south is tropical, with mainly even temperatures. Typhoons in central provinces.

PEOPLE AND SOCIETY
Partitioned in 1954, the communist north reunited the nation after the Vietnam War, in which two million people died. Women outnumber men, largely because of war deaths. Resettling of lowlanders in mountain regions has put pressure on farming and forest resources. Family life is based on kinship groups within village clans.

THE ECONOMY
After years of stagnation, the economy is recovering. Government seeking transfer to market economy. Growing steel, oil, gas, car industries.

FACTFILE
Official Name Socialist Republic of Viet-Nam

Date of Formation 1976

Capital Hanoi

Population 76.2 million

Total Area
329,560 sq km (127,243 sq miles)

Density
231 people per sq km

Languages
Vietnamese*, other

Religions Buddhist 55%, Catholic 7%, Muslim 1%, other 37%

Ethnic Mix Vietnamese 88%, Chinese 4%, Thai 2%, other 6%

Government
Single-party republic

Currency Dong = 10 hao = 100 xu

MALAYSIA

MALAYSIA'S THREE **separate** territories stretch over 2,000 km (1,240 miles) from the Malay Peninsula to the northern area of the island of Borneo.

GEOGRAPHY
Peninsular Malaysia (Malaya) has mountain ranges along its axis. Almost three-quarters of the land is tropical rainforest or swamp forest. States of Sabah and Sarawak in Borneo are rugged and forested.

CLIMATE
Equatorial. Warm, with year-round rainfall. Heaviest rain March–May and September–November.

PEOPLE AND SOCIETY
Indigenous Malays are the largest ethnic group, but Chinese have traditionally controlled most economic activity. Malays favoured in education and jobs since 1970s, in order to address imbalance. Labour shortages attract many immigrants from other Southeast Asian states.

THE ECONOMY
Rapid growth since 1980s. Successful electronics, car industries. Leading producer of rubber, palm oil, pepper, tin, tropical hardwoods.

FACTFILE
Official Name Malaysia
Date of Formation 1957 / 1965
Capital Kuala Lumpur
Population 20.6 million
Total Area
  329,750 sq km (127,317 sq miles)
Density
  62 people per sq km
Languages
  Malay*, Chinese*, Tamil
Religions Muslim 53%, Buddhist and Confucian 30%, other 17%
Ethnic Mix Malay and aborigine 60%, Chinese 30%, Indian 8%, other 2%
Government
  Federal constitutional monarchy
Currency Ringgit = 100 cents

INDONESIA

THE WORLD'S **largest** archipelago, Indonesia's 13,677 islands are scattered over 5,000 km (3,000 miles), from the Indian Ocean to the Pacific Ocean.

GEOGRAPHY
Mountains, tropical swamps, rainforests and over 200 volcanoes, many still active. Most larger islands have coastal lowlands.

CLIMATE
Predominantly tropical monsoon. Hilly areas are cooler. June–September dry season.

PEOPLE AND SOCIETY
A mosaic of different cultures and languages. Islam, urbanization and national language, Bahasa Indonesia, are unifying factors. Papuans of Irian Jaya, East Timorese and Aceh of north Sumatra, denied autonomy, are all in conflict with government.

Rice terraces on Bali, one of Indonesia's 13,677 islands.

THE ECONOMY
Varied resources, especially oil, coal and gas. Timber, minerals (bauxite and nickel), fishing, are all important. Rice is main cash and subsistence crop for the rural population.

FACTFILE
Official Name Republic of Indonesia
Date of Formation 1949 / 1963
Capital Jakarta
Population 200.6 million
Total Area 1,904,570 sq km
  (735,555 sq miles)
Density
  105 people per sq km
Languages Bahasa Indonesia*, 250 (est.) languages or dialects
Religions Muslim 87%, Christian 10%, Hindu 2%, Buddhist 1%
Ethnic Mix Javanese 45%, Sundanese 14%, Madurese 8%, other 33%
Government
  Multiparty republic
Currency Rupiah = 100 sen

SINGAPORE

A CITY STATE **linked** to the southernmost tip of the Malay Peninsula by a causeway, Singapore is one of Asia's most important commercial centres.

GEOGRAPHY
Little remains of the original vegetation on Singapore island. The other 54 much smaller islands are swampy jungle.

CLIMATE
Equatorial. Hot and humid, with heavy rainfall all year round.

PEOPLE AND SOCIETY
Dominated by the Chinese, who make up three-quarters of the community. English-speaking Straits Chinese and newer Mandarin-speakers are now well integrated. There is a significant foreign workforce. Society is highly regulated and government campaigns to improve public behaviour are frequent. Crime is limited and punishment can be severe.

Singapore's financial centre. More than a quarter of Singapore's GDP is generated by financial and business services.

THE ECONOMY
Highly successful financial, banking and manufacturing sectors. Produces 50% of the world's computer disk drives. All food and energy has to be imported.

FACTFILE
Official Name Republic of Singapore
Date of Formation 1965
Capital Singapore
Population 2.9 million
Total Area
  620 sq km (239 sq miles)
Density
  4677 people per sq km
Languages
  Malay*, Chinese*, other
Religions Buddhist 30%, Christian 20%, Muslim 17%, other 33%
Ethnic Mix Chinese 76%, Malay 15%, South Asian 7%, other 2%
Government
  Multiparty republic
Currency
  Singapore $ = 100 cents

BRUNEI

LYING ON **the** northwestern coast of the island of Borneo, Brunei is surrounded and divided in two by the Malaysian state of Sarawak.

GEOGRAPHY
Mostly dense lowland rainforest and mangrove swamps. Mountains in the southeast.

CLIMATE
Tropical. Six-month rainy season with very high humidity.

PEOPLE AND SOCIETY
Malays benefit from positive discrimination. Many in Chinese community are stateless. Independent from the UK since 1984, Brunei is ruled by decree of the Sultan. In 1990, 'Malay Muslim Monarchy' was introduced, promoting Islamic values as state ideology. Women less restricted than in some Muslim states.

THE ECONOMY
Oil and natural gas reserves have brought one of the world's highest standards of living. Massive overseas investments. Major consumer of high-tech hi-fi, video recorders, Western designer clothes.

FACTFILE
Official Name The Sultanate of Brunei
Date of Formation 1984
Capital Bandar Seri Begawan
Population 300,000
Total Area
  5,770 sq km (2,228 sq miles)
Density
  52 people per sq km
Languages
  Malay*, English, Chinese
Religions Muslim 63%, Buddhist 14%, Christian 10%, other 13%
Ethnic Mix Malay 69%, Chinese 18%, other 13%
Government
  Absolute monarchy
Currency Brunei $ = 100 cents

PHILIPPINES

AN ARCHIPELAGO of 7,107 islands between the South China Sea and the Pacific. After 21 years of dictatorship, democracy was restored in 1986.

GEOGRAPHY
Larger islands are forested and mountainous. Over 20 active volcanoes. Frequent earthquakes.

CLIMATE
Tropical. Warm and humid all year round. Typhoons occur in rainy season, June–October.

PEOPLE AND SOCIETY
Over 100 ethnic groups. Most Filipinos are of Malay origin, and Christian. Catholic Church is the dominant cultural force. It opposes state-sponsored family planning programmes designed to curb accelerating population growth. Women have traditionally played a prominent part in society. Many enter the professions. Half the population live on the poverty line.

THE ECONOMY
Now open to considerable outside investment. Agricultural productivity is generally rising. Power failures limit scope for expansion. Weak infrastructure.

FACTFILE
Official Name Republic of the Philippines

Date of Formation 1946

Capital Manila

Population 69 million

Total Area 300,000 sq km (115,831 sq miles)

Density 230 people per sq km

Languages Pilipino*, English*, other

Religions Catholic 83%, Protestant 9%, Muslim 5%, other 3%

Ethnic Mix Filipino 96%, Chinese 2%, other 2%

Government Multiparty republic

Currency Peso = 100 centavos

TAIWAN

THE ISLAND republic of Taiwan lies 130 km (80 miles) off the southeast coast of mainland China. China considers it to be one of its provinces.

GEOGRAPHY
Mountain region covers two-thirds of the island. Highly fertile lowlands and coastal plains.

CLIMATE
Tropical monsoon. Hot and humid. Typhoons July–September. Snow falls in mountains in winter.

PEOPLE AND SOCIETY
Most Taiwanese are Han Chinese, descendants of 17th-century settlers from the mainland. Taiwan came into existence in 1949, when the government was expelled from Beijing (then Peking) by the communists under Mao. 100,000 Nationalists arrived and established themselves as ruling class. Taiwan is diplomatically isolated and cannot gain representation at the UN.

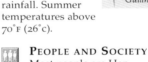

Wen Wu temple lies on the shores of Sun Moon Lake in the mountains of central Taiwan.

THE ECONOMY
One of the world's most successful economies, based on small, adaptable manufacturing companies. Goods include televisions calculators, footwear.

FACTFILE
Official Name Republic of China (Taiwan)

Date of Formation 1949

Capital Taipei

Population 21.1 million

Total Area 36,179 sq km (13,969 sq miles)

Density 584 people per sq km

Languages Mandarin*, other

Religions Buddhist, Confucian and Taoist 93%, Christian 5%, other 2%

Ethnic Mix Taiwanese 84%, mainland Chinese 14%, other 2%

Government Multiparty republic

Currency New Taiwan $ = 100 cents

CHINA

CHINA COVERS a vast area of East Asia. From the founding of Communist China in 1949, until his death in 1976, Mao Zedong dominated the nation.

GEOGRAPHY
Great mountains and plateau in west. Arid basin in north and northeast. Deserts in northwest. South is mountainous. Rolling hills and plains in east.

CLIMATE
North and west are mainly arid. South and east warmer and more humid, with year-round rainfall. Summer temperatures above 70°F (26°C).

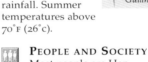

The famous limestone hills of Guilin in southern China.

PEOPLE AND SOCIETY
Most people are Han Chinese. Rest of population belong to one of 55 minority nationalities, or recognized ethnic groups. One-child family policy no longer applies to minorities after some small groups brought close to extinction. Han still face controls.

THE ECONOMY
Moving rapidly towards a market-oriented economy. Vast mineral reserves. Increasingly diversified industrial sector. Low wage costs. Self-sufficient in food.

FACTFILE
Official Name People's Republic of China

Date of Formation 1949/1950

Capital Beijing

Population 1234.3 million

Total Area 9,396,960 sq km (3,628,166 sq miles)

Density 131 people per sq km

Languages Mandarin*, other

Religions Confucianist 20%, Buddhist 6%, Taoist 2%, other 72%

Ethnic Mix Han 93%, Zhuang 1%, Hui 1%, other 5%

Government Single-party republic

Currency Yuan = 10 jiao = 100 fen

NORTH KOREA

NORTH KOREA comprises the northern half of the Korean peninsula. A communist state since 1948, it is largely isolated from the outside world.

GEOGRAPHY
Mostly mountainous, with fertile plains in the southwest.

CLIMATE
Continental. Warm summers and cold winters, especially in the north, where snow is common.

PEOPLE AND SOCIETY
People live severely regulated lives. Divorce is non-existent and extra-marital sex highly frowned upon. Women form 57% of the work force, but are also expected to run the home. From an early age, children are looked after in state-run nurseries. Korean Workers' Party is only legal political party. Membership is essential for advancement. The political elite enjoy a privileged lifestyle.

THE ECONOMY
Economy has suffered badly in 1990s, since end of aid from China and former Soviet Union. Manufacturing, agriculture and mining all in decline. Electricity shortage is a problem.

FACTFILE
Official Name Democratic People's Republic of Korea

Date of Formation 1948

Capital Pyongyang

Population 24.3 million

Total Area 120,540 sq km (46,540 sq miles)

Density 202 people per sq km

Languages Korean*, Chinese

Religions Traditional beliefs 16%, Ch'ondogyo 14%, Buddhist 2%, non-religious 68%

Ethnic Mix Korean 99%, other 1%

Government Single-party republic

Currency Won = 100 chon

SOUTH KOREA

SOUTH KOREA occupies the southern half of the Korean peninsula. Under US sponsorship, it was separated from the communist North in 1948.

GEOGRAPHY
Over 80% is mountainous and two-thirds is forested. Flattest and most populous parts lie along west coast and in the extreme south.

CLIMATE
Four distinct seasons. Winters are dry, and bitterly cold. Summers are hot and humid.

PEOPLE AND SOCIETY
Inhabited by a single ethnic group for the last 2,000 years. Tiny Chinese community. Family life is a central and clearly defined part of Korean society. Women's role is traditional; it is not respectable for those who are married to have jobs. Since the inconclusive Korean War (1950–53), North and South Korea have remained mutually hostile

THE ECONOMY
World's biggest ship-builder. High demand from China for Korean goods, especially cars. Electronics, household appliances also important.

FACTFILE
Official Name Republic of Korea
Date of Formation 1948
Capital Seoul
Population 45.4 million
Total Area
99,020 sq km (38,232 sq miles)
Density
458 people per sq km
Languages
Korean*, Chinese
Religions Mahayana Buddhist 47%, Protestant 38%, Catholic 11%, Confucian 3%, other 1%
Ethnic Mix Korean 99.9%, other (mainly Chinese) 0.1%
Government
Multiparty republic
Currency Won = 100 chon

JAPAN

JAPAN COMPRISES four principal islands and over 3,000 smaller ones. With the emperor as constitutional head, Japan is now the world's most powerful economy.

GEOGRAPHY
Predominantly mountainous, and wooded, with small fertile areas. Lies on a fault line. Frequent earthquakes and volcanic eruptions. Pacific coast vulnerable to tsunamis – giant waves.

CLIMATE
Generally temperate oceanic. Spring is warm and sunny, summer hot and humid, with high rainfall. In northwest, winters are very cold, with heavy snowfall.

PEOPLE AND SOCIETY

Racially homogenous society. People define themselves by the company they work for, not the job they do. Women mostly play a traditional role running the home. Education system is highly pressurized.

The Ginza District of central Tokyo lit by neon signs at night. Japan's cities are among the world's safest.

THE ECONOMY
World's most competitive producer of high-tech electronic products and cars. Commitment to long-term research and development. Revolutionary management and production methods.

FACTFILE
Official Name Japan
Date of Formation 1868 / 1945
Capital Tokyo
Population 125.4 million
Total Area
377,800 sq km (145,869 sq miles)
Density
332 people per sq km
Languages Japanese*, Korean, Chinese
Religions Shinto and Buddhist 76%, Buddhist 16%, other (including Christian) 8%
Ethnic Mix Japanese 99.4%, other (mostly Korean) 0.6%
Government
Constitutional monarchy
Currency Yen = 100 sen

AUSTRALIA

AN ISLAND continent located between the Indian and Pacific oceans, Australia was settled by Europeans 200 years ago. The focus has shifted away from Europe towards Asia.

GEOGRAPHY
Western half arid plateaus, and vast deserts. Eastern lowlands and river systems drain into Lake Eyre. Great Dividing Range in east. In the north are tropical rainforests.

CLIMATE
Interior, west and south are arid and very hot in summer. Central desert areas can reach 50°C (120°F). The north is hot throughout the year. East, south-east and southwest coasts are temperate.

PEOPLE AND SOCIETY

Immigration after 1945 brought many Europeans to Australia. Since 1970s, 50% of immigrants have been Asian. Aborigines, the first inhabitants, are sidelined economically and socially. 1990s recession increased gap between rich and poor.

Green Island on Australia's Great Barrier Reef in the far north of Queensland. The reef stretches more than 200 km down the coast.

THE ECONOMY
Efficient mining and agricultural industries. Successful tourist industry. Investor in booming Southeast Asian economies.

FACTFILE
Official Name Commonwealth of Australia
Date of Formation 1901
Capital Canberra
Population 18.3 million
Total Area 7,686,850 sq km (2,967,893 sq miles)
Density 2 people per sq km
Languages English*, Greek, Italian, Malay, Bahasa Indonesia, Vietnamese, Aboriginal, other
Religions Protestant 60%, Catholic 26%, other 14%
Ethnic Mix Caucasian 95%, Asian 4%, Aboriginal and other 1%
Government Parliamentary democracy
Currency Australian $ = 100 cents

VANUATU

AN ARCHIPELAGO of 82 islands and islets in the Pacific Ocean, it was ruled jointly by Britain and France from 1906 until independence in 1980.

GEOGRAPHY
Mountainous and volcanic, with coral beaches and dense rainforest. Cultivated land along coasts.

CLIMATE
Tropical. Temperatures and rainfall decline from north to south.

PEOPLE AND SOCIETY
Indigenous Melanesians form a majority. 80% of the population live on 16 main islands. People are among the most traditional in the Pacific local social and religious customs are strong, despite centuries of missionary influence. Subsistence farming and fishing are the main activities. Women have lower social status than men and payment of bride-price is common.

THE ECONOMY
Copra and cocoa are the largest exports. Recent upsurge in tourist industry. Offshore financial services are also important.

FACTFILE
Official Name Republic of Vanuatu
Date of Formation 1980
Capital Port-Vila
Population 200,000
Total Area
12,190 sq km (4,706 sq miles)
Density
16 people per sq km
Languages Bislama (Melanesian pidgin)*, English*, French*, other
Religions Protestant 77%, Catholic 15%, traditional beliefs 8%
Ethnic Mix Ni-Vanuatu 98%, European 1%, other 1%
Government
Multiparty republic
Currency
Vatu = 100 centimes

FIJI

A VOLCANIC archipelago
in the southern Pacific Ocean,
Fiji comprises two large
islands and 880 islets.
From 1874 to 1970, it was
a British colony.

GEOGRAPHY
Main islands are
mountainous, fringed by coral
reefs. Remainder are limestone and
coral formations.

CLIMATE
Tropical.
High temperatures
year round.
Cyclones are
a hazard.

PEOPLE AND SOCIETY
The British
introduced
workers from
India in the late 19th century,
and by 1946 their descendants
outnumbered the Native Fijian
population. In 1987, the Indian-
dominated government was
overthrown by Native Fijians.
Many Indo-Fijians left the country.
Civilian rule returned in 1990, and
a new constitution discriminating
against Indo-Fijians was
introduced.

THE ECONOMY
Well-diversified economy
based on sugar production, gold
mining, timber and commercial
fishing. Tourists are returning after
a drop in numbers after the coups.

FACTFILE

Official Name Republic of Fiji

Date of Formation 1970

Capital Suva

Population 800,000

Total Area
  18,270 sq km (7,054 sq miles)

Density
  44 people per sq km

Languages English*, Fijian*, Hindi,
  Urdu, Tamil, Telugu

Religions Christian 52%, Hindu
  38%, Muslim 8%, other 2%

Ethnic Mix Native Fijian 49%,
  Indo-Fijian 46%, other 5%

Government
  Multiparty republic

Currency
  Fiji $ = 100 cents

PAPUA NEW GUINEA

ACHIEVING INDEPENDENCE
from Australia in 1975,
PNG occupies the eastern
section of the island of
New Guinea and several
other island groups.

GEOGRAPHY
Mountainous and forested
mainland, with broad, swampy
river valleys. 40 active volcanoes in
the north. Around 600 outer islands.

CLIMATE
Hot and
humid in lowlands,
cooling towards
highlands, where
snow can fall on
highest peaks.

*Papua New Guinea's 600 outer
islands are mainly high, volcanic
islands, fringed by coral reefs.*

PEOPLE AND SOCIETY
Around 750
language groups –
the highest number in the world –
and even more tribes. Main social
distinction is between lowlanders,
who have frequent contact with
the outside world, and the
very isolated, but increasingly
threatened, highlanders who
live by hunter-gathering. Great
tensions exist between highland
tribes – anyone who is not
a wontok (of one's tribe) is
seen as potentially hostile.

THE ECONOMY
Significant quantities of gold,
copper, silver. Oil and natural gas
reserves. Secessionist violence on
Bougainville deters investors.

FACTFILE

Official Name The Independent
  State of Papua New Guinea

Date of Formation 1975

Capital Port Moresby

Population 4.4 million

Total Area 462,840 sq km
  (178,700 sq miles)

Density
  10 people per sq km

Languages Pidgin English*,
  Motu*, Papuan, 750 (est.)
  native languages

Religions
  Christian 66%, other 34%

Ethnic Mix Papuan 85%, other 15%

Government
  Parliamentary democracy

Currency Kina = 100 toea

SOLOMON ISLANDS

THE SOLOMONS
archipelago comprises
several hundred islands
scattered in the southwestern
Pacific. Independence from
Britain came in 1978.

GEOGRAPHY
The six largest islands are
volcanic, mountainous and thickly
forested. Flat coastal plains
provide the only cultivable land.

CLIMATE
Northern islands are hot and
humid all year round; further south
a cool season develops. November–
April wet season brings cyclones.

PEOPLE AND SOCIETY
Most Solomon Islanders are
Melanesian. Around 87 native
languages are spoken, but
Pidgin English is used as a
contact language between
tribes. Most people live
by shifting, subsistence
agriculture in small rural
villages. Villagers work
collectively on community
projects and there is much
sharing among clans.
Animist beliefs exist
alongside Christianity.

*Unloading seed coconuts
near Munda on New
Georgia in the Solomons'
southern chain.*

THE ECONOMY
Main products are
palm oil, copra, cocoa,
fish and timber. Bauxite
deposits found on Rennell island,
but islanders persuaded the
government that exploiting
them would destroy the island.

FACTFILE

Official Name Solomon Islands

Date of Formation 1978

Capital Honiara

Population 400,000

Total Area
  289,000 sq km (111,583 sq miles)

Density
  1 people per sq km

Languages English*, Pidgin English,
  87 (est.) native languages

Religions
  Christian 91%, other 9%

Ethnic Mix Melanesian 94%,
  other (Polynesian, Chinese,
  European) 6%

Government
  Parliamentary democracy

Currency Solomon Is. $ = 100 cents

PALAU

THE PALAU archipelago,
a group of over 300 islands,
lies in the western Pacific
Ocean. In 1994, it became
the world's newest
independent state.

GEOGRAPHY
Terrain varies from thickly-
forested mountains to limestone
and coral reefs. Babeldaob, the
largest island, is volcanic, with
many rivers and waterfalls.

CLIMATE
Hot and wet. Little variation
in daily and seasonal temperatures.
February–April is the dry season.

PEOPLE AND SOCIETY
Palau was the last remaining
US-administered UN Trust
Territory of the
Pacific Islands,
until 1994. Only
nine islands are
inhabited and
two-thirds of the
population live
in Oreor. Society is
matrilineal; women
choose which
males will be the
clan chiefs. Local
traditions remain
strong, despite
US influence.

THE ECONOMY
Subsistence level. Main crops
are coconuts and cassava. Revenue
from fishing licences and tourism.
Heavily reliant on US aid.

FACTFILE

Official Name Republic of Palau

Date of Formation 1994

Capital Oreor

Population 16,500

Total Area
  497 sq km (192 sq miles)

Density
  33 people per sq km

Languages Palauan*, English*,
  Sonsorolese-Tobian, other

Religions Christian (mainly
  Catholic) 70%, traditional beliefs
  30%

Ethnic Mix Palaun 99%,
  other (mainly Filipino) 1%

Government
  Multiparty republic

Currency US $ = 100 cents

MICRONESIA

THE FEDERATED States of Micronesia, situated in the western Pacific, comprise 607 islands and atolls grouped into four main island states.

GEOGRAPHY
Mixture of high volcanic islands with forested interiors, and low-lying coral atolls. Some islands have coastal mangrove swamps.

CLIMATE
Tropical, with high humidity. Very heavy rainfall outside the January–March dry season.

PEOPLE AND SOCIETY
Part of the US-administered UN Trust Territory of the Pacific Islands, until independence in 1979, but it still relies on US aid, which funds food stamps, schools and hospitals. Most islanders live without electricity or running water. Society is traditionally matrilineal.

THE ECONOMY
Fishing and copra production are the mainstays. Construction industry is largest private-sector activity. High unemployment.

FACTFILE
Official Name Federated States of Micronesia

Date of Formation 1986

Capital Palikir

Population 104,000

Total Area
2,900 sq km (1,120 sq miles)

Density
36 people per sq km

Languages English*, Trukese, Pohnpeian, Mortlockese, other

Religions Catholic 50%, Protestant 48%, other 2%

Ethnic Mix Micronesian 99%, other 1%

Government
Republic

Currency US $ = 100 cents

MARSHALL ISLANDS

UNDER US rule as part of the UN Trust Territory of the Pacific Islands until independence in 1986, the Marshall Islands comprise a group of 34 atolls.

GEOGRAPHY
Narrow coral rings with sandy beaches enclosing lagoons. Those in the south have thicker vegetation. Kwajalein is the world's largest atoll.

CLIMATE
Tropical oceanic, cooled year-round by northeast trade winds.

PEOPLE AND SOCIETY
Majuro Atoll is the main commercial centre, and is home to almost half the population. Tensions are high due to poor living conditions. Life on the outlying islands is still traditional, based around subsistence agriculture and fishing. Society is matrilineal; chiefly titles descend through the mother.

Ebeye Island in the Marshalls where population pressures have led to the disappearance of most tree and grass cover.

THE ECONOMY
Almost totally dependent on US aid and the rent paid by the US for its missile base on Kwajalein Atoll. Revenue from Japan for use of Marshallese waters for tuna-fishing. Copra and coconut oil are the only significant agricultural exports.

FACTFILE
Official Name Republic of the Marshall Islands

Date of Formation 1986

Capital No official capital

Population 54,000

Total Area
181 sq km (70 sq miles)

Density
298 people per sq km

Languages
English*, Marshallese*

Religions Protestant 80%, Catholic 15%, other 5%

Ethnic Mix Marshallese 90%, other Pacific islanders 10%

Government
Republic

Currency US $ = 100 cents

NAURU

NAURU LIES in the Pacific, 4,000 km (2,480 miles) northeast of Australia. Phosphate deposits have made its citizens among the richest in the world.

GEOGRAPHY
Low-lying coral atoll, with a fertile coastal belt. Coral cliffs encircle an elevated interior plateau.

CLIMATE
Equatorial, moderated by sea breezes. Occasional long droughts.

PEOPLE AND SOCIETY
Native Nauruans are of mixed Micronesian and Polynesian origin. Most live in simple, traditional houses and spend their money on luxury cars and consumer goods. Government provides free welfare and education. Diet of imported processed foods has caused widespread obesity and diabetes. Mining is left to an imported labour force, mainly from Kiribati. Many young attend boarding school in Australia.

Nauru is almost circular with a single 19-km ring road.

THE ECONOMY
Phosphate, the only resource, is sold to Pacific Rim countries for use as a fertilizer. Deposits are near exhaustion. Huge investments in Australian and Hawaiian property. Possible future as a tax haven.

FACTFILE
Official Name Republic of Nauru

Date of Formation 1968

Capital No official capital

Population 11,000

Total Area
21.2 sq km (8.2 sq miles)

Density
519 people per sq km

Languages
Nauruan*, English, other

Religions
Christian 95%, other 5%

Ethnic Mix Nauruan 58%, other Pacific islanders 26%, Chinese 8%, European 8%

Government
Parliamentary democracy

Currency Australian $ = 100 cents

KIRIBATI

PART OF the British colony of the Gilbert and Ellice Islands until independence in 1979, Kiribati comprises 33 islands in the mid-Pacific Ocean.

GEOGRAPHY
Three groups of tiny, very low-lying coral atolls scattered across 5 million sq km (1,930,000 sq miles) of ocean. Most have central lagoons.

CLIMATE
Central islands have maritime equatorial climate. Those to north and south are tropical, with constant high temperatures.

PEOPLE AND SOCIETY
Locals still refer to themselves as Gilbertese. Apart from the inhabitants of Banaba, who employed anthropologists to establish their racial distinction, almost all people are Micronesian. Most are poor subsistence farmers. The islands are effectively ruled by traditional chiefs, though there is a party system based on the British model.

THE ECONOMY
Until 1980, when deposits ran out, phosphate from Banaba provided 80% of exports. Since then, coconuts, copra, fish, have become main exports, but the islands are heavily dependent on foreign aid.

FACTFILE
Official Name Republic of Kiribati

Date of Formation 1979

Capital Bairiki

Population 77,000

Total Area
710 sq km (274 sq miles)

Density
108 people per sq km

Languages
English*, Kiribati, other

Religions Catholic 53%, Protestant (mainly Congregational) 40%, other Christian 4%, other 3%

Ethnic Mix
I-Kiribati 98%, other 2%

Government Multiparty republic

Currency Australian $ = 100 cents

TUVALU

A TINY isolated state, linked to the Gilbert Islands as a British colony until independence in 1978, Tuvalu's nine islands lie in the central Pacific.

GEOGRAPHY
Coral atolls, none more than 4.6 metres (15 feet) above sea level. Poor soils restrict vegetation to bush, coconut palms and breadfruit trees.

CLIMATE
Hot all year round. Heavy annual rainfall. Hurricane season brings many violent storms.

PEOPLE AND SOCIETY
People are mostly Polynesian, related to the Samoans and Tongans. Almost half the population live on Funafuti Atoll, where government jobs are centred. Life is communal and traditional. Most people live by subsistence farming, digging pits out of the coral to grow crops. Fresh water is precious due to frequent droughts.

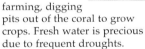

THE ECONOMY
World's smallest economy. Fish stocks exploited mainly by foreign boats in return for licensing fees. Exports are few; copra, stamps and garments. Aid is crucial.

FACTFILE
Official Name Tuvalu

Date of Formation 1978

Capital Fongafale

Population 9,000

Total Area
26 sq km (10 sq miles)

Density
346 people per sq km

Languages Tuvaluan, Kiribati, other (no official language)

Religions
Protestant 97%, other 3%

Ethnic Mix Tuvaluan 95%, other (inc. Micronesian, I-Kiribati) 5%

Government
Constitutional monarchy

Currency
Australian $ = 100 cents

SAMOA

THE SOUTHERN Pacific islands of Samoa gained independence from New Zealand in 1962. Four of the nine islands are inhabited.

GEOGRAPHY
Comprises two large islands and seven smaller ones. Two largest islands have rainforested, mountainous interiors surrounded by coastal lowlands and coral reefs.

CLIMATE
Tropical, with high humidity. Cooler May–November. Hurricane season December–March.

PEOPLE AND SOCIETY
Ethnic Samoans are world's second largest Polynesian group, after the Maoris. Extended family groups own 80% of the land. Each family has an elected chief, who looks after its political and social interests. Large-scale migration to the US and New Zealand reflects lack of jobs and attractions of Western lifestyle.

The capital of Samoa, Apia, lies on Upolu, the second largest island.

THE ECONOMY
Agricultural products include taro, coconut cream, cocoa and copra. Growth of service sector since 1989 launch of offshore banking. Dependent on aid and expatriate remittances.

FACTFILE
Official Name Independent State of Samoa

Date of Formation 1962

Capital Apia

Population 200,000

Total Area
2,840 sq km (1,027 sq miles)

Density
70 people per sq km

Languages
Samoan*, English*

Religions Protestant (mostly Congregational) 74%, Catholic 26%

Ethnic Mix Samoan 93%, mixed European and Polynesian 7%

Government Parliamentary state

Currency Tala = 100 sene

TONGA

TONGA IS an archipelago of 170 islands, 45 of which are inhabited, in the South Pacific. Politics is effectively controlled by the king.

GEOGRAPHY
Easterly islands are generally low and fertile. Those in the west are higher and volcanic in origin.

CLIMATE
Tropical oceanic. Temperatures range between 20°C (68°F) and 30°C (86°F) all year round. Heavy rainfall, especially February–March.

New Zealand has many volcanoes, some of which are still active. Mount Taranaki on North Island is now extinct.

PEOPLE AND SOCIETY
The last remaining Polynesian monarchy, and the only Pacific state never brought under foreign rule. All land is property of the crown, but is administered by nobles who allot it to the common people. Respect for traditional institutions and values remains high, although younger, Westernized Tongans are starting to question some attitudes.

THE ECONOMY
Most people are subsistence farmers. Commercial production of coconuts, cassava and passion fruit. Tourism is increasing slowly.

FACTFILE
Official Name Kingdom of Tonga

Date of Formation 1970

Capital Nuku'alofa

Population 98,000

Total Area
750 sq km (290 sq miles)

Density
131 people per sq km

Languages
Tongan*, English

Religions Protestant 82% (mainly Methodist), Catholic 18%

Ethnic Mix Tongan 98%, mixed European and Polynesian 2%

Government
Constitutional monarchy

Currency
Pa'anga = 100 seniti

NEW ZEALAND

LYING SOUTHEAST of Australia, New Zealand comprises the North and South Islands, separated by the Cook Strait, and many smaller islands.

GEOGRAPHY
North Island has mountain ranges, valleys and volcanic central plateau. South Island is mostly mountainous, with eastern lowlands.

CLIMATE
Generally temperate and damp. Extreme north is almost sub-tropical; southern winters are cold.

PEOPLE AND SOCIETY
Maoris were the first settlers, 1,200 years ago. Today's majority European population is descended mainly from British migrants who settled after 1840. Maoris' living and education standards are generally lower than average. Tense relations beween the two groups in recent years. Government now negotiating settlement of Maori land claims.

THE ECONOMY
Modern agricultural sector; world's biggest exporter of wool, cheese, butter and meat. Growing manufacturing industry. Tourism.

FACTFILE
Official Name The Dominion of New Zealand

Date of Formation 1947

Capital Wellington

Population 3.6 million

Total Area
268,680 sq km (103,730 sq miles)

Density
13 people per sq km

Languages English*, Maori, other

Religions Protestant 62%, Catholic 18%, other 20%

Ethnic Mix European 88%, Maori 9%, other (inc. Malay, Chinese) 3%

Government
Constitutional monarchy

Currency NZ $ = 100 cents

GAZETTEER OF INTERNATIONAL ORGANIZATIONS

THIS LISTING GIVES the full names of a number of international organizations. Most have been set up for the purpose of fostering social and economic ties between countries – usually with close geographic links. The full names are followed by the date of establishment or foundation, an indication of membership where appropriate and a summary of the organization's aims and functions.

ACC
Arab Co-operation Council
Established 1989
Members – Egypt, Iraq, Jordan, Yemen; promotes Arab economic co-operation

ACP
African, Caribbean and Pacific Countries
Established 1976
Members – 70 developing countries; preferential economic and aid relationship with the EU

ACS
Association of Caribbean States
Established 1994
Members – 24 Caribbean countries; promotes economic, scientific and cultural co-operation in the region

ADB
Asian Development Bank
Established 1966
Members – 39 Asian-Pacific countries and territories, 16 non-regional countries; encourages regional development

AfDB
African Development Bank
Established 1963
Members – 52 African countries, 24 non-African countries; encourages African economic development

AFESD **Arab Fund for Economic and Social Development**
Established 1968
Members – 20 Arab countries and the PLO; promotes social and economic development in Arab states

AL
Arab League
Established 1945
Members – 21 Arab countries and the PLO; forum to promote Arabic co-operation on social, political and military issues

ALADI
Latin American Integration Association
Established 1960
Members – 11 South American countries; promotes trade and regional integration

AMAZON PACT
Established 1978
Members – Bolivia, Brazil, Colombia, Ecuador, Guyana, Peru, Surinam, Venezuela; promotes the harmonious development of the Amazon region

AG
Andean Pact (Acuerdo de Cartegena)
Established 1969
Members – Bolivia, Colombia, Ecuador, Peru and Venezuela; promotes development through integration

AMF
Arab Monetary Fund
Established 1977
Members – 19 countries and the PLO; promotes monetary and economic co-operation

AMU
Arab Maghreb Union
Established 1989
Members – Algeria, Libya, Mauritania, Morocco, Tunisia; promotes integration and economic co-operation among North African Arab states

APEC
Asia-Pacific Economic Co-operation
Established 1989
Members – 18 Pacific Rim countries; promotes regional economic co-operation

ASEAN
Association of Southeast Asian Nations
Established 1967
Members – Brunei, Burma, Indonesia, Laos, Malaysia, Philippines, Singapore, Thailand, Vietnam; promotes economic, social and cultural co-operation

BADEA **Arab Bank for Economic Development in Africa**
Established 1974 (as an agency of the Arab League)
Members – 17 Arab countries and the PLO; promotes economic development in Africa

BDEAC **Central African States Development Bank**
Established 1976
Members – Cameroon, Central African Republic, Chad, Congo, Equatorial Guinea, France, Gabon, Germany, Kuwait; furthers economic development

BENELUX
Benelux Economic Union
Established 1958
Members – Belgium, Luxembourg, Netherlands; develops economic ties between member countries

BOAD
West African Development Bank
Established 1973
Members – Benin, Burkina, Ivory Coast, Mali, Niger, Senegal, Togo; promotes economic development and integration

BSEC
Black Sea Economic Co-operation Group
Established 1992
Members – Albania, Armenia, Azerbaijan, Bulgaria, Georgia, Greece, Moldavia, Romania, Russia, Turkey, Ukraine; furthers regional stability through economic co-operation

CACM
Central American Common Market
Established 1960
Members – Costa Rica, El Salvador, Guatemala, Honduras, Nicaragua; furthers economic ties between members; one of its institutions is the BCIE – Central American Bank for Economic Integration

CAEU
Council of Arab Economic Unity
Established 1964
Members – 11 Arab countries and the PLO; encourages economic integration

CARICOM **Caribbean Community and Common Market**
Established 1973
Members – 13 Caribbean countries and Montserrat; fosters economic ties in the Caribbean

CBSS
Council of the Baltic Sea States
Established 1992
Members – Denmark, Estonia, Finland, Germany, Latvia, Lithuania, Norway, Poland, Russia, Sweden; promotes co-operation among Baltic Sea states

CDB
Caribbean Development Bank
Established 1969
Members – 20 Caribbean countries, 5 non-Caribbean countries; promotes regional development

CE
Council of Europe
Established 1949
Members – 40 European countries; promotes unity and quality of life in Europe

CEEAC **Economic Community of Central African States**
Established 1983
Members – 10 Central African countries; promotes regional co-operation, and aims to establish a Central African common market

CEFTA **Central European Free Trade Agreement**
Established 1992
Members – Czech Republic, Hungary, Poland, Romania, Slovakia, Slovenia; promotes trade and co-operation

CEI **Central European Initiative**
Established 1991 (evolved from Hexagonal Group)
Members – Austria, Bosnia & Herzegovina, Bulgaria, Belorussia, Croatia, Czech Republic, Hungary, Italy, Moldavia, Poland, Slovakia, Slovenia, Ukraine, Yugoslavia; promotes economic and political co-operation, within the OSCE

CEMAC **Economic and Monetary Community of Central Africa**
Established 1994
Members – 6 Central African members of the franc zone; customs union (replaced UDEAC)

CEPGL **Economic Community of the Great Lakes Countries**
Established 1976
Members – Burundi, Congo (Zaire), Rwanda; promotes regional economic co-operation

CERN **European Organization for Nuclear Research**
Established 1953
Members – 23 European countries; provides for collaboration in nuclear research for peaceful purposes

CILSS **Permanent Inter-state Committee for Drought Control in the Sahel**
Established 1973
Members – 9 African countries in the Sahel region; promotes prevention of drought and crop failure in the region

CIS
Commonwealth of Independent States
Established 1991
(as successor of the Soviet Union)
Members – Armenia, Azerbaijan, Belorussia, Georgia, Kazakhstan, Kyrgyzstan, Moldavia, Russia, Tajikistan, Turkmenistan, Ukraine, Uzbekistan; promotes inter-state relationships

COMESA **Common Market for Eastern and Southern Africa**
Established 1993 (replacing PTA)
Members – 24 African countries; promotes economic development and co-operation

COMMONWEALTH
(evolved from British Empire)
Established 1931
Members – 53 countries; develops relationships and contacts between its members (Nigeria suspended 1995, Fiji re-admitted in 1997)

CP **Colombo Plan**
Established 1951
Members – Australia, Japan, New Zealand, USA (donors) and 20 Asia-Pacific countries; encourages economic and social development in Asia-Pacific region

DAMASCUS DECLARATION
Established 1991
Members – Bahrain, Egypt, Kuwait, Oman, Qatar, Saudi Arabia, Syria, UAE; a loose association, formed after the Gulf War, which aims to secure the stability of the region

EBRD **European Bank for Reconstruction and Development**
Established 1991
Members – 58 countries; helps transition of former communist European states to market economies

ECO
Economic Co-operation Organization
Established 1985
Members – Iran, Pakistan, Turkey and 7 Central Asian states; aims at co-operation in economic, social and cultural affairs

ECOWAS **Economic Community of West African States**
Established 1975
Members – 16 West African countries; promotes regional economic co-operation

EEA **European Economic Area**
Established 1994
Members – the 15 members of the EU and all the members of EFTA, except Switzerland; aims to include EFTA members in the EU single market

EFTA
European Free Trade Association
Established 1960
Members – Iceland, Norway, Liechtenstein, Switzerland; promotes economic co-operation

ESA
European Space Agency
Established 1973
Members – 14 European countries; promotes co-operation in space research for peaceful purposes

EU European Union
Established 1992;
Members – 15 countries; aims to integrate the economies of member states and promote co-operation and co-ordination of policies

FZ Franc zone
Members – 15 African states, France and Monaco; aims to form monetary union among countries whose currencies are linked to the French franc.

GCC Gulf Co-operation Council
Established 1981
Members – Bahrain, Kuwait, Oman, Qatar, Saudi Arabia, UAE; promotes co-operation in economic, political and social affairs

G3 Group of 3
Established 1987
Members – Colombia, Mexico, Venezuela; aims to remove trade restrictions

G5 Group of 5
Finance ministers of France, Germany, Japan, UK, USA, meeting informally to establish agenda of G7

G7 Group of 7
Established 1975
Members – Canada, France, Germany, Italy, Japan, UK, USA; the seven major industrialized countries

G10 Group of 10
Established 1962
Members – G7 members, plus Belgium, the Netherlands, Sweden and Switzerland (now 11 members); ministers meet to discuss monetary issues

G15 Group of 15
Established 1989
Members – 15 developing countries; meets annually to further co-operation among developing countries

G24 Group of 24
Members – the 24 countries within the IMF which represent the interests of developing countries

GEPLACEA Latin American and Caribbean Sugar Exporting Countries
Established 1974
Members – 23 countries; a forum for consultation on the production and sale of sugar

IMF International Monetary Fund
Established 1945
Members – 181 countries (voting rights of Congo (Zaire) and Sudan are currently suspended); promotes international monetary co-operation, balanced growth of trade and exchange rate stability; provides credit resources to members experiencing balance-of-trade difficulties

IBRD International Bank for Reconstruction and Development (also known as the World Bank)
Established 1945
Members – 178 countries; UN agency providing economic development loans

IDB Islamic Development Bank
Established 1975 (agency of the OIC)
Members – 47 countries and the PLO; promotes economic development on Islamic principles among Muslim communities

IGADD Inter-Governmental Authority on Drought and Development
Established 1986
Members – Djibouti, Eritrea, Ethiopia, Kenya, Somalia, Sudan, Uganda; promotes co-operation on drought-related matters

IOC Indian Ocean Commission
Established 1982
Members – Comoros, France (representing Réunion), Madagascar, Mauritius, Seychelles; promotes regional co-operation

IWC International Whaling Commission
Established 1946
Members – 40 countries; reviews conduct of whaling throughout world; co-ordinates and funds whale research

LCBC Lake Chad Basin Commission
Established 1964
Members – Cameroon, CAR, Chad, Niger, Nigeria; encourages economic and environmental development in Lake Chad region

MEKONG RIVER COMMISSION
Established 1995 (replacing the 1958 interim Mekong Secretariat)
Members – Cambodia, Laos, Thailand, Vietnam; accord on the sustainable development of Mekong River basin

MERCOSUR Southern Common Market
Established 1991
Members – Argentina, Brazil, Paraguay, Uruguay; promotes economic co-operation

MRU Mano River Union
Established 1973
Members – Guinea, Liberia, Sierra Leone; aims to create customs and economic union

NACC North Atlantic Co-operation Council
Established 1991
Members – 36 countries (members of NATO and former members of Warsaw Pact); forum for co-operation on political and security issues

NAFTA North American Free Trade Agreement
Established 1994
Members – Canada, Mexico, USA; free-trade zone

NAM Non-Aligned Movement
Established 1961
Members – 111 countries; fosters political and military co-operation away from traditional Eastern or Western blocs

NATO North Atlantic Treaty Organization
Established 1949
Members – 16 countries; promotes mutual defence co-operation. Since January 1994, NATO's *Partnerships for Peace* programme has provided a loose framework for co-operation with former members of the Warsaw Pact and the ex-Soviet republics. In 1997, Czech Republic, Hungary and Poland were the first former Warsaw Pact members invited to join.

NC Nordic Council
Established 1952
Members – Denmark, Finland, Iceland, Norway, Sweden; promotes cultural and environmental co-operation in Scandinavia

OAPEC Organization of Arab Petroleum Exporting Countries
Established 1968
Members – Algeria, Bahrain, Egypt, Iraq, Kuwait, Libya, Qatar, Saudi Arabia, Syria, UAE; aims to promote the interests of member countries and increase co-operation in the petroleum industry

OAS Organization of American States
Established 1948
Members – 34 American countries; promotes security, economic and social development in the Americas

OAU Organization of African Unity
Established 1963
Members – 53 African countries; promotes unity and co-operation

OECD Organization for Economic Co-operation and Development
Established 1961
Members – 29 industrialized democracies; forum for co-ordinating economic policies

OECS Organization of Eastern Caribbean States
Established 1981
Members – Antigua & Barbuda, Dominica, Grenada, Montserrat, St Kitts & Nevis, St Lucia, St Vincent & the Grenadines; promotes political, economic and defence co-operation

OIC Organization of the Islamic Conference
Established 1971
Members – 53 Islamic countries; furthers Islamic solidarity and co-operation

OMVG Gambia River Development Organization
Established 1978
Members – The Gambia, Guinea, Guinea-Bissau, Senegal; promotes integrated development of the Gambia River basin

OPANAL Agency for the Prohibition of Nuclear Weapons in Latin America and the Caribbean
Established 1969
Members – 26 countries; aims to ensure compliance with the Treaty of Tlatelolco (banning nuclear weapons from South America and the Caribbean)

OPEC Organization of the Petroleum Exporting Countries
Established 1960
Members – Algeria, Gabon, Indonesia, Iran, Iraq, Kuwait, Libya, Nigeria, Qatar, Saudi Arabia, UAE, Venezuela; aims to co-ordinate oil policies to ensure fair and stable prices

OSCE Organization for Security and Co-operation in Europe
Established 1972 (as CSCE; renamed 1994)
Members – 53 countries; aims to strengthen democracy and human rights, and settle disputes peacefully

PARTNERSHIPS FOR PEACE (PfP)
see NATO

RG Rio Group
Established 1987 (evolved from Contadora Group, established 1948)
Members – Argentina, Bolivia, Brazil, Chile, Colombia, Ecuador, Mexico, Paraguay, Peru, Uruguay, Venezuela; forum for Latin American issues

SAARC South Asian Association for Regional Co-operation
Established 1985
Members – Bangladesh, Bhutan, India, Maldives, Nepal, Pakistan, Sri Lanka; encourages economic, social and cultural co-operation

SACU Southern African Customs Union
Established 1969
Members – 5 countries; promotes co-operation in trade and customs matters among southern African states

SADC Southern African Development Community
Established 1992
Members – Angola, Botswana, Lesotho, Malawi, Mauritius, Mozambique, Namibia, South Africa, Swaziland, Tanzania, Zambia, Zimbabwe; promotes economic integration

SAN JOSÉ GROUP
Established 1988
Members – Costa Rica, El Salvador, Guatemala, Honduras, Nicaragua, Panama; a 'complementary, voluntary and gradual' economic union

SELA Latin American Economic System
Established 1975
Members – 27 countries; promotes economic and social development through regional co-operation

SPC South Pacific Commission
Established 1948
Members – 28 countries and territories; a forum for dialogue between Pacific countries and powers administering Pacific territories

SPF South Pacific Forum
Established 1971
Members – 15 countries and territories; develops regional political co-operation

UEMOA West African Economic and Monetary Union
Established 1994
Members – 7 countries; aims for convergence of monetary policies and economic union

UN United Nations
Established 1945
Members – 184 countries; permanent members of the Security Council – China, France, Russia, UK, USA; aims to maintain international peace and security and to promote co-operation over economic, social, cultural and humanitarian problems. Agencies include the regional commissions of the UN's Economic and Social Council: ECA (Economic Commission for Africa – established 1958); ECE (Economic Commission for Europe – established 1947); ECLAC (Economic Commission for Latin America and the Caribbean – established 1948); ESCAP (Economic and Social Commission for Asia and the Pacific – established 1947); ESCWA (Economic and Social Commission for Western Asia – established 1973)

WEU Western European Union
Established 1954
Members – 10 countries; a forum for European military co-operation

WTO World Trade Organisation
Established 1995 (as the successor to GATT – General Agreement on Tariffs and Trade)
Members – 131 countries; aims to liberalize trade through multilateral trade agreements

Aachen – Alexandria

INDEX

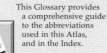

Glossary of Abbreviations

This Glossary provides a comprehensive guide to the abbreviations used in this Atlas, and in the Index.

abbrev abbreviation
Afr. Afrikaans
Alb. Albanian
Amh. Amharic
anc. ancient
Ar. Arabic
Arm. Armenian
Az. Azerbaijani

B
Basq. Basque
Bel. Belorussian
Ben. Bengali
Bibl. Biblical
Bret. Breton
Bul. Bulgarian
Bur. Burmese

C
Cam. Cambodian
Cant. Cantonese
Cast. Castilian
Cat. Catalan
Chin. Chinese
Cro. Croat
Cz. Czech

D
Dan. Danish
Dut. Dutch

E
Eng. English
Est. Estonian
est. estimated

F
Faer. Faeroese
Fij. Fijian
Fin. Finnish
Flem. Flemish
Fr. French
Fris. Frisian

G
Geor. Georgian
Ger. German
Gk. Greek
Guj. Gujarati

H
Haw. Hawaiian
Heb. Hebrew
Hind. Hindi
hist. historical
Hung. Hungarian

I
Icel. Icelandic
Ind. Indonesian
Inuit Inuit
Ir. Irish
It. Italian

J
Jap. Japanese

K
Kaz. Kazakh
Kir. Kirghiz
Kor. Korean
Kurd. Kurdish

L
Lao. Laotian
Lapp. Lappis
Lat. Latin
Latv. Latvian
Lith. Lithuanian
Lus. Lusatian

M
Mac. Macedonian
Mal. Malay
Malg. Malagasy
Malt. Maltese
Mong. Mongolia

N
Nepali. Nepali
Nor. Norwegian

O
off. officially

P
Pash. Pashtu
Per. Persian
Pol. Polish
Port. Portuguese
prev. previously

R
Rmsch. Romansch
Roman. Romanian
Rus. Russian

S
SCr. Serbian & Croatian
Serb. Serbian
Slvk. Slovak
Slvn. Slovene
Som. Somali
Sp. Spanish
Swa. Swahili
Swe. Swedish

T
Taj. Tajik
Th. Thai
Tib. Tibetan
Turk. Turkish
Turkm. Turkmenistan

U
Uigh. Uighur
Ukr. Ukrainian
Uzb. Uzbek

V
var. variant
Vtn. Vietnamese

W
Wel. Welsh

X
Xh. Xhosa

Y
Yugo. Yugoslavia

Index

A

Aachen 110 A4 Dut. Aken, Fr. Aix-la-Chapelle; anc. Aquae Grani, Aquisgranum. Nordrhein-Westfalen, W Germany
Aaiún see Laâyoune
Aalborg see Ålborg
Aalen 111 B6 Baden-Württemberg, S Germany
Aalsmeer 102 C3 Noord-Holland, C Netherlands
Aalst 103 B6 Fr. Alost. Oost-Vlaanderen, C Belgium
Aalten 102 E4 Gelderland, E Netherlands
Aalter 103 B5 Oost-Vlaanderen, NW Belgium
Äänekoski 101 D5 Keski-Suomi, C Finland
Aar see Aare
Aare 111 A7 var. Aar. River W Switzerland
Aarhus see Århus
Aat see Ath
Aba 91 G5 Abia, S Nigeria
Aba 93 E5 Haut-Zaïre, NE Congo (Zaire)
Abā as Su'ūd see Najrān
Abaco Island see Great Abaco
Ābādān 136 C4 Khūzestān, SW Iran
Abai see Blue Nile
Abakan 130 D4 Respublika Khakasiya, S Russian Federation
Abancay 76 D4 Apurímac, SE Peru
Abariringa see Kanton
Abashiri 146 D2 var. Abasiri. Hokkaidō, NE Japan
Abasiri see Abashiri
Ābaya Hāyk' 89 C5 Eng. Lake Margherita, It. Abbaia. Lake SW Ethiopia
Ābay Wenz see Blue Nile
Abbeville 106 C2 anc. Abbatis Villa. Somme, N France
'Abd al 'Azīz, Jabal 134 D2 mountain range NE Syria
Abéché 92 C3 var. Abécher, Abeshr. Ouaddaï, SE Chad
Abécher see Abéché
Abela see Ávila
Abemama 160 D2 var. Apamama; prev. Roger Simpson Island. Atoll Tungaru, W Kiribati
Abengourou 91 E5 E Ivory Coast
Aberdeen 104 D3 anc. Devana. NE Scotland, UK
Aberdeen 61 E2 South Dakota, N USA
Aberdeen 62 B2 Washington, NW USA
Abergwaun see Fishguard
Abertawe see Swansea
Aberystwyth 105 C6 W Wales, UK
Abeshr see Abéché
Abhā 137 B6 'Asīr, SW Saudi Arabia
Abidavichy 123 D7 Rus. Obidovichi. Mahilyowskaya Voblasts', E Belorussia
Abidjan 91 E5 S Ivory Coast
Abilene 65 F3 Texas, SW USA
Abingdon see Pinta, Isla
Abkhazia 133 E1 autonomous republic NW Georgia
Åbo 101 D6 Turku-Pori, SW Finland
Aboisso 91 E5 SE Ivory Coast
Abo, Massif d' 92 B1 mountain range NW Chad
Abomey 91 F5 S Benin
Abou-Déïa 92 C3 Salamat, SE Chad
Abrantes 108 B3 var. Abrántes. Santarém, C Portugal
Abrolhos Bank 72 E4 undersea feature W Atlantic Ocean
Abrova 123 B6 Rus. Obrovo. Brestskaya Voblasts', SW Belorussia
Abrud 124 B4 Ger. Gross-Schlatten, Hung. Abrudbánya. Alba, SW Romania
Abruzzese, Appennino 112 C4 mountain range C Italy
Absaroka Range 60 B2 mountain range Montana/Wyoming, NW USA
Abū aḍ Ḍuhūr 134 B3 Fr. Aboudouhour. Idlib, NW Syria
Abu Dhabi see Abū Ẓaby
Abu Hamed 88 C3 River Nile, N Sudan
Abū Ḥardān 134 E3 var. Hajîne. Dayr az Zawr, E Syria
Abuja 91 G4 country capital (Nigeria) Federal Capital District, C Nigeria
Abū Kamāl 134 E3 Fr. Abou Kémal. Dayr az Zawr, E Syria
Abula see Ávila
Abunã, Rio 78 C2 var. Río Abuná. River Bolivia/Brazil
Abut Head 167 B6 headland South Island, NZ
Ābuyē Mēda 88 D4 mountain C Ethiopia
Abū Ẓabī see Abū Ẓaby
Abū Ẓaby 137 C5 var. Abū Ẓabī, Eng. Abu Dhabi. Country capital (UAE) Abū Ẓaby, C UAE
Abyla see Ávila
Acalayong 93 A5 SW Equatorial Guinea
Acaponeta 66 D4 Nayarit, C Mexico
Acapulco 67 E5 var. Acapulco de Juárez. Guerrero, S Mexico
Acapulco de Juárez see Acapulco
Acarai Mountains 75 F4 Sp. Serra Acaraí. Mountain range Brazil/Guyana
Acarigua 74 D2 Portuguesa, N Venezuela
Accra 91 E5 country capital (Ghana) SE Ghana
Achacachi 77 E4 La Paz, W Bolivia
Acklins Island 70 C2 island SE Bahamas
Aconcagua, Cerro 80 B4 mountain W Argentina
Açores see Azores
A Coruña 108 B1 Cast. La Coruña, Eng. Corunna; anc. Caronium. Galicia, NW Spain
Acre 78 C2 off. Estado do Acre. State W Brazil
Açu 79 G2 var. Assu. Rio Grande do Norte, E Brazil
Acuña 66 D2 var. Villa Acuña. Coahuila de Zaragoza, NE Mexico
Ada 65 G2 Oklahoma, C USA
Ada 116 D3 Serbia, N Yugoslavia
Adalia, Gulf of see Antalya Körfezi
Adama see Nazrēt
Adamawa Highlands 92 B4 plateau NW Cameroon
'Adan 137 B7 Eng. Aden. SW Yemen
Adana 132 D4 var. Seyhan. Adana, S Turkey
Adapazarı 132 B2 prev. Ada Bazar. Sakarya, NW Turkey
Adare, Cape 170 B4 headland Antarctica
Ad Dahnā' 136 C4 desert E Saudi Arabia
Ad Dakhla 86 A4 var. Dakhla. SW Western Sahara
Ad Dalanj see Dilling
Ad Damar see Ed Damer
Ad Damazīn see Ed Damazin
Ad Dāmir see Ed Damer
Ad Dammān 136 C4 var. Dammām. Ash Sharqīyah, NE Saudi Arabia
Ad Dāmūr see Damoûr
Ad Dawḥah 136 C4 Eng. Doha. Country capital (Qatar) C Qatar
Aḍ Ḍiffah see Libyan Plateau
Addis Ababa see Ādīs Ābeba
Addu Atoll 148 A5 atoll S Maldives
Adelaide 165 B6 state capital South Australia
Aden see 'Adan
Aden, Gulf of 137 C7 gulf SW Arabian Sea
Adige 112 C2 Ger. Etsch. River N Italy
Adirondack Mountains 57 F2 mountain range New York, NE USA
Ādīs Ābeba 89 C5 Eng. Addis Ababa. Country capital (Ethiopia) C Ethiopia
Adıyaman 133 E4 Adıyaman, SE Turkey
Adjud 124 C4 Vrancea, E Romania
Admiralty Islands 160 B3 island group N PNG
Adra 109 E5 Andalucía, S Spain
Adrar 86 D3 C Algeria
Adrar des Iforas see Ifôghas, Adrar des
Adrian 56 C3 Michigan, N USA
Adriatic Sea 119 E2 Alb. Deti Adriatik, It. Mare Adriatico, SCr. Jadransko More, Slvn. Jadransko Morje. Sea N Mediterranean Sea
Adycha 131 F2 river NE Russian Federation
Aegean Sea 121 C5 Gk. Aigaíon Pélagos, Aigaío Pélagos, Turk. Ege Denizi. Sea NE Mediterranean Sea
Aegviidu 122 D2 Ger. Charlottenhof. Harjumaa, NW Estonia
Aelana see Al 'Aqabah
Aelok see Ailuk Atoll
Aelōnlaplap see Ailinglaplap Atoll
Aeolian Islands see Eolie, Isole
Afar Depression see Danakil Desert
Afghanistan 138 C4 off. Islamic State of Afghanistan, Per. Dowlat-e Eslāmī-ye Afghānestān; prev. Republic of Afghanistan. Country C Asia
Afmadow 89 D6 Jubbada Hoose, S Somalia
Africa 84 continent
Africa, Horn of 84 E4 physical region Ethiopia/Somalia
Africana Seamount 157 A6 undersea feature SW Indian Ocean
'Afrīn 134 B2 Ḥalab, N Syria
Afyon 132 B3 prev. Afyonkarahisar. Afyon, W Turkey
Agadez 91 G3 prev. Agadès. Agadez, C Niger
Agadir 86 B3 SW Morocco
Agana 160 B1 var. Agaña. Dependent territory capital (Guam) NW Guam
Āgaro 89 C5 W Ethiopia
Agassiz Fracture Zone 159 G5 tectonic feature S Pacific Ocean
Agathónisi 121 D6 island Dodekánisos, Greece, Aegean Sea
Agde 107 C6 anc. Agatha. Hérault, S France
Agedabia see Ajdābiyā
Agen 107 B5 anc. Aginnum. Lot-et-Garonne, SW France
Aghri Dagh see Büyükağrı Dağı
Agiá 120 B4 var. Ayiá. Thessalía, C Greece
Agialoúsa 118 D4 var. Yenierenköy. NE Cyprus
Agía Marína 121 E6 Léros, Dodekánisos, Greece, Aegean Sea
Ágios Nikólaos 121 D8 var. Áyios Nikólaos. Kríti, Greece, E Mediterranean Sea
Āgra 150 D3 Uttar Pradesh, N India
Ağrı 133 F3 var. Karaköse; prev. Karakılısse. Ağrı, NE Turkey
Agri Dagi see Büyükağrı Dağı
Agrigento 113 C7 Gk. Akragas; prev. Girgenti. Sicilia, Italy, C Mediterranean Sea
Agriovótano 121 C5 Évvoia, C Greece
Agropoli 113 D5 Campania, S Italy
Aguachica 74 B2 Cesar, N Colombia
Aguadulce 69 F5 Coclé, S Panama
Agua Prieta 66 B1 Sonora, NW Mexico
Aguascalientes 66 D4 Aguascalientes, C Mexico
Aguaytía 76 C3 Ucayali, C Peru
Aguilas 109 E4 Murcia, SE Spain
Aguililla 66 D4 Michoacán de Ocampo, SW Mexico
Agulhas Basin 85 D8 undersea feature SW Indian Ocean
Agulhas Plateau 83 D6 undersea feature SW Indian Ocean
Ahaggar 91 F2 high plateau region SE Algeria
Ahlen 110 B4 Nordrhein-Westfalen, W Germany
Ahmadābād 150 C4 var. Ahmedabad. Gujarāt, W India
Ahmadnagar 150 C5 var. Ahmednagar. Mahārāshtra, W India
Ahmedabad see Ahmadābād
Ahmednagar see Ahmadnagar
Ahuachapán 68 B3 Ahuachapán, W El Salvador
Ahvāz 136 C3 var. Ahwāz; prev. Nāsiri. Khūzestān, SW Iran
Ahvenanmaa see Åland
Ahwāz see Ahvāz
Aïdin see Aydın
Aígina 121 C6 var. Aíyina, Egina. Aígina, C Greece
Aígio 121 B5 var. Egio; prev. Aíyion. Dytikí Ellás, S Greece
Aiken 59 E2 South Carolina, SE USA
Ailigandí 69 G4 San Blas, NE Panama
Ailinglaplap Atoll 160 D2 var. Aelōnlaplap. Atoll Ralik Chain, S Marshall Islands
Ailuk Atoll 160 D1 var. Aelok. Atoll Ratak Chain, NE Marshall Islands
Ainaži 122 D3 Est. Heinaste, Ger. Hainasch. Limbaži, N Latvia
'Aïn Ben Tili 90 D1 Tiris Zemmour, N Mauritania
Aintab see Gaziantep
Aïoun el Atrous see 'Ayoûn el 'Atroûs
Aïoun el Atroûss see 'Ayoûn el 'Atroûs
Aiquile 77 F4 Cochabamba, C Bolivia
Aïr see Aïr, Massif de l'
Air du Azbine see Aïr, Massif de l'
Aïr, Massif de l' 91 G2 var. Aïr, Air du Azbine, Asben. Mountain range NC Niger
Aiud 124 B4 Ger. Strassburg, Hung. Nagyenyed; prev. Engeten. Alba, SW Romania
Aix see Aix-en-Provence
Aix-en-Provence 107 D6 var. Aix; anc. Aquae Sextiae. Bouches-du-Rhône, SE France
Aíyina see Aígina
Aíyion see Aígio
Aizkraukle 122 C4 Aizkraukle, S Latvia
Ajaccio 107 E7 Corse, France, C Mediterranean Sea
Ajaria 133 F2 autonomous republic SW Georgia
Aj Bogd Uul 142 D2 mountain SW Mongolia
Ajdābiyā 87 G2 var. Agedabia, Ajdābiyah. NE Libya
Ajdābiyah see Ajdābiyā
Ajjinena see El Geneina
Ajmer 150 D3 var. Ajmere. Rājasthān, N India
Ajmere see Ajmer
Ajo 64 A3 Arizona, SW USA
Akaba see Al 'Aqabah
Akamagaseki see Shimonoseki
Akasha 88 B3 Northern, N Sudan
Akchâr 90 C2 desert W Mauritania
Akhalts'ikhe 133 F2 SW Georgia
Akhisar 132 A3 Manisa, W Turkey
Akhmīm 88 B2 anc. Panopolis. C Egypt
Akhtubinsk 127 C7 Astrakhanskaya Oblast', SW Russian Federation
Akimiski Island 54 C3 island Northwest Territories, C Canada
Akinovka 125 F4 Zaporiz'ka Oblast', S Ukraine
Akita 146 D4 Akita, Honshū, C Japan
Akjoujt 90 C2 prev. Fort-Repoux. Inchiri, W Mauritania
Akkeshi 146 E2 Hokkaidō, NE Japan
Aklavik 52 D3 Northwest Territories, NW Canada
Akmola 130 C4 Kaz. Aqmola; prev. Akmolinsk, Tselinograd. Akmola, N Kazakhstan
Akpatok Island 55 E1 island Northwest Territories, E Canada
Akra Dhrepanon see Drépano, Ákra
Akra Kanestron see Palioúri, Ákra
Akron 56 D4 Ohio, N USA
Akrotiri see Akrotírion
Akrotírion 118 C5 var. Akrotiri. UK air base S Cyprus
Aksai Chin 140 B2 Chin. Aksayqin. Disputed region China/India
Aksaray 132 C4 Aksaray, C Turkey
Akşehir 132 B4 Konya, W Turkey
Aktau 130 A4 Kaz. Aqtaū; prev. Shevchenko. Mangistau, W Kazakhstan
Aktsyabrski 123 C7 Rus. Oktyabr'skiy; prev. Karpilovka. Homyel'skaya Voblasts', SE Belorussia
Aktyubinsk 130 B4 Kaz. Aqtöbe. Aktyubinsk, NW Kazakhstan
Akula 93 C5 Equateur, NW Congo (Zaire)
Akureyri 99 E4 Nordhurland Eystra, N Iceland
Akyab see Sittwe
Alabama 67 G1 off. State of Alabama; also known as Camellia State, Heart of Dixie, The Cotton State, Yellowhammer State. State S USA
Alabama River 58 C3 river Alabama, S USA
Alaca 132 C3 Çorum, N Turkey
Alagoas 79 G2 off. Estado de Alagoas. State E Brazil
Alajuela 69 E4 Alajuela, C Costa Rica
Alakanuk 52 C2 Alaska, USA
Al 'Alamayn see El 'Alamein
Al 'Amārah 136 C3 var. Amara. E Iraq
Alamo 63 D6 Nevada, W USA
Alamogordo 64 D3 New Mexico, SW USA
Alamosa 60 C5 Colorado, C USA
Åland 101 C6 var. Aland Islands, Fin. Ahvenanmaa. Island group SW Finland
Aland Islands see Åland
Aland Sea see Ålands Hav
Ålands Hav 101 C6 var. Aland Sea. Strait Baltic Sea/Gulf of Bothnia
Alanya 132 C4 Antalya, S Turkey
Alappuzha see Alleppey
Al 'Aqabah 135 B8 var. Akaba, Aqaba, 'Aqaba; anc. Aelana, Elath. Ma'ān, SW Jordan
Alaşehir 132 A4 Manisa, W Turkey
Al 'Ashārah 134 E3 var. Ashara. Dayr az Zawr, E Syria
Alaska 52 C3 off. State of Alaska; also known as Land of the Midnight Sun, The Last Frontier, Seward's Folly; prev. Russian America. State NW USA
Alaska, Gulf of 52 C4 var. Golfo de Alasca. Gulf Canada/USA
Alaska Peninsula 52 C3 peninsula Alaska, USA
Alaska Range 50 B2 mountain range Alaska, USA
Al-Asnam see Chlef
Al Awaynāt see Al 'Uwaynāt
Al 'Aynā 135 B7 Al Karak, W Jordan
Alazeya 131 G2 river NE Russian Federation
Al Bāb 134 B2 Ḥalab, N Syria
Albacete 109 E3 Castilla-La Mancha, C Spain
Al Baghdādī 136 B3 var. Khān al Baghdādī. SW Iraq
Al Bāha see Al Bāḥah
Al Bāḥah 137 B5 var. Al Bāha. Al Bāḥah, SW Saudi Arabia
Al Baḥr al Mayyit see Dead Sea
Alba Iulia 124 B4 Ger. Weissenburg, Hung. Gyulafehérvár; prev. Bălgrad, Karlsburg, Károly-Fehérvár. Alba, W Romania
Albania 117 C7 off. Republic of Albania, Alb. Republika e Shqipërisë, Shqipëria; prev. People's Socialist Republic of Albania. Country SE Europe
Albany 54 C3 river Ontario, S Canada
Albany 57 F3 state capital New York, NE USA
Albany 58 D3 Georgia, SE USA
Albany 62 B3 Oregon, NW USA
Albany 163 B7 Western Australia
Al Bāridah 134 C4 var. Bāridah. Ḥimṣ, C Syria
Al Başrah 136 C3 Eng. Basra; hist. Busra, Bussora. SE Iraq
Al Batrūn see Batroûn
Al Bayḍā' 87 G2 var. Beida. NE Libya
Albemarle Island see Isabela, Isla
Albemarle Sound 59 G1 inlet W Atlantic Ocean
Albergaria-a-Velha 108 B2 Aveiro, N Portugal
Albert 106 C3 Somme, N France
Alberta 53 E4 province SW Canada
Albert Edward Nyanza see Edward, Lake
Albert, Lake 89 B6 var. Albert Nyanza, Lac Mobutu Sese Seko. Lake Uganda/Congo (Zaire)
Albert Lea 61 F3 Minnesota, N USA
Albert Nyanza see Albert, Lake
Albi 107 C6 anc. Albiga. Tarn, S France
Ålborg 96 D3 var. Aalborg, Ålborg-Nørresundby; anc. Alburgum. Nordjylland, N Denmark
Ålborg-Nørresundby see Ålborg
Alborz, Reshteh-ye Kūhhā-ye 136 C2 Eng. Elburz Mountains. Mountain range N Iran
Albuquerque 64 D2 New Mexico, SW USA
Al Burayqah see Marsá al Burayqah
Alburgum see Ålborg
Albury 165 C7 New South Wales, SE Australia
Alcácer do Sal 108 B4 Setúbal, W Portugal
Alcalá de Henares 109 E3 Ar. Alkal'a; anc. Complutum. Madrid, C Spain
Alcamo 113 C7 Sicilia, Italy, C Mediterranean Sea
Alcañiz 109 F2 Aragón, NE Spain
Alcántara, Embalse de 108 C3 reservoir W Spain
Alcaudete 108 D4 Andalucía, S Spain
Alcázar see Ksar-el-Kebir
Alcoi see Alcoy
Alcoy 109 F4 var. Alcoi. País Valenciano, E Spain
Aldabra Group 95 G2 island group SW Seychelles
Aldan 131 F3 river NE Russian Federation
al Dar al Baida see Rabat
Alderney 106 A2 island Channel Islands
Aleg 90 C3 Brakna, SW Mauritania
Aleksandropol' see Gyumri
Aleksin 127 B5 Tul'skaya Oblast', W Russian Federation
Aleksinac 116 E4 Serbia, SE Yugoslavia
Alençon 106 B3 Orne, N France
Alenquer 79 E2 Pará, NE Brazil
Aleppo see Ḥalab
Alert 53 F1 Ellesmere Island, Northwest Territories, N Canada
Alès 107 C6 prev. Alais. Gard, S France
Aleşd 124 B3 Hung. Élesd. Bihor, SW Romania
Alessandria 112 B2 Fr. Alexandrie. Piemonte, N Italy
Ålesund 101 A5 Møre og Romsdal, S Norway
Aleutian Basin 129 G3 undersea feature Bering Sea
Aleutian Islands 52 A3 island group Alaska, USA
Aleutian Range 50 A2 mountain range Alaska, USA
Aleutian Trench 129 H3 undersea feature S Bering Sea
Alexander Archipelago 52 D4 island group Alaska, USA
Alexander City 58 D2 Alabama, S USA
Alexander Island 170 A3 island Antarctica
Alexandra 167 B7 Otago, South Island, NZ
Alexándreia 120 B4 var. Alexándria. Kentrikí Makedonía, N Greece
Alexandria 88 B1 Ar. Al Iskandarīyah. N Egypt
Alexándria see Alexándreia
Alexandria 58 B3 Louisiana, S USA
Alexandria 61 F2 Minnesota, N USA

Alexandria – Aoukâr

Alexandria 124 C5 Teleorman, S Romania
Alexandroúpoli 120 D3 var. Alexandroupolis, Turk. Dedeagaç, Dedeagach. Anatolikí Makedonía kai Thráki, NE Greece
Alexandroúpolis see Alexandroúpoli
Al Fāshir see El Fasher
Alfatar 120 E1 Razgradska Oblast, NE Bulgaria
Alfeiós 121 B6 prev. Alfiós, anc. Alpheius, Alpheus. River S Greece
Alföld see Great Hungarian Plain
Alga 130 B4 Kaz. Algha. Aktyubinsk, NW Kazakhstan
Algarve 108 B4 cultural region S Portugal
Algeciras 108 C5 Andalucía, SW Spain
Algemesí 109 F3 País Valenciano, E Spain
Al-Genain see El Geneina
Alger 87 E1 var. Algiers, El Djazaïr, Al Jazair. Country capital (Algeria) N Algeria
Algeria 86 C3 off. Democratic and Popular Republic of Algeria. Country N Africa
Algerian Basin 96 C5 var. Balearic Plain undersea feature W Mediterranean Sea
Al Ghābah 137 E5 var. Ghaba. C Oman
Alghero 113 A5 Sardegna, Italy, C Mediterranean Sea
Al Ghurdaqah see Hurghada
Algiers see Alger
Al Golea see El Goléa
Algona 61 F3 Iowa, C USA
Al Ḥajār al Gharbī 137 D5 mountain range N Oman
Al Ḥasakah 134 D2 var. Al Hasijah, El Haseke, Fr. Hassetché. Al Ḥasakah, NE Syria
Al Hasijah see Al Ḥasakah
Al Ḥillah 136 B3 var. Hilla. C Iraq
Al Ḥisā 135 B7 Aṭ Ṭafīlah, W Jordan
Al Ḥudaydah 137 B6 Eng. Hodeida. W Yemen
Al Hufūf 136 C4 var. Hofuf. Ash Sharqīyah, NE Saudi Arabia
Aliákmonas 120 B4 prev. Aliákmon, anc. Haliacmon. River N Greece
Alíartos 121 C5 Stereá Ellás, C Greece
Alicante 109 F4 Cat. Alacant;. País Valenciano, SE Spain
Alice 65 G5 Texas, SW USA
Alice Springs 164 A4 Northern Territory, C Australia
Aliki see Alykí
Alima 93 B6 river C Congo
Alindao 92 C4 Basse-Kotto, S Central African Republic
Aliquippa 56 D4 Pennsylvania, NE USA
Alistráti 120 C3 Kentrikí Makedonía, NE Greece
Alivéri 121 C5 var. Alivérion. Évvoia, C Greece
Alivérion see Alivéri
Al Jabal al Akhḍar 87 G2 mountain range NE Libya
Al Jabal ash Sharqī see Anti-Lebanon
Al Jafr 135 B7 Ma'ān, S Jordan
Al Jaghbūb 87 H3 NE Libya
Al Jahrā' 136 C4 var. Al Jahrah, Jahra. C Kuwait
Al Jahrah see Al Jahrā'
Al Jawf 136 B4 var. Jauf. Al Jawf, NW Saudi Arabia
Al Jazair see Alger
Al Jazīrah 134 E2 physical region Iraq/Syria
Al Jīzah see El Gîza
Al Junaynah see El Geneina
Al Karak 135 B7 var. El Kerak, Karak, Kerak; anc. Kir Moab, Kir of Moab. Al Karak, W Jordan
Al-Kasr al-Kebir see Ksar-el-Kebir
Al Khalīl see Hebron
Al Khārijah see El Khârga
Al Khufrah 87 H4 SE Libya
Al Khums 87 F2 var. Homs, Khoms, Khums. NW Libya
Alkmaar 102 C2 Noord-Holland, NW Netherlands
Al Kūt 136 C3 var. Kūt al 'Amārah, Kut al Imara. E Iraq
Al-Kuwait see Al Kuwayt
Al Kuwayt 136 C4 var. Al-Kuwait, Eng. Kuwait, Kuwait City; prev. Qurein. Country capital (Kuwait) E Kuwait
Al Lādhiqīyah 134 A3 Eng. Latakia, Fr. Lattaquié; anc. Laodicea, Laodicea ad Mare. Al Lādhiqīyah, W Syria
Allahābād 151 E3 Uttar Pradesh, N India
Allanmyo 152 B4 Magwe, C Burma
Allegheny Plateau 57 E3 mountain range New York/Pennsylvania, NE USA
Allentown 57 F4 Pennsylvania, NE USA
Alleppey 148 C3 var. Alappuzha; prev. Alleppi. Kerala, SW India
Alleppi see Alleppey
Alliance 60 D3 Nebraska, C USA
Al Līth 137 B5 Makkah, SW Saudi Arabia
Alma-Ata see Almaty
Almada 108 B4 Setúbal, W Portugal
Al Madīnah 137 A5 Eng. Medina. Al Madīnah, W Saudi Arabia
Al Mafraq 135 B6 var. Mafraq. Al Mafraq, N Jordan
Al Mahdīyah see Mahdia
Al Mahrah 137 C6 mountain range E Yemen
Al Majma'ah 136 B4 Ar Riyāḍ, C Saudi Arabia
Al Mālikīyah 134 E1 Al Ḥasakah, NE Syria
Al Manāmah 136 C4 Eng. Manama. Country capital (Bahrain) N Bahrain
Al Manāṣif 134 E3 mountain range E Syria
Almansa 109 F4 Castilla-La Mancha, C Spain
Al Marj 87 G2 var. Barka, It. Barce. NE Libya
Almaty 130 C5 var. Alma-Ata. Country capital (Kazakhstan) Almaty, SE Kazakhstan
Al Mawṣil 136 B2 Eng. Mosul. N Iraq
Al Mayādīn 134 D3 var. Mayadin, Fr. Meyadine. Dayr az Zawr, E Syria
Al Mazra' see Al Mazra'ah
Al Mazra'ah 135 B6 var. Al Mazra', Mazra'a. Al Karak, W Jordan
Almelo 102 E3 Overijssel, E Netherlands
Almendra, Embalse de 108 C2 reservoir Castilla-León, NW Spain
Almendralejo 108 C4 Extremadura, W Spain
Almere 102 C3 var. Almere-stad. Flevoland, C Netherlands
Almere-stad see Almere
Almería 109 E5 Ar. Al-Mariyya; anc. Unci, Lat. Portus Magnus. Andalucía, S Spain
Al'met'yevsk 127 D5 Respublika Tatarstan, W Russian Federation
Al Mīnā' see El Mina
Al Minyā see El Minya
Almirante 69 E4 Bocas del Toro, NW Panama
Al Mudawwarah 135 B8 Ma'ān, SW Jordan
Al Mukallā 137 C6 var. Mukalla. SE Yemen
Al Obayyid see El Obeid
Alofi 161 F4 dependent territory capital (Niue) W Niue
Aloja 122 D3 Limbaži, N Latvia
Alónnisos 121 C5 island Vóreioi Sporádes, Greece, Aegean Sea
Álora 108 D5 Andalucía, S Spain
Alor, Kepulauan 155 E5 island group E Indonesia
Al Oued see El Oued
Alpen see Alps
Alpena 56 D2 Michigan, N USA
Alpes see Alps
Alpha Cordillera 171 B3 var. Alpha Ridge. Undersea feature Arctic Ocean
Alpha Ridge see Alpha Cordillera
Alphen see Alphen aan den Rijn
Alphen aan den Rijn 102 C3 var. Alphen. Zuid-Holland, C Netherlands
Alpi see Alps
Alpine 65 E4 Texas, SW USA
Alpi Transilvaniei see Carpaţii Meridionali
Alps 118 C1 Fr. Alpes, Ger. Alpen, It. Alpi. Mountain range C Europe
Al Qaḍārif see Gedaref
Al Qāmishlī 134 E1 var. Kamishli, Qamishly. Al Ḥasakah, NE Syria
Al Qaṣrayn see Kasserine
Al Qayrawān see Kairouan
Al-Qsar see Ksar-el-Kebir
Al Qubayyāt see Qoubaïyât
Al Qunayṭirah 135 B5 var. El Kuneitra, El Quneitra, Kuneitra, Qunaytra. Al Qunayṭirah, SW Syria
Al Quṣayr 134 B4 var. El Quseir, Quṣayr, Fr. Kousseir. Ḥimṣ, W Syria
Al Quwayrah 135 B8 var. El Quweira. Ma'ān, SW Jordan
Alsace 106 E3 cultural region NE France
Alsdorf 110 A4 Nordrhein-Westfalen, W Germany
Alt see Olt
Alta 100 D2 Fin. Alattio. Finnmark, N Norway
Altai see Altai Mountains
Altai Mountains 142 C2 var. Altai, Chin. Altay Shan, Rus. Altay. Mountain range Asia/Europe
Altamaha River 59 E3 river Georgia, SE USA
Altamira 79 E2 Pará, NE Brazil
Altamura 113 E5 anc. Lupatia. Puglia, SE Italy
Altar, Desierto de 66 A1 var. Sonoran Desert. Desert Mexico/USA see also Sonoran Desert
Altay 142 C2 Chin. A-le-t'ai, Mong. Sharasume; prev. Ch'eng-hua, Chenghwa. Xinjiang Uygur Zizhiqu, NW China
Altay see Altai Mountains
Altay 142 D2 Govĭ-Altay, W Mongolia
Altay Shan see Altai Mountains
Altin Köprü 136 B3 var. Altun Kupri. N Iraq
Altiplano 77 F4 physical region W South America
Alton 56 B5 Illinois, N USA
Alton 56 B4 Missouri, C USA
Altoona 57 E4 Pennsylvania, NE USA
Alto Paraná see Paraná
Altun Kupri see Altin Köprü
Altun Shan 142 C3 var. Altyn Tagh. Mountain range NW China
Altus 65 F2 Oklahoma, C USA
Altyn Tagh see Altun Shan
Al Ubayyiḍ see El Obeid
Alūksne 122 D3 Ger. Marienburg. Alūksne, NE Latvia
Al 'Ulā 136 A4 Al Madīnah, NW Saudi Arabia
Al 'Umarī 135 C6 'Ammān, E Jordan
Alupka 125 F5 Respublika Krym, S Ukraine
Alushta 125 F5 Respublika Krym, S Ukraine
Al 'Uwaynāt 87 F4 var. Al Awaynāt. SW Libya
Alva 65 F1 Oklahoma, C USA
Alvarado 67 F4 Veracruz-Llave, E Mexico
Alvin 65 H4 Texas, SW USA
Al Wajh 136 A4 Tabūk, NW Saudi Arabia
Alwar 150 D3 Rājasthān, N India
Al Wari'ah 136 C4 Ash Sharqīyah, N Saudi Arabia
Alykí 120 C4 var. Aliki. Thásos, N Greece
Alytus 123 B5 Pol. Olita. Alytus, S Lithuania
Alzette 103 D8 river S Luxembourg
Amadeus, Lake 163 D5 seasonal lake Northern Territory, C Australia
Amadi 89 B5 Western Equatoria, SW Sudan
Amadjuak Lake 53 G3 lake Baffin Island, Northwest Territories, N Canada
Amakusa-nada 147 A7 gulf Kyūshū, SW Japan
Åmål 101 B6 Älvsborg, S Sweden
Amami-guntō 146 A3 island group SW Japan
Amami-Ō-shima 146 A3 island S Japan
Amantea 113 D6 Calabria, SW Italy
Amapá 79 E1 Amapá, NE Brazil
Amara see Al 'Amārah
Amarapura 152 B3 Mandalay, C Burma
Amarillo 65 E2 Texas, SW USA
Amay 103 C6 Liège, E Belgium
Amazon 79 E1 Sp. Amazonas. River Brazil/Peru
Amazon Basin 78 D2 basin N South America
Amazon, Mouths of the 79 F1 delta NE Brazil
Ambam 93 B5 Sud, S Cameroon
Ambanja 95 G2 Antsirañana, N Madagascar
Ambarchik 131 G2 Respublika Sakha (Yakutiya), NE Russian Federation
Ambato 76 B1 Tungurahua, C Ecuador
Ambérieu-en-Bugey 107 D5 Ain, E France
Amboasary 95 F4 Toliara, S Madagascar
Ambon 155 F4 prev. Amboina, Amboyna. Pulau Ambon, E Indonesia
Ambositra 95 G3 Fianarantsoa, SE Madagascar
Ambrim see Ambrym
Ambriz 94 A1 Bengo, NW Angola
Ambrym 160 D4 var. Ambrim. Island C Vanuatu
Amchitka Island 52 A2 island Aleutian Islands, Alaska, USA
Amdo 142 C5 Xizang Zizhiqu, W China
Ameland 102 D1 Fris. It Amelân. Island Waddeneilanden, N Netherlands
America-Antarctica Ridge 83 C7 undersea feature S Atlantic Ocean
American Falls Reservoir 62 E4 reservoir Idaho, NW USA
American Samoa 161 E4 US unincorporated territory W Polynesia
Amersfoort 102 D3 Utrecht, C Netherlands
Ames 61 F3 Iowa, C USA
Amfilochía 121 A5 var. Amfilokhía. Dytikí Ellás, C Greece
Amfilokhía see Amfilochía
Amga 131 F3 river NE Russian Federation
Amherst 55 F4 Nova Scotia, SE Canada
Amida see Diyarbakır
Amiens 106 C3 anc. Ambianum, Samarobriva. Somme, N France
Amíndaion see Amýntaio
Amindeo see Amýntaio
Amīndīvi Islands 148 A2 island group Lakshadweep, India, N Indian Ocean
Amirante Islands 95 G1 var. Amirantes Group. Island group C Seychelles
Amirantes Group see Amirante Islands
Amistad Reservoir 65 F4 var. Presa de la Amistad. Reservoir Mexico/USA
'Ammān 135 B6 var. Amman; anc. Philadelphia, Bibl. Rabbah Ammon, Rabbath Ammon. Country capital (Jordan) 'Ammān, NW Jordan
Amman see 'Ammān
Ammassalik 98 D4 var. Angmagssalik. S Greenland
Ammóchostos 118 D5 var. Famagusta, Gazimağusa. E Cyprus
Āmol 136 D2 var. Amul. Māzandarān, N Iran
Amorgós 121 D6 island Kykládes, Greece, Aegean Sea
Amorgós 121 D6 Amorgós, Kykládes, Greece, Aegean Sea
Amos 54 D4 Québec, SE Canada
Amourj 90 D3 Hodh ech Chargui, SE Mauritania
Amoy see Xiamen
Ampato, Nevado 77 E4 mountain S Peru
Amposta 109 F2 Cataluña, NE Spain
Amrāvati 150 D4 prev. Amraoti. Mahārāshtra, C India
Amritsar 150 D2 Punjab, N India
Amstelveen 102 C3 Noord-Holland, C Netherlands
Amsterdam 102 C3 country capital (Netherlands) Noord-Holland, C Netherlands
Amsterdam Island 157 C6 island NE French Southern and Antarctic Territories
Am Timan 92 C3 Salamat, SE Chad
Amu Darya 138 D2 Rus. Amudar'ya, Taj. Dar"yoi Amu, Turkm. Amyderya, Uzb. Amudaryo; anc. Oxus. River C Asia
Amu-Dar'ya 139 E3 Lebapskiy Velayat, NE Turkmenistan
Amul see Āmol
Amund Ringnes Island 53 F2 island Northwest Territories, N Canada
Amundsen Basin see Fram Basin
Amundsen Gulf 53 E2 gulf Northwest Territories, N Canada
Amundsen Plain 170 A4 undersea feature S Pacific Ocean
Amundsen-Scott 170 B3 US research station Antarctica
Amundsen Sea 170 A4 sea S Pacific Ocean
Amuntai 154 D4 prev. Amoentai. Borneo, C Indonesia
Amur 131 G4 Chin. Heilong Jiang. River China/Russian Federation
Amvrosiyivka 125 H3 Rus. Amvrosiyevka. Donets'ka Oblast', SE Ukraine
Amýntaio 120 B4 var. Amindeo; prev. Amíndaion. Dytikí Makedonía, N Greece
Anabar 131 E2 river NE Russian Federation
An Abhainn Mhór see Blackwater
Anaco 75 E2 Anzoátegui, NE Venezuela
Anaconda 60 B2 Montana, NW USA
Anacortes 62 B1 Washington, NW USA
Anadolu Dağları see Doğu Karadeniz Dağları
Anadyr' 131 G1 river NE Russian Federation
Anadyr' 131 H1 Chukotskiy Avtonomnyy Okrug, NE Russian Federation
Anadyr, Gulf of see Anadyrskiy Zaliv
Anadyrskiy Zaliv 131 H1 Eng. Gulf of Anadyr. Gulf NE Russian Federation
Anáfi 121 D7 anc. Anaphe. Island Kykládes, Greece, Aegean Sea
'Ānah see 'Annah
Anaheim 62 E2 California, W USA
Anaiza see 'Unayzah
Analalava 95 G2 Mahajanga, NW Madagascar
Anamur 132 C5 İçel, S Turkey
Anantapur 148 C2 Andhra Pradesh, S India
Anápolis 79 F3 Goiás, C Brazil
Anār 136 D3 Kermān, C Iran
Anatolia 132 C4 plateau C Turkey
Anatom 160 D5 var. Aneityum; prev. Kéamu. Island S Vanuatu
Añatuya 80 C3 Santiago del Estero, N Argentina
An Bhearú see Barrow
Anchorage 52 C3 Alaska, USA
Ancona 112 C3 Marche, C Italy
Ancud 81 B6 prev. San Carlos de Ancud. Los Lagos, S Chile
Åndalsnes 101 A5 Møre og Romsdal, S Norway
Andalucía 108 D4 cultural region S Spain
Andalusia 58 C3 Alabama, S USA
Andaman Islands 140 B4 island group India, NE Indian Ocean
Andaman Sea 140 C4 sea NE Indian Ocean
Andenne 103 C6 Namur, SE Belgium
Anderlues 103 B7 Hainaut, S Belgium
Anderson 56 C4 Indiana, N USA
Andes 80 B3 mountain range W South America
Andhra Pradesh 151 E5 state E India
Andijon 139 F2 Rus. Andizhan. Andijon Wiloyati, E Uzbekistan
Andikíthira see Antikýthira
Andipaxi see Antípaxoi
Andípsara see Antípsara
Ándissa see Ántissa
Andkhvoy 138 D3 Fāryāb, N Afghanistan
Andorra 107 A7 off. Principality of Andorra, Cat. Valls d'Andorra, Fr. Vallée d'Andorre. Country SW Europe
Andorra see Andorra la Vella
Andorra la Vella 107 A8 var. Andorra, Fr. Andorre la Vielle, Sp. Andorra la Vieja. Country capital (Andorra) C Andorra
Andorra la Vieja see Andorra la Vella
Andorre la Vielle see Andorra la Vella
Andover 105 D7 S England, UK
Andøya 100 C2 island C Norway
Andreanof Islands 52 A3 island group Aleutian Islands, Alaska, USA
Andrews 65 E3 Texas, SW USA
Andrew Tablemount 156 A4 var. Gora Andryu. Undersea feature W Indian Ocean
Andria 113 D5 Puglia, SE Italy
An Droichead Nua see Newbridge
Ándros 121 C6 island Kykládes, Greece, Aegean Sea
Ándros 121 D6 Ándros, Kykládes, Greece, Aegean Sea
Andros Island 70 B2 island NW Bahamas
Andros Town 70 C1 Andros Island, NW Bahamas
Aneityum see Anatom
Änewetak see Enewetak Atoll
Angara 131 E4 river C Russian Federation
Angarsk 131 E4 Irkutskaya Oblast', S Russian Federation
Ånge 101 C5 Västernorrland, C Sweden
Ángel de la Guarda, Isla 66 B2 island NW Mexico
Angeles 155 E1 off. Angeles City. Luzon, N Philippines
Angel Falls see Ángel, Salto
Ángel, Salto 75 E3 Eng. Angel Falls. Waterfall E Venezuela
Ångermanälven 100 C4 river N Sweden
Angermünde 110 D3 Brandenburg, NE Germany
Angers 106 B4 anc. Juliomagus. Maine-et-Loire, NW France
Anglesey 105 C5 island NW Wales, UK
Anglet 107 A6 Pyrénées-Atlantiques, SW France
Angleton 65 H4 Texas, SW USA
Angmagssalik see Ammassalik
Ang Nam Ngum 152 C4 lake C Laos
Angola 94 B2 off. Republic of Angola; prev. People's Republic of Angola, Portuguese West Africa. Country SW Africa
Angola Basin 85 B5 undersea feature E Atlantic Ocean
Angostura, Presa de la 67 G5 reservoir SE Mexico
Angoulême 107 B5 anc. Iculisma. Charente, W France
Angoumois 107 B5 cultural region W France
Angren 139 F2 Toshkent Wiloyati, E Uzbekistan
Anguilla 71 G3 UK dependent territory E West Indies
Anguilla Cays 70 B2 islets SW Bahamas
Anhui 144 C5 var. Anhui Sheng, Anhwei, Wan. Admin. region province E China
Anhui Sheng see Anhui
Anhwei see Anhui
Anina 124 A4 Ger. Steierdorf, Hung. Stájerlakanina; prev. Staierdorf-Anina, Steierdorf-Anina, Steyerlak-Anina. Caraş-Severin, SW Romania
Anjou 106 B4 cultural region NW France
Anjouan 95 F2 var. Nzwani, Johanna Island. Island SE Comoros
Ankara 132 C3 prev. Angora, anc. Ancyra. Country capital (Turkey) Ankara, C Turkey
Ankeny 61 F3 Iowa, C USA
Anklam 110 D2 Mecklenburg-Vorpommern, NE Germany
Anykščiai 122 C4 Anykščiai, E Lithuania
An Longfort see Longford
An Mhuir Cheilteach see Celtic Sea
Annaba 87 E1 prev. Bône. NE Algeria
An Nafūd 136 B4 desert NW Saudi Arabia
'Annah 136 B3 var. 'Ānah. NW Iraq
An Najaf 136 B3 var. Najaf. S Iraq
Annamitique, Chaîne 152 D4 mountain range C Laos
Annapolis 57 F4 state capital Maryland, NE USA
Annapurna 151 E3 mountain C Nepal
An Nāqūrah see En Nâqoûra
Ann Arbor 56 C3 Michigan, N USA
An Nāṣirīyah 136 C3 var. Nasiriya. SE Iraq
Annecy 107 D5 anc. Anneciacum. Haute-Savoie, E France
An Nīl al Azraq see Blue Nile
Anniston 58 D2 Alabama, S USA
Annotto Bay 70 B4 C Jamaica
An Ómaigh see Omagh
Anqing 144 D5 Anhui, E China
Anse La Raye 71 F1 NW Saint Lucia
Anshun 144 B6 Guizhou, S China
Ansongo 91 E3 Gao, E Mali
An Srath Bán see Strabane
Antakya 132 D4 anc. Antioch, Antiochia. Hatay, S Turkey
Antalaha 95 G2 Antsirañana, NE Madagascar
Antalya 132 B4 prev. Adalia, anc. Attaleia, Bibl. Attalia. Antalya, SW Turkey
Antalya, Gulf of see Antalya Körfezi
Antalya Körfezi 132 B4 var. Gulf of Adalia, Eng. Gulf of Antalya. Gulf SW Turkey
Antananarivo 95 G3 prev. Tananarive. Country capital (Madagascar) Antananarivo, C Madagascar
Antarctica 170 B3 continent
Antarctic Peninsula 170 A2 peninsula Antarctica
Antep see Gaziantep
Antequera 108 D5 anc. Anticaria, Antiquaria. Andalucía, S Spain
Antequera see Oaxaca
Antibes 107 D6 anc. Antipolis. Alpes-Maritimes, SE France
Anticosti, Île d' 55 F3 Eng. Anticosti Island. Island Québec, E Canada
Antigua 71 G3 island S Antigua and Barbuda, Leeward Islands
Antigua and Barbuda 71 G3 country E West Indies
Antikýthira 121 B7 var. Andikíthira. Island S Greece
Anti-Lebanon 134 B4 var. Jebel esh Sharqi, Ar. Al Jabal ash Sharqī, Fr. Anti-Liban. Mountain range Lebanon/Syria
Anti-Liban see Anti-Lebanon
Antípaxoi 121 A5 var. Andipaxi. Island Iónioi Nísoi, Greece, C Mediterranean Sea
Antipodes Islands 158 D5 island group S NZ
Antípsara 121 D5 var. Andípsara. Island E Greece
Ántissa 121 D5 var. Ándissa. Lésvos, E Greece
An tIúr see Newry
Antofagasta 80 B2 Antofagasta, N Chile
Antony 106 E2 Hauts-de-Seine, N France
Antserana see Antsirañana
An tSionainn see Shannon
Antsirañana 95 G2 var. Antserana; prev. Antsirane, Diégo-Suarez. Antsirañana, N Madagascar
Antsirane see Antsirañana
Antsohihy 95 G2 Mahajanga, NW Madagascar
An-tung see Dandong
Antwerp see Antwerpen
Antwerpen 103 C5 Eng. Antwerp, Fr. Anvers. Antwerpen, N Belgium
Anuradhapura 148 D3 North Central Province, C Sri Lanka
Anyang 144 C4 Henan, C China
A'nyêmaqên Shan 142 D4 mountain range C China
Anzio 113 C5 Lazio, C Italy
Aomori 146 D3 Aomori, Honshū, C Japan
Aóos see Vjosës, Lumi i
Aosta 112 A1 anc. Augusta Praetoria. Valle d'Aosta, NW Italy
Ao Thai see Thailand, Gulf of
Aoukâr 90 D3 var. Aouker. Plateau C Mauritania

Baardheere – Beatrice

Baardheere *89 D6 var.* Bardere, *It.* Bardera. Gedo, SW Somalia
Baarle-Hertog *103 C5* Antwerpen, N Belgium
Baarn *102 C3* Utrecht, C Netherlands
Babadag *124 D5* Tulcea, SE Romania
Babahoyo *76 B2 prev.* Bodegas. Los Ríos, C Ecuador
Bābā, Kūh-e *139 E4 mountain range* C Afghanistan
Babayevo *126 B4* Vologodskaya Oblast', NW Russian Federation
Babeldaob *160 A1 var.* Babeldaop, Babelthuap. *Island* N Palau
Babeldaop *see* Babeldaob
Bab el Mandeb *137 B7 strait* Gulf of Aden/Red Sea
Babelthuap *see* Babeldaob
Bá Bheanntraí *see* Bantry Bay
Babruysk *123 D7 Rus.* Bobruysk. Mahilyowskaya Voblasts', E Belorussia
Babuyan Channel *155 E1 channel* N Philippines
Babuyan Island *155 E1 island* N Philippines
Bacabal *79 F2* Maranhão, E Brazil
Bacău *124 C4 Hung.* Bákó. Bacău, NE Romania
Băc Giang *152 D3* Ha Băc, N Vietnam
Bacheykava *123 D5 Rus.* Bocheykovo. Vitsyebskaya Voblasts', N Belorussia
Back *53 F3 river* Northwest Territories, N Canada
Bačka Palanka *116 D3 prev.* Palanka. Serbia, NW Yugoslavia
Bačka Topola *116 D3 Hung.* Topolya; prev. *Hung.* Bácstopolya. Serbia, N Yugoslavia
Bac Liêu *153 D6 var.* Vinh Loi. Minh Hai, S Vietnam
Bacolod *141 E4 off.* Bacolod City. Negros, C Philippines
Bacolod City *see* Bacolod
Bácsszenttamás *see* Srbobran
Badajoz *108 C4 anc.* Pax Augusta. Extremadura, W Spain
Baden-Baden *111 B6 anc.* Aurelia Aquensis. Baden-Württemberg, SW Germany
Bad Freienwalde *110 D3* Brandenburg, NE Germany
Bad Hersfeld *110 B4* Hessen, C Germany
Bad Homburg *see* Bad Homburg vor der Höhe
Bad Homburg vor der Höhe *111 B5 var.* Bad Homburg. Hessen, W Germany
Bá Dhún na nGall *see* Donegal Bay
Bad Ischl *111 D7* Oberösterreich, N Austria
Bad Krozingen *111 A6* Baden-Württemberg, SW Germany
Badlands *60 D2 physical region* North Dakota, N USA
Badu Island *164 C1 island* Queensland, NE Australia
Bad Vöslau *111 E6* Niederösterreich, NE Austria
Baetic Cordillera *see* Béticos, Sistemas
Baetic Mountains *see* Béticos, Sistemas
Bafatá *90 C4* C Guinea-Bissau
Baffin Bay *53 G2 bay* Canada/Greenland
Baffin Island *53 G2 island* Northwest Territories, NE Canada
Bafing *90 C3 headstream* W Africa
Bafoussam *92 A4* Ouest, W Cameroon
Bafra *132 D2* Samsun, N Turkey
Bāft *136 D4* Kermān, S Iran
Bagaces *68 D4* Guanacaste, NW Costa Rica
Bagdad *see* Baghdād
Bagé *79 E5* Rio Grande do Sul, S Brazil
Baghdād *136 B3 var.* Bagdad, *Eng.* Baghdad. *Country capital* (Iraq) C Iraq
Baghlān *139 E3* Baghlān, NE Afghanistan
Bago *see* Pegu
Bagoé *90 D4 river* Ivory Coast/Mali
Bagrationovsk *122 A4 Ger.* Preussisch Eylau. Kaliningradskaya Oblast', W Russian Federation
Bagrax Hu *see* Bosten Hu
Baguio *155 E1 off.* Baguio City. Luzon, N Philippines
Bagzane, Monts *91 F3 mountain* N Niger
Bahama Islands *see* Bahamas
Bahamas *70 C2 off.* Commonwealth of the Bahamas. *Country* N West Indies
Bahamas *51 D6 var.* Bahama Islands. *Island group* N West Indies
Bahāwalpur *150 C2* Punjab, E Pakistan
Bahia *79 F3 off.* Estado da Bahia. *State* E Brazil
Bahía Blanca *81 C5* Buenos Aires, E Argentina
Bahía, Islas de la *68 C1 Eng.* Bay Islands. *Island group* N Honduras
Bahir Dar *88 C4 var.* Bahr Dar, Bahrdar Giyorgis. NW Ethiopia
Bahraich *151 E3* Uttar Pradesh, N India
Bahrain *136 C4 off.* State of Bahrain, Dawlat al Bahrayn, *Ar.* Al Baḩrayn; *prev.* Bahrein, *anc.* Tylos or Tyros. *Country* SW Asia
Baḩr al Milḩ *see* Razāzah, Buḩayrat ar
Baḩrat Lūt *see* Dead Sea
Bahrat Tabariya *see* Tiberias, Lake
Bahr Dar *see* Bahir Dar
Bahrdar Giyorgis *see* Bahir Dar
Bahr el Azraq *see* Blue Nile
Bahr el Jebel *see* White Nile
Bahret Lut *see* Dead Sea
Bahr Tabariya, Sea of *see* Tiberias, Lake
Bahushewsk *123 E6 Rus.* Bogushëvsk. Vitsyebskaya Voblasts', NE Belorussia
Baia Mare *124 B3 Ger.* Frauenbach, *Hung.* Nagybánya; *prev.* Neustadt. Maramureș, NW Romania
Baia Sprie *124 B3 Ger.* Mittelstadt, *Hung.* Felsőbánya. Maramureș, NW Romania
Baïbokoum *92 B4* Logone-Oriental, SW Chad
Baidoa *see* Baydhabo
Baie-Comeau *55 E3* Québec, SE Canada
Baikal, Lake *see* Baykal, Ozero
Baile Átha Luain *see* Athlone
Bailén *108 D4* Andalucía, S Spain
Baile na Mainistreach *see* Newtownabbey
Băilești *124 B5* Dolj, SW Romania
Ba Illi *92 B3* Chari-Baguirmi, SW Chad
Bainbridge *58 D3* Georgia, SE USA
Bā'ir *see* Bāyir
Baireuth *see* Bayreuth
Bairiki *160 D2 country capital* (Kiribati) Tarawa, NW Kiribati
Bairnsdale *165 C7* Victoria, SE Australia
Baishan *145 E3 prev.* Hunjiang. Jilin, NE China
Baiyin *144 B4* Gansu, C China
Baja *115 C7* Bács-Kiskun, S Hungary
Baja California *64 A4 Eng.* Lower California. *Peninsula* NW Mexico
Baja California *66 B2 state* NW Mexico
Bajo Boquete *see* Boquete
Bajram Curri *117 D5* Kukës, N Albania
Bakala *92 C4* Ouaka, C Central African Republic
Bakan *see* Shimonoseki
Baker and Howland Islands *161 E2 US unincorporated territory* W Polynesia
Baker Lake *53 F3* Northwest Territories, N Canada
Bakersfield *63 C7* California, W USA
Bakharden *138 C3 Turkm.* Bäherden; *prev.* Bakherden. Akhalskiy Velayat, C Turkmenistan
Bakhchysaray *125 F5 Rus.* Bakhchisaray. Respublika Krym, S Ukraine
Bakhmach *125 F1* Chernihivs'ka Oblast', N Ukraine
Bākhtarān *136 C3 prev.* Kermānshāh, Qahremānshahr. Kermānshāhān, W Iran
Bakı *133 H2 Eng.* Baku. *Country capital* (Azerbaijan) E Azerbaijan
Bakony *115 C7 Eng.* Bakony Mountains, *Ger.* Bakonywald. *Mountain range* W Hungary
Baku *see* Bakı
Balabac Island *145 C8 island* W Philippines
Balabac Strait *154 D2 var.* Selat Balabac. *Strait* Malaysia/Philippines
Ba'labakk *see* Baalbek
Balaguer *109 F2* Cataluña, NE Spain
Balakovo *127 C6* Saratovskaya Oblast', W Russian Federation
Bālā Morghāb *138 D4* Laghmān, NW Afghanistan
Balashov *127 B6* Saratovskaya Oblast', W Russian Federation
Balaton *C7 var.* Lake Balaton, *Ger.* Plattensee. *Lake* W Hungary
Balaton, Lake *see* Balaton
Balbina, Represa *78 D1 reservoir* NW Brazil
Balboa *69 G4* Panamá, C Panama
Balcarce *81 D5* Buenos Aires, E Argentina
Balclutha *167 B7* Otago, South Island, NZ
Baldy Mountain *60 C1 mountain* Montana, NW USA
Bâle *see* Basel
Baleares, Islas *109 G3 Eng.* Balearic Islands. *Island group* Spain, W Mediterranean Sea
Balearic Islands *see* Baleares, Islas
Balearic Plain *see* Algerian Basin
Baleine, Rivière à la *55 E2 river* Québec, E Canada
Balen *103 C5* Antwerpen, N Belgium
Bāleshwar *151 F4 prev.* Balasore. Orissa, E India
Bali *154 D5 island* C Indonesia
Balıkesir *132 A3* Balıkesir, W Turkey
Balīkh, Nahr *134 C2 river* N Syria
Balikpapan *154 D4* Borneo, C Indonesia
Balkan Mountains *120 C2 Bul./SCr.* Stara Planina. *Mountain range* Bulgaria/Yugoslavia
Balkh *139 E3 anc.* Bactra. Balkh, N Afghanistan
Balkhash *130 C5 Kaz.* Balqash. Zhezkazgan, SE Kazakhstan
Balkhash, Lake *see* Balkhash, Ozero
Balkhash, Ozero *130 C5 Eng.* Lake Balkhash, *Kaz.* Balqash. *Lake* SE Kazakhstan
Balladonia *163 C6* Western Australia
Ballarat *165 C7* Victoria, SE Australia
Balleny Islands *170 B5 island group* Antarctica
Ballinger *65 F3* Texas, SW USA
Balochistān *see* Baluchistān
Balș *124 B5* Olt, S Romania
Balsas *79 F2* Maranhão, E Brazil
Balsas, Río *67 E5 var.* Río Mexcala. *River* S Mexico
Bal'shavik *123 D7 Rus.* Bol'shevik. Homyel'skaya Voblasts', SE Belorussia
Balta *124 D3* Odes'ka Oblast', SW Ukraine
Bălți *124 D3 Rus.* Bel'tsy. N Moldavia
Baltic Sea *101 C7 Ger.* Ostee, *Rus.* Baltiskoye More. *Sea* N Europe
Baltimore *57 F4* Maryland, NE USA
Baluchistān *150 B3 var.* Balochistān, Beluchistan. *Admin. region province* SW Pakistan
Balvi *122 D4* Balvi, NE Latvia
Balykchy *139 G2 Kir.* Ysyk-Köl; *prev.* Issyk-Kul', Rybach'ye. Issyk-Kul'skaya Oblast', NE Kyrgyzstan
Balzers *110 E2* S Liechtenstein
Bam *136 E4* Kermān, SE Iran
Bamako *90 D4 country capital* (Mali) Capital District, SW Mali
Bambari *92 C4* Ouaka, C Central African Republic
Bamberg *111 C5* Bayern, SE Germany
Bamenda *92 A4* Nord-Ouest, W Cameroon
Banaba *160 D2 var.* Ocean Island. *Island* Tungaru, W Kiribati
Bandaaceh *154 A3 var.* Banda Atjeh; *prev.* Koetaradja, Kutaradja, Kutaraja. Sumatera, W Indonesia
Banda Atjeh *see* Bandaaceh
Bandama *90 D5 var.* Bandama Fleuve. *River* S Ivory Coast
Bandama Fleuve *see* Bandama
Bandar 'Abbās *see* Bandar-e 'Abbās
Bandarbeyla *89 E5 var.* Bender Beila, Bender Beyla. Bari, NE Somalia
Bandar-e 'Abbās *136 D4 var.* Bandar 'Abbās; *prev.* Gombroon. Hormozgān, S Iran
Bandar-e Būshehr *136 C4 var.* Būshehr, *Eng.* Bushire. Būshehr, S Iran
Bandar-e Khamīr *136 D4* Hormozgān, S Iran
Bandar-e Langeh *136 D4 var.* Bandar-e Lengeh, Lingeh. Hormozgān, S Iran
Bandar-e Lengeh *see* Bandar-e Langeh
Bandar Kassim *see* Boosaaso
Bandarlampung *154 C4 prev.* Tanjungkarang, Teloekbetoeng, Telukbetung. Sumatera, W Indonesia
Bandar Maharani *see* Muar
Bandar Masulipatnam *see* Machilīpatnam
Bandar Seri Begawan *154 D3 prev.* Brunei Town. *Country capital* (Brunei) N Brunei
Bandar Sri Aman *see* Sri Aman
Banda Sea *155 F5 var.* Laut Banda. *Sea* E Indonesia
Bandırma *132 A3 var.* Penderma. Balıkesir, NW Turkey
Bandundu *93 C6 prev.* Banningville. Bandundu, W Congo (Zaire)
Bandung *154 C5 prev.* Bandoeng. Jawa, C Indonesia
Bangalore *148 C2* Karnātaka, S India
Bangassou *92 D4* Mbomou, SE Central African Republic
Banggai, Kepulauan *155 E4 island group* C Indonesia
Banghāzī *87 G2 Eng.* Bengazi, Benghazi, *It.* Bengasi. NE Libya
Bangka, Pulau *154 C4 island* W Indonesia
Bangkok *see* Krung Thep
Bangkok, Bight of *see* Krung Thep, Ao
Bangladesh *151 G3 off.* People's Republic of Bangladesh; *prev.* East Pakistan. *Country* S Asia
Bangor *105 B5 Ir.* Beannchar. E Northern Ireland, UK
Bangor *57 G2* Maine, NE USA
Bangor *105 C6* NW Wales, UK
Bangui *93 B5 country capital* (Central African Republic) Ombella-Mpoko, SW Central African Republic
Bangweulu, Lake *89 B8 var.* Lake Bengweulu. *Lake* N Zambia
Ban Hat Yai *see* Hat Yai
Ban Hin Heup *152 C4* Viangchan, C Laos
Ban Houayxay *see* Houayxay
Ban Houei Sai *see* Houayxay
Ban Hua Hin *153 C6 var.* Hua Hin. Prachuap Khiri Khan, SW Thailand
Bani *90 D3 river* S Mali
Banias *see* Bāniyās
Banī Suwayf *see* Beni Suef
Bāniyās *134 B3 var.* Banias, Baniyas, Paneas. Ṭarṭūs, W Syria
Baniyas *see* Bāniyās
Banja Luka *116 B3* NW Bosnia and Herzegovina
Banjarmasin *154 D4 prev.* Bandjarmasin. Borneo, C Indonesia
Banjul *90 B3 prev.* Bathurst. *Country capital* (Gambia) W Gambia
Banks Island *53 E2 island* Banks Island, Northwest Territories, NW Canada
Banks Islands *160 D4 Fr.* Îles Banks. *Island group* N Vanuatu
Banks Lake *62 B1 reservoir* Washington, NW USA
Banks Peninsula *167 C6 peninsula* South Island, NZ
Banks Strait *165 C8 strait* SW Tasman Sea
Bānkura *151 F4* West Bengal, NE India
Ban Mak Khaeng *see* Udon Thani
Banmo *see* Bhamo
Bañolas *see* Banyoles
Ban Pak Phanang *see* Pak Phanang
Ban Sichon *see* Sichon
Banská Bystrica *115 C6 Ger.* Neusohl, *Hung.* Beszterczebánya. Stredné Slovensko, C Slovakia
Bantry Bay *105 A7 Ir.* Bá Bheanntraí. *Bay* SW Ireland
Banya *120 E2* Burgaska Oblast, E Bulgaria
Banyak, Kepulauan *154 A3 prev.* Kepulauan Banjak. *Island group* NW Indonesia
Banyo *92 B4* Adamaoua, NW Cameroon
Banyoles *109 G2 var.* Bañolas. Cataluña, NE Spain
Banzare Seamounts *157 C7 undersea feature* S Indian Ocean
Baoji *144 B4 var.* Pao-chi, Paoki. Shaanxi, C China
Baoro *92 B4* Nana-Mambéré, W Central African Republic
Baoshan *144 A6 var.* Pao-shan. Yunnan, SW China
Baotou *143 F3 var.* Pao-t'ou, Paotow. Nei Mongol Zizhiqu, N China
Ba'qūbah *136 B3 var.* Qubba. C Iraq
Baquerizo Moreno *see* Puerto Baquerizo Moreno
Bar *117 C5 It.* Antivari. Montenegro, SW Yugoslavia
Baraawe *89 D6 It.* Brava. Shabeellaha Hoose, S Somalia
Baraji, Hirfanli *132 C3 lake* C Turkey
Bārāmati *150 C5* Mahārāshtra, W India
Baranavichy *123 B6 Pol.* Baranowicze, *Rus.* Baranovichi. Brestskaya Voblasts', SW Belorussia
Barbados *71 G1 country* SE West Indies
Barbastro *109 F2* Aragón, NE Spain
Barbate de Franco *108 C5* Andalucía, S Spain
Barbuda *71 G3 island* N Antigua and Barbuda
Barcaldine *164 C4* Queensland, E Australia
Barce *see* Al Marj
Barcelona *109 G2 anc.* Barcino, Barcinona. Cataluña, E Spain
Barcelona *75 E2* Anzoátegui, NE Venezuela
Barcoo *see* Cooper Creek
Barcs *115 C7* Somogy, SW Hungary
Bardaï *92 C1* Borkou-Ennedi-Tibesti, N Chad
Bardejov *115 D5 Ger.* Bartfeld, *Hung.* Bártfa. Východné Slovensko, NE Slovakia
Bardera *see* Baardheere
Bardere *see* Baardheere
Bareilly *151 E3 var.* Bareli. Uttar Pradesh, N India
Bareli *see* Bareilly
Barendrecht *102 C4* Zuid-Holland, SW Netherlands
Barentin *106 C3* Seine-Maritime, N France
Barentsberg *99 G2* Spitsbergen, W Svalbard
Barentsøya *99 G2 island* E Svalbard
Barents Sea *126 C2 Nor.* Barents Havet, *Rus.* Barentsevo More. *Sea* Arctic Ocean
Barents Trough *97 E1 undersea feature* SW Barents Sea
Bar Harbor *57 H2* Mount Desert Island, Maine, NE USA
Bari *113 E5 var.* Bari delle Puglie; *anc.* Barium. Puglia, SE Italy
Bāridah *see* Al Bāridah
Bari delle Puglie *see* Bari
Barikot *see* Barīkowṭ
Barīkowṭ *139 F4 var.* Barikot. Kunar, NE Afghanistan
Barillas *68 A2 var.* Santa Cruz Barillas. Huehuetenango, NW Guatemala
Barinas *74 C2* Barinas, W Venezuela
Barisal *151 G4* Khulna, S Bangladesh
Barisan, Pegunungan *154 B4 mountain range* Sumatera, W Indonesia
Barito, Sungai *154 D4 river* Borneo, C Indonesia
Barium *see* Bari
Barka *see* Al Marj
Barkly Tableland *164 B3 plateau* Northern Territory/Queensland, N Australia
Bârlad *124 D4 prev.* Bîrlad. Vaslui, E Romania
Barlavento, Ilhas de *90 A2 var.* Windward Islands. *Island group* N Cape Verde
Bar-le-Duc *106 D3 var.* Bar-sur-Ornain. Meuse, NE France
Barlee, Lake *163 B6 lake* Western Australia
Barlee Range *162 A4 mountain range* Western Australia
Barletta *113 D5 anc.* Barduli. Puglia, SE Italy
Barlinek *114 B3 Ger.* Berlinchen. Gorzów, W Poland
Barmouth *105 C6* NW Wales, UK
Barnaul *130 D4* Altayskiy Kray, C Russian Federation
Barnet *105 A7* SE England, UK
Barnstaple *105 C7* SW England, UK
Baroghil Pass *139 F3 var.* Kowtal-e Barowghīl. *Pass* Afghanistan/Pakistan
Baron'ki *123 E7 Rus.* Boron'ki. Mahilyowskaya Voblasts', E Belorussia
Barquisimeto *74 C2* Lara, NW Venezuela
Barra *104 B3 island* NW Scotland, UK
Barra de Río Grande *69 E3* Región Autónoma Atlántico Sur, E Nicaragua
Barragem de Sobradinho *see* Sobradinho, Represa de
Barranca *76 C3* Lima, W Peru
Barrancabermeja *74 B2* Santander, N Colombia
Barranquilla *74 B1* Atlántico, N Colombia
Barreiro *108 B4* Setúbal, W Portugal
Barrier Range *165 C6 hill range* New South Wales, SE Australia
Barrow *105 B6 Ir.* An Bhearú. *River* SE Ireland
Barrow *52 D2* Alaska, USA
Barrow-in-Furness *105 C5* NW England, UK
Barrow Island *162 A4 island* Western Australia
Barstow *63 C7* California, W USA
Bar-sur-Ornain *see* Bar-le-Duc
Bartang *139 F3 river* SE Tajikistan
Bartica *75 F3* N Guyana
Bartın *132 C2* Zonguldak, N Turkey
Bartlesville *65 G1* Oklahoma, C USA
Bartoszyce *114 D2 Ger.* Bartenstein. Olsztyn, N Poland
Baruun-Urt *143 F2* Sühbaatar, E Mongolia
Barú, Volcán *69 E5 var.* Volcán de Chiriquí. *Volcano* W Panama
Barwon River *165 D5 river* New South Wales, SE Australia
Barysaw *123 D6 Rus.* Borisov. Minskaya Voblasts', NE Belorussia
Basarabeasca *124 D4 Rus.* Bessarabka. SE Moldavia
Basel *111 A7 Eng.* Basle, *Fr.* Bâle. Basel-Stadt, NW Switzerland
Basilan *155 E3 island* SW Philippines
Basle *see* Basel
Basra *see* Al Baṣrah
Bassano del Grappa *112 C2* Veneto, NE Italy
Bassein *152 A4 var.* Pathein. Irrawaddy, SW Burma
Basse-Terre *71 G4 dependent territory capital* (Guadeloupe) Basse Terre, SW Guadeloupe
Basse Terre *71 G4 island* W Guadeloupe
Basseterre *71 G3 country capital* (Saint Kitts and Nevis) Saint Kitts, Saint Kitts and Nevis
Bassikounou *90 D3* Hodh ech Chargui, SE Mauritania
Bass Strait *165 C7 strait* SE Australia
Bassum *110 B3* Niedersachsen, NW Germany
Bastia *107 E7* Corse, France, C Mediterranean Sea
Bastogne *103 D7* Luxembourg, SE Belgium
Bastrop *58 B2* Louisiana, S USA
Bastyn' *123 B7 Rus.* Bostyn'. Brestskaya Voblasts', SW Belorussia
Basuo *see* Dongfang
Bata *93 A5* NW Equatorial Guinea
Batabanó, Golfo de *70 A2 gulf* W Cuba
Batajnica *116 D3* Serbia, N Yugoslavia
Batangas *155 E2 off.* Batangas City. Luzon, N Philippines
Bătdâmbâng *153 C5 prev.* Battambang. Bătdâmbâng, NW Cambodia
Batéké, Plateaux *93 B6 plateau* S Congo
Bath *105 D7 hist.* Akermanceaster, *anc.* Aquae Calidae, Aquae Solis. SW England, UK
Bathinda *150 D2* Punjab, NW India
Bathsheba *71 G1* E Barbados
Bathurst *55 F4* New Brunswick, SE Canada
Bathurst *165 D6* New South Wales, SE Australia
Bathurst Island *162 D2 island* Northern Territory, N Australia
Bathurst Island *53 F2 island* Parry Islands, Northwest Territories, N Canada
Bāṭin, Wādī al *136 C4 dry watercourse* SW Asia
Batman *133 E4 var.* Iluh. Batman, SE Turkey
Batna *87 E2* NE Algeria
Baton Rouge *58 B3 state capital* Louisiana, S USA
Batroûn *134 A4 var.* Al Batrūn. N Lebanon
Batticaloa *148 D3* Eastern Province, E Sri Lanka
Battipaglia *113 D5* Campania, S Italy
Bat'umi *133 F2* W Georgia
Batu Pahat *154 B3 prev.* Bandar Penggaram. Johor, Peninsular Malaysia
Bauchi *91 G4* Bauchi, NE Nigeria
Bauer Basin *169 F3 undersea feature* E Pacific Ocean
Bauska *122 C3 Ger.* Bauske. Bauska, S Latvia
Bautzen *110 D4 Lus.* Budyšin. Sachsen, E Germany
Bavarian Alps *111 C7 Ger.* Bayrische Alpen. *Mountain range* Austria/Germany
Bavispe, Río *66 C2 river* NW Mexico
Bawîti *88 B2* N Egypt
Bawku *91 E4* N Ghana
Bayamo *70 C3* Granma, E Cuba
Bayan Har Shan *142 D4 var.* Bayan Khar. *Mountain range* C China
Bayanhongor *142 D2* Bayanhongor, C Mongolia
Bayan Khar *see* Bayan Har Shan
Bayano, Lago *69 G4 lake* E Panama
Bay City *56 C3* Michigan, N USA
Bay City *65 G4* Texas, SW USA
Baydhabo *89 D6 var.* Baydhowa, Isha Baydhabo, *It.* Baidoa. Bay, SW Somalia
Baydhowa *see* Baydhabo
Bayern *111 C6 cultural region* SE Germany
Bayeux *106 B3 anc.* Augustodurum. Calvados, N France
Bāyir *135 C7 var.* Bā'ir. Ma'ān, S Jordan
Baykal, Ozero *131 E4 Eng.* Lake Baikal. *Lake* S Russian Federation
Baymak *127 D6* Respublika Bashkortostan, W Russian Federation
Bayonne *107 A6 anc.* Lapurdum. Pyrénées-Atlantiques, SW France
Bayramaly *138 D3 prev.* Bayram-Ali. Maryyskiy Velayat, S Turkmenistan
Bayreuth *111 C5 var.* Baireuth. Bayern, SE Germany
Bayrūt *see* Beyrouth
Baytown *65 H4* Texas, SW USA
Baza *109 E4* Andalucía, S Spain
Beagle Channel *81 C8 channel* Argentina/Chile
Béal Feirste *see* Belfast
Beannchar *see* Bangor
Bear Lake *62 E4 lake* Idaho/Utah, NW USA
Beas de Segura *109 E4* Andalucía, S Spain
Beata, Isla *71 E3 island* SW Dominican Republic
Beatrice *61 F4* Nebraska, C USA

Chain Ridge – Clark Fork

Chain Ridge *156 B4 undersea feature* W Indian Ocean
Chajul *68 B2* Quiché, W Guatemala
Chakhānsūr *138 D5* Nīmrūz, SW Afghanistan
Chala *76 D4* Arequipa, SW Peru
Chalatenango *68 C3* Chalatenango, N El Salvador
Chalcidice *see* Chalkidikí
Chalcis *see* Chalkída
Chálki *121 E7 island* Dodekánisos, Greece, Aegean Sea
Chalkída *121 C5 var.* Halkida; *prev.* Khalkís, *anc.* Chalcis. Evvoia, E Greece
Chalkidikí *120 C4 var.* Khalkidhikí; *anc.* Chalcidice. *Peninsula* NE Greece
Challans *106 B4* Vendée, NW France
Challapata *77 F4* Oruro, SW Bolivia
Challenger Deep *168 B3 undersea feature* W Pacific Ocean
Challenger Fracture Zone *169 F4 tectonic feature* SE Pacific Ocean
Châlons-en-Champagne *106 D3 prev.* Châlons-sur-Marne, *hist.* Arcae Remorum, *anc.* Carolopois. Marne, NE France
Chalon-sur-Saône *106 D4 anc.* Cabillonum. Saône-et-Loire, C France
Cha Mai *see* Thung Song
Chaman *150 B2* Baluchistān, SW Pakistan
Chambéry *107 D5 anc.* Camberia. Savoie, E France
Champagne *106 D3* Yukon Territory, W Canada
Champaign *56 B4* Illinois, N USA
Champasak *153 D5* Champasak, S Laos
Champlain, Lake *57 F2 lake* Canada/USA
Champotón *67 G4* Campeche, SE Mexico
Chanak *see* Çanakkale
Chañaral *80 B3* Atacama, N Chile
Chanchiang *see* Zhanjiang
Chandeleur Islands *58 C3 island group* Louisiana, S USA
Chandīgarh *150 D2* Punjab, N India
Chandrapur *151 E5* Mahārāshtra, C India
Changan *see* Xi'an
Changane *95 E3 river* S Mozambique
Changchun *144 D3 var.* Ch'angch'un, Ch'ang-ch'un; *prev.* Hsinking. Jilin, NE China
Ch'angch'un *see* Changchun
Chang Jiang *144 B5 var.* Yangtze Kiang, *Eng.* Yangtze. *River* C China
Changkiakow *see* Zhangjiakou
Chang, Ko *153 C6 island* S Thailand
Changsha *144 C5 var.* Ch'angsha, Ch'ang-sha. Hunan, S China
Ch'angsha *see* Changsha
Changzhi *144 C4* Shanxi, C China
Chaniá *121 C7 var.* Hania, Khaniá, *Eng.* Canea; *anc.* Cydonia. Kríti, Greece, E Mediterranean Sea
Chañi, Nevado de *80 B2 mountain* NW Argentina
Chankiri *see* Çankırı
Channel Islands *105 C8 Fr.* Îles Normandes. *Island group* S English Channel
Channel Islands *63 B8 island group* California, W USA
Channel-Port aux Basques *55 G4* Newfoundland, Newfoundland and Labrador, SE Canada
Channel, The *see* English Channel
Channel Tunnel *106 C2 tunnel* France/UK
Chantabun *see* Chanthaburi
Chantaburi *see* Chanthaburi
Chantada *108 C1* Galicia, NW Spain
Chanthaburi *153 C6 var.* Chantabun, Chantaburi. Chantaburi, S Thailand
Chanute *61 F5* Kansas, C USA
Chaouèn *see* Chefchaouen
Chaoyang *144 D3* Liaoning, NE China
Chapala, Lago de *66 D4 lake* C Mexico
Chapan, Gora *138 B3 mountain* C Turkmenistan
Chapayevsk *127 C6* Samarskaya Oblast', W Russian Federation
Chaplynka *125 F4* Khersons'ka Oblast', S Ukraine
Charcot Seamounts *96 B3 undersea feature* E Atlantic Ocean
Chardzhev *138 D3 prev.* Chardzhou, Chardzhui, Leninsk-Turkmenski, *Turkm.* Chärjew. Lebapskiy Velayat, E Turkmenistan
Charente *107 B5 cultural region* W France
Charente *107 B5 river* W France
Chari *92 B3 var.* Shari. *River* Central African Republic/Chad
Chārīkār *139 E4* Parwān, NE Afghanistan
Charity *75 F2* NW Guyana
Charkhlik *see* Ruoqiang
Charkhliq *see* Ruoqiang
Charleroi *103 C7* Hainaut, S Belgium
Charlesbourg *55 E4* Québec, SE Canada
Charles de Gaulle *106 E1 international airport* (Paris) Seine-et-Marne, N France
Charles Island *54 D1 island* Northwest Territories, NE Canada
Charles Island *see* Santa María, Isla
Charleston *56 D5 state capital* West Virginia, NE USA
Charleston *59 F2* South Carolina, SE USA
Charleville *165 D5* Queensland, E Australia
Charleville-Mézières *106 D3* Ardennes, N France
Charlie-Gibbs Fracture Zone *82 B2 tectonic feature* N Atlantic Ocean
Charlotte *59 E1* North Carolina, SE USA
Charlotte Amalie *71 F3 prev.* Saint Thomas. *Dependent territory capital* (Virgin Islands (US)) Saint Thomas, N Virgin Islands (US)
Charlotte Harbor *59 E5 inlet* Florida, SE USA
Charlottesville *57 E5* Virginia, NE USA
Charlottetown *55 F4* Prince Edward Island, Prince Edward Island, SE Canada
Charsk *130 D5* Semipalatinsk, E Kazakhstan
Charters Towers *164 D3* Queensland, NE Australia
Chartres *106 C3 anc.* Autricum, Civitas Carnutum. Eure-et-Loir, C France
Charus Nuur *142 C2 lake* NW Mongolia
Chashniki *123 D5 Rus.* Chashniki. Vitsyebskaya Voblasts', N Belorussia
Châteaubriant *106 B4* Loire-Atlantique, NW France
Châteaudun *106 C3* Eure-et-Loir, C France
Châteauroux *106 C4 prev.* Indreville. Indre, C France
Château-Thierry *106 C3* Aisne, N France
Châtelet *103 C7* Hainaut, S Belgium
Châtelherault *see* Châtellerault
Châtellerault *106 B4 var.* Châtelherault. Vienne, W France
Chatham Island *see* San Cristóbal, Isla
Chatham Island Rise *see* Chatham Rise
Chatham Islands *159 E5 island group* NZ, SW Pacific Ocean
Chatham Rise *158 D5 var.* Chatham Island Rise. *Undersea feature* S Pacific Ocean
Chatkal Range *139 F2 Rus.* Chatkal'skiy Khrebet. *Mountain range* Kyrgyzstan/Uzbekistan
Chattahoochee River *58 D3 river* SE USA
Chattanooga *58 D1* Tennessee, S USA
Chatyr-Tash *139 G2* Narynskaya Oblast', C Kyrgyzstan
Châu Đốc *153 D6 var.* Chauphu, Chau Phu. An Giang, S Vietnam
Chauk *152 A3* Magwe, W Burma
Chaumont *106 D4 prev.* Chaumont-en-Bassigny. Haute-Marne, N France
Chau Phu *see* Châu Đốc
Chaves *108 C2 anc.* Aquae Flaviae. Vila Real, N Portugal
Chávez, Isla *see* Santa Cruz, Isla
Chavusy *123 E6 Rus.* Chausy. Mahilyowskaya Voblasts', E Belorussia
Chaykovskiy *127 D5* Permskaya Oblast', NW Russian Federation
Cheb *115 A5 Ger.* Eger. Západní Čechy, W Czech Republic
Cheboksary *127 C5* Chuvashskaya Respublika, W Russian Federation
Cheboygan *56 C2* Michigan, N USA
Chechaouèn *see* Chefchaouen
Chech, Erg *90 D1 desert* Algeria/Mali
Che-chiang *see* Zhejiang
Cheduba Island *152 A4 island* W Burma
Chefchaouen *86 C2 var.* Chaouèn, Chechaouèn, *Sp.* Xauen. N Morocco
Chefoo *see* Yantai
Cheju-do *145 E4 Jap.* Saishū; *prev.* Quelpart. *Island* S South Korea
Cheju Strait *145 E4 strait* S South Korea
Chekiang *see* Zhejiang
Cheleken *138 B2* Balkanskiy Velayat, W Turkmenistan
Chelkar *130 B4* Aktyubinsk, W Kazakhstan
Chełm *114 E4 Rus.* Kholm. Chełm, SE Poland
Chełmno *114 C3 Ger.* Culm, Kulm. Toruń, N Poland
Cheltenham *105 D6* C England, UK
Chelyabinsk *130 C3* Chelyabinskaya Oblast', C Russian Federation
Chemnitz *110 D4 prev.* Karl-Marx-Stadt. Sachsen, E Germany
Chenāb *150 C2 river* India/Pakistan
Chengchiatun *see* Liaoyuan
Ch'eng-chou *see* Zhengzhou
Chengchow *see* Zhengzhou
Chengde *144 D3 var.* Jehol. Hebei, E China
Chengdu *144 B5 var.* Chengtu, Ch'eng-tu. Sichuan, C China
Chenghsien *see* Zhengzhou
Ch'eng-tu *see* Chengdu
Chennai *see* Madras
Chen Xian *see* Chenzhou
Chen Xiang *see* Chenzhou
Chenzhou *144 C6 var.* Chenxian, Chen Xian, Chen Xiang. Hunan, S China
Chepelare *120 C3* Plovdivska Oblast, S Bulgaria
Chepén *76 B3* La Libertad, C Peru
Cher *106 C4 river* C France
Cherbourg *106 B3 anc.* Carusbur. Manche, N France
Cherepovets *126 B4* Vologodskaya Oblast', NW Russian Federation
Chergui, Chott ech *86 D2 salt lake* NW Algeria
Cherkasy *125 E2 Rus.* Cherkassy. Cherkas'ka Oblast', C Ukraine
Cherkessk *127 B7* Karachayevo-Cherkesskaya Respublika, SW Russian Federation
Chernihiv *125 E1 Rus.* Chernigov. Chernihivs'ka Oblast', NE Ukraine
Chernivtsi *124 C3 Ger.* Czernowitz, *Rom.* Cernăuţi, *Rus.* Chernovtsy. Chernivets'ka Oblast', W Ukraine
Cherno More *see* Black Sea
Chernoye More *see* Black Sea
Chernyakhovsk *122 A4 Ger.* Insterburg. Kaliningradskaya Oblast', W Russian Federation
Cherry Hill *57 F4* New Jersey, NE USA
Cherski Range *see* Cherskogo, Khrebet
Cherskiy *131 G2* Respublika Sakha (Yakutiya), NE Russian Federation
Cherskogo, Khrebet *131 F2 var.* Cherski Range. *Mountain range* NE Russian Federation
Chervonohrad *124 C2 Rus.* Chervonograd. L'vivs'ka Oblast', NW Ukraine
Chervyen' *123 D6 Rus.* Cherven'. Minskaya Voblasts', C Belorussia
Cherykaw *123 E7 Rus.* Cherikov. Mahilyowskaya Voblasts', E Belorussia
Chesapeake Bay *57 F5 inlet* NE USA
Chesha Bay *see* Chëshskaya Guba
Chëshskaya Guba *172 D5 var.* Archangel Bay, Chesha Bay, Dvina Bay. *Bay* NW Russian Federation
Chester *105 C6 Wel.* Caerleon; *hist.* Legaceaster, *Lat.* Deva, Devana Castra. C England, UK
Chetumal *67 H4 var.* Payo Obispo. Quintana Roo, SE Mexico
Cheviot Hills *104 D4 hill range* England/Scotland, UK
Cheyenne *60 D4 state capital* Wyoming, C USA
Cheyenne River *60 D3 river* South Dakota/Wyoming, N USA
Chhapra *151 F3 prev.* Chapra. Bihār, N India
Chiai *144 D6 var.* Chia-i, Chiayi, Kiayi, Jiayi, *Jap.* Kagi. C Taiwan
Chia-i *see* Chiai
Chiang-hsi *see* Jiangxi
Chiang Mai *152 B4 var.* Chiangmai, Chiengmai, Kiangmai. Chiang Mai, NW Thailand
Chiangmai *see* Chiang Mai
Chiang Rai *152 C3 var.* Chianpai, Chienrai, Muang Chiang Rai. Chiang Rai, NW Thailand
Chiang-su *see* Jiangsu
Chian-ning *see* Nanjing
Chianpai *see* Chiang Rai
Chianti *112 C3 cultural region* C Italy
Chiapa *see* Chiapa de Cerzo
Chiapa de Cerzo *67 G5 var.* Chiapa. Chiapas, SE Mexico
Chiayi *see* Chiai
Chiba *146 B1 var.* Tiba. Chiba, Honshū, S Japan
Chibougamau *54 D3* Québec, SE Canada
Chicago *56 B3* Illinois, N USA
Ch'i-ch'i-ha-erh *see* Qiqihar
Chickasha *65 G2* Oklahoma, C USA
Chiclayo *76 B3* Lambayeque, NW Peru
Chico *63 B5* California, W USA
Chico, Río *81 B6 river* S Argentina
Chico, Río *81 B7 river* SE Argentina
Chicoutimi *55 E4* Québec, SE Canada
Chiengmai *see* Chiang Mai
Chienrai *see* Chiang Rai
Chiesanuova *112 D2* SW San Marino
Chieti *112 D4 var.* Teate. Abruzzi, C Italy
Chifeng *143 G2 var.* Ulanhad. Nei Mongol Zizhiqu, N China
Chih-fu *see* Yantai
Chihli *see* Hebei
Chihli, Gulf of *see* Bo Hai
Chihuahua *66 C2* Chihuahua, NW Mexico
Childress *65 F2* Texas, SW USA
Chile *80 B3 off.* Republic of Chile. *Country* SW South America
Chile Basin *73 A5 undersea feature* E Pacific Ocean
Chile Chico *81 B6* Aisén, W Chile
Chile Rise *73 A7 undersea feature* SE Pacific Ocean
Chililabombwe *94 D2* Copperbelt, C Zambia
Chi-lin *see* Jilin
Chillán *81 B5* Bío Bío, C Chile
Chillicothe *56 D4* Ohio, N USA
Chiloé, Isla de *81 A6 var.* Isla Grande de Chiloé. *Island* W Chile
Chilpancingo *67 E5 var.* Chilpancingo de los Bravos. Guerrero, S Mexico
Chilpancingo de los Bravos *see* Chilpancingo
Chilung *144 D6 var.* Keelung, *Jap.* Kirun, Kirun'; *prev. Sp.* Santissima Trinidad. N Taiwan
Chimán *69 G5* Panamá, E Panama
Chimborazo *76 A1 volcano* C Ecuador
Chimbote *76 C3* Ancash, W Peru
Chimboy *138 D1 Rus.* Chimbay. Qoraqalpoghiston Respublikasi, NW Uzbekistan
Chimoio *95 E3* Manica, C Mozambique
China *140 C2 off.* People's Republic of China, *Chin.* Chung-hua Jen-min Kung-ho-kuo, Zhonghua Renmin Gongheguo; *prev.* Chinese Empire. *Country* E Asia
Chi-nan *see* Jinan
Chinandega *68 C3* Chinandega, NW Nicaragua
Chincha Alta *76 D4* Ica, SW Peru
Chin-chiang *see* Quanzhou
Chin-chou *see* Jinzhou
Chinchow *see* Jinzhou
Chindwin *152 B2 river* N Burma
Ch'ing Hai *see* Qinghai Hu
Chingola *94 D2* Copperbelt, C Zambia
Ching-Tao *see* Qingdao
Chinguetti *90 C2 var.* Chinguetti. Adrar, C Mauritania
Chin Hills *152 A3 mountain range* W Burma
Chinhsien *see* Jinzhou
Chinnereth *see* Tiberias, Lake
Chinook Trough *129 H4 undersea feature* N Pacific Ocean
Chioggia *112 C2 anc.* Fossa Claudia. Veneto, NE Italy
Chíos *121 D5 var.* Hios, Khíos, *It.* Scio, *Turk.* Sakiz-Adasi. Chíos, E Greece
Chíos *121 D5 var.* Khíos. *Island* E Greece
Chipata *94 D2 prev.* Fort Jameson. Eastern, E Zambia
Chiquián *76 C3* Ancash, W Peru
Chiquimula *68 B2* Chiquimula, SE Guatemala
Chīrāla *148 D1* Andhra Pradesh, E India
Chirchiq *139 E2 Rus.* Chirchik. Toshkent Wiloyati, E Uzbekistan
Chiriquí, Golfo de *69 E5 Eng.* Chiriqui Gulf. *Gulf* SW Panama
Chiriquí, Laguna de *69 E5 lagoon* NW Panama
Chirripó Grande, Cerro *68 D4 var.* Cerro Chirripó. *Mountain* SE Costa Rica
Chisec *68 B2* Alta Verapaz, C Guatemala
Chisholm *61 F1* Minnesota, N USA
Chisimaio *see* Kismaayo
Chisimayu *see* Kismaayo
Chişinău *124 D4 Rus.* Kishinev. *Country capital* (Moldavia) C Moldavia
Chita *131 F4* Chitinskaya Oblast', S Russian Federation
Chitato *94 C1* Lunda Norte, NE Angola
Chitina *52 D3* Alaska, USA
Chitose *146 D2 var.* Titose. Hokkaidō, NE Japan
Chitré *69 F5* Herrera, S Panama
Chittagong *151 G4 Ben.* Chāttagām. Chittagong, SE Bangladesh
Chitungwiza *94 D3 prev.* Chitangwiza. Mashonaland East, NE Zimbabwe
Chlef *86 D2 var.* Ech Cheliff, Ech Chleff; *prev.* Al-Asnam, El Asnam, Orléansville. NW Algeria
Chocolate Mountains *63 D8 mountain range* California, W USA
Chodzież *114 C3* Piła, NW Poland
Choele Choel *81 C5* Río Negro, C Argentina
Choiseul *160 C3 var.* Lauru. *Island* NW Solomon Islands
Ch'ok'ē *88 C4 var.* Choke Mountains. *Mountain range* NW Ethiopia
Choke Mountains *see* Ch'ok'ē
Cholet *106 B4* Maine-et-Loire, NW France
Choluteca *68 C3* Choluteca, S Honduras
Choluteca, Río *68 C3 river* SW Honduras
Choma *94 D2* Southern, S Zambia
Chomutov *114 A4 Ger.* Komotau. Severní Čechy, NW Czech Republic
Chona *129 E2 river* C Russian Federation
Chon Buri *153 C5 prev.* Bang Pla Soi. Chon Buri, S Thailand
Chone *76 A1* Manabí, W Ecuador
Ch'ŏngjin *145 E3* NE North Korea
Chongqing *144 B5 var.* Ch'ung-ching, Ch'ung-ch'ing, Chungking, Pahsien, Tchongking, Yuzhou. Sichuan, C China
Chonnacht *see* Connaught
Chonos, Archipiélago de los *81 A6 island group* S Chile
Chorne More *see* Black Sea
Chornomors'ke *125 E4 Rus.* Chernomorskoye. Respublika Krym, S Ukraine
Chortkiv *124 C2 Rus.* Chortkov. Ternopil's'ka Oblast', W Ukraine
Chorum *see* Çorum
Chorzów *115 C5 Ger.* Königshütte; *prev.* Królewska Huta. Katowice, S Poland
Chōshi *147 D5 var.* Tyôsi. Chiba, Honshū, S Japan
Choszczno *114 B3 Ger.* Arnswalde. Gorzów, W Poland
Chota Nāgpur *151 E4 plateau* N India
Chott el-Hodna *see* Hodna, Chott El
Chott Melrhir *see* Melghir, Chott
Choûm *90 C2* Adrar, C Mauritania
Choybalsan *143 F2* Dornod, E Mongolia
Christchurch *167 C6* Canterbury, South Island, NZ
Christiana *70 B5* C Jamaica
Christiansand *see* Kristiansand
Christianshåb *see* Qasigiannguit
Christiansund *see* Kristiansund
Christmas Island *157 D5 Australian external territory* E Indian Ocean
Christmas Ridge *159 E1 undersea feature* C Pacific Ocean
Chuan *see* Sichuan
Ch'uan-chou *see* Quanzhou
Chubut *73 B7 off.* Provincia de Chubut. Admin. region *province* S Argentina
Chubut, Río *81 B6 river* SE Argentina
Ch'u-chiang *see* Shaoguan
Chūgoku-sanchi *147 B6 mountain range* Honshū, SW Japan
Chuí *see* Chuy
Chukai *see* Cukai
Chukchi Plain *171 B2 undersea feature* Arctic Ocean
Chukchi Plateau *50 C2 undersea feature* Arctic Ocean
Chukchi Sea *50 B2 Rus.* Chukotskoye More. *Sea* Arctic Ocean
Chula Vista *63 C8* California, W USA
Chulucanas *76 B2* Piura, NW Peru
Chulym *130 D4 river* C Russian Federation
Chumphon *153 C6 var.* Jumporn. Chumphon, SW Thailand
Ch'unch'ŏn *145 E4 Jap.* Shunsen. N South Korea
Ch'ung-ching *see* Chongqing
Chungking *see* Chongqing
Chunya *131 E3 river* C Russian Federation
Chuquicamata *80 B2* Antofagasta, N Chile
Chur *111 B7 Fr.* Coire, *It.* Coira, *Rmsch.* Cuera, Quera; *anc.* Curia Rhaetorum. Graubünden, E Switzerland
Churchill *54 B2 river* Manitoba/Saskatchewan, C Canada
Churchill *55 F2 river* Newfoundland and Labrador, E Canada
Churchill *53 G4* Manitoba, C Canada
Chuska Mountains *64 C1 mountain range* Arizona/New Mexico, SW USA
Chusovoy *127 D5* Permskaya Oblast', NW Russian Federation
Chuuk Islands *160 B2 var.* Hogoley Islands; *prev.* Truk Islands. *Island group* Caroline Islands, C Micronesia
Chuy *80 E4 var.* Chuí. Rocha, E Uruguay
Chyhyryn *125 E2 Rus.* Chigirin. Cherkas'ka Oblast', N Ukraine
Ciadîr-Lunga *124 D4 var.* Ceadâr-Lunga, *Rus.* Chadyr-Lunga. S Moldavia
Cide *132 C2* Kastamonu, N Turkey
Ciechanów *114 D3 prev.* Zichenau. Ciechanów, C Poland
Ciego de Ávila *70 C2* Ciego de Ávila, C Cuba
Ciénaga *74 B1* Magdalena, N Colombia
Cienfuegos *70 B2* Cienfuegos, C Cuba
Cieza *109 E4* Murcia, SE Spain
Cihanbeyli *132 C3* Konya, C Turkey
Cikobia *161 E4 prev.* Thikombia. *Island* N Fiji
Cilacap *154 C5 prev.* Tjilatjap. Jawa, C Indonesia
Cill Airne *see* Killarney
Cill Chainnigh *see* Kilkenny
Cill Mhantáin *see* Wicklow
Cincinnati *56 C4* Ohio, N USA
Ciney *103 C7* Namur, SE Belgium
Cinto, Monte *107 E7 mountain* Corse, France, C Mediterranean Sea
Cipolletti *81 B5* Río Negro, C Argentina
Cirebon *154 C4 prev.* Tjirebon. Jawa, S Indonesia
Cirò Marina *113 E6* Calabria, S Italy
Cisnădie *124 B4 Ger.* Heltau, *Hung.* Nagydisznód. Sibiu, SW Romania
Citlaltépetl *see* Orizaba, Volcán Pico de
Citrus Heights *63 B5* California, W USA
Ciudad Bolívar *75 E2 prev.* Angostura. Bolívar, E Venezuela
Ciudad Cortés *see* Cortés
Ciudad Darío *68 D3 var.* Dario. Matagalpa, W Nicaragua
Ciudad de Dolores Hidalgo *see* Dolores Hidalgo
Ciudad de Guatemala *68 B2 Eng.* Guatemala City; *prev.* Santiago de los Caballeros. *Country capital* (Guatemala) Guatemala, C Guatemala
Ciudad del Carmen *see* Carmen
Ciudad del Este *80 E2 prev.* Cuidad Presidente Stroessner, Presidente Stroessner, Puerto Presidente Stroessner. Alto Paraná, SE Paraguay
Ciudad Delicias *see* Delicias
Ciudad de México *see* México
Ciudad de Panamá *see* Panamá
Ciudad Guayana *75 E2 prev.* San Tomé de Guayana, Santo Tomé de Guayana. Bolívar, NE Venezuela
Ciudad Guzmán *66 D4* Jalisco, SW Mexico
Ciudad Hidalgo *67 G5* Chiapas, SE Mexico
Ciudad Juárez *66 C1* Chihuahua, N Mexico
Ciudad Lerdo *66 D3* Durango, C Mexico
Ciudad Madero *67 E3 var.* Villa Cecilia. Tamaulipas, C Mexico
Ciudad Mante *67 E3* Tamaulipas, C Mexico
Ciudad Miguel Alemán *67 E2* Tamaulipas, C Mexico
Ciudad Obregón *66 B2* Sonora, NW Mexico
Ciudad Ojeda *74 C1* Zulia, NW Venezuela
Ciudad Porfirio Díaz *see* Piedras Negras
Ciudad Quesada *see* Quesada
Ciudad Real *108 D3* Castilla-La Mancha, C Spain
Ciudad-Rodrigo *108 C3* Castilla-León, N Spain
Ciudad Valles *67 E3* San Luis Potosí, C Mexico
Ciudad Victoria *67 E3* Tamaulipas, C Mexico
Ciutadella *see* Ciutadella de Menorca
Ciutadella de Menorca *109 H3 var.* Ciutadella. Menorca, Spain, W Mediterranean Sea
Civitanova Marche *112 D3* Marche, C Italy
Civitavecchia *112 C4 anc.* Centum Cellae, Trajani Portus. Lazio, C Italy
Claremore *65 G1* Oklahoma, C USA
Clarence *167 C5 river* South Island, NZ
Clarence *167 C5* Canterbury, South Island, NZ
Clarence Town *70 D2* Long Island, C Bahamas
Clarinda *61 F4* Iowa, C USA
Clarion Fracture Zone *169 E2 tectonic feature* NE Pacific Ocean
Clarión, Isla *66 A5 island* W Mexico
Clark Fork *60 A1 river* Idaho/Montana, NW USA

Damachava – Drăgăşani

Damachava 123 A6 var. Damachova, Pol. Domaczewo, Rus. Domachëvo. Brestskaya Voblasts', SW Belorussia
Damachova see Damachava
Damān 150 C4 Damān and Diu, W India
Damara 92 C4 Ombella-Mpoko, S Central African Republic
Damas see Dimashq
Damasco see Dimashq
Damascus see Dimashq
Damāvand, Qolleh-ye 136 D3 mountain N Iran
Dammām see Ad Dammān
Damoûr 135 A5 var. Ad Dāmūr. W Lebanon
Dampier 162 A4 Western Australia
Dampier, Selat 155 F4 strait Irian Jaya, E Indonesia
Damqawt 137 D6 var. Damqut. E Yemen
Damqut see Damqawt
Damxung 142 C5 Xizang Zizhiqu, W China
Danakil Desert 88 D4 var. Afar Depression, Danakil Plain. Desert E Africa
Danakil Plain see Danakil Desert
Danané 90 D5 W Ivory Coast
Đă Năng 153 E5 prev. Tourane. Quang Nam-Đa Năng, C Vietnam
Danborg see Daneborg
Dandong 144 D3 var. Tan-tung; prev. An-tung. Liaoning, NE China
Daneborg 99 E3 var. Danborg. N Greenland
Dänew see Deynau
Dangerous Archipelago see Tuamotu, Îles
Danghara 139 E3 Rus. Dangara. SW Tajikistan
Danghe Nanshan 142 D3 mountain range W China
Dangla see Tanggula Shan
Dângrêk, Chuŏr Phnum 153 D5 var. Phanom Dang Raek, Phanom Dong Rak, Fr. Chaîne des Dangrek. Mountain range Cambodia/Thailand
Dangriga 68 C1 prev. Stann Creek. Stann Creek, E Belize
Danish West Indies see Virgin Islands (US)
Danlí 68 D2 El Paraíso, S Honduras
Danmarksstraedet see Denmark Strait
Dannenberg 110 C3 Niedersachsen, N Germany
Dannevirke 166 D4 Manawatu-Wanganui, North Island, NZ
Danube 97 E4 Bul. Dunav, Cz. Dunaj, Ger. Donau, Hung. Duna, Rom. Dunărea. River C Europe
Danville 57 E5 Virginia, NE USA
Dan Xian see Danxian
Danxian 144 C7 var. Dan Xian, Nada. Hainan, S China
Danziger Bucht see Danzig, Gulf of
Danzig, Gulf of 114 C2 var. Gulf of Gdańsk, Ger. Danziger Bucht, Pol. Zakota Gdańska, Rus. Gdan'skaya Bukhta. Gulf N Poland
Daqm see Duqm
Dar'ā 135 B5 var. Der'a, Fr. Déraa. Dar'ā, SW Syria
Darabani 124 C3 Botoşani, NW Romania
Daraut-Korgon see Daroot-Korgon
Dardanelli see Çanakkale
Dar es Salaam 89 C7 Dar es Salaam, E Tanzania
Darfield 167 C6 Canterbury, South Island, NZ
Darfur 88 A4 var. Darfur Massif. Cultural region W Sudan
Darfur Massif see Darfur
Darhan 143 E2 Selenge, N Mongolia
Darien, Gulf of 74 A2 Sp. Golfo del Darién. Gulf S Caribbean Sea
Darién, Serranía del 69 H5 mountain range Colombia/Panama
Dario see Ciudad Darío
Darjeeling see Darjiling
Darjiling 151 F3 prev. Darjeeling. West Bengal, NE India
Darling River 165 C6 river New South Wales, SE Australia
Darlington 105 D5 N England, UK
Darmstadt 111 B5 Hessen, SW Germany
Darnah 87 G2 var. Dérna. NE Libya
Darnley, Cape 170 D2 headland Antarctica
Daroca 109 E2 Aragón, NE Spain
Daroot-Korgon 139 F3 var. Daraut-Kurgan. Oshskaya Oblast', SW Kyrgyzstan
Dartford 105 B8 SE England, UK
Dartmoor 105 C7 moorland SW England, UK
Dartmouth 55 F4 Nova Scotia, SE Canada
Darvaza 138 C2 Turkm. Derweze. Akhalskiy Velayat, C Turkmenistan
Darwin 162 D2 prev. Palmerston, Port Darwin. Territory capital Northern Territory, N Australia
Darwin, Isla 76 A4 var. Culpepper Island. Island W Ecuador
Daryācheh-ye Hāmūn see Şāberī, Hāmūn-e
Daryācheh-ye Sīstān see Şāberī, Hāmūn-e
Daryā-ye Morghāb see Murgab
Daryā-ye Pāmīr see Pamir
Daryoi Pomir see Pamir
Dashkawka 123 D6 Rus. Dashkovka. Mahilyowskaya Voblasts', E Belorussia
Dashkhovuz 138 C2 Turkm. Dashhowuz; prev. Tashauz. Dashkhovuzskiy Velayat, N Turkmenistan
Datong 144 C3 var. Tatung, Ta-t'ung. Shanxi, C China
Daugavpils 122 D4 Ger. Dünaburg; prev. Rus. Dvinsk. Municipality Daugvapils, SE Latvia
Daung Kyun 153 B6 island S Burma
Dauphiné 107 D5 cultural region E France
Dāvangere 148 C2 Karnātaka, W India
Davao 155 F3 off. Davao City. Mindanao, S Philippines
Davao Gulf 155 F3 gulf Mindanao, S Philippines
Davenport 61 G3 Iowa, C USA
David 69 E5 Chiriquí, W Panama
Davie Ridge 157 A5 undersea feature W Indian Ocean
Davis 170 D3 Australian research station Antarctica
Davis Sea 170 D3 sea Antarctica
Davis Strait 98 B3 strait Baffin Bay/Labrador Sea
Dawei see Tavoy
Dax 107 B6 var. Ax; anc. Aquae Augustae, Aquae Tarbelicae. Landes, SW France
Dayr az Zawr 134 D3 var. Deir ez Zor. Dayr az Zawr, E Syria
Dayton 56 C4 Ohio, N USA
Daytona Beach 59 E4 Florida, SE USA
De Aar 94 C5 Northern Cape, C South Africa
Dead Sea 135 B6 var. Bahret Lut, Lacus Asphaltites, Ar. Al Baḩr al Mayyit, Baḩrat Lūt, Heb. Yam HaMelaḥ. Salt lake Israel/Jordan
Dealnu see Tana
Deán Funes 80 C3 Córdoba, C Argentina
Death Valley 63 C7 valley California, W USA
Debar 117 D6 Ger. Dibra, Turk. Debre. W FYR Macedonia
De Bildt see De Bilt
De Bilt 102 C3 var. De Bildt. Utrecht, C Netherlands
Debrecen 115 D6 Ger. Debreczin, Rom. Debreţin; prev. Debreczen. Hajdú-Bihar, E Hungary
Decatur 58 C1 Alabama, S USA
Decatur 56 B4 Illinois, N USA
Deccan 150 D5 Hind. Dakshin. Plateau C India
Děčín 114 B4 Ger. Tetschen. Severní Čechy, NW Czech Republic
Dedeagaç see Alexandroúpoli
Dedeagach see Alexandroúpoli
Dedemsvaart 102 E3 Overijssel, E Netherlands
Dee 104 C3 river NE Scotland, UK
Deering 52 C2 Alaska, USA
Deggendorf 111 D6 Bayern, SE Germany
Değirmenlik 118 C5 N Cyprus
Deh Bīd 136 D3 Fārs, C Iran
Dehli see Delhi
Deh Shū 138 D5 var. Deshu. Helmand, S Afghanistan
Deinze 103 B5 Oost-Vlaanderen, NW Belgium
Deir ez Zor see Dayr az Zawr
Deirgeirt, Loch see Derg, Lough
Dej 124 B3 Hung. Dés; prev. Deés. Cluj, NW Romania
Dékoa 92 C4 Kémo, C Central African Republic
De Land 59 E4 Florida, SE USA
Delano 63 C7 California, W USA
Delārām 138 D5 Farāh, SW Afghanistan
Delaware 57 F4 off. State of Delaware; also known as Blue Hen State, Diamond State, First State. State NE USA
Delaware 56 D4 Ohio, N USA
Delft 102 B4 Zuid-Holland, W Netherlands
Delfzijl 102 E1 Groningen, NE Netherlands
Delgo 88 B3 Northern, N Sudan
Delhi 150 D3 var. Dehli, Hind. Dilli; hist. Shahjahanabad. Delhi, N India
Delicias 66 D2 var. Ciudad Delicias. Chihuahua, N Mexico
Déli-Kárpátok see Carpaţii Meridionali
Delmenhorst 110 B3 Niedersachsen, NW Germany
Del Rio 65 F4 Texas, SW USA
Deltona 59 E4 Florida, SE USA
Demba 93 D6 Kasai Occidental, C Congo (Zaire)
Dembia 92 D4 Mbomou, SE Central African Republic
Demchok var. Dêmqog. Disputed region China/India see also Dêmqog
Demchok 142 A4 var. Dêmqog. China/India see also Dêmqog
Demerara Plain 72 C2 undersea feature W Atlantic Ocean
Deming 64 C3 New Mexico, SW USA
Demmin 110 C2 Mecklenburg-Vorpommern, NE Germany
Demopolis 58 C2 Alabama, S USA
Dêmqog var. Demchok. Disputed region China/India see also Demchok
Denali see McKinley, Mount
Dender 103 B6 Fr. Dendre. River W Belgium
Denekamp 102 E3 Overijssel, E Netherlands
Den Haag see 's-Gravenhage
Den Ham 102 E3 Overijssel, E Netherlands
Denham 163 A5 Western Australia
Den Helder 102 C2 Noord-Holland, NW Netherlands
Denia 109 F4 País Valenciano, E Spain
Deniliquin 165 C7 New South Wales, SE Australia
Denison 61 F3 Iowa, C USA
Denison 65 G2 Texas, SW USA
Denizli 132 B4 Denizli, SW Turkey
Denmark 101 A7 off. Kingdom of Denmark, Dan. Danmark; anc. Hafnia. Country N Europe
Denmark Strait 98 D4 var. Danmarksstraedet. Strait Greenland/Iceland
Dennery 71 F1 E Saint Lucia
Denow 139 E3 Rus. Denau. Surkhondaryo Wiloyati, S Uzbekistan
Denpasar 154 D5 prev. Paloe. Bali, C Indonesia
Denton 65 G2 Texas, SW USA
D'Entrecasteaux Islands 160 B3 island group SE PNG
Denver 60 D4 state capital Colorado, C USA
Der'a see Dar'ā
Déraa see Dar'ā
Dera Ghāzi Khān 150 C2 var. Dera Ghāzikhān. Punjab, C Pakistan
Dera Ghāzikhān see Dera Ghāzi Khān
Đeravica 117 D5 mountain S Yugoslavia
Derbent 127 B8 Respublika Dagestan, SW Russian Federation
Derby 105 D6 C England, UK
Dereli see Gönoi
Derg, Lough 105 A6 Ir. Loch Deirgeirt. Lake W Ireland
Derhachi 125 G2 Rus. Dergachi. Kharkivs'ka Oblast', E Ukraine
De Ridder 58 A3 Louisiana, S USA
Dérna see Darnah
Derry see Londonderry
Derventa 116 B3 N Bosnia and Herzegovina
Deschutes River 62 B3 river Oregon, NW USA
Desē 88 C4 var. Desse, It. Dessie. N Ethiopia
Deseado, Río 81 B7 river S Argentina
Desertas, Ilhas 86 A2 island group Madeira, Portugal, NE Atlantic Ocean
Deshu see Deh Shū
Desierto de Altar see Sonoran Desert
Des Moines 61 F3 state capital Iowa, C USA
Desna 125 E2 river Russian Federation/Ukraine
Dessau 110 C4 Sachsen-Anhalt, E Germany
Desse see Desē
Dessie see Desē
Detroit 56 D3 Michigan, N USA
Detroit Lakes 61 F2 Minnesota, N USA
Deurne 103 D5 Noord-Brabant, SE Netherlands
Deva 124 B4 Ger. Diemrich, Hung. Déva. Hunedoara, W Romania
Đevđelija see Gevgelija
Deventer 102 D3 Overijssel, E Netherlands
Devils Lake 61 E1 North Dakota, N USA
Devoll see Devollit, Lumi i
Devollit, Lumi i 117 D6 var. Devoll. River SE Albania
Devon Island 53 F2 prev. North Devon Island. Island Parry Islands, Northwest Territories, NE Canada
Devonport 165 C8 Tasmania, SE Australia
Devrek 132 C2 Zonguldak, N Turkey
Dexter 61 H5 Missouri, C USA
Deynau 138 D3 var. Dyanev, Turkm. Dänew. Lebapskiy Velayat, NE Turkmenistan
Dezfūl 136 C3 var. Dizful. Khūzestān, SW Iran
Dezhou 144 D4 Shandong, E China
Dhaka 151 G4 prev. Dacca. Country capital (Bangladesh) Dhaka, C Bangladesh
Dhanbād 151 F4 Bihār, NE India
Dhekélia 118 C5 Eng. Dhekelia. Gk. Dekéleia. UK air base SE Cyprus
Dhidhimótikhon see Didymóteicho
Dhíkti Ori see Díkti
Dhodhekánisos see Dodekánisos
Dhomokós see Domokós
Dhráma see Dráma
Dhuusa Marreeb 89 E5 var. Dusa Marreb, It. Dusa Mareb. Galguduud, C Somalia
Diakovár see Đakovo
Diamantina, Chapada 79 F3 mountain range E Brazil
Diamantina Fracture Zone 157 E6 tectonic feature E Indian Ocean
Diarbekr see Diyarbakır
Dibrugarh 151 H3 Assam, NE India
Dickinson 60 D2 North Dakota, N USA
Didimotiho see Didymóteicho
Didymóteicho 120 D3 var. Dhidhimótikhon, Didimotiho. Anatolikí Makedonía kai Thráki, NE Greece
Diégo-Suarez see Antsirañana
Diekirch 103 D7 Diekirch, C Luxembourg
Điện Biên 152 D3 var. Bien Bien, Dien Bien Phu. Lai Châu, N Vietnam
Dien Bien Phu see Điện Biên
Diepenbeek 103 D6 Limburg, NE Belgium
Diepholz 110 B3 Niedersachsen, NW Germany
Dieppe 106 C2 Seine-Maritime, N France
Dieren 102 D4 Gelderland, E Netherlands
Differdange 103 D8 Luxembourg, SW Luxembourg
Digne 107 D6 var. Digne-les-Bains. Alpes-de-Haute-Provence, SE France
Digne-les-Bains see Digne
Digoin 106 C4 Saône-et-Loire, C France
Digul, Sungai 155 H5 prev. Digoel. River Irian Jaya, E Indonesia
Dihang see Brahmaputra
Dijon 106 D4 anc. Dibio. Côte d'Or, C France
Dikhil 88 D4 SW Djibouti
Dikson 130 D2 Taymyrskiy (Dolgano-Nenetskiy) Avtonomnyy Okrug, N Russian Federation
Díkti 121 D8 var. Dhíkti Ori. Mountain range Kríti, Greece, E Mediterranean Sea
Dili 155 F5 var. Dilli, Dilly. Timor, C Indonesia
Dilia 91 G3 var. Dillia. River SE Niger
Di Linh 153 E6 Lâm Đông, S Vietnam
Dilli see Delhi
Dilli see Dili
Dillia see Dilia
Dilling 88 B4 var. Ad Dalanj. Southern Kordofan, C Sudan
Dillon 60 B2 Montana, NW USA
Dilly see Dili
Dilolo 93 D7 Ngounié, S Gabon
Dimashq 135 B5 var. Ash Shām, Esh Sham, Eng. Damascus, Fr. Damas, It. Damasco. Country capital (Syria) Dimashq, SW Syria
Dimitrovgrad 120 D3 Khaskovska Oblast, S Bulgaria
Dimitrovgrad 127 C6 Ul'yanovskaya Oblast', W Russian Federation
Dimovo 120 B1 Oblast Montana, NW Bulgaria
Dinajpur 151 F3 Rajshahi, NW Bangladesh
Dinan 106 B3 Côtes d'Armor, NW France
Dinant 103 C7 Namur, S Belgium
Dinar 132 B4 Afyon, SW Turkey
Dinara see Dinaric Alps
Dinaric Alps 116 C4 var. Dinara. Mountain range Bosnia and Herzegovina/Croatia
Dindigul 148 C3 Tamil Nādu, SE India
Dingle Bay 105 A6 Ir. Bá an Daingin. Bay SW Ireland
Dinguiraye 90 C4 Haute-Guinée, N Guinea
Diourbel 90 B3 W Senegal
Dirē Dawa 89 D5 E Ethiopia
Dirk Hartog Island 163 A5 island Western Australia
Disappointment, Lake 162 C4 salt lake Western Australia
Dispur 151 G3 Assam, NE India
Divinópolis 79 F4 Minas Gerais, SE Brazil
Divo 90 D5 S Ivory Coast
Diyarbakır 133 E4 var. Diarbekr; anc. Amida. Diyarbakır, SE Turkey
Dizful see Dezfūl
Djajapura see Jayapura
Djakovica see Đakovica
Djakovo see Đakovo
Djambala 93 B6 Plateaux, C Congo
Djambi see Jambi
Djanet 87 E4 prev. Fort Charlet. SE Algeria
Djéblé see Jablah
Djelfa 86 D2 var. El Djelfa. N Algeria
Djéma 92 D4 Haut-Mbomou, E Central African Republic
Djérablous see Jarābulus
Djerba see Jerba, Île de
Djérem 92 B4 river C Cameroon
Djevdjelija see Gevgelija
Djibouti 88 D4 off. Republic of Djibouti, var. Jibuti; prev. French Somaliland, French Territory of the Afars and Issas, Fr. Côte Française des Somalis, Territoire Français des Afars et des Issas. Country E Africa
Djibouti 88 D4 var. Jibuti. Country capital (Djibouti) E Djibouti
Djourab, Erg du 92 C2 dunes N Chad
Djúpivogur 99 E5 Austurland, SE Iceland
Dnieper 97 F4 Bel. Dnyapro, Rus. Dnepr, Ukr. Dnipro. River E Europe
Dnieper Lowland 125 E2 Bel. Prydnyaprowskaya Nizina, Ukr. Prydniprovs'ka Nyzovyna. Lowlands Belorussia/Ukraine
Dniester 97 E4 Rom. Nistru, Rus. Dnestr, Ukr. Dnister; anc. Tyras. River Moldavia/Ukraine
Dnipro see Dnieper
Dniprodzerzhyns'k 125 F3 Rus. Dneprodzerzhinsk; prev. Kamenskoye. Dnipropetrovs'ka Oblast', E Ukraine
Dniprodzerzhyns'ke Vodoskhovyshche 125 F3 Rus. Dneprodzerzhinskoye Vodokhranilishche. Reservoir C Ukraine
Dnipropetrovs'k 125 F3 Rus. Dnepropetrovsk; prev. Yekaterinoslav. Dnipropetrovs'ka Oblast', E Ukraine
Dniprorudne 125 F3 Rus. Dneprorudnoye. Zaporiz'ka Oblast', SE Ukraine
Doba 92 C4 Logone-Oriental, S Chad
Döbeln 110 D4 Sachsen, E Germany
Doberai, Jazirah 155 G4 Dut. Vogelkop. Peninsula Irian Jaya, E Indonesia
Doboj 116 C3 N Bosnia and Herzegovina
Dobre Miasto 114 D2 Ger. Guttstadt. Olsztyn, N Poland
Dobrich 120 E1 Rom. Bazargic; prev. Tolbukhin. Varnenska Oblast, NE Bulgaria
Dobrush 123 D7 Homyel'skaya Voblasts', SE Belorussia
Dodecánese see Dodekánisos
Dodekánisos 121 D6 var. Nóties Sporádes, Eng. Dodecanese; prev. Dhodhekánisos. Island group SE Greece
Dodge City 61 E5 Kansas, C USA
Dodoma 85 D5 country capital (Tanzania) Dodoma, C Tanzania
Dodoma 89 C7 region C Tanzania
Dogana 112 E1 NE San Marino
Dōgo 147 B6 island Oki-shotō, SW Japan
Dogondoutchi 91 F3 Dosso, SW Niger
Doğubayazıt 133 F3 Ağrı, E Turkey
Doğu Karadeniz Dağları 133 E3 var. Anadolu Dağları. Mountain range NE Turkey
Doha see Ad Dawḩah
Doire see Londonderry
Dokkum 102 D1 Friesland, N Netherlands
Dokuchayevs'k 125 G3 var. Dokuchayevsk. Donets'ka Oblast', SE Ukraine
Dokuchayevsk see Dokuchayevs'k
Doldrums Fracture Zone 82 C4 tectonic feature W Atlantic Ocean
Dôle 106 D4 Jura, E France
Dolisie 93 B6 prev. Loubomo. Le Niari, S Congo
Dolomites see Dolomitiche, Alpi
Dolomiti see Dolomitiche, Alpi
Dolomitiche, Alpi 112 C1 var. Dolomiti, Eng. Dolomites. Mountain range NE Italy
Dolores 80 D4 Buenos Aires, E Argentina
Dolores 68 B1 Petén, N Guatemala
Dolores 80 D4 Soriano, SW Uruguay
Dolores Hidalgo 67 E4 var. Ciudad de Dolores Hidalgo. Guanajuato, C Mexico
Dolyna 124 B2 Rus. Dolina. Ivano-Frankivs'ka Oblast', W Ukraine
Dolyns'ka 125 F3 Rus. Dolinskaya. Kirovohrads'ka Oblast', S Ukraine
Domachëvo see Damachava
Domaczewo see Damachava
Dombås 101 B5 Oppland, S Norway
Domel Island see Letsôk-aw Kyun
Domeyko 80 B3 Atacama, N Chile
Dominica 71 H4 off. Commonwealth of Dominica. Country E West Indies
Dominica Channel see Martinique Passage
Dominican Republic 71 E2 country C West Indies
Domokós 121 B5 var. Dhomokós. Stereá Ellás, C Greece
Don 127 B6 var. Duna, Tanais. River SW Russian Federation
Donau see Danube
Donauwörth 111 C6 Bayern, S Germany
Don Benito 108 C3 Extremadura, W Spain
Doncaster 105 D5 anc. Danum. N England, UK
Dondo 94 B1 Cuanza Norte, NW Angola
Donegal 105 B5 Ir. Dún na nGall. NW Ireland
Donegal Bay 105 A5 Ir. Bá Dhún na nGall. Bay NW Ireland
Donets 125 G2 river Russian Federation/Ukraine
Donets'k 125 G3 Rus. Donetsk; prev. Stalino. Donets'ka Oblast', E Ukraine
Dongfang 144 B7 var. Basuo. Hainan, S China
Dongguan 144 C6 Guangdong, S China
Đông Ha 152 E4 Quang Tri, C Vietnam
Đông Hơi 152 D4 Quang Binh, C Vietnam
Dongliao see Liaoyuan
Dongola 88 B3 var. Donqola, Dunqulah. Northern, N Sudan
Dongou 93 C5 La Likouala, NE Congo
Dongting Hu 144 C5 var. Tung-t'ing Hu. Lake S China
Donostia-San Sebastián 109 E1 País Vasco, N Spain
Donqola see Dongola
Doolow 89 D5 SE Ethiopia
Doornik see Tournai
Door Peninsula 56 C2 peninsula Wisconsin, N USA
Dooxo Nugaaleed 89 E5 var. Nogal Valley. Valley E Somalia
Dordogne 107 B5 cultural region SW France
Dordogne 107 B5 river W France
Dordrecht 102 C4 var. Dordt, Dort. Zuid-Holland, SW Netherlands
Dordt see Dordrecht
Dorohoi 124 C3 Botoşani, NE Romania
Dorotea 100 C4 Västerbotten, N Sweden
Dorre Island 163 A5 island Western Australia
Dort see Dordrecht
Dortmund 110 A4 Nordrhein-Westfalen, W Germany
Dos Hermanas 108 C4 Andalucía, S Spain
Dospad Dagh see Rhodope Mountains
Dospat 120 C3 Plovdivska Oblast, SW Bulgaria
Dothan 58 D3 Alabama, S USA
Dotnuva 122 B4 Kėdainiai, C Lithuania
Douai 106 C2 prev. Douay, anc. Duacum. Nord, N France
Douala 93 A5 var. Duala. Littoral, W Cameroon
Douglas 105 C5 dependent territory capital (Isle of Man) E Isle of Man
Douglas 64 C3 Arizona, SW USA
Douglas 60 D3 Wyoming, C USA
Douro 108 B2 Sp. Duero. River Portugal/Spain see also Duero
Dover 105 E7 Fr. Douvres; Lat. Dubris Portus. SE England, UK
Dover 57 F4 state capital Delaware, NE USA
Dover, Strait of 106 C2 var. Straits of Dover, Fr. Pas de Calais. Strait England, UK/France
Dover, Straits of see Dover, Strait of
Dovrefjell 101 B5 plateau S Norway
Downpatrick 105 B5 Ir. Dún Pádraig. SE Northern Ireland, UK
Dözen 147 B6 island Oki-shotō, SW Japan
Drač see Durrës
Drachten 102 D2 Friesland, N Netherlands
Drăgăşani 124 B5 Vâlcea, SW Romania

Ernākulam – French Polynesia

Ernākulam *148 C3* Kerala, SW India
Erode *148 C2* Tamil Nādu, SE India
Erquelinnes *103 B7* Hainaut, S Belgium
Er-Rachidia *86 C2 var.* Ksar al Soule. E Morocco
Er Rahad *88 B4 var.* Ar Rahad. Northern Kordofan, C Sudan
Erromango *160 D4 island* S Vanuatu
Ertis *see* Irtysh
Erzgebirge *111 C5 Cz.* Krušné Hory, *Eng.* Ore Mountains. *Mountain range* Czech Republic/Germany *see also* Krušné Hory
Erzincan *133 E3 var.* Erzinjan. Erzincan, E Turkey
Erzinjan *see* Erzincan
Erzurum *133 E3 prev.* Erzerum. Erzurum, NE Turkey
Esbjerg *101 A7* Ribe, W Denmark
Escaldes *107 A8* C Andorra
Escanaba *56 C2* Michigan, N USA
Esch-sur-Alzette *103 D8* Luxembourg, S Luxembourg
Escondido *63 C8* California, W USA
Escuinapa *66 D3 var.* Escuinapa de Hidalgo. Sinaloa, C Mexico
Escuinapa de Hidalgo *see* Escuinapa
Escuintla *67 G5* Chiapas, SE Mexico
Escuintla *68 B2* Escuintla, S Guatemala
Eşfahān *136 C3 Eng.* Isfahan; *anc.* Aspadana. Eşfahān, C Iran
Esh Sham *see* Dimashq
Esh Sharā *see* Ash Sharāh
Eskişehir *132 B3 var.* Eskishehr. Eskişehir, W Turkey
Eskishehr *see* Eskişehir
Eslāmābād *136 C3 var.* Eslāmābād-e Gharb; *prev.* Harunabad, Shāhābād. Kermānshāhān, W Iran
Eslāmābād-e Gharb *see* Eslāmābād
Esmeraldas *76 A1* Esmeraldas, N Ecuador
Esna *see* Isna
Espanola *64 D1* New Mexico, SW USA
Esperance *163 B7* Western Australia
Esperanza *170 A2 Argentinian research station* Antarctica
Esperanza *66 B2* Sonora, NW Mexico
Espinal *74 B3* Tolima, C Colombia
Espinhaço, Serra do *72 D4 mountain range* SE Brazil
Espírito Santo *79 F4 off.* Estado do Espírito Santo. *State* E Brazil
Espiritu Santo *160 C4 var.* Santo. *Island* W Vanuatu
Espoo *101 D6 Swe.* Esbo. Uusimaa, S Finland
Esquel *81 B6* Chubut, SW Argentina
Essaouira *86 B2 prev.* Mogador. W Morocco
Es Semara *see* Smara
Essen *110 A4 var.* Essen an der Ruhr. Nordrhein-Westfalen, W Germany
Essen *103 C5* Antwerpen, N Belgium
Essen an der Ruhr *see* Essen
Essequibo River *75 F3 river* C Guyana
Es Suweida *see* As Suwaydā'
Estacado, Llano *65 E2 plain* New Mexico/Texas, SW USA
Estados, Isla de los *81 C8 prev. Eng.* Staten Island. *Island* S Argentina
Estância *79 G3* Sergipe, E Brazil
Estelí *68 D3* Estelí, NW Nicaragua
Estella *109 E1* Navarra, N Spain
Estepona *108 D5* Andalucía, S Spain
Estevan *53 F5* Saskatchewan, S Canada
Estonia *122 D2 off.* Republic of Estonia, *Est.* Eesti Vabariik, *Ger.* Estland, *Latv.* Igaunija; *prev.* Estonian SSR, *Rus.* Estonskaya SSR. *Country* NE Europe
Estrela, Serra da *108 C3 mountain range* C Portugal
Estremoz *108 C4* Évora, S Portugal
Esztergom *115 C6 Ger.* Gran; *anc.* Strigonium. Komárom-Esztergom, N Hungary
Étalle *103 D8* Luxembourg, SE Belgium
Etāwah *150 D3* Uttar Pradesh, N India
Ethiopia *89 C5 off.* Federal Democratic Republic of Ethiopia; *prev.* Abyssinia, People's Democratic Republic of Ethiopia. *Country* E Africa
Ethiopian Highlands *89 C5 var.* Ethiopian Plateau. *Plateau* N Ethiopia
Ethiopian Plateau *see* Ethiopian Highlands
Etna, Monte *113 C7 Eng.* Mount Etna. *Volcano* Sicilia, Italy, C Mediterranean Sea
Etna, Mount *see* Etna, Monte
Etosha Pan *94 B3 salt lake* N Namibia
Etoumbi *93 B5* Cuvette, NW Congo
Et Tafila *see* Aṭ Ṭafīlah
Ettelbrück *103 D8* Diekirch, C Luxembourg
'Eua *161 E5 prev.* Middleburg Island. *Island* Tongatapu Group, SE Tonga
Euboea *see* Évvoia
Eucla *163 D6* Western Australia
Euclid *56 D3* Ohio, N USA
Eufaula Lake *65 G1 var.* Eufaula Reservoir. *Reservoir* Oklahoma, C USA
Eufaula Reservoir *see* Eufaula Lake
Eugene *62 B3* Oregon, NW USA
Eupen *103 D6* Liège, E Belgium
Euphrates *128 B4 Ar.* Al Furāt, *Turk.* Firat Nehri. *River* SW Asia
Eureka *63 A5* California, W USA
Eureka *60 A1* Montana, NW USA
Europa Point *109 H5 headland* S Gibraltar
Europe *50 E1 continent*
Eutin *110 C2* Schleswig-Holstein, N Germany
Euxine Sea *see* Black Sea
Evansdale *61 G3* Iowa, C USA
Evanston *56 B3* Illinois, N USA
Evanston *60 B4* Wyoming, C USA
Evansville *56 B5* Indiana, N USA
Eveleth *61 G1* Minnesota, N USA
Everard, Lake *165 A6 salt lake* South Australia
Everest, Mount *142 B5 Chin.* Qomolangma Feng, *Nep.* Sagarmatha. *Mountain* China/Nepal
Everett *62 B2* Washington, NW USA
Everglades, The *59 F5 wetland* Florida, SE USA
Evje *101 A6* Aust-Agder, S Norway
Évora *108 B4 anc.* Ebora, *Lat.* Liberalitas Julia. Évora, C Portugal
Évreux *106 C3 anc.* Civitas Eburovicum. Eure, N France
Évros *see* Maritsa
Évry *106 E2* Essonne, N France
Évvoia *117 E8 Lat.* Euboea. *Island* C Greece
Ewarton *70 B5* C Jamaica
Excelsior Springs *61 F4* Missouri, C USA
Exe *105 C7 river* SW England, UK
Exeter *105 C7 anc.* Isca Damnoniorum. SW England, UK
Exmoor *105 C7 moorland* SW England, UK
Exmouth *105 C7* SW England, UK
Exmouth *162 A4* Western Australia
Exmouth Gulf *162 A4 gulf* Western Australia
Exmouth Plateau *157 E5 undersea feature* E Indian Ocean
Extremadura *108 C3 cultural and historical region* W Spain
Exuma Cays *70 C1 islets* C Bahamas
Exuma Sound *70 C1 sound* C Bahamas
Eyre Mountains *167 A7 mountain range* South Island, NZ
Eyre North, Lake *165 A5 salt lake* South Australia
Eyre Peninsula *165 A6 peninsula* South Australia
Eyre South, Lake *165 A5 salt lake* South Australia

F

Faadhippolhu Atoll *148 B4 var.* Fadiffolu, Lhaviyani Atoll. *Atoll* N Maldives
Fabens *64 D3* Texas, SW USA
Fada *92 C2* Borkou-Ennedi-Tibesti, E Chad
Fada-Ngourma *91 E4* E Burkina
Fadiffolu *see* Faadhippolhu Atoll
Faenza *112 C3 anc.* Faventia. Emilia-Romagna, N Italy
Faeroe-Iceland Ridge *96 C1 undersea feature* NW Norwegian Sea
Faeroe-Shetland Trough *96 C2 undersea feature* NE Atlantic Ocean
Faeroes Islands *99 E5 Dan.* Færøerne, *Faer.* Føroyar. *Danish external territory* N Atlantic Ocean
Faetano *112 E2* E San Marino
Făgăraş *124 C4 Ger.* Fogarasch, *Hung.* Fogaras. Braşov, C Romania
Fagibina, Lake *see* Faguibine, Lac
Fagne *103 C7 hill range* S Belgium
Faguibine, Lac *91 E3 var.* Lake Fagibina. *Lake* NW Mali
Fahlun *see* Falun
Fahraj *136 E4* Kermān, SE Iran
Faial *108 A5 var.* Ilha do Faial. *Island* Azores, Portugal, NE Atlantic Ocean
Fairbanks *52 D3* Alaska, USA
Fairfield *63 B6* California, W USA
Fair Isle *104 D2 island* NE Scotland, UK
Fairlie *167 B6* Canterbury, South Island, NZ
Fairmont *61 F3* Minnesota, N USA
Faisalābād *150 C2 prev.* Lyallpur. Punjab, NE Pakistan
Faizābād *see* Feyzābād
Faizābād *151 E3* Uttar Pradesh, N India
Fakaofo Atoll *161 F3 island* SE Tokelau
Falam *152 A3* Chin State, W Burma
Falconara Marittima *112 C3* Marche, C Italy
Falkland Islands *81 D7 var.* Falklands, Islas Malvinas. *UK dependent territory* SW Atlantic Ocean
Falkland Plateau *73 D7 var.* Argentine Rise. *Undersea feature* SW Atlantic Ocean
Falklands *see* Falkland Islands
Fallbrook *63 C8* California, W USA
Falmouth *105 C7* SW England, UK
Falmouth *70 A4* W Jamaica
Falster *101 B8 island* SE Denmark
Fălticeni *124 C3 Hung.* Falticsén. Suceava, NE Romania
Falun *101 C6 var.* Fahlun. Kopparberg, C Sweden
Famagusta *see* Ammóchostos
Famagusta Bay *see* Kólpos Ammóchostos
Famenne *103 C7 physical region* SE Belgium
Fang *152 C3* Chiang Mai, NW Thailand
Fano *112 C3 anc.* Colonia Julia Fanestris, Fanum Fortunae. Marche, C Italy
Farafangana *95 G4* Fianarantsoa, SE Madagascar
Farāh *138 D4 var.* Farah, Fararud. Farāh, W Afghanistan
Farāh Rūd *138 D4 river* W Afghanistan
Faranah *90 C4* Haute-Guinée, S Guinea
Fararud *see* Farāh
Farasān, Jazā'ir *137 A6 island group* SW Saudi Arabia
Farewell, Cape *166 C4 headland* South Island, NZ
Farghona *139 F2 Rus.* Fergana; *prev.* Novyy Margilan. Farghona Wiloyati, E Uzbekistan
Fargo *61 F2* North Dakota, N USA
Faribault *61 F2* Minnesota, N USA
Farīdābād *150 D3* Haryāna, N India
Farkhor *139 E3 Rus.* Parkhar. SW Tajikistan
Farmington *61 G5* Missouri, C USA
Farmington *64 C1* New Mexico, SW USA
Faro *108 B5* Faro, S Portugal
Farquhar Group *95 G2 island group* S Seychelles
Fastiv *125 E2 Rus.* Fastov. Kyyivs'ka Oblast', NW Ukraine
Fauske *100 C3* Nordland, C Norway
Faxaflói *98 D5 Eng.* Faxa Bay. *Bay* W Iceland
Faya *92 C2 prev.* Faya-Largeau, Largeau. Borkou-Ennedi-Tibesti, N Chad
Fayetteville *58 A1* Arkansas, C USA
Fayetteville *59 F1* North Carolina, SE USA
Fdérick *see* Fdérik
Fdérik *90 C2 var.* Fdérick, *Fr.* Fort Gouraud. Tiris Zemmour, NW Mauritania
Fear, Cape *59 F2 headland* Bald Head Island, North Carolina, SE USA
Fécamp *106 B3* Seine-Maritime, N France
Federation of the separate territories of *see* Malaysia
Fehérgyarmat *115 E6* Szabolcs-Szatmár-Bereg, E Hungary
Fehmarn *110 C2 island* N Germany
Fehmarn Belt *110 C2 Ger.* Fehmarnbelt. *Strait* Denmark/Germany
Feijó *78 C2* Acre, W Brazil
Feilding *166 D4* Manawatu-Wanganui, North Island, NZ
Feira *see* Feira de Santana
Feira de Santana *79 G3 var.* Feira. Bahia, E Brazil
Felanitx *109 G3 anc.* Canati, Felaniche. Mallorca, Spain, W Mediterranean Sea
Felidhu Atoll *148 B4 atoll* C Maldives
Felipe Carrillo Puerto *67 H4* Quintana Roo, SE Mexico
Felixstowe *105 E6* E England, UK
Femunden *101 B5 lake* S Norway
Fengcheng *144 D3 var.* Feng-cheng, Fenghwangcheng. Liaoning, NE China
Feng-cheng *see* Fengcheng
Fenghwangcheng *see* Fengcheng
Fengtien *see* Liaoning
Fenoarivo *95 G3* Toamasina, E Madagascar
Fens, The *105 E6 wetland* E England, UK
Feodosiya *125 F5 var.* Kefe, *It.* Kaffa; *anc.* Theodosia. Respublika Krym, S Ukraine
Féres *120 D3* Anatolikí Makedonía kai Thráki, NE Greece
Fergus Falls *61 F2* Minnesota, N USA
Ferkessédougou *90 D4* N Ivory Coast
Fermo *112 C4 anc.* Firmum Picenum. Marche, C Italy
Fernandina, Isla *76 A4 var.* Narborough Island. *Island* Galapagos Islands, Ecuador, E Pacific Ocean
Fernando de Noronha *79 H2 island* E Brazil
Fernando Po *see* Bioco, Isla de
Fernando Póo *see* Bioco, Isla de
Ferrara *112 C2 anc.* Forum Alieni. Emilia-Romagna, N Italy
Ferreñafe *76 B3* Lambayeque, W Peru
Ferro *see* Hierro
Ferrol *108 B1 var.* El Ferrol; *prev.* El Ferrol del Caudillo. Galicia, NW Spain
Ferwerd *102 D1 Fris.* Ferwert. Friesland, N Netherlands
Fès *86 C2 Eng.* Fez. N Morocco
Feteşti *124 D5* Ialomiţa, SE Romania
Fethiye *132 B4* Muğla, SW Turkey
Fetlar *104 D1 island* NE Scotland, UK
Feyzābād *139 F3 var.* Faizabad, Faizābād, Feyzābād, Fyzabad. Badakhshān, NE Afghanistan
Fianarantsoa *95 F3* Fianarantsoa, C Madagascar
Fianga *92 B4* Mayo-Kébbi, SW Chad
Fier *117 C6 var.* Fieri. Fier, SW Albania
Fieri *see* Fier
Figeac *107 C5* Lot, S France
Figig *see* Figuig
Figueira da Foz *108 B3* Coimbra, W Portugal
Figueres *109 G2* Cataluña, E Spain
Figuig *86 D2 var.* Figig. E Morocco
Fiji *161 E5 off.* Sovereign Democratic Republic of Fiji, *Fij.* Viti. *Country* SW Pacific Ocean
Filadelfia *68 D4* Guanacaste, W Costa Rica
Filiaşi *124 B5* Dolj, SW Romania
Filipstad *101 B6* Värmland, C Sweden
Finale Ligure *112 A3* Liguria, NW Italy
Finchley *105 A7* SE England, UK
Findlay *56 C4* Ohio, N USA
Finike *132 B4* Antalya, SW Turkey
Finland *100 D4 off.* Republic of Finland, *Fin.* Suomen Tasavalta, Suomi. *Country* N Europe
Finland, Gulf of *101 D6 Est.* Soome Laht, *Fin.* Suomenlahti, *Ger.* Finnischer Meerbusen, *Rus.* Finskiy Zaliv, *Swe.* Finska Viken. *Gulf* E Baltic Sea
Finnmarksvidda *100 D2 physical region* N Norway
Finsterwalde *110 D4* Brandenburg, E Germany
Fiordland *167 A7 physical region* South Island, NZ
Fiorina *112 E1* NE San Marino
Firenze *112 C3 Eng.* Florence; *anc.* Florentia. Toscana, C Italy
Fischbacher Alpen *111 E7 mountain range* E Austria
Fish *94 B4 var.* Vis. *River* S Namibia
Fishguard *105 C6 Wel.* Abergwaun. SW Wales, UK
Fisterra, Cabo *108 B1 headland* NW Spain
Fitzroy Crossing *162 C3* Western Australia
Fitzroy River *162 C3 river* Western Australia
Flagstaff *64 B2* Arizona, SW USA
Flanders *103 A6 Dut.* Vlaanderen, *Fr.* Flandre. *Cultural region* Belgium/France
Flathead Lake *60 B1 lake* Montana, NW USA
Flat Island *144 C8 island* NE Spratly Islands
Flatts Village *58 B5 var.* The Flatts Village. C Bermuda
Flensburg *110 B2* Schleswig-Holstein, N Germany
Flinders Island *165 C8 island* Furneaux Group, Tasmania, SE Australia
Flinders Ranges *165 B6 mountain range* South Australia
Flinders River *164 C3 river* Queensland, NE Australia
Flin Flon *53 F5* Manitoba, C Canada
Flint *56 C3* Michigan, N USA
Flint Island *161 G4 island* Line Islands, E Kiribati
Floreana, Isla *see* Santa María, Isla
Florence *see* Firenze
Florence *58 C1* Alabama, S USA
Florence *59 F2* South Carolina, SE USA
Florencia *74 B4* Caquetá, S Colombia
Florentia *see* Firenze
Flores *108 A5 island* Azores, Portugal, NE Atlantic Ocean
Flores *155 E5 island* Nusa Tenggara, C Indonesia
Flores *68 B1* Petén, N Guatemala
Flores Sea *154 D5 Ind.* Laut Flores. *Sea* C Indonesia
Floriano *79 F2* Piauí, E Brazil
Florianópolis *79 F5 prev.* Destêrro. *State capital* Santa Catarina, S Brazil
Florida *59 E4 off.* State of Florida; also known as Peninsular State, Sunshine State. *State* SE USA
Florida *80 D4* Florida, S Uruguay
Florida Bay *59 E5 bay* Florida, SE USA
Florida Keys *59 E5 island group* Florida, SE USA
Florida, Straits of *70 B1 strait* Atlantic Ocean/Gulf of Mexico
Flórina *120 B4 var.* Phlórina. Dytikí Makedonía, N Greece
Florissant *61 G4* Missouri, C USA
Floúda, Ákra *121 D7 headland* Astypálaia, Kykládes, Greece, Aegean Sea
Foča *116 C4* SE Bosnia and Herzegovina
Focşani *124 C4* Vrancea, E Romania
Foggia *113 D5* Puglia, SE Italy
Fogo *90 A3 island* Ilhas de Sotavento, SW Cape Verde
Foix *107 B6* Ariège, S France
Folégandros *121 C7 island* Kykládes, Greece, Aegean Sea
Foleyet *54 C4* Ontario, S Canada
Foligno *112 C4* Umbria, C Italy
Folkestone *105 E7* SE England, UK
Fond du Lac *56 B2* Wisconsin, N USA
Fongafale *161 E3 var.* Funafuti. *Country capital* (Tuvalu) Funafuti Atoll, SE Tuvalu
Fonseca, Gulf of *68 C3 Sp.* Golfo de Fonseca. *Gulf* Central America
Fontainebleau *106 C3* Seine-et-Marne, N France
Fontenay-le-Comte *106 B4* Vendée, NW France
Fontvieille *107 B8* SW Monaco
Fonyód *115 C7* Somogy, W Hungary
Foochow *see* Fuzhou
Forchheim *111 C5* Bayern, SE Germany
Forel, Mont *98 D4 mountain* SE Greenland
Forfar *104 C3* E Scotland, UK
Forge du Sud *see* Dudelange
Forlì *112 C3 anc.* Forum Livii. Emilia-Romagna, N Italy
Formentera *109 G4 anc.* Ophiusa, *Lat.* Frumentum. *Island* Islas Baleares, Spain, W Mediterranean Sea
Formosa *80 D2* Formosa, NE Argentina
Formosa, Serra *79 E3 mountain range* C Brazil
Formosa Strait *see* Taiwan Strait
Forrest City *58 B1* Arkansas, C USA
Fort Albany *54 C3* Ontario, C Canada
Fortaleza *79 G2 prev.* Ceará. *State capital* Ceará, NE Brazil
Fortaleza *77 F2* Pando, N Bolivia
Fort-Bayard *see* Zhanjiang
Fort-Cappolani *see* Tidjikja
Fort Collins *60 D4* Colorado, C USA
Fort Davis *65 E3* Texas, SW USA
Fort-de-France *71 H4 prev.* Fort-Royal. *Dependent territory capital* (Martinique) W Martinique
Fort Dodge *61 F3* Iowa, C USA
Fortescue River *162 A4 river* Western Australia
Fort Frances *54 B4* Ontario, S Canada
Fort Good Hope *53 E3 var.* Good Hope. Northwest Territories, NW Canada
Fort Gouraud *see* Fdérik
Forth *104 C4 river* C Scotland, UK
Forth, Firth of *104 C4 estuary* E Scotland, UK
Fort-Lamy *see* Ndjamena
Fort Lauderdale *59 F5* Florida, SE USA
Fort Liard *53 E4 var.* Liard. Northwest Territories, W Canada
Fort Madison *61 G4* Iowa, C USA
Fort McMurray *53 E4* Alberta, C Canada
Fort McPherson *52 D3 var.* McPherson. Northwest Territories, NW Canada
Fort Morgan *60 D4* Colorado, C USA
Fort Myers *59 F5* Florida, SE USA
Fort Nelson *53 E4* British Columbia, W Canada
Fort Peck Lake *60 C1 reservoir* Montana, NW USA
Fort Pierce *59 F4* Florida, SE USA
Fort Providence *53 E4 var.* Providence. Northwest Territories, W Canada
Fort St.John *53 E4* British Columbia, W Canada
Fort Scott *61 F5* Kansas, C USA
Fort Severn *54 C2* Ontario, C Canada
Fort-Shevchenko *130 A4* Mangistau, W Kazakhstan
Fort Simpson *53 E4 var.* Simpson. Northwest Territories, W Canada
Fort Smith *53 E4 district capital* Northwest Territories, W Canada
Fort Smith *58 B1* Arkansas, C USA
Fort Stockton *65 E3* Texas, SW USA
Fort-Trinquet *see* Bîr Mogreïn
Fort Vermilion *53 E4* Alberta, W Canada
Fort Walton Beach *58 C3* Florida, SE USA
Fort Wayne *56 C4* Indiana, N USA
Fort William *104 C3* N Scotland, UK
Fort Worth *65 G2* Texas, SW USA
Fort Yukon *52 D3* Alaska, USA
Fougamou *93 A6* Ngounié, C Gabon
Fougères *106 B3* Ille-et-Vilaine, NW France
Fou-hsin *see* Fuxin
Foulwind, Cape *167 B5 headland* South Island, NZ
Foumban *92 A4* Ouest, NW Cameroon
Fou-shan *see* Fushun
Foveaux Strait *167 A8 strait* S NZ
Foxe Basin *53 G3 sea* Northwest Territories, N Canada
Fox Glacier *167 B6* West Coast, South Island, NZ
Fox Mine *53 F4* Manitoba, C Canada
Fraga *109 F2* Aragón, NE Spain
Fram Basin *171 C3 var.* Amundsen Basin. *Undersea feature* Arctic Ocean
France *106 B4 off.* French Republic, *It./Sp.* Francia; *prev.* Gaul, Gaule, *Lat.* Gallia. *Country* W Europe
Franceville *93 B6 var.* Massoukou, Masuku. Haut-Ogooué, E Gabon
Francfort prev *see* Frankfurt am Main
Franche-Comté *106 D4 cultural region* E France
Francis Case, Lake *61 E3 reservoir* South Dakota, N USA
Francisco Escárcega *67 G4* Campeche, SE Mexico
Francistown *94 D3* North East, NE Botswana
Franconian Jura *see* Fränkische Alb
Frankenalb *see* Fränkische Alb
Frankenstein *see* Ząbkowice Śląskie
Frankenstein in Schlesien *see* Ząbkowice Śląskie
Frankfort *56 C5 state capital* Kentucky, S USA
Frankfort on the Main *see* Frankfurt am Main
Frankfurt *see* Frankfurt am Main
Frankfurt am Main *111 B5 var.* Frankfurt, *Fr.* Francfort; prev. *Eng.* Frankfort on the Main. Hessen, SW Germany
Frankfurt an der Oder *110 D3* Brandenburg, E Germany
Fränkische Alb *111 C6 var.* Frankenalb, *Eng.* Franconian Jura. *Mountain range* S Germany
Franklin *58 C1* Tennessee, S USA
Franklin D.Roosevelt Lake *62 C1 reservoir* Washington, NW USA
Frantsa-Iosifa, Zemlya *130 D1 Eng.* Franz Josef Land. *Island group* N Russian Federation
Franz Josef Land *see* Frantsa-Iosifa, Zemlya
Fraserburgh *104 D3* NE Scotland, UK
Fraser Island *164 E4 var.* Great Sandy Island. *Island* Queensland, E Australia
Fredericksburg *57 E5* Virginia, NE USA
Fredericton *55 F4* New Brunswick, SE Canada
Frederikshåb *see* Paamiut
Fredrikstad *101 B6* Østfold, S Norway
Freeport *70 C1* Grand Bahama Island, N Bahamas
Freeport *65 H4* Texas, SW USA
Freetown *90 C4 country capital* (Sierra Leone) W Sierra Leone
Freiburg *see* Freiburg im Breisgau
Freiburg im Breisgau *111 A6 var.* Freiburg, *Fr.* Fribourg-en-Brisgau. Baden-Württemberg, SW Germany
Fremantle *163 A6* Western Australia
Fremont *61 F4* Nebraska, C USA
French Guiana *75 H3 var.* Guiana, Guyane. *French overseas department* N South America
French Polynesia *159 F4 French overseas territory* C Polynesia

Karaginskiy, Ostrov – Kirkkoniemi

Karaginskiy, Ostrov *131 H2 island* E Russian Federation
Karak *see* Al Karak
Kara-Kala *138 C3 var.* Garrygala. Balkanskiy Velayat, W Turkmenistan
Karakax *see* Moyu
Karakılısse *see* Ağrı
Karakol *139 G2 prev.* Przheval'sk. Issyk-Kul'skaya Oblast', NE Kyrgyzstan
Karakol *139 G2 var.* Karakolka. Issyk-Kul'skaya Oblast', NE Kyrgyzstan
Karakolka *see* Karakol
Karakoram Range *150 D1 mountain range* C Asia
Karaköse *see* Ağrı
Kara Kum *see* Garagumy
Kara Kum Canal *see* Garagumskiy Kanal
Karakumskiy Kanal *see* Garagumskiy Kanal
Karamai *see* Karamay
Karaman *132 C4* Karaman, S Turkey
Karamay *142 B2 var.* Karamai, Kelamayi, *prev. Chin.* K'o-la-ma-i. Xinjiang Uygur Zizhiqu, NW China
Karamea Bight *167 B5 gulf* South Island, NZ
Karapelit *120 E1 Rom.* Stejarul. Varnenska Oblast, NE Bulgaria
Kara-Say *139 G2* Issyk-Kul'skaya Oblast', NE Kyrgyzstan
Karasburg *94 B4* Karas, S Namibia
Kara Sea *see* Karskoye More
Karatau *130 C5 Kaz.* Qarataū. Zhambyl, S Kazakhstan
Karavás *121 B7* Kýthira, S Greece
Karbalā' *136 B3 var.* Kerbala, Kerbela. S Iraq
Kardhítsa *see* Kardítsa
Kardítsa *121 B5 var.* Kardhítsa. Thessalía, C Greece
Kärdla *122 C2 Ger.* Kertel. Hiiumaa, W Estonia
Karet *see* Kâgheṭ
Kargı *132 C2* Çorum, N Turkey
Kargilik *see* Yecheng
Kariba *94 D2* Mashonaland West, N Zimbabwe
Kariba, Lake *94 D3 reservoir* Zambia / Zimbabwe
Karibib *94 B3* Erongo, C Namibia
Karies *see* Karyés
Karigasniemi *100 D2 Lapp.* Garegegasnjárga. Lappi, N Finland
Karimata, Selat *154 C4 strait* W Indonesia
Karīmnagar *150 D5* Andhra Pradesh, C India
Karin *88 D4* Woqooyi Galbeed, N Somalia
Kariot *see* Ikaría
Káristos *see* Kárystos
Karkinits'ka Zatoka *125 E4 Rus.* Karkinitskiy Zaliv. *Gulf* S Ukraine
Karkūk *see* Kirkūk
Karlovac *116 B3 Ger.* Karlstadt, *Hung.* Károlyváros. Karlovac, C Croatia
Karlovy Vary *115 A5 Ger.* Karlsbad; *prev. Eng.* Carlsbad. Západní Čechy, W Czech Republic
Karlskrona *101 C7* Blekinge, S Sweden
Karlsruhe *111 B6 var.* Carlsruhe. Baden-Württemberg, SW Germany
Karlstad *101 B6* Värmland, C Sweden
Karnāl *150 D2* Haryāna, N India
Karnātaka *148 C1 var.* Kanara; *prev.* Maisur, Mysore. Admin. region *state* W India
Karnobat *120 D2* Burgaska Oblast, E Bulgaria
Karnul *see* Kurnool
Karpaten *see* Carpathian Mountains
Kárpathos *121 E7 It.* Scarpanto; *anc.* Carpathos, Carpathus. *Island* SE Greece
Kárpathos *121 E7* Kárpathos, SE Greece
Karpaty *see* Carpathian Mountains
Karpenísi *121 B5 prev.* Karpenísion. Stereá Ellás, C Greece
Kars *133 F2 var.* Qars. Kars, NE Turkey
Kārsava *122 D4 Ger.* Karsau; *prev.* Rus. Korsovka. Ludza, E Latvia
Karskiye Vorota, Proliv *126 E2 Eng.* Kara Strait. *Strait* N Russian Federation
Karskoye More *130 D2 Eng.* Kara Sea. *Sea* Arctic Ocean
Karyés *120 C4 var.* Karies. Ágion Óros, N Greece
Kárystos *121 C6 var.* Káristos. Évvoia, C Greece
Kasai *93 C6 var.* Cassai, Kassai. *River* Angola / Congo (Zaire)
Kasaji *93 D7* Shaba, S Congo (Zaire)
Kasama *94 D1* Northern, N Zambia
Kāsaragod *148 B2* Kerala, SW India
Kāshān *136 C3* Eṣfahān, C Iran
Kashi *142 A3 Chin.* Kaxgar, K'o-shih, *Uigh.* Kashgar. Xinjiang Uygur Zizhiqu, NW China
Kasongo *93 D6* Maniema, E Congo (Zaire)
Kasongo-Lunda *93 C7* Bandundu, SW Congo (Zaire)
Kásos *121 D7 island* S Greece
Kaspiysk *127 B8* Respublika Dagestan, SW Russian Federation
Kassai *see* Kasai
Kassala *88 C4* Kassala, E Sudan
Kassel *110 B4 prev.* Cassel. Hessen, C Germany
Kasserine *87 E2 var.* Al Qaşrayn. W Tunisia
Kastamonu *132 C2 var.* Castamoni, Kastamuni. Kastamonu, N Turkey
Kastamuni *see* Kastamonu
Kastaneá *120 B4* Kentrikí Makedonía, N Greece
Kastélli *121 C7* Kríti, Greece, E Mediterranean Sea
Kastoría *120 B4* Dytikí Makedonía, N Greece
Kástro *121 C6* Sífnos, Kykládes, Greece, Aegean Sea
Kastsyukovichy *123 E7 Rus.* Kostyukovichi. Mahilyowskaya Voblasts', E Belorussia
Kastsyukowka *123 D7 Rus.* Kostyukovka. Homyel'skaya Voblasts', SE Belorussia
Kasulu *89 B7* Kigoma, W Tanzania
Kasumiga-ura *147 D5 lake* Honshū, S Japan
Katahdin, Mount *57 G1mountain* Maine, NE USA
Katalla *52 C3* Alaska, USA
Katana *see* Qaṭanā
Katanning *163 B7* Western Australia
Katawaz *see* Zarghūn Shahr
Katchall Island *149 F3 island* Nicobar Islands, India, NE Indian Ocean
Kateríni *120 B4* Kentrikí Makedonía, N Greece
Katha *152 B2* Sagaing, N Burma
Katherine *164 A2* Northern Territory, N Australia
Kathmandu *140 C3 prev.* Kantipur. *Country capital* (Nepal) Central, C Nepal
Katikati *166 D3* Bay of Plenty, North Island, NZ
Katima Mulilo *94 C3* Caprivi, NE Namibia
Katiola *90 D4* C Ivory Coast
Káto Achaïa *121 B5 var.* Kato Ahaia, Káto Akhaía. Dytikí Ellás, S Greece
Kato Ahaia *see* Káto Achaïa
Káto Akhaía *see* Káto Achaïa
Katoúna *121 A5* Dytikí Ellás, C Greece
Katowice *115 C5 Ger.* Kattowitz. Katowice, S Poland
Katsina *91 G3* Katsina, N Nigeria
Kattaqürghon *139 E2 Rus.* Kattakurgan. Samarqand Wiloyati, C Uzbekistan
Kattavía *121 E7* Ródos, Dodekánisos, Greece, Aegean Sea
Kattegat *101 B7 Dan.* Kattegatt. *Strait* N Europe
Kauai *63 A7 Haw.* Kaua'i. *Island* Hawaiian Islands, Hawaii, USA, C Pacific Ocean
Kaufbeuren *111 C6* Bayern, S Germany
Kaunas *122 B4 Ger.* Kauen, *Pol.* Kowno; *prev.* Rus. Kovno. Kaunas, C Lithuania
Kavadarci *117 E6 Turk.* Kavadar. C FYR Macedonia
Kavajë *117 C6 It.* Cavaia, Kavaja. Tiranë, W Albania
Kavála *120 C3 prev.* Kaválla. Anatolikí Makedonía kai Thráki, NE Greece
Kāvali *148 D2* Andhra Pradesh, E India
Kavango *see* Cubango
Kavaratti Island *148 A3 island* Lakshadweep, India, N Indian Ocean
Kavarna *120 E2* Varnenska Oblast, NE Bulgaria
Kavengo *see* Cubango
Kavīr, Dasht-e *136 D3 var.* Great Salt Desert. *Salt pan* N Iran
Kavīr-e Lūt *see* Lūt, Dasht-e
Kawagoe *147 D5* Saitama, Honshū, S Japan
Kawasaki *146 A2* Kanagawa, Honshū, S Japan
Kawerau *166 E3* Bay of Plenty, North Island, NZ
Kaya *91 E3* C Burkina
Kayan *152 B4* Yangon, SW Burma
Kayan, Sungai *154 D3 prev.* Kajan. *River* Borneo, C Indonesia
Kayes *90 C3* Kayes, W Mali
Kayseri *132 D3 var.* Kaisaria; *anc.* Caesarea Mazaca, Mazaca. Kayseri, C Turkey
Kazach'ye *131 F2* Respublika Sakha (Yakutiya), NE Russian Federation
Kazakhskiy Melkosopochnik *130 C4 Eng.* Kazakh Uplands, Kirghiz Steppe, *Kaz.* Saryarqa. *Uplands* C Kazakhstan
Kazakhstan *130 B4 off.* Republic of Kazakhstan, *var.* Kazakstan, *Kaz.* Qazaqstan, Qazaqstan Respublikasy; *prev.* Kazakh Soviet Socialist Republic, *Rus.* Kazakhskaya SSR. *Country* C Asia
Kazakh Uplands *see* Kazakhskiy Melkosopochnik
Kazan' *127 C5* Respublika Tatarstan, W Russian Federation
Kazanlŭk *120 D2 prev.* Kazanlik. Khaskovska Oblast, C Bulgaria
Kazbegi *see* Kazbek
Kazbek *133 F1 var.* Kazbegi, *Geor.* Mqinvartsveri. *Mountain* N Georgia
Kāzerūn *136 D4* Fārs, S Iran
Kazvin *see* Qazvīn
Kéa *121 C6 prev.* Kéos, *anc.* Ceos. *Island* Kykládes, Greece, Aegean Sea
Kéa *121 C6* Kéa, Kykládes, Greece, Aegean Sea
Kea, Mauna *63 B8 mountain* Hawaii, USA, C Pacific Ocean
Kéamu *see* Anatom
Kearney *61 E4* Nebraska, C USA
Keban Barajı *133 E3 reservoir* C Turkey
Kebkabiya *88 A4* Northern Darfur, W Sudan
Kebnekaise *100 C3 mountain* N Sweden
Kecskemét *115 D7* Bács-Kiskun, C Hungary
Kediri *154 D5* Jawa, C Indonesia
Keelung *see* Chilung
Keetmanshoop *94 B4* Karas, S Namibia
Kefallinía *121 A5 var.* Kefallonía. *Island* Iónioi Nísoi, Greece, C Mediterranean Sea
Kefallonía *see* Kefallinía
Kefe *see* Feodosiya
Kehl *111 A6* Baden-Württemberg, SW Germany
Keila *122 D2 Ger.* Kegel. Harjumaa, NW Estonia
Keïta *91 F3* Tahoua, C Niger
Keitele *100 D4 lake* C Finland
Keith *165 B7* South Australia
Këk-Art *139 G2 prev.* Alaykel', Alay-Kuu. Oshskaya Oblast', SW Kyrgyzstan
Kékes *115 C6 mountain* N Hungary
Kelamayi *see* Karamay
Kelang *see* Klang
Kelat *see* Kalāt
Kelifskiy Uzboy *138 D3 salt marsh* E Turkmenistan
Kelkit Çayı *133 E3 river* N Turkey
Kelmė *122 B4* Kelmė, C Lithuania
Kélo *92 B4* Tandjilé, SW Chad
Kelowna *53 E5* British Columbia, SW Canada
Kelso *62 B2* Washington, NW USA
Keluang *154 B3 var.* Kluang. Johor, Peninsular Malaysia
Kem' *126 B3* Respublika Kareliya, NW Russian Federation
Kemah *133 E3* Erzincan, E Turkey
Kemaman *see* Cukai
Kemerovo *130 D4 prev.* Shcheglovsk. Kemerovskaya Oblast', C Russian Federation
Kemi *100 D4* Lappi, NW Finland
Kemijärvi *100 D3 Swe.* Kemiträsk. Lappi, N Finland
Kemijoki *100 D3 river* NW Finland
Kemin *139 G2 prev.* Bystrovka. Chuyskaya Oblast', N Kyrgyzstan
Kempele *100 D4* Oulu, C Finland
Kempten *111 B7* Bayern, S Germany
Kendal *105 D5* NW England, UK
Kendari *155 E4* Sulawesi, C Indonesia
Kenedy *65 G4* Texas, SW USA
Kenema *90 C4* SE Sierra Leone
Këneurgench *138 C2 Turkm.* Köneürgench; *prev.* Kunya-Urgench. Dashkhovuzskiy Velayat, N Turkmenistan
Kenge *93 C6* Bandundu, SW Congo (Zaire)
Keng Tung *152 C3 var.* Kentung. Shan State, E Burma
Kénitra *86 C2 prev.* Port-Lyautey. NW Morocco
Kennett *61 H5* Missouri, C USA
Kennewick *62 C2* Washington, NW USA
Kenora *54 A3* Ontario, S Canada
Kenosha *56 B3* Wisconsin, N USA
Kentau *130 B5* Yuzhnyy Kazakhstan, S Kazakhstan
Kentucky *56 C5 off.* Commonwealth of Kentucky; also known as The Bluegrass State. *State* C USA
Kentucky Lake *56 B5 reservoir* Kentucky / Tennessee, S USA
Kentung *see* Keng Tung
Kenya *89 C6 off.* Republic of Kenya. *Country* E Africa
Keokuk *61 G4* Iowa, C USA
Kępno *114 C4* Kalisz, C Poland
Keppel Island *see* Niuatoputapu
Kepulauan Sangihe *see* Sangir, Kepulauan
Kerak *see* Al Karak
Kerala *148 C2 state* S India
Kerasunt *see* Giresun
Keratea *see* Keratéa
Keratéa *121 C6 var.* Keratea. Attikí, C Greece
Kerbala *see* Karbalā'
Kerbela *see* Karbalā'
Kerch *125 G5 Rus.* Kerch'. Respublika Krym, SE Ukraine
Kerchens'ka Protska *see* Kerch Strait
Kerchenskiy Proliv *see* Kerch Strait
Kerch Strait *125 G4 var.* Bosporus Cimmerius, Enikale Strait, *Rus.* Kerchenskiy Proliv, *Ukr.* Kerchens'ka Protska. *Strait* Black Sea / Sea of Azov
Kerguelen *157 C7 island* C French Southern and Antarctic Territories
Kerguelen Plateau *157 C7 undersea feature* S Indian Ocean
Kerí *121 A6* Zákynthos, Iónioi Nísoi, Greece, C Mediterranean Sea
Kerikeri *166 D2* Northland, North Island, NZ
Kerkenah, Îles de *118 D4 var.* Kerkenna Islands, *Ar.* Juzur Qarqannah. *Island group* E Tunisia
Kerkenna Islands *see* Kerkenah, Îles de
Kerki *138 D3* Lebapskiy Velayat, E Turkmenistan
Kérkira *see* Kérkyra
Kerkrade *103 D6* Limburg, SE Netherlands
Kerkuk *see* Kirkūk
Kérkyra *120 A4 var.* Kérkira, *Eng.* Corfu. *Island* Iónioi Nísoi, Greece, C Mediterranean Sea
Kermadec Islands *168 C4 island group* NZ, SW Pacific Ocean
Kermadec Trench *159 E4 undersea feature* SW Pacific Ocean
Kermān *136 D3 var.* Kirman; *anc.* Carmana. Kermān, C Iran
Kerrville *65 F4* Texas, SW USA
Kerulen *143 E2 Chin.* Herlen He, *Mong.* Herlen Gol. *River* China / Mongolia
Kerýneia *118 C5 var.* Girne, Kyrenia. N Cyprus
Kesennuma *146 D4* Miyagi, Honshū, C Japan
Keszthely *115 C7* Zala, SW Hungary
Ketchikan *52 D4* Revillagigedo Island, Alaska, USA
Kettering *105 D6* C England, UK
Kettering *56 C4* Ohio, N USA
Keuruu *101 D5* Keski-Suomi, C Finland
Keweenaw Peninsula *56 B1 peninsula* Michigan, N USA
Key Largo *59 F5* Key Largo, Florida, SE USA
Key West *59 E5* Florida Keys, Florida, SE USA
Khabarovsk *131 G4* Khabarovskiy Kray, SE Russian Federation
Khairpur *150 B3* Sind, SE Pakistan
Khalīj al 'Aqabah *see* Aqaba, Gulf of
Khalīj al 'Arabī *see* Gulf, The
Khalīj-e Fars *see* Gulf, The
Khalkidhikí *see* Chalkidikí
Khalkís *see* Chalkída
Khambhāt, Gulf of *150 C4 Eng.* Gulf of Cambay. *Gulf* W India
Khamīs Mushayt *137 B6 var.* Hamīs Musait. 'Asīr, SW Saudi Arabia
Khānābād *139 E3* Kunduz, NE Afghanistan
Khān al Baghdādī *see* Al Baghdādī
Khandwa *150 D4* Madhya Pradesh, C India
Khanh *see* Soc Trăng
Khaniá *see* Chaniá
Khanka, Lake *145 E2 var.* Hsing-k'ai Hu, Lake Hanka, *Chin.* Xingkai Hu, *Rus.* Ozero Khanka. *Lake* China / Russian Federation
Khanthabouli *152 D4 prev.* Savannakhét. Savannakhét, S Laos
Khanty-Mansiysk *130 C3 prev.* Ostyako-Voguls'k. Khanty-Mansiyskiy Avtonomnyy Okrug, C Russian Federation
Khān Yūnis *135 A7 var.* Khān Yūnus. S Gaza Strip
Khān Yūnus *see* Khān Yūnis
Khanzi *see* Ghanzi
Kharagpur *151 F4* West Bengal, NE India
Kharbin *see* Harbin
Kharkiv *125 G2 Rus.* Khar'kov. Kharkivs'ka Oblast', NE Ukraine
Kharmanli *120 D3* Khaskovska Oblast, S Bulgaria
Khartoum *88 B4 var.* El Khartûm, Khartum. *Country capital* (Sudan) Khartoum, C Sudan
Khartum *see* Khartoum
Khasavyurt *127 B8* Respublika Dagestan, SW Russian Federation
Khāsh, Dasht-e *138 D5 Eng.* Khash Desert. *Desert* SW Afghanistan
Khashim Al Qirba *see* Khashm el Girba
Khashm al Qirbah *see* Khashm el Girba
Khashm el Girba *88 C4 var.* Khashim Al Qirba, Khashm al Qirbah. Kassala, E Sudan
Khaskovo *120 D3* Khaskovska Oblast, S Bulgaria
Khaydarkan *139 F2 var.* Khaydarken. Oshskaya Oblast', SW Kyrgyzstan
Khaydarken *see* Khaydarkan
Khelat *see* Kalāt
Kherson *125 E4* Khersons'ka Oblast', S Ukraine
Kheta *131 E2 river* N Russian Federation
Khíos *see* Chíos
Khiwa *138 D2 Rus.* Khiva. Khorazm Wiloyati, W Uzbekistan
Khmel'nyts'kyy *124 C2 Rus.* Khmel'nitskiy; *prev.* Proskurov. Khmel'nyts'ka Oblast', W Ukraine
Khodasy *123 E6 Rus.* Khodosy. Mahilyowskaya Voblasts', E Belorussia
Khodoriv *124 C2 Pol.* Chodorów, *Rus.* Khodorov. L'vivs'ka Oblast', NW Ukraine
Khodzhent *see* Khŭjand
Khoi *see* Khvoy
Khojend *see* Khŭjand
Khokand *see* Qŭqon
Kholm *139 E3 var.* Tashqurghan, *Pash.* Khulm. Balkh, N Afghanistan
Khoms *see* Al Khums
Khong Sedone *see* Muang Khôngxédôn
Khon Kaen *152 D4 var.* Muang Khon Kaen. Khon Kaen, E Thailand
Khor *131 G4* Khabarovskiy Kray, SE Russian Federation
Khorat *see* Nakhon Ratchasima
Khorugh *139 F3 Rus.* Khorog. S Tajikistan
Khotan *see* Hotan
Khouribga *86 B2* C Morocco
Khovd *see* Hovd
Khowst *139 F4* Paktīā, E Afghanistan
Khoy *see* Khvoy
Khoyniki *123 D8 Rus.* Khoyniki. Homyel'skaya Voblasts', SE Belorussia
Khrebet Kolymskiy *see* Kolyma Range
Khrebet Kopetdag *see* Koppeh Dāgh
Khrebet Lomonsova *see* Lomonosov Ridge
Khudzhand *see* Khŭjand
Khŭjand *139 E2 var.* Khodzhent, Khojend, *Rus.* Khudzhand; *prev.* Leninabad, *Taj.* Leninobod. N Tajikistan
Khulm *see* Kholm
Khulna *151 G4* Khulna, SW Bangladesh
Khums *see* Al Khums
Khust *124 B3 Cz.* Chust, Husté, *Hung.* Huszt. Zakarpats'ka Oblast', W Ukraine
Khvoy *136 C2 var.* Khoi, Khoy. Āzarbāyjān-e Bākhtarī, NW Iran
Khyber Pass *150 C1 var.* Kowtal-e Khaybar. *Pass* Afghanistan / Pakistan
Kiangmai *see* Chiang Mai
Kiang-ning *see* Nanjing
Kiangsi *see* Jiangxi
Kiangsu *see* Jiangsu
Kiáto *121 B6 prev.* Kiáton. Pelopónnisos, S Greece
Kiayi *see* Chiai
Kibangou *93 B6* Le Niari, SW Congo
Kibombo *93 D6* Maniema, E Congo (Zaire)
Kičevo *117 D6* SW FYR Macedonia
Kidderminster *105 D6* C England, UK
Kiel *110 B2* Schleswig-Holstein, N Germany
Kielce *114 D4 Rus.* Keltsy. Kielce, SE Poland
Kieler Bucht *110 B2 bay* N Germany
Kiev *see* Kyyiv
Kiffa *90 C3* Assaba, S Mauritania
Kigali *89 B6 country capital* (Rwanda) C Rwanda
Kigoma *89 B7* Kigoma, W Tanzania
Kihnu *122 C2 var.* Kihnu Saar, *Ger.* Kühnö. *Island* SW Estonia
Kihnu Saar *see* Kihnu
Kii-suidō *147 C7 strait* S Japan
Kikinda *116 D3 Ger.* Grosskikinda, *Hung.* Nagykikinda; *prev.* Velika Kikinda. Serbia, N Yugoslavia
Kikládhes *see* Kykládes
Kikwit *93 C6* Bandundu, W Congo (Zaire)
Kilien Mountains *see* Qilian Shan
Kilimane *see* Quelimane
Kilimanjaro *89 C7 var.* Uhuru Peak. *Mountain* NE Tanzania
Kilimanjaro *85 E5 region* E Tanzania
Kilingi-Nõmme *122 D3 Ger.* Kurkund. Pärnumaa, SW Estonia
Kilis *132 D4* Gaziantep, S Turkey
Kiliya *124 D4 Rom.* Chilia-Nouă. Odes'ka Oblast', SW Ukraine
Kilkenny *105 B6 Ir.* Cill Chainnigh. S Ireland
Kilkís *120 B3* Kentrikí Makedonía, N Greece
Killarney *105 A6 Ir.* Cill Airne. SW Ireland
Killeen *65 G3* Texas, SW USA
Kilmain *see* Quelimane
Kilmarnock *104 C4* W Scotland, UK
Kilwa *see* Kilwa Kivinje
Kilwa Kivinje *89 C7 var.* Kilwa. Lindi, SE Tanzania
Kimberley *94 C4* Northern Cape, C South Africa
Kimberley Plateau *162 C3 plateau* Western Australia
Kimch'aek *145 E3 prev.* Sŏngjin. E North Korea
Kinabalu, Gunung *154 D3 mountain* East Malaysia
Kindersley *53 F5* Saskatchewan, S Canada
Kindia *90 C4* Guinée-Maritime, SW Guinea
Kindley Field *58 A4 air base* E Bermuda
Kindu *93 D6 prev.* Kindu-Port-Empain. Maniema, C Congo (Zaire)
Kineshma *127 C5* Ivanovskaya Oblast', W Russian Federation
King Island *165 B8 island* Tasmania, SE Australia
Kingman *64 A1* Arizona, SW USA
Kingman Reef *161 E2 US territory* C Pacific Ocean
Kingsford Smith *164 E2 international airport* (Sydney) New South Wales, SE Australia
King's Lynn *105 E6 var.* Bishop's Lynn, Kings Lynn, Lynn, Lynn Regis. E England, UK
King Sound *162 B3 sound* Western Australia
Kingsport *59 E1* Tennessee, S USA
Kingston *70 B5 country capital* (Jamaica) E Jamaica
Kingston *57 F3* New York, NE USA
Kingston *54 D5* Ontario, SE Canada
Kingston upon Hull *105 D5 var.* Hull. E England, UK
Kingston upon Thames *105 A8* SE England, UK
Kingstown *71 H4 country capital* (Saint Vincent and the Grenadines) Saint Vincent, Saint Vincent and the Grenadines
Kingsville *65 G5* Texas, SW USA
King William Island *53 F3 island* Northwest Territories, N Canada Arctic Ocean
Kinrooi *103 D5* Limburg, NE Belgium
Kinshasa *93 B6 prev.* Léopoldville. *Country capital* (Congo (Zaire)) Kinshasa, W Congo (Zaire)
Kintyre *104 B4 peninsula* W Scotland, UK
Kinyeti *89 B5 mountain* S Sudan
Kiparissía *see* Kyparissía
Kipili *89 B7* Rukwa, W Tanzania
Kipushi *93 D8* Shaba, SE Congo (Zaire)
Kirdzhali *see* Kŭrdzhali
Kirghiz Range *139 F2 Rus.* Kirgizskiy Khrebet; *prev.* Alexander Range. *Mountain range* Kazakhstan / Kyrgyzstan
Kirghiz Steppe *see* Kazakhskiy Melkosopochnik
Kiriath-Arba *see* Hebron
Kiribati *161 F2 off.* Republic of Kiribati. *Country* C Pacific Ocean
Kırıkhan *132 D4* Hatay, S Turkey
Kırıkkale *132 C3* Kırıkkale, C Turkey
Kirin *see* Jilin
Kirinyaga *89 C6 prev.* Mount Kenya. *Volcano* C Kenya
Kirishi *126 B4 var.* Kirisi. Leningradskaya Oblast', NW Russian Federation
Kirisi *see* Kirishi
Kiritimati *161 G2 prev.* Christmas Island. *Atoll* Line Islands, E Kiribati
Kirkenes *100 E2 var.* Kirkkoniemi. Finnmark, N Norway
Kirkkoniemi *see* Kirkenes

INDEX

Lüdwigsfelde – Manzanillo

Lüdwigsfelde *110 D3* Brandenburg, NE Germany
Ludwigshafen *111 B5* var. Ludwigshafen am Rhein. Rheinland-Pfalz, W Germany
Ludwigshafen am Rhein see Ludwigshafen
Ludza *122 D4* Ger. Ludsan. Ludza, E Latvia
Luebo *93 C6* Kasai Occidental, SW Congo (Zaire)
Luena *94 C2* var. Lwena, Port. Luso. Moxico, E Angola
Lufira *93 E7* river SE Congo (Zaire)
Lufkin *65 H3* Texas, SW USA
Luga *126 A4* Leningradskaya Oblast', NW Russian Federation
Lugano *111 B8* Ger. Lauis. Ticino, S Switzerland
Lugenda, Rio *95 E2* river N Mozambique
Lugo *108 C1* anc. Lugus Augusti. Galicia, NW Spain
Lugoj *124 A4* Ger. Lugosch, Hung. Lugos. Timiş, W Romania
Luhans'k *125 H3* Rus. Lugansk; prev. Voroshilovgrad. Luhans'ka Oblast', E Ukraine
Luimneach see Limerick
Lukapa see Lucapa
Lukenie *93 C6* river C Congo (Zaire)
Lukovit *120 C2* Loveshka Oblast, NW Bulgaria
Łuków *114 E4* Ger. Bogendorf. Siedlce, E Poland
Lukuga *93 D7* river SE Congo (Zaire)
Luleå *100 D4* Norrbotten, N Sweden
Luleälven *100 C3* river N Sweden
Lulonga *93 C5* river NW Congo (Zaire)
Lulua *93 D7* river S Congo (Zaire)
Lumbo *95 F2* Nampula, NE Mozambique
Lumsden *167 A7* Southland, South Island, NZ
Lund *101 B7* Malmöhus, S Sweden
Lüneburg *110 C3* Niedersachsen, N Germany
Lungkiang see Qiqihar
Lungué-Bungo *94 C2* var. Lungwebungu. River Angola/Zambia see also Lungwebungu
Lungwebungu see Lungué-Bungo
Luninyets *123 B7* Pol. Łuniniec, Rus. Luninets. Brestskaya Voblasts', SW Belorussia
Lunteren *102 D4* Gelderland, C Netherlands
Luong Nam Tha see Louangnamtha
Luoyang *144 C4* var. Honan, Lo-yang. Henan, C China
Lúrio *95 F2* Nampula, NE Mozambique
Lúrio, Rio *95 E2* river NE Mozambique
Lusaka *94 D2* country capital (Zambia) Lusaka, SE Zambia
Lushnja see Lushnjë
Lushnjë *117 C6* var. Lushnja. Fier, C Albania
Luso see Luena
Lūt, Dasht-e *136 D3* var. Kavīr-e Lūt. Desert E Iran
Luton *105 D6* SE England, UK
Łutselk'e *53 F4* prev. Snowdrift. Northwest Territories, W Canada
Luts'k *124 C1* Pol. Łuck, Rus. Lutsk. Volyns'ka Oblast', NW Ukraine
Lutzow-Holm Bay see Lützow Holmbukta
Lützow Holmbukta *170 C2* var. Lutzow-Holm Bay. Bay Antarctica
Luuq *89 D6* It. Lugh Ganana. Gedo, SW Somalia
Luvua *93 D7* river SE Congo (Zaire)
Luwego *89 C8* river S Tanzania
Luxembourg *103 D8* off. Grand Duchy of Luxembourg, var. Lëtzebuerg, Luxemburg. Country NW Europe
Luxembourg *103 D8* country capital (Luxembourg) Luxembourg, S Luxembourg
Luxor *88 B2* Ar. Al Uqşur. E Egypt
Luza *126 C4* Kirovskaya Oblast', NW Russian Federation
Luz, Costa de la *108 C5* coastal region SW Spain
Luzern *111 B7* Fr. Lucerne, It. Lucerna. Luzern, C Switzerland
Luzon *155 E1* island N Philippines
Luzon Strait *141 E3* strait Philippines/Taiwan
L'viv *124 B2* Ger. Lemberg, Pol. Lwów, Rus. L'vov. L'vivs'ka Oblast', W Ukraine
Lwena see Luena
Lyakhavichy *123 B6* Rus. Lyakhovichi. Brestskaya Voblasts', SW Belorussia
Lycksele *100 C4* Västerbotten, N Sweden
Lycopolis see Asyût
Lyel'chytsy *123 C7* Rus. Lel'chitsy. Homyel'skaya Voblasts', SE Belorussia
Lyepyel' *123 D5* Rus. Lepel'. Vitsyebskaya Voblasts', N Belorussia
Lyme Bay *105 C7* bay S England, UK
Lynchburg *57 E5* Virginia, NE USA
Lynn Regis see King's Lynn
Lyon *107 D5* Eng. Lyons; anc. Lugdunum. Rhône, E France
Lyozna *123 E6* Rus. Liozno. Vitsyebskaya Voblasts', NE Belorussia
Lypovets' *124 D2* Rus. Lipovets. Vinnyts'ka Oblast', C Ukraine
Lysychans'k *125 H3* Rus. Lisichansk. Luhans'ka Oblast', E Ukraine
Lyttelton *167 C6* Canterbury, South Island, NZ
Lyubotyn *125 G2* Rus. Lyubotin. Kharkivs'ka Oblast', E Ukraine
Lyulyakovo *120 E2* prev. Keremitlik. Burgaska Oblast, E Bulgaria
Lyusina *123 B6* Rus. Lyusino. Brestskaya Voblasts', SW Belorussia

M

Ma'ān *135 B7* Ma'ān, SW Jordan
Maardu *122 D2* Ger. Maart. Harjumaa, NW Estonia
Ma'aret-en-Nu'man see Ma'arrat an Nu'mān
Ma'arrat an Nu'mān *134 B3* var. Ma'aret-en-Nu'man, Fr. Maarret enn Naamâne. Idlib, NW Syria
Maarret enn Naamâne see Ma'arrat an Nu'mān
Maaseik *103 D5* prev. Maeseyck. Limburg, NE Belgium
Maastricht *103 D6* var. Maestricht; anc. Traietum ad Mosam, Traiectum Tungorum. Limburg, SE Netherlands
Macao *144 C6* Chin. Aomen, Port. Macau. Portugese special territory E Asia
Macapá *79 E1* state capital Amapá, N Brazil
Macassar see Ujungpandang
MacCluer Gulf see Berau, Teluk
Macdonnell Ranges *162 D4* mountain range Northern Territory, C Australia
Macedonia, FYR *117 D6* off. the Former Yugoslav Republic of Macedonia, var. Macedonia, Mac. Makedonija, abbrev. FYR Macedonia, FYROM. Country SE Europe
Maceió *79 G3* state capital Alagoas, E Brazil
Machachi *76 B1* Pichincha, C Ecuador
Machala *76 B2* El Oro, SW Ecuador
Machanga *95 E3* Sofala, E Mozambique
Machilīpatnam *148 D1* var. Bandar Masulipatnam. Andhra Pradesh, E India
Machiques *74 C2* Zulia, NW Venezuela
Macías Nguema Biyogo see Bioco, Isla de
Măcin *124 D5* Tulcea, SE Romania
Macizo de las Guayanas see Guiana Highlands
Mackay *164 D4* Queensland, NE Australia
Mackay, Lake *162 C4* salt lake Northern Territory/Western Australia
Mackenzie *53 E3* river Northwest Territories, NW Canada
Mackenzie Bay *170 D3* bay Antarctica
Mackenzie Mountains *52 D3* mountain range Northwest Territories, NW Canada
Macleod, Lake *162 A4* lake Western Australia
Macomb *56 A4* Illinois, N USA
Macomer *113 A5* Sardegna, Italy, C Mediterranean Sea
Macon *58 D2* Georgia, SE USA
Macon *61 G4* Missouri, C USA
Mâcon *107 D5* anc. Matisco, Matisco Ædourum. Saône-et-Loire, C France
Macquarie Ridge *170 C5* undersea feature SW Pacific Ocean
Macuspana *67 G4* Tabasco, SE Mexico
Ma'dabā *135 B6* var. Mādabā, Madeba; anc. Medeba. 'Ammān, NW Jordan
Madagascar *95 F3* off. Democratic Republic of Madagascar, Malg. Madagasikara; prev. Malagasy Republic. Country W Indian Ocean
Madagascar *95 F3* island W Indian Ocean
Madagascar Basin *85 E7* undersea feature W Indian Ocean
Madagascar Plateau *85 E7* var. Madagascar Ridge, Madagascar Rise, Rus. Madagaskarskiy Khrebet. Undersea feature W Indian Ocean
Madagascar Ridge see Madagascar Plateau
Madagascar Rise see Madagascar Plateau
Madagaskarskiy Khrebet see Madagascar Plateau
Madang *160 B3* Madang, N PNG
Madanīyīn see Médenine
Made *102 C4* Noord-Brabant, S Netherlands
Madeba see Ma'dabā
Madeira *86 A2* var. Ilha de Madeira. Island Portugal, NE Atlantic Ocean
Madeira *86 A2* var. Madeira, Port. Arquipélago da Madeira. Island group Portugal, NE Atlantic Ocean
Madeira Plain *82 C3* undersea feature E Atlantic Ocean
Madeira, Rio *78 D2* Sp. Río Madera. River Bolivia/Brazil see also Madera, Río
Madeleine, Îles de la *55 F4* Eng. Magdalen Islands. Island group Québec, E Canada
Madera *63 B6* California, W USA
Madhya Pradesh *151 E4* prev. Central Provinces and Berar. Admin. region state C India
Madīnat ath Thawrah *134 C2* var. Ath Thawrah. Ar Raqqah, N Syria Asia
Madison *56 B3* state capital Wisconsin, N USA
Madison *61 F3* South Dakota, N USA
Madiun *154 D5* prev. Madioen. Jawa, C Indonesia
Madona *122 D4* Ger. Modohn. Madona, E Latvia
Madras see Tamil Nādu
Madras *148 D2* var. Chennai. Tamil Nādu, S India
Madre de Dios *72 B4* off. Departamento de Madre de Dios. Department E Peru
Madre de Dios, Río *77 E3* river Bolivia/Peru
Madre del Sur, Sierra *67 E5* mountain range S Mexico
Madre, Laguna *67 F3* lagoon NE Mexico
Madre, Laguna *65 G5* lake Texas, SW USA
Madre Occidental, Sierra *66 C3* var. Western Sierra Madre. Mountain range C Mexico
Madre Oriental, Sierra *67 E3* var. Eastern Sierra Madre. Mountain range C Mexico
Madrid *108 D3* country capital (Spain) Madrid, C Spain
Madurai *148 C3* prev. Madura, Mathurai. Tamil Nādu, S India
Madura, Pulau *154 D5* prev. Madoera. Island C Indonesia
Maebashi *147 D5* var. Maebasi, Mayebashi. Gunma, Honshū, S Japan
Maebasi see Maebashi
Mae Nam Khong see Mekong
Mae Nam Nan *152 C4* river NW Thailand
Mae Nam Yom *152 C4* river W Thailand
Maestricht see Maastricht
Maewo *160 D4* prev. Aurora. Island C Vanuatu
Mafia *89 D7* island E Tanzania
Mafraq see Al Mafraq
Magadan *131 G3* Magadanskaya Oblast', E Russian Federation
Magangué *74 B2* Bolívar, N Colombia
Magdalena *72 A2* off. Departamento del Magdalena. Province N Colombia
Magdalena *77 F3* Beni, N Bolivia
Magdalena *66 B1* Sonora, NW Mexico
Magdalena, Isla *66 B3* island W Mexico
Magdalena, Río *74 B2* river C Colombia
Magdeburg *110 C4* Sachsen-Anhalt, C Germany
Magelang *154 C5* Jawa, C Indonesia
Magellan, Strait of *81 B8* Sp. Estrecho de Magallanes. Strait Argentina/Chile
Magerøy see Magerøya
Magerøya *100 D1* var. Magerøy. Island N Norway
Maggiore, Lake *112 B1* It. Lago Maggiore. Lake Italy/Switzerland
Maglaj *116 C3* N Bosnia and Herzegovina
Maglie *113 E6* Puglia, SE Italy
Magna *60 B4* Utah, W USA
Magnesia see Manisa
Magnitogorsk *130 B4* Chelyabinskaya Oblast', C Russian Federation
Magta' Lahjar *90 C3* var. Magta Lahjar, Magta' Lahjar, Magta Lahjar. Brakna, SW Mauritania
Magway see Magwe
Magwe *152 A3* var. Magway. Magwe, W Burma
Mahajanga *95 F2* var. Majunga. Mahajanga, NW Madagascar
Mahakam, Sungai *154 D4* var. Koetai, Kutai. River Borneo, C Indonesia
Mahalapye *94 D3* var. Mahalatswe. Central, SE Botswana
Mahalatswe see Mahalapye
Mahān *136 D3* Kermān, E Iran
Mahanādi *151 F4* river E India
Mahārāshtra *150 D5* state W India
Mahbés see El Mahbas
Mahbūbnagar *150 D5* Andhra Pradesh, C India
Mahdia *87 F2* var. Al Mahdīyah, Mehdia. NE Tunisia
Mahé *95 H1* island Inner Islands, NE Seychelles
Mahia Peninsula *166 E4* peninsula North Island, NZ
Mahilyow *123 D6* Rus. Mogilëv. Mahilyowskaya Voblasts', E Belorussia
Mahmūd-e 'Erāqī see Maḩmūd-e Rāqī
Maḩmūd-e Rāqī *139 E4* var. Mahmūd-e 'Erāqī. Kāpīsā, NE Afghanistan
Mahón *109 H3* Cat. Maó, Eng. Port Mahon; anc. Portus Magonis. Menorca, Spain, W Mediterranean Sea
Maicao *74 C1* La Guajira, N Colombia
Mai Ceu see Maych'ew
Mai Chio see Maych'ew
Maidstone *105 E7* SE England, UK
Maiduguri *91 H4* Borno, NE Nigeria
Maimāna see Meymaneh
Main *111 B5* river C Germany
Mai-Ndombe, Lac *93 C6* prev. Lac Léopold II. Lake W Congo (Zaire)
Maine *57 G2* off. State of Maine; also known as Lumber State, Pine Tree State. State NE USA
Maine *106 B3* cultural region NW France
Maine, Gulf of *57 H2* gulf NE USA
Main Island see Bermuda
Mainland *104 C2* island Orkney, N Scotland, UK
Mainland *104 D1* island Shetland, NE Scotland, UK
Mainz *111 B5* Fr. Mayence. Rheinland-Pfalz, SW Germany
Maio *90 A3* var. Mayo. Island Ilhas de Sotavento, SE Cape Verde
Maisur see Karnātaka
Maisur see Mysore
Maizhokunggar *142 C5* Xizang Zizhiqu, W China
Maíz, Islas del *69 E3* var. Corn Islands. Island group SE Nicaragua
Mājro see Majuro Atoll
Majunga see Mahajanga
Majuro Atoll *160 D2* var. Mājro. Atoll Ratak Chain, SE Marshall Islands
Makale see Mek'elē
Makarov Basin *171 B3* undersea feature Arctic Ocean
Makarska *116 B4* It. Macarsca. Split-Dalmacija, SE Croatia
Makasar see Ujungpandang
Makassar see Ujungpandang
Makassar Strait *154 D4* Ind. Selat Makasar. Strait C Indonesia
Makay *95 F3* var. Massif du Makay. Mountain range SW Madagascar
Makeni *90 C4* C Sierra Leone
Makhachkala *130 A4* prev. Petrovsk-Port. Respublika Dagestan, SW Russian Federation
Makin *160 D2* prev. Pitt Island. Atoll Tungaru, W Kiribati
Makira see San Cristobal
Makiyivka *125 G3* Rus. Makeyevka; prev. Dmitriyevsk. Donets'ka Oblast', E Ukraine
Makkah *137 A5* Eng. Mecca. Makkah, W Saudi Arabia
Makkovik *55 F2* Newfoundland and Labrador, NE Canada
Makó *115 D7* Rom. Macău. Csongrád, SE Hungary
Makoua *93 B5* Cuvette, C Congo
Makran Coast *136 E4* coastal region SE Iran
Makrany *123 A6* Rus. Mokrany. Brestskaya Voblasts', SW Belorussia
Mākū *136 B2* Āẕarbāyjān-e Bākhtarī, NW Iran
Makurdi *91 G4* Benue, C Nigeria
Mala see Malaita
Malabār Coast *148 B3* coast SW India
Malabo *93 A5* prev. Santa Isabel. Country capital (Equatorial Guinea) Isla de Bioco, NW Equatorial Guinea
Malacca see Melaka
Malacca, Strait of *154 B3* Ind. Selat Malaka. Strait Indonesia/Malaysia
Malacky *115 C6* Hung. Malacka. Západné Slovensko, W Slovakia
Maladzyechna *123 C5* Pol. Molodeczno, Rus. Molodechno. Minskaya Voblasts', C Belorussia
Málaga *108 D5* anc. Malaca. Andalucía, S Spain
Malagarasi River *89 B7* river W Tanzania
Malaita *160 C3* var. Mala. Island N Solomon Islands
Malakal *89 B5* Upper Nile, S Sudan
Malakula see Malekula
Malang *154 D5* Jawa, C Indonesia
Malange see Malanje
Malanje *94 B1* var. Malange. Malanje, NW Angola
Mälaren *101 C6* lake C Sweden
Malatya *133 E4* anc. Melitene. Malatya, SE Turkey
Mala Vyska *125 E3* Rus. Malaya Viska. Kirovohrads'ka Oblast', S Ukraine
Malawi *95 E1* off. Republic of Malaŵi; prev. Nyasaland, Nyasaland Protectorate. Country S Africa
Malawi, Lake see Nyasa, Lake
Malay Peninsula *140 D4* peninsula Malaysia/Thailand
Malaysia *154 B3* var. Federation of Malaysia; prev. the separate territories of Federation of Malaya, Sarawak and Sabah (North Borneo) and Singapore. Country SE Asia
Malaysia, Federation of see Malaysia
Malbork *114 C2* Ger. Marienburg, Marienburg in Westpreussen. Elbląg, N Poland
Malchin *110 C3* Mecklenburg-Vorpommern, N Germany
Malden *61 H5* Missouri, C USA
Malden Island *161 G3* prev. Independence Island. Atoll E Kiribati
Maldives *148 A4* off. Maldivian Divehi, Republic of Maldives. Country N Indian Ocean
Male' *148 B4* Male' Atoll, C Maldives
Male' Atoll *148 B4* var. Kaafu Atoll. Atoll C Maldives
Malekula *160 D4* var. Malakula; prev. Mallicolo. Island W Vanuatu
Malesína *121 C5* Stereá Ellás, E Greece
Malheur Lake *62 C3* lake Oregon, NW USA
Mali *91 E3* off. Republic of Mali, Fr. République du Mali; prev. French Sudan, Sudanese Republic. Country W Africa
Malik, Wadi al see Milk, Wadi el
Mali Kyun *153 B5* var. Tavoy Island. Island Mergui Archipelago, S Burma
Malindi *89 D7* Coast, SE Kenya
Malko Tŭrnovo *120 E3* Burgaska Oblast, SE Bulgaria
Mallaig *104 B3* N Scotland, UK
Mallawi *88 B2* C Egypt
Mallicolo see Malekula
Mallorca *109 G3* Eng. Majorca; anc. Baleares Major. Island Islas Baleares, Spain, W Mediterranean Sea
Malmberget *100 C3* Norrbotten, N Sweden
Malmédy *103 D6* Liège, E Belgium
Malmö *101 B7* Malmöhus, S Sweden
Maļoeļap see Maloelap Atoll
Maloelap Atoll *160 D1* var. Maļoeļap. Atoll E Marshall Islands
Małopolska *114 D4* plateau S Poland
Malozemel'skaya Tundra *126 D3* physical region NW Russian Federation
Malta *113 C8* off. Republic of Malta. Country C Mediterranean Sea
Malta *113 C8* island Malta, C Mediterranean Sea
Malta *60 C1* Montana, NW USA
Malta *122 D4* Rēzekne, SE Latvia
Malta Channel *113 C8* It. Canale di Malta. Strait Italy/Malta
Maluku *155 F4* Dut. Molukken, Eng. Moluccas; prev. Spice Islands. Island group E Indonesia
Malung *101 B6* Kopparberg, C Sweden
Malyn *124 D2* Rus. Malin. Zhytomyrs'ka Oblast', N Ukraine
Mamberamo, Sungai *155 H4* river Irian Jaya, E Indonesia
Mambij see Manbij
Mamonovo *122 A4* Ger. Heiligenbeil. Kaliningradskaya Oblast', W Russian Federation
Mamoré, Rio *77 F3* river Bolivia/Brazil
Mamou *90 C4* Moyenne-Guinée, W Guinea
Mamoudzou *95 F2* dependent territory capital (Mayotte) C Mayotte
Mamuno *94 C3* Ghanzi, W Botswana
Manacor *109 G3* Mallorca, Spain, W Mediterranean Sea
Manado *155 F3* prev. Menado. Sulawesi, C Indonesia
Managua *68 D3* country capital (Nicaragua) Managua, W Nicaragua
Managua, Lago de *68 C3* var. Xolotlán. Lake W Nicaragua
Manakara *95 G4* Fianarantsoa, SE Madagascar
Manama see Al Manāmah
Mananjary *95 G3* Fianarantsoa, SE Madagascar
Manapouri, Lake *167 A7* lake South Island, NZ
Manar see Mannar
Manas, Gora *139 E2* mountain Kyrgyzstan/Uzbekistan
Manaus *78 D2* prev. Manáos. State capital Amazonas, NW Brazil
Manavgat *132 B4* Antalya, SW Turkey
Manbij *134 C2* var. Mambij, Fr. Membidj. Ḩalab, N Syria
Manchester *105 D5* Lat. Mancunium. NW England, UK
Manchester *57 G3* New Hampshire, NE USA
Man-chou-li see Manzhouli
Manchuria *141 E1* cultural region NE China
Máncio Lima see Japiim
Mand see Mand, Rūd-e
Mandalay *152 B3* Mandalay, C Burma
Mandan *61 E2* North Dakota, N USA
Mandeville *70 B5* C Jamaica
Mándra *121 C6* Attikí, C Greece
Mand, Rūd-e *136 D4* var. Mand. River S Iran
Mandurah *163 A6* Western Australia
Manduria *113 E5* Puglia, SE Italy
Mandya *148 C2* Karnātaka, C India
Manfredonia *113 D5* Puglia, SE Italy
Mangai *93 C6* Bandundu, W Congo (Zaire)
Mangaia *161 G5* island group S Cook Islands
Mangalia *124 D5* anc. Callatis. Constanţa, SE Romania
Mangalmé *92 C3* Guéra, SE Chad
Mangalore *148 B2* Karnātaka, W India
Mangaung see Bloemfontein
Mango see Sansanné-Mango
Mangoky *95 F3* river W Madagascar
Manhattan *61 F4* Kansas, C USA
Manicouagan, Réservoir *54 D3* lake Québec, E Canada
Manihiki *161 G4* atoll N Cook Islands
Manihiki Plateau *159 E3* undersea feature C Pacific Ocean
Maniitsoq *98 C3* var. Manîtsoq, Dan. Sukkertoppen. S Greenland
Manila *155 E1* off. City of Manila. Country capital (Philippines) Luzon, N Philippines
Manisa *132 A3* var. Manissa; prev. Saruhan, anc. Magnesia. Manisa, W Turkey
Manissa see Manisa
Manitoba *53 F5* province S Canada
Manitoba, Lake *53 F5* lake Manitoba, S Canada
Manitoulin Island *54 C4* island Ontario, S Canada
Manîtsoq see Maniitsoq
Manizales *74 B3* Caldas, W Colombia
Manjimup *163 A7* Western Australia
Mankato *61 F3* Minnesota, N USA
Manlleu *109 G2* Cataluña, NE Spain
Manly *164 E1* New South Wales, SE Australia
Manmād *150 C5* Mahārāshtra, W India
Mannar *148 C3* var. Manar. Northern Province, NW Sri Lanka
Mannar, Gulf of *148 C3* gulf India/Sri Lanka
Mannheim *111 B5* Baden-Württemberg, SW Germany
Manono *93 E7* Shabo, SE Congo (Zaire)
Manosque *107 D6* Alpes-de-Haute-Provence, SE France
Manra *161 F3* prev. Sydney Island. Atoll Phoenix Islands, C Kiribati
Mansa *94 D2* prev. Fort Rosebery. Luapula, N Zambia
Mansel Island *53 G3* island Northwest Territories, NE Canada
Mansfield *56 D4* Ohio, N USA
Manta *76 A2* Manabí, W Ecuador
Manteca *63 B6* California, W USA
Mantova *112 B2* Eng. Mantua, Fr. Mantoue. Lombardia, NW Italy
Manuae *161 G4* island S Cook Islands
Manukau see Manurewa
Manurewa *166 D3* var. Manukau. Auckland, North Island, NZ
Manzanares *109 E3* Castilla-La Mancha, C Spain
Manzanillo *66 D4* Colima, SW Mexico

Miahutlán de Porfirio Díaz – Moŭng Roessei

Miahuatlán de Porfirio Díaz *see* Miahuatlán
Miami *59 F5* Florida, SE USA
Miami *65 G1* Oklahoma, C USA
Miami Beach *59 F5* Florida, SE USA
Mīāneh *136 C2 var.* Miyāneh. Āzarbāyjān-e Khāvarī, NW Iran
Mianyang *144 B5* Sichuan, C China
Miastko *114 C2 Ger.* Rummelsburg in Pommern. Słupsk, NW Poland
Mi Chai *see* Nong Khai
Michalovce *115 E5 Ger.* Grossmichel, *Hung.* Nagymihály. Východné Slovensko, E Slovakia
Michigan *56 C1 off.* State of Michigan; also known as Great Lakes State, Lake State, Wolverine State. *State* N USA
Michigan, Lake *56 C2 lake* N USA
Michurinsk *127 B5* Tambovskaya Oblast', W Russian Federation
Micoud *71 F2* SE Saint Lucia
Micronesia *160 B1 off.* Federated States of Micronesia. *Country* W Pacific Ocean
Micronesia *160 C1 island group* W Pacific Ocean
Mid-Atlantic Cordillera *see* Mid-Atlantic Ridge
Mid-Atlantic Ridge *82 C3 var.* Mid-Atlantic Cordillera, Mid-Atlantic Rise, Mid-Atlantic Swell. *Undersea feature* Atlantic Ocean
Mid-Atlantic Rise *see* Mid-Atlantic Ridge
Mid-Atlantic Swell *see* Mid-Atlantic Ridge
Middelburg *103 B5* Zeeland, SW Netherlands
Middelharnis *102 B4* Zuid-Holland, SW Netherlands
Middelkerke *103 A5* West-Vlaanderen, W Belgium
Middle America Trench *51 B7 undersea feature* E Pacific Ocean
Middle Andaman *149 F2 island* Andaman Islands, India, NE Indian Ocean
Middlesboro *56 C5* Kentucky, S USA
Middlesbrough *105 D5* N England, UK
Middletown *57 F4* New Jersey, NE USA
Middletown *57 F3* New York, NE USA
Mid-Indian Basin *157 C5 undersea feature* N Indian Ocean
Mid-Indian Ridge *157 C5 var.* Central Indian Ridge. *Undersea feature* C Indian Ocean
Midland *56 C3* Michigan, N USA
Midland *54 D5* Ontario, S Canada
Midland *65 E3* Texas, SW USA
Mid-Pacific Mountains *168 C2 var.* Mid-Pacific Seamounts. *Undersea feature* NW Pacific Ocean
Mid-Pacific Seamounts *see* Mid-Pacific Mountains
Midway Islands *168 D2 US territory* C Pacific Ocean
Miechów *115 D5* Kielce, S Poland
Międzyrzec Podlaski *114 E3* Biała Podlaska, E Poland
Międzyrzecz *114 B3 Ger.* Meseritz. Gorzów, W Poland
Mielec *115 D5* Rzeszów, SE Poland
Miercurea-Ciuc *124 C4 Ger.* Szeklerburg, *Hung.* Csíkszereda. Harghita, C Romania
Mieres *108 D1* Asturias, NW Spain
Mieresch *see* Mureș
Mī'ēso *89 D5 var.* Meheso, Miesso. C Ethiopia
Miesso *see* Mī'ēso
Miguel Asua *66 D3 var.* Miguel Auza. Zacatecas, C Mexico
Miguel Auza *see* Miguel Asua
Mijdrecht *102 C3* Utrecht, C Netherlands
Mikashevichy *123 C7 Pol.* Mikaszewicze, *Rus.* Mikashevichi. Brestskaya Voblasts', SW Belorussia
Mikhaylovka *127 B6* Volgogradskaya Oblast', SW Russian Federation
Míkonos *see* Mýkonos
Mikre *120 C2* Loveshka Oblast, C Bulgaria
Mikun' *126 D4* Respublika Komi, NW Russian Federation
Mikuni-sanmyaku *147 D5 mountain range* Honshū, N Japan
Mikura-jima *147 D6 island* E Japan
Milagro *76 B2* Guayas, SW Ecuador
Milan *see* Milano
Milange *95 E2* Zambézia, NE Mozambique
Milano *112 B2 Eng.* Milan, *Ger.* Mailand; *anc.* Mediolanum. Lombardia, N Italy
Milas *132 A4* Muğla, SW Turkey
Milashavichy *123 C7 Rus.* Milashevichi. Homyel'skaya Voblasts', SE Belorussia
Mildura *165 C6* Victoria, SE Australia
Mile *see* Mili Atoll
Miles *165 D5* Queensland, E Australia
Miles City *60 C2* Montana, NW USA
Milford Haven *105 C6 prev.* Milford. SW Wales, UK
Milford Sound *167 A6 inlet* South Island, NZ
Milford Sound *167 A6* Southland, South Island, NZ
Mili Atoll *160 D2 var.* Mile. *Atoll* Ratak Chain, SE Marshall Islands
Mil'kovo *131 H3* Kamchatskaya Oblast', E Russian Federation
Milk River *60 C1 river* Montana, NW USA
Milk River *53 E5* Alberta, SW Canada
Milk, Wadi el *88 B4 var.* Wadi al Malik. *River* C Sudan
Milledgeville *59 E2* Georgia, SE USA
Mille Lacs Lake *61 F2 lake* Minnesota, N USA
Millerovo *127 B6* Rostovskaya Oblast', SW Russian Federation
Mílos *121 C7 island* Kykládes, Greece, Aegean Sea
Mílos *121 C6* Mílos, Kykládes, Greece, Aegean Sea
Milton *167 B7* Otago, South Island, NZ
Milton Keynes *105 D6* SE England, UK
Milwaukee *56 B3* Wisconsin, N USA
Min *see* Fujian
Mīnā' Qābūs *156 B3* NE Oman
Minas Gerais *79 F3 off.* Estado de Minas Gerais. *State* E Brazil
Minatitlán *67 F4* Veracruz-Llave, E Mexico
Minbu *152 A3* Magwe, W Burma
Minch, The *104 B3 var.* North Minch. *Strait* NW Scotland, UK
Mindanao *155 F2 island* S Philippines
Mindanao Sea *see* Bohol Sea
Mindelheim *111 C6* Bayern, S Germany
Mindello *see* Mindelo
Mindelo *90 A2 var.* Mindello; *prev.* Porto Grande. São Vicente, N Cape Verde
Minden *110 B4 anc.* Minthun. Nordrhein-Westfalen, NW Germany
Mindoro *155 E2 island* N Philippines
Mindoro Strait *155 E2 strait* W Philippines
Mineral Wells *65 F2* Texas, SW USA
Mingäçevir *133 G2 Rus.* Mingechaur, Mingechevir. C Azerbaijan
Mingāora *150 C1 var.* Mingora, Mongora. North-West Frontier Province, N Pakistan
Mingora *see* Mingāora
Minho *108 B2 former province* N Portugal
Minho *see* Miño
Minicoy Island *148 B3 island* SW India
Minius *see* Miño
Minna *91 G4* Niger, C Nigeria
Minneapolis *61 F2* Minnesota, N USA
Minnesota *61 F2 off.* State of Minnesota; also known as Gopher State, New England of the West, North Star State. *State* N USA
Miño *108 B2 var.* Mino, Minius, *Port.* Minho. *River* Portugal/Spain *see also* Minho
Mino *see* Miño
Minot *61 E1* North Dakota, N USA
Minsk *123 C6 country capital* (Belorussia) Minskaya Voblasts', C Belorussia
Minskaya Wzvyshsha *123 C6 mountain range* C Belorussia
Minto, Lac *54 D2 lake* Québec, C Canada
Minya *see* El Minya
Miraflores *66 C3* Baja California Sur, W Mexico
Miranda de Ebro *109 E1* La Rioja, N Spain
Miri *154 D3* Sarawak, East Malaysia
Mirim Lagoon *79 E5 var.* Lake Mirim, *Sp.* Laguna Merín. *Lagoon* Brazil/Uruguay
Mirim, Lake *see* Mirim Lagoon
Mírina *see* Mýrina
Mīrjāveh *136 E4* Sīstān va Balūchestān, SE Iran
Mirny *170 C3 Russian research station* Antarctica
Mirnyy *131 F3* Respublika Sakha (Yakutiya), NE Russian Federation
Mīrpur Khās *150 B3* Sind, SE Pakistan
Mirtóo Pélagos *121 C6 Eng.* Mirtoan Sea; *anc.* Myrtoum Mare. *Sea* S Greece
Miskito Coast *see* Mosquito Coast
Miskitos, Cayos *69 E2 island group* NE Nicaragua
Miskolc *115 D6* Borsod-Abaúj-Zemplén, NE Hungary
Misool, Pulau *155 F4 island* Maluku, E Indonesia
Mişrātah *87 F2 var.* Misurata. NW Libya
Mission *65 G5* Texas, SW USA
Mississippi *58 B2 off.* State of Mississippi; also known as Bayou State, Magnolia State. *State* SE USA
Mississippi Delta *58 B4 delta* Louisiana, S USA
Mississippi River *51 C6 river* C USA
Missoula *60 B1* Montana, NW USA
Missouri *61 F5 off.* State of Missouri; also known as Bullion State, Show Me State. *State* C USA
Missouri River *61 E3 river* C USA
Mistassini, Lac *54 D3 lake* Québec, SE Canada
Mistelbach an der Zaya *111 E6* Niederösterreich, NE Austria
Misti, Volcán *77 E4 mountain* S Peru
Misurata *see* Mişrātah
Mitchell *165 D5* Queensland, E Australia
Mitchell *61 E3* South Dakota, N USA
Mitchell, Mount *59 E1 mountain* North Carolina, SE USA
Mitchell River *164 C2 river* Queensland, NE Australia
Mi Tho *see* My Tho
Mitilíni *see* Mytilíni
Mito *147 D5* Ibaraki, Honshū, S Japan
Mits'iwa *see* Massawa
Mitú *74 C4* Vaupés, SE Colombia
Mitumba, Monts *93 E7 var.* Chaîne des Mitumba, Mitumba Range. *Mountain range* E Congo (Zaire)
Mitumba Range *see* Mitumba, Monts
Miyako *146 D4* Iwate, Honshū, C Japan
Miyako-jima *147 D6 island* Sakishima-shotō, SW Japan
Miyakonojō *147 B8 var.* Miyakonzyô. Miyazaki, Kyūshū, SW Japan
Miyakonzyô *see* Miyakonojō
Miyāneh *see* Mīāneh
Miyazaki *147 B8* Miyazaki, Kyūshū, SW Japan
Mizil *124 C5* Prahova, SE Romania
Miziya *120 C1* Oblast Montana, NW Bulgaria
Mizpé Ramon *135 A7* Southern, S Israel
Mjøsa *101 B6 var.* Mjøsen. *Lake* S Norway
Mjøsen *see* Mjøsa
Mladenovac *116 D4* Serbia, C Yugoslavia
Mława *114 D3* Ciechanów, C Poland
Mljet *117 B5 It.* Meleda; *anc.* Melita. *Island* S Croatia
Mmabatho *94 C4* North-West, N South Africa
Moab *60 B5* Utah, W USA
Moab, Kir of *see* Al Karak
Moa Island *164 C1 island* Queensland, NE Australia
Moanda *93 B6 var.* Mouanda. Haut-Ogooué, SE Gabon
Moba *93 E7* Shaba, E Congo (Zaire)
Mobay *see* Montego Bay
Mobaye *93 C5* Basse-Kotto, S Central African Republic
Moberly *61 G4* Missouri, C USA
Mobile *58 C3* Alabama, S USA
Mobutu Sese Seko, Lac *see* Albert, Lake
Mochudi *94 C4* Kgatleng, SE Botswana
Mocímboa da Praia *95 F2 var.* Vila de Mocímboa da Praia. Cabo Delgado, N Mozambique
Môco *94 B2 var.* Morro de Môco. *Mountain* W Angola
Mocoa *74 A4* Putumayo, SW Colombia
Mocuba *95 E3* Zambézia, NE Mozambique
Modena *112 B3 anc.* Mutina. Emilia-Romagna, N Italy
Modesto *63 B6* California, W USA
Modica *113 C7 anc.* Motyca. Sicilia, Italy, C Mediterranean Sea
Modriča *116 C3* N Bosnia and Herzegovina
Moe *165 C7* Victoria, SE Australia
Moero, Lac *see* Mweru, Lake
Mogadishu *see* Muqdisho
Mogilno *114 C3* Bydgoszcz, C Poland
Mohammedia *86 C2 prev.* Fédala. NW Morocco
Mohave, Lake *63 D7 reservoir* Arizona/Nevada, W USA
Mohawk River *57 F3 river* New York, NE USA
Mohéli *95 F2 var.* Mwali, Mohilla, Mohila, *Fr.* Moili. *Island* S Comoros
Mohila *see* Mohéli
Mohilla *see* Mohéli
Mohns Ridge *99 F3 undersea feature* Greenland Sea/Norwegian Sea
Moho *77 E4* Puno, SW Peru
Mohoro *89 C7* Pwani, E Tanzania
Mohyliv-Podil's'kyy *124 D3 Rus.* Mogilev-Podol'skiy. Vinnyts'ka Oblast', C Ukraine
Moi *101 A6* Rogaland, S Norway
Moili *see* Mohéli
Mo i Rana *100 C3* Nordland, C Norway
Mõisaküla *122 D3 Ger.* Moiseküll. Viljandimaa, S Estonia
Moissac *107 B6* Tarn-et-Garonne, S France
Mojácar *109 E5* Andalucía, S Spain
Mojave Desert *63 D7 plain* California, W USA
Moktama *see* Martaban
Mol *103 C5 prev.* Moll. Antwerpen, N Belgium
Moldavia *124 D3 off.* Republic of Moldova, *var.* Moldova; *prev.* Moldavian SSR, *Rus.* Moldavskaya SSR. *Country* SE Europe
Molde *101 A5* Møre og Romsdal, S Norway
Moldo-Too, Khrebet *139 G2 prev.* Khrebet Moldotau. *Mountain range* C Kyrgyzstan
Moldova Nouă *124 A4 Ger.* Neumoldowa, *Hung.* Újmoldova. Caraș-Severin, SW Romania
Moldoveanul *see* Vârful Moldoveanu
Molfetta *113 E5* Puglia, SE Italy
Mollendo *77 E4* Arequipa, SW Peru
Mölndal *101 B7* Göteborg och Bohus, S Sweden
Molochans'k *125 G4 Rus.* Molochansk. Zaporiz'ka Oblast', SE Ukraine
Molodezhnaya *170 C2 Russian research station* Antarctica
Molokai *63 B8 Haw.* Moloka'i. *Island* Hawaii, USA, C Pacific Ocean
Molokai Fracture Zone *169 E2 tectonic feature* NE Pacific Ocean
Molopo *94 C4 seasonal river* Botswana/South Africa
Mólos *121 B5* Stereá Ellás, C Greece
Moluccas *see* Maluku
Molucca Sea *155 F4 Ind.* Laut Maluku. *Sea* E Indonesia
Mombasa *89 D7 international airport* Coast, SE Kenya
Mombasa *89 D7* Coast, SE Kenya
Mombetsu *see* Monbetsu
Momchilgrad *120 D3 prev.* Mastanli. Khaskovska Oblast, S Bulgaria
Møn *101 B8 prev.* Möen. *Island* SE Denmark
Monaco *107 E6 off.* Principality of Monaco. *Country* W Europe
Monaco *107 C7 var.* Monaco-Ville; *anc.* Monoecus. *Country capital* (Monaco) S Monaco
Monaco, Port de *107 C8 bay* S Monaco
Monaco-Ville *see* Monaco
Monahans *65 E3* Texas, SW USA
Mona, Isla *71 E3 island* W Puerto Rico
Mona Passage *71 E3 Sp.* Canal de la Mona. *Channel* Dominican Republic/Puerto Rico
Monbetsu *146 D2 var.* Mombetsu, Monbetu. Hokkaidō, NE Japan
Monbetu *see* Monbetsu
Moncalieri *112 A2* Piemonte, NW Italy
Monchegorsk *126 C2* Murmanskaya Oblast', NW Russian Federation
Monclova *66 D2* Coahuila de Zaragoza, NE Mexico
Moncton *55 F4* New Brunswick, SE Canada
Mondovì *112 A2* Piemonte, NW Italy
Monfalcone *112 D2* Friuli-Venezia Giulia, NE Italy
Monforte *108 C1* Galicia, NW Spain
Mongo *92 C3* Guéra, C Chad
Mongolia *142 C2 Mong.* Mongol Uls. *Country* E Asia
Mongolia, Plateau of *140 D1 plateau* E Mongolia
Mongora *see* Mingāora
Mongu *94 C2* Western, W Zambia
Monkchester *see* Newcastle upon Tyne
Monkey Bay *95 E2* Southern, SE Malawi
Monkey River *see* Monkey River Town
Monkey River Town *68 C2 var.* Monkey River. Toledo, SE Belize
Monoecus *see* Monaco
Mono Lake *63 C6 lake* California, W USA
Monóvar *109 F4* País Valenciano, E Spain
Monroe *58 B2* Louisiana, S USA
Monrovia *90 C5 country capital* (Liberia) W Liberia
Mons *103 B6 Dut.* Bergen. Hainaut, S Belgium
Monselice *112 C2* Veneto, NE Italy
Montagnes Rocheuses *see* Rocky Mountains
Montana *60 B1 off.* State of Montana; also known as Mountain State, Treasure State. *State* NW USA
Montana *120 C2 prev.* Ferdinand, Mikhaylovgrad. Oblast Montana, NW Bulgaria
Montargis *106 C4* Loiret, C France
Montauban *107 B6* Tarn-et-Garonne, S France
Montbéliard *106 D4* Doubs, E France
Mont Cenis, Col du *107 D5 pass* E France
Mont-de-Marsan *107 B6* Landes, SW France
Monteagudo *77 G4* Chuquisaca, S Bolivia
Monte-Carlo *107 C8* NE Monaco
Monte Caseros *80 D3* Corrientes, NE Argentina
Monte Cristi *70 D3 var.* San Fernando de Monte Cristi. NW Dominican Republic
Montegiardino *112 E2* SE San Marino
Montego Bay *70 A4 var.* Mobay. W Jamaica
Montélimar *107 D5 anc.* Acunum Acusio, Montilium Adhemari. Drôme, E France
Montemorelos *67 E3* Nuevo León, NE Mexico
Montenegro *117 C5 Serb.* Crna Gora. Admin. region *republic* SW Yugoslavia
Monte Patria *80 B3* Coquimbo, N Chile
Monterey *see* Monterrey
Monterey *63 B6* California, W USA
Monterey Bay *63 A6 bay* California, W USA
Montería *74 B2* Córdoba, NW Colombia
Montero *77 G4* Santa Cruz, C Bolivia
Monterrey *67 E3 var.* Monterey. Nuevo León, NE Mexico
Montes Claros *79 F3* Minas Gerais, SE Brazil
Montevideo *80 D4 country capital* (Uruguay) Montevideo, S Uruguay
Montevideo *61 F2* Minnesota, N USA
Montgenèvre, Col de *107 D5 pass* France/Italy
Montgomery *58 D2 state capital* Alabama, S USA
Monthey *111 A7* Valais, SW Switzerland
Montluçon *106 C4* Allier, C France
Montoro *108 D4* Andalucía, S Spain
Montpelier *57 G2 state capital* Vermont, NE USA
Montpellier *107 C6* Hérault, S France
Montréal *55 E4 Eng.* Montreal. Québec, SE Canada
Montrose *60 C5* Colorado, C USA
Montrose *104 D3* E Scotland, UK
Montserrat *71 G3 var.* Emerald Isle. *UK dependent territory* E West Indies
Monywa *152 B3* Sagaing, C Burma
Monza *112 B2* Lombardia, N Italy
Monze *94 D2* Southern, S Zambia
Monzón *109 F2* Aragón, NE Spain
Moonie *165 D5* Queensland, E Australia
Moora *163 A6* Western Australia
Moore *65 G1* Oklahoma, C USA
Moore, Lake *163 B6 lake* Western Australia
Moorhead *61 F2* Minnesota, N USA
Moose *54 C3 river* Ontario, S Canada
Moosehead Lake *57 G1 lake* Maine, NE USA
Moosonee *54 C3* Ontario, SE Canada
Mopti *91 E3* Mopti, C Mali
Moquegua *77 E4* Moquegua, SE Peru
Mora *101 C5* Kopparberg, C Sweden
Morales *68 C2* Izabal, E Guatemala
Morant Bay *70 B5* E Jamaica
Moratalla *109 E4* Murcia, SE Spain
Morava *115 C5 var.* March. *River* C Europe *see also* March
Morava *see* Velika Morava
Moravia *115 B5* Iowa, C USA
Moray Firth *104 C3 inlet* N Scotland, UK
Morea *see* Pelopónnisos
Moreau River *60 D2 river* South Dakota, N USA
Moree *165 D5* New South Wales, SE Australia
Morelia *67 E4* Michoacán de Ocampo, S Mexico
Morena, Sierra *108 C4 mountain range* S Spain
Moreni *124 C5* Dâmbovița, S Romania
Mórfou *118 C5* W Cyprus
Morgan City *58 B3* Louisiana, S USA
Morghāb, Daryā-ye *138 D4 var.* Murgap Deryasy, *Rus.* Murgab. *River* Afghanistan/Turkmenistan
Morioka *146 D4* Iwate, Honshū, C Japan
Morlaix *106 A3* Finistère, NW France
Mornington Abyssal Plain *83 A7 undersea feature* SE Pacific Ocean
Mornington Island *164 B2 island* Wellesley Islands, Queensland, N Australia
Morocco *86 B3 off.* Kingdom of Morocco, *Ar.* Al Mamlakah. *Country* N Africa
Morocco *see* Marrakech
Morogoro *89 C7* Morogoro, E Tanzania
Moro Gulf *155 E3 gulf* S Philippines
Morón *70 C2* Ciego de Ávila, C Cuba
Mörön *142 D2* Hövsgöl, N Mongolia
Morondava *95 F3* Toliara, W Madagascar
Moroni *95 F2 country capital* (Comoros) Grande Comore, NW Comoros
Morotai, Pulau *155 F3 island* Maluku, E Indonesia
Morotiri *see* Marotiri
Morrinsville *166 D3* Waikato, North Island, NZ
Morris *61 F2* Minnesota, N USA
Morris Jesup, Kap *99 E1 headland* N Greenland
Morro de Môco *see* Môco
Morvan *106 D4 physical region* C France
Moscow *see* Moskva
Moscow *62 C2* Idaho, NW USA
Mosel *111 A5 Fr.* Moselle. *River* W Europe *see also* Moselle
Moselle *103 E8 Ger.* Mosel. *River* W Europe *see also* Mosel
Moselle *106 D3 department* NE France
Mosgiel *167 B7* Otago, South Island, NZ
Moshi *89 C7* Kilimanjaro, NE Tanzania
Mosjøen *100 B4* Nordland, C Norway
Moskva *127 B5 Eng.* Moscow. *Country capital* (Russian Federation) Gorod Moskva, W Russian Federation
Moskva *139 E3 Rus.* Moskovskiy; *prev.* Chubek. SW Tajikistan
Mosonmagyaróvár *115 C6 Ger.* Wieselburg-Ungarisch-Altenburg; *prev.* Moson and Magyaróvár, *Ger.* Wieselburg and Ungarisch-Altenburg. Győr-Moson-Sopron, NW Hungary
Mosquito Coast *69 E3 var.* Miskito Coast. *Coastal region* E Nicaragua
Mosquitos, Golfo de los *69 F4 Eng.* Mosquito Gulf. *Gulf* N Panama
Moss *101 B6* Østfold, S Norway
Mosselbaai *94 C5 var.* Mosselbai, *Eng.* Mossel Bay. Western Cape, SW South Africa
Mossendjo *93 B6* Le Niari, SW Congo
Mossoró *79 G2* Rio Grande do Norte, NE Brazil
Most *114 A4 Ger.* Brüx. Severní Čechy, NW Czech Republic
Mosta *118 B5 var.* Musta. C Malta
Mostaganem *86 D2 var.* Mestghanem. NW Algeria
Mostar *116 C4* S Bosnia and Herzegovina
Mosul *see* Al Mawşil
Mota del Cuervo *109 E3* Castilla-La Mancha, C Spain
Motagua, Río *68 B2 river* Guatemala/Honduras
Motril *108 D5* Andalucía, S Spain
Motru *124 B4* Gorj, SW Romania
Motueka *167 C5* Tasman, South Island, NZ
Motul *67 H3 var.* Motul de Felipe Carrillo Puerto. Yucatán, SE Mexico
Motul de Felipe Carrillo Puerto *see* Motul
Mouanda *see* Moanda
Mouhoun *see* Black Volta
Mouila *93 A6* Ngounié, C Gabon
Mould Bay *53 E2* Prince Patrick Island, Northwest Territories, N Canada
Moulins *106 C4* Allier, C France
Moulmein *152 B4 var.* Maulmain, Mawlamyine. Mon State, S Burma
Moundou *92 B4* Logone-Occidental, SW Chad
Moŭng Roessei *153 D5* Bătdâmbâng, W Cambodia

Ouessant, Île d' – Petrozsény

Ouessant, Île d' 106 A3 Eng. Ushant. Island NW France
Ouésso 93 B5 La Sangha, NW Congo
Oujda 86 D2 Ar. Oudjda, Ujda. NE Morocco
Oujeft 90 C2 Adrar, C Mauritania
Oulu 100 D4 Swe. Uleåborg. Oulu, C Finland
Oulujärvi 100 D4 Swe. Uleträsk. Lake C Finland
Oulujoki 100 D4 Swe. Uleälv. River C Finland
Ounasjoki 100 D3 river N Finland
Ounianga Kébir 92 C2 Borkou-Ennedi-Tibesti, N Chad
Oup see Auob
Oupeye 103 D6 Liège, E Belgium
Our 103 D6 river NW Europe
Ourense 108 C1 Cast. Orense; Lat. Aurium. Galicia, NW Spain
Ourique 108 B4 Beja, S Portugal
Ourthe 103 D7 river E Belgium
Ouse 105 D5 river N England, UK
Outer Hebrides 104 B3 var. Western Isles. Island group NW Scotland, UK
Outer Islands 95 G1 island group SW Seychelles
Outes 108 B1 Galicia, NW Spain
Ouvéa 160 D5 island Îles Loyauté, NE New Caledonia
Ouyen 165 C6 Victoria, SE Australia
Ovalle 80 B3 Coquimbo, N Chile
Ovar 108 B2 Aveiro, N Portugal
Overflakkee 102 B4 island SW Netherlands
Overijse 103 C6 Vlaams Brabant, C Belgium
Oviedo 108 C1 anc. Asturias. Asturias, NW Spain
Ovruch 124 D1 Zhytomyrs'ka Oblast', N Ukraine
Owando 93 B5 prev. Fort-Rousset. Cuvette, C Congo
Owase 147 C6 Mie, Honshū, SW Japan
Owatonna 61 F3 Minnesota, N USA
Owen Fracture Zone 156 B4 tectonic feature W Arabian Sea
Owen, Mount 167 C5 mountain South Island, NZ
Owensboro 56 B5 Kentucky, S USA
Owen Stanley Range 160 B3 mountain range S PNG
Owerri 91 G5 Imo, S Nigeria
Owo 91 F5 Ondo, SW Nigeria
Owyhee River 62 C4 river Idaho/Oregon, NW USA
Oxford 105 D6 Lat. Oxonia. S England, UK
Oxford 167 C6 Canterbury, South Island, NZ
Oxkutzcab 67 H4 Yucatán, SE Mexico
Oxnard 63 B7 California, W USA
Oyama 147 D5 Tochigi, Honshū, S Japan
Oyem 93 B5 Woleu-Ntem, N Gabon
Oyo 93 B6 Cuvette, C Congo
Oyo 91 F4 Oyo, W Nigeria
Ozark 58 D3 Alabama, S USA
Ozark Plateau 61 G5 plain Arkansas/Missouri, C USA
Ozarks, Lake of the 61 F5 reservoir Missouri, C USA
Ozbourn Seamount 168 D4 undersea feature W Pacific Ocean
Ózd 115 D6 Borsod-Abaúj-Zemplén, NE Hungary
Ozero Khanka see Khanka, Lake
Ozero Ubsu-Nur see Uvs Nuur
Ozieri 113 A5 Sardegna, Italy, C Mediterranean Sea

P

Paamiut 98 B4 var. Pâmiut, Dan. Frederikshåb. S Greenland
Pa-an 152 B4 Karen State, S Burma
Pabna 151 G4 Rajshahi, W Bangladesh
Pachuca 67 E4 var. Pachuca de Soto. Hidalgo, C Mexico
Pachuca de Soto see Pachuca
Pacific-Antarctic Ridge 170 B5 undersea feature S Pacific Ocean
Pacific Ocean 168 D3 ocean
Padalung see Phatthalung
Padang 154 B4 Sumatera, W Indonesia
Paderborn 110 B4 Nordrhein-Westfalen, NW Germany
Padma see Brahmaputra
Padova 112 C2 Eng. Padua; anc. Patavium. Veneto, NE Italy
Padre Island 65 G5 island Texas, SW USA
Padua see Padova
Paducah 56 B5 Kentucky, S USA
Paeroa 166 D3 Waikato, North Island, NZ
Páfos 118 C5 var. Paphos. W Cyprus
Pag 116 A3 It. Pago. Island C Croatia
Page 64 B1 Arizona, SW USA
Pago Pago 161 F4 dependent territory capital (American Samoa) Tutuila, W American Samoa
Pahiatua 166 D4 Manawatu-Wanganui, North Island, NZ
Pahsien see Chongqing
Paide 122 D2 Ger. Weissenstein. Järvamaa, N Estonia
Paihia 166 D2 Northland, North Island, NZ
Päijänne 101 D5 lake S Finland
Paine, Cerro 81 A7 mountain S Chile
Painted Desert 64 B1 desert Arizona, SW USA
Paisley 104 C4 W Scotland, UK
País Valenciano 109 F3 cultural region NE Spain
País Vasco 109 E1 cultural region N Spain
Paita 76 B3 Piura, NW Peru
Pakanbaru see Pekanbaru
Pakaraima Mountains 75 E3 var. Serra Pacaraim, Sierra Pacaraima. Mountain range N South America
Pakistan 150 A2 off. Islamic Republic of Pakistan, var. Islami Jamhuriya e Pakistan. Country S Asia
Paknam see Samut Prakan
Pakokku 152 A3 Magwe, C Burma
Pak Phanang 153 C7 var. Ban Pak Phanang. Nakhon Si Thammarat, SW Thailand
Pakruojis 122 C4 Pakruojis, N Lithuania
Paks 115 C7 Tolna, S Hungary
Paksé see Pakxé
Pakxé 153 D5 var. Paksé. Champasak, S Laos
Palafrugell 109 G2 Cataluña, NE Spain
Palagruža 117 B5 It. Pelagosa. Island SW Croatia
Palaiá Epídavros 121 C6 Pelopónnisos, S Greece
Palaiseau 106 D2 Essonne, N France
Palamós 109 G2 Cataluña, NE Spain
Palamuse 122 E2 Ger. Sankt-Bartholomäi. Jõgevamaa, E Estonia
Pālanpur 150 C4 Gujarāt, W India
Palapye 94 D3 Central, SE Botswana
Palau 160 A2 var. Belau. Country W Pacific Ocean
Palawan 155 E2 island W Philippines
Palawan Passage 154 D2 passage W Philippines
Paldiski 122 D2 prev. Baltiski, Eng. Baltic Port, Ger. Baltischport. Harjumaa, NW Estonia
Palembang 154 B4 Sumatera, W Indonesia
Palencia 108 D2 anc. Palantia, Pallantia. Castilla-León, NW Spain
Palermo 113 C7 Fr. Palerme; anc. Panhormus, Panormus. Sicilia, Italy, C Mediterranean Sea
Pāli 150 C3 Rājasthān, N India
Palikir 160 C2 country capital (Micronesia) Pohnpei, E Micronesia
Palimé see Kpalimé
Palioúri, Ákra 120 C4 var. Akra Kanestron. Headland N Greece
Palk Strait 148 C3 strait India/Sri Lanka
Palliser, Cape 167 D5 headland North Island, NZ
Palma 109 G3 var. Palma de Mallorca. Mallorca, Spain, W Mediterranean Sea
Palma del Río 108 D4 Andalucía, S Spain
Palma de Mallorca see Palma
Palmar Sur 69 E5 Puntarenas, SE Costa Rica
Palma Soriano 70 C3 Santiago de Cuba, E Cuba
Palm Beach 164 E1 New South Wales, SE Australia
Palmer 170 A2 US research station Antarctica
Palmer Land 170 A3 physical region Antarctica
Palmerston 161 F4 island S Cook Islands
Palmerston North 166 D4 Manawatu-Wanganui, North Island, NZ
Palmi 113 D7 Calabria, SW Italy
Palmira 74 B3 Valle del Cauca, W Colombia
Palm Springs 63 D7 California, W USA
Palmyra see Tudmur
Palmyra Atoll 161 G2 US privately owned unincorporated territory C Pacific Ocean
Palo Alto 63 B6 California, W USA
Palu 155 E4 prev. Paloe. Sulawesi, C Indonesia
Pamiers 107 B6 Ariège, S France
Pamir var. Daryā-ye Pāmīr, Taj. Dar"yoi Pomir. River Afghanistan/Tajikistan see also Pāmīr, Daryā-ye
Pamirs 139 F3 Pash. Daryā-ye Pāmīr, Rus. Pamir. Mountain range C Asia
Pâmiut see Paamiut
Pamlico Sound 59 G1 sound North Carolina, SE USA
Pampa 65 E1 Texas, SW USA
Pampas 80 C4 plain C Argentina
Pamplona 109 E1 Basq. Iruñea; prev. Pampeluna, anc. Pompaelo. Navarra, N Spain
Pamplona 74 C2 Norte de Santander, N Colombia
Panaji 148 B1 var. Pangim, Panjim, New Goa. Goa, W India
Panama 69 G5 off. Republic of Panama. Country Central America
Panamá 69 G4 var. Ciudad de Panamá, Eng. Panama City. Country capital (Panama) Panamá, C Panama
Panama Basin 51 C8 undersea feature E Pacific Ocean
Panama Canal 69 F4 canal E Panama
Panama City see Panamá
Panama City 58 D3 Florida, SE USA
Panamá, Golfo de 69 G5 var. Gulf of Panama. Gulf S Panama
Panama, Gulf of see Panamá, Golfo de
Panamá, Isthmus of see Panamá, Istmo de
Panamá, Istmo de 69 G4 Eng. Isthmus of Panama; prev. Isthmus of Darien. Isthmus E Panama
Panay Island 155 E2 island C Philippines
Pančevo 116 D3 Ger. Pantschowa, Hung. Pancsova. Serbia, N Yugoslavia
Paneas see Bāniyās
Panevėžys 122 C4 Panevėžys, C Lithuania
Pangim see Panaji
Pangkalpinang 154 C4 Pulau Bangka, W Indonesia
Pang-Nga see Phang-Nga
Panjim see Panaji
Pánormos 121 C7 Kríti, Greece, E Mediterranean Sea
Pantanal 79 E3 var. Pantanalmato-Grossense. Swamp SW Brazil
Pantanalmato-Grossense see Pantanal
Pantelleria, Isola di 113 B7 island SW Italy
Pánuco 67 E3 Veracruz-Llave, E Mexico
Pao-chi see Baoji
Paoki see Baoji
Paola 118 B5 E Malta
Pao-shan see Baoshan
Pao-t'ou see Baotou
Paotow see Baotou
Papagayo, Golfo de 68 C4 gulf NW Costa Rica
Papakura 166 D3 Auckland, North Island, NZ
Papantla 67 F4 var. Papantla de Olarte. Veracruz-Llave, E Mexico
Papantla de Olarte see Papantla
Papeete 161 H4 dependent territory capital (French Polynesia) Tahiti, W French Polynesia
Paphos see Páfos
Papilė 122 B3 Akmenė, NW Lithuania
Papillion 61 F4 Nebraska, C USA
Papua, Gulf of 160 B3 gulf S PNG
Papua New Guinea 160 B3 off. Independent State of Papua New Guinea; prev. Territory of Papua and New Guinea, abbrev. PNG. Country NW Melanesia
Papuk 116 C3 mountain range NE Croatia
Pará 79 E2 off. Estado do Pará. State NE Brazil
Pará see Belém
Paracel Islands 141 E3 disputed territory SE Asia
Paraćin 116 D4 Serbia, C Yugoslavia
Paragua, Río 75 E3 river SE Venezuela
Paraguay 80 D2 var. Río Paraguay. River C South America
Paraguay 80 C2 country C South America
Paraguay, Río see Paraguay
Paraíba 79 G2 off. Estado da Paraíba; prev. Parahiba, Parahyba. State E Brazil
Parakou 91 F4 C Benin
Paramaribo 75 G3 country capital (Surinam) Paramaribo, N Surinam
Paramushir, Ostrov 131 H3 island SE Russian Federation
Paraná 79 E5 off. Estado do Paraná. State S Brazil
Paraná 73 C5 var. Alto Paraná. River C South America
Paraná 79 E4 Entre Ríos, E Argentina
Paranéstio 120 C3 Anatolikí Makedonía kai Thráki, NE Greece
Paraparaumu 167 D5 Wellington, North Island, NZ
Parchim 110 C3 Mecklenburg-Vorpommern, N Germany
Parczew 114 E4 Biała Podlaska, E Poland
Pardubice 115 B5 Ger. Pardubitz. Východní Čechy, C Czech Republic
Parechcha 123 B5 Rus. Porech'ye. Hrodzyenskaya Voblasts', NE Belorussia
Parecis, Chapada dos 78 D3 var. Serra dos Parecis. Mountain range W Brazil
Parepare 155 E4 Sulawesi, C Indonesia
Párga 121 A5 Ípeiros, W Greece
Paria, Gulf of 75 E1 var. Golfo de Paria. Gulf Trinidad and Tobago/Venezuela
Parika 75 F2 NE Guyana
Paris 106 D1 anc. Lutetia, Lutetia Parisiorum, Parisii. Country capital (France) Paris, N France
Paris 65 G2 Texas, SW USA
Parkersburg 56 D4 West Virginia, NE USA
Parkes 165 D6 New South Wales, SE Australia
Parma 112 B2 Emilia-Romagna, N Italy
Parnahyba see Parnaíba
Parnaíba 79 F2 var. Parnahyba. Piauí, E Brazil
Pärnu 122 D2 Ger. Pernau, Latv. Pērnava; prev. Rus. Pernov. Pärnumaa, SW Estonia
Pärnu 122 D2 var. Parnu Jõgi, Ger. Pernau. River SW Estonia
Pärnu-Jaagupi 122 D2 Ger. Sankt-Jakobi. Pärnumaa, SW Estonia
Parnu Jõgi see Pärnu
Pärnu Laht 122 D2 Ger. Pernauer Bucht. Bay SW Estonia
Páros 121 C6 island Kykládes, Greece, Aegean Sea
Páros 121 D6 Páros, Kykládes, Greece, Aegean Sea
Parral see Hidalgo del Parral
Parral 80 B4 Maule, C Chile
Parramatta 164 D1 New South Wales, SE Australia
Parras 66 D3 var. Parras de la Fuente. Coahuila de Zaragoza, NE Mexico
Parras de la Fuente see Parras
Parsons 61 F5 Kansas, C USA
Pasadena 63 C7 California, W USA
Pasadena 65 H4 Texas, SW USA
Paşcani 124 C3 Hung. Páskán. Iaşi, NE Romania
Pasco 62 C2 Washington, NW USA
Pas de Calais see Dover, Strait of
Pasewalk 110 D3 Mecklenburg-Vorpommern, NE Germany
Pasinler 133 F3 Erzurum, NE Turkey
Pasłęk 114 D2 Ger. Preußisch Holland. Elbląg, N Poland
Pasni 150 A3 Baluchistān, SW Pakistan
Paso de Indios 81 B6 Chubut, S Argentina
Passau 111 D6 Bayern, SE Germany
Passo del Brennero see Brenner Pass
Passo Fundo 79 E5 Rio Grande do Sul, S Brazil
Pastavy 123 C5 Pol. Postawy, Rus. Postavy. Vitsyebskaya Voblasts', NW Belorussia
Pastaza, Río 76 B2 river Ecuador/Peru
Pasto 74 A4 Nariño, SW Colombia
Pasvalys 122 C4 Pasvalys, N Lithuania
Patagonia 73 B7 physical region Argentina/Chile
Patalung see Phatthalung
Patani see Pattani
Patavium see Padova
Patea 166 D4 Taranaki, North Island, NZ
Paterson 57 F3 New Jersey, NE USA
Pathein see Bassein
Pátmos 121 D6 island Dodekánisos, Greece, Aegean Sea
Patna 151 F3 var. Azimabad. Bihār, N India
Patnos 133 F3 Ağrı, E Turkey
Patos, Lagoa dos 79 E5 lagoon S Brazil
Pátra 121 B5 Eng. Patras; prev. Pátrai. Dytikí Ellás, S Greece
Pattani 153 C7 var. Patani. Pattani, SW Thailand
Pattaya 153 C5 Chon Buri, S Thailand
Patuca, Río 68 D2 river E Honduras
Pau 107 B6 Pyrénées-Atlantiques, SW France
Paulatuk 53 E3 Northwest Territories, NW Canada
Paungde 152 B4 Pegu, C Burma
Pavia 112 B2 anc. Ticinum. Lombardia, N Italy
Pāvilosta 122 B3 Liepāja, W Latvia
Pavlikeni 120 D2 Loveshka Oblast, N Bulgaria
Pavlodar 130 C4 Pavlodar, NE Kazakhstan
Pavlohrad 125 G3 Rus. Pavlograd. Dnipropetrovs'ka Oblast', E Ukraine
Pawn 152 B3 river C Burma
Paxoí 121 A5 island Iónioi Nísoi, Greece, C Mediterranean Sea
Payo Obispo see Chetumal
Paysandú 80 D4 Paysandú, W Uruguay
Pazar 133 E2 Rize, NE Turkey
Pazardzhik 120 C3 prev. Tatar Pazardzhik. Plovdivska Oblast, SW Bulgaria
Pearl River 58 B3 river Louisiana/Mississippi, S USA
Pearsall 65 F4 Texas, SW USA
Peć 117 D5 Alb. Pejë, Turk. Ipek. Serbia, S Yugoslavia
Pechora 126 D3 river NW Russian Federation
Pechora 126 D3 Respublika Komi, NW Russian Federation
Pechorskoye More 126 D2 Eng. Pechora Sea. Sea NW Russian Federation
Pecos 65 E3 Texas, SW USA
Pecos River 65 E3 river New Mexico/Texas, SW USA
Pécs 115 C7 Ger. Fünfkirchen; Lat. Sopianae. Baranya, SW Hungary
Pedra Lume 90 A3 Sal, NE Cape Verde
Pedro Cays 70 C3 island group S Jamaica
Pedro Juan Caballero 80 D2 Amambay, E Paraguay
Peer 103 D5 Limburg, NE Belgium
Pegasus Bay 167 C6 bay South Island, NZ
Pegu 152 B4 var. Bago. Pegu, SW Burma
Pehuajó 80 C4 Buenos Aires, E Argentina
Pei-ching see Beijing
Peine 110 B3 Niedersachsen, C Germany
Pei-p'ing see Beijing
Peipus, Lake E3 Est. Peipsi Järv, Ger. Peipus-See, Rus. Chudskoye Ozero. Lake Estonia/Russian Federation
Peiraías 121 C6 prev. Piraiévs, Eng. Piraeus. Attikí, C Greece
Pèk 152 D4 var. Xieng Khouang; prev. Xiangkhoang. Xiangkhoang, N Laos
Pekalongan 154 C4 Jawa, C Indonesia
Pekanbaru 154 B3 var. Pakanbaru. Sumatera, W Indonesia
Pekin 56 B4 Illinois, N USA
Peking see Beijing
Pelagie, Isole 113 B8 island group SW Italy
Pelly Bay 53 G3 Northwest Territories, N Canada
Peloponnese see Pelopónnisos
Peloponnesus see Pelopónnisos
Pelopónnisos 121 B6 var. Morea, Eng. Peloponnese; anc. Peloponnesus. Peninsula S Greece
Pematangsiantar 154 B3 Sumatera, W Indonesia
Pemba 95 F2 prev. Port Amelia, Porto Amélia. Cabo Delgado, NE Mozambique
Pemba 89 D7 island E Tanzania
Pembroke 54 D4 Ontario, SE Canada
Penang see George Town
Penang see Pinang, Pulau
Penas, Golfo de 81 A7 gulf S Chile
Penderma see Bandırma
Pendleton 62 C3 Oregon, NW USA
Pend Oreille, Lake 62 D2 lake Idaho, NW USA
Peneius see Pineiós
Peng-pu see Bengbu
Peniche 108 B3 Leiria, W Portugal
Péninsule de la Gaspésie see Gaspé, Péninsule de
Pennine Alps 111 A8 Fr. Alpes Pennines, It. Alpi Pennine; Lat. Alpes Penninae. Mountain range Italy/Switzerland
Pennine Chain see Pennines
Pennines 105 D5 var. Pennine Chain. Mountain range N England, UK
Pennsylvania 56 D3 off. Commonwealth of Pennsylvania; also known as The Keystone State. State NE USA
Penobscot River 57 G2 river Maine, NE USA
Penong 165 A6 South Australia
Penonomé 69 F5 Coclé, C Panama
Penrhyn 161 G3 atoll N Cook Islands
Penrhyn Basin 159 F3 undersea feature C Pacific Ocean
Penrith 164 D1 New South Wales, SE Australia
Penrith 105 D5 NW England, UK
Pensacola 58 C3 Florida, SE USA
Pentecost 160 D4 Fr. Pentecôte. Island C Vanuatu
Penza 127 C6 Penzenskaya Oblast', W Russian Federation
Penzance 105 C7 SW England, UK
Peoria 56 B4 Illinois, N USA
Perchtoldsdorf 111 E6 Niederösterreich, NE Austria
Percival Lakes 162 C4 lakes Western Australia
Perdido, Monte 109 F1 mountain NE Spain
Perece Vela Basin see West Mariana Basin
Pereira 74 B3 Risaralda, W Colombia
Pergamino 80 C4 Buenos Aires, E Argentina
Périgueux 107 C5 anc. Vesuna. Dordogne, SW France
Perito Moreno 81 B6 Santa Cruz, S Argentina
Perlas, Archipiélago de las 69 G5 Eng. Pearl Islands. Island group SE Panama
Perlas, Laguna de 69 E3 Eng. Pearl Lagoon. Lagoon E Nicaragua
Perleberg 110 C3 Brandenburg, N Germany
Perm' 130 C3 prev. Molotov. Permskaya Oblast', NW Russian Federation
Pernambuco 79 G2 off. Estado de Pernambuco. State E Brazil
Pernambuco Abyssal Plain see Pernambuco Plain
Pernambuco Plain 83 C5 var. Pernambuco Abyssal Plain. Undersea feature E Atlantic Ocean
Pernau see Pärnu
Pernik 120 B2 prev. Dimitrovo. Sofiyska Oblast, W Bulgaria
Perote 67 F4 Veracruz-Llave, E Mexico
Perovsk see Kzyl-Orda
Perpignan 107 C6 Pyrénées-Orientales, S France
Perryton 65 F1 Texas, SW USA
Perryville 61 H5 Missouri, C USA
Persian Gulf see Gulf, The
Perth 163 A6 state capital Western Australia
Perth 104 C4 C Scotland, UK
Perth Basin 157 E6 undersea feature SE Indian Ocean
Peru 76 C3 off. Republic of Peru. Country W South America
Peru see Beru
Peru Basin 83 A5 undersea feature E Pacific Ocean
Peru-Chile Trench 72 A4 undersea feature E Pacific Ocean
Perugia 112 C4 Fr. Pérouse; anc. Perusia. Umbria, C Italy
Péruwelz 103 B6 Hainaut, SW Belgium
Pervomays'k 125 E3 prev. Ol'viopol'. Mykolayivs'ka Oblast', S Ukraine
Pervyy Kuril'skiy Proliv 131 H3 strait E Russian Federation
Pesaro 112 C3 anc. Pisaurum. Marche, C Italy
Pescara 112 D4 anc. Aternum, Ostia Aterni. Abruzzi, C Italy
Peshāwar 150 C1 North-West Frontier Province, N Pakistan
Peshkopi 117 C6 var. Peshkopia, Peshkopija. Dibër, NE Albania
Peshkopia see Peshkopi
Peshkopija see Peshkopi
Peski Karakumy see Garagumy
Pessac 107 B5 Gironde, SW France
Petach-Tikva see Petaḥ Tiqwa
Petah Tiqva see Petaḥ Tiqwa
Petaḥ Tiqwa 135 A6 var. Petach-Tikva, Petah Tiqva. Tel Aviv, C Israel
Pétange 103 D8 Luxembourg, SW Luxembourg
Petchaburi see Phetchaburi
Peterborough 105 E6 prev. Medeshamstede. E England, UK
Peterborough 54 D5 Ontario, SE Canada
Peterborough 165 B6 South Australia
Peterhead 104 D3 NE Scotland, UK
Peter I Island 170 A3 Norwegian dependency Antarctica
Petermann Bjerg 99 E3 mountain C Greenland
Petersburg 57 E5 Virginia, NE USA
Peters Mine 75 F3 var. Peter's Mine. N Guyana
Peto 67 H4 Yucatán, SE Mexico
Petoskey 56 C2 Michigan, N USA
Petra see Wādī Mūsā
Petrich 120 C3 Sofiyska Oblast, SW Bulgaria
Petrinja 116 B3 Sisak-Moslavina, C Croatia
Petrodvorets 126 A4 Fin. Pietarhovi. Leningradskaya Oblast', NW Russian Federation
Petrograd see Sankt-Peterburg
Petropavlovsk 130 C4 Kaz. Petropavl. Severnyy Kazakhstan, N Kazakhstan
Petropavlovsk-Kamchatskiy 131 H3 Kamchatskaya Oblast', E Russian Federation
Petroşani 124 B4 var. Petroşeni, Ger. Petroschen, Hung. Petrozsény. Hunedoara, W Romania
Petroschen see Petroşani
Petroşeni see Petroşani
Petrozavodsk 130 B2 Fin. Petroskoi. Respublika Kareliya, NW Russian Federation
Petrozsény see Petroşani

Prizren – Reggio Calabria

Prizren *117 D5 Alb.* Prizreni. Serbia, S Yugoslavia
Probolinggo *154 D5* Jawa, C Indonesia
Progreso *67 H3* Yucatán, SE Mexico
Prokhladnyy *127 B8* Kabardino-Balkarskaya Respublika, SW Russian Federation
Prokuplje *117 D5* Serbia, SE Yugoslavia
Prome *152 B4 var.* Pyè. Pegu, C Burma
Promyshlennyy *126 E3* Respublika Komi, NW Russian Federation
Prostějov *115 C5 Ger.* Prossnitz, *Pol.* Prościejów. Jižní Morava, SE Czech Republic
Provence *107 D6 cultural region* SE France
Providence *see* Fort Providence
Providence *57 G3 state capital* Rhode Island, NE USA
Providencia, Isla de *69 F3 island* NW Colombia
Provideniya *172 B1* Chukotskiy Avtonomnyy Okrug, NE Russian Federation
Provo *60 B4* Utah, W USA
Prudhoe Bay *52 D2* Alaska, USA
Prusa *see* Bursa
Pruszków *114 D3 Ger.* Kaltdorf. Warszawa, C Poland
Prut *124 D4 Ger.* Pruth. *River* E Europe
Pruzhany *123 B6 Pol.* Prużana. Brestskaya Voblasts', SW Belorussia
Prydniprovs'ka Vysochyna *125 G3 Rus.* Pridneprovskaya Vozvyshennost'. *Mountain range* NW Ukraine
Prydz Bay *170 D3 bay* Antarctica
Pryluky *125 E2 Rus.* Priluki. Chernihivs'ka Oblast', NE Ukraine
Prymors'k *125 G4 Rus.* Primorsk; *prev.* Primorskoye. Zaporiz'ka Oblast', SE Ukraine
Przemyśl *115 E5 Rus.* Peremyshl. Przemyśl, SE Poland
Psará *121 D5 island* E Greece
Psël *125 F2 river* Russian Federation/Ukraine
Pskov *130 B2 Ger.* Pleskau, *Latv.* Pleskava. Pskovskaya Oblast', W Russian Federation
Pskov, Lake *E3 Est.* Pihkva Järv, *Ger.* Pleskauer See, *Rus.* Pskovskoye Ozero. *Lake* Estonia/Russian Federation
Ptsich *123 C7 Rus.* Ptich'. *River* SE Belorussia
Ptsich *123 C7 Rus.* Ptich'. Homyel'skaya Voblasts', SE Belorussia
Ptuj *111 E7 Ger.* Pettau; *anc.* Poetovio. NE Slovenia
Pucallpa *76 C3* Ucayali, C Peru
Puck *114 C2* Gdańsk, N Poland
Pudasjärvi *100 D4* Oulu, C Finland
Puducheri *see* Pondicherry
Puebla *67 F4 var.* Puebla de Zaragoza. Puebla, S Mexico
Puebla de Zaragoza *see* Puebla
Pueblo *60 D5* Colorado, C USA
Puerto Acosta *77 E4* La Paz, W Bolivia
Puerto Aisén *81 B6* Aisén, S Chile
Puerto Ángel *67 F5* Oaxaca, SE Mexico
Puerto Ayacucho *74 D3* Amazonas, SW Venezuela
Puerto Baquerizo Moreno *76 B4 var.* Baquerizo Moreno. Galapagos Islands, Ecuador, E Pacific Ocean
Puerto Barrios *68 C2* Izabal, E Guatemala
Puerto Bello *see* Portobelo
Puerto Berrío *74 B2* Antioquia, C Colombia
Puerto Cabello *74 D1* Carabobo, N Venezuela
Puerto Cabezas *69 E2 var.* Bilwi. Región Autónoma Atlántico Norte, NE Nicaragua
Puerto Carreño *74 D3* Vichada, E Colombia
Puerto Cortés *68 C2* Cortés, NW Honduras
Puerto Cumarebo *74 C1* Falcón, N Venezuela
Puerto Deseado *81 C7* Santa Cruz, SE Argentina
Puerto Escondido *67 F5* Oaxaca, SE Mexico
Puerto Francisco de Orellana *76 B1 var.* Coca. Napo, N Ecuador
Puerto Gallegos *see* Río Gallegos
Puerto Inírida *74 D3 var.* Obando. Guainía, E Colombia
Puerto La Cruz *75 E1* Anzoátegui, NE Venezuela
Puerto Lempira *69 E2* Gracias a Dios, E Honduras
Puerto Limón *see* Limón
Puertollano *108 D4* Castilla-La Mancha, C Spain
Puerto López *74 C1* La Guajira, N Colombia
Puerto Maldonado *77 E3* Madre de Dios, E Peru
Puerto México *see* Coatzacoalcos
Puerto Montt *81 B5* Los Lagos, C Chile
Puerto Natales *81 B7* Magallanes, S Chile
Puerto Obaldía *69 H5* San Blas, NE Panama
Puerto Plata *71 E3 var.* San Felipe de Puerto Plata. N Dominican Republic
Puerto Princesa *155 E2 off.* Puerto Princesa City. Palawan, W Philippines
Puerto Rico *71 F3 off.* Commonwealth of Puerto Rico; *prev.* Porto Rico. *US commonwealth territory* C West Indies
Puerto Rico *72 B1 island* C West Indies
Puerto Rico Trench *72 B1 undersea feature* NE Caribbean Sea
Puerto San José *see* San José
Puerto San Julián *81 B7 var.* San Julián. Santa Cruz, SE Argentina
Puerto Suárez *77 H4* Santa Cruz, E Bolivia
Puerto Vallarta *66 D4* Jalisco, SW Mexico
Puerto Varas *81 B5* Los Lagos, C Chile
Puerto Viejo *69 E4* Heredia, NE Costa Rica
Puertoviejo *see* Portoviejo
Puget Sound *62 B1 sound* Washington, NW USA
Puglia *113 E5 Eng.* Apulia. *Cultural region* SE Italy
Pukaki, Lake *167 B6 lake* South Island, NZ
Pukekohe *166 D3* Auckland, North Island, NZ
Puket *see* Phuket
Pukhavichy *123 C6 Rus.* Pukhovichi. Minskaya Voblasts', C Belorussia
Pula *116 A3 It.* Pola; *prev.* Pulj. Istra, NW Croatia
Pulaski *56 D5* Virginia, NE USA
Pulau Butung *see* Buton, Pulau
Puławy *114 D4 Ger.* Neu Amerika. Lublin, E Poland
Pul-i-Khumri *see* Pol-e Khomrī
Pullman *62 C2* Washington, NW USA
Pułtusk *114 D3* Ciechanów, C Poland
Puná, Isla *76 A2 island* SW Ecuador
Pune *150 C5 prev.* Poona. Mahārāshtra, W India
Punjab *150 C2 prev.* West Punjab, Western Punjab. *Province* E Pakistan
Puno *77 E4* Puno, SE Peru
Punta Alta *81 C5* Buenos Aires, E Argentina
Punta Arenas *81 B8 prev.* Magallanes. Magallanes, S Chile
Punta Gorda *69 E4* Región Autónoma Atlántico Sur, SE Nicaragua
Punta Gorda *68 C2* Toledo, SE Belize
Puntarenas *68 D4* Puntarenas, W Costa Rica
Punto Fijo *74 C1* Falcón, N Venezuela
Pupuya, Nevado *77 E4 mountain* W Bolivia
Puri *151 F5 var.* Jagannath. Orissa, E India
Puriramya *see* Buriram
Purmerend *102 C3* Noord-Holland, C Netherlands
Purus, Rio *78 C2 Sp.* Río Purús. *River* Brazil/Peru
Pusan *145 E4 off.* Pusan-gwangyŏksi, *var.* Busan, *Jap.* Fusan. SE South Korea
Püspökladány *115 D6* Hajdú-Bihar, E Hungary
Putorana Mountains *see* Putorana, Plato
Putorana, Plato *130 D3 var.* Gory Putorana, *Eng.* Putorana Mountains. *Mountain range* N Russian Federation
Puttalam *148 C3* North Western Province, W Sri Lanka
Puttgarden *110 C2* Schleswig-Holstein, N Germany
Putumayo, Río *74 B5 var.* Rio Içá. *River* NW South America *see also* Içá, Rio
Putumayo, Río *see* Içá, Rio
Puurmani *122 D2 Ger.* Talkhof. Jõgevamaa, E Estonia
Pyatigorsk *127 B7* Stavropol'skiy Kray, SW Russian Federation
P"yatykhatky *125 F3 Rus.* Pyatikhatki. Dnipropetrovs'ka Oblast', E Ukraine
Pyè *see* Prome
Pyetrykaw *123 C7 Rus.* Petrikov. Homyel'skaya Voblasts', SE Belorussia
Pyinmana *152 B4* Mandalay, C Burma
Pýlos *121 B6 var.* Pilos. Pelopónnisos, S Greece
P'yŏngyang *145 E3 var.* P'yŏngyang-si, *Eng.* Pyongyang. *Country capital* (North Korea) SW North Korea
P'yŏngyang-si *see* P'yŏngyang
Pyramid Lake *63 C5 lake* Nevada, W USA
Pyrenees *118 B2 Fr.* Pyrénées, *Sp.* Pirineos; *anc.* Pyrenaei Montes. *Mountain range* SW Europe
Pýrgos *121 B6 var.* Pírgos. Dytikí Ellás, S Greece
Pyryatyn *125 E2 Rus.* Piryatin. Poltavs'ka Oblast', NE Ukraine
Pyrzyce *114 B3 Ger.* Pyritz. Szczecin, NW Poland
Pyu *152 B4* Pegu, C Burma
Pyuntaza *152 B4* Pegu, SW Burma

Q

Qā' al Jafr *135 C7 lake* S Jordan
Qaanaaq *98 D1 var.* Qânâq, *Dan.* Thule. N Greenland
Qābis *see* Gabès
Qacentina *see* Constantine
Qafṣah *see* Gafsa
Qagan Us *see* Dulan
Qaidam Pendi *142 C4 basin* C China
Qal'aikhum *139 F3 Rus.* Kalaikhum. S Tajikistan
Qal'at Bīshah *137 B5* 'Asīr, SW Saudi Arabia
Qamdo *142 D5* Xizang Zizhiqu, W China
Qamishly *see* Al Qāmishlī
Qânâq *see* Qaanaaq
Qaqortoq *98 C4 Dan.* Julianehåb. S Greenland
Qara Qum *see* Garagumy
Qarkilik *see* Ruoqiang
Qarokŭl *139 F3 Rus.* Karakul'. E Tajikistan
Qars *see* Kars
Qarshi *139 E3 Rus.* Karshi; *prev.* Bek-Budi. Qashqadaryo Wiloyati, S Uzbekistan
Qasigianguit *see* Qasigiannguit
Qasigiannguit *98 C3 var.* Qasigianguit, *Dan.* Christianshåb. C Greenland
Qasr Farâfra *88 B2* W Egypt
Qaṭanā *135 B5 var.* Katana. Dimashq, S Syria
Qatar *136 C4 off.* State of Qatar, *Ar.* Dawlat Qaṭar. *Country* SW Asia
Qattara Depression *see* Qaṭṭāra, Monkhafad el
Qaṭṭâra, Monkhafad el *88 A1 var.* Munkhafaḍ al Qaṭṭārah, *Eng.* Qattara Depression. *Desert* NW Egypt
Qazimämmäd *133 H3 Rus.* Kazi Magomed. SE Azerbaijan
Qazvīn *136 C2 var.* Kazvin. Zanjān, NW Iran
Qena *88 B2 var.* Qinā; *anc.* Caene, Caenepolis. E Egypt
Qeqertarssuaq *see* Qeqertarsuaq
Qeqertarsuaq *98 C3 var.* Qeqertarssuaq, *Dan.* Godhavn. S Greenland
Qeqertarsuaq *98 C3 island* W Greenland
Qeqertarsuup Tunua *98 C3 Dan.* Disko Bugt. *Inlet* W Greenland
Qerveh *see* Qorveh
Qeshm *136 D4 var.* Jazīreh-ye Qeshm, Qeshm Island. *Island* S Iran
Qeshm Island *see* Qeshm
Qian *see* Guizhou
Qilian Shan *142 D3 var.* Kilien Mountains. *Mountain range* N China
Qimusseriarsuaq *98 C2 Dan.* Melville Bugt, *Eng.* Melville Bay. *Bay* NW Greenland
Qinā *see* Qena
Qing *see* Qinghai
Qingdao *144 D4 var.* Ching-Tao, Ch'ing-tao, Tsingtao, Tsintao, *Ger.* Tsingtau. Shandong, E China
Qinghai *142 C4 var.* Chinghai, Koko Nor, Qing, Qinghai Sheng, Tsinghai. Admin. region *province* C China
Qinghai Hu *142 D4 var.* Ch'ing Hai, Tsing Hai, *Mong.* Koko Nor. *lake* C China
Qinghai Sheng *see* Qinghai
Qingzang Gaoyuan *142 B4 var.* Xizang Gaoyuan, *Eng.* Plateau of Tibet. *Plateau* W China
Qinhuangdao *144 D3* Hebei, E China
Qinzhou *144 B6* Guangxi Zhuangzu Zizhiqu, S China
Qiong *see* Hainan
Qiqihar *144 D2 var.* Ch'i-ch'i-ha-erh, Tsitsihar; *prev.* Lungkiang. Heilongjiang, NE China
Qira *142 B4* Xinjiang Uygur Zizhiqu, NW China
Qitai *142 C3* Xinjiang Uygur Zizhiqu, NW China
Qīzān *see* Jīzān
Qizil Orda *see* Kzyl-Orda
Qizil Qum *see* Kyzyl Kum
Qizilrabot *139 G3 Rus.* Kyzylrabot. SE Tajikistan
Qom *136 C3 var.* Kum, Qum. Markazī, N Iran
Qomul *see* Hami
Qondūz *see* Kunduz
Qorveh *136 C3 var.* Qerveh, Qurveh. Kordestān, W Iran
Qoubaïyât *134 B4 var.* Al Qubayyāt. N Lebanon
Qoussantîna *see* Constantine
Quang Ngai *153 E5 var.* Quangngai, Quang Nghia. Quang Ngai, C Vietnam
Quangngai *see* Quang Ngai
Quang Nghia *see* Quang Ngai
Quanzhou *144 D6 var.* Ch'uan-chou, Tsinkiang; *prev.* Chin-chiang. Fujian, SE China
Quanzhou *144 C6* Guangxi Zhuangzu Zizhiqu, S China
Qu'Appelle *53 F5 river* Saskatchewan, S Canada
Quarles, Pegunungan *155 E4 mountain range* Sulawesi, C Indonesia
Quarnero *see* Kvarner
Quartu Sant' Elena *113 A6* Sardegna, Italy, C Mediterranean Sea
Quba *133 H2 Rus.* Kuba. N Azerbaijan
Qubba *see* Ba'qūbah
Québec *55 E4 var.* Quebec. Québec, SE Canada
Québec *54 D3 var.* Quebec. Admin. region *province* SE Canada
Queen Charlotte Islands *52 C5 Fr.* Îles de la Reine-Charlotte. *Island group* British Columbia, SW Canada
Queen Charlotte Sound *52 C5 sea area* British Columbia, W Canada
Queen Elizabeth Islands *53 F2 Fr.* Îles de la Reine-Élisabeth. *Island group* Northwest Territories, N Canada
Queensland *164 B4 state* N Australia
Queenstown *94 D5* Eastern Cape, S South Africa
Queenstown *167 B7* Otago, South Island, NZ
Quelimane *95 E3 var.* Kilimane, Kilmain, Quilimane. Zambézia, NE Mozambique
Quepos *69 E4* Puntarenas, S Costa Rica
Querétaro *67 E4* Querétaro de Arteaga, C Mexico
Quesada *69 E4 var.* Ciudad Quesada, San Carlos. Alajuela, N Costa Rica
Quetta *150 B2* Baluchistān, SW Pakistan
Quetzalcoalco *see* Coatzacoalcos
Quetzaltenango *see* Quezaltenango
Quezaltenango *68 A2 var.* Quetzaltenango. Quezaltenango, W Guatemala
Quibdó *74 A3* Chocó, W Colombia
Quilimane *see* Quelimane
Quillabamba *76 D3* Cusco, C Peru
Quilon *148 C3 var.* Kolam, Kollam. Kerala, SW India
Quimper *106 A3 anc.* Quimper Corentin. Finistère, NW France
Quimperlé *106 A3* Finistère, NW France
Quincy *56 A4* Illinois, N USA
Qui Nhon *see* Quy Nhơn
Quissico *95 E4* Inhambane, S Mozambique
Quito *76 B1 country capital* (Ecuador) Pichincha, N Ecuador
Qullai Garmo *see* Kommunizm, Qullai
Qum *see* Qom
Qunaytra *see* Al Qunayṭirah
Qŭqon *139 F2 var.* Khokand, *Rus.* Kokand. Farghona Wiloyati, E Uzbekistan
Qurein *see* Al Kuwayt
Qŭrghonteppa *139 E3 Rus.* Kurgan-Tyube. SW Tajikistan
Qurlurtuuq *see* Coppermine
Qurveh *see* Qorveh
Quşayr *see* Al Quşayr
Quy Nhơn *153 E5 var.* Quinhon, Qui Nhon. Binh Định, C Vietnam
Qyteti Stalin *see* Kuçovë
Qyzylorda *see* Kzyl-Orda

R

Raab *116 B1 Hung.* Rába. *River* Austria/Hungary *see also* Rába
Raahe *100 D4 Swe.* Brahestad. Oulu, W Finland
Raalte *102 D3* Overijssel, E Netherlands
Raamsdonksveer *102 C4* Noord-Brabant, S Netherlands
Raasiku *122 D2 Ger.* Rasik. Harjumaa, NW Estonia
Rába *115 B7 Ger.* Raab. *River* Austria/Hungary *see also* Raab
Rabat *86 C2 var.* al Dar al Baida. *Country capital* (Morocco) NW Morocco
Rabat *see* Victoria
Rabat *118 B5* W Malta
Rabbah Ammon *see* 'Ammān
Rabbath Ammon *see* 'Ammān
Rabinal *68 B2* Baja Verapaz, C Guatemala
Rabka *115 D5* Nowy Sącz, S Poland
Râbniţa *see* Rîbniţa
Rabyanāh, Ramlat *87 G4 var.* Rebiana Sand Sea, ṣaḥrā' Rabyanāh. *Desert* SE Libya
Race, Cape *55 H3 headland* Newfoundland, Newfoundland and Labrador, E Canada
Rach Gia *153 D6* Kiên Giang, S Vietnam
Rach Gia, Vinh *153 D6 bay* S Vietnam
Racine *56 B3* Wisconsin, N USA
Rădăuţi *124 C3 Ger.* Radautz, *Hung.* Rádóc. Suceava, N Romania
Radom *114 D4* Radom, C Poland
Radomsko *114 D4 Rus.* Novoradomsk. Piotrków, C Poland
Radomyshl' *124 D2* Zhytomyrs'ka Oblast', N Ukraine
Radoviš *117 E6 prev.* Radovište. E FYR Macedonia
Radviliškis *122 B4* Radviliškis, N Lithuania
Radzyń Podlaski *114 E4* Biała Podlaska, E Poland
Rae-Edzo *53 E4* Northwest Territories, NW Canada
Raetihi *166 D4* Manawatu-Wanganui, North Island, NZ
Rafa *see* Rafah
Rafaela *80 C3* Santa Fe, E Argentina
Rafah *135 A7 var.* Rafa, Rafaḥ, *Heb.* Rafiaḥ, Raphiah. SW Gaza Strip
Rafaḥ *see* Rafah
Rafḥah *136 B4* Al Ḥudūd ash Shamālīyah, N Saudi Arabia
Rafiaḥ *see* Rafah
Raga *89 A5* Western Bahr el Ghazal, SW Sudan
Ragged Island Range *70 C2 island group* S Bahamas
Ragusa *113 C7* Sicilia, Italy, C Mediterranean Sea
Rahachow *123 D7 Rus.* Rogachëv. Homyel'skaya Voblasts', SE Belorussia
Rahaeng *see* Tak
Rahaţ, Ḩarrat *137 B5 lavaflow* W Saudi Arabia
Rahīmyār Khān *150 C3* Punjab, SE Pakistan
Raiatea *161 G4 island* Îles Sous le Vent, W French Polynesia
Rāichūr *148 C1* Karnātaka, C India
Rainier, Mount *50 A4 volcano* Washington, NW USA
Rainy Lake *54 A4 lake* Canada/USA
Raipur *151 E4* Madhya Pradesh, C India
Rājahmundry *151 E5* Andhra Pradesh, E India
Rajang *see* Rajang, Batang
Rajang, Batang *154 D3 var.* Rajang. *River* East Malaysia
Rājapālaiyam *148 C3* Tamil Nādu, SE India
Rājasthān *150 C3 state* NW India
Rājkot *150 C4* Gujarāt, W India
Rāj Nāndgaon *151 E4* Madhya Pradesh, C India
Rajshahi *151 G3 prev.* Rampur Boalia. Rajshahi, W Bangladesh
Rakahanga *161 F3 atoll* N Cook Islands
Rakaia *167 B6 river* South Island, NZ
Rakka *see* Ar Raqqah
Rakke *122 E2* Lääne-Virumaa, NE Estonia
Rakvere *122 E2 Ger.* Wesenberg. Lääne-Virumaa, N Estonia
Ralik Chain *160 D1 island group* Ralik Chain, W Marshall Islands
Ramadi *see* Ar Ramādī
Ramlat Ahl Wahībah *see* Wahībah, Ramlat Āl
Ramlat Al Wahaybah *see* Wahībah, Ramlat Āl
Râmnicu Sărat *124 C4 prev.* Râmnicul-Sărat, Rîmnicu-Sărat. Buzău, E Romania
Râmnicu Vâlcea *124 B4 prev.* Rîmnicu Vîlcea. Vâlcea, C Romania
Ramree Island *152 A4 island* W Burma
Ramtha *see* Ar Ramthā
Rancagua *80 B4* Libertador, C Chile
Rānchi *151 F4* Bihār, N India
Randers *101 B7* Århus, C Denmark
Rangiora *167 C6* Canterbury, South Island, NZ
Rangitaiki *166 D4 river* North Island, NZ
Rangoon *see* Yangon
Rangpur *151 G3* Rajshahi, N Bangladesh
Rankin Inlet *53 G3* Northwest Territories, C Canada
Ranong *153 B6* Ranong, SW Thailand
Rapa Nui *see* Easter Island
Raphiah *see* Rafah
Rapid City *60 D3* South Dakota, N USA
Räpina *122 E3 Ger.* Rappin. Põlvamaa, SE Estonia
Rapla *122 D2 Ger.* Rappel. Raplamaa, NW Estonia
Rarotonga *161 G5 island* S Cook Islands, C Pacific Ocean
Ras al 'Ain *see* Ra's al 'Ayn
Ra's al 'Ayn *134 D1 var.* Ras al 'Ain. Al Ḥasakah, N Syria
Ra's an Naqb *135 B7* Ma'ān, S Jordan
Raseiniai *122 B4* Raseiniai, C Lithuania
Ras Hafun *see* Xaafuun, Raas
Rasht *136 C2 var.* Resht. Gīlān, NW Iran
Râşnov *124 C4 prev.* Rîşno, Rozsnyó, *Hung.* Barcarozsnyó. Braşov, C Romania
Ratak Chain *160 D1 island group* Ratak Chain, E Marshall Islands
Ratan *101 C5* Jämtland, C Sweden
Rat Buri *see* Ratchaburi
Ratchaburi *153 C5 var.* Rat Buri. Ratchaburi, W Thailand
Rat Islands *52 A2 island group* Aleutian Islands, Alaska, USA
Ratlām *150 D4 prev.* Rutlam. Madhya Pradesh, C India
Ratnapura *148 D4* Sabaragamuwa Province, S Sri Lanka
Raton *64 D1* New Mexico, SW USA
Rättvik *101 C5* Kopparberg, C Sweden
Raudhatain *see* Ar Rawḍatayn
Raufarhöfn *99 E4* Nordhurland Eystra, NE Iceland
Raukawa *see* Cook Strait
Raukumara Range *166 E3 mountain range* North Island, NZ
Rauma *101 D5 Swe.* Raumo. Turku-Pori, SW Finland
Raurkela *151 F4 prev.* Rourkela. Orissa, E India
Ravenna *112 C3* Emilia-Romagna, N Italy
Rāvi *150 C2 river* India/Pakistan
Rāwalpindi *150 C1* Punjab, NE Pakistan
Rawa Mazowiecka *114 D4* Skierniewice, C Poland
Rawicz *114 C4 Ger.* Rawitsch. Leszno, W Poland
Rawlins *60 C3* Wyoming, C USA
Rawson *81 C6* Chubut, SE Argentina
Rayak *134 B4 var.* Rayaq, Riyāq. E Lebanon
Rayaq *see* Rayak
Rayleigh *59 F1 state capital* North Carolina, SE USA
Rayong *153 C5* Rayong, S Thailand
Razāzah, Buḩayrat ar *136 B3 var.* Baḩr al Milḩ. *Lake* C Iraq
Razgrad *120 D2* Razgradska Oblast, NE Bulgaria
Razim, Lacul *124 D5 prev.* Lacul Razelm. *Lagoon* NW Black Sea
Reading *57 F4* Pennsylvania, NE USA
Reading *105 D7* S England, UK
Realicó *80 C4* La Pampa, C Argentina
Reăng Kesei *153 D5* Bătdâmbâng, W Cambodia
Rebecca, Lake *163 C6 lake* Western Australia
Rebiana Sand Sea *see* Rabyanāh, Ramlat
Rebun-tō *146 C2 island* NE Japan
Rechytsa *123 D7 Rus.* Rechitsa. Brestskaya Voblasts', SW Belorussia
Recife *79 G2 prev.* Pernambuco. *State capital* Pernambuco, E Brazil
Recklinghausen *110 A4* Nordrhein-Westfalen, W Germany
Recogne *103 C7* Luxembourg, SE Belgium
Reconquista *80 D3* Santa Fe, C Argentina
Red Deer *53 E5* Alberta, SW Canada
Redding *63 B5* California, W USA
Redon *106 B4* Ille-et-Vilaine, NW France
Red River *152 C2 var.* Yuan, *Chin.* Yuan Jiang, *Vtn.* Sông Hông Hà. *River* China/Vietnam
Red River *61 E1 river* Canada/USA
Red River *58 B3 river* Louisiana, S USA
Red River *51 C6 river* S USA
Red Sea *88 C3 anc.* Sinus Arabicus. *Sea* Africa/Asia
Red Wing *61 G2* Minnesota, N USA
Reefton *167 C5* West Coast, South Island, NZ
Reese River *63 C5 river* Nevada, W USA
Refahiye *133 E3* Erzincan, C Turkey
Regensburg *111 C6 Eng.* Ratisbon, *Fr.* Ratisbonne; *hist.* Ratisbona, *anc.* Castra Regina, Reginum. Bayern, SE Germany
Regenstauf *111 C6* Bayern, SE Germany
Reggane *86 D3* C Algeria
Reggio *see* Reggio nell' Emilia
Reggio Calabria *see* Reggio di Calabria

Shensi – Sop Hao

Shensi see Shaanxi
Shenyang 144 D3 Chin. Shen-yang, Eng. Moukden, Mukden; prev. Fengtien. Liaoning, NE China
Shepetivka 124 D2 Rus. Shepetovka. Khmel'nyts'ka Oblast', NW Ukraine
Shepparton 165 C7 Victoria, SE Australia
Sherbrooke 55 E4 Québec, SE Canada
Shereik 88 C3 River Nile, N Sudan
Sheridan 60 C2 Wyoming, C USA
Sherman 65 G2 Texas, SW USA
's-Hertogenbosch 102 C4 Fr. Bois-le-Duc, Ger. Herzogenbusch. Noord-Brabant, S Netherlands
Shetland Islands 104 D1 island group NE Scotland, UK
Shibarghān see Sheberghān
Shiberghān see Sheberghān
Shibetsu 146 D2 var. Sibetu. Hokkaidō, NE Japan
Shibh Jazīrat Sīnā' see Sinai
Shibushi-wan 147 B8 bay SW Japan
Shigatse see Xigazê
Shih-chia-chuang see Shijiazhuang
Shihezi 142 C2 Xinjiang Uygur Zizhiqu, NW China
Shihmen see Shijiazhuang
Shijiazhuang 144 C4 var. Shih-chia-chuang; prev. Shihmen. Hebei, E China
Shikārpur 150 B3 Sind, S Pakistan
Shikoku 147 C7 var. Sikoku. Island SW Japan
Shikoku Basin 141 F2 var. Sikoku Basin. Undersea feature N Philippine Sea
Shikotan, Ostrov 146 E2 Jap. Shikotan-tō. Island NE Russian Federation
Shilabo 89 D5 SE Ethiopia
Shiliguri 151 F3 prev. Siliguri. West Bengal, NE India
Shilka 131 F4 river S Russian Federation
Shimbir Berris see Shimbiris
Shimbiris 88 E4 var. Shimbir Berris. Mountain N Somalia
Shimoga 148 C2 Karnātaka, W India
Shimonoseki 147 A7 var. Simonoseki; hist. Akamagaseki, Bakan. Yamaguchi, Honshū, SW Japan
Shinano-gawa 147 C5 var. Sinano Gawa. River Honshū, C Japan
Shīndand 138 D4 Farāh, W Afghanistan
Shingū 147 C6 var. Singû. Wakayama, Honshū, SW Japan
Shinjō 146 D4 var. Sinzyô. Yamagata, Honshū, C Japan
Shinyanga 89 C7 Shinyanga, NW Tanzania
Shiprock 64 C1 New Mexico, SW USA
Shīrāz 136 D4 var. Shīrāz. Fārs, S Iran
Shivpuri 150 D3 Madhya Pradesh, C India
Shizugawa 146 D4 Miyagi, Honshū, NE Japan
Shizuoka 147 D6 var. Sizuoka. Shizuoka, Honshū, S Japan
Shklow 123 D6 Rus. Shklov. Mahilyowskaya Voblasts', E Belorussia
Shkodër 117 C5 var. Shkodra, It. Scutari, SCr. Skadar. Shkodër, NW Albania
Shkodra see Shkodër
Shkubinit, Lumi i 117 C6 var. Shkumbî, Shkumbin. River C Albania
Shkumbî see Shkubinit, Lumi i
Shkumbin see Shkubinit, Lumi i
Sholāpur see Solāpur
Shostka 125 F1 Sums'ka Oblast', NE Ukraine
Show Low 64 B2 Arizona, SW USA
Shpola 125 E3 Cherkas'ka Oblast', N Ukraine
Shreveport 58 A2 Louisiana, S USA
Shrewsbury 105 D6 hist. Scrobesbyrig'. W England, UK
Shu 130 C5 Kaz. Shū. Zhambyl, SE Kazakhstan
Shuang-liao see Liaoyuan
Shumagin Islands 52 B3 island group Alaska, USA
Shumen 120 D2 Varnenska Oblast, NE Bulgaria
Shumilina 123 E5 Rus. Shumilino. Vitsyebskaya Voblasts', NE Belorussia
Shuqrah 137 B7 var. Shaqrā. SW Yemen
Shwebo 152 B3 Sagaing, C Burma
Shyichy 123 C7 Rus. Shiichi. Homyel'skaya Voblasts', SE Belorussia
Shymkent 130 B5 prev. Chimkent. Yuzhnyy Kazakhstan, S Kazakhstan
Shyshchytsy 123 C6 Rus. Shishchitsy. Minskaya Voblasts', C Belorussia
Si see Syr Darya
Siam, Gulf of see Thailand, Gulf of
Sian see Xi'an
Siang see Brahmaputra
Siangtan see Xiangtan
Šiauliai 122 B4 Ger. Schaulen. Šiauliai, N Lithuania
Sibay 127 D6 Respublika Bashkortostan, W Russian Federation
Šibenik 116 B4 It. Sebenico. Šibenik, S Croatia
Siberia see Sibir'
Siberut, Pulau 154 A4 prev. Siberoet. Island Kepulauan Mentawai, W Indonesia
Sibetu see Shibetsu
Sibi 150 B2 Baluchistān, SW Pakistan
Sibir' 131 E3 var. Siberia. Physical region NE Russian Federation
Sibiti 93 B6 La Lékoumou, S Congo
Sibiu 124 B4 Ger. Hermannstadt, Hung. Nagyszeben. Sibiu, C Romania
Sibolga 154 B3 Sumatera, W Indonesia
Sibu 154 D3 Sarawak, East Malaysia
Sibut 92 C4 prev. Fort-Sibut. Kémo, S Central African Republic
Sibuyan Sea 155 E2 sea C Philippines
Sichon 153 C6 var. Ban Sichon, Si Chon. Nakhon Si Thammarat, SW Thailand
Sichuan 144 B5 var. Chuan, Sichuan Sheng, Ssu-ch'uan, Szechuan, Szechwan. Admin. region province C China
Sichuan Pendi 144 B5 depression C China
Sichuan Sheng see Sichuan
Sicilia 113 C7 Eng. Sicily; anc. Trinacria. Island Italy, C Mediterranean Sea
Sicilian Channel see Sicily, Strait of
Sicily see Sicilia
Sicily, Strait of 113 B7 var. Sicilian Channel. Strait C Mediterranean Sea
Sicuani 77 E4 Cusco, S Peru
Sidári 120 A4 Kérkyra, Iónioi Nísoi, Greece, C Mediterranean Sea
Sidas 154 C4 Borneo, C Indonesia
Siderno 113 D7 Calabria, SW Italy
Sîdi Barrâni 88 A1 NW Egypt
Sidi Bel Abbès 86 D2 var. Sidi bel Abbès, Sidi-Bel-Abbès. NW Algeria
Sidirókastro 120 C3 prev. Sidhirókastron. Kentrikí Makedonía, NE Greece
Sidley, Mount 170 B4 mountain Antarctica
Sidney 60 D1 Montana, NW USA
Sidney 60 D4 Nebraska, C USA
Sidney 56 C4 Ohio, N USA
Sidon see Saïda
Sidra see Surt
Siedlce 114 E3 Ger. Sedlez, Rus. Sesdlets. Siedlce, E Poland
Siegen 110 B4 Nordrhein-Westfalen, W Germany
Siemiatycze 114 E3 Białystok, E Poland
Siena 112 B3 Fr. Sienne; anc. Saena Julia. Toscana, C Italy
Sieradz 114 C4 Sieradz, C Poland
Sierpc 114 D3 Płock, C Poland
Sierra de Soconusco see Sierra Madre
Sierra Leone 90 C4 off. Republic of Sierra Leone. Country W Africa
Sierra Leone Basin 82 C4 undersea feature E Atlantic Ocean
Sierra Leone Ridge see Sierra Leone Rise
Sierra Leone Rise 82 C4 var. Sierra Leone Ridge, Sierra Leone Schwelle. Undersea feature E Atlantic Ocean
Sierra Leone Schwelle see Sierra Leone Rise
Sierra Madre 68 B2 var. Sierra de Soconusco. Mountain range Guatemala/Mexico
Sierra Madre see Madre Occidental, Sierra
Sierra Nevada 63 C6 mountain range W USA
Sierra Pacaraima see Pakaraima Mountains
Sierra Vieja 64 D3 mountain range Texas, SW USA
Sierra Vista 64 B3 Arizona, SW USA
Sífnos 121 C6 anc. Siphnos. Island Kykládes, Greece, Aegean Sea
Sigli 154 A3 Sumatera, W Indonesia
Siglufjördhur 99 E4 Nordhurland Vestra, N Iceland
Signal Peak 64 A2 mountain Arizona, SW USA
Signan see Xi'an
Signy 170 A2 UK research station South Orkney Islands, Antarctica
Siguatepeque 68 C2 Comayagua, W Honduras
Siguiri 90 D4 Haute-Guinée, NE Guinea
Siilinjärvi 100 E4 Kuopio, C Finland
Siirt 133 F4 var. Sert; anc. Tigranocerta. Siirt, SE Turkey
Sikandarabad see Secunderābād
Sikasso 90 D4 Sikasso, S Mali
Sikeston 61 H5 Missouri, C USA
Sikhote-Alin', Khrebet 131 G4 mountain range SE Russian Federation
Siking see Xi'an
Siklós 115 C7 Baranya, SW Hungary
Sikoku see Shikoku
Sikoku Basin see Shikoku Basin
Šilalė 122 B4 Šilalė, W Lithuania
Silchar 151 G3 Assam, NE India
Silesia 114 B4 Montana, NW USA
Silifke 132 C4 anc. Seleucia. İçel, S Turkey
Siling Co 142 C5 lake W China
Silinhot see Xilinhot
Silistra 120 E1 var. Silistria; anc. Durostorum. Razgradska Oblast, NE Bulgaria
Silistria see Silistra
Sillamäe 122 E2 Ger. Sillamäggi. Ida-Virumaa, NE Estonia
Šilutė 122 B4 Ger. Heydekrug. Šilutė, W Lithuania
Silvan 133 E4 Dıyarbakır, SE Turkey
Silverek 133 E4 Şanlıurfa, SE Turkey
Simanggang see Sri Aman
Simanichy 123 C7 Rus. Simonichi. Homyel'skaya Voblasts', SE Belorussia
Simav 132 B3 Kütahya, W Turkey
Simav Çayı 132 A3 river NW Turkey
Simeto 113 C7 river Sicilia, Italy, C Mediterranean Sea
Simeulue, Pulau 154 A3 island NW Indonesia
Simferopol' 125 F5 Respublika Krym, S Ukraine
Simitli 120 C3 Sofiyska Oblast, SW Bulgaria
Şimleu Silvaniei 124 B3 Hung. Szilágsomlyó; prev. Şimlăul Silvaniei, Şimleul Silvaniei. Sălaj, NW Romania
Simonoseki see Shimonoseki
Simpelveld 103 D6 Limburg, SE Netherlands
Simplon Pass 111 B8 pass S Switzerland
Simpson see Fort Simpson
Simpson Desert 164 B4 desert Northern Territory/South Australia
Sīnā' see Sinai
Sinai 88 C2 var. Sinai Peninsula, Ar. Shibh Jazīrat Sīnā', Sīnā'. Physical region NE Egypt
Sinaia 124 C4 Prahova, SE Romania
Sinai Peninsula see Sinai
Sinano Gawa see Shinano-gawa
Sincelejo 74 B2 Sucre, NW Colombia
Sind 150 B3 var. Sindh. Admin. region province SE Pakistan
Sindelfingen 111 B6 Baden-Württemberg, SW Germany
Sindh see Sind
Sindi 122 D2 Ger. Zintenhof. Pärnumaa, SW Estonia
Sines 108 B4 Setúbal, S Portugal
Singan see Xi'an
Singapore 154 A1 off. Republic of Singapore. Country SE Asia
Singapore 154 B3 country capital (Singapore) S Singapore
Singen 111 B6 Baden-Württemberg, S Germany
Singida 89 C7 Singida, C Tanzania
Singkang 155 E4 Sulawesi, C Indonesia
Singkawang 154 C3 Borneo, C Indonesia
Singora see Songkhla
Singû see Shingū
Sining see Xining
Siniscola 113 A5 Sardegna, Italy, C Mediterranean Sea
Sinj 116 B4 Split-Dalmacija, SE Croatia
Sinkiang see Xinjiang Uygur Zizhiqu
Sinkiang Uighur Autonomous Region see Xinjiang Uygur Zizhiqu
Sinnamarie see Sinnamary
Sinnamary 75 H3 var. Sinnamarie. N French Guiana
Sînnicolau Mare see Sânnicolau Mare
Sinoie, Lacul 124 D5 prev. Lacul Sinoe. Lagoon SE Romania
Sinop 132 D2 anc. Sinope. Sinop, N Turkey
Sinsheim 111 B6 Baden-Württemberg, SW Germany
Sint Maarten 71 G3 Eng. Saint Martin. Island N Netherlands Antilles
Sint-Michielsgestel 102 C4 Noord-Brabant, S Netherlands
Sint-Niklaas 103 B5 Fr. Saint-Nicolas. Oost-Vlaanderen, N Belgium
Sint-Pieters-Leeuw 103 B6 Vlaams Brabant, C Belgium
Sintra 108 B3 prev. Cintra. Lisboa, W Portugal
Sinujiif 89 E5 Nugaal, NE Somalia
Sinus Aelaniticus see Aqaba, Gulf of
Sinyang see Xinyang
Sinzyô see Shinjō
Sion 111 A7 Ger. Sitten; anc. Sedunum. Valais, SW Switzerland
Sioux City 61 F3 Iowa, C USA
Sioux Falls 61 F3 South Dakota, N USA
Siping 144 D3 var. Ssu-p'ing, Szeping; prev. Ssu-p'ing-chieh. Jilin, NE China
Siple, Mount 170 A4 mountain Siple Island, Antarctica
Siquirres 69 E4 Limón, E Costa Rica
Siracusa 113 D7 Eng. Syracuse. Sicilia, Italy, C Mediterranean Sea
Sir Darya see Syr Darya
Sir Edward Pellew Group 164 B2 island group Northern Territory, NE Australia
Siret 124 C3 var. Siretul, Ger. Sereth, Rus. Seret, Ukr. Siret. River Romania/Ukraine
Siret see Siret
Siretul see Siret
Sirikit Reservoir 152 C4 lake N Thailand
Sīrjān 136 D4 prev. Sa'īdābād. Kermān, S Iran
Sirna see Sýrna
Şırnak 133 F4 Şırnak, SE Turkey
Síros see Sýros
Sirte see Surt
Sirte, Gulf of see Surt, Khalīj
Sisak 116 B3 var. Siscia, Ger. Sissek, Hung. Sziszek; anc. Segestica. Sisak-Moslavina, C Croatia
Siscia see Sisak
Sisimiut 98 C3 var. Holsteinborg, Holsteinsborg, Holstenborg, Holstensborg. S Greenland
Sissek see Sisak
Sistema Penibético see Béticos, Sistemas
Siteía 121 D8 var. Sitía. Kríti, Greece, E Mediterranean Sea
Sitges 109 G2 Cataluña, NE Spain
Sitía see Siteía
Sittang 152 B4 var. Sittoung. River S Burma
Sittard 103 D5 Limburg, SE Netherlands
Sittoung see Sittang
Sittwe 152 A3 var. Akyab. Arakan State, W Burma
Siuna 68 D3 Región Autónoma Atlántico Norte, NE Nicaragua
Siut see Asyût
Sivas 132 D3 anc. Sebastia, Sebaste. Sivas, C Turkey
Sivers'kyy Donets' 125 G2 Rus. Severskiy Donets. River Russian Federation/Ukraine see also Severskiy Donets
Siwa 88 A2 var. Sīwah. NW Egypt
Sīwah see Siwa
Six-Fours-les-Plages 107 D6 Var, SE France
Siyäzän 133 H2 Rus. Siazan'. NE Azerbaijan
Sizuoka see Shizuoka
Sjar see Sääre
Sjælland B8 Eng. Zealand, Ger. Seeland. Island E Denmark
Sjenica 117 D5 Turk. Seniça. Serbia, SW Yugoslavia
Skadar see Shkodër
Skagerak see Skagerrak
Skagerrak 101 A6 var. Skagerak. Channel N Europe
Skagit River 62 B1 river Washington, NW USA
Skalka 100 C3 lake N Sweden
Skaudvilė 122 B4 Tauragė, SW Lithuania
Skegness 105 E6 E England, UK
Skellefteå 100 D4 Västerbotten, N Sweden
Skellefteälven 100 C4 river N Sweden
Ski 101 B6 Akershus, S Norway
Skíathos 121 C5 Skíathos, Vóreioi Sporádes, Greece, Aegean Sea
Skidal' 123 B5 Rus. Skidel'. Hrodzyenskaya Voblasts', W Belorussia
Skiftet 122 C1 Fin. Kihti. Strait Gulf of Bothnia/Gulf of Finland
Skíros see Skýros
Skópelos 121 C5 Skópelos, Vóreioi Sporádes, Greece, Aegean Sea
Skopje 117 D6 var. Üsküb, Turk. Üsküp; prev. Skoplje, anc. Scupi. Country capital (FYR Macedonia) N FYR Macedonia
Skoplje see Skopje
Skovorodino 131 F4 Amurskaya Oblast', SE Russian Federation
Skuodas 122 B3 Ger. Schoden, Pol. Szkudy. Skuodas, NW Lithuania
Skye, Isle of 104 B3 island NW Scotland, UK
Skýros 121 C5 var. Skíros. Skýros, Vóreioi Sporádes, Greece, Aegean Sea
Skýros 121 C5 var. Skíros; anc. Scyros. Island Vóreioi Sporádes, Greece, Aegean Sea
Slagelse 101 B7 Vestsjælland, E Denmark
Slatina 124 B5 Olt, S Romania
Slavonska Požega 116 C3 prev. Požega, Ger. Poschega, Hung. Pozsega. Požega-Slavonija, NE Croatia
Slavonski Brod 116 C3 Ger. Brod, Hung. Bród; prev. Brod, Brod na Savi. Brod-Posavina, NE Croatia
Slavuta 124 C2 Khmel'nyts'ka Oblast', NW Ukraine
Slawharad 123 E7 Rus. Slavgorod. Mahilyowskaya Voblasts', E Belorussia
Sławno 114 C2 Słupsk, NW Poland
Sléibhte Chill Mhantáin see Wicklow Mountains
Slēmānī see As Sulaymānīyah
Sliema 118 B5 N Malta
Sligeach see Sligo
Sligo 105 A5 Ir. Sligeach. NW Ireland
Sliven 120 D2 var. Slivno. Burgaska Oblast, E Bulgaria
Slivnitsa 120 B2 Sofiyska Oblast, W Bulgaria
Slivno see Sliven
Slobozia 124 C5 Ialomiţa, SE Romania
Slonim 123 B6 Pol. Słonim, Rus. Slonim. Hrodzyenskaya Voblasts', W Belorussia
Slovakia 115 C6 off. Slovenská Republika, Ger. Slowakei, Hung. Szlovákia, Slvk. Slovensko. Country C Europe
Slovenia 111 D8 off. Republic of Slovenia, Ger. Slowenien, Slvn. Slovenija. Country SE Europe
Slovenské Rudohorie 115 D6 Eng. Slovak Ore Mountains, Ger. Slowakisches Erzgebirge, Ungarisches Erzgebirge. Mountain range C Slovakia
Slov"yans'k 125 G3 Rus. Slavyansk. Donets'ka Oblast', E Ukraine
Słubice 114 B3 Ger. Frankfurt. Gorzów, W Poland
Sluch 124 D1 river NW Ukraine
Słupsk 114 C2 Ger. Stolp. Słupsk, NW Poland
Slutsk 123 C6 Rus. Slutsk. Minskaya Voblasts', S Belorussia
Smallwood Reservoir 55 F2 lake Newfoundland and Labrador, S Canada
Smara 86 B3 var. Es Semara. N Western Sahara
Smarhon' 123 C5 Pol. Smorgonie, Rus. Smorgon'. Hrodzyenskaya Voblasts', W Belorussia
Smederevo 116 D4 Ger. Semendria. Serbia, N Yugoslavia
Smederevska Palanka 116 D4 Serbia, C Yugoslavia
Smila 125 E2 Rus. Smela. Cherkas'ka Oblast', C Ukraine
Smiltene 122 D3 Ger. Smilten. Valka, N Latvia
Smøla 100 A4 island W Norway
Smolensk 127 A5 Smolenskaya Oblast', W Russian Federation
Snake 50 B4 river Yukon Territory, NW Canada
Snake River 62 C3 river NW USA
Snake River Plain 62 D4 plain Idaho, NW USA
Sneek 102 D2 Friesland, N Netherlands
Sněžka 114 B4 Ger. Schneekoppe. Mountain N Czech Republic
Śniardwy, Jezioro D3 Ger. Spirdingsee. Lake NE Poland
Snina 115 E5 Hung. Szinna. Východné Slovensko, E Slovakia
Snowdonia 105 C6 mountain range NW Wales, UK
Snyder 65 F3 Texas, SW USA
Sobradinho, Represa de 79 F2 var. Barragem de Sobradinho. Reservoir E Brazil
Sochi 127 A7 Krasnodarskiy Kray, SW Russian Federation
Société, Archipel de la 161 G4 var. Archipel de Tahiti, Îles de la Société, Eng. Society Islands. Island group W French Polynesia
Society Islands see Société, Archipel de la
Socorro 64 D2 New Mexico, SW USA
Socorro, Isla 66 B5 island W Mexico
Socotra see Suquţrā
Soc Trăng 153 D6 var. Khanh. Soc Trăng, S Vietnam
Socuéllamos 109 E3 Castilla-La Mancha, C Spain
Sodankylä 100 D3 Lappi, N Finland
Sodari see Sodiri
Söderhamn 101 C5 Gävleborg, C Sweden
Södertälje 101 C6 Stockholm, C Sweden
Sodiri 88 B4 var. Sawdirī, Sodari. Northern Kordofan, C Sudan
Sofia see Sofiya
Sofiya 120 C2 var. Sophia, Eng. Sofia; Lat. Serdica. Country capital (Bulgaria) Grad Sofiya, W Bulgaria
Sogamoso 74 B3 Boyacá, C Colombia
Sognefjorden 101 A5 fjord NE North Sea
Sohâg 88 B2 var. Sawhāj, Suliag. C Egypt
Sohar see Şuḩār
Sohm Plain 82 B3 undersea feature NW Atlantic Ocean
Sohrau see Żory
Sokal' 124 C2 Rus. Sokal. L'vivs'ka Oblast', NW Ukraine
Söke 132 A4 Aydın, SW Turkey
Sokhumi 133 E1 Rus. Sukhumi. NW Georgia
Sokodé 91 F4 C Togo
Sokol 126 C4 Vologodskaya Oblast', NW Russian Federation
Sokółka 114 E3 Białystok, NE Poland
Sokolov 115 A5 Ger. Falkenau an der Eger; prev. Falknov nad Ohří. Západní Čechy, W Czech Republic
Sokone 90 B3 W Senegal
Sokoto 91 F4 river NW Nigeria
Sokoto 91 F3 Sokoto, NW Nigeria
Sokotra see Suquţrā
Solāpur 140 B3 var. Sholāpur. Mahārāshtra, W India
Solca 124 C3 Ger. Solka. Suceava, N Romania
Sol, Costa del 108 D5 coastal region S Spain
Soldeu 107 B7 NE Andorra
Solec Kujawski 114 C3 Bydgoszcz, W Poland
Soledad see East Falkland
Soledad 74 B1 Anzoátegui, NE Venezuela
Solikamsk 130 C3 Permskaya Oblast', NW Russian Federation
Sol'-Iletsk 127 D6 Orenburgskaya Oblast', W Russian Federation
Solingen 110 A4 Nordrhein-Westfalen, W Germany
Sollentuna 101 C6 Stockholm, C Sweden
Solok 154 B4 Sumatera, W Indonesia
Solomon Islands 160 C3 prev. British Solomon Islands Protectorate. Country W Pacific Ocean
Solomon Islands 160 C3 island group PNG/Solomon Islands
Solomon Sea 160 B3 sea W Pacific Ocean
Soltau 110 B3 Niedersachsen, NW Germany
Sol'tsy 126 A4 Novgorodskaya Oblast', W Russian Federation
Solwezi 94 D2 North Western, NW Zambia
Sōma 146 D4 Fukushima, Honshū, C Japan
Somalia 89 D5 off. Somali Democratic Republic, Som. Jamuuriyada Demuqraadiga Soomaaliyeed, Soomaaliya; prev. Italian Somaliland, Somaliland Protectorate. Country E Africa
Somali Basin 85 E5 undersea feature W Indian Ocean
Sombor 116 C3 Hung. Zombor. Serbia, NW Yugoslavia
Someren 103 D5 Noord-Brabant, SE Netherlands
Somerset 58 A5 var. Somerset Village. W Bermuda
Somerset 56 C5 Kentucky, S USA
Somerset Island 53 F2 island Queen Elizabeth Islands, Northwest Territories, NW Canada
Somerset Island 58 A5 island W Bermuda
Somerset Village see Somerset
Somers Islands see Bermuda
Somerton 64 A2 Arizona, SW USA
Someş 124 B3 var. Somesch, Someşul, Szamos, Ger. Samosch. River Hungary/Romania
Somesch see Someş
Someşul see Someş
Somme 106 C2 river N France
Somotillo 68 C3 Chinandega, NW Nicaragua
Somoto 68 D3 Madriz, NW Nicaragua
Songea 89 C8 Ruvuma, S Tanzania
Sông Hông Hà see Red River
Songkhla 153 C7 var. Songkla, Mal. Singora. Songkhla, SW Thailand
Songkla see Songkhla
Sông Srepok see Srêpôk, Tônle
Sông Tiên Giang see Mekong
Sonoran Desert 64 A3 var. Desierto de Altar. Desert Mexico/USA see also Altar, Desierto de
Sonsonate 68 B3 Sonsonate, W El Salvador
Soochow see Suzhou
Sop Hao 152 D3 Houaphan, N Laos

Syracuse – The Pas

Syracuse 57 E3 New York, NE USA
Syrdariya see Syr Darya
Syr Darya 130 B4 var. Sai Hun, Sir Darya, Syrdarya, Kaz. Syrdariya, Rus. Syrdar'ya, Uzb. Sirdaryo; anc. Jaxartes. River C Asia
Syria 134 B3 off. Syrian Arab Republic, var. Siria, Syrie, Ar. Al-Jumhūrīyah al-'Arabīyah as-Sūrīyah, Sūrīya. Country SW Asia
Syrian Desert 135 D5 Ar. Al Hamad, Bādiyat ash Shām. Desert SW Asia
Sýrna 121 E7 var. Sirna. Island Kykládes, Greece, Aegean Sea
Sýros 121 C6 var. Síros. Island Kykládes, Greece, Aegean Sea
Syvash, Zatoka 125 F4 Rus. Zaliv Syvash. Inlet S Ukraine
Syzran' 127 C6 Samarskaya Oblast', W Russian Federation
Szamos see Someş
Szamotuły 114 B3 Poznań, W Poland
Szczecin 114 B3 Eng./Ger. Stettin. Szczecin, NW Poland
Szczecinek 114 B2 Ger. Neustettin. Koszalin, NW Poland
Szczeciński, Zalew 114 A2 var. Stettiner Haff, Ger. Oderhaff. Bay Germany/Poland
Szczytno 114 D3 Ger. Ortelsburg. Olsztyn, NE Poland
Szechuan see Sichuan
Szechwan see Sichuan
Szeged 115 D7 Ger. Szegedin, Rom. Seghedin. Csongrád, SE Hungary
Székesfehérvár 115 C6 Ger. Stuhlweissenberg; anc. Alba Regia. Fejér, W Hungary
Szekszárd 115 C7 Tolna, S Hungary
Szenttamás see Srbobran
Szeping see Siping
Sziszek see Sisak
Szolnok 115 D6 Jász-Nagykun-Szolnok, C Hungary
Szombathely 115 B6 Ger. Steinamanger; anc. Sabaria, Savaria. Vas, W Hungary
Szprotawa 114 B4 Ger. Sprottau. Zielona Góra, W Poland

T

Table Rock Lake 65 G1 reservoir Arkansas/Missouri, C USA
Tábor 115 B5 Jižní Čechy, SW Czech Republic
Tabora 89 B7 Tabora, W Tanzania
Tabrīz 136 C2 var. Tebriz; anc. Tauris. Āžarbāyjān-e Khāvarī, NW Iran
Tabuaeran 161 G2 prev. Fanning Island. Atoll Line Islands, E Kiribati
Tabūk 136 A4 Tabūk, NW Saudi Arabia
Täby 101 C6 Stockholm, C Sweden
Tachov 115 A5 Ger. Tachau. Západní Čechy, W Czech Republic
Tacloban 155 F2 off. Tacloban City. Leyte, C Philippines
Tacna 77 E4 Tacna, SE Peru
Tacoma 62 B2 Washington, NW USA
Tacuarembó 80 D4 prev. San Fructuoso. Tacuarembó, C Uruguay
Tademaït, Plateau du 86 D3 plateau C Algeria
Tadmor see Tudmur
Tadmur see Tudmur
Tādpatri 148 C2 Andhra Pradesh, E India
Taegu 145 E4 off. Taegu-gwangyŏksi, var. Daegu, Jap. Taikyū. SE South Korea
Taejŏn 145 E4 off. Taejŏn-gwangyŏksi, Jap. Taiden. C South Korea
Tafassâsset, Ténéré du 91 G2 desert N Niger
Tafila see Aţ Ţafilah
Taganrog 127 A7 Rostovskaya Oblast', SW Russian Federation
Taganrog, Gulf of 125 G4 Rus. Taganrogskiy Zaliv, Ukr. Tahanroz'ka Zatoka. Gulf Russian Federation/Ukraine
Taguatinga 79 F3 Tocantins, C Brazil
Tagus 108 C3 Port. Rio Tejo, Sp. Río Tajo. River Portugal/Spain
Tagus Plain 96 A4 undersea feature E Atlantic Ocean
Tahat 87 E4 mountain SE Algeria
Tahiti 161 H4 island Îles du Vent, W French Polynesia
Tahlequah 65 G1 Oklahoma, C USA
Tahoe, Lake 63 B5 lake California/Nevada, W USA
Tahoua 91 F3 Tahoua, W Niger
T'aichung 144 D6 Jap. Taichū; prev. Taiwan. C Taiwan
Taieri 167 B7 river South Island, NZ
Taihape 166 D4 Manawatu-Wanganui, North Island, NZ
Tailem Bend 165 B7 South Australia
T'ainan 144 D6 Jap. Tainan; prev. Dainan. S Taiwan
T'aipei 144 D6 Jap. Taihoku; prev. Daihoku. Country capital (Taiwan) N Taiwan
Taiping 154 B3 Perak, Peninsular Malaysia
Taiwan 144 D6 off. Republic of China, var. Formosa, Formo'sa. Country E Asia
T'aiwan Haihsia see Taiwan Strait
Taiwan Haixia see Taiwan Strait
Taiwan Strait 144 D6 var. Formosa Strait, Chin. T'aiwan Haihsia, Taiwan Haixia. Strait China/Taiwan
Taiyuan 144 C4 prev. T'ai-yuan, T'ai-yüan, Yangku. Shanxi, C China
Ta'izz 137 B7 SW Yemen
Tajikistan 139 E3 off. Republic of Tajikistan, Rus. Tadzhikistan, Taj. Jumhurii Tojikiston; prev. Tajik S.S.R. Country C Asia
Tak 152 C4 var. Rahaeng. Tak, W Thailand
Takao see Kaohsiung
Takaoka 147 C5 Toyama, Honshū, SW Japan
Takapuna 166 D2 Auckland, North Island, NZ
Takhiatosh 138 C2 Rus. Takhiatash. Qoraqalpoghiston Respublikasi, W Uzbekistan
Takhtakŭpir 138 D1 Rus. Takhtakupyr. Qoraqalpoghiston Respublikasi, NW Uzbekistan
Takikawa 146 D2 Hokkaidō, NE Japan
Takla Makan Desert see Taklimakan Shamo
Taklimakan Shamo 142 B3 Eng. Takla Makan Desert. Desert NW China
Takow see Kaohsiung
Takutea 161 G4 island S Cook Islands
Talachyn 123 D6 Rus. Tolochin. Vitsyebskaya Voblasts', NE Belorussia
Talamanca, Cordillera de 69 E5 mountain range S Costa Rica
Talara 76 B2 Piura, NW Peru
Talas 139 F2 Talasskaya Oblast', NW Kyrgyzstan
Talaud, Kepulauan 155 F3 island group E Indonesia
Talavera de la Reina 108 D3 anc. Caesarobriga, Talabriga. Castilla-La Mancha, C Spain
Talca 80 B4 Maule, C Chile
Talcahuano 81 B5 Bío Bío, C Chile
Taldykorgan 130 C5 Kaz. Taldyqorghan; prev. Taldy-Kurgan. Taldykorgan, SE Kazakhstan
Ta-lien see Dalian
Taliq-an see Tāloqān
Tal'ka 123 C6 Rus. Tal'ka. Minskaya Voblasts', C Belorussia
Tallahassee 58 D3 prev. Muskogean. State capital Florida, SE USA
Tall al Abyaḑ see At Tall al Abyaḑ
Tallinn 122 D2 Ger. Reval, Rus. Tallin; prev. Revel. Country capital (Estonia) Harjumaa, NW Estonia
Tall Kalakh 134 B4 var. Tell Kalakh. Ḩimş, C Syria
Tallulah 58 B2 Louisiana, S USA
Talnakh 130 D3 Taymyrskiy (Dolgano-Nenetskiy) Avtonomnyy Okrug, N Russian Federation
Tal'ne 125 E3 Rus. Tal'noye. Cherkas'ka Oblast', C Ukraine
Taloga 65 F1 Oklahoma, C USA
Tāloqān 139 E3 var. Taliq-an. Takhār, NE Afghanistan
Talsi 122 C3 Ger. Talsen. Talsi, NW Latvia
Taltal 80 B2 Antofagasta, N Chile
Talvik 100 D2 Finnmark, N Norway
Tamabo, Banjaran 154 D3 mountain range East Malaysia
Tamale 91 E4 C Ghana
Tamana 161 E3 prev. Rotcher Island. Atoll Tungaru, W Kiribati
Tamanrasset 87 E4 var. Tamenghest. S Algeria
Tamar 105 C7 river SW England, UK
Tamar see Tudmur
Tamatave see Toamasina
Tamazunchale 67 E4 San Luis Potosí, C Mexico
Tambacounda 90 C3 SE Senegal
Tambov 127 B6 Tambovskaya Oblast', W Russian Federation
Tambura 89 B5 Western Equatoria, SW Sudan
Tamchaket see Tâmchekket
Tâmchekket 90 C3 var. Tamchaket. Hodh el Gharbi, S Mauritania
Tamenghest see Tamanrasset
Tamiahua, Laguna de 67 F4 lagoon E Mexico
Tamil Nādu 148 C3 prev. Madras. State SE India
Tam Ky 153 E5 Quang Nam-Đa Nǎng, C Vietnam
Tampa 59 E4 Florida, SE USA
Tampa Bay 59 E4 bay Florida, SE USA
Tampere 101 D5 Swe. Tammerfors. Häme, SW Finland
Tampico 67 E3 Tamaulipas, C Mexico
Tamworth 165 D6 New South Wales, SE Australia
Tana 100 D2 var. Tenojoki, Fin. Teno, Lapp. Dealnu. River Finland/Norway see also Teno
Tana 100 D2 Finnmark, N Norway
Tanabe 147 C7 Wakayama, Honshū, SW Japan
T'ana Hāyk' 88 C4 Eng. Lake Tana. Lake NW Ethiopia
Tanais see Don
Tanami Desert 162 D3 desert Northern Territory, N Australia
Ţăndărei 124 D5 Ialomiţa, SE Romania
Tandil 81 D5 Buenos Aires, E Argentina
Tanega-shima 147 B8 island Nansei-shotō, SW Japan
Tane Range 152 B4 Bur. Tanen Taunggyi. Mountain range W Thailand
Tanezrouft 86 D4 desert Algeria/Mali
Ţanf, Jabal aţ 134 D4 mountain SE Syria
Tanga 85 E5 Tanga, E Tanzania
Tanga 89 C7 region E Tanzania
Tanganyika, Lake 89 B7 lake E Africa
Tangeh-ye Hormoz see Hormuz, Strait of
Tanger 86 C2 var. Tangiers, Tangier, Fr./Ger. Tangerk, Sp. Tánger; anc. Tingis. NW Morocco
Tangerk see Tanger
Tanggula Shan 142 C4 var. Dangla, Tangla Range. Mountain range W China
Tangier see Tanger
Tangiers see Tanger
Tangla Range see Tanggula Shan
Tangra Yumco 142 B5 var. Tangro Tso. Lake W China
Tangro Tso see Tangra Yumco
Tangshan 144 D3 var. T'ang-shan. Hebei, E China
T'ang-shan see Tangshan
Tanimbar, Kepulauan 155 F5 island group Maluku, E Indonesia
Tanna 160 D4 island S Vanuatu
Tan-Tan 86 B3 SW Morocco
Tan-tung see Dandong
Tanzania 89 C7 off. United Republic of Tanzania, Swa. Jamhuri ya Muungano wa Tanzania; prev. German East Africa, Tanganyika and Zanzibar. Country E Africa
Taoudenit see Taoudenni
Taoudenni 91 E2 var. Taoudenit. Tombouctou, N Mali
Tapa 122 E2 Ger. Taps. Lääne-Virumaa, NE Estonia
Tapachula 67 G5 Chiapas, SE Mexico
Tapajós, Rio 79 E2 var. Tapajóz. River NW Brazil
Tapajóz see Tapajós, Rio
Ţarābulus 87 F2 var. Ţarābulus al Gharb, Eng. Tripoli.Country capital (Libya) NW Libya
Tarābulus see Tripoli
Ţarābulus al Gharb see Ţarābulus
Ţarābulus ash Shām see Tripoli
Taraclia 124 D4 Rus. Tarakilya. S Moldavia
Taranaki, Mount 166 C4 var. Egmont. Mountain North Island, NZ
Tarancón 109 E3 Castilla-La Mancha, C Spain
Taranto 113 E5 var. Tarentum. Puglia, SE Italy
Taranto, Golfo di 113 E6 Eng. Gulf of Taranto. Gulf S Italy
Tarapoto 76 C2 San Martín, N Peru
Tarare 107 D5 Rhône, E France
Tarascon 107 D6 Bouches-du-Rhône, SE France
Tarawa 160 D2 atoll Tungaru, W Kiribati
Tarazona 109 E2 Aragón, NE Spain
Tarbes 107 B6 anc. Bigorra. Hautes-Pyrénées, S France
Tarcoola 165 A6 South Australia
Taree 165 D6 New South Wales, SE Australia
Tarentum see Taranto
Târgovişte 124 C5 prev. Tîrgovişte. Dâmboviţa, S Romania
Târgu Jiu 124 B4 prev. Tîrgu Jiu. Gorj, W Romania
Târgul-Neamţ see Târgu-Neamţ
Târgu Mureş 124 B4 prev. Oşorhei, Tîrgu Mures, Ger. Neumarkt, Hung. Marosvásárhely. Mureş, C Romania
Târgu-Neamţ 124 C3 var. Târgul-Neamţ; prev. Tîrgu-Neamţ. Neamţ, NE Romania
Târgu Ocna 124 C4 Hung. Aknavásár; prev. Tîrgu Ocna. Bacău, E Romania
Târgu Secuiesc 124 C4 Ger. Neumarkt, Szekler Neumarkt, Hung. Kezdivásárhely; prev. Chezdi-Oşorheiu, Târgul-Săcuiesc, Tîrgu Secuiesc. Covasna, E Romania
Tarija 77 G5 Tarija, S Bolivia
Tarīm 137 C6 C Yemen
Tarim Basin 140 C2 basin NW China
Tarim He 142 B3 river NW China
Tarma 76 C3 Junín, C Peru
Tarn 107 C6 cultural region S France
Tarn 107 C6 river S France
Tarnobrzeg 114 D4 Tarnobrzeg, SE Poland
Tarnów 115 D5 Tarnów, SE Poland
Tarragona 109 G2 anc. Tarraco. Cataluña, E Spain
Tàrrega 109 F2 var. Tarrega. Cataluña, NE Spain
Tarsus 132 C4 İçel, S Turkey
Tartu 122 D3 Ger. Dorpat; prev. Rus. Yurev, Yur'yev. Tartumaa, SE Estonia
Ţarţūs 134 A3 Fr. Tartouss; anc. Tortosa. Ţarţūs, W Syria
Ta Ru Tao, Ko 153 B7 island S Thailand
Tarvisio 112 D2 Friuli-Venezia Giulia, NE Italy
Tashi Chho Dzong see Thimphu
Tashkent see Toshkent
Tash-Kumyr 139 F2 Kir. Tash-Kömür. Dzhalal-Abadskaya Oblast', W Kyrgyzstan
Tashqurghan see Kholm
Tasikmalaya 154 C5 prev. Tasikmalaja. Jawa, C Indonesia
Tasman Basin 158 C5 var. East Australian Basin. Undersea feature S Tasman Sea
Tasman Bay 167 C5 inlet South Island, NZ
Tasmania 165 B8 prev. Van Diemen's Land. State SE Australia
Tasmania 168 B4 island SE Australia
Tasman Plateau 158 C5 var. South Tasmania Plateau. Undersea feature SW Tasman Sea
Tasman Sea 158 C5 sea SW Pacific Ocean
Tassili-n-Ajjer 87 E4 plateau E Algeria
Tatabánya 115 C6 Komárom-Esztergom, NW Hungary
Tathlīth 137 B5 'Asīr, S Saudi Arabia
Tatra Mountains 115 D5 Ger. Tatra, Hung. Tátra, Pol./Slvk. Tatry. Mountain range Poland/Slovakia
Ta-t'ung see Datong
Tatvan 133 F3 Bitlis, SE Turkey
Ta'ū 161 F4 var. Tau. Island Manua Islands, E American Samoa
Tau see Ta'ū
Taukum, Peski 139 G1 desert SE Kazakhstan
Taumarunui 166 D4 Manawatu-Wanganui, North Island, NZ
Taungdwingyi 152 B3 Magwe, C Burma
Taunggyi 152 B3 Shan State, C Burma
Taunton 105 C7 SW England, UK
Taupo 166 D3 Waikato, North Island, NZ
Taupo, Lake 166 D3 lake North Island, NZ
Tauragė 122 B4 Ger. Tauroggen. Tauragė, SW Lithuania
Tauranga 166 D3 Bay of Plenty, North Island, NZ
Tauris see Tabrīz
Tavas 132 B4 Denizli, SW Turkey
Tavira 108 C5 Faro, S Portugal
Tavoy 153 B5 var. Dawei. Tenasserim, S Burma
Tavoy Island see Mali Kyun
Tawakoni, Lake 65 G2 reservoir Texas, SW USA
Tawau 154 D3 Sabah, East Malaysia
Ţawkar see Tokar
Tawzar see Tozeur
Taxco 67 E4 var. Taxco de Alarcón. Guerrero, S Mexico
Taxco de Alarcón see Taxco
Tay 104 C3 river C Scotland, UK
Taylor 65 G3 Texas, SW USA
Taymā' 136 A4 Tabūk, NW Saudi Arabia
Taymyr, Ozero 131 E2 lake N Russian Federation
Taymyr, Poluostrov 131 E2 peninsula N Russian Federation
Taz 130 D3 river N Russian Federation
T'bilisi 133 G2 Eng. Tiflis. Country capital (Georgia) SE Georgia
T'bilisi 128 B4 international airport S Georgia
Tchien see Zwedru
Tchongking see Chongqing
Tczew 114 C2 Ger. Dirschau. Gdańsk, N Poland
Te Anau 167 A7 Southland, South Island, NZ
Te Anau, Lake 167 A7 lake South Island, NZ
Teapa 67 G4 Tabasco, SE Mexico
Teate see Chieti
Tebingtinggi 154 B3 Sumatera, N Indonesia
Tebriz see Tabrīz
Techirghiol 124 D5 Constanţa, SE Romania
Tecomán 66 D4 Colima, SW Mexico
Tecpan 67 E5 var. Tecpan de Galeana. Guerrero, S Mexico
Tecpan de Galeana see Tecpan
Tecuci 124 C4 Galaţi, E Romania
Tedzhen 138 C3 Turkm. Tejen. Akhalskiy Velayat, S Turkmenistan
Tedzhen see Harīrūd
Tees 105 D5 river N England, UK
Tefé 78 D2 Amazonas, N Brazil
Tegal 154 C4 Jawa, C Indonesia
Tegelen 103 D5 Limburg, SE Netherlands
Tegucigalpa 68 C3 country capital (Honduras) Francisco Morazán, SW Honduras
Teheran see Tehrān
Tehrān 136 C3 var. Teheran. Country capital (Iran) Tehrān, N Iran
Tehuacán 67 F4 Puebla, S Mexico
Tehuantepec 67 F5 var. Santo Domingo Tehuantepec. Oaxaca, SE Mexico
Tehuantepec, Golfo de 67 F5 var. Gulf of Tehuantepec. Gulf S Mexico
Tehuantepec, Gulf of see Tehuantepec, Golfo de
Tehuantepec, Isthmus of see Tehuantepec, Istmo de
Tehuantepec, Istmo de 67 F5 var. Isthmus of Tehuantepec. Isthmus SE Mexico
Tejen see Harīrūd
Te Kao 166 C1 Northland, North Island, NZ
Tekax 67 H4 var. Tekax de Álvaro Obregón. Yucatán, SE Mexico
Tekax de Álvaro Obregón see Tekax
Tekeli 130 C5 Taldykorgan, SE Kazakhstan
Tekirdağ 132 A2 It. Rodosto; anc. Bisanthe, Raidestos, Rhaedestus. Tekirdağ, NW Turkey
Te Kuiti 166 D3 Waikato, North Island, NZ
Tela 68 C2 Atlántida, NW Honduras
Telanaipura see Jambi
Tel Aviv-Jaffa see Tel Aviv-Yafo
Tel Aviv-Yafo 135 A6 var. Tel Aviv-Jaffa. Tel Aviv, C Israel
Teles Pirés see São Manuel, Rio
Telish 120 C2 prev. Azizie. Loveshka Oblast, NW Bulgaria
Tell Abiad see At Tall al Abyaḑ
Tell Abyad see At Tall al Abyaḑ
Tell Kalakh see Tall Kalakh
Tell Shedadi see Ash Shadādah
Telšiai 122 B3 Ger. Telschen. Telšiai, NW Lithuania
Temerin 116 D3 Serbia, N Yugoslavia
Temirtau 130 C4 prev. Samarkandski, Samarkandskoye. Karaganda, C Kazakhstan
Tempio Pausania 113 A5 Sardegna, Italy, C Mediterranean Sea
Temple 65 G3 Texas, SW USA
Temuco 81 B5 Araucanía, C Chile
Temuka 167 B6 Canterbury, South Island, NZ
Tenasserim 153 B6 Tenasserim, S Burma
Ténenkou 90 D3 Mopti, C Mali
Ténéré 91 G3 physical region C Niger
Tenerife 86 A3 island Islas Canarias, Spain, NE Atlantic Ocean
Tengger Shamo 143 E3 desert N China
Tengréla 90 D4 var. Tingréla. N Ivory Coast
Tenkodogo 91 E4 S Burkina
Tennant Creek 164 A3 Northern Territory, C Australia
Tennessee 58 C1 off. State of Tennessee; also known as The Volunteer State. State SE USA
Tennessee River 58 C1 river S USA
Teno see Tana
Tenojoki see Tana
Tepelena see Tepelenë
Tepelenë 117 C7 var. Tepelena, It. Tepeleni. Gjirokastër, S Albania
Tepeleni see Tepelenë
Tepic 66 D4 Nayarit, C Mexico
Teplice 114 A4 Ger. Teplitz; prev. Teplice-Šanov, Teplitz-Schönau. Severní Čechy, NW Czech Republic
Tequila 66 D4 Jalisco, SW Mexico
Teraina 161 G2 prev. Washington Island. Atoll Line Islands, E Kiribati
Teramo 112 C4 anc. Interamna. Abruzzi, C Italy
Tercan 133 E3 Erzincan, NE Turkey
Terceira 108 A5 var. Ilha Terceira. Island Azores, Portugal, NE Atlantic Ocean
Teresina 79 F2 var. Therezina. State capital Piauí, NE Brazil
Termia see Kýthnos
Términos, Laguna de 67 G4 lagoon SE Mexico
Termiz 139 E3 Rus. Termez. Surkhondaryo Wiloyati, S Uzbekistan
Termoli 112 D4 Molise, C Italy
Terneuzen 103 B5 var. Neuzen. Zeeland, SW Netherlands
Terni 112 C4 anc. Interamna Nahars. Umbria, C Italy
Ternopil' 124 C2 Pol. Tarnopol, Rus. Ternopol'. Ternopil's'ka Oblast', W Ukraine
Terracina 113 C5 Lazio, C Italy
Terrassa 109 G2 Cast. Tarrasa. Cataluña, E Spain
Terre Adélie 170 C4 disputed region SE Antarctica
Terre Haute 56 B4 Indiana, N USA
Territoire du Yukon see Yukon Territory
Terschelling 102 C1 Fris. Skylge. Island Waddeneilanden, N Netherlands
Teruel 109 F3 anc. Turba. Aragón, E Spain
Tervel 120 E1 prev. Kurtbunar, Rom. Curtbunar. Varnenska Oblast, NE Bulgaria
Tervueren see Tervuren
Tervuren 103 C6 var. Tervueren. Vlaams Brabant, C Belgium
Teseney 88 C4 var. Tessenei. W Eritrea
Tessalit 91 E2 Kidal, NE Mali
Tessaoua 91 G3 Maradi, S Niger
Tessenderlo 103 C5 Limburg, NE Belgium
Tessenei see Teseney
Testigos, Islas los 75 E1 island group N Venezuela
Tete 95 E2 Tete, NW Mozambique
Teterow 110 C3 Mecklenburg-Vorpommern, NE Germany
Tétouan 86 C2 var. Tetouan, Tetuán. N Morocco
Tetovo 117 D5 Alb. Tetova, Tetovë, Turk. Kalkandelen. NW FYR Macedonia
Tetuán see Tétouan
Tevere 112 C4 Eng. Tiber. River C Italy
Teverya 135 B5 var. Tiberias. Northern, N Israel
Te Waewae Bay 167 A7 bay South Island, NZ
Texarkana 58 A2 Arkansas, C USA
Texarkana 65 H2 Texas, SW USA
Texas 65 F3 off. State of Texas; also known as The Lone Star State. State S USA
Texas City 65 H4 Texas, SW USA
Texel 102 C2 island Waddeneilanden, NW Netherlands
Texoma, Lake 65 G2 reservoir Oklahoma/Texas, C USA
Teziutlán 67 F4 Puebla, S Mexico
Thaa Atoll see Kolhumadulu Atoll
Thai Binh 152 D3 Thai Binh, N Vietnam
Thailand 153 C5 off. Kingdom of Thailand, Th. Prathet Thai; prev. Siam. Country SE Asia
Thailand, Gulf of 153 C6 var. Gulf of Siam, Th. Ao Thai, Vtn. Vinh Thai Lan. Gulf SE Asia
Thai Nguyên 152 D3 Bắc Thai, N Vietnam
Thakhèk 152 D4 prev. Muang Khammouan. Khammouan, C Laos
Thamarīd see Thamarīt
Thamarīt 137 D6 var. Thamarīd, Thumrayt. SW Oman
Thames 105 B8 river S England, UK
Thames 166 D3 Waikato, North Island, NZ
Thanh Hoa 152 D3 Vinh Phu, N Vietnam
Thanintari Taungdan see Bilauktaung Range
Thar Desert 150 C3 var. Great Indian Desert, Indian Desert. Desert India/Pakistan
Tharthār, Buḩayrat ath 136 B3 lake C Iraq
Thásos 120 C4 island E Greece
Thásos 120 C4 Thásos, E Greece
Thaton 152 B4 Mon State, S Burma
Thayetmyo 152 A4 Magwe, C Burma
The Crane 71 H2 var. Crane. S Barbados
The Dalles 62 B3 Oregon, NW USA
The Flatts Village see Flatts Village
The Hague see 's-Gravenhage
Theodosia see Feodosiya
The Pas 53 F5 Manitoba, C Canada

Waterford – Yining

Waterford *105 B6 Ir.* Port Láirge. S Ireland
Waterloo *61 G3* Iowa, C USA
Watertown *57 F2* New York, NE USA
Watertown *61 F2* South Dakota, N USA
Waterville *57 G2* Maine, NE USA
Watford *105 A7* SE England, UK
Watsa *93 E5* Haut-Zaïre, NE Congo (Zaire)
Watts Bar Lake *reservoir* Tennessee, S USA
Wau *89 B5 var.* Wāw. Western Bahr el Ghazal, S Sudan
Waukegan *56 B3* Illinois, N USA
Waukesha *56 B3* Wisconsin, N USA
Wausau *56 B2* Wisconsin, N USA
Waverly *61 G3* Iowa, C USA
Wavre *103 C6* Walloon Brabant, C Belgium
Wāw *see* Wau
Wawa *54 C4* Ontario, S Canada
Waycross *59 E3* Georgia, SE USA
Wearmouth *see* Sunderland
Webster City *61 F3* Iowa, C USA
Weddell Plain *170 A2 undersea feature* SW Atlantic Ocean
Weddell Sea *170 A2 sea* SW Atlantic Ocean
Weener *110 A3* Niedersachsen, NW Germany
Weert *103 D5* Limburg, SE Netherlands
Weesp *102 C3* Noord-Holland, C Netherlands
Węgorzewo *114 D2 Ger.* Angerburg. Suwałki, NE Poland
Weimar *110 C4* Thüringen, C Germany
Weissenburg *111 C6* Bayern, SE Germany
Weiswampach *103 D7* Diekirch, N Luxembourg
Wejherowo *114 C2* Gdańsk, NW Poland
Welchman Hall *71 G1* C Barbados
Weldiya *88 C4 var.* Waldia, *It.* Valdia. N Ethiopia
Welkom *94 D4* Free State, C South Africa
Welle *see* Uele
Wellesley Islands *164 B2 island group* Queensland, N Australia
Wellington *167 D5 country capital* (NZ) Wellington, North Island, NZ
Wellington *see* Wellington, Isla
Wellington *61 F5* Kansas, C USA
Wellington, Isla *81 A7 var.* Wellington. *Island* S Chile
Wells *62 D4* Nevada, W USA
Wellsford *166 D2* Auckland, North Island, NZ
Wells, Lake *163 C5 lake* Western Australia
Wels *111 D6 anc.* Ovilava. Oberösterreich, N Austria
Wembley *105 A8* SE England, UK
Wemmel *103 B6* Vlaams Brabant, C Belgium
Wenatchee *62 B2* Washington, NW USA
Wenchi *91 E4* W Ghana
Wen-chou *see* Wenzhou
Wenchow *see* Wenzhou
Wenmen Island *see* Wolf, Isla
Wenzhou *144 D5 var.* Wen-chou, Wenchow. Zhejiang, SE China
Werda *94 C4* Kgalagadi, S Botswana
Werkendam *102 C4* Noord-Brabant, S Netherlands
Weser *110 B3 river* NW Germany
Wessel Islands *164 B1 island group* Northern Territory, N Australia
West Antarctica *see* Lesser Antarctica
West Bank *135 A6 disputed region* SW Asia
West Bend *56 B3* Wisconsin, N USA
West Bengal *151 F4 state* NE India
West Cape *167 A7 headland* South Island, NZ
West Des Moines *61 F3* Iowa, C USA
Westerland *110 B2* Schleswig-Holstein, N Germany
Western Australia *162 B4 state* W Australia
Western Desert *see* Sahara el Gharbîya
Western Dvina *101 E7 Bel.* Dzvina, *Ger.* Düna, *Latv.* Daugava, *Rus.* Zapadnaya Dvina. *River* W Europe
Western Ghats *150 C5 mountain range* SW India
Western Isles *see* Outer Hebrides
Western Sahara *86 B3 UK disputed territory* N Africa
Westerschelde *103 B5 Eng.* Western Scheldt; *prev.* Honte. *Inlet* S North Sea
West Falkland *81 C7 var.* Gran Malvina. *Island* W Falkland Islands
West Fargo *61 F2* North Dakota, N USA
West Irian *see* Irian Jaya
West Mariana Basin *158 B1 var.* Perece Vela Basin. *Undersea feature* W Pacific Ocean
West Memphis *58 B1* Arkansas, C USA
West New Guinea *see* Irian Jaya
Weston-super-Mare *105 D7* SW England, UK
West Palm Beach *59 F4* Florida, SE USA
Westport *167 C5* West Coast, South Island, NZ
West River *see* Xi Jiang
West Siberian Plain *see* Zapadno-Sibirskaya Ravnina
West Virginia *56 D4 off.* State of West Virginia; also known as The Mountain State. *State* NE USA
Wetar, Pulau *155 F5 island* Kepulauan Damar, E Indonesia
Wetzlar *111 B5* Hessen, W Germany
Wevok *52 C2 var.* Wewuk. Alaska, USA
Wewuk *see* Wevok
Wexford *105 B6 Ir.* Loch Garman. SE Ireland
Weyburn *53 F5* Saskatchewan, S Canada
Weymouth *105 D7* S England, UK
Wezep *102 D3* Gelderland, E Netherlands
Whakatane *166 E3* Bay of Plenty, North Island, NZ
Whale Cove *53 G3* Northwest Territories, C Canada
Whangarei *166 D2* Northland, North Island, NZ
Wharton Basin *157 D5 var.* West Australian Basin. *Undersea feature* E Indian Ocean
Whataroa *167 B6* West Coast, South Island, NZ
Wheatland *60 D3* Wyoming, C USA
Wheeler Peak *64 D1 mountain* New Mexico, SW USA
Wheeling *56 D4* West Virginia, NE USA
Whitby *105 D5* N England, UK
Whitefish *60 B1* Montana, NW USA
Whitehaven *105 C5* NW England, UK
Whitehorse *52 D4 territory capital* Yukon Territory, W Canada
White Nile *88 B4 Ar.* Al Baḩr al Abyaḑ, An Nīl al Abyaḑ, Bahr el Jebel. *River* SE Sudan
White Nile *88 B4 var.* Bahr el Jebel. *River* S Sudan
White River *60 D3 river* South Dakota, N USA
White Sea *see* Beloye More
White Volta *91 E4 var.* Nakambé, *Fr.* Volta Blanche. *River* Burkina/Ghana
Whitianga *166 D2* Waikato, North Island, NZ
Whitney, Mount *63 C6 mountain* California, W USA
Whitsunday Group *164 D3 island group* Queensland, E Australia
Whyalla *165 B6* South Australia
Wichita *61 F5* Kansas, C USA
Wichita Falls *65 F2* Texas, SW USA
Wichita River *65 F2 river* Texas, SW USA
Wickenburg *64 B2* Arizona, SW USA
Wicklow *105 B6 Ir.* Cill Mhantáin. *Cultural region* E Ireland
Wicklow Mountains *105 B6 Ir.* Sléibhte Chill Mhantáin. *Mountain range* E Ireland
Wieliczka *115 D5* Kraków, S Poland
Wieluń *114 C4* Sieradz, C Poland
Wien *111 E6 Eng.* Vienna, *Hung.* Bécs, *Slvk.* Vídeň, *Slvn.* Dunaj; *anc.* Vindobona. *Country capital* (Austria) Wien, NE Austria
Wiener Neustadt *111 E6* Niederösterreich, E Austria
Wierden *102 E3* Overijssel, E Netherlands
Wiesbaden *111 B5* Hessen, W Germany
Wight, Isle of *105 D7 island* S England, UK
Wijchen *102 D4* Gelderland, SE Netherlands
Wijk bij Duurstede *102 D4* Utrecht, C Netherlands
Wilcannia *165 C6* New South Wales, SE Australia
Wilhelm, Mount *160 B3 mountain* C PNG
Wilhelm-Pieck-Stadt *see* Guben
Wilhelmshaven *110 B3* Niedersachsen, NW Germany
Wilkes Barre *57 F3* Pennsylvania, NE USA
Wilkes Land *170 C4 physical region* Antarctica
Willard *64 D2* New Mexico, SW USA
Willcox *64 C3* Arizona, SW USA
Willebroek *103 B5* Antwerpen, C Belgium
Willemstad *71 E5 dependent territory capital* (Netherlands Antilles) Curaçao, Netherlands Antilles
Williston *60 D1* North Dakota, N USA
Wilmington *57 F4* Delaware, NE USA
Wilmington *59 F2* North Carolina, SE USA
Wilmington *56 C4* Ohio, N USA
Wilrijk *103 C5* Antwerpen, N Belgium
Winchester *105 D7 hist.* Wintanceaster, *Lat.* Venta Belgarum. S England, UK
Winchester *57 E4* Virginia, NE USA
Windhoek *94 B3 Ger.* Windhuk. *Country capital* (Namibia) Khomas, C Namibia
Windorah *164 C4* Queensland, C Australia
Windsor *57 G3* Connecticut, NE USA
Windsor *164 D1* New South Wales, SE Australia
Windsor *54 C5* Ontario, S Canada
Windsor *105 D7* S England, UK
Windward Islands *71 H4 island group* E West Indies
Windward Islands *see* Barlavento, Ilhas de
Windward Passage *70 D3 Sp.* Paso de los Vientos. *Channel* Cuba/Haiti
Winisk *54 C2 river* Ontario, S Canada
Winisk *54 C2* Ontario, C Canada
Winnebago, Lake *56 B2 lake* Wisconsin, N USA
Winnemucca *63 C5* Nevada, W USA
Winnipeg *53 G5* Manitoba, S Canada
Winnipeg, Lake *53 G5 lake* Manitoba, C Canada
Winnipegosis, Lake *54 A3 lake* Manitoba, C Canada
Winona *61 G3* Minnesota, N USA
Winschoten *102 E2* Groningen, NE Netherlands
Winsen *110 B3* Niedersachsen, N Germany
Winston Salem *59 E1* North Carolina, SE USA
Winsum *102 D1* Groningen, NE Netherlands
Winterswijk *102 E4* Gelderland, E Netherlands
Winterthur *111 B7* Zürich, NE Switzerland
Winton *164 C4* Queensland, E Australia
Winton *167 A7* Southland, South Island, NZ
Wisconsin *56 A2 off.* State of Wisconsin; also known as The Badger State. *State* N USA
Wisconsin Rapids *56 B2* Wisconsin, N USA
Wisconsin River *56 B3 river* Wisconsin, N USA
Wisła *114 C2 Eng.* Vistula, *Ger.* Weichsel. *River* C Poland
Wismar *110 C2* Mecklenburg-Vorpommern, N Germany
Wittenberge *110 C3* Brandenburg, N Germany
Wittlich *111 A5* Rheinland-Pfalz, SW Germany
Wittstock *110 C3* Brandenburg, NE Germany
W.J. van Blommesteinmeer *75 G3 reservoir* E Surinam
Władysławowo *114 C2* Gdańsk, N Poland
Włocławek *114 C3 Ger./Rus.* Vlotslavsk. Włocławek, C Poland
Włodawa *114 E4 Rus.* Vlodava. Chełm, SE Poland
Wlotzkasbaken *94 B3* Erongo, W Namibia
Wodonga *165 C7* Victoria, SE Australia
Wodzisław Śląski *115 C5 Ger.* Loslau. Katowice, S Poland
Wōjjā *see* Wotje Atoll
Woking *105 D7* SE England, UK
Wolf, Isla *76 A4 var.* Wenmen Island. *Island* W Ecuador
Wolfsberg *111 D7* Kärnten, SE Austria
Wolfsburg *110 C3* Niedersachsen, N Germany
Wolgast *110 D2* Mecklenburg-Vorpommern, NE Germany
Wollaston Lake *53 F4* Saskatchewan, C Canada
Wollongong *165 D6* New South Wales, SE Australia
Wolvega *102 D2 Fris.* Wolvegea. Friesland, N Netherlands
Wolverhampton *105 D6* C England, UK
Wŏnsan *145 E3* SE North Korea
Woodburn *62 B3* Oregon, NW USA
Woodland *63 B5* California, W USA
Woodruff *56 B2* Wisconsin, N USA
Woods, Lake of the *54 A3 Fr.* Lac des Bois. *Lake* Canada/USA
Woodville *166 D4* Manawatu-Wanganui, North Island, NZ
Woodward *65 F1* Oklahoma, C USA
Worcester *105 D6 hist.* Wigorna Ceaster. W England, UK
Worcester *57 G3* Massachusetts, NE USA
Worcester *94 C5* Western Cape, SW South Africa
Workington *105 C5* NW England, UK
Worland *60 C3* Wyoming, C USA
Worms *111 B5 anc.* Augusta Vangionum, Borbetomagus, Wormatia. Rheinland-Pfalz, SW Germany
Worms *see* Vormsi
Worthington *61 F3* Minnesota, N USA
Wotje Atoll *160 D1 var.* Wōjjā. *Atoll* Ratak Chain, E Marshall Islands
Woudrichem *102 C4* Noord-Brabant, S Netherlands
Wrangel Island *see* Vrangelya, Ostrov
Wrangel Plain *171 B2 undersea feature* Arctic Ocean
Wrocław *114 C4 Eng./Ger.* Breslau. Wrocław, SW Poland
Września *114 C3* Poznań, C Poland
Wuchang *see* Wuhan
Wuday 'ah *137 C6* Najrān, S Saudi Arabia
Wuhai *143 E3* Nei Mongol Zizhiqu, N China
Wuhan *144 C5 var.* Han-kou, Han-k'ou, Hanyang, Wuchang, Wu-han; *prev.* Hankow. Hubei, C China
Wuhsi *see* Wuxi
Wuhsien *see* Suzhou
Wuhu *144 D5 var.* Wu-na-mu. Anhui, E China
Wujlān *see* Ujelang Atoll
Wukari *91 G4* Taraba, E Nigeria
Wuliang Shan *144 A6 mountain range* SW China
Wu-lu-k'o-mu-shi *see* Ürümqi
Wu-lu-mu-ch'i *see* Ürümqi
Wu-na-mu *see* Wuhu
Wuppertal *110 A4 prev.* Barmen-Elberfeld. Nordrhein-Westfalen, W Germany
Würzburg *111 B5* Bayern, SW Germany
Wusih *see* Wuxi
Wuxi *144 D5 var.* Wuhsi, Wu-hsi, Wusih. Jiangsu, E China
Wuyi Shan *141 E3 mountain range* SE China
Wye *105 C6 Wel.* Gwy. *River* England/Wales, UK
Wyndham *162 D3* Western Australia
Wyoming *60 B3 off.* State of Wyoming; also known as The Equality State. *State* C USA
Wyoming *56 C3* Michigan, N USA
Wyszków *114 D3 Ger.* Probstberg. Ostrołęka, NE Poland

X

Xaafuun, Raas *88 E4 var.* Ras Hafun. *Headland* NE Somalia
Xaçmaz *133 H2 Rus.* Khachmas. N Azerbaijan
Xaignabouli *152 C4 prev.* Muang Xaignabouri, *Fr.* Sayaboury. Xaignabouli, N Laos
Xai-Xai *95 E4 prev.* João Belo, Vila de João *Bel.* Gaza, S Mozambique
Xalapa *67 F4 var.* Jalapa, Jalapa Enríquez. Veracruz-Llave, SE Mexico
Xam Nua *152 D3 var.* Sam Neua. Houaphan, N Laos
Xankändi *133 G3 Rus.* Khankendi; *prev.* Stepanakert. SW Azerbaijan
Xánthi *120 C3* Anatolikí Makedonía kai Thráki, NE Greece
Xátiva *109 F3 var.* Jativa; *anc.* Setabis. País Valenciano, E Spain
Xauen *see* Chefchaouen
Xeres *see* Jeréz de la Frontera
Xiaguan *see* Dali
Xiamen *144 D6 var.* Hsia-men; *prev.* Amoy. Fujian, SE China
Xi'an *144 C4 var.* Changan, Sian, Signan, Siking, Singan, Xian. Shaanxi, C China
Xian *see* Xi'an
Xiangkhoang *see* Pèk
Xiangtan *144 C5 var.* Hsiang-t'an, Siangtan. Hunan, S China
Xiao Hinggan Ling *144 D2 Eng.* Lesser Khingan Range. *Mountain range* NE China
Xichang *144 B5* Sichuan, C China
Xieng Khouang *see* Pèk
Xieng Ngeun *see* Muong Xiang Ngeun
Xigaze *see* Xigazê
Xigazê *142 C5 var.* Jih-k'a-tse, Shigatse, Xigaze. Xizang Zizhiqu, W China
Xi Jiang *140 D3 var.* Hsi Chiang, *Eng.* West River. *River* S China
Xilinhot *143 F2 var.* Silinhot. Nei Mongol Zizhiqu, N China
Xilokastro *see* Xylókastro
Xin *see* Xinjiang Uygur Zizhiqu
Xingkai Hu *see* Khanka, Lake
Xingu, Rio *79 E2 river* C Brazil
Xingxingxia *142 D3* Xinjiang Uygur Zizhiqu, NW China
Xining *143 E4 var.* Hsining, Hsi-ning, Sining. *Province capital* Qinghai, C China
Xinjiang *see* Xinjiang Uygur Zizhiqu
Xinjiang Uygur Zizhiqu *142 B3 var.* Sinkiang, Sinkiang Uighur Autonomous Region, Xin, Xinjiang. Admin. region *autonomous region* NW China
Xinpu *see* Lianyungang
Xinxiang *144 C4* Henan, C China
Xinyang *144 C5 var.* Hsin-yang, Sinyang. Henan, C China
Xinzo de Limia *108 C2* Galicia, NW Spain
Xiqing Shan *140 D2 mountain range* C China
Xizang *see* Xizang Zizhiqu
Xizang Gaoyuan *see* Qingzang Gaoyuan
Xizang Zizhiqu *142 B4 var.* Thibet, Tibetan Autonomous Region, Xizang, *Eng.* Tibet. Admin. region *autonomous region* W China
Xolotlán *see* Managua, Lago de
Xuddur *89 D5 var.* Hudur, *It.* Oddur. Bakool, SW Somalia
Xuwen *144 C7* Guangdong, S China
Xuzhou *144 D4 var.* Hsu-chou, Suchow, Tongshan; *prev.* T'ung-shan. Jiangsu, E China
Xylókastro *121 B5 var.* Xilokastro. Pelopónnisos, S Greece

Y

Ya'an *144 B5 var.* Yaan. Sichuan, C China
Yabēlo *89 C5* S Ethiopia
Yablis *69 E2* Región Autónoma Atlántico Norte, NE Nicaragua
Yablonovyy Khrebet *131 F4 mountain range* S Russian Federation
Yabrai Shan *143 E3 mountain range* NE China
Yafran *87 F2* NW Libya
Yaghan Basin *83 B7 undersea feature* SE Pacific Ocean
Yahotyn *125 E2 Rus.* Yagotin. Kyyivs'ka Oblast', N Ukraine
Yahualica *66 D4* Jalisco, SW Mexico
Yakima *62 B2* Washington, NW USA
Yakima River *62 B2 river* Washington, NW USA
Yakoruda *120 C3* Sofiyska Oblast, SW Bulgaria
Yaku-shima *147 B8 island* Nansei-shotō, SW Japan
Yakutat *52 D4* Alaska, USA
Yakutsk *131 F3* Respublika Sakha (Yakutiya), NE Russian Federation
Yala *153 C7* Yala, SW Thailand
Yalizava *123 D6 Rus.* Yelizovo. Mahilyowskaya Voblasts', E Belorussia
Yalong Jiang *144 A5 river* C China
Yalova *132 B3* İstanbul, NW Turkey
Yalpuh, Ozero *124 D4 Rus.* Ozero Yalpug. *Lake* SW Ukraine
Yalta *125 F5* Respublika Krym, S Ukraine
Yalu *141 E2 Chin.* Yalu Jiang, *Jap.* Oryokko, *Kor.* Amnok-kang. *River* China/North Korea
Yamaguchi *147 B7 var.* Yamaguti. Yamaguchi, Honshū, SW Japan
Yamaguti *see* Yamaguchi
Yamal, Poluostrov *130 D2 peninsula* N Russian Federation
Yambio *89 B5 var.* Yambiyo. Western Equatoria, S Sudan
Yambiyo *see* Yambio
Yambol *120 D2 Turk.* Yanboli. Burgaska Oblast, E Bulgaria
Yamdena, Pulau *155 G5 prev.* Jamdena. *Island* Kepulauan Tanimbar, E Indonesia
Yam HaMelaḩ *see* Dead Sea
Yam Kinneret *see* Tiberias, Lake
Yamoussoukro *90 D5 country capital* (Ivory Coast) C Ivory Coast
Yamuna *150 D3 prev.* Jumna. *River* N India
Yana *131 F2 river* NE Russian Federation
Yanbu 'al Baḩr *137 A5* Al Madīnah, W Saudi Arabia
Yangambi *93 D5* Haut-Zaïre, N Congo (Zaire)
Yangchow *see* Yangzhou
Yangiyŭl *139 E2 Rus.* Yangiyul'. Toshkent Wiloyati, E Uzbekistan
Yangon *152 B4 Eng.* Rangoon. *Country capital* (Burma) Yangon, S Burma
Yangtze *see* Chang Jiang
Yangtze Kiang *see* Chang Jiang
Yangzhou *144 D5 var.* Yangchow. Jiangsu, E China
Yankton *61 E3* South Dakota, N USA
Yannina *see* Ioánnina
Yanskiy Zaliv *129 F2 bay* N Russian Federation
Yantai *144 D4 var.* Yan-t'ai; *prev.* Chefoo, Chih-fu. Shandong, E China
Yan-t'ai *see* Yantai
Yaoundé *93 B5 var.* Yaunde. *Country capital* (Cameroon) Centre, S Cameroon
Yap *160 A1 island* Caroline Islands, W Micronesia
Yapanskoye More *see* Japan, Sea of
Yapen, Pulau *155 G4 prev.* Japen. *Island* E Indonesia
Yap Trench *158 B2 var.* Yap Trough. *Undersea feature* SE Philippine Sea
Yap Trough *see* Yap Trench
Yapurá *see* Caquetá, Río
Yapurá *see* Japurá, Rio
Yaqui, Río *66 C2 river* NW Mexico
Yaransk *127 C5* Kirovskaya Oblast', NW Russian Federation
Yarega *126 D4* Respublika Komi, NW Russian Federation
Yarkant *see* Shache
Yarlung Zangbo Jiang *see* Brahmaputra
Yarmouth *see* Great Yarmouth
Yarmouth *55 F5* Nova Scotia, SE Canada
Yaroslavl' *126 B4* Yaroslavskaya Oblast', W Russian Federation
Yarumal *74 B2* Antioquia, NW Colombia
Yasyel'da *123 B7 river* SW Belorussia
Yatsushiro *147 A7 var.* Yatusiro. Kumamoto, Kyūshū, SW Japan
Yatusiro *see* Yatsushiro
Yaunde *see* Yaoundé
Yavarí *see* Javari, Rio
Yaviza *69 H5* Darién, SE Panama
Yavoriv *124 B2 Pol.* Jaworów, *Rus.* Yavorov. L'vivs'ka Oblast', NW Ukraine
Yazd *136 D3 var.* Yezd. Yazd, C Iran
Yazoo City *58 B2* Mississippi, S USA
Yding Skovhøj *101 A7 hill* C Denmark
Ýdra *121 C6 var.* Ídhra. *Island* S Greece
Ye *153 B5* Mon State, S Burma
Yecheng *142 A3 var.* Kargilik. Xinjiang Uygur Zizhiqu, NW China
Yefremov *127 B5* Tul'skaya Oblast', W Russian Federation
Yekaterinburg *130 C3 prev.* Sverdlovsk. Sverdlovskaya Oblast', C Russian Federation
Yelets *127 B5* Lipetskaya Oblast', W Russian Federation
Yell *104 D1 island* NE Scotland, UK
Yellowknife *53 E4 territory capital* Northwest Territories, W Canada
Yellow River *see* Huang He
Yellow Sea *144 D4 Chin.* Huang Hai, *Kor.* Hwang-Hae. *Sea* E Asia
Yellowstone River *60 C2 river* Montana/Wyoming, NW USA
Yel'sk *123 C7 Rus.* Yel'sk. Homyel'skaya Voblasts', SE Belorussia
Yelwa *91 F4* Kebbi, W Nigeria
Yemen *137 C7 off.* Republic of Yemen, *Ar.* Al Jumhūrīyah al Yamanīyah, Al Yaman. *Country* SW Asia
Yemva *126 D4 prev.* Zheleznodorozhnyy. Respublika Komi, NW Russian Federation
Yenakiyeve *125 G3 Rus.* Yenakiyevo; *prev.* Ordzhonikidze, Rykovo. Donets'ka Oblast', E Ukraine
Yenangyaung *152 A3* Magwe, W Burma
Yendi *91 E4* NE Ghana
Yengisar *142 A3* Xinjiang Uygur Zizhiqu, NW China
Yenierenköy *see* Agialoúsa
Yenisey *130 D3 river* Mongolia/Russian Federation
Yenping *see* Nanping
Yeovil *105 D7* SW England, UK
Yeppoon *164 D4* Queensland, E Australia
Yerevan *133 F3 var.* Erevan, *Eng.* Erivan. *Country capital* (Armenia) C Armenia
Yeu, Île d' *106 A4 island* NW France
Yevlax *133 G2 Rus.* Yevlakh. C Azerbaijan
Yevpatoriya *125 F5* Respublika Krym, S Ukraine
Yeya *125 H4 river* SW Russian Federation
Yezd *see* Yazd
Yezyaryshcha *123 E5 Rus.* Yezerishche. Vitsyebskaya Voblasts', NE Belorussia
Yiannitsá *see* Giannitsá
Yichang *144 C5* Hubei, C China
Yıldızeli *132 D3* Sivas, N Turkey
Yinchuan *144 B4 var.* Yinch'uan, Yin-ch'uan, Yinchwan. Ningxia, N China
Yinchwan *see* Yinchuan
Yin-hsien *see* Ningbo
Yining *142 B2 var.* I-ning, *Uigh.* Gulja, Kuldja. Xinjiang Uygur Zizhiqu, NW China

MAP FINDER

NORTH & WEST ASIA *128-129*

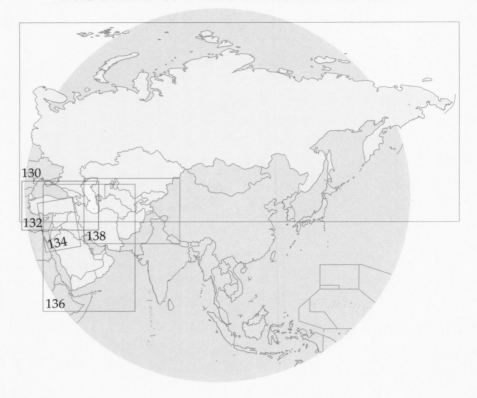

SOUTH & EAST ASIA *140-141*

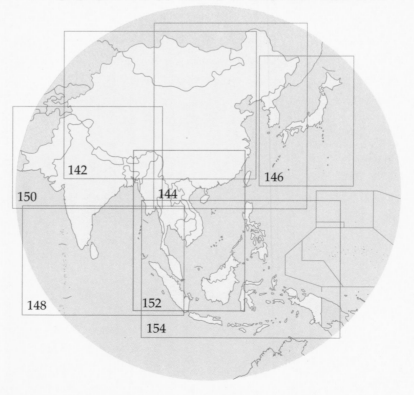